D1238745

Handbook of Cognitive, Social, and Neuropsychological Aspects of Learning Disabilities

Volume II

Handbook of Cognitive, Social, and Neuropsychological Aspects of Learning Disabilities

Volume II

Edited by

Stephen J. Ceci
Cornell University

LEA LAWRENCE ERLBAUM ASSOCIATES, PUBLISHERS

1987   Hillsdale, New Jersey   London

Lawrence Erlbaum Associates, Inc., Publishers
365 Broadway
Hillsdale, New Jersey 07642

Library of Congress Cataloging-in-Publication Data
(Revised for volume 2)

Handbook of cognitive, social, and neuropsychological
aspects of learning disabilities.

Includes indexes.
1. Learning disabillities—Handbooks, manuals, etc.—
Collective work. I. Ceci, Stephen J. [DMLM: 1. Learning
Disorders—in infancy & childhood. WS 110 H2363]
RJ506.L4H36   1986   616.92'89   85-32547
ISBN 0-89859-682-3 (v. 1)
ISBN 0-89859-797-8 (v. 2)

Printed in the United States of America
10   9   8   7   6   5   4   3   2   1

Contents

PART I: MICROLEVEL COGNITIVE ASPECTS OF LEARNING DISABILITIES

Chapter 1   **An Information-Processing Framework for Understanding Reading Disability**
Louise C. Spear and Robert J. Sternberg   **3**

Chapter 2   **The Nature of Reading Disability: Toward an Integrative Framework**
Frederick J. Morrison   **33**

Chapter 3   **In Search of the Attentional Deficit**
Kathleen L. McNellis   **63**

Chapter 4   **An Interactive Model of Strategic Processing**
Mitchell Rabinowitz and Michelen T. H. Chi   **83**

Commentary: **How Shall We Conceptualize the Language Problems of Learning-Disabled Children?**
Stephen J. Ceci and Jacquelyn G. Baker   **103**

PART II: MACROLEVEL COGNITIVE ASPECTS OF LEARNING DISABILITIES

Chapter 5   **Patterns of Motivation and Reading Skills in Underachieving Children**
Evelyn R. Oka and Scott G. Paris   **115**

Chapter 6   **Metacognition, Motivation, and Controlled Performance**
               John G. Borkowski, Mary Beth Johnston, and Molly K.Reid   **147**

Chapter 7   **Elaborative Learning Strategies for the Inefficient Learner**
               Michael Pressley and Joel R. Levin   **175**

Commentary: **The Four M's—Memory Strategies, Metastrategies, Monitoring, and Motivation**
               Patricia E. Worden   **213**

PART III: SOCIOEMOTIONAL ASPECTS
           OF LEARNING DISABILITIES

Chapter 8   **Affect and Cognition in Learning Disabilities**
               David Goldstein and William D. Dundon   **233**

Chapter 9   **Psychosocial Aspects of Learning Disabilities**
               Maribeth Montgomery Kasik, David A. Sabatino, and Patricia Spoentgen   **251**

Chapter 10   **Social Cognitive Factors in Learning-Disabled Children's Social Problem**
               Ruth Pearl   **273**

Commentary: **Socioemotional Factors in Learning Disabilities**
               Elaine Walker   **295**

PART IV: NEUROPSYCHOLOGICAL ASPECTS
          OF LEARNING DISABILITIES

Chapter 11   **Natural Histories in Learning Disabilities: Neuropsychological Difference / Environmental Demand**
               Jane M. Holmes   **303**

Chapter 12   **Learning Disability With and Without Attention Deficit Disorder**
               Elizabeth H. Aylward and Dennis Whitehouse   **321**

Chapter 13   **Event-Related Potentials of RDs During Memory Scanning**
Phillip J. Holcomb, Peggy T. Ackerman, and Roscoe A. Dykman   **343**

Commentary: **Brain Function and Learning Disabilities**
Karl Pribram and Diane McGuinness   **369**

Author Index   **375**
Subject Index   **387**

This volume is dedicated to my parents, John A. and Gilda R., who provided a foundation to be able to tackle this enterprise. In a large way, this book is theirs.

List of Contributors

Peggy T. Ackerman, *University of Arkansas for Medical Sciences*

Elizabeth H. Aylward, *John F. Kennedy Institute for Handicapped Children, Johns Hopkins University*

Jacquelyn G. Baker, *Cornell University*

John G. Borkowski, *University of Notre Dame*

Stephen J. Ceci, *Cornell University*

Michelene T. H. Chi, *University of Pittsburgh*

William D. Dundon, *Temple University*

Roscoe A. Dykman, *University of Arkansas for Medical Sciences*

David Goldstein, *Temple University and The Irving Schwartz Institute for Children and Youth*

Phillip J. Holcomb, *University of Arkansas for Medical Sciences*

Jane M. Holmes, *Children's Hospital, Boston and Harvard Medical School*

Mary Beth Johnston, *University of Notre Dame*

Maribeth Montgomery Kasik, *Governor's State University*

Joel R. Levin, *University of Wisconsin*

Diane McGuinness, *Stanford University*

Kathleen L. McNellis, *Cornell University*

Frederick J. Morrison, *University of Alberta*

Evelyn R. Oka, *University of Michigan*

Scott G. Paris, *University of Michigan*

Ruth Pearl, *University of Illinois, Chicago*

Michael Pressley, *University of Western Ontario*

Karl Pribram, *Stanford University*

Mitchell Rabinowitz, *University of Illinois Chicago Circle*

Molly K. Reid, *University of Notre Dame*

David A. Sabatino, *University of Wisconsin-Stout*

Louise C. Spear, *Yale University*

Patricia Spoentgen, *University of Wisconsin-Stout*

Robert J. Sternberg, *Yale University*

Elaine Walker, *Cornell University*

Dennis Whitehouse, *John F. Kennedy Institute for Handicapped Children, Johns Hopkins University*

Patricia E. Worden, *California State University, Fullerton*

Foreword

This is the companion volume to the *Handbook of Cognitive, Social, and Neuropsychological Aspects of Learning Disabilities-Vol. 1.* As such, it is a continuation of the theme and approach taken in the first volume. There are four thematic sections, comprised of three to four chapters each, dealing with cognitive (micro-level and macro-level), social, and neurological characteristics of learning-disabled individuals. In the Preface to volume 1 of the *Handbook,* I described the development of these first two volumes. It is not necessary to rehash those details here, but I do think one feature deserves mentioning again. It is the use of critical commentaries.

Each thematic section is followed by a critical/integrative commentary written by an active researcher in the area. These commentaries should prove to be immensely useful to researchers, as they are replete with insights and linkages that make for exciting reading. Often during the course of putting together these first two volumes I came to regret this commentary feature. There were several reasons for the regret. First, the use of commentators enormously complicated the production schedule because the individual chapters had to be sent to the commentators for analysis and this alone added several months delay to their publication. In the event that an individual chapter was returned to the author for revisions, the others could not be sent on to the commentator or publisher because all of the chapters were needed to typeset the correct page numbers, indices, and so on. And second, frequently an author and commentator disagreed about something stated by the author or commentator and refereeing such disputes added additional delays (and occasionally resulted in some bruised feelings). But I am glad I did not abandon the commentary concept. It is the one feature that is unique to the *Handbooks* and it is responsible for the high level of scholarship found in the chapters.

The authors of the individual chapters were told their chapters would be sent to active researchers in their area for a "no holds barred" treatment. This was not meant to frighten persons but simply to help our field consolidate the gains it has made over the past decade by having outside researchers make connections between the arguments found in the chapters and basic theory. Readers can judge for themselves how successful this assignment has been. But, regardless how one feels about the quality of the commentaries, it is beyond question that they helped elevate the quality of the chapters. Authors knew their ideas would be subjected to critical peer scrutiny and this probably served to boost the quality of these contributions beyond the level normally encountered in an edited volume. Even more importantly, the commentators helped me to filter acceptable from unacceptable chapters and frequently advised me to return a manuscript to its author(s) and give them the opportunity to expand their treatment to include ideas introduced by the commentator. Although this resulted in delays and disagreements, this was a truly exciting process to witness. I observed chapters in the process of major improvement. My gratitude to the commentators is genuine.

My hunch is that these *Handbooks* will come to be regarded as the learning-disability counterpart to the prestigeous *Attention and Performance* series in cognition that Lawrence Erlbaum Associates also publishes. There are over 900 different references in this second volume and over 2,100 in the two volumes together! Moreover, the review chapters one encounters in these volumes are the very finest to be found anywhere. I found myself inspired and often provoked by them, which is not something one can claim of most reviews. The difference was that these authors were commissioned to write theoretical–integrative reviews, not merely redescribe findings they previously have published. Surely they will come to be cited widely and will figure into more than a few doctoral dissertation proposals.

Finally, I encourage readers to peruse chapters that are not part of their traditional areas of concentration. For example, if you regard yourself as a cognitively oriented researcher, try reading the social and neuropsychological chapters. A treasure trove of surprises lay in wait if we, as researchers, would occassionally venture out of the narrow confines of our areas of concentration and begin building bridges with other areas. The problems exhibited by learning-disabled individuals are panoramic in scope and their resolution will require broad visions and frequent bridge-crossing. In this regard, the first volume of the *Handbooks* contains many exciting chapters by top researchers and commentaries by renowned basic researchers (e.g., Pribram, Farnham-Diggory, Vellutino, etc.). They should be read by all serious workers in the area.

Stephen J. Ceci
Ithaca, NY

MICROLEVEL COGNITIVE ASPECTS OF LEARNING DISABILITIES

1 An Information-Processing Framework for Understanding Reading Disability

Louise C. Spear
Yale University and Southern Connecticut State University

Robert J. Sternberg
Yale University

Several years ago, when the senior author of this chapter taught in a resource room for learning-disabled children, she made a disturbing discovery. This discovery involved the reading-disabled youngsters, who comprised the majority of the children in the program. All these youngsters entered the program with poor decoding skills, but once exposed to the intensive phonic program used in the resource room, they generally learned to decode individual words with alacrity; that is, they could grasp phonic rules, memorize sounds for various letters and letter combinations, and apply the rules and sounds when reading individual words. The disturbing thing, particularly to someone who had had excessive faith in the curative powers of a phonic approach to teaching reading, was that the children continued to be poor readers. Now, however, their difficulties involved higher level aspects of reading. Their oral reading was discontinuous, effortful, and sometimes painfully slow; their reading comprehension was frequently poor; and the older children lacked the study strategies so important for success in content area subjects such as social studies and science.

It soon became clear to the co-author that remediation of reading disability was going to be a considerably more complex and lengthy process than she had originally thought. The presence of the higher level reading deficits also raised some troubling theoretical questions. In particular, did the reading-disabled children start out with high-level cognitive deficits that became obvious only as more demanding reading tasks were encountered? If so, the distinction between these kinds of individuals and the mentally retarded, so firmly maintained by

3

professionals in the field of learning disabilities, became much harder to defend. Or were the higher level deficits of the reading-disabled children somehow the result of their lower level reading problems? If the latter case were true, how did the higher level deficits arise and how might instruction repair them?

In this chapter, we seek to resolve some of those questions by examining a wide range of experimental findings. Although there is no lack of research on the subject of reading disability, much of it is so labyrinthine and contradictory as to cause a Talmudic scholar to throw up his hands in despair. Borrowing an analogy, which has been used elsewhere in regard to verbal comprehension (Sternberg & Powell, 1983), but which is equally apt for reading disability, we can liken research in this field to the Indian folktale about the blind men and the elephant. In the folktale, one blind man feels the elephant's trunk and proclaims that the elephant is just like a snake; another feels the elephant's side and asserts that the elephant is like a wall; and so on, with each blind man contributing a different, only partially correct opinion on the nature of the elephant. Clearly, a theoretical framework is needed that will be specific enough to be helpful to both researchers and practitioners but broad enough to enable us to see the whole elephant. In this regard, verbal deficit theory (Vellutino, 1979) is a major step in the right direction. Information-processing models of reading (LaBerge & Samuels, 1974) and interactive–compensatory models (Perfetti & Roth, 1980; Stanovich, 1980) also have important implications for the study of individual differences in reading. This chapter attempts to combine findings related to these and other models into a coherent theoretical framework for understanding reading disability.

We have restricted ourselves to reading disability, rather than also considering learning disabilities in other areas such as mathematics, for two reasons. First, reading disability has been the focus of most learning-disabilities research, although in recent years this has started to change. In addition, the learning-disabilities category is so heterogeneous that a single framework for comprehending it is beyond the scope of the chapter, if not doomed to failure from the start. We also need to explain what we mean by the term *reading disability* (RD). In using this term, we refer to individuals who have a specific deficit in reading, coupled with average or above-average intelligence. (Although we would agree, theoretically, that RD can also occur in individuals of below-average intelligence, the difficulties inherent in disentangling the reading deficits from general cognitive deficits preclude the consideration of the low-intelligence population for the present.) We further conceptualize reading disability as an intrinsic deficit, one not caused by (but perhaps exacerbated by) external factors such as poor teaching, environmental deprivation, and so on; or by other handicapping conditions, such as sensory impairment or emotional disturbance. This exclusionary "definition" of RD is, of course, highly traditional (Johnson & Myklebust, 1967; Kirk, 1962; Orton, 1937). Essentially, it is the same as the federal register (PL 94–142) definition used by public schools in this country to identify children with learning disabilities (LD). This traditional way of conceptualizing LD and RD has obvious shortcomings, but given the state of the art, it is probably as good a definition as any other.

The problem of defining a sample is but one of many methodological difficulties involved in interpreting and carrying out research on reading disability. Many of the studies that presently exist are difficult to interpret because of incomplete information about the sample and other methodological flaws. If researchers begin to include standard information about certain "marker variables" (Keogh, Major, Omori, Gandara, & Reid, 1980), future studies will be much easier to interpret. Some excellent guidelines for conducting research in this area have been suggested by Vellutino (1979). In our view, some minimal requirements are as follows: IQ scores, with means and standard deviations, should be provided for both the reading-disabled and control groups; reading achievement scores, with means and standard deviations, should also be provided for both groups; all groups should receive the same IQ and achievement measures; the researcher should control IQ in the statistical analyses, or at least match the groups on IQ; and the reading-disabled group should be significantly below grade level in reading—at least 1 year below grade level for children in grades one through four, and at least 2 years below grade level for children in fifth grade and above. A nonverbal IQ measure is highly desirable, especially for older reading-disabled individuals, but is not often used by researchers. Similarly, although statistical control of IQ (e.g., through the use of multiple- and partial-correlation methods) is more desirable than IQ matching, because regression-to-the-mean causes serious problems with the latter, until very recently it has been only rarely employed by researchers.

Some authors (e.g., Hall & Humphreys, 1982) have raised questions about the validity of other aspects of reading-disability research, such as questioning the inclusion of children who are behind in mathematics as well as in reading. However, we think it is important to acknowledge the extraordinary practical difficulties involved in doing research on learning disabilities, in general, and reading disability, in particular. It would be possible to become so zealous about methodology that one would never actually complete any new work. Our argument is not with the technical correctness of these authors' criticisms, but with what can reasonably be accomplished. Moreover, the problems discussed so far, which are specific to research on reading disability, are in addition to a host of other difficulties attendant on conducting any research in schools: getting administrators to return one's phone calls, getting parental permission, scheduling, attrition, and so forth.

Finally, a few words about the organization of this chapter are in order. In the next section, we review some of the major results of existing research on reading disability. As many other detailed reviews of the literature in this field already exist (e.g., Vellutino, 1979; Worden, 1983), we have concentrated on summarizing and organizing a range of findings, rather than elaborating on results in any one particular area. The third and final section of the chapter presents a theoretical framework for understanding these results, along with some practical implications for those who work with reading-disabled individuals.

LITERATURE REVIEW

This literature review comprises three levels of organization. The first level is topical; the results are grouped according to the type of skill studied and whether the processing required is primarily *top-down* or *bottom-up* in nature. Top-down processing is conceptually driven, or guided by higher level processes, whereas bottom-up processing is data-driven, or guided by lower level processes. (A crucial point to bear in mind, however, and one to which we return to later, is that bottom-up deficits may affect top-down processing, and vice versa.) The findings we review fall into three skill areas: reading, language, and memory. Thus, the first section of the review deals with reading skills that involve top-down processing (e.g., comprehension), and the second section deals with reading skills that involve bottom-up processing (e.g., decoding of single words). Subsequent sections are Language: Top-down Processing, Language: Bottom-up Processing, Memory: Top-down Processing, and Memory: Bottom-up Processing.

In a second tier of organization within each skill area, results are further grouped according to whether the reading-disabled group's performance was statistically comparable to that of the control group's, or instead, statistically deficient. We believe that accounting for the areas of sameness is especially crucial for theoretical purposes, as the areas of deficit are often open to interpretation that depends on the overall pattern of sameness and difference.

A third level of grouping organizes the results as *high confidence, middle confidence,* or *low confidence.* We made judgments about confidence levels not only by considering the criteria discussed earlier for reading-disability research, but also by considering the extent to which the results have been replicated, especially by more than one group of researchers. Although our identification of some of the skill areas is open to debate, the confidence judgments will doubtless inspire the most controversy. Many times these judgments were not easily made. Without them, however, it is impossible to make any sense of the findings in this field.

Finally, we have included two tables that summarize the results of the literature review. Table 1.1 summarizes research findings involving skills that require primarily top-down processing. Table 1.2 summarizes research findings involving skills that require primarily bottom-up processing. Frequent reference to the tables during the literature review should prove helpful to the reader.

TABLE 1.1
Performance of Disabled Readers in Top-Down Areas

	Areas That Are Not Deficient	*Areas of Deficit*
High confidence	Use of content to speed word recognition General language comprehension Organization of long-term memory	Reading comprehension Use of reading strategies
Middle confidence	Automatic semantic processing	Knowledge about orthographic structure Purposive semantic processing Strategic short-term memory deficits
Low confidence		Use of partial information

TABLE 1.2
Performance of Disabled Readers in Bottom-Up Areas

	Areas That Are Not Deficient	*Areas of Deficit*
High confidence	Basic visual information processing	Word recognition and decoding Automatization of decoding Awareness of the sound structure of speech
Middle confidence		Use of a phonetic code in short-term memory
Low confidence	Use of the sentence boundary as a recoding cue Naming speed	

READING: TOP-DOWN PROCESSING

Areas in Which the Reading-Disabled Perform as Well as Normals

High Confidence: Use of Context to Speed Word Recognition. (See Table 1.1.) According to top-down models of reading, people generate hypotheses about text as they read, focusing on the decoding of individual words only when the hypothesis fails to be confirmed (Goodman, 1976; Smith, 1973). According to this view, then, proficient reading is driven by higher level comprehension processes, not by lower level, bottom-up processes such as the decoding of single words. A corollary of this view is that poor readers fail to make use of context, which is a higher level, comprehension-based skill, to aid in word recognition. However, the lack of evidence to support the hypothesis-testing models has been noted elsewhere (Stanovich, 1982). Recent research indicates that disabled readers not only are capable of using context to facilitate word recognition but actually rely on context to speed decoding more than do good readers (Allington & Strange, 1977; Perfetti, 1982; Perfetti & Roth, 1980; Stanovich, 1980; Stanovich & West, 1979; Weber, 1970).

These findings do not contradict previous findings that disabled readers perform more poorly on measures of contextual sensitivity and knowledge, such as a cloze procedure or a sentence completion task. Rather, they indicate that during actual reading, good readers have no need to use context to aid decoding, because they recognize words so rapidly that the processing of other types of cues does not have time to be completed. Disabled readers, on the other hand, need to supplement their slow decoding abilities by relying on context. (We offer evidence regarding the deficient decoding abilities of disabled readers later.) Thus, it appears that good readers acquire greater knowledge regarding context, as one would expect, but they use this knowledge minimally, if at all, to speed ongoing word recognition.

Two points should be raised here. First, in order to make use of context during reading, the reader must be able to recognize some minimal number of words in the text; otherwise, there is no inferred "context" of which to make use. The youngest or most severely disabled readers may therefore fail to show a context effect, especially if the reading materials are too difficult for them. Second, we should acknowledge that many of the researchers who have found context effects in disabled readers have used readers who were only moderately impaired. However, there is no evidence to suggest that these findings would not apply to more severely impaired readers.

Areas of Deficit for Disabled Readers

High Confidence: Reading Comprehension.   (See Table 1.1.) Even when reading material that they can decode accurately, disabled readers frequently show reading comprehension deficits (Cromer, 1970; Levin, 1973; Oaken, Wiener, & Cromer, 1971; Smiley, Oakley, Worthen, Campione, & Brown, 1977). Vellutino (1979) has presented convincing evidence that these deficits are not attributable to poorer general language comprehension, provided IQ is controlled, as in the study by Oaken et al. (1971). Instead, the reading comprehension problems of disabled readers may be partially accounted for by their differential use of strategies during reading. For instance, Wong (1982) had reading-disabled, normal, and gifted children read a series of "story units" and select 12 units to serve as potential retrieval cues. The reading-disabled youngsters were less thorough in considering the cues and showed less tendency to check their selections. Other evidence suggests that disabled readers are less efficient at scanning text (Garner & Reis, 1981), more passive in their approach to reading (Bransford, Stein, & Vye, 1982), less likely to use elaborative encoding to aid comprehension (Pearson & Camperell, 1981), and less able to adjust their reading strategies to suit varying purposes for reading (Forrest & Waller, 1979).

However, the relationship between strategy use and reading disability is not as straightforward as it might initially appear. For one thing, it is important to distinguish between knowledge about a given strategy and spontaneous use of that strategy in a particular situation. Disabled readers may have knowledge about a strategy, yet may still fail to employ the strategy on their own, perhaps because they do not perceive its utility. Also, it is necessary to consider normal developmental trends in strategy acquisition. Paris and Lindauer (1982) have noted that normal children acquire strategic knowledge gradually with formal schooling, and that younger children will not freely adopt strategies whose usefulness is unclear to them. There is evidence that even in good readers, many strategies develop fairly late. Awareness of text structure (e.g., ability to differentiate main idea sentences from supporting details) and the use of this awareness to facilitate recall are one example of strategic knowledge that appears rather slow in developing. For instance, Taylor and Samuels (1983) identified 72% of good readers in fifth and sixth grades as lacking awareness of text organization. Moreover, if one accepts Durkin's (1979) finding that a negligible amount of time is actually spent teaching reading comprehension in the schools (in contrast to the amount of time allocated in the schedule or the number of pages devoted to it in the curriculum guide), it seems reasonable to assume that little direct instruction on strategy use takes place in most classrooms. Our own experience in the schools would do nothing to contradict this assumption.

The point of the preceding discussion for understanding the disabled reader is that the disabled reader's lack of strategy use must be at least partially due to the reading failure itself; that is, because of their prolonged difficulty in learning to read, these youngsters do not profit sufficiently from the experiences with text through which normal children seem to induce and practice strategies. A recent study by Taylor and Williams (1983) supports this conclusion as it relates to one aspect of strategy acquisition, the awareness of text organization. These authors found that when the disabled readers were matched on reading level to a group of younger normal readers, both groups showed the same sensitivity to text features.

Relatively few studies involving strategy instruction have been done with disabled readers. However, some of this initial research indicates that strategy training fails to make up for reading comprehension differences between reading-disabled and normal subjects (Worden, 1983). Automatization failure (see Table 1.2) is an alternative explanation for these differences (LaBerge & Samuels, 1974; Perfetti & Lesgold, 1977; Sternberg & Wagner, 1982). According to this view, even after disabled readers have learned to decode accurately, decoding continues to require conscious effort. Decoding therefore consumes attentional resources that are free for higher level comprehension processes in the normal reader, who has automatized decoding. Similarly, we have seen that disabled readers can use context to speed word recognition, but this extra processing has a cost: Disabled readers' comprehension suffers because they have fewer free attentional resources. Although training on high-speed word-recognition techniques has sometimes failed to make up for comprehension differences between good and poor readers (Samuels & LaBerge, 1983), it is important to differentiate speed from automatization. The existence of one does not necessarily imply the existence of the other. It is also particularly crucial to rule out IQ differences in this type of research. Nevertheless, it is likely that both automatization failure and lack of strategy use, and perhaps other factors as well, play a role in the reading comprehension problems of disabled readers.

Middle Confidence: Knowledge About Orthographic Structure. (See Table 1.1.) Another line of research indicates that reading-disabled children have deficient knowledge about the orthographic structure of words, that is, deficient knowledge about sound–symbol relationships and phonic rules. Compared to good readers, disabled readers have more difficulty reading pseudowords that conform to complex rather than simple phonic rules, and they have more difficulty automatizing the decoding of phonetically complex but regular words (Manis, 1981; Morrison & Manis, 1982). Shankweiler and Liberman (1972) found that in reading pseudowords, disabled readers were most likely to make errors on vowels, whose sounds tend to be the most variable parts of words and the parts for which knowledge about phonic rules is most helpful. Baron and Strawson (1976) categorized children as *Phoenicians* or *Chinese*, based on whether they used a phonetic or sight–word strategy, and found the former (the children using a phonetic strategy) to be better readers.

Two methodological problems found in many of these studies involve the classification of the words or pseudowords given to the children to read, and the failure to specify the reading approach to which the children previously have been exposed. As an example of the first problem, it is not clear why Manis (1981) classifies "lute" as a regular word of high complexity, but "gannet" as a word of low complexity. With regard to the second problem, the type of reading instruction children have received will presumably affect their knowledge of orthographic structure and their strategies for recognizing individual words. For instance, most youngsters in regular classrooms are exposed to a sight–word approach to reading, which encourages a whole-word strategy for recognizing individual words and requires children to infer many phonic rules. However, children in special education or remedial reading classes often are taught according to a synthetic–phonic approach in which phonic rules are explicitly taught and a "sounding-out" strategy is emphasized. Knowing which approach the children in a given study have received is central to the interpretation of these findings.

It has been argued (Morrison & Manis, 1982) that the lack of orthographic knowledge on the part of disabled readers is evidence of a larger difficulty with learning complex or irregular rule systems. One problem with this argument is that it fails to explain why many disabled readers have no obvious difficulties with language acquisition, which, like reading, involves mastering a system of highly complex rules and relationships. Moreover, to a much greater extent than reading, language acquisition requires a child to infer rules and relationships that are never explicitly taught. The "rule-learning" view also fails to explain the existence of at least some reading disability cases in other, more phonetically regular languages than English (Stevenson, Stigler, Lucker, Lee, Hsu, & Kitamura, 1982).

Summary

Available evidence strongly suggests that reading-disabled children can use context to facilitate word recognition. In fact, during actual reading, disabled readers appear to rely on context to a much greater extent than do good readers. However, reading-disabled children are clearly deficient in two other top-down aspects of reading: comprehension and knowledge about the orthographic structure of words.

READING: BOTTOM-UP PROCESSING

Areas in Which Disabled Readers Perform as Well as Normals

High-Confidence: Basic Visual Information-Processing.   (See Table 1.2.) An impressive number of studies on the visual information-processing skills of disabled readers has been done. Most of these studies have failed to find differences between disabled and normal readers (Holmes & McKeever, 1979; Liberman & Shankweiler, 1978; Perfetti, Finger, & Hogaboam, 1978; Vellutino, Steger, Kaman, & DeSetto, 1975). These findings contradict the traditional historical belief, still held by most laymen as well as some professionals, that disabled readers sustain visual perceptual deficits—for example, that they perceive letters and words backwards. Research suggestive of a visual perceptual deficit in disabled readers is usually confounded by a failure to rule out linguistic and memory factors, as well as the effects of poor reading itself. Relatively recent advances in experimental techniques have provided particularly convincing evidence regarding the soundness of the visual information-processing abilities of disabled readers. Morrison, Giordani, and Nagy (1977) provide a good example of this type of experiment. Using the partial report technique, these investigators found that for delay intervals between 0 and 300 msec—the duration of the purely perceptual visual information store—the recognition accuracy of reading-disabled subjects for visual stimuli did not differ from that of normal subjects. Other research in this area has been exhaustively reviewed by Vellutino (1979). As a final piece of evidence, it is worth noting the lack of success of visual perceptual training programs, which were commonly used with reading-disabled children in the 1960s and early 1970s. Most researchers have found that perceptual training programs fail to improve academic performance (Hammill, 1972; Smead, 1977). Furthermore, many of the perceptual tests used to "diagnose" RD fail even to correlate with academic performance (Hammill, 1972; Newcomer, 1975).

Low Confidence: Use of the Sentence Boundary As a Recoding Cue.   (See Table 1.2.) Perfetti, Goldman, and various of their colleagues have done a series of experiments investigating the use of the sentence boundary as a recoding cue during reading (Goldman, Hogaboam, Bell, & Perfetti, 1980; Perfetti & Goldman, 1976). Readers generally use sentence boundaries as occasions for converting the actual words of the text, which are being held in working memory, to a nonverbatim representation in long-term memory. However, if the sentence is long or complex, the limits of working memory are reached before the reader completes the sentence, so recoding occurs prior to the sentence boundary. The aforementioned research indicates that like good readers, disabled readers also use sentence boundaries as recoding cues. However, disabled readers reach the limits of working memory sooner than do good readers and are therefore more likely to have to recode before finishing a sentence. Perfetti and Goldman attribute the working memory limitations of disabled readers to inefficient verbal coding processes.

We have classified this finding as *low confidence* for several reasons. First, not all the experiments in the series control for intelligence. Second, further replication of the finding by other authors is needed. Finally, Goldman et al. (1980) note that the sentence boundary cue is probably less consistent for reading than for listening, because readers can control the rate of input of text but listeners cannot do the same for spoken words.

Areas of Deficit for Disabled Readers

High Confidence: Word Recognition.   (See Table 1.2.) Researchers have consistently found disabled readers to have difficulty reading individual words (Barron, 1978; Calfee, Chapman, & Venezky, 1972; Firth, 1972; McCormick & Samuels, 1979; Perfetti, Finger, & Hogaboam, 1978; Perfetti & Hogaboam, 1975; Shankweiler & Liberman, 1972). Both speed and accuracy differences have been found, and the differences are especially large in the case of long, phonetically complex words (Perfetti, Finger, & Hogaboam, 1978). Reading disability is clearly associated with less efficient word decoding/word recognition, rather than with, for instance, reading comprehension deficits only. In our own work with 10 to 12-year-old disabled readers (Spear & Sternberg, in preparation), we have found a task measuring decoding accuracy to discriminate reliably between disabled and normal readers.

Summary

Contrary to traditional belief, disabled readers sustain no impairment in their basic visual information-processing ability. However, these individuals are consistently found to have difficulty reading single words. Even when they have attained levels of decoding accuracy comparable to those of normal readers, their rate of decoding continues to be deficient.

LANGUAGE: TOP-DOWN PROCESSING

Thus far we have considered the performance of disabled readers in some top-down and bottom-up aspects of reading. We turn now to a different but related area, that of language. First we discuss top-down language processing in disabled readers, then bottom-up language processing.

Areas in Which Disabled Readers Perform as Well as Normals

Middle Confidence: Automatic Semantic Processing. (See Table 1.1.) Readers and listeners respond more rapidly to semantically related words than to semantically unrelated words. For instance, in a lexical decision task involving pairs of letter strings, both children and adults respond to semantically related pairs such as "cat" and "dog" faster than to semantically unrelated pairs such as "cat" and "fruit." Ceci (1982) terms this type of meaning-based facilitation, which occurs without effort or awareness, "automatic semantic processing." Ceci has found learning-disabled and normal youngsters to perform similarly on various measures of automatic semantic processing (Ceci, 1982, 1983), although sometimes he dismisses as unimportant differences that are quite large for this type of research (e.g., Ceci, 1982, Experiment 1). His subjects are described as "language/learning disabled" rather than as reading-disabled or dyslexic. They tend to have large verbal-performance discrepancies on the WISC and deficits in areas such as listening comprehension as well as reading (Ceci, 1983). His results may therefore better characterize the child who is more generally impaired in language, rather than the specifically reading-disabled child.

Areas of Deficit for the Disabled Readers

Middle Confidence: Purposive Semantic Processing.   (See Table 1.1.) In contrast to automatic semantic processing, purposive semantic processing requires conscious planning and intent (Ceci, 1983; Simpson & Lorsbach, 1983). Ceci (1982, 1983) used a priming task to demonstrate that learning-disabled children were deficient in the use of purposive semantic processing. The task required children to name slides of familiar objects. The purposive condition involved the use of semantically related primes (e.g., "here's an animal" before the subject saw a picture of a horse), whereas the automatic condition employed semantically unrelated primes (e.g., "here's an animal" before the subject saw a picture of a banana). Learning-disabled 10-year-olds were like normal 4-year-olds in their failure to show large reaction-time increases for the semantically unrelated primes, or as large a facilitation as normal 10-year-olds when the primes were semantically related. In contrast, normal 10-year-olds sustained relatively large penalties from unrelated primes, and large benefits from related ones, suggesting that they were deliberately employing the primes to aid themselves in rapid naming of the slides. With a different procedure using lists of semantically related and unrelated words, Ceci (1985) has obtained similar results.

As noted earlier, Ceci's results may not be characteristic of children who are specifically disabled in reading, but rather of children who are more generally language-impaired. Also, Ceci (1985) fails to report IQ data on his nondisabled subjects, making firm conclusions impossible.

Summary

Ceci's research suggests that children classified as "language/learning disabled" sustain deficits in purposive semantic processing, but not in automatic semantic processing. It is not clear to what extent his findings apply to reading-disabled youngsters who lack more generalized language difficulties.

LANGUAGE: BOTTOM-UP PROCESSING

Areas in Which Disabled Readers Perform as Well as Normals

Low Confidence: Naming Speed.   (See Table 1.2.) Naming speed is another type of automatic process that has been frequently studied by researchers interested in reading disability. The results in this area are especially conflicting, which is why we have labeled our conclusion that disabled and normal readers are similar in naming speed as *low confidence*. Perfetti, Finger, and Hogaboam (1978) found that disabled third-grade readers did not differ from nondisabled third graders in their speed of naming colors, digits, and pictures, but only on their speed of naming words (i.e., reading). Stanovich (1981) obtained similar results. However, Denckla and Rudel (1976), Spring (1976), and Spring and Capps (1974) have found general naming speed differences between disabled and normal readers.

One explanation of these conflicting findings has to do with sampling differences: Perfetti's and Stanovich's subjects tended to be less severely disabled in reading than those of Denckla and Rudel. In addition, the accuracy of the continuous-list procedure employed by both Denckla and Rudel (1976) and Spring and Capps (1974) is questionable (see Stanovich, 1981, for further discussion). Thus, experimental methodology is a second explanation of the discrepant findings. Finally, a number of investigators have failed to find differences in naming speed between disabled readers and other clinical populations (such as nondisabled hyperactive youngsters) who read normally (Ackerman & Dykman, 1982). It seems likely to us that the characteristic reading-disabled child in public school—one with a specific reading deficit—is usually not deficient in speed of naming stimuli other than words. This type of youngster is in contrast to the type of youngster likely to be found in a clinic setting, who may well sustain a more general level of impairment, including a name retrieval deficit.

Areas of Deficit for Disabled Readers

High Confidence: Awareness of the Sound Structure of Speech. (See Table 1.2.) Disabled readers are much less aware than are normal readers of the phonemic and syllabic structure of spoken language. For example, disabled readers have been found deficient at Pig Latin games and rhyming tasks (Bradley & Bryant, 1978; Savin, 1972), at segmenting words into syllables (Liberman, Shankweiler, Fischer, & Carter, 1974), and at segmenting words into phonemes (Calfee, Lindamood, & Lindamood, 1973; Fox & Routh, 1975; Rosner & Simon, 1971). For the syllable segmentation task, the experimenter typically asks the child to tap out the number of syllables he hears in a word such as "butterfly"; the analogous phoneme segmentation task might involve counting the number of sounds heard in a word such as "ship" (three). Therefore, in contrast to the standard auditory discrimination tests often used with disabled readers, these tasks require explicit awareness of the syllabic and phonemic structure of speech. Other evidence regarding the syllabic and phonemic awareness of young or disabled readers has been reviewed at length by Golinkoff (1978), Liberman and Shankweiler (1978), and Rozin and Gleitman (1977).

Of course, one would expect children to acquire greater awareness of the sound structure of spoken words as they learn to read. Some confounding of phonemic awareness with reading skill can therefore be anticipated. Indeed, Morais, Cary, Alegria, and Bertelson (1979) found that illiterate adults performed poorly on a phonemic awareness task. However, whereas phonemic awareness appears to be partly a by-product of learning to read, there is considerable evidence that it is also causally related to the acquisition of reading skill. For instance, Helfgott (1976) found kindergarteners' ability to segment one-syllable words to be strongly predictive of their first-grade reading level. Perfetti, Beck, and Hughes (1981) found that gains in phonemic synthesis (a blending task) preceded gains in reading, but gains in phonemic analysis (a phoneme deletion task) followed gains in reading. These researchers concluded that less sophisticated kinds of phonemic knowledge enable reading progress, whereas more sophisticated kinds of phonemic knowledge, such as that measured by the phoneme deletion task, are a result of reading progress. In addition, several investigators (Litcher & Roberge, 1979; Williams, 1980) have found that training on various kinds of phonemic tasks improves reading skill. Finally, syllabic awareness, which appears to be less confounded with reading instruction than with phonemic awareness (Alegria, Pignot, & Morais, 1982), has also been found to be a strong predictor of first-grade reading ability (Mann & Liberman, 1982).

Summary

It is clear that, at least in the early grades, disabled readers are much less aware of the sound structure of spoken language than are normal readers. Particularly convincing are the findings that deficits in phonemic and syllabic awareness actually precede the reading difficulty. However, we have concluded that disabled readers probably do not have naming speed deficits, although we concede that the evidence in this area is especially contradictory.

MEMORY: TOP-DOWN PROCESSING

We now turn to the final skill area to be considered, that of memory. We follow our earlier pattern of first discussing top-down processing, followed by a discussion of bottom-up processing, which concludes the review section of the chapter.

Areas in Which Disabled Readers Perform as Well as Normals

High Confidence: Organization of Long-Term Memory. (See Table 1.1.) The organization of long-term memory is evidently intact in reading-disabled individuals. Using a variety of stimuli—lists of words, pictures, and prose materials—researchers have generally found that the quantity of material recalled by disabled readers, but not its organization, is deficient. For example, Berger and Perfetti (1977) compared disabled and normal fifth-grade readers on paraphrase recall and literal question answering, using stimulus stories presented orally in one condition and in writing in another condition. They found that the normal readers' performance exceeded that of the disabled readers by equal amounts for both tasks and in both conditions. Although the disabled readers recalled less, their recall patterns did not differ from those of the normal readers. Similar results were obtained by Worden, Malmgren, and Gabourie (1982), who used stories based on the story grammar of Mandler and Johnson (1977) with adult disabled and nondisabled subjects. Again, although the disabled subjects recalled less (in this case, dramatically less) than did the normal subjects, their patterns of recall of the various story constituents did not differ. Other authors (Dallago & Moely, 1980; Torgesen, 1977) have obtained comparable results using lists of words rather than stories.

In a number of studies, the lowered quantity of material recalled by disabled readers has been accounted for by deficits in short-term memory (e.g., Bauer, 1979). Perfetti and Lesgold (1977) have proposed that verbal coding problems in short-term memory (STM) result in a "bottleneck" for reading-disabled individuals (that is, slower coding in STM affects the ability of disabled readers to hold larger units of discourse, such as clauses and sentences, in working memory; faulty integration of these larger units results in impaired comprehension and recall). Evidence that mere repetition of stimulus materials can raise the recall of disabled readers to normal levels (Worden, Malmgren, & Gabourie, 1982; Worden & Nakamura, 1982) lends support to the "STM bottleneck" hypothesis.

Two cautionary notes should be raised here. First, a number of these studies, particularly the ones by Worden and her colleagues (Worden, Malmgren, & Gabourie, 1982; Worden & Nakamura, 1982), failed to control for IQ. However, one would expect any IQ differences to favor the nondisabled readers. Nevertheless, no differences in the organization of long-term recall have been found. Furthermore, studies that have controlled for IQ, such as the ones by Perfetti and his colleagues, have obtained similar results.

The second cautionary note involves the existence of a number of studies that have found disabled and normal readers to differ in their recall of more important propositions in a passage (Hansen, 1978; Smiley, Oakley, Worthen, Campione, & Brown, 1977; Wong, 1979). These results might appear to contradict our conclusion that disabled readers have no deficits in the organization of long-term memory. However, these studies used only one presentation of the stimulus materials, so it is possible that repetition would have elevated the performance of the reading-disabled group (see Worden, 1983, for further discussion). In addition, differential use of reading strategies—especially as a result of differential reading experience—may be the culprit here, and not the structure of long-term memory itself.

Areas of Deficit for Disabled Readers

Middle Confidence: Strategic Deficits in Short-Term Memory. (See Table 1.1.) We discussed earlier the possible role of short-term memory deficiencies in the long-term recall problems of the reading disabled. The exact nature of these short-term memory deficits is a matter of some dispute. One opinion, that of Perfetti and others, attributes the inferior STM performance of disabled readers to inefficient verbal coding. This is a bottom-up view of the problem, about which we have more to say later.

However, another view, more top-down in nature, attributes the short-term memory problems of disabled readers to strategic deficits, such as failure to mentally group items to aid recall, or failure to employ verbal rehearsal (Bauer, 1982; Torgesen & Goldman, 1977). It has been noted, for instance, that slowing the rate of presentation of items on a short-term recall task, or lengthening the interval between presentation and recall, worsens the performance of reading-disabled youngsters (Bauer, 1979; Torgesen & Houck, 1980). These are precisely the conditions under which the use of strategies may come into play. Nonstrategic accounts for the differences can also be devised, however: Torgesen and Houck (1980) suggested a more rapid decay of the stimulus trace as one such explanation.

Although a moderate amount of evidence for strategic short-term memory deficits in disabled readers exists, we must again counsel caution in interpreting the relationship between strategy use and reading disability. We would raise here the same issues raised earlier in examining the role of strategy use in reading comprehension: the need to differentiate knowledge about a strategy from its spontaneous use; the need to consider normal developmental trends in strategy acquisition; and the need to consider the impact of reading failure itself on strategy acquisition. A number of training studies have found training to benefit disabled and normal readers equally (see Worden, 1983, for a review), indicating that strategic STM deficits are not the primary, or at least not the only, factor distinguishing reading-disabled children from normal readers.

Summary

Long-term memory organization is apparently intact in disabled readers who clearly have short-term memory deficits. One explanation for these deficits involves faulty strategy use. However, several studies have found that strategy training benefits disabled and normal readers to the same extent. Strategic differences are thus probably not the primary factor in disabled readers' poor short-term memory performance.

MEMORY: BOTTOM-UP PROCESSING

Areas of Deficit for Disabled Readers

Middle-Confidence: Phonetic Coding in Short-Term Memory. (See Table 1.2.) Previously, we have repeatedly alluded to verbal coding problems in STM as an explanation for the difficulties of disabled readers in various areas. Here, we discuss some of the research evidence regarding these problems. First, we should begin by noting that there is considerable evidence that the short-term memory difficulties of disabled readers are restricted to memory for materials that can be coded verbally, such as letters, words, pictures, and numbers (see Vellutino, 1979, for an extensive review). Disabled readers have usually not differed from normal readers in their short-term memory for nonsense doodles or pictures of unfamiliar faces (Katz, Shankweiler, & Liberman, 1981; Liberman, Mann, Shankweiler, & Werfelman, 1983). Additional evidence indicates that, at least in the early stages of reading, disabled youngsters do not make efficient use of a phonetic code in STM (Byrne & Shea, 1979; Hogaboam & Perfetti, 1978; Mann, Liberman, & Shankweiler, 1980; Shankweiler, Liberman, Mark, Fowler, & Fischer, 1979). In other words, reading-disabled children have difficulty using an auditory or sound type of code to process visual material such as letters and words. Proficient readers are thought to rely heavily on this kind of speech code, even during silent reading (see Crowder, 1982, for further discussion).

The lack of an efficient phonetic code in STM has generally been inferred through the use of a memory task involving phonetically confusable (i.e., rhyming) materials. Shankweiler, Liberman, Mark, Fowler, and Fischer (1979) provide a good example of this type of study. Disabled and nondisabled second-grade readers were asked to recall strings of phonetically confusable (e.g., b, c, g, t) and strings of phonetically nonconfusable (e.g., f, h, q, w) consonants. Although the good readers recalled more letters than did the disabled readers, they were more heavily penalized by phonetic confusability. Furthermore, the differences were not attributable to differences in verbal rehearsal. These results have been replicated using lists of phonetically confusable words (Byrne & Shea, 1979) and sentences (Mann, Liberman, & Shankweiler, 1980). It should be emphasized that in most of these experiments, the disabled-reader group was affected by the phonetic confusability manipulation, but not to the same extent as the good reader group. The problem thus has appeared to involve deficient phonetic coding, rather than the complete absence of phonetic coding. As in the case of phonemic awareness, there is even some evidence that verbal short-term memory problems and phonetic coding problems actually presage reading difficulties. For example, Mann and Liberman (1982) found that a verbal STM task and a phonetic coding measure involving rhyming words, but not a nonverbal test of short-term memory, predicted reading achievement at the end of first grade.

However, a number of recent experiments (Hall, Wilson, Humphreys, Tinzmann, & Bowyer, 1983; Wolford & Fowler, 1983) dispute the phonetic coding hypothesis. In the Hall et al. (1983) study, disabled readers in second, third, and fourth grades were found to be as susceptible to phonetic confusability manipulations as normal readers. These investigators attribute earlier findings of deficient phonetic coding in disabled readers to a floor effect, stemming from the fact that the overall difficulty of the serial-recall task is usually greater for disabled than for normal readers. On the other hand, Wolford and Fowler (1983) obtained results similar to those of Shankweiler et al. (1979) in phonetic confusability manipulations but also found disabled readers to make more visual confusions on a visual whole-report task. Thus, these researchers suggest that the problems of disabled readers are more general than deficient phonetic coding. They propose that disabled readers fail to make use of partial information, a hypothesis that implies that reading disability is characterized by top-down kinds of cognitive deficits.

Both Hall et al. (1983) and Wolford and Fowler (1983) used readers who were not very disabled in reading. Nevertheless, their results raise some serious questions abut the phonetic coding hypothesis. It may be that only more severely impaired readers show a true phonetic coding deficit. In particular, perhaps phonetic coding deficiencies are characteristic of disabled readers only at the beginning stages of reading, and once a certain level of reading skill is acquired— e.g., a second- or third-grade level—phonetic coding deficits disappear. (But see Alegria, Pignot, & Morais, 1982, who failed to find phonetic coding deficits even in first graders.)

Of course, as Hall et al. (1983) suggest, it may also be the case that the phonetic coding deficits of disabled readers are largely artifactual. In addition, phonetic coding measures are susceptible to the same confounds with reading skill and reading approach as measures of phonemic awareness. These confounds are not an issue with kindergarten subjects, such as those employed in the Mann and Liberman (1982) study, provided that the subjects have not yet learned to read. Nevertheless, when subjects are older and especially if they have been exposed to a phonic approach to reading, the phonetic coding measure is much less reliable in discriminating disabled from normal readers (e.g., Beverly & Perfetti, 1982). Thus, although the use of a phonetic code may be causally related to reading skill, it is probably also partly a result of reading skill.

There is also some evidence that disabled readers make greater use of a semantic code in short-term memory than do normal readers (Beverly & Perfetti, 1982; Byrne & Shea, 1979); that is, disabled readers may have a greater tendency than do normal readers to code items in terms of meaning. This finding is even less consistent than the one for phonetic coding. If accurate, however, the *semantic coding* result fits nicely with the findings regarding disabled readers' greater reliance on context to speed word recognition: Disabled readers may tend to rely generally on meaning to compensate for deficient phonetic abilities.

Summary

Disabled readers have difficulty with short-term memory for material that can be coded verbally. One specific area of deficit may involve faulty use of phonetic coding in short-term memory, although research on phonetic coding in disabled readers has yielded some mixed findings.

General Summary and Conclusions

The bulk of available evidence indicates that the deficits of disabled readers are verbal rather than nonverbal and cognitive rather than perceptual in nature. Disabled readers clearly have difficulty with a number of skills involving bottom-up processing: phonemic awareness, syllabic awareness, the ability to read individual words accurately and rapidly, and perhaps also the use of a phonetic code in short-term memory. (See Table 1.2.) Except for slow decoding, these difficulties tend to be characteristic of disabled readers at beginning, rather than later, stages of reading.

In addition, disabled readers manifest problems with some skills involving top-down processing, particularly reading comprehension and knowledge about the orthographic structure of words. (See Table 1.1.) These higher level difficulties are typical of the older disabled reader. There is little evidence that disabled readers start out with top-down processing problems; it seems more likely that their difficulties in these areas are related to the earlier bottom-up processing deficits. This contention is supported by the observation that disabled readers' top-down processing abilities in a number of areas central to reading, such as the organization of long-term memory, general language comprehension, and the ability to use context to speed word recognition, are apparently intact. (However, the preceding analysis probably does not hold true for youngsters with more general types of language difficulties, such as those studied by Ceci and by Denckla and Rudel.)

AN INFORMATION-PROCESSING FRAMEWORK FOR UNDERSTANDING READING DISABILITY

Our plan for this final section of the chapter is to present an information-processing framework and then to discuss a few practical implications of the framework for teachers of disabled readers. Before we begin, however, it is appropriate to again acknowledge several antecedents of our framework. Our view of reading, especially on the role of automatization in reading, has been heavily influenced by the model of LaBerge and Samuels (1974). We have also been influenced by interactive–compensatory models of reading (Perfetti & Roth, 1980; Stanovich, 1980), which hold that intact higher level processes can compensate for deficient lower level ones, and vice versa. Finally, our thinking in this particular area has been shaped by our own componential view of intelligence (Sternberg, 1985).

The Framework

In our view, reading disability must be conceptualized in terms of at least two stages. The earlier stage is characterized by bottom-up kinds of problems in learning to read individual words; the later stage, by problems with top-down kinds of reading skills, such as comprehension. However, we maintain that the poor performance of disabled readers in these top-down areas is not attributable to a true top-down processing deficit. Instead, the primary reading deficit sustained by disabled readers, and one source of their deficits in the second stage of the framework, is their difficulty in learning to decode or recognize single words. (Recall our earlier assertion that bottom-up deficits may interfere with top-down processing.) Reading disability is thus a bottom-up type of disorder. One could imagine other patterns of reading difficulties, such as comprehension deficits in the absence of a history of decoding problems, but these patterns are not characteristic of reading-disabled children.

Word recognition and decoding skills are the primary focus of reading instruction in the early grades. Two possible precursors of reading failure at this level have been identified. These are lack of phonemic or syllabic awareness, and, somewhat less reliably, faulty use of phonetic coding in short-term memory. It is not difficult to see how each of these precursors might be causally related to the disability. For instance, a child with poor awareness of the sound structure of speech could be expected to have trouble mapping visual symbols (letters) to their spoken word equivalents, which is precisely what is required by decoding. The tendency of schools to use a sight–word method to teach reading would exacerbate the problem. Because the use of a phonetic code is a particularly efficient way to maintain information in short-term memory, difficulty establishing such a code could also impede a child's efforts to learn to read individual words. In addition, given the heterogeneous nature of the reading disability population, it is quite likely that other precursors of the condition exist. Probably not all of these precursors are present in all children with reading disability. However, for the present, the bulk of the evidence points toward the importance of phonemic awareness and, to a lesser degree, phonetic coding.

At the beginning of this section, we asserted that in the initial stage, reading disability is characterized by bottom-up kinds of problems in learning to read individual words, but that in the later stage, problems with top-down kinds of reading skills, such as comprehension, are common. In other words, disabled readers have trouble both "learning to read" and "reading to learn" (Chall, 1979). Thus far our framework has dealt with the learning-to-read stage typical of children functioning at a first- or second-grade level in reading (of course, the disabled child at this level may be chronologically much older). But what of the reading-to-learn stage, when children must apply the basic mechanics of reading to acquire information? This stage is typical of children functioning at a third- or fourth-grade level and higher. As we have seen, the difficulties of disabled readers do not seem to vanish magically with the acquisition of basic word recognition and decoding skills. Although earlier difficulties with phonemic awareness and use of a phonetic code in short-term memory seem to ameliorate after a second- or third-grade reading level has been attained, other difficulties arise to take their place. We turn now to a consideration of these higher level reading deficits.

We propose two main sources for these difficulties with more advanced reading skills, neither of which involves a true top-down processing deficit. The first source is simply the original constellation of bottom-up deficits (difficulties with decoding words, using a phonetic code in short-term memory, and becoming aware of the sound structure of speech), which drag a host of secondary problems in their wake. For instance, coding problems in STM could directly affect comprehension through the "bottleneck" mechanism proposed by Perfetti and discussed earlier in this chapter. Early reading failure would also deprive the child of the opportunity to learn various comprehension and memory strategies, which normal children appear to induce as they acquire skill in reading. In addition, reading-disabled children would lack knowledge about the orthographic structure of words, not because of a general problem with learning rules, but because they could not decode a sufficient number of words to make inferences about orthographic structure, or because they had not acquired enough skill to have learned to attend to orthographic features. Of course, these secondary deficits would create problems of their own, in a mushrooming of academic failure.

We think the preceding explanation sufficient to account partially, but not wholly, for the higher level reading problems of disabled readers. A second factor involves the failure of these youngsters to automatize the reading of individual words. Even when these children can decode accurately, they do not decode as effortlessly or as rapidly as normal readers. Thus, they are forced to divert to decoding mental resources that could otherwise be allocated to comprehension. They may also use intact higher level processes to compensate for inefficient decoding, (e.g., using context to speed word recognition), but this mode of compensation also consumes mental resources at the expense of comprehension, metacomprehension, and other higher level skills. The failure to automatize is not a general one, however. In some areas involving automatic processes, such as rapid naming of colors, pictures, and digits, disabled readers appear to function as well as normals. Instead, the automatization failure appears to be associated specifically with the reading of words.

Some investigators have argued that both the orthography (i.e., the writing system used in a language) and the phonetic regularity of a language play a crucial role in the genesis of reading disability. These investigators maintain that reading disability is very infrequent in countries with more phonetic languages than English, such as Spanish, or in languages in which the written symbols stand for syllables rather than sounds, such as Japanese. Although we agree with these researchers that language and orthography play an important role in reading disability, we think that this role has less to do with the frequency of the disorder than with its essential character. In other words, the underlying information-processing deficits that are problematic will vary depending on the language and orthography. Therefore, in some languages, "reading disability"—depending on how one defines it—might well involve more general cognitive deficits, including some true top-down processing deficits (e.g., Stevenson et al., 1982). In this sense, the analysis we have given here is quite specific to English and similar languages.

Our framework differs in varying ways and to varying degrees from the views of other researchers interested in reading disability. It is most different from a view such as Wolford's, which is not only a strongly top-down view of reading disability but which maintains that processing is deficient in the nonverbal as well as the verbal domain. Another essentially top-down view differing from our own is that of Ceci. On the other hand, the first stage of our framework is relatively compatible with the view associated with the Haskins Laboratories group of investigators, such as Liberman, Mann, and Shankweiler, although the second stage of the framework, with its emphasis on the role of automatization, is one feature which distinguishes our view from theirs. However, the emphasis on automatization is consistent with the view of LaBerge and Samuels (1974). A number of other researchers whose work we have reviewed here, such as Worden and Morrison, have done research that is highly relevant to specific parts of the framework. We differ from these researchers primarily in having chosen to take a broader look at reading disability—a breadth that necessarily comes at the expense of some detail—and in emphasizing the role of bottom-up deficits in creating the higher level difficulties of disabled readers. In summary, then, the features that tend to distinguish our framework from the views of other investigators are its relatively broad scope, the inclusion of a second stage involving automatization failure, and the emphasis on the bottom-up nature of reading disability.

Practical Implications of the Framework

The preceding discussion answered the theoretical questions raised at the beginning of this chapter. Specifically, we contend that disabled readers' difficulties with reading comprehension and other higher level reading skills are a result of failure to automatize the reading of individual words, as well as a result of the original bottom-up processing deficits, namely, poor word decoding, lack of awareness of the sound structure of speech, and perhaps faulty phonetic coding in short-term memory. As we do not think that reading disability is related to a top-down or more general cognitive deficit, at least not for English speakers and readers, we view it as sharply distinct from mental retardation. Our own work (Spear & Sternberg, in preparation) is highly consistent with the framework. We have found that 10-to-12-year-old disabled readers differ from normal readers on measures of their ability to read single words but not on measures of perceptual speed, nonverbal analogical reasoning, or their ability to use context to determine the meanings of unfamiliar words. However, what of the practical implications of the framework? What does it suggest for those engaged in providing instruction to disabled readers?

Though not a cure-all, a phonic approach to reading still seems a logical course for the teacher to take in beginning reading instruction. This approach is desirable because it makes explicit the relationship between speech sounds and written words, an understanding of which is crucial to reading an alphabetic orthography, and it teaches the various sound–symbol relationships directly. Most phonic programs also include rules for decoding, and learning these does not appear to be a problem for disabled readers provided that the rules are directly taught. Activities promoting awareness of spoken language are also advisable, especially with young children. Games involving rhyming and alliteraton, counting the number of syllables in a spoken word, and blending sounds together, are all examples of these kinds of activities; many others can be found in Engelmann (1969). In addition, because spoken language and general language comprehension are areas of strength for disabled readers, the use of supplementary language experience activities often works well. (In "language experience," the child dictates stories for the teacher to write, then learns the words in his story through repeated tracing and saying of the word; see Fernald, 1943, for a classic description of the method.)

Once the child has learned to decode accurately, automatic and rapid decoding must be developed. LaBerge and Samuels (1974) have suggested repeated drill and practice to promote automatization. We have also used timed speed drills of written words, similar to the kinds of drills teachers frequently use to help children memorize multiplication and division tables. Certainly these techniques have reasonable face validity. Whether they actually work, however, and to what degree, is still uncertain.

Finally, teachers must be aware of the need to fill in the gaps in knowledge that may be created by a reading disability; that is, instruction must address the secondary deficits, particularly in the case of the older disabled child. Directly teaching study skills, such as how to take notes, and reading comprehension strategies, such as paying close attention to chapter and section headings, would be some examples. As we have indicated, the evidence regarding strategy training is sparse, and what exists often suggests no unique benefits of training to disabled readers. However, what we advocate are commonsense measures—teaching skills that disabled readers would have acquired in the classroom, were they not hampered by poor word decoding. Although these measures cannot be expected to cure a reading disability, they should help to improve a child's performance in some specific problem areas.

The framework that we have proposed here suggests reasons for cautious optimism on the part of practitioners working with disabled readers. On the one hand, it is clear that reading disability poses a complex configuration of problems that cannot be ameliorated with one simple procedure. We are uncertain how to remediate some of the most crucial problems, such as automatization failure, and even uncertain whether these problems can be remediated at all. On the other hand, disabled readers do learn a great deal, in spite of our mistakes. They do not appear to sustain the kinds of higher level cognitive deficits that would affect their ability to grasp ideas or to see relationships and that would impair their overall academic functioning in an even more pervasive way. The more we researchers learn about this complicated and baffling disorder, the better we understand it, the more optimistic practitioners can be about finding the best methods for helping disabled readers.

ACKNOWLEDGMENTS

We thank the many researchers who provided us with reprints and copies of unpublished manuscripts, especially Steve Ceci, Scott Paris, Charles Perfetti, Keith Stanovich, George Wolford, and Patricia Worden.

REFERENCES

Ackerman, P., & Dykman, R. A. (1982). Automatic and effortful information-processing deficits in children with learning and attention disorders. *Topics in Learning and Learning Disabilities, 2,* 12–22.

Alegria, J., Pignot, E., & Morais, J. (1982). Phonetic analysis of speech and memory codes in beginning readers. *Memory and Cognition, 10,* 451–456.

Allington, R. L., & Strange, M. (1977). Effects of grapheme substitutions in connected text upon reading behaviors. *Visible Language, 11,* 285–289.

Baron, J., & Strawson, C. (1976). Use of orthographic and word-specific knowledge in reading words aloud. *Journal of Experimental Psychology: Human Perception and Performance, 2,* 386–393.

Barron, R. W. (1978). Access to the meanings of printed words: Some implications for reading and learning to read. In F. Murray (Ed.), *The recognition of words: IRA series on the development of the reading process.* Newark, DE: International Reading Association.

Bauer, R. H. (1979). Memory, acquisition, and category clustering in learning disabled children. *Journal of Experimental Child Psychology, 27,* 365–383.

Bauer, R. H. (1982). Information processing as a way of diagnosing and understanding learning disabilities. *Topics in Learning and Learning Disabilities, 2,* 33–45.

Berger, N. S., & Perfetti, C. A. (1977). Reading skill and memory for spoken and written discourse. *Journal of Reading Behavior, IX,* 7–16.

Beverly, S. E., & Perfetti, C. A. (1982, April). *Phonemic and semantic processes of skilled and less skilled beginning readers.* Paper presented at the annual meeting of the American Educational Research Association, New York.

Bradley, L., & Bryant, P. E. (1978). Difficulties in auditory organization as a possible cause of reading backwardness. *Nature, 271,* 746–747.

Bransford, J. D., Stein, B. S., & Vye, N. J. (1982). Helping students learn how to learn from written texts. In M. Singer (Ed.), *Competent reader, disabled reader: Research and application.* Hillsdale, NJ: Lawrence Erlbaum Associates.

Byrne, B., & Shea, P. (1979). Semantic and phonetic memory codes in beginning readers. *Memory and Cognition, 7,* 333–338.

Calfee, R. C., Chapman, R., & Venezky, R. L. (1972). How a child needs to think to learn to read. In L. W. Gregg (Ed.), *Cognition and learning in memory.* New York: Wiley.

Calfee, R. C., Lindamood, P., & Lindamood, C. (1973). Acoustic phonetic skills and reading: Kindergarten through twelfth grade. *Journal of Educational Psychology, 64,* 293–298.

Ceci, S. J. (1982). Extracting meaning from stimuli: Automatic and purposive processing characteristics of the language-based learning disabled. *Topics in Learning and Learning Disabilities, 2,* 46–53.

Ceci, S. J. (1983). An investigation of the semantic processing characteristics of normal and language/learning disabled children. *Developmental Psychology, 19,* 427–439.

Ceci, S. J. (1985). *A developmental study of learning disabilities and memory.* Unpublished manuscript.

Chall, J. S. (1979). The great debate: Ten years later, with a modest proposal for reading stages. In L. B. Resnick & P. L. Weaver (Eds.), *Theory and practice of early reading, 1.* Hillsdale, NJ: Lawrence Erlbaum Associates.

Cromer, W. (1970). The difference model: A new explanation for some reading difficulties. *Journal of Educational Psychology, 61,* 471–483.

Crowder, R. G. (1982). *The psychology of reading.* New York: Oxford University Press.

Dallago, M. L. P., & Moely, B. E. (1980). Free recall in boys of normal and poor reading levels as a function of task manipulations. *Journal of Experimental Child Psychology, 30,* 62–78.

Denckla, M. P., & Rudel, R. (1976). Rapid automatized naming: Dyslexia differentiated from other learning disabilities. *Neuropsychologia, 14,* 471–479.

Durkin, D. (1979). What classroom observations reveal about reading comprehension instruction. *Reading Research Quarterly, (XIV)4,* 481–533.

Engelmann, S. (1969). *Preventing failure in the primary grades.* Chicago: Science Research Associates.

Fernald, G. (1943). *Remedial techniques in basic school subjects.* New York: McGraw–Hill.

Firth, I. (1972). *Components of reading disability.* Unpublished doctoral dissertation, University of New South Wales.

Forrest, D. L., & Waller, T. G. (1979, April). *Cognitive and metacognitive aspects of reading.* Paper presented at the biennial meeting of the Society for Research in Child Development, San Francisco.

Fox, B., & Routh, D. K. (1975). Analyzing spoken language into words, syllables, and phonemes: A developmental study. *Journal of Psycholinguistic Research, 4,* 331–342.

Garner, R., & Reis, R. (1981). Monitoring and resolving comprehension obstacles: An investigation of spontaneous text lookbacks among upper-grade good and poor comprehenders. *Reading Research Quarterly, 16,* 569–582.

Goldman, S. R., Hogaboam, T. W., Bell, L. C., & Perfetti, C. A. (1980). Short-term retention of discourse during reading. *Journal of Educational Psychology, 72,* 647–655.

Golinkoff, R. (1978). Phonemic awareness skills and reading achievement. In F. B. Murray & J. J. Pikulski (Eds.), *The acquisition of reading: Cognitive, linguistic, and perceptual prerequisites*. Baltimore: University Park Press.

Goodman, K. S. (1976). Reading: A psycholinguistic guessing game. In H. Singer & R. Ruddell (Eds.), *Theoretical models and processes of reading*. Newark, DE: International Reading Association.

Hall, J. W., & Humphreys, M. S. (1982). Research on specific learning disabilities: Deficits and remediation. *Topics in Learning and Learning Disabilities, 2*, 68–78.

Hall, J. W., Wilson, K. P., Humphreys, M. S., Tinzmann, M. B., & Bowyer, P. M. (1983). Phonemic-similarity effects in good vs. poor readers. *Memory and Cognition, 11*, 520–527.

Hammill, D. D. (1972). Training visual perceptual processes. *Journal of Learning Disabilities, 5*, 35–46.

Hansen, C. L. (1978). Story retelling used with average and learning disabled readers as a measure of reading comprehension. *Learning Disability Quarterly, 1*, 62–69.

Helfgott, J. (1976). Phonemic segmentation and blending skills of kindergarten children: Implications for beginning reading acquisition. *Contemporary Educational Psychology, 1*, 157–169.

Hogaboam, T. W., & Perfetti, C. A. (1978). Reading skill and the role of verbal experience in decoding. *Journal of Educational Psychology, 70*, 717–729.

Holmes, D. R., & McKeever, W. F. (1979). Material-specific serial memory deficit in adolescent dyslexics. *Cortex, 15*, 51–62.

Johnson, D. J., & Myklebust, H. R. (1967). *Learning disabilities: Educational principles and practices*. New York: Grune & Stratton.

Katz, R. B., Shankweiler, D., & Liberman, I. Y. (1981). Memory for item order and phonetic recoding in the beginning reader. *Journal of Experimental Child Psychology, 32*, 474–484.

Keogh, B. K., Major, S. M., Omori, H., Gandara, P., & Reid, H. P. (1980). Proposed markers in learning disabilities research. *Journal of Abnormal Child Psychology, 8*, 21–31.

Kirk, S. A. (1962). *Educating exceptional children*. Boston: Houghton–Mifflin.

LaBerge, D., & Samuels, S. J. (1974). Toward a theory of automatic information processing in reading. *Cognitive Psychology, 6*, 293–323.

Levin, J. R. (1973). Inducing comprehension in poor readers: A test of a recent model. *Journal of Educational Psychology, 65*, 19–24.

Liberman, I. Y., Mann, V. A., Shankweiler, D., & Werfelman, M. (1983). Children's memory for recurring linguistic and nonlinguistic material in relation to reading ability. *Cortex, 20*, 50–61.

Liberman, I. Y., & Shankweiler, D. (1978). Speech, the alphabet and teaching to read. In L. Resnick & P. Weaver (Eds.), *Theory and practice of early reading*. New York: Wiley.

Liberman, I. Y., Shankweiler, D., Fischer, F. W., & Carter, B. (1974). Explicit syllable and phoneme segmentation in the young child. *Journal of Experimental Child Psychology, 18*, 201–212.

Litcher, J. H., & Roberge, L. P. (1979). First-grade intervention for reading achievement of high-risk children. *Bulletin of the Orton Society, 29*, 238–244.

Mandler, J. M., & Johnson, N. S. (1977). Remembrance of things parsed: Story structure and recall. *Cognitive Psychology, 9*, 111–151.

Manis, F. R. (1981). *Rule knowledge and the acquisition of word identification skills in normal and disabled readers*. Unpublished doctoral dissertation, University of Minnesota.

Mann, V. A., & Liberman, I. Y. (1982). *Phonological awareness and verbal short-term memory: Can they presage early reading problems?* (Status Report on Speech Research SR-70). New Haven, CT: Haskins Laboratories.

Mann, V. A., Liberman, I. Y., & Shankweiler, D. (1980). Children's memory for sentences and word strings in relation to reading ability. *Memory and Cognition, 8*, 329–335.

McCormick, C., & Samuels, S. J. (1979). Word recognition by second graders: The unit of perception and interrelationships among accuracy, laatency, and comprehension. *Journal of Reading Behavior, 11,* 107–118.

Morais, J., Carey, L., Alegria, J., & Bertelson, P. (1979). Does awareness of speech as a sequence of phones arise spontaneously? *Cognition, 7,* 323–331.

Morrison, F. J., Giordani, B., & Nagy, J. (1977). Reading disabilities: An information-processing analysis. *Science, 196,* 77–79.

Morrison, F. J., & Manis, F. R. (1982). Cognitive processes and reading disability: A critique aand proposal. In C. J. Brainerd & M. Pressley (Eds.), *Verbal processes in children.* New York: Springer-Verlag.

Newcomer, P. (1975). The ITPA and academic achievement. *Academic Therapy Quarterly, 10,* 401–406.

Oaken, R., Wiener, M., & Cromer, W. (1971). Identification, organization, and reading comprehension for good and poor readers. *Journal of Educational Psychology, 62,* 71–78.

Orton, S. T. (1937). *Reading, writing, and speech problems in children.* New York: Norton.

Paris, S. G., & Lindauer, B. K. (1982). The development of cognitive skills during childhood. In B. W. Wolman (Ed.), *Handbook of developmental psychology.* Englewood Cliffs, NJ: Prentice–Hall.

Pearson, P. D., & Camperell, K. (1981). Comprehension of text structures. In J. T. Guthrie (Ed.), *Comprehension and teaching.* Newark, DE: International Reading Association.

Perfetti, C. A. (1982). Discourse context, word identification and reading ability. In J. F. LeNy & W. Kintsch (Eds.), *Language and comprehension.* Amsterdam: North–Holland.

Perfetti, C. A., Beck, I., & Hughes, C. (1981, April). *Phonemic knowledge and learning to read.* Paper presented at SRCD Symposium, Boston.

Perfetti, C. A., Finger, E., & Hogaboam, T. W. (1978). Sources of vocalization latency differences between skilled and less-skilled readers. *Journal of Educational Psychology, 70,* 730–739.

Perfetti, C. A., & Goldman, S. R. (1976). Discourse memory and reading comprehension skill. *Journal of Verbal Learning and Verbal Behavior, 14,* 33–42.

Perfetti, C. A., & Hogaboam, T. (1975). The relationship between single word decoding and reading comprehension skill. *Journal of Educational Psychology, 67,* 461–469.

Perfetti, C. A., & Lesgold, A. M. (1977). Discourse comprehension and sources of individual differences. In M. Just & P. Carpenter (Eds.), *Cognitive processes in comprehension.* Hillsdale, NJ: Lawrence Erlbaum Associates.

Perfetti, C. A., & Roth, S. (1980). Some of the interactive processes in reading and their role in reading skill. In A. Lesgold & C. Perfetti (Eds.), *Interactive processes in reading.* Hillsdale, NJ: Lawrence Erlbaum Associates.

Rosner, J., & Simon, D. P. (1971). The auditory analysis test: An initial report. *Journal of Learning Disabilities, 4,* 40–48.

Rozin, P., & Gleitman, L. R. (1977). The structure and acquisition of reading: The reading process and the acquisition of the alphabetic principle. In A. S. Reber & D. L. Scarborough (Eds.), *Toward a psychology of reading: The proceedings of the CUNY conferences* (pp. 113–133). New York: Wiley.

Samuels, S. J., & LaBerge, D. (1983). A theory of automaticity in reading: Looking back: A retrospective analysis of the LaBerge–Samuels reading model. In L. M. Gentile, M. L. Kamil, & J. S. Blanchard (Eds.), *Reading research revisited.* Columbus, OH: Merrill.

Savin, H. B. (1972). What the child knows about speech when he starts to learn to read. In J. Kavanagh & I. Mattingly (Eds.), *Language by ear and by eye.* Cambridge: MIT Press.

Shankweiler, D., & Liberman, I. Y. (1972). Misreading: A search for causes. In J. Kavanagh & I. Mattingly (Eds.), *Language by ear and by eye.* Cambridge: MIT Press.

Shankweiler, D., Liberman, I. Y., Mark, L. S., Fowler, C. A., & Fischer, F. W. (1979). The speech code and learning to read. *Journal of Experimental Psychology: Human Learning and Memory, 5,* 531–545.

Simpson, G. B., & Lorsbach, T. C. (1983). The development of automatic and conscious components of contextual facilitation. *Child Development, 54,* 760–772.

Smead, V. S. (1977). Ability training and task analysis in diagnostic–prescriptive teaching. *Journal of Special Education, 11,* 114–125.

Smiley, S. S., Oakley, D. D., Worthen, D., Campione, J. C., & Brown, A. L. (1977). Recall of thematically relevant material by adolescent good and poor readers as a function of written versus oral presentation. *Journal of Educational Psychology, 69,* 381–389.

Smith, F. (1973). *Psycholinguistics and reading.* New York: Holt, Rinehart, & Winston.

Spear, L. C., & Sternberg, R. J. (in preparation). *Information-processing abilities of disabled and nondisabled readers.*

Spring, C. (1976). Encoding speed and memory span in dyslexic children. *Journal of Special Education, 10,* 35–40.

Spring, C., & Capps, C. (1974). Encoding speed, rehearsal, and probed recall of dyslexic boys. *Journal of Educational Psychology, 66,* 780–786.

Stanovich, K. E. (1980). Toward an interactive–compensatory model of individual differences in the development of reading fluency. *Reading Research Quarterly, 1,* 32–71.

Stanovich, K. E. (1981). Relationships between word decoding speed, general name-retrieval ability, and reading progress in first-grade children. *Journal of Educational Psychology, 73,* 809–815.

Stanovich, K. E. (1982). Individual differences in the cognitive processes of reading: Word decoding. *Journal of Learning Disabilities, 15,* 485–493.

Stanovich, K. E., & West, R. F. (1979). Mechanisms of sentence context effects in reading: Automatic activation and conscious attention. *Memory and Cognition, 7,* 77–85.

Sternberg, R. J. (1985). *Beyond IQ: A triarchic theory of human intelligence.* New York: Cambridge University Press.

Sternberg, R. J., & Powell, J. S. (1983). Comprehending verbal comprehension. *American Psychologist, 38,* 878–893.

Sternberg, R. J., & Wagner, R. K. (1982). Automatization failure in learning disabilities. *Topics in Learning and Learning Disabilities, 2,* 1–11.

Stevenson, H. W., Stigler, J. W., Lucker, G. W., Lee, S., Hsu, C., & Kitamura, S. (1982). Reading disabilities: The case of Chinese, Japanese, and English. *Child Development, 53,* 1164–1181.

Taylor, B. M., & Samuels, S. J. (1983). Children's use of text structure in the recall of expository material. *American Educational Research Journal, 20,* 517–528.

Taylor, M. B., & Williams, J. P. (1983). Comprehension of learning disabled readers: Task and text variations. *Journal of Educational Psychology, 75,* 584–601.

Torgesen, J. K. (1977). Memorization processes in reading-disabled children. *Journal of Educational Psychology, 79,* 571–578.

Torgesen, J. K., & Goldman, T. (1977). Verbal rehearsal and short-term memory in reading-disabled children. *Child Development, 48,* 56–60.

Torgesen, J. K., & Houck, D. G. (1980). Processing deficiencies in children who perform poorly on the digit span test. *Journal of Educational Psychology, 72,* 141–160.

Vellutino, F. R. (1979). *Dyslexia: Theory and research.* Cambridge, MA: MIT Press.

Vellutino, F. R., Steger, J. A., Kaman, M., & DeSetto, L. (1975). Visual form perception in deficient and normal readers as a function of age and orthographic linguistic familiarity. *Cortex, 11,* 22–30.

Weber, R. M. (1970). First graders' use of grammatical context in reading. In H. Levin & Williams (Eds.), *Basic studies in reading.* New York: Basic Books.

Williams, J. P. (1980). Teaching decoding with an emphasis on phoneme analysis and phoneme blending. *Journal of Educational Psychology, 72,* 1–15.

Wolford, G., & Fowler, C. A. (1983). The perception and use of information in good and poor readers. In T. Tighe & B. Shepp (Eds.), *Perception, cognition, and development.* Hillsdale, NJ: Lawrence Erlbaum Associates.

Wong, B. Y. L. (1979). Increasing retention of main ideas through questioning strategies. *Learning Disability Quarterly, 2,* 42–47.

Wong, B. Y. L. (1982). Strategic behaviors in selecting retrieval cues in gifted, normal achieving and learning disabled children. *Journal of Learning Disabilities, 15,* 33–37.

Worden, P. E. (1983). Memory strategy instruction with the learning disabled. In M. Pressley & J. R. Levin (Eds.), *Cognitive strategies: Developmental, educational, and treatment-related issues,* New York: Springer–Verlag.

Worden, P. E., Malmgren, I., & Gabourie, P. (1982). Memory for stories in learning disabled adults. *Journal of Learning Disabilities, 15,* 145–152.

Worden, P. E., & Nakamura, G. V. (1982). Story comprehension and recall in learning-disabled vs. normal college students. *Journal of Educational Psychology, 74,* 633–641.

2 The Nature of Reading Disability: Toward an Integrative Framework

Frederick J. Morrison
University of Alberta

For almost a century, scientists have labored to comprehend the riddle of reading disability. Recent years have witnessed solid progress in discriminating disabled readers from other poor readers and learners (Rutter & Yule, 1975), in isolating the nature of their reading problems (Manis & Morrison, 1984; Vellutino, 1979; see also Spear & Sternberg, this volume) and in critically examining the cognitive bases of the disorder (Morrison & Manis, 1982; Vellutino, 1979). Advances on all these fronts have provided not only a firmer empirical base for investigating reading disability, but also a more comprehensive and integrative framework for understanding the nature of this puzzling disorder.

At this juncture, further progress in understanding reading disability requires integration of information from a broad spectrum of disciplines. This chapter represents an attempt to provide a coherent explanation of the nature of reading disability that incorporates a broad range of psychological, educational, medical, and anthropological data about disabled readers. The chapter begins with some guiding assumptions that have shaped and directed our efforts. Next, a description is provided of the major data that need to be included in an adequate explanation of the disorder. Subsequently we present our integrative conceptualization of the nature of reading disability, including some recent empirical tests of our major hypotheses. The chapter concludes with some thoughts about future work in the area.

GUIDING ASSUMPTIONS

Although some uniformity in perspective has been achieved among scientists studying reading disability, surprising discrepancies still exist in fundamental aspects of research on the problem. We focus on two areas, both to make clear our own working definitions and assumptions and to highlight the need for greater agreement on some of these issues.

Who Is a Reading-Disabled Child?

There has existed for some time a standard set of descriptors and exclusionary criteria for who is and is not a reading-disabled child (see e.g., Rourke, 1975). These characteristics have served in essence as a working definition for scientists in the field. In practice, however, selection of subjects for research has included a rather broad spectrum of poor readers, some if not most of whom are probably not "specifically reading disabled." Two areas are of particular importance. First is the *range of IQ scores* included in the disabled sample. Although the majority of recent work has selected disabled readers with a cut-off IQ score of 85 or 90, one recent study included children with IQs of 80 (Siegel & Ryan, 1984). A separate investigation regarded as "normal" any poor reader with an IQ score of 70 or above, presumably because they could not be called "retarded" (Stevenson, Stigler, Lucker, Lee, Hsu, & Kitamura, 1982). Nevertheless, recent research (Rutter & Yale, 1975) has clearly revealed major differences between groups or poor readers above and below the IQ range of 85–90. The groups manifested notable differences in sex ratios, in neurological status, and in patterns of achievement in reading versus mathematics. Hence, in our opinion, it is imperative in research on specific reading disability that a relatively conservative IQ cut-off be employed. In our own research (including that presented here) we have attempted whenever possible to select disabled readers with a full-scale IQ score of *at least 90*. Such a selection procedure, we feel, minimizes the risk of including nondisabled readers in the research sample.

The second issue focuses on the status of achievement in other academic areas, specifically *mathematics achievement*. Until very recently, almost no research investigations of specific reading disability included in their selection criteria that the poor readers be achieving at a higher (perhaps even grade) level in mathematics. Hence truly disabled readers have been grouped together with normal IQ but generally underachieving children. In a recent study Hall, Wilson, Humphreys, Tinzmann, & Bowyer (1983) demonstrated different patterns of memory performance between these two groups. Notwithstanding some important statistical problems that arise in this area (most critically that of regression to the mean, which is not insurmountable), in our view mathematics achievement should be considered in selecting subjects for a reading-disabled sample. In our most recent work, we have been comparing performance of the two groups of poor readers and our preliminary results reveal differences between the groups in both level and pattern of cognitive and reading performance. Typically, we include in our reading-disabled sample children who are at least 1 year ahead in mathematics achievement. In our general underachiever group we include children whose math–reading achievement levels differ by less than 1 year *and* who have demonstrated that small degree of discrepancy throughout elementary school. If, for example, a child had a strong math–reading discrepancy in Grade 4 that had disappeared by Grade 6, he would be considered for the reading-disabled sample.

The Question of Heterogeneity

Perhaps the single most confused issue in theory and practice is whether reading disability constitutes a heterogeneous group of underlying cognitive disorders. The vast majority of educators and practitioners take heterogeneity for granted, accepting the view that different disabled readers suffer from fundamentally different cognitive problems: Some have memory deficits, others have language deficits, whereas still others have serial-ordering problems. Some preliminary investigations claimed to uncover different subtypes of disabled readers (Boder, 1973; Doehring, Trites, Patel, & Fiedorowicz, 1981; Mattis, French, & Rapin, 1975; Rourke, 1978), though disappointingly little communality emerged from these efforts. In addition, serious logical and methodological flaws were noted (see Vellutino, 1979).

In contrast, the majority of recent cognitive research in the area has focused on disabled readers as a whole, comparing their performance with chronological age- and sometimes reading age-matched normal readers on a broad range of cognitive and reading tasks (see Morrison & Manis, 1982). In general, a reasonably consistent pattern of findings has emerged from these group comparisons. The clear implication of obtaining these kinds of reliable results is that reading-disabled children constitute an identifiable and relatively homogeneous group whose performance as a group can be reliably discriminated from comparable normal readers.

Clearly the issue of heterogeneity is not settled. Important logical and methodological problems require careful attention (see Morrison, 1986, for consideration of some issues). In our own research, we have been proceeding on the more parsimonious assumption that reading disability constitutes a relatively homogeneous disorder whose general nature can be discerned by examining disabled readers as a whole.

PIECES IN THE COGNITIVE PUZZLE

Having fleshed out some of the assumptions guiding our recent work, it is useful here to describe the data or phenomena that we feel need to be included in an adequate account of reading disability. We do so for two reasons. First such a description will reinforce our call for more integrative theoretical efforts. Second, however, beyond differences in working definitions like those elucidated earlier, researchers have not agreed on what constitutes the important phenomena to be explained in understanding reading disability. It is our view that recent empirical work has resulted in some degree of consensus on the pieces of the puzzle that require inclusion in a final account of the disorder (see also Spear & Sternberg, this volume).

General Findings

In this group are included such straightforward issues as the specificity of the disorder, the severity of the disorder, and the math–reading discrepancy (as a separate but related issue to specificity). First, in general terms, understanding reading disability requires consideration of why the problem is limited primarily (if not exclusively) to reading activity. Such consideration does not deny that other areas of deficit exist, especially if their are associated (as cause, effect, or correlate) of the reading disorder (see Morrison, 1984, for further discussion). Nevertheless, the question of why reading is affected and not math, and not general intellectual status must be addressed. For those who consider such a degree of specificity to be spurious or deceptive, alternative explanations must be offered.

Second an adequate account must explain how a child with a normal IQ could suffer so severe a problem as do many disabled readers. To be in Grade 7 or 8 and reading at a Grade-2 level constitutes a datum of importance, in our view. Equally crucial are the gradations in severity observed among age-matched disabled readers.

Finally, the reading–math discrepancy deserves a central place in explanatory efforts. Though clearly part of the "specificity" problem, the reading–math discrepancy holds a special place for theories of the underlying cognitive disorder. Elucidation of the important psychological or processing differences between reading and mathematics performance or acquisition may hold a key to unlocking the cognitive mystery.

Cognitive Abilities

Elementary Information Processes

Until recently, the dominant focus in work on reading disability has been on basic cognitive operations. Reading-disabled children were generally conceived to suffer a deficit in the execution of one or more elementary processes involved in perceiving, remembering, or attending to information. Perhaps the most significant progress in the past decade has been the accumulation of solid evidence that disabled readers do not differ from normal readers in elementary information processing. Be it perceptual identification or discrimination, serial ordering, cross-modal integration, selective or sustained attention and basic short-term memory capacity, disabled readers have been shown to equal performance of normal readers (see Morrison & Manis, 1982, and Vellutino, 1979, for review).

One basic process, *phonetic coding*, did emerge initially as a possible problem for disabled readers. A series of studies by Liberman, Shankweiler, and their colleagues (Mann, Liberman, & Shankweiler, 1980; Shankweiler, Liberman, Mark, Fowler, & Fischer, 1979) as well as others (Byrne & Shea, 1979; Hogaboam & Perfetti, 1978) demonstrated that reading-disabled children did not code information into a phonetic or verbal form as accurately or as rapidly or as efficiently (if at all) as normal readers. Nonexistent, or poor, or slow phonetic coding could easily explain why disabled readers failed to learn to read. Despite its explanatory power and the weight of selected evidence, the case for phonetic coding has become weakened in recent years. A series of studies (Bisanz, Das, & Mancini, in press; Hall, Wilson, Humphreys, Tinzmann, & Bowyer, 1983; Morrison, Giordani, & Nagy, 1977; Wolford & Fowler, 1984) have documented that (a) disabled readers do phonetically code incoming information, though perhaps not as readily or rapidly as normal readers, and (b) differences between normal and disabled readers in rapid processing and memory tasks are not limited to those tasks requiring phonetic coding. For example Wolford and Fowler (1984) found that in a Sperling-type full-report task relying exclusively on visual processing operations, normal readers outperformed disabled readers. Additional evidence suggests that differences initially attributed to use of phonetic coding processes in normal readers and its absence in disabled readers stemmed from differences in use of a rapid serial-processing strategy (Schwantes, 1979), in rehearsal strategies (Bisanz et al., in press), in level-of-performance artifacts (Hall et al., 1983) or in strategic use of partial information (Wolford & Fowler, 1984).

Despite the contradictory evidence, aspects of phonetic coding do emerge as powerful discriminators of performance between normal and disabled readers and need to be included in a complete explanation. The great question at this point is whether the fundamental process of phonetic recoding of incoming information is the key deficit in reading disability or whether it reflects or is part of a deeper cognitive disorder.

It should be noted that reports of deficiencies in basic processes continue to appear. In particular, deficits have been observed in very basic visual processes, such as speed of processing (Di Lollo, Hanson, & McIntyre, 1983), duration of visual persistence for high spatial frequencies (Badcock & Lovegrove, 1981; Lovegrove, Heddle, & Slaghuis, 1980), and in oculomotor control of eye movements (Pavlidis, 1981, 1983). At least in the latter case, subsequent experiments (Olson, Kliegl, & Davidson, 1983; Stanley, Smith, & Howell, in press) failed to confirm the earlier work. Olson et al. (1983), found no differences between disabled and normal readers in number of saccades, percentage of regressions, or stability of fixations in a visual-tracking task. They suggested that procedural differences across studies in recruiting disabled readers may account for the discrepant findings. A similar explanation may apply to other recent research on basic visual-processing deficiencies. The most comprehensive interpretation of these new data is that a very small percentage of poor readers may exhibit unusual elementary-processing problems but that the vast majority of disabled readers do not differ from normal readers in elementary cognitive operations.

Aspects of Processing That Are Deficient

It is certainly the case that, even in simple information-processing tasks, disabled readers perform more poorly than normal readers (Bauer, 1979; Manis & Morrison, 1982; Morrison, Giordani, & Nagy, 1977; Schwantes, 1979; Wolford & Fowler, 1984). For example, in one study utilizing a partial-report procedure, Morrison et al. (1977) found that although no performance differences emerged in the 0–300 msec delay interval, normal readers outperformed disabled readers in the 450–2000 msec range. In addition, Bauer (1979) found a lack of reader group differences in the magnitude of the recency effect in free recall but a greater primacy effect for normal versus disabled readers.

In general, two major classes of processing differences have emerged: use of a serial-scanning routine in rapid visual-processing tasks and use of strategies to rehearse, maintain, and organize information in short-term memory.

Serial Scanning. Both developmental and reader group comparisons have confirmed that differences across age and reading ability in the longer delay intervals of the partial-report task stem from use by older children and better readers of a serial-scanning routine. For example, Schwantes (1979) demonstrated that older children and better readers switched to a left-to-right scanning strategy for a linear array of eight letters when the delay interval increased beyond the persistence of the visual sensory register. Although the cause of these differences has not been pinpointed, the similarity in performance between younger normal and older disabled readers suggests that skills like serial scanning are acquired and/or perfected during the elementary school years. It is also hard to escape the conclusion that such skills develop as a by-product of learning to read.

Short-term Memory Strategies. A similar pattern of developmental and reader ability differences has emerged from studies of short-term memory. A major factor underlying short-term memory capacity is the degree of organized cumulative rehearsal. A series of studies has shown that changes across age (Ornstein & Naus, 1978) and reading ability (Bauer, 1979) in memory capacity are a direct function of differences in organized rehearsal. As with serial scanning, parallel results for developmental and reader ability differences suggest that use of rehearsal strategies too is learned and/or facilitated during elementary school. Yet in the case of learning rehearsal skills, it is not as easy to view growth of mental rehearsal as a simple by-product of acquiring reading skills. Other factors like knowledge or metamemory probably play a role. Nevertheless most models of reading comprehension do postulate a short-term memory store in which information must be maintained and recycled for subsequent integration and semantic processing.

Language Processes

Beyond elementary deficits in phonetic coding, discussed earlier, some investigators have suggested that disabled readers may suffer a global pervasive problem in general language functioning (Siegel & Ryan, 1984; Vellutino & Scanlon, 1982). Whereas most authors concede that disabled readers do not manifest major deficits during elementary school when the reading disorder is diagnosed, they claim that (a) significant delays in language acquisition were manifest during preschool years, and (b) more subtle linguistic problems persist into the school years and influence aspects of reading acquisition, including word learning (see Vellutino & Scanlon, 1982, for more details).

Two linguistic processes have received most attention: phonemic awareness and syntactic development. Although problems in semantic development have occasionally been highlighted, deficiencies in this area have not been consistently observed (Siegel & Ryan, 1984; Spear & Sternberg, this volume). When uncovered, semantic problems appear to stem from more fundamental syntactic or phonological disorders (Vellutino & Scanlon, 1982).

Phonemic Awareness.   Some authors have suggested that one prerequisite to learning adequate decoding skills in English is the need to acquire an ability to analyze the phonemic structure of spoken words (Liberman, Shankweiler, Liberman, Fowler, & Fischer, 1977; Rozin & Gleitman, 1977). Although most 5-year-olds are able to make subtle phonological distinctions in speech perception and production (Gibson & Levin, 1975; Rozin & Gleitman, 1977), a more explicit level of awareness of phonemic structure may be necessary in order to map the alphabetic code onto the spoken language.

There is evidence that beginning readers experience some problems segmenting words into their constituent phonemes (Calfee, Chapman, & Venezky, 1972; Liberman, Shankweiler, Fischer, & Carter, 1974; Rosner & Simon, 1971). Moreover children with reading difficulties perform poorly on tests of speech segmentation. Rosner and Simon (1971) found that reading achievement was moderately correlated with performance on the Auditory Analysis Test, which requires children to pronounce words before and after a specific phoneme is deleted from them (e.g., *man* would be pronounced /an/ after the phoneme /m/

is deleted from it). Correlations were highest in the first few years of elementary school and attenuated somewhat by fifth and sixth grade. Liberman et al. (1977) found the ability of 5-year-olds to indicate the number of phonemic segments in a word by tapping on a table was a strong predictor of later scores on the Wide Range Achievement Test.

Clearly the correlation between reading achievement and phonemic analysis skills does not necessarily imply that difficulties in phonemic analysis are a major source of reading difficulties among disabled readers. One problem is that few studies of phonemic analysis report the IQ scores of subjects. Thus, it is unclear what proportion of the variance in phonemic analysis skills between good and poor readers is associated with IQ differences and what proportion with reading ability differences. Further the direction of causality between analysis and reading achievement cannot be ascertained. It is equally likely that learning to read is a prerequisite for the development of phonemic segmentation skills (Morrison & Manis, 1982). Children may be aided in their analysis of abstract phonemes by being exposed to concrete representations of those phonemes in print.

A recent study by Bradley and Bryant (1978) appears to satisfy both of these objections. They required normal and disabled readers to indicate which of four spoken words did not belong in a list (e.g., *weed, need, peel, deed*). Disabled readers performed more poorly on this task than normal readers. Of interest in this study was the fact that the normal reader group was 4 years younger than the disabled group but read at the same level. Hence, differences between the groups could not be attributed to greater reading experience on the part of normal readers. The findings revealed a specific deficit in phonemic analysis in the disabled readers. Similar conclusions have been drawn recently by Helfgott (1976) and Triemen and Baron (1980).

Nevertheless there is substantial evidence that exposure to written material and experience with reading significantly influence the growth of phonemic awareness and other linguistic skills (Ehri, in press). In one recent study (Morais, Carey, Alegria, & Bertelson, 1979), two groups within a backward peasant community in Portugal were compared on a phoneme awareness task. Though neither of the groups had learned to read as children, one group that had received literacy training as adults was much better at adding or deleting a phoneme from a spoken nonsense word.

Taken together, findings on phonemic awareness suggest that phonemic awareness may influence and be influenced by reading ability and experience. (Perfetti, Beck, & Hughes, 1981). Nevertheless, it is not easy to see how problems in the subtle discrimination of the phonemic segments of words could produce the severity of the disorder observed in most reading-disabled children. As noted earlier, the impact of early individual differences in phonemic awareness probably persists for only the earliest stages of reading acquisition (Rosner & Simon, 1971). Subsequent disorders appear to stem directly from lack of experience with written materials.

Notwithstanding the empirical and logical difficulties with the concept of phonemic awareness as a cause of reading disability, the failure of most disabled readers to acquire phonemic awareness skills has been amply documented and requires explanation.

Syntactic Development.   It has been suggested, most recently by Vellutino and Scanlon (1982), that early syntactic disorders could influence later reading performance, even acquisition of word-decoding skills. Some tentative findings have revealed subtle syntactic deficits in disabled readers (see Morrison & Manis, 1982, and Vellutino & Scanlon, 1982, for reviews).

In one study, Fry, Johnson, and Muehl (1970) required 7- and 8-year-old normal and poor readers to tell a story about each of 20 pictures. The syntactic structure of normal readers' productions was found to be more flexible and more complex than that of poor readers. Also normal readers made greater use of clauses to elaborate the meaning of subjects and verbs. In addition, Wiig, Semel, and Crouse (1973) found 9-year-old poor readers to be inferior to normal readers in morphological usage (Berko, 1958) and concluded that poor readers had not mastered morphological rules as well as normal readers. Finally, Vogel (1974) found differences between normal and disabled 7- and 8-year-old readers on tasks measuring comprehension of syntax and knowledge of morphology. However, because most of the studies employed *concurrent* measures of reading and syntactic skills, as with phonemic awareness, caution must be exercised in establishing a direction of causality. It is possible that reader ability differences in syntactic knowledge result from differential exposure to reading materials, rather than from an independent problem in acquiring syntactic rules and relationships.

Nevertheless a recent series of studies by Siegel and Ryan (1984) obtained further evidence of difficulties in syntactic and morphological knowledge in disabled readers, but with a significant qualifier; namely that deficits were most pronounced with irregular and complex linguistic constructions. For example, in one task presented orally with an accompanying picture the child had to fill in the missing word in "The man is planting a tree. Here the tree has been___." The correct response — "planted" — is a regular construction. Other items required irregular constructions, as in "The thief is stealing the jewels. These are the jewels that he _____." Only the youngest disabled children (7 and 8) had problems with the regular constructions. However both younger and older disabled readers had significantly more difficulty than normal readers with the irregular constructions.

On balance, existing evidence does suggest that syntactic skills may be deficient in disabled readers. Most important, the syntactic problem may be limited to or most pronounced with irregular or complex linguistic constructions. As such, the syntactic deficit may represent a more fundamental cognitive disorder relating to acquisition of rules for irregular or complex syntactic or morphologic forms. Although such findings are particularly seductive for our own view (explicated later), the data in this area are still preliminary, and further work is needed.

Reading Skills

Major insights into reading disability have been gained recently by examining the pattern of reading skills possessed by the disabled reader. Findings have revealed that not all aspects of reading are deficient and those areas that are problematic present a coherent picture that point to possible underlying sources of the problem (Manis & Morrison, 1985).

Perception and Discrimination of Letters

Disabled readers do not appear to experience major problems in learning the letters of the alphabet. Comparisons of good and poor readers in first grade reveal no major differences in visual letter recognition (Shankweiler, 1964). By age 4 or 5, most children perform close to perfect on visual matching of letters (Calfee, Chapman, & Venezky, 1972). Although consistent discrimination of letters differing only in orientation (e.g., *b*, *d* and *p*, *q*) develops more slowly (Gibson, Gibson, Pick, & Osser, 1962), poor readers have not been shown to differ from normal readers in their tendency to make visual reversal errors (Liberman, Shankweiler, Orlando, Harris, & Bell-Berti, 1971; Lyle & Goyen, 1968).

Word Processing

It is in the domain of word learning and word decoding that disabled readers show the most marked problems (Guthrie & Siefert, 1977; Shankweiler & Liberman, 1972). Further, of the three properties of words relevant to reading—graphic, orthographic, and phonological characteristics (Gibson & Levin, 1975)—it is phonological processing (and especially grapheme–phoneme translation) that most clearly differentiates disabled from normal readers.

Graphic Characteristics.   In contrast to the extensive research on letter discriminaton, processing of graphic characteristics at the word level (e.g., length, shape) has not received much attention. Nevertheless, the limited research to date does not provide strong evidence of visual word-processing deficits in disabled readers. Good and poor readers equated for IQ have been shown to perform equivalently on grapheme–grapheme matching tasks (Snowling, 1980; Steinheiser & Guthrie, 1978) and on tasks requiring copying of familiar words presented tachistoscopically (Vellutino, Steger, & Kandel, 1972). In addition, Katz and Wicklund (1971) showed that good and poor readers scanned for target words in two and three word displays at the same rate.

On balance, difficulties in processing the graphic characteristics of letters and words do not appear to be a major source of difficulty beyond the early years of reading instruction (Gibson & Levin, 1975), nor do they constitute a serious problem for disabled readers.

Orthographic Characteristics.   Orthographic structure refers to the fact that some letters are more likely to occur in certain positions than others. For example, *e* is more likely to occur in the terminal position of a three-letter word than it is in the first position. Orthographic structure also exists because certain sequences of letters are legal in English (e.g., initial *th*, or terminal *oat*) and others are not (e.g., initial *ht*, or terminal *aot*).

Sensitivity to orthographic structure has been studied by comparing the speed with which children search for a target letter through arrays of words (*board, chair*), orthographically regular nonwords, or pseudowords (*droab, raich*) and random letter strings (rbdoa, hrcai). Typically, subjects search more quickly through arrays of words and pseudowords than through arrays of random letters, presumably because subjects use their knowledge of probable letter sequences and positions to reduce processing time (e.g., Juola, Schadler, Chabot, & McCaughey, 1978). By second or third grade, children and adults show a similar percentage decrease in search rate from random letter strings to strings with orthographic structure (Krueger, Keen, & Rublevich, 1974). Stanovich and West (1979) examined the effects of orthographic structure on visual search in good and poor readers. Subjects searched for word targets rather than letter targets. The authors found that although good and poor readers in the third grade both showed pronounced effects of orthographic structure the magnitude of the effects did not differ between the two groups. However, the reading groups differed by less than 1 year in reading ability on the average. It is unknown whether similar results would be found in a more severely disabled population or with younger age groups. One problem with the visual search task, and with other tasks employing similar logic (see Barron, 1981, for a discussion of research with other tasks) is the fact that orthographic structure is confounded with word familiarity and pronounceability. Words are more familiar than random letter strings. Although the familiarity factor can be eliminated by comparing responses to pseudowords and random letter strings, pseudowords are clearly more pronounceable than random letter strings, and this may facilitate processing (Santa, 1976–1977).

An alternative approach is to define orthographic structure in terms of statistical redundancy rather than pronounceability (Mason, 1975; Massaro & Taylor, 1980). Statistical redundancy is based on the frequency with which letters occur in certain positions or in certain sequences. Mason (1975), using summed single-letter positional frequency as a measure of orthographic structure in a visual letter search task found that sixth-grade good readers were more sensitive to this form of orthographic redundancy than were sixth-grade poor readers. Massaro and Taylor (1980) presented words varying orthogonally in summed single-letter positional frequency and pronounceability but failed to find any interactions of these variables with reading ability in a sixth-grade sample. Reader ability differences did occur when measures of bigram and trigram frequency were used. However, subjects in their experiment again did not vary greatly in reading ability, which may have attenuated group differences in sensitivity to orthographic structure.

In conclusion, there is little evidence of a strong association between reading ability and processing of orthographic structure. However, more research employing disabled readers as subjects is necessary before any conclusions can be drawn about the role of orthographic structure in the word-decoding problems of the disabled reader.

Phonological Characteristics.   One or more aspects of phonological processing appears to be a major stumbling block for the reading-disabled child. Whether one favors a rule-based symbol–sound translation process (Calfee, Venezky, & Chapman, 1969; Firth, 1972; Fowler, Shankweiler, & Liberman, 1979) or a whole-word analogy strategy (Glushko, 1979; see following for further discussion) several pieces of research have documented that recoding printed words into their phonological counterparts represents a serious problem for disabled readers. For example disabled readers typically lag several years behind normal readers in pronouncing pseudowords according to symbol–sound rules (Calfee et al., 1969; Firth, 1972; Venezky, Chapman, & Calfee, 1972). In addition, Shankweiler and Liberman (1972) found that in word pronunciation disabled readers made proportionately more errors on vowel segments than on consonants, whereas errors of good readers on the two segments were roughly equivalent. The authors noted that reading vowels may be more difficult because the pronunciation rules for vowels versus consonants are more complex and may take longer to acquire. Mason's (1976) analysis of pronunciation errors in oral-reading tasks revealed that increases in reading skills were associated with a different pattern of errors. Less skilled (not disabled) readers tended to apply short vowel rules to the pronunciation of vowels regardless of the graphemic environment of the vowel (e.g., *lit* for *light, ran* for *rain*). More advanced readers made proportionately more vowel errors involving long vowel sounds (e.g., *sweet* for *sweat, played* for *plaid*), indicating greater awareness of the variability of vowel pronunciation.

Overall, coupled with the findings on phonemic coding reviewed earlier, the accumulating evidence points very directly at phonological characteristics of words or phonological processing of words as a central datum to be explained.

Growth of Automatic Word-decoding Skills.   Beyond the problems they experience in decoding words accurately, disabled readers are slower to develop rapid, efficient decoding skills. For example Perfetti and Hogaboam (1975) required good and poor readers in third and fifth grades to name high- and low-frequency words and pronounceable nonwords rapidly. Poor readers at both age levels were almost as fast as good readers on high-frequency words but much slower on low-frequency words and nonwords. Subsequently Hogaboam and Perfetti (1978) investigated changes in pseudoword-naming speed across several exposures. After only three exposures, naming speed of good readers for pseudowords was as fast as for high-frequency real words. In contrast pseudoword-naming speed of poor readers remained slower than real word latencies even after 18 exposures. To the extent that high-frequency words are processed automatically (Laberge & Samuels, 1974), the evidence clearly points to a deficiency in the growth of automatic word-decoding skills in disabled readers. Similar results have been found by Manis and Morrison (1984).

Semantic Processing of Words.   Having established a problem in the visual-phonological coding process for words, the question arises whether a related or independent problem in semantically processing words exists. Although the question has not been extensively studied to date, existing evidence suggests that disabled readers do not differ from normal readers in automatic activation of semantic codes for words (Ceci, 1982, 1983). In contrast, disabled readers do not appear to consciously activate semantic codes to aid them in processing words to the same degree as normal readers (Ceci, 1983). Although the implication of the latter result is unclear, the existence of automatic semantic access in disabled readers confirms that elementary semantic processing of words is not severely deficient in reading-disabled children.

Reading Comprehension

Almost by definition, measures of reading comprehension show major differences between normal and disabled readers (Vellutino, 1979). Nevertheless, not all aspects of comprehension are deficient and the pattern of strengths and weaknesses may provide important clues to the cause of the comprehension problem. For example Vellutino (1979) has ruled out problems in general language as underlying the difficulty for most normal IQ disabled readers. In addition, several studies of word reading in context have demonstrated that disabled readers use sentence context to aid word decoding (Perfetti, 1982), and, further, some investigators (Stanovich, 1980) have suggested that disabled readers use context to a greater extent than normal readers to facilitate word decoding. Finally Waller (1976) found that poor readers comprehended the overall meaning of passages but remembered details less well.

Other aspects of comprehension are clearly deficient. Disabled readers have been shown to be inferior to good readers on memory for words in a passage (Perfetti & Goldman, 1976) and less effective at retaining specific words in a sentence recognition task (Waller, 1976). Further, disabled readers have shown less elaborative encoding while reading (Pearson & Camperell, 1981) and have been described as less efficient and more passive in approaching text (Bransford, Stein, & Vye, 1982; Garner & Ries, 1981).

Taken together, findings on reading comprehension present a mixed picture of strengths and weaknesses. Although understanding of the total pattern is far from complete, some investigators attribute at least part of the comprehension problem to word-decoding deficits. For example Perfetti and Lesgold (1978) obtained evidence consistent with the view that poor memory for words in a text stems from slow verbal coding. Similar interpretations have been offered by Stanovich (1980) and Morrison and Manis (1982). However research equating good and poor readers on word-decoding processes still revealed comprehension problems in poor readers (Fleisher, Jenkins, & Pany, 1979; Guthrie, 1973). On balance, although some residual problems in comprehension can be expected, existing evidence favors the view that comprehension per se is not deficient in disabled readers but arises as a necessary consequence of problems at the word-decoding level.

AN INTEGRATIVE FRAMEWORK

As illustrated in the foregoing sections, examination of the cognitive, linguistic, and reading skills of disabled readers as well as some general findings surrounding the disorder encompass a broadly based set of scientific pieces in a giant cognitive puzzle. Until recently, explanatory efforts have focused rather narrowly on selected cognitive, or reading, or linguistic aspects of the problem (Vellutino, 1979; Wolford, 1985). Progress at this point requires a broader more comprehensive framework encompassing the wider array of solid scientific evidence that has emerged in the last decade. A few years ago, in an attempt to move toward a broader perspective, we formulated a theoretical framework for understanding the nature and course of reading disability (Morrison, 1980; Morrison & Manis, 1982). Briefly our proposal contained four central ideas (Morrison & Manis, 1982):

1. The fundamental problem experienced by the disabled reader lies in acquiring knowledge about words, in particular, knowledge of spelling–sound correspondences. Difficulties in acquiring word knowledge stem from the child's failure to master the complex, irregular system of rules governing symbol–sound correspondences in English. The rule-learning difficulty in reading may represent a problem in learning complex or irregular rule systems in general.

2. Failure to learn the rules and regularities linking English orthography and phonology prevents the child from developing rapid, automated word-decoding operations.

3. Having to expend effort at simply decoding words for meaning, the disabled reader has little residual capacity to devote to higher order reading skills and comprehension.

4. Differences observed between normal and disabled readers in cognitive processing tasks represent a failure by disabled readers to develop processing skills (rapid encoding and serial scanning as well as rehearsal skills), which are themselves the result of acquisition of higher order reading and comprehension skills.

We have discussed the background and rationale for the preceding reconceptualization elsewhere (Manis & Morrison, 1984; Morrison & Manis, 1982). Although some authors have raised questions about the current perspective (Sternberg & Wagner, 1982; Vellutino & Scanlon, 1982), we feel that the focus on word-learning problems provides a crucial insight into the fundamental source of the reading problem and helps to explain the majority of cognitive, linguistic, and reading problems experienced by the disabled reader. Given the centrality that word-decoding problems hold in our view, we have focused our recent efforts primarily (though not exclusively) on understanding what word knowledge is and those aspects of word learning that pose the greatest difficulty for the disabled reader.

What Constitutes Word Knowledge?

We have focused on three major kinds of knowledge that could potentially influence word decoding.

Conditional Versus Unconditional Rules.   Children learn that pronunciation of some English orthographic units depends on the graphemic environment or on the position of the graphemic unit in the word. We have called these *conditional correspondences.* For example, short and long vowels are conditional because their correct pronunciation is contingent or conditional upon identifiable variations or rules in the graphemic environment (e.g., can vs. cane, or hop vs. hope as an example of the silent "e" rule). Other correspondences, here called unconditional, do not vary in pronunciation as a function of identifiable contingencies in the graphemic environment (e.g., *ow* as in blow, brow, grown, clown or *ea* in treat, great, breath, breather, feather). Pronunciation of these units appears to require whole-word paired-associate learning. Another way to characterize the aforementioned distinction is between one-to-one (unconditional) correspondences versus rule-based (conditional) correspondences.

Consistent Versus Inconsistent Rules.   Beyond dealing with different types of correspondences, children develop sensitivity to irregularities in the symbol–sound translation process. Some correspondences are *relatively* consistent, e.g., initial consonants like m, n, p, & t (in children's readers at least) and vowel digraphs such as *ee* (in keep, keen), *ai* (in mail, maid), or *oa* (in loaf, load).

Other correspondences have significant numbers of exceptions (here called inconsistent), e.g., medial *o* (in moth vs. both or in love vs. stove).

Consistent Versus Inconsistent Words.   Recently some investigators have argued that the process of translating from print to sound may not require use of symbol–sound correspondences at all (Baron, 1979). When pronouncing an unfamiliar word, for example, a reader may make implicit or explicit analogies to visually similar words the reader already knows. Glushko (1979) proposed a model of how an analogy strategy might work. According to the model, presentation of a word automatically activates in memory a "neighborhood" of visually similar words and their corresponding phonological codes. Some words activate "neighbors" whose pronunciations are all consistent—e.g., *meal* activates *deal, seal, real,* etc. Other words produce inconsistent phonological codes for neighboring words in memory—e.g., *meat* activates *seat,* and *neat* but also *sweat* and *great.* Glushko (1979) and, later, Bauer and Stanovich (1980) found that adult subjects pronounced consistent words faster than inconsistent words, supporting the notion that adult readers at least store and utilize knowledge of consistencies at the word level.

From our perspective on the nature of reading disability as failure to master the irregularities of the English system, these three variables—rule conditionality, rule consistency, and word consistency—provided some direct tests of our hypothesis. Overall we would predict that disabled readers would be more adversely affected than normal readers when reading words with conditional versus unconditional correspondence rules, inconsistent versus consistent rules, or with inconsistent versus consistent words.

Experiment 1: Word Pronunciation in Normal and Disabled Readers As a Function of Rule Conditionality, Rule Consistency, and Word Consistency

In one experiment, Manis and Morrison (1984) required normal and disabled readers to pronounce 64 words displayed on a video screen. The words varied along three dimensions (which can be seen in Table 2.1)—rule conditionality, rule consistency, and word consistency. The conditionality dimension referred to the presence or absence of conditional rules for vowel pronunciation (e.g., *ee* in keep and *ai* in mail are unconditional, whereas medial *i* or *o* is conditional). Rule *consistency* was based on the number of exceptions to spelling–sound correspondence rules contained in the Berdiansky, Cronnell, and Koehler (1969) norms. A vowel unit was classified as consistent if it had fewer than 10% exceptions and inconsistent if it had greater than 10%—hence *ee* in keep and *ai* in mail follow consistent rules whereas *ea* in heap or hear and *ow* in crowd or crown are inconsistent. Word consistency referred to whether a word activated alternative pronunciations. Hence *mail* and *store* are considered consistent, because

TABLE 2.1
Examples of Words Used in Experiment 1

| | Rule and Word Consistency | | | |
| | Consistent Rule | | Inconsistent Rule | |
	Consistent Word	Inconsistent Word	Consistent Word	Inconsistent Word
Unconditional rules	keep	keen	heap	hear
	mail	maid	crowd	crown
	loaf	load	count	couch
Conditional rules	dime	dive	mock	moth
	cane	cave	store	stove
	told	toll	hunt	hush

TABLE 2.2
Mean Word Pronunciation Latency (in Msec) and Accuracy As a
Function of Word Consistency

| | Word Consistency | | | |
	Consistent		Inconsistent	
Disabled readers	1198	(85.4%)	1200	(81.8%)
Reading age controls	1026	(90.9%)	1027	(86.2%)
Chronological age controls	605	(98.9%)	599	(93.1%)

they activate only one phonological code, whereas *maid* and *stove* are inconsistent, because they activate competing phonological codes (*said* and *love*).

Subjects were 20 disabled readers in fifth and sixth grades (mean IQ = 96; mean reading level = 3.4) and two groups of 20 normal readers: a chronological age (C.A.) control group of fifth–sixth graders (mean IQ = 100; mean reading level = 7.2) and a reading age (R.A.) control group of first, second, and third graders (mean IQ = 103; mean reading level 3.5). Subjects were required to pronounce the 64 presented words as accurately and rapidly as possible.

If we consider first the effects of word consistency collapsed across the other two variables, Table 2.2 reveals that for all three groups of children, accuracy of pronunciation of consistent words was significantly better than inconsistent words, but disabled readers were not differentially affected by word consistency. Surprisingly, no significant differences were obtained in reaction time to consistent versus inconsistent words for any reading groups.

Turning to the effects of rule consistency (see Table 2.3), accuracy of pronunciation of words with inconsistent versus consistent rules was not different for either group of normal readers, although for disabled readers, words with inconsistent rules produced poorer performance than words with consistent rules.

TABLE 2.3
Mean Word Pronunciation Latency (in Msec) and Accuracy As a
Function of Rule Consistency

	Consistent		Inconsistent	
Disabled readers	1107	(86.6%)	1290	(80.7%)
Reading age control	1001	(89.3%)	1052	(87.7%)
Chronological age controls	599	(96.9%)	606	(93.7%)

TABLE 2.4
Mean Word Pronunciation Latency (in Msec) and Accuracy As a
Function of Rule Conditionality

	Unconditional		Conditional	
Disabled readers	1167	(83.7%)	1231	(83.6%)
Reading age controls	1053	(90.8%)	1000	(86.3%)
Chronological age controls	600	(96.8%)	604	(95.2%)

Nevertheless, results are somewhat confounded because of the presence of a ceiling effect, especially for older readers. Shifting to the reaction-time data, for older normal readers (C.A. controls) words with inconsistent rules were pronounced slightly but nonsignificantly more slowly than words with consistent rules (606 vs. 599 msec, respectively). However, for both younger normal readers (R.A. controls) and disabled readers, inconsistent rules produced reliably longer reaction times than consistent rules. Most important the difference between inconsistent and consistent rules was significantly greater for disabled readers (193 msec) than for the reading-age-matched controls (51 msec). The findings for rule consistency then support the hypothesis that disabled readers have differentially greater difficulty with words following inconsistent rules than do normal readers.

Finally Table 2.4 depicts the results for rule conditionality. In this case, very little difference emerged for any group in accuracy of processing words with conditional versus unconditional rules. Looking at reaction time, the older normal children were unaffected by conditional versus unconditional rules (604 vs. 600 msec). For disabled readers, however, words with conditional rules took longer to pronounce than words with unconditional rules (1231 vs. 1167 msec). In contrast for younger normal readers conditional rules actually produced slightly shorter pronunciation latencies than did unconditional rules (1000 vs. 1053).

With the exception of the surprising finding for younger normal readers the combined results for rule conditionality and consistency confirmed the view that one source of the disabled reader's problem lies in mastering the complex, irregular system of rules governing symbol–sound correspondence in English.

Even compared with beginning normal readers, older disabled readers performed relatively more poorly with inconsistent and conditional rules.

The findings for rule consistency revealed the usefulness of a developmental perspective. Although older normal readers were unaffected by the rule consistency manipulation, younger normal readers took significantly longer on words with inconsistent rules. This finding suggests that acquisition and use of rule knowledge in word decoding may be important in the early stages of learning to read but diminish in importance in later years as word decoding becomes more unitized or automated.

Experiment 2: The Interactive Effects of Word Frequency and Word Consistency on Pronunciation Latency

Returning to the effects of *word* consistency, we were quite puzzled at the failure to obtain differences in reaction time between consistent and inconsistent words, in contrast to Glushko (1979) and Bauer and Stanovich (1980). One possible explanation was offered recently by Seidenberg, Waters, Barnes, and Tanenhaus (in press), who found that for adults the effects of word consistency differed depending on the word's frequency. Inconsistent words in their study took longer than consistent words only if the words were low frequency. Because in our studies with children we typically used relatively high-frequency words, we wondered what would happen if we looked at the effects of word consistency separately for low- and high-frequency words.

Accordingly, we recently conducted a study in which children were required to pronounce 42 words, which varied in word consistency (consistent–inconsistent, as defined by Glushko) and word frequency (low–high, taken from the Carroll, Davies, and Richman (1971) norms for children's readers). The low-frequency set comprised words with less than 25 occurrences per million words, whereas the high-frequency set contained words with greater than 100 occurrences per million.

Subjects were fourth-, fifth-, and sixth-grade disabled readers reading at least 1½ years below grade level, and two groups of normal readers, matched on IQ (mean IQ = 99)—a C.A. match and an R.A. match group. As in the previous experiment, subjects were asked to read the words presented singly on a video screen as accurately and rapidly as possible. Figure 2.1 depicts the results first for high-frequency words, where mean reaction time is graphed as a function of word consistency for the three groups of readers. The numbers in parentheses depict accuracy of pronunciation in the different conditions. As can be seen, for older normal readers, reaction time to high-frequency words did not differ for consistent versus inconsistent words (showing a difference of 19 msec). In contrast, for younger normal and older disabled readers, inconsistent words took significantly longer than consistent words. Most critically, although younger

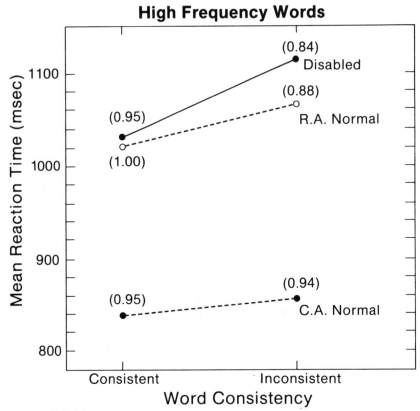

FIG. 2.1 Mean reaction time (and accuracy in parentheses) on high-frequency words as a function of word consistency for the three groups of readers.

normal and disabled readers did not differ on consistent words, the disabled readers took longer to pronounce inconsistent words than did younger normal readers (about 40 msec). If we look now at the effects for low-frequency words (Fig. 2.2), for older normal readers, low-frequency inconsistent words take longer than consistent words (a difference of 70 msec). In addition, for younger normal readers and for disabled readers, the degree of difference between consistent and inconsistent words is significantly greater than for older normal readers.

Taken together the results of this last study show several things. First they confirm the results of Seidenberg et al. that for older normal readers, a word consistency effect is limited primarily to low-frequency words. Second, for beginning normal readers, inconsistent words even of high frequency are pronounced more slowly than consistent words. Finally older disabled readers continue to lag behind even beginning normal readers in speed of pronunciation of inconsistent words. As such, the results support the notion that disabled readers suffer particular difficulty on words with inconsistent pronunciations.

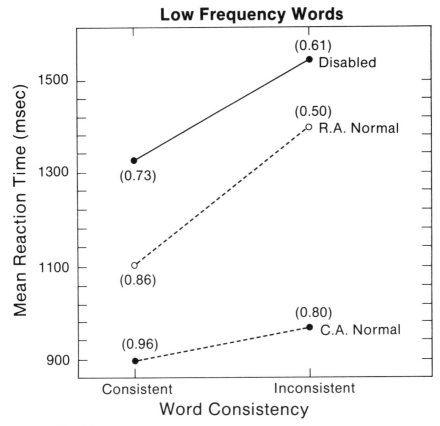

FIG. 2.2 Mean reaction time (and accuracy in parentheses) on low-frequency words as a function of word consistency for the three groups of readers.

Overall, the results of these initial efforts have confirmed our belief that difficulties in acquiring certain aspects of word knowledge constitute a major source of the disabled reader's failure to progress beyond rudimentary word decoding. Whether the problem lies in learning correspondence rules or in developing word representations and analogy skills (or all of the aforementioned), we are persuaded that the key to understanding reading disability lies in probing the acquisition of word knowledge and of word-decoding skills.

Experiment 3: Evidence From a Nonreading Task

In addition to examining word-decoding operations, we have been curious about whether problems in mastering the complex, irregular system of correspondence rules might represent a more general cognitive problem learning rule systems that are irregular or otherwise ambiguous. To test this hypothesis, Savage (in

Manis & Morrison, 1984) devised a paired-associate task in which children had to learn symbol–word pairs. The stimuli are shown in Table 2.5. Four separate conditions were run, in an attempt to roughly stimulate the kinds of learning involved in acquiring word knowledge. Specifically, two types of correspondences (or associations) were included: *one-to-one associations,* in which the symbol–word pairs were learned as straightforward paired associates; *rule-based* associations, in which one symbol was paired with two separate words, which stood in the relation "opposite" e.g., ←. was associated with boy while ←* was associated with girl. Discovery of the higher order rule relating symbols to words

Table 2.5
The four groups of symbol-word correspondences used in
Experiment 3.

Artificial Symbol - Word Correspondences

Consistent One-to-One	Inconsistent One-to-One
←. Boy	←. Boy
◯* Day	←* Day
8. Cat	8. Cat
Ψ* Mother	8* Mother
∧∧. Summer	∧∧. Summer
✗* Plant	∧∧* Plant
▢. White	▢. White
+++* Rich	▢* Rich
⊕. New	⊕. New
I* Hot	⊕* Hot
△. Bad	△. Bad
◡* Soft	△* Soft

Consistent Rule	Inconsistent Rule
←. Boy	←. Boy
←* Girl	←* Girl
8. Cat	8. Cat
8* Dog	8* Mother
∧∧. Summer	∧∧. Summer
∧∧* Winter	∧∧* Winter
▢. White	▢. White
▢* Black	▢* Black
⊕. New	⊕. New
⊕* Old	⊕* Hot
△. Bad	△. Bad
△* Good	△* Good

could facilitate learning of the paired associates. The one-to-one and rule-based associations were considered roughly analogous to learning unconditional and conditional rules in word decoding. The second dimension on which the pairs varied was consistency of association; *Consistent associations* contained symbols that were paired with only one word; *inconsistent associations* contained symbols that were paired with more than one word (but distinguished by different subscripts) or that violated the "opposites" rule (e.g., ← with boy–girl vs. 8 with cat–mother). The consistency dimension was deemed analogous to learning consistent versus inconsistent rules in word decoding.

Thirty-six disabled and normal readers in Grades 4 through 6 served as subjects. Children were required to learn 12 symbol–word pairs across four study–test trial sequences. During the study phase, each symbol was presented visually on a separate page and the associated word was presented auditorally. To ensure that the child had attended to the study trial, an immediate test was given after presentation of each pair. Following each of the four sets of study trials, test trials were presented in which each symbol was presented and the child was asked to say which word had been shown with that symbol. The four experimental conditions were run as a between-subjects manipulation.

The results are shown in Fig. 2.3, where mean number of correct responses is graphed as a function of test trials (one through four) for normal and disabled readers in the four different conditions. Looking first at the consistent/one-to-one condition, it is clear that normal and disabled readers did not differ in learning the simple, regular paired associates. The slight advantage for disabled readers was nonsignificant. Likewise, normal and disabled readers did not differ in learning the inconsistent/one-to-one pairs. Notice, moreover, that performance in that condition was extremely low. Moving to the consistent/rule condition, normal readers did outperform disabled readers and the difference was statistically significant by Trial 4. Finally in the inconsistent/rule condition, normal readers clearly outperformed disabled readers.

The pattern of findings from this experiment suggests several things. First, disabled readers do not differ from normal readers in basic paired-associate learning ability. With pairs governed by consistent one-to-one associations, performance of disabled readers equalled that of normal readers. Likewise, even when the one-to-one associations were inconsistent, the two reading groups performed equivalently. Second, differences between normal and disabled readers began to emerge in conditions involving abstraction of some higher order rule governing the symbol–word pairs. The most dramatic difference occurred when subjects were learning pairs governed by a higher order rule, but in which the rule was inconsistent. The findings confirmed those of the word–decoding studies in showing disabled readers to experience greatest difficulty with associations or correspondences that are rule based or conditional, and inconsistent. Finally, the findings are relevant to a persistent problem in comparisons of normal

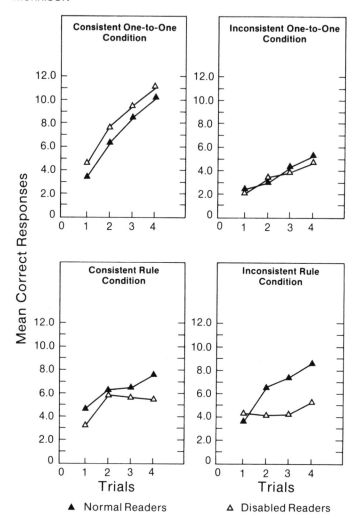

FIG. 2.3 Mean number of correct responses of normal versus disabled readers across four test trials in the four experimental conditions.

and disabled readers. Specifically, it is often the case that, in manipulating variables like word consistency or rule consistency, one also varies task complexity or difficulty. Because disabled readers most often perform more poorly relative to normal readers on the more difficult tasks, it is possible that the difficulty of the task and not the variable manipulated is producing the difference. In the present experiment, findings for the inconsistent/one-to-one condition refute this interpretation. Performance in that condition was lowest of all, but performance of disabled readers equalled that of normal readers. Hence differences observed between normal and disabled readers in the two rule conditions could not have resulted simply from the greater difficulty of those tasks.

In summary, our work to date on word-decoding skills confirms our belief that disabled readers suffer particular difficulty in mastering the complex, irregular system of correspondence rules in English, over and above that expected as part of the normal process of learning to read across age. Further we have obtained preliminary evidence that the word-learning problem may represent a more fundamental problem mastering symbol systems with irregular or ambiguous rules.

Whatever the deeper, underlying cognitive disorder responsible for the rule-learning problem turns out to be, the present results suggest that the key to unravelling the mystery of reading disability lies in understanding the acquisition and use of word-decoding skills.

OVERVIEW AND CONCLUSIONS

Although we emphasized word learning in the previous section, it should be clear that our conceptualization attempts to incorporate the broad range of major findings outlined earlier. In essence, we view the disabled reader as coming to the task of reading with a relatively intact set of cognitive and linguistic skills with the exception that some residual deficits in language skills persist, especially those involved in processing irregular syntax or morphology. Although acquisition of knowledge about letters proceeds relatively smoothly, the disabled reader first encounters serious problems when attempting to learn to decode English words. Although processing of regular, high-frequency words develops relatively smoothly, the disabled reader encounters major problems attempting to deal with inconsistent words and the irregular rules governing them. Having to continually and laboriously decode words consciously with great effort, the disabled reader fails to progress to the stage where word processing becomes effortless, perhaps unconscious. Being stuck at the word level, the child does not practice nor perfect the rapid encoding, scanning, and rehearsal skills that come as a byproduct of reading experience. Naturally higher level skills involved in comprehension will lag far behind those of normal readers.

Regarding the specificity of the disorder to reading, we have seen that a host of related problems can be discerned that at first glance bear little resemblance to reading—serial scanning, mental rehearsal, linguistic processing of irregular constructions. Nevertheless the current framework provides a coherent explanation of these seemingly disparate phenomena. In so doing reading disability does emerge as a relatively specific disorder because in our opinion, with one exception it is unique in requiring children to acquire a highly inconsistent symbol system. Only selected aspects of language acquisition require similar kinds of learning and we have seen preliminary evidence (Siegel & Ryan, 1984) that it is precisely those elements that most strongly differentiate the language skills of disabled readers from those of normal readers. In contrast, learning of elementary arithmetic skills consists of mastering a relatively straightforward and consistent set of symbols, relations, and manipulations.

The disability can at times be extremely severe because the acquisition sequence from word learning to word automatization to comprehension skills is hampered at the very outset, hence leaving the disabled reader at a most primitive reading level.

Whatever the ultimate fate of this conceptualization, however, the important point is that future efforts must be directed toward a broader, more integrative perspective. At this juncture, progress depends on a wider vision that encompasses the insights of all those disciplines that have been struggling to arrange the puzzle pieces into an identifiable and coherent picture.

ACKNOWLEDGMENTS

The author acknowledges in particular the contribution of Franklin R. Manis to the ideas and research presented in this chapter. Preparation of this chapter was supported in part by a grant from the National Sciences and Engineering Research Council of Canada.

REFERENCES

Badcock, D., & Lovegrove, W. (1981). The effects of contrast, stimulus and spatial frequency on visible persistence in normal and specifically disabled readers. *Journal of Experimental Psychology: Human Perception and Performance, 1*, 495–505.

Baron, J. (1979). Orthographic and word specific mechanisms in children's reading of words. *Child Development, 50*, 60–72.

Barron, R. W. (1981). Development of visual word recognition: A review. In G. E. MacKinnon & T. G.Waller (Eds.), *Reading research: Advances in theory and practice* (Vol. 3). New York: Academic Press.

Bauer, D. W., & Stanovich, K. E. (1980). Lexical access and the spelling-to-sound regularity effect. *Memory and Cognition, 8*(5), 424–432.

Bauer, R. H. (1979). Memory, acquisition, and category clustering in learning-disabled children. *Journal of Experimental Child Psychology, 21*, 365–383.

Berdiansky, B., Cronnell, B., & Koehler, J. A. (1969). *Spelling–sound relations and primary form–class descriptions for speech-comprehension vocabularies of 6–9 year olds* (Tech. Rep. No. 15). Los Angeles: Southwest Regional Laboratory for Educational Research and Development.

Berko, J. (1958). The child's learning of English morphology. *Word, 14*, 150–177.

Bisanz, G. L., Das, J. P., & Mancini, G. (in press). Children's memory for phonemically confusable and nonconfusable letters: Changes with age and reading ability. *Child Development*.

Bradley, L., & Bryant, P. E. (1978). Difficulties in auditory organization as a possible cause of reading backwardness. *Nature, 271,* 746–747.

Bransford, J. D., Stein, B. S., & Vye, N. J. (1982). Helping students learn how to learn from written texts. In M. Singer (Ed.), *Competent reader, disabled reader: Research and application.* Hillsdale, NJ: Lawrence Erlbaum Associates.

Byrne, B., & Shea, P. (1979). Semantic and phonetic memory codes in beginning readers. *Memory and Cognition, 7,* 333–338.

Calfee, R. C., & Chapman, R. S. (1972). How a child needs to think to learn to read. In L. W. Gregg (Ed.), *Cognition in learning and memory.* New York: Wiley.

Calfee, R. C., Venezky, R. L., & Chapman, R. S. (1969). *Pronunciation of synthetic words with predictable and unpredictable letter–sound correspondences* (Tech. Rep. No. 71). Madison, WI: Wisconsin Research and Development Center for Cognitive Learning.

Carroll, J. B., Davies, P., & Richman, B. (1971). *American heritage word frequency book.* New York: Houghton Mifflin.

Ceci, S. J. (1982). Extracting meaning from stimuli: Automatic and purposive processing characteristics of the language-based learning disabled. *Topics in Learning and Learning Disabilities,* 46–53.

Ceci, S. J. (1983). An investigation of the semantic processing characteristics of normal and language/learning disabled children. *Developmental Psychology, 19,* 427–439.

Di Lollo, V., Hanson, D., & McIntyre, J. S. (1983). Initial stages of visual information processing in dyslexia. *Journal of Experimental Psychology: Human Perception and Performance, 9(6),* 923–935.

Doehring, D. G., Trites, R. L., Patel, P. G., & Fiedorowicz, A. M. (1981). *Reading disabilities: The interaction of reading, language and neuropsychological deficits.* New York: Academic Press.

Ehri, L. C. (in press). How orthography alters spoken language competencies in children. In J. Downing & R. Valtin (Eds.), *Language awareness and learning to read.* New York: Springer–Verlag.

Firth, I. (1972). *Components of reading disability.* Doctoral dissertation, University of New South Wales, New South Wales.

Fleisher, L. S., Jenkins, J. R., & Pany, D. (1979). Effects on poor readers' comprehension of training in rapid decoding. *Reading Research Quarterly, 15,* 30–48.

Fowler, C. A., Shankweiler, D., & Liberman, I. Y. (1979). Apprehending spelling patterns for vowels: A developmental study. *Language and Speech, 22(3),* 243–252.

Fry, M. A., Johnson, C. S., & Muehl, S. (1970). Oral language production in relation to reading achievement among select second graders. In D. J. Bakker & P. Satz (Eds.), *Specific reading disability: Advances in theory and method.* Rotterdam: Rotterdam University Press.

Garner, R., & Ries, R. (1981). Monitoring and resolving comprehension obstacles: An investigation of spontaneous text lookbacks among upper grade good and poor comprehenders. *Reading Research Quarterly, 16,* 569–582.

Gibson, E. J., Gibson, J. J., Pick, A. D., & Osser, R. (1962). A developmental study of the discrimination of letter-like forms. *Journal of Comparative and Physiological Psychology, 55,* 897–906.

Gibson, E. J., & Levin, H. (1975). *The psychology of reading.* Cambridge, MA: MIT Press.

Glushko, R. J. (1979). The organization and activation of orthographic knowledge in reading aloud. *Journal of Experimental Psychology: Human Perception and Performance, 5(4),* 674–691.

Guthrie, J. T. (1973). Reading comprehension and syntactic responses in good and poor readers. *Journal of Educational Psychology, 65,* 294–299.

Guthrie, J. T., & Seifert, M. (1977). Letter-sound complexity in learning to identify words. *Journal of Educational Psychology, 69,* 686–696.

Hall, J. W., Wilson, K. P., Humphreys, M. S., Tinzmann, M. B., & Bowyer, P. M. (1983). Phonemic similarity effects in good vs. poor readers. *Memory & Cognition, 11*(5), 520–527.

Helfgott, J. (1976). Phonemic segmentation and blending skills of kindergarten children: Implications for beginning reading acquisition. *Contemporary Education Psychology, 1,* 157–169.

Hogaboam, T.W., & Perfetti, C. A. (1978). Reading skill and the role of verbal experience in decoding. *Journal of Educational Psychology, 70,* 717–729.

Juloa, J. F., Schadler, M., Chabot, R. J., & McCaughey, M. W. (1978). The development of visual information processing skills related to reading. *Journal of Experimental Child Psychology, 25,* 459–476.

Katz, L., & Wicklund, D. A. (1971). Word scanning rate for good and poor readers. *Journal of Educational Psychology, 62,* 138–140.

Katz, L., & Wicklund, D. A. (1972). Letter scanning rate for good and poor readers in grades two and six. *Journal of Educational Psychology, 63,* 363–367.

Krueger, L. E., Keen, R. H., & Rublevich, B. (1974). Letter search through words and nonwords by adults and fourth-grade children. *Journal of Experimental Psychology, 102*(5), 845–849.

Laberge, D., & Samuels, S. J. (1974). Toward a theory of automatic information processing in reading. *Cognitive Psychology, 6,* 293–323.

Liberman, I. Y., Shankweiler, D., Fischer, F. W., & Carter, B. (1974). Explicit syllable and phoneme segmentation in the young child. *Journal of Experimental Child Psychology, 18,* 210–212.

Liberman, I. Y., Shankweiler, K., Liberman, A. M., Fowler, C., & Fischer, F. W. (1977). Phonetic segmentation and recoding in the beginning reader. In A. S. Reber & D. Scarborough (Eds.), *Toward a psychology of reading: The proceedings of the CUNY conferences* (pp. 1–22). Hillsdale, NJ: Lawrence Erlbaum Associates.

Liberman, I. Y., Shankweiler, D., Orlando, C., Harris, K. S., & Bell-Berti, F. (1971). Letter confusions and reversals of sequence in the beginning reader: Implications for Orton's theory of developmental dyslexia. *Cortex, 7,* 127–142.

Lovegrove, W. J., Heddle, M., & Slaghuis, W. (1980). Reading disability, spatial frequency deficits in visual information store. *Neuropsychologia, 18,* 111–115.

Lyle, J. G., & Goyen, J. (1968). Visual recognition, developmental lag, and strephosymbolia in reading retardation. *Journal of Abnormal Psychology, 73,* 25–29.

Manis, F. R., & Morrison, F. J. (1982). Processing of identity and position information in normal and disabled readers. *Journal of Experimental Child Psychology, 33,* 74–86.

Manis, F. R., & Morrison, F. J. (1985). Reading disability: A deficit in rule learning? In L. S. Siegel & F. J. Morrison (Eds.), *Cognitive development in atypical children.* New York: Springer–Verlag.

Mann, V.A., Liberman, I. Y., & Shankweiler, D. (1980). Children's memory for sentences and word strings in relation to reading ability. *Memory and Cognition, 8,* 329–335.

Mason, M. (1975). Reading ability and letter search time: Effects of orthographic structure defined by single-letter positional frequency. *Journal of Experimental Psychology: General, 104,* 146–166.

Mason, J. M. (1976). Overgeneralization in learning to read. *Journal of Reading Behavior, 8,* 173–182.

Massaro, D. W., & Taylor, G. A. (1980). Reading ability and utilization of orthographic structure in reading. *Journal of Educational Psychology, 72*(6), 730–742.

Mattis, S., French, J., & Rapin, I. (1975). Dyslexia in children and young adults: Three independent neuropsychological syndrommes. *Developmental Medicine and Child Neurology, 17,* 150–163.

Morais, J., Carey, L., Alegria, J., & Bertelsch, P. (1979). Does awareness of speech as a sequence of phones arise spontaneously? *Cognition, 7,* 323–331.

Morrison, F. J. (1980, November). *The nature of reading disability: Toward a reconceptualization.* Paper presented at the meeting of the Psychononomic Society, St. Louis.

Morrison, F. J. (1984). Learning and not learning to read. *Remedial and Special Education, 5*(3), 20–27.

Morrison, F. J. (1985). The nature of reading disability. In F. J. Morrison, C. Lord, & D. P. Keating (Eds.), *Applied developmental psychology*. San Francisco: Academic Press.

Morrison, F. J., Giordani, B., & Nagy, I. (1977). Reading disability: An information processing analysis. *Science, 196,* 77–79.

Morrison, F. J., & Manis, F. R. (1982). Cognitive processes and reading disability: A critique and proposal. In C. J. Brainerd & M. I. Pressley (Eds.), *Verbal processes in children*. New York: Springer–Verlag.

Olson, R. K., Kliegl, R., & Davidson, B. J. (1983). Dyslexic and normal readers' eye movements. *Journal of Experimental Psychology: Human Perception and Performance, 9*(5), 816–825.

Ornstein, P. A. (1978). Rehearsal processes in children's memory. In P. A. Ornstein (Ed.). *Memory development in children*. Hillsdale, NJ: Lawrence Erlbaum Associates.

Ornstein, P. A., & Naus, M. J. (1978). Rehearsal processes in children's memory. In P. A. Ornstein (Ed.), *Memory development in children* (pp. 69–100). Hillsdale, NJ: Lawrence Erlbaum Associates.

Pavlidis, G. T. (1981). Do eye movements hold the key to dyslexia? *Neuropsychologia, 19,* 57–64.

Pavlidis, G. T. (1983). The dyslexia syndrome and its objective diagnosis by erratic eye movements. In K. Rayne (Ed.), *Eye movements in reading: Perceptual and language processes*. New York: Academic Press.

Pearson, P. D., & Camperell, A. D. (1981). Comprehension of text structures. In J. T. Guthrie (Ed.), *Comprehension and teaching*. Newark, DE: International Reading Association.

Perfetti, C. A. (1982). Discourse context, word identification and reading ability. In J. F. Le Ny and W. Kintsch (Eds.), *Language and comprehension*. Amsterdam: North Holland.

Perfetti, C. A., Beck, I., & Hughes, C. (1981, April). *Phonemic knowledge and learning to read*. Paper presented at the meeting of Society for Research in Child Development. Boston.

Perfetti, C. A., & Goldman, S. R. (1976). Discourse memory and reading comprehension skill. *Journal of Verbal Learning and Verbal Behavior, 14,* 33–42.

Perfetti, C. A., & Hogaboam, T. (1975). Relationship between single-word decoding and reading comprehension skill. *Journal of Educational Psychology, 67,* 461–469.

Perfetti, C. A., & Lesgold, A. M. (1978). Discourse comprehension and sources of individual differences. In M. J. Just & P. A. Carpenter (Eds.), *Cognitive processes in comprehension*. Hillsdale, NJ: Lawrence Erlbaum Associates.

Rosner, J., & Simon, D. P. (1971). The auditory analysis test: An initial report. *Journal of Learning Disabilities, 4,* 40–48.

Rourke, B. (1975). Brain-behaviour relationships in children with learning disabilities: A research program, *30,* 911–920.

Rourke, B. (1978). Reading, spelling, arithmetic disabilities: A neuropsychological perspective. In H. R. Myklebust (Ed.), *Progress in learning disabilities* (pp. 97–120). New York: Grune & Stratton.

Rozin, P., & Gleitman, L. R. (1977). The structure and acquisition of reading II: The reading process and the acquisition of the alphabetic principle. In A. S. Reber & D. L. Scarborough (Eds.), *Toward a psychology of reading: The proceedings of the CUNY Conferences* (pp. 110–137). Hillsdale, NJ: Lawrence Erlbaum Associates.

Rutter, M., & Yule, W. (1975). The concept of specific reading retardation. *Journal of Child Psychiatry, 16,* 181–197.

Santa, C. M. (1976–77). Spelling patterns and the development of flexible word recognition strategies. *Reading Research Quarterly, 2,* 125–144.

Schwantes, F. M. (1979). Cognitive scanning processes in children. *Child Development, 50,* 1136–1143.

Schwantes, F. M. (1980). Cognitive scanning processes in children. *Child Development, 50,* 1136–1143.

Seidenberg, M. S., Waters, G. S., Barnes, M. A., & Tanenhaus, M. K. (in press). When does irregular spelling or pronunciation influence word recognition? *Journal of Verbal Learning and Verbal Behavior*.

Shankweiler, D. (1964). Developmental dyslexia: A critique and review of recent evidence. *Cortex, 1*, 53–62.

Shankweiler, D., & Liberman, I. (1972). Misreading: A search for causes. In J. Kavanaugh & I. Mattingly (Eds.), *Language by ear and by eye.* Cambridge, MA: MIT Press.

Shankweiler, D., Liberman, I. Y., Mark, L. S., Fowler, C. A., & Fischer, F. W. (1979). The speech code and learning to read. *Journal of Experimental Psychology: Human Learning and Memory, 5,* 531–545.

Siegel, L. S., & Ryan, E. B. (1984). Reading disability as a language disorder. *Remedial and Special Education, 5*(3), 28–33.

Snowling, M. J. (1980). The development of grapheme–phoneme correspondence in normal and dyslexic readers. *Journal of Experimental Child Psychology, 29,* 294–305.

Stanley, G., Smith, G. A., & Howell, E. A. (in press). Eye movements and sequential tracking in dyslexic and control children. *British Journal of Psychology.*

Stanovich, K. E., & West, R. F. (1979). Mechanisms of sentence context effects in reading: Automatic activation and conscious attention. *Memory and Cognition, 1,* 77–85.

Stanovich, K. E. (1980). Toward an interactive–compensatory model of individual differences in the development of reading fluency. *Reading Research Quarterly, 1,* 32–71.

Steinheiser, F., & Guthrie, J. T. (1978). Reading ability and efficiency of graphemic–phonemic encoding. *Journal of General Psychology, 99,* 281–291.

Sternberg, R. J., & Wagner, R. K. (1982). Automatization failure in learning disabilities. *Topics in Learning and Learning Disabilities, 2,* 1–11.

Stevenson, H. W., Stigler, J. W., Lucker, G. W., Lee, S., Hsu, C., & Kitamura, S. (1982). Reading disabilities: The case of Chinese, Japanese, and English. *Child Development, 53*(5), 1164–1182.

Trieman, R., & Baron, J. (1980). Segmental analysis ability: Development and relation to reading ability. In T. Waller & G. MacKinnon (Eds.), *Reading research: Advances in theory and practice* (Vol. 2). New York: Academic Press.

Vellutino, F. R. (1979). *Dyslexia: Theory and research.* Cambridge, MA: MIT Press.

Vellutino, F. R., & Scanlon, D. M. (1982). Verbal processing in poor and normal readers. In C. J. Brainerd & M. Pressley (Eds.), *Verbal processes in children* (pp. 189–265). New York: Springer–Verlag.

Vellutino, F. R., Steger, J. A., & Kandel, G. (1972). Reading disability: An investigation of the perceptual deficit hypothesis. *Cortex, 8,* 106–118.

Venezky, R. L., Chapman, R. S., & Calfee, R. C. (1972). *The development of letter–sound generalizations from second through sixth grade* (Tech. Rep. 231). Madison, WI: Wisconsin Research and Development Center for Cognitive Learning.

Vogel, S. A. (1974). Syntactic abilities in normal and dyslexic children. *Journal of Learning Disabilities, 7,* 103–109.

Walford, G. (1985). Information-processing approaches to reading disability. In L. S. Siegel & F. J. Morrison (Eds.), *Cognitive development in atypical children* (pp. 27–44). New York: Springer–Verlag.

Waller, T. G. (1976). Children's recognition memory for written sentences: A comparison of good and poor readers. *Child Development, 47,* 90–95.

Wiig, E. H., Semel, M. S., & Crouse, M. B. (1973). The use of English morphology by high-risk and learning disabled children. *Journal of Learning Disabilities, 6,* 457–465.

Wolford, G., & Fowler, C. A. (1984). Differential use of partial information by good and poor readers. *Developmental Review, 4,* 15–35.

3 In Search of the Attentional Deficit

Kathleen L. McNellis
Cornell University

The idea of an attentional deficit as the central syndrome affecting learning-disabled (LD) children was popularized by Dykman, Ackerman, Clements, and Peters (1971). Since then the idea has become widely accepted by researchers in the field, both for its simple, perhaps simplistic intuitive appeal, and because of the large number of studies that claim to support it. Unfortunately, evidence for this disorder is quite difficult to substantiate, because a close look at the attention literature with LD children reveals as much disarray as does the rest of the literature with LD subjects. The problems one encounters in this literature are myriad, but they can be sorted into three general categories. There are problems with the sampling and labeling of LD subjects, problems with the definitions and measurement of attention employed, and there are a variety of methodological problems. These are discussed in turn. This chapter demonstrates that there is no support for the notion of an attentional deficit as a central syndrome affecting LD children; it also outlines new research that will substantiate this claim.

The first problem one encounters in the literature is the sampling/labeling problem. In many studies purporting to have LD children it is impossible to know who the subjects really were. Only recently have many researchers begun to separate "hyperactive" from "LD" populations, although the children described by these terms are often very separate and distinct groups. In principle, a hyperactive diagnosis implies nothing whatsoever about a child's learning achievement or potential, whereas an LD label implies nothing about a child's activity. And although the DSM III describes an "Attentional Deficit Disorder with Hyperactivity" (ADDH) syndrome for some hyperactive children, there is no evidence for global attentional deficits in LD populations, as this chapter demonstrates.

Another major sampling error involves the misuse or nonuse of intelligence test scores. Although children labeled LD should have normal range IQs of 85 and above, Kirk and Elkins (1975) found in a survey of over 3,000 LD children that the median IQ was 93, and that 35% had IQs below 90. Simple calculations reveal that only 9% of children in the general population would be expected to have IQs in the 85 to 90 range. Even more troubling was the finding of Keogh, Major-Kingsley, Omori-Gordon, and Reid (1982), who did an exhaustive computer search of experimental studies with LD populations. They located more than 4,000 such studies and found that more than 30% of the studies they sampled did not report IQ scores at all. The possibility is distinct, therefore, that LD/non-LD performance differences in many studies may be caused by sampling errors involving the inclusion of individuals with low IQs, as well as hyperactive children.

The second problem with the LD attention literature has to do with the notion of attention itself, and with what constitutes evidence for a deficit in attention. Faulty attention, in the most global sense of the term, can explain poor performance on any task. Such a notion is therefore useless as an experimental hypothesis. Some researchers prefer to explore one or more of the "components" of attention in order to provide support for the attentional deficit notion. The components studied vary somewhat, but the trend is to include "arousal," "vigilance," and "selective attention" as three of the most common components (e.g., Samuels & Edwall, 1981; Tarver & Hallahan, 1974). Typically, each group of researchers devises one experiment with one task on which LD/non-LD differences are demonstrated. It can certainly be argued, as does Koppel (1979), that poor performance on one task designed to measure one component of attention does not substantiate the claim of across-the-board attentional deficits. In fact, such a claim could only be supported with evidence, using one carefully selected LD population, that showed both poor LD performance on a number of attention tasks and significant correlations among performance scores on the various tasks. Without such correlations, one cannot conclude that the various experimental tasks, given to separate LD groups, are tapping the same "thing" called attention at all, regardless of what the various researchers may claim to be measuring. Nevertheless, disparate studies that show LD/non-LD differences on diverse tasks, measuring different components of attention, with different research populations, are taken collectively to support the claim of global attentional deficits in LD children (e.g., Bryan & Bryan, 1980; Hallahan, 1975; Keogh & Margolis, 1976). Such claims are simply not warranted. No researcher has demonstrated correlations among performance scores on various attention tasks with a single, nonhyperactive LD population. Pelham (1979) did administer multiple attention tasks to a single group of subjects. Notably, he did not find clear-cut attentional differences between LD and non-LD children, nor did he find correlations among performance scores on his tasks. This study is discussed in more detail in a later section.

The final sort of problems one encounters in this literature are methodological. Although individual studies exhibit a variety of problems, there are some problems of a more general nature that seem to be epidemic in the LD attention literature. One quite serious problem is that rarely, if ever, are baseline differences in performance between the LD/non-LD groups equated; another is that group IQ differences are almost never eliminated or controlled (see discussion in Douglas & Peters, 1979). Moreover, the attention tasks used in many experiments are frequently heavily memory-loaded or otherwise strategy-dependent, such that any poor student would be expected to perform poorly. Finally, the dependent measure of attention is often reaction time (RT). Whereas RT may be a fair approximation of the attending behavior of a college sophomore, it may not be a realistic measure of the capabilities of an unmotivated youngster. These problems are elaborated in the sections that follow.

THE COMPONENTS OF ATTENTION

Arousal

It has been suggested by many psychologists (e.g., Kahneman, 1973) that there are optimal levels of physiological arousal that correspond with the difficulty levels of various tasks. A subject's attention is inferred from his physiological state, which is measured by reaction time, heart rate, EEG, pupil size, and so forth. It is reasoned by some that if LD children are less reactive than non-LD children in performing certain tasks, then they are exhibiting attentional disorders. (See Rosenthal & Allen, 1978, for a review.) LD researchers who study the arousal component of attention often work in the psychiatric tradition. A major problem with much of this research is that the LD subjects who participate in these studies are usually clinical referrals to medical school research laboratories. The children often have neurological soft signs and very unacceptable classroom behavior. Hyperactive children are routinely included in the research samples. The researchers typically record physiologic measures and reaction times while the children perform complicated tasks. Not surprisingly, LD children are often found to perform poorly in such circumstances (e.g., Dykman, Ackerman, & Oglesby, 1979).

Among the researchers who work in the psychiatric tradition, reaction time is a very common dependent measure. Rosenthal and Allen (1978) reported that RTs of LD children are usually found to be slower than those of non-LD children, that greater individual variability is often found, and that there is a greater likelihood that the RTs of LD youngsters will increase over time in continuous performance tasks. This latter finding suggests that some factor other than a unified attentional dysfunction may be affecting response time. One cannot help but wonder whether a very interesting reward (say, brief glimpses at pictures of nudes) would eliminate possible group differences in reaction time, in these failure-oriented LD youngsters.

The EEG has been another measure employed by those who work with clinical populations. However, in a major review of the neurologic tests given to these children, Coles (1978) concluded that neither the EEG nor any of the tests in the standard neurologic battery could conclusively discriminate LD from non-LD children. In practice though, very few LD children are ever given these tests because very few children are referred to medical schools. Moreover, even if LD/non-LD differences on these tests are sometimes found in such populations, it would not be safe to generalize from such findings to the average LD child. Yet, this is often done.

Vigilance

Vigilance, or sustained attention, is another component common to many theories of attention. Learning-disabled children generally perform poorly on tasks designed to measure this. A typical task consists of isolating the child for 20 to 30 minutes with a panel of flashing lights or a rotating drum displaying letters. The child must make a rapid response to a particular pattern of lights or sequence of letters. The poor performance of LD children on these tasks is commonly offered as evidence of an attentional deficit (e.g., Anderson, Halcomb, & Doyle, 1973). One could certainly make the case, however, that many factors—interest, motivation, desire to conform, and so forth—can contribute substantially to a child's score on a vigilance task. It is reasonable then to suggest that a significant portion of what is measured on such tasks may be things other than attention. Such tasks do measure a behavior pattern that is related to academic success, however, because obedience and willingness to persevere in tedium will certainly help a child succeed in school. But one must certainly question whether failure-oriented LD children would be likely to demonstrate their optimal performance capabilities in such dull, repetive tasks.

Thus, although sustained attention tasks may frequently yield LD/non-LD differences, it may be that the tasks are not appropriate for the measurement of attention with these subjects. Such tasks may merely highlight obvious motivational differences between groups, rather than illustrating any differences in actual attentional capabilities. Such studies tell us very little about the optimal performance of LD children, because they do not provide optimal circumstances in which the children might demonstrate their abilities. It seems reasonable to suggest, therefore, that the results of both arousal studies with clinical LD populations and tedious vigilance tasks with unmotivated, atypical youngsters cannot be taken as very strong support for the notion of attentional deficits in LD children.

Selective Attention

Tasks designed to measure the selective component of attention are the most common in developmental psychology. LD/non-LD performance differences on these tasks are offered as the best evidence of the attentional deficit syndrome. An unquestioned assumption among those who use these tasks is the belief that these tasks are measuring the same unitary component, factor, or ability. This ability is variously called selective attention, distractibility, focusing, discriminability, or stimulus selection, with selective attention the most common term.

There are two general types of experimental paradigms that are used to measure the selective attention deficit. LD children appear to have trouble in tasks with proximal or embedded kinds of distractors in which the extraneous or incidental information appears to affect their performance on a central task. And they also appear to perform more poorly than non-LD children on tasks which measure the central and incidental information directly; that is, LD children are said to pay more attention to the incidental information and less attention to the central information than non-LD children. They are thought to be deficient at selective attention because they inefficiently trade-off some central information for the incidental (e.g., Ross, 1976).

The Proximal/Embedded Tasks

Stroop Tasks.   It is frequently claimed that LD children have trouble with stroop tasks. The classic color Stroop (Stroop, 1935) requires the subject to name the ink color of color words that are printed in discrepant ink hues. A closer look at the research that is cited, however, reveals that the results are somewhat ambiguous. Silverman, Davids, and Andrews (1963) is frequently cited, although an examination of their data shows that when they corrected for base rate differences in naming speed, a significant difference in distractibility did not occur for their "underachievers" until the fifth trial. A trial consisted of reading a color interference card with 100 words on it. It is reasonable to suppose that the underachievers may have lost interest in the task by the 400th word or so. Eakins and Douglas (1971) claimed to show differences between poor and good readers, but they failed to control for group differences in baseline naming speed. If they had, it appears that their effect would have disappeared.

A nonreading version of the Stroop task, "The Fruit Distraction Task," or Fruit Stroop, has also been used (e.g., Santostephano, Rutledge, & Randall, 1965). The distraction condition in this task involves naming the real-world color of inappropriately colored fruit pictures, such as a purple banana. Studies with this paradigm have generally used "poor readers" (not necessarily with normal IQs), and results have been mixed. A variety of conflicting results are reported by Alwitt (1966), Campbell (1969), Denney (1974), and Santostephano et al. (1965). It is still unsettled how a well-selected sample of LD children would perform on this task, although one would expect them to perform more poorly than controls if they evidenced a deficit in selective attention.

The Picture–Word Stroop.   Another type of Stroop-like task involves words embedded in pictures. The child's task is to ignore the embedded words and to name the pictures as fast as possible. It has been shown that children as young as late first grade show Stroop-like interference on this task, and that naming latencies increase, in order, as nonsense words, words unrelated to the pictures, and words from categories related to the pictures are embedded; that is, interference increases as the distractor words become more semantically related to the pictures. The same pattern of interference is found for adults, although overall latencies tend to decrease with age (Ehri, 1977; Golinkoff & Rosinski, 1976; Guttentag & Haith, 1978; Rosinski, 1977; Rosinski, Golinkoff, & Kukish, 1975).

A few of these studies have used "poor readers" and have found the same semantically related interference effects, although the overall response latencies are generally longer than for the controls. However, the poor readers in these studies seem to be never more than 1½ years below grade level in reading (Golinkoff & Rosinski, 1976; Pace & Golinkoff, 1976). Frequently, no reading scores at all are reported for the poor readers (Ehri, 1976; Ehri & Wilce, 1979; Guttentag & Haith, 1978). Because we cannot safely assume that all these poor readers had normal range IQs, it would be interesting to administer this task to a carefully selected sample of learning-disabled children. Given that LD children might have slower baseline picture-naming latencies (RTs), if they were to exhibit a selective attention deficit in performing this task, then the amount of interference they experience would be greater than overall slower baseline picture-naming speed would predict.

The Bender Test.   Some versions of the Bender Visual Motor Gestalt Test (Bender, 1946) have also been used to support the notion of the selective attention deficit. The test requires children to replicate nine simple, geometric designs. The Bender has been popular with reading specialists for years, although many now believe that it is not particularly good at discriminating poor readers from good ones (Coles, 1978). There is some evidence though that when the Bender test is made more distracting, LD children have trouble with it. Sabatino and Ysseldyke (1972) drew extraneous backgrounds around the simple Bender figures and found that a sample of 143 nonreading third graders with normal range IQs performed significantly worse than a group of matched controls. Their performance with the standard Bender figures was equivalent to that of the controls, however.

Other researchers have worked with the standardized *Background Interference Procedure* (BIP) for the Bender test (Canter, 1966). In this test the extraneous background stimuli are on the sheet of paper onto which the subject copies the

Bender designs. The subject copies the figures twice, once onto a white sheet of paper, once onto a sheet with wavy, intersecting BIP lines on it. The difference between the score on the standard Bender test and the score on the BIP paper is the measure of distraction, or selective attention efficiency/inefficiency.

Fabian and Jacobs (1981) found that their sample of 14- to 18-year-old LD adolescents performed significantly worse in the BIP condition than did the normal 8- to 12-year-olds in the BIP manual tables. Other studies with this test have used populations that were more clinical. There is some evidence that this test can identify "hyperactive" children (Adams, Hayden, & Canter, 1974); children with "cerebral dysfunction" (Kenny, 1971); and "minimally brain damaged children" (Hayden, Talmadge, Hall, & Schiff, 1970). Because all these labels are frequently used to describe LD children, one might presume that LD children would perform poorly on this test if they are more distractible, and suffer from a selective attention deficit.

The Embedded Figures Test.   Results of studies with the Embedded Figures Test (EFT) and the Children's Embedded Figures Test (CEFT) (Witkin, Oltman, Raskin, & Karp, 1971) have also been used as support for the notion of a selective attention deficit. These tests are said to measure a relatively stable perceptual style known as "field dependence/independence." The task is to find and outline a simple geometric form that is obscured in an embedding background of lines and shading. LD children are often found to be field dependent on these tests, and field dependent children are thought to have trouble with stimulus selection. Many LD researchers consider this to be evidence of a deficit in selective attention.

Results of experiments with LD subjects have been mixed, however. Both Goldman and Hardin (1982) with the CEFT and Spellacy and Peter (1978) with the EFT found LD children performed significantly worse than non-LDs. Scott and Moore (1980) found no LD/non-LD group differences on the CEFT. Tarver and Maggiore (1979) found no LD/non-LD group differences either. Cowen and Harway (1976) also found no LD/non-LD group differences, but a subgroup of their LD sample with "visual/perceptual problems," as measured on subtests of the Illinois Test of Psycholinguistic Abilities, performed significantly worse than non-LDs on the CEFT. There does appear to be a trend for LD/non-LD group differences. However, it must be noted that the EFT is known to correlate moderately with IQ (Witkin et al., 1971), so there is some possibility that IQ differences between groups may have contributed to group performance differences in some of the studies cited.

Selective Listening.   LD children are also said to demonstrate an attentional deficit in selective listening tasks. The child's task is to select and repeat one of two different auditory messages that are presented simultaneously. Mulberg and Whitman (1978) found that reading-disabled (normal IQ) children performed poorly on this task. The children made more intrusions from the unattended ear and more errors shadowing, or repeating, the selected message. On the other hand, Pelham (1979) found that a group of reading-disabled children did not experience more overall distraction in a selective listening task, but they had problems only in the speeded conditions of the task. Lasky and Tobin (1973) found a group of 11 "pre-LD" first graders to be not distracted from following the instructions on an audio tape by a white noise distractor, but they were more distracted than controls by a tape of a competing linguistic message.

It is not unreasonable, however, to expect that poor students would perform poorly on complicated, unnatural tasks like selective listening. Bryan and Bryan (1980) argue that many extraneous factors may contribute to a child's poor performance on auditory tasks: the child's age, the complexity of the task, the type of task, the responses demanded, and the child's verbal skills. All of these may interfere with the researchers' ability to measure attention in selective-listening tasks with young, atypical subjects.

The Central/Incidental Studies

The second type of studies that are cited as evidence for the selective attention deficit involve paradigms that measure the central and incidental information directly. If one conceptualizes selective attention as a trade off between central and incidental information, as many researchers do, and if LD youngsters have a deficit in selective attention, then they should pay relatively more attention to incidental information and less attention to central information than non-LD children. Higher incidental recall by LD children has been found in two studies. Diekel and Friedman (1976) gave non-LD and LD children a difficult IBM card-sorting task. They found that the LD children made more errors in sorting the cards (the central task) and that they also remembered more extraneous markings on the cards (the incidental measure). Likewise, Mondani and Tutko (1969), in a widely cited study, found underachievers more likely to notice and recall extraneous doodles on a questionnaire. There was no measure of central recall in this study, however.

In both of these studies, although the amount of incidental information recalled by the LD groups was greater than that recalled by the controls, it was not demonstrated that the LD children were unable to select the central information. It might have been the case that the card sorting was difficult to do, and the questionnaire was difficult to read, so the LD children directed their attention to less aversive incidental stimuli. This is not a demonstration of attentional deficit, because in neither case was there a baseline measure of performance on the central task without the distractors. If LDs are trading central for incidental information, it is crucial to measure their performance on the central task without the distractors, so that one can measure whether their central performance is impaired by the addition of the incidental distractors. And even if the central performance is impaired, the burden of proof would be on the researcher to show that the child can not, as opposed to will not, attend to the central display. This criticism can be leveled against many of the studies that purport to show selective attention deficits.

The Hagen Paradigm.   The most widely cited evidence for the selective attention deficit in LD children comes from studies with Hagen's (1967) Incidental Learning Paradigm. The task requires that a child remember the positions of animal pictures in a repeatedly presented, random, seven-card array, and that the child later recall the incidental pictures that had been paired with the animals. Critiques of this paradigm have been put forward by many researchers, notably Douglas and Peters (1979) and Lane (1980). Nevertheless, results of studies with this paradigm are still presented as evidence for the selective attention deficit. Suffice it to say that Hagen himself claims that strategies such as verbal rehearsal confound the measurement of attention with this task (Hagen & Kail, 1975). Furthermore, when LD children are taught verbal rehearsal strategies their performance approximates that of non-LDs (e.g., Tarver, Hallahan, Kauffman, & Ball, 1976).

If one were to allow that the Hagen task measured selective attention, and one wished to substantiate an LD deficiency, it would be necessary to show that LD children pay relatively more attention than do non-LDs to the incidental information on this task. A variety of researchers have repeatedly used this task and they have never been able to demonstrate this: Copeland and Wisniewski (1981); Dawson, Hallahan, Reeve, and Ball (1980); Hallahan, Gajar, Cohen, and Tarver (1978); Hallahan, Kauffman, and Ball (1973); Heins, Hallahan, Tarver, and Kauffman (1976); Mercer, Cullinan, Hallahan, and LaFleur (1975); Pelham (1979); Tarver, Hallahan, Cohen, and Kauffman (1977); Tarver et al. (1976); Tarver and Maggiore (1979); Quay and Weld (1980). Incidental recall scores are never found to be significantly different between groups; in fact, they are often lower for the LD groups. Moreover, the correlations between central and incidental recall almost never appear to differ significantly. Memory for the central stimuli is the only real difference that is consistently found. One exception was a study by Pelham and Ross (1977), which did find incidental recall to be higher for the LD group, but the researchers used a nonstandard administration of the task.

Surprisingly, all the aforementioned studies are cited as evidence for the alleged selective attention deficit of LD children. In order to provide some support for this claim, Hallahan created the "Index of Selective Attention Efficiency": the percentage of central recall minus the percentage of incidental recall (%C–%I; Hallahan, 1975). Nevertheless, significant %C–%I group differences are reported in only two of these studies (Copeland & Wisniewski, 1981; Hallahan et al., 1978), and trends are reported for only two others (Dawson et al., 1980; Tarver et al., 1977).

Yet another problem with this literature is that there is never a baseline measure of central recall without the incidental distractor pictures. Therefore, given the typical finding of equal incidental recall scores between LD/non-LD groups, one cannot assume that the central recall of LD children has been differentially affected by the distractor pictures at all. Rather, one can only safely assume that LD and non-LD children attend about equally to the incidental information, and that they may differ in their purposeful central recall strategies.

SUMMARY AND NEW EVIDENCE AGAINST A SELECTIVE ATTENTION DEFICIT

Although results of studies with the Hagen paradigm have been the most commonly presented evidence for the alleged selective attention deficit of LD children, such studies have consistently demonstrated only lower central memory scores for LD children. The other type of experiments that have been offered as support for the selective attention deficit are experiments in which recall for incidental, proximal or embedded distractors is not measured directly, although the presence of these distractors seems to disrupt the central performance of LD children more so than non-LD children. In this tradition there is some evidence that LD children are more distracted by Stroop interference, by embedded figures, by extraneous backgrounds on Bender figures, and on several experimenter-designed tasks that have these sorts of properties. Admittedly, there are problems with some of these studies, and the results have been mixed in several cases, but if there is such a thing as a selective attention deficit it should show up on several tests designed to measure this deficit convergently. Hagen and Kail (1975) claim that performance on these sorts of tasks should correlate, because these tasks are assumed to measure a common ability. And, as was discussed earlier, such correlations are necessary in order to demonstrate that the tasks actually measure the same thing, a thing that we call attention.

One researcher who examined correlations among performance scores on several selective attention tasks was Pelham (1979). As was mentioned previously, he did not find clear-cut LD/non-LD differences on four attentional tasks, and he did not find significant correlations among the tasks. His task were in different modalities, however, and this may have attenuated some of his correlations. Moreover, results of two of his four tasks might have been interpreted as supporting the notion of a selective attention deficit, although he argued against such an interpretation. Finally, an examination of his data reveals that his task reliabilities were low ($M = .32$), and that two of his six correlations were not significantly different from their theoretical ceilings. Such problems make clear interpretations of his data difficult.

One must conclude, therefore, that the evidence for a selective attention deficit in LD children is certainly less than satisfactory, although the issue is not entirely resolved. Unambiguous empirical testing of such a notion has not previously been done. Moreover, the very notion of selective attention as a unitary factor or ability on which there are stable, individual differences can also be challenged.

Researchers who study the development of selective attention find that the age at which selective attention appears to be efficient depends on a number of variables including which tasks the subjects are given, and how the tasks are explained to them (e.g., Sexton & Geffen, 1979). Eleanor Gibson has repeatedly argued that infants are selective from birth, and that selection efficiency depends upon task appropriate skills and expectancies (e.g., Gibson & Rader, 1979). It is reasonable, therefore, to suppose that diverse selective attention tasks do not uniformly measure a thing called selective attention, but that different tasks require different specific strategies, prior knowledge, coordination, and skills, all of which affect a child's performance on these tasks. Sensible research hypotheses, therefore, are: (a) that systematic LD/non-LD differences in selective attention performance cannot be demonstrated, and (b) that different selective attention tasks do not measure a unitary ability.

A test of these hypotheses (McNellis, 1984) was recently completed. Five selective attention tasks were employed, all in the visual modality, all with proximal or embedded distractors. On all these tasks previous researchers had shown some evidence for LD/non-LD performance differences. Included were a Stroop Color-Word task, a picture–word Stroop task with four types of distractors, a modified version of the Group Embedded Figures Test, and the Bender Background Interference procedure. There was also an experimenter-designed, central/incidental task similar to the Hagen task but modified to decrease the memory load and make it less strategy dependent. In this task, the "picture–picture Stroop task," the child had to name rapidly seven animal pictures, which were repeatedly presented in random order, and to ignore seven pictures of household objects, which were embedded in or proximal to the central animal pictures. As a separate measure, the children were later asked to recall the central and the incidental pictures.

Each task was designed to have a "baseline" and at least one "distractor" condition. In the case of the three Stroop-like tasks, the baseline conditions involved rapidly naming the colors or pictures with no distractors present. In the Bender and the modified Embedded Figures Test the baseline measures were the number of errors that the child made in finding or reproducing the figures without extraneous background lines or shading. In this manner, it was possible to test whether performance in the baseline condition was significantly different from performance in the distractor condition. More important, the effects of possible group differences in performance in the baseline condition could be statistically removed from the distractor condition to yield a more precise measure of "selective attention." For example, although the Stroop-like tasks had reaction time measures, the effects of possible slower baseline RTs in the LD group could be removed.

It was predicted that although LD children might perform more poorly than controls in the raw baseline and distractor conditions of the five tasks, they would not perform more poorly on the selective attention measures, when the effects of differences in baseline performance were removed. Also, it was hypothesized that performance in the baseline conditions would correlate, and might correlate with reading ability. However, selective attention measures would be uncorrelated, and would not correlate with reading ability. This would demonstrate that the children were performing in a systematic manner on the tasks themselves, but that only the selective attention measures of the tasks were uncorrelated. Finally, it was predicted that LD children would not trade-off central information for incidental in the recall measure of the picture–picture Stroop task; that is, they would not exhibit higher incidental memory scores at the expense of lower central memory scores.

Sixty-seven children, 36 LDs and 31 non-LD controls, participated in the study. IQ scores, and scores on standardized reading tests administered within approximately 1 month of the experiment were available for all LD children. The LD children were selected to have normal-range IQs of 84 and above ($M = 98$, $SD = 10.91$). Their reading scores averaged 1.9 years below grade level. Because IQ tests are not given to normally achieving children, reading level was used as a fair approximation of normal-range IQ for the nonLD children. The 31 non-LD children had, on the average, reading scores that were within 1 month of their grade level. Parental occupation information was available for most of the children and this was used as a rough measure of socioeconomic status (Davis, Smith, & Stephenson, 1980). The children were matched as closely as possible in age, IQ or achievement, SES, and race. The groups differed significantly in sex, however, and this was taken into account in the data analysis, as was the greater variability in age of the LD group.

The results of the experiment showed that the tasks were sufficiently distracting for the children. An analysis of the raw data showed that the distracting (D) conditions were significantly more difficult than the nondistracting (ND) baseline conditions for all five tasks for the nonLD children, and for four of the five tasks for the LD children. Moreover, as was predicted, LD children performed more poorly than non-LDs in both the raw baseline and distractor measures on four of the five tasks.

As was mentioned previously, it was necessary to devise a method whereby the effects of possible group differences in performance in the baseline conditions could be statistically removed from the distractor conditions. This would provide the measure of selective attention. Simple D minus ND difference scores, or D/ND ratios could not be used because such measures are inherently unreliable, because they assume equal, linear relationships between D and ND for all tasks, and because correlations among variables transformed in this manner may be spurious (Cohen & Cohen, 1983, chaps. 2, 10).

Therefore, the data from all 67 children were combined and multiple regression equations were computed for each of the five tasks. For each task possible baseline, sex, and age differences in performance were removed from performance in the distractor condition. The residuals from these regression lines (the

Residualized Gain Scores) were the data of comparison, the measure of selective attention. Thus, the selective attention measures were that portion of the distractor score that was not predicted by baseline performance, age, or sex. (This method is discussed in Cronbach & Furby, 1970.)

The first major hypothesis of the investigation was that LD/non-LD differences would not be demonstrated on multiple selective attention tasks. To test this hypothesis, t tests were used to measure the mean difference of the residuals, the selective attention measures, between LD/non-LD groups. This procedure is directly analogous to analysis of covariance, with sex, age, and baseline performance as the covariates, and the distraction scores as the dependent variable. This method is more useful than analysis of covariance, however, because the regression equations yield residuals, which can be used for group comparisons, for power calculations, for correlations, for reliability calculations, and for computing theoretical ceilings on the observed correlations. Results of the t tests showed no significant differences between the groups on any of the five selective attention measures, although the Bender BIP approached significance, t (64) = 1.82, $p < .08$, two-tailed. The average p-value for the tests of group differences on the five tasks was .48.

One can safely assume that no real population differences existed between the LD and non-LD groups on the selective attention measures of the five tasks, because the power analyses demonstrated that there was sufficient statistical power to detect differences on any task, had any differences existed. The average power to detect a mean group difference as small as 15% on any task was found to be .80. All tests were thus sufficiently powerful to detect a difference, yet none was found.

The second major prediction of the study was that selective attention would not appear to be a stable, unitary factor or ability. If the five tasks are measuring the same ability, as many developmental psychologists have suggested, then performance on the selective attention measures should correlate. Correlations were computed among the five selective attention measures and only 1 of the 10 intercorrelations was significant, with an uncorrected α of .05. The average correlation among the tasks was only .11. Moreover, the Omnibus Null Hypothesis, that all rs might really be zero, could not be rejected, $\chi^2(10) = 13.91$, $.10 < p < .25$ (Cohen & Cohen, 1983, p. 58).

To ensure that unreliability in the five selective attention tasks did not cause the correlations to be so low, split-half or odd–even reliabilities were computed for each of the five tasks. These reliabilities were used to compute the theoretical ceilings for each of the 10 intercorrelations. Each correlation was then compared to its theoretical ceiling, and all were found to be significantly below their ceilings, at least $p < .01$, in all cases. One can conclude, therefore, that the low intercorrelations among the tasks were not caused by lack of reliability in the selective attention tasks, rather, that the tasks do not appear to be measuring a unitary factor or ability. Additional support for this assertion comes from an exploratory Principal Components Analysis, which indicated that five separate factors are required to explain the data. These findings cast serious doubt on the notion of selective attention as a unitary ability on which there are stable individual differences.

Performance in the baseline conditions was examined next. This was done in order to ensure that the subjects were not performing randomly in all task conditions, but that only the selective attention measures were uncorrelated. Five new regression equations were generated, which removed the effects of differences in age and sex from the baseline scores. This allowed for direct comparison with the selective attention measures. It was predicted that the baseline measures would intercorrelate, although selective attention measures would not, and that baseline measures might correlate with reading ability, although selective attention measures would not.

These hypotheses were confirmed. Performance in the baseline condition proved to be quite systematic. The average of the 10 intercorrelations among baseline measures was .35, and 7 out of 10 were significant. The Group Embedded Figures Test accounted for the 3 nonsignificant correlations, as it appeared only to correlate with the Bender BIP test. Recall that the average correlation among the selective attention measures was only .11, however. Correlations between baseline performance and reading level also provided proof that the data were systematic. The average correlation of reading level with the 5 baseline measures was $-.23$, with 3 out of 5 significant. The mean correlation of selective attention and reading ability was only $-.08$, however, and none were significant. (These correlations are negative because the dependent measures in the five tasks are errors and latencies.)

In addition to the predictions about the five selective attention measures, there was an additional prediction about the central (C) and incidental (I) recall measures on the picture–picture Stroop task. Unlike the Hagen task, the recall measures on this task could not be substantially affected by strategy or rehearsal, because the task was primarily a Stroop task. Therefore, it was predicted that although LD children might recall somewhat less central information, they would not recall more incidental information than the non-LDs; that is, they would not trade-off central information for incidental. An analysis of the raw recall scores showed that, surprisingly, LD children recalled slightly more central and incidental information than non-LDs. These differences were not significant, however, when effects of differences in age and sex were removed.

Another measure that was used to compare LD/non-LD groups on the recall measure of this task was Hallahan's "Index of Selective Attention Efficiency," %C–%I. This difference score was computed for the raw central and incidental recall data for the LDs and the non-LDs. If this index measures selective attention efficiency, and if non-LDs are more efficient than LDs, then one would expect this index to yield group differences. No significant differences between groups were found. Moreover, if %C–%I can be taken as a measure of selective attention, one might expect it to correlate with the five other selective attention measures, the residuals for the five tasks. This analysis was also done. The average correlation of %C–%I, after the effects of age and sex differences were removed, with the other selective attention measures was .05. None of the correlations were significant. Thus, there is convincing data to support the position that LD children do not appear to differ from non-LD children in either central or incidental recall, when strategy variables such as rehearsal are not confounding the task. The final prediction of the study was confirmed.

CONCLUSIONS AND IMPLICATIONS

This chapter has been an attempt to outline the major evidence for the central syndrome that is said to affect LD children, the attentional deficit disorder. It was argued that evidence from studies with the arousal and vigilance components of attention does not provide clear-cut support for the attentional deficit notion, because such measures are confounded with many other variables, such as motivation, that hamper the measurement of attention with young, atypical subjects. Next, the evidence from selective attention studies was reviewed in some detail. These studies appeared to indicate a tendency for poorer LD performance on a variety of tasks, although some methodological problems with these studies were discussed. Critically, none of the studies reviewed, with one exception, had even attempted to question whether these various attention tasks were really measuring the same "thing" called selective attention at all.

Finally, some recent research with LD children (McNellis, 1984) was outlined. No evidence was found for the alleged selective attention deficit in learning-disabled children in this study, although evidence from studies with the selective component of attention had previously proved to be the best evidence for the alleged attentional deficit disorder of LD children. Five selective attention tasks were used in this experiment, and on only one task, the Bender BIP, was there even a tendency for LD children to demonstrate more distraction than the non-LDs. Each test had enough statistical power to detect group differences, yet no differences emerged. A sixth measure of central and incidental recall, which has often been used as a measure of selective attention, also failed to demonstrate significant group differences. These central and incidental recall scores were examined several different ways, and no measure yielded significant LD/non-LD differences.

On all these tasks, or tasks very similar to them, other researchers have sometimes demonstrated LD/non-LD differences. One reason that group differences were not found in this study may be because the subjects were selected and matched on IQ or achievement, SES, race, sex, grade, and age as carefully as practical restraints in real-world research would allow. The greater age variability of the LD children was taken into account in the data analysis, as was the inevitable sex difference between groups. Finally, baseline performance differences between the groups were controlled. This was particularly important because three of the tasks required a reaction time response. Other researchers who use selective attention measures with LD populations rarely match groups on all these variables, nor do they routinely use multiple regression to control for differences that may exist. Other researchers may have found group differences on similar tasks because their samples may not have been as carefully selected; because their tasks, notably the Hagen task, may have been confounded by other cognitive variables; or because they may not have controlled for baseline response differences between groups. One can, however, assert with a fair degree of confidence that the reason that no LD/non-LD differences were found on these five selective attention measures is that no population differences exist.

The second major finding of the study was that there were no significant correlations among the selective attention measures, although baseline performance scores for the tasks were correlated. The tasks had been designed to be highly similar to one another to increase the chance of intercorrelation. All tasks were visual, and all required attending to a central visual stimulus in the face of proximal or embedded distractors. Furthermore, the low observed correlations were not caused by lack of reliability in the data. All observed correlations were significantly and substantially below their theoretical ceilings. It appeared that the five tasks were not measuring a unitary selective attention ability, because performance on the selective attention measures was uncorrelated.

The major implications of the study concern the nature of selective attention itself and its relationship with developmental psychology. The results of the study indicate that developmental psychologists have been willy-nilly researching an "ability" that may not exist. Neither these data, nor those of Pelham (1979), who used a different battery of tests and a different subject pool, were able to demonstrate correlations in performance among several selective attention measures. Previous developmental researchers have each used a single type of selective attention measure, and their findings are as diverse as their tasks and instructions. Psychologists and educators are going to have to look somewhere other than at "attention" to find a single syndrome that may typify learning-disabled children.

ACKNOWLEDGMENT

This study was supported in part by the Cornell Comprehensive Cognitive Psychology Training Program, under NIMH Grant 5T32 MH15777.

REFERENCES

Adams, J., Hayden, B. S., & Canter, A. (1974). The relationship between the Canter Background Interference Procedure and the hyperkinetic behavior syndrome. *Journal of Learning Disabilities*, *1*, 110–115.

Alwitt, L. F. (1966). Attention in a visual task among non-readers and readers. *Perceptual and Motor Skills, 23,* 361–362.

Anderson, R. P., Halcomb, C. G., & Doyle, R. B. (1973). The measurement of attentional deficits. *Exceptional Children, 39,* 534–539.

Bender, L. (1946). *The Visual–Motor Gestalt test.* New York: American Orthopsychiatric Association.

Bryan, T. H., & Bryan, J. H. (1980). Learning disorders. In H. E. Rie & E. D. Rie (Eds.), *Handbook of minimal brain dysfunction: A critical view* (pp. 456–482). New York: Wiley.

Cambell, S. (1969). *Cognitive styles in normal and hyperactive children.* Unpublished doctoral dissertation, McGill University, Montreal.

Canter, A. (1966). A background interference procedure to increase sensitivity of the Bender Gestalt test to organic brain disorder. *Journal of Consulting Psychology, 30,* 91–97.

Cohen, J., & Cohen, P. (1983). *Applied multiple regression/correlation analysis for the behavioral sciences* (2nd ed.). Hillsdale, NJ: Lawrence Erlbaum Associates.

Coles, G. S. (1978). The learning disabilities test battery: Empirical and social issues. *Harvard Educational Review, 48,* 313–337.

Copeland, A. P., & Wisniewski, N. M. (1981). Learning disability and hyperactivity: Deficits in selective attention. *Journal of Experimental Child Psychology, 32,* 88–101.

Cowen, R. J., & Harway, N. I. (1976). Field dependence in visually and non-visually involved learning disabled children. *Perceptual and Motor Skills, 43,* 67–74.

Cronbach, L., & Furby, L. (1970). How should we measure change or should we? *Psychological Bulletin, 74,* 68–80.

Davis, J., Smith, T., & Stephenson, C. B. (1980). Occupational classification distributions. *General social surveys, 1972–1980: Cumulative codebook.* Chicago: National Opinion Research Center.

Dawson, M. M., Hallahan, D. P., Reeve, R. E., & Ball, D. W. (1980). The effect of reinforcement and verbal rehearsal on selective attention in learning disabled children. *Journal of Abnormal Child Psychology, 8,* 133–144.

Denney, D. R. (1974). Relationship of three cognitive style dimensions to elementary reading abilities. *Journal of Educational Psychology, 66,* 702–709.

Diekel, S. M., & Friedman, M. P. (1976). Selective attention in children with learning disabilities. *Perceptual and Motor Skills, 42,* 675–678.

Douglas, V. I., & Peters, K. G. (1979). Toward a clearer definition of the attentional deficit of hyperactive children. In G. A. Hale & M. Lewis (Eds.), *Attention and cognitive development* (pp. 173–247). New York: Plenum.

Dykman, R. A., Ackerman, P. T., Clements, S. D., & Peters, J. E. (1971). Specific learning disabilities: An attentional deficit syndrome. In H. R. Myklebust (Ed.), *Progress in learning disabilities* (Vol. 2, pp. 56–93). New York: Grune & Stratton.

Dykman, R. A., Ackerman, P. T., & Oglesby, D. M. (1979). Selective and sustained attention in hyperactive, learning-disabled, and normal boys. *Journal of Nervous and Mental Disease, 16,* 288–297.

Eskins, S., & Douglas, V. I. (1971). "Automatization" and oral reading problems in children. *Journal of Learning Disabilities, 4,* 26–32.

Ehri, L. C. (1976). Do words really interfere in naming pictures? *Child Development, 47,* 502–505.

Ehri, L. C. (1977). Do adjectives and functors interfere as much as nouns in naming pictures? *Child Development, 48,* 697–701.

Ehri, L. C., & Wilce, L. S. (1979). Does word training increase or decrease interference in a Stroop task? *Journal of Experimental Child Psychology, 27,* 352–364.

Fabian, J. J., & Jacobs, V. W. (1981). Discrimination of neurological impairment in the learning disabled adolescent. *Journal of Learning Disabilities, 14,* 594–596.

Gibson, E. J., & Rader, N. (1979). Attention: The perceiver as performer. In G. A. Hale & M. Lewis (Eds.), *Attention and cognitive development* (pp. 1–21). New York: Plenum.

Goldman, R. L., & Hardin, V. B. (1982). The social perception of learning disabled and non-learning disabled children. *The Exceptional Child, 29,* 57–63.

Golinkoff, R. M., & Rosinski, R. R. (1976). Decoding, semantic processing and reading comprehension skill. *Child Development, 47,* 252–258.

Guttentag, R. E., & Haith, M. M. (1978). Automatic processing as a function of age and reading ability. *Child Development, 49,* 707–716.

Hagen, J. W. (1967). The effect of distraction on selective attention. *Child Development, 38,* 685–694.

Hagen, J. W., & Kail, R. V. (1975). The role of attention in perceptual and cognitive development. In W. M. Cruickshank & D. P. Hallahan (Eds.), *Perceptual and learning disabilities in children: Vol. 2. Research and theory* (pp. 165–192). New York: Syracuse University Press.

Hallahan, D. P. (1975). Distractibility in the learning disabled child. In W. M. Cruickshank & D. P. Hallahan (Eds.), *Perceptual and learning disabilities in children: Vol. 2. Research and theory* (pp. 195–218). New York: Syracuse University Press.

Hallahan, D. P., Gajar, A. H., Cohen, S. B., & Tarver, S. G. (1978). Selective attention and locus of control in learning disabled and normal children. *Journal of Learning Disabilities, 11,* 231–236.

Hallahan, D. P., Kauffman, J. M., & Ball, D. W. (1973). Selective attention and cognitive tempo of low and high achieving sixth grade males. *Perceptual and Motor Skills, 36,* 579–583.

Hayden, B. S., Talmadge, M., Hall, M., & Schiff, D. (1970). Diagnosing minimal brain damage in children: A comparison of two Bender scoring systems. *Merril–Palmer Quarterly, 16,* 278–285.

Heins, E. D., Hallahan, D. P., Tarver, S. G., & Kauffman, J. M. (1976). Relationship between cognitive tempo and selective attention in learning disabled children. *Perceptual and Motor Skills, 42,* 233–234.

Kahneman,, D. (1973). *Attention and effort.* Englewood Cliffs, NJ: Prentice-Hall.

Kenny, T. J. (1971). Background interference procedure: A means of assessing neurological dysfunction in school-age children. *Journal of Consulting Clinical Psychology, 37,* 44–46.

Keogh, B. K., Major-Kingsley, S. M., Omori-Gordon, H., & Reid, H. P. (1982). *A system of marker variables for the field of learning disabilities.* Syracuse: Syracuse University Press.

Keogh, B. K., & Margolis, J. (1976). Learn to labor and to wait: Attentional problems of children with learning disorders. *Journal of Learning Disabilities, 9,* 18–26.

Kirk, S. A., & Elkins, J. (1975). Characteristics of children enrolled in the child service demonstration centers. *Journal of Learning Disabilities, 8,* 630–637.

Koppel, S. (1979). Testing the attentional deficit notion. *Journal of Learning Disabilities, 12,* 43–48.

Lane, D. M. (1980). Theoretical notes: Incidental learning and the development of selective attention. *Psychological Review, 87,* 316–319.

Lasky, E. Z., & Tobin, H. (1973). Linguistic and nonlinguistic competing message effects. *Journal of Learning Disabilities, 6,* 243–251.

McNellis, K. L. (1984). *The selective attention deficit in learning disabled children.* Unpublished doctoral dissertation, Cornell University, Ithaca, NY.

Mercer, C. D., Cullinan, D., Hallahan, D. P., & LaFleur, N. K. (1975). Modeling and attention-retention in learning disordered children. *Journal of Learning Disabilities, 8,* 440–450.

Mondani, M. S., & Tutko, T. A. (1969). Relationship of academic underachievement to incidental learning. *Journal of Consulting Clinical Psychology, 33,* 558–560.

Mulberg, W., & Whitman, R. D. (1978, February). *Selective attention in good and poor readers: Hope for the left hemisphere.* Paper presented at the International Neuropsychology Society Convention, Minneapolis.

Pace, A. J., & Golinkoff, R. M. (1976). Relationship between word difficulty and access of single-word meaning by skilled and less skilled readers. *Journal of Educational Psychology, 68,* 760–767.

Pelham, W. E. (1979). Selective attention deficits in poor readers? Dichotic listening, speeded classification, and auditory and visual central and incidental learning tasks. *Child Development, 50,* 1050–1061.

Pelham, W. E., & Ross, A. O. (1977). Selective attention in children with reading problems: A developmental study of incidental learning. *Journal of Abnormal Child Psychology, 5,* 1–7.

Quay, L. C., & Weld, G. L. (1980). Visual and auditory selective attention and reflection-impulsivity in normal and learning disabled boys at two age levels. *Journal of Abnormal Child Psychology, 8,* 117–125.

Rosenthal, R. H., & Allen, T. W. (1978). An examination of attention, arousal, and learning dysfunctions of hyperkinetic children. *Psychological Bulletin, 85,* 689–715.

Rosinski, R. R. (1977). Picture–word interference is semantically based. *Child Development, 48,* 643–647.

Rosinski, R. R., Golinkoff, R. M., & Kukish, K. S. (1975). Automatic semantic processing in a picture–word interference task. *Child Development, 46,* 247–253.

Ross, A. O. (1976). *Psychological aspects of learning disabilities and reading disorders.* New York: McGraw–Hill.

Sabatino, D. A., & Ysseldyke, J. E. (1972). Effect of extraneous "background" on visual–perceptual performance of readers and nonreaders. *Perceptual and Motor Skills, 35,* 323–328.

Samuels, S. J., & Edwall, G. (1981). The role of attention in reading with implications for the learning disabled student. *Journal of Learning Disabilities, 14,* 353–361.

Santostephano, S., Rutledge, L., & Randall, D. (1965). Cognitive styles and reading disability. *Psychology in the Schools, 2,* 57–62.

Scott, N. A., & Moore, W. A. (1980). Differences in locus of control orientation between normal and learning disabled boys. *Psychological Reports, 46,* 795–801.

Sexton, M. A., & Geffen, G. (1979). Development of three strategies of attention in dichotic monitoring. *Developmental Psychology, 15,* 299–310.

Silverman, M., Davids, A., & Andrews, J. M. (1963). Powers of attention and academic achievement. *Perceptual and Motor Skills, 17,* 243–249.

Spellacy, F., & Peter, B. (1978). Dyscalculia and elements of the developmental Gerstmann Syndrome in school children. *Cortex, 14,* 197–206.

Stroop, J. R. (1935). Studies of interference in serial verbal reactions. *Journal of Experimental Psychology, 18,* 643–662.

Tarver, S. G., & Hallahan, D. P. (1974). Attentional deficits in children with learning disabilities: A review. *Journal of Learning Disabilities, 7,* 560–569.

Tarver, S. G., Hallahan, D. P., Cohen, S. B., & Kauffman, J. M. (1977). The development of visual selective attention and verbal rehearsal in learning disabled boys. *Journal of Learning Disabilities, 10,* 491–500.

Tarver, S. G., Hallahan, D. P., Kauffman, J. M., & Ball, D. W. (1976). Verbal rehearsal and selective attention in children with learning disabilities: A developmental lag. *Journal of Experimental Child Psychology, 22,* 375–385.

Tarver, S. G., & Maggiore, R. (1979). Cognitive development in learning disabled boys. *Learning Disabilities Quarterly, 2,* 78–84.

Witkin, H., Oltman, P., Raskin, E., & Karp, J. (1971). *A manual for the embedded figures test.* Palo Alto, CA: Consulting Psychologists Press.

4

An Interactive Model of
Strategic Processing

Mitchell Rabinowitz
University of Illinois at Chicago

Michelene T. H. Chi
Learning Research and Development Center

With the popularization of an information-processing approach to the study of cognition, developmental and cognitive psychologists have been interested in specifying the processes (or processing deficiencies) that determine the level and characteristics of performance. For example, when either very competent or very poor performance is exhibited, what are the processes or processing deficiencies that influence the level of performance? In order to explore this issue, a comparative approach contrasting performance from such groups as novices and experts within a given domain, children of different ages, or learning-disabled and nondisabled children is often used. This methodology permits the uncovering of particular processes that are responsible for variations in performance proficiency. Such research is of interest to psychologists and practitioners working with learning-disabled children who want to understand the causes of the low levels of performance, as well as suggest possible methods of remediation.

In this chapter, we assert one commonly accepted view: that learning-disabled children who show no apparent brain damage perform poorly because of deficiencies in strategic processing. Although this premise is widely accepted, the reasons why we observe such differences in the use of strategies are still being debated. We propose a possible explanation for such variations in strategic processing by addressing the relationship between existing knowledge in semantic memory and the use of cognitive strategies. Specifically, we argue that both the decision to use a strategy and the efficiency in which a strategy can be used are based on a complex interaction with the conceptual knowledge to which the strategy is to be applied. The influence of this knowledge on processing is illustrated with the aid of a computer simulation environment in which a spreading activation memory system is modeled.

STRATEGIC DEFICIENCIES

At a general level, strategies are often described as procedures that are used as an aid in the performance of a given task. Examples of different strategies abound in the psychological literature as do different definitions. Strategies can be powerful in that they are ideally suited for use on one particular task; or weak, in that they can be used generally across a wide variety of tasks (Newell, 1979). For the initial purpose of this chapter, the important characteristics of strategies are that they are *goal-oriented* processes (Brown, Bransford, Ferrara, & Campione, 1983; Chi, 1985) that are *intentionally* invoked (Paris, 1978, in press). Additional characteristics of strategic processes are specified as this chapter progresses.

Much comparative research has indicated that poorer performance is often associated with problems related to the use of strategic processes; i.e., either optimal strategies are not used or there is inefficient use of the strategies. In most instances, older children who efficiently use good strategies perform considerably better on tasks than younger children who are less efficient at strategy use or who are nonstrategic. The contrast between learning-disabled children and nondisabled children of the same age often mimics those differences between younger and older children; that is, learning-disabled children are less efficient or exhibit a deficiency in the use of strategic processing (Bauer, 1982, 1984; Campione, Brown, & Ferrara, 1982; Ceci, 1982, 1984; Worden, 1983).

Evidence showing deficiencies in learning-disabled children's strategic processing comes from research investigating differences in memory performance. Torgesen and Goldman (1977) asked learning-disabled and normal second graders to learn the sequence in which the experimenter pointed to a series of pictures. A 15-sec delay period was used to observe any evidence of overt rehearsing, such as lip movements or whispered words. Learning-disabled children showed less evidence of overt rehearsal and recalled less than their normal peers. Later training in the use of overt rehearsal, however, eliminated recall differences between the two ability groups.

Similarly, other researchers have linked ineffective rehearsal strategies with poor memory performance in the learning-disabled children. For example, Bauer (1977, 1979) showed that following a short delay after the presentation of a list of items, recall within the primacy portion of the serial position curve was less for learning-disabled children than for normal children. The recall of items from this portion of the list has been shown to be very dependent on effective rehearsal. The recall of items at other points of the curve was similar for the two groups. This finding suggests that normal children used rehearsal to maintain the items in memory. In addition, increasing the delay between presentation and recall negatively affected the recall of the learning-disabled children much more than the recall of the normal children (Bauer, 1977, 1979; Torgesen & Houck, 1980). Because maintaining performance level is also dependent on effective rehearsal strategies, this finding, then, is also consistent with the differential rehearsal usage interpretation.

Another common finding from memory research is that children whose recall is poor oftentimes do not utilize available knowledge to aid memorization. For example, when learning-disabled children were asked to free recall a list of categorizable words, they consistently were less likely to use category structure to organize the materials. This finding was indexed by the direct observation of the learning-disabled child's studying behavior (Torgesen, 1977) as well as by lower clustering scores, which measure the tendency of subjects to group items from the same category together during recall (Bauer, 1979, 1982; Wong, Wong, & Foth, 1977). As with rehearsal, training the learning-disabled child to use a categorization strategy had the effect of dramatically increasing memory performance (Dallago & Moely, 1980; Torgesen, 1977). One interpretation of this finding is that learning-disabled children possess the categorical knowledge necessary to organize the list categorically but simply do not use that knowledge. Flavell (1971) has characterized this failure as a production deficiency.[1]

That strategy training is effective in improving memory performance is considered to provide additional support for the hypothesis that variations in the use of strategies underlie group differences in performance. (See Campione, Brown, & Ferrara, 1982, for an excellent discussion of this argument.) Presumably, if these strategies are important in determining the proficiency of performance, then prompting people who perform poorly to use the strategies should have the effect of improving their performance. Performance should not be affected by prompting, however, for subjects already performing well, for this skill should be redundant with what the person is already doing. As stated earlier, a number of studies have shown that when learning-disabled children are presented with a categorizable list to memorize and are prompted to use the categorical organization as an aid for memorization, both the amount recalled and clustering scores increase significantly. This indicates that these children do have the necessary knowledge to use this strategy and can do so if encouraged. These results also indicate that the use of strategic processing enables much higher levels of performance.

Care must be taken to distinguish between the deficient and the inefficient use of a strategy. Deficient use implies problems concerning strategy choice; that is, a strategy that should be used is not being used. Inefficient use of a strategy implies that a strategy being used is not being used well. The preceding

---

[1]An alternate interpretation, as we later argue, is that children's knowledge is not organized in a way that makes this knowledge easily accessible (see Chi, in press; Rabinowitz, 1984).

review indicates that learning-disabled children are deficient in the use of some strategies and inefficient in the use of others. These two issues are discussed separately within the chapter. Although we are able to make this distinction, however, it often is difficult to tell on the basis of performance whether problems arise because of deficient use or inefficient use of strategies.

The amount of evidence that indicates problems in strategic processing for children who perform poorly on these memory tasks is quite extensive. In fact, most researchers would agree that learning-disabled children, or younger children in comparison to older children or adults, are deficient in such processing. What is currently under debate, however, is why we observe these differences in processing. In essence, what are the factors that contribute to these group differences in strategic processing?

AVAILABILITY VERSUS ACCESSIBILITY OF KNOWLEDGE

In this section, we argue that the decision to use strategies as well as the efficiency of such strategies are affected by variations in the *accessibility* of relevant conceptual knowledge. Conceptual knowledge is often described in terms of a specific representational system—a spreading activation memory system (Anderson, 1983; Anderson & Pirolli, 1984; Collins & Loftus, 1975). Some common assumptions associated with such an architecture are that concepts are represented as nodes within the system and the nodes are interconnected by associative links that can vary in strength. When an item is encountered, the corresponding concept in memory is activated. Activation then spreads from that concept to related concepts. The amount of activation that spreads depends on the strength of the associative links between concepts, with stronger associations leading to stronger activations.

This spread of activation within the knowledge base is thought to occur automatically and not be under the conscious control of the learner. Thus, whereas strategic behavior might be characterized as goal-oriented, the automatic spread of activation within the knowledge base cannot. Whether activation will spread from concept to concept in memory is determined by the level of initial activation and the existence of associative links, and not necessarily the intentions of the person. Any given concept can initially become activated through a variety of goal-oriented (strategic) or nongoal-oriented (spread of activation) processes. Once the concept becomes active, however, it will spread activation to its neighbors regardless of the goal-oriented behavior going on. Thus, the spread of activation affects the activation levels of concepts in a manner that is independent of any specific goal-oriented or strategic behavior.

The proposal that strategic processing is dependent on the *availability* of relevant knowledge is acknowledged, at least to some extent, by practically everyone conducting research pertaining to strategic processing. Unfortunately, knowledge is often only considered in an all-or-none manner with the distinction being between knowledge that is available and information that is unavailable because of lack of knowledge. With such a dichotomy, the role that knowledge can play in accounting for variations in strategic processing becomes minimal and, thus, variations in the observance of strategies are often considered to be independent of the factor of conceptual knowledge.

For example, with the acceptance of this dichotomy, it is often considered to be sufficient to show that knowledge was available but not used, in order to eliminate knowledge as a possible explanatory construct underlying differences in performance. In the typical training study, removal of performance differences is attempted through instruction and application of certain strategies. The underlying assumption is that the person has the relevant knowledge needed to take advantage of the instruction, and prompting the use of that strategy should remove or reduce differences in performance. To the extent that such training is successful, this obviates the need to further consider knowledge as a relevant factor. Clearly, such results imply that subjects had the knowledge relevant for the task. We suggest in this chapter that there may be alternative conclusions and interpretations.

One alternative interpretation considers metacognitive factors to be important. For example, Worden (1983) stated that "To the extent that strategy instruction elevates performance to normal levels, the rehearsal deficits could be metacognitive in origin" (p. 136). She further stated, "The study of metamemory may yield information relevant to the view of the learning-disabled child as an inactive learner whose major problem is only that he or she is less prone to employ the strategic memory behaviors that normal children spontaneously execute" (p. 139).

According to such a view, it is deficient knowledge about different types of strategies, rather than conceptual knowledge, that might account for the variations we observe in the use of strategies. As a result of this line of reasoning, much research has recently been conducted investigating the nature and training of metacognitive skills (Brown et al., 1983).

Before accepting a metacognitive account of variations in strategic processing wholeheartedly, an issue that still needs to be addressed is what constitutes "available knowledge." As we stated earlier, the availability of knowledge is often discussed in terms of an all-or-none proposition—either knowledge is available to be used or not. A situation can easily be imagined, however, in which a person must search long and hard for a piece of previously encoded information before that information is retrieved. Alternately, some information seems to be easily accessible and quickly retrieved. Although two pieces of information might both be available, they might vary markedly in their accessibility.

Clearly, a distinction needs to be made between the *availability* and the *accessibility* of knowledge (Mandler, 1967; Tulving & Pearlstone, 1966). Using the framework of a spreading activation memory system where concepts are represented as nodes and relations are represented via labeled associative links, the issue of availability of knowledge can be conceived of as whether or not concepts and their relations are explicitly represented in memory. Accessibility can then be thought of in terms of the strength of the relations or associative links.

The distinction can be made more concrete by looking at the example presented in Fig. 4.1. In this figure, three different representations of the relationship between the concepts of *cat* and *animal*[2] are displayed. In each of these representations there are nodes representing the concept of *cat* and *animal*, and a labeled (ISA) associative link representing the relationship between the two concepts. Thus, in terms of the availability of knowledge, these three representations are equivalent. However, these three representations vary in terms of the strength of the associative link—in 1A, the strength is equal to .9; in 1B, the strength equals .5; in 1C, .1.

Upon presentation of the word *cat* to the subject, the node representing this concept in all three representations would be activated. Activation would then spread along the associative links to related concepts—in this case, to ANIMAL. With representation 1A, because of the strong weight of the associative link, the activation level of the node ANIMAL will automatically rise substantially. Thus, given the activation of CAT, the relationship with ANIMAL would automatically become very accessible. With 1B, the activation level of ANIMAL

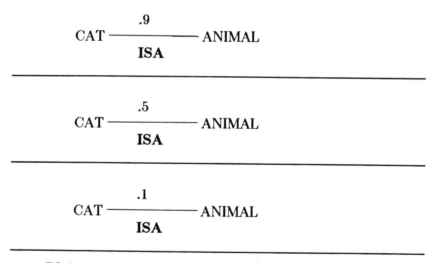

FIG. 4.1 The concept CAT can be related to ANIMAL by an ISA link of varying strength, such as .9, .5, or .1.

---

[2]We use the convention of using upper case letters when referring to the label of a node and italics when referring to stimuli.

would rise somewhat, given the moderate strength of the associative link, but the information would still not be as accessible as in 1A. Finally, with representation 1C, activation would still spread from CAT to ANIMAL, but because of the weak associative link, the activation level of ANIMAL will not change much. Given the activation of CAT, in this case, the relationship with ANIMAL would still be relatively inaccessible.

The previously discussed situation may be illustrated by use of a computer simulation of a spreading activation memory system. First, however, some of the basic assumptions associated with the simulation need to be specified. Consistent with our conception of spreading activation systems, concepts are represented within the simulation as nodes, which are interconnected by associative links. Associative links can be either excitatory or inhibitory. Excitatory links, represented by positive weights, will increase the level of activation of neighbors. Inhibitory links, represented by negative weights, will decrease the activation level of neighbors. In Fig. 4.1, all of the associative links are excitatory.

In a quiet system, where no information has yet been presented and, thus, no nodes are active, all nodes have an activation level equivalent to their *resting state.* Upon presentation of an item, the activation level of the node representing that item rises from the resting state. Once the activation level of the node has exceeded a *threshold point,* that node will start to spread activation to its neighbors. A node with an activation level below threshold will have no influence on the activation level of any other node. The amount of activation that is spread from node to node is dependent on two factors: first, the strength of the associative link and second, the level of activation of the node. The greater the strength of the associative link or the greater the level of activation of a node, the greater the amount of activation that will be spread. The probability of one's being aware of the activation of a concept increases as the level of activation increases above the threshold value.[3] In addition, once a node starts to become active, there is always a tendency for that node to *decay* back to its original (resting state) level of activation, unless it is reactivated. One final assumption associated with this simulation is that time can be broken up into discrete units called cycles. At each cycle, the activation level of each node is updated on the basis of the values on the previous cycle. This is a matter of computational convenience and should not really be considered a fundamental psychological assumption. The reader may refer to McClelland and Rumelhart (1981) for a more detailed description of the system upon which this one is based.

Figure 4.2 displays a set of patterns of activation corresponding to the representations depicted in Fig. 4.1. Figure 4.2A corresponds to the representation of CAT and ANIMAL with the associative link of .9; Fig. 4.2B corresponds to the representation with the weight of .5; and Fig. 4.2C, to the representation

---

[3]This allows for the possibility that a node can be above threshold, affecting the activation levels of related nodes but still not be easily accessible to consciousness.

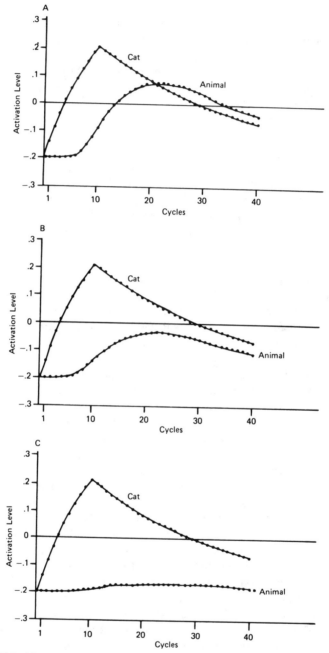

FIG. 4.2 Activation level as a function of cycles, for associative weights of .9 (2A), .5 (2B), and .1 (2C).

with the weight of .1. For purposes of this illustration, the resting state of all nodes was set to $-.2$ and their threshold levels were set to zero. All three patterns of activation simulate the situation where the item *cat* is being presented. Excitation of the node CAT occurs during cycles 1–10 in the simulation and each CAT node receives the same amount of activation. During this time the activation level of each CAT node rises from the resting level of $-.2$ to an activation level of .21 at cycle 10. After cycle 10, *cat* is no longer being presented so the activation levels of the CAT nodes start to decay back to their resting state. As can be seen from the graphs, at cycle 4, the activation level of CAT exceeds the threshold point and it is at this time that activation spreads from the node CAT to the node ANIMAL. At cycle 5, the activation level of the node representing ANIMAL starts to rise from its resting state. In Fig. 4.2A, you can see that because of the strong weight of the associative link (.9), the activation level of ANIMAL rises relatively rapidly and the activation of this node also exceeds threshold at cycle 14. At this time, both CAT and ANIMAL are above threshold and, thus, would allow with some probability for the relationship between these two concepts to be noticed.

In Fig. 4.2B, where the associative link was set at a value of .5, the activation level of ANIMAL also starts to rise at cycle 5. But because of the weaker strength of the associative link, this node's level of activation rises at a slower rate and never exceeds its threshold point. Thus, the relationship between *cat* and *animal* will not be noticed because ANIMAL never became activated above threshold. In Fig. 4.2C, because of the very weak strength of the associative link (.1), the activation level of ANIMAL hardly rises at all. In this case, the relationship between CAT and ANIMAL will also not be noticed. These examples, then, illustrate that the relative accessibility of information depends not only on the availability of knowledge, but also on how strongly associated the concepts are. Assuming that individual and developmental differences exist in the strength of association, such a model could be used to interpret findings concerning available but inaccessible knowledge.

SPECIFIC-CONTEXT AND GENERAL-CONTEXT STRATEGIES

Specific-Context Strategies

At this point, in order to discuss how variations in the accessibility of knowledge might affect strategy use, we first make a distinction between specific-context and general-context strategies. Briefly, a general-context strategy is one that is exhibited in situations in which a person chooses to use a strategy simply on the basis of the general constraints of the task. Within this situation, the person makes the decision to use a strategy at the start of the task (for example, before the actual materials are presented). The decision to initiate a specific-context strategy, however, is made in response to a specific, rather than a general, situation. The decision to use a specific-context strategy is *not* made at the start of the task; rather, it is driven by the result of noticing similarities, differences or gaps in the materials being worked on. The use of specific-context strategies strongly relies on perceiving relations among the materials. For example, the use of a categorization strategy in a free recall task that was discussed earlier is dependent on noticing the categorical relations inherent within the list (Lange, 1978; Ornstein & Naus, in press). Why would the learner choose to use a categorization strategy if the categorical relations among the items were never noticed? We are arguing that the tendency to use many strategies is dependent on the ability to perceive relations within materials and that the noticing of relationships will vary with differences in the accessibility of knowledge. Thus, even when knowledge is available, variations in the accessibility of knowledge can still play a role in producing variability in the use of specific-context strategies.

Effort and the Decision to Use Specific-Context Strategies. The training studies discussed earlier have shown that available relevant knowledge can be made accessible. In fact, each of the three representations presented earlier have inherent the requisite categorical knowledge relating *cat* and *animal* and this knowledge can be made accessible. For example, if the amount of activation of the node CAT or the amount of time the node was to remain above threshold were to increase, greater amounts of activation would then spread from CAT to its neighbors. One way to accomplish this is to pay more attention or concentrate harder when the item is being presented. This should affect the level of activation a node reaches upon initial excitation. The amount of activation that spreads from any node is dependent on *both* the strength of the associative link *and* the level of activation of a node. In Fig. 4.2, the pattern of activation for the node CAT is identical in all three graphs—each reaches a peak at .21 at cycle 10. This level of activation is more than sufficient to allow the activation level of ANIMAL to rise over threshold when the associative link has a weight of .9, but not enough when the associative link has weights of either .5 or .1. In Fig. 4.3, it is shown that if the activation level of CAT were to reach .26, given the associative link with the weight .5, enough activation would spread from CAT to ANIMAL to enable ANIMAL to exceed the threshold point. It is assumed that more effort would be required of the subject to enable a node to reach an activation level of .26 than of .21. However, an activation level for CAT of .26 would still not allow the activation level of ANIMAL to exceed threshold if the associative link is .1. The activation of CAT needs to reach an even higher level, when the associative weight is .1, to allow ANIMAL to exceed the threshold point. In other words, this would require even more effort on the part of the subject. Thus, with more weakly associated knowledge bases, learners might have to work harder to attain the same endpoint.

A second way of enabling the noticing of the relationship between CAT and ANIMAL is to increase the amount of rehearsal. Increasing rehearsal should

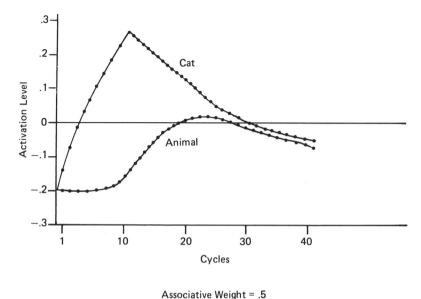

Associative Weight = .5

FIG. 4.3 Activation level of CAT with an associative weight of .5 to ANIMAL.

affect activation in two ways—it would reactivate a node (CAT), thereby counteracting the node's tendency to decay back to its resting state. Both of these
effects would enable a concept to remain active for a longer period of time and
would allow more activation to spread between nodes, increasing the probability
that the relationship could be noticed. CAT only needed to be activated once
with representation 1A to enable ANIMAL to obtain a level of activation that
exceeds threshold. Given the same amount of activation of the concept CAT,
this was not sufficient to enable ANIMAL to reach the same end point with
representation 1B and 1C. Greater amounts of rehearsal would be required with
the latter two representations with more rehearsal being required for 1C than 1B
to enable the activation level of ANIMAL to exceed threshold. Given that rehearsal
is an effortful process, a person with representation 1C would have to work
harder than a person with representation 1B to obtain the same end point. Similarly, the person with representation 1B would have to work harder than the
person with representation 1A. Training studies might be effective because they
compel the subjects to work harder, thus increasing the probability that relatively
inaccessible knowledge is made accessible.

General-Context Strategies

Increasing cognitive effort, then, can compensate for more weakly associated
or less accessible knowledge. Increased effort might increase the possibility of
accessing knowledge relevant to the decision of strategy choice, although such

processing cannot account for all the variations found in strategic processing. There will still be situations where students fail even following extra effort.

Some students must have more knowledge about strategies and their constraints, and thus will be able to perceive the contexts in which certain strategies should be applied. Our definition of a specific-context strategy proposed in the preceding section projects a view of the learner as someone who, while working on a task, notices similarities or incongruities within the materials, and on this basis decides to use a strategy. With the free recall of categorizable lists of words, the noticing of the categorical relations within the list was considered to be a prerequisite to the decision to use a goal-oriented strategy of trying to categorize the items. If the learner was not able to notice the categorical relations within the list, the decision to use the categorization strategy would not be made.[4] We have argued that both the *availability* and *accessibility* of relevant knowledge would affect whether such relations would be noticed.

However, the decision to be strategic can also be made in a very different manner (that is, the learner could approach the task with a preconceived notion of what strategy or strategies should be used). Good studiers sometimes approach the learning task in such a way. For example, in a recent study conducted by Rabinowitz, Gobbo, and Glaser, individual differences in studying skills among college students were investigated. Subjects in this experiment were asked to read and study two passages—one pertaining to rice growing, the other to Victoria, Australia—so that they would be able to answer questions about the passages later on. In addition, all subjects were asked to read aloud and were asked to verbalize what they were thinking so that protocols of the studying behavior could be obtained. One subject, JM, started the studying of the rice growing passage in the following manner: "What I usually do is look over the layout of the article, seeing if there's any type of subtitles. There's like, rice requirements, planting management, and harvesting and drying advice." At this point, she then began to read the passage. For the Victoria passage, she started off the task in a similar way: "Okay, I'm gonna look over it and see what it's about. It's about Victoria. Subdivisions are physical features—the only subdivisions they have are underlined anyway—talks about the soil, river flow." The decision to use this outlining strategy was made prior to looking at the specific nature of the materials. There was no way in which the specific information presented in the passage, or how that information related to prior knowledge, could have influenced the decision.

A general-context strategy, then, requires some knowledge of the general constraints of the task and context under which it can be applied. Such knowledge (or general-context strategies) can be obtained from prior experience working

---

[4]Conversely, one could decide a priori to use a categorization strategy (as in the case of a student or subject being told to do so). But such a decision will not have a facilitative effect on recall if no categorical relations can be perceived in the stimulus materials.

on a task. Such a situation could arise with the free recall task, for example, if the learner has had prior experience with the task. Given the situation where a learner has to consecutively memorize three lists of categorizable items, after noticing the categorical relations on the first two lists, the learner might decide, before any items were presented from the third list, to try to categorize the items in the last list. The decision to use the categorization strategy on the first two lists is seen to be dependent on noticing the categorical relations within the list and thus upon the availability and accessibility of knowledge. The decision to use the categorization strategy on the third list was not; the learner made the decision to use the strategy before any of the items were presented. With the third list, the decision to use the strategy was made on the basis of knowledge of the strategy and knowledge of the general constraints of the task. In this last situation, then, prior conceptual knowledge did not play a primary role towards the decision to use the categorization strategy. Knowledge played a secondary role by enabling the invention of the strategy in the first place, but it was not directly involved in the decision with the third list. By our definition then, a specific-context strategy can become a general-context strategy.

Knowledge of strategies can also be acquired from explicit instruction. An excellent example of such a training procedure comes from the work of Palincsar and Brown (1984). Using a fairly elaborate procedure (it required three sessions to train teachers to use it), these researchers instructed students who had problems with reading comprehension on how to strategically detect important information within text, to detect incongruities, to ask predicting questions, and to summarize. As a result of the training, students' reading comprehension increased dramatically and this increase even transferred to very different types of reading materials. The knowledge of the strategies, then, had a very definite effect on the children's strategic behavior. Thus, explicit knowledge of strategies can increase students' tendency to be strategic. With such knowledge, however, the decision to use a strategy can be made at the beginning of the task or before the learner has viewed the materials.

Thus, the students trained by Palincsar and Brown have learned to decide, at the start of the reading assignment, to try to pick out the main ideas, ask questions of the text, etc. This decision process is very different from the one in which the student starts to read the text, realizes that he or she doesn't understand something, and then decides to try and ask questions or summarize. The later decision will be based somewhat on the accessibility of relevant conceptual knowledge, the former decision will not be. It would be interesting to note whether the students trained by Palincsar and Brown used the taught strategies selectively (i.e., with hard to understand materials, but not easy materials), or indiscriminately (with all types of materials). To apply a general-context strategy selectively, one has to be able to perceive relations within the specific materials that suggest the use of the strategy.

Given this distinction as well as possible interaction between general-context and specific-context strategies, how does one characterize the deficiencies in strategy use by the learning-disabled child? Are such deficiencies primarily deficiencies in the use of general-context strategies, of specific-context strategies, or both? The decision to use a general-context strategy is seen to be based primarily on metacognitive knowledge whereas the decision to use a specific-context strategy is primarily based on the accessibility of relevant conceptual knowledge. We propose that an efficient learner is one who not only possesses both kinds of strategies, but who can also handle the interaction of the two.

Although we have suggested that people do, in fact, use general-content strategies, and that use of these strategies can improve performance, the relationship between the use of these strategies alone and the exhibition of competent performance does not seem to be very strong. Available research has shown only modest correlations between metacognitive knowledge and strategy use (Brown et al., 1983; Cavanaugh & Perlmutter, 1982; Flavell & Wellman, 1977). This suggests that many of the strategies being used are specific-context strategies. In addition, it should be asked whether people make explicit judgments about task demands and available strategies every time they face a task. If so, then the theoretical motivation underlying strategy choice decisions needs to be better specified. Do people consider all possible strategies that are applicable to the task? As a general explanation of variations in strategy use, the metacognitive approach seems less promising than it once appeared. This is true in regard to both the learning-disabled population as well as the nondisabled population. In light of these uncertainties, it seems worthwhile to pursue the possibility that variations in strategic processing are primarily variations in the use of specific-context strategies. The interaction between conceptual knowledge and strategy choice needs to be investigated more carefully.

Knowledge and Characteristics of Strategic Processing

As of this point, we have centered our discussion primarily on variations in the tendency to use a strategy, emphasizing the strong correlation, in many cases, between performance proficiency and the tendency to employ strategic processes. However, knowledge of the conceptual relations might affect characteristics of strategy use, such as efficiency, as well as the decision to use a strategy.

Rabinowitz (1984), for example, tested the hypothesis that variation in accessibility of categorical knowledge affects the effectiveness of an organizational strategy. In this experiment, second and fifth graders were asked to memorize two categorizable lists of words. One list consisted of items that were highly representative of their respective categories (e.g., dog for animals); the other consisted of items that were less representative (e.g., goat). In addition, subjects were given one of three types of memory instructions: standard free recall, repetition, or categorization instructions. In the categorization condition, subjects were informed of the categorical nature of the list and were instructed to try and group the items by categories. As expected, performance was better for subjects in the categorization condition than for subjects in the repetition and standard free recall conditions. However, the interesting finding is that the subjects in the categorization condition benefited more with the high representative list than with the less representative list. The ability to group items by category depended on the representativeness of the exemplars to their related superordinates. The categorical relations within the high list might be considered to be more accessible than those in the less representative list.

This interaction between knowledge and the characteristics of strategy use can also be illustrated with reference to rehearsal processes. For example, Ornstein, Naus, and Liberty (1975, Experiment 1) presented third, sixth, and eighth graders with a list of 18 unrelated words to memorize. The subjects were asked to rehearse aloud as each item was presented and then to recall the words in any order. In this situation, then, the decision to use a rehearsal strategy was made for all subjects by the requirement to rehearse aloud. However, Ornstein et al. (1975) observed a developmental difference in the manner in which the children rehearsed the items; that is, although all children used a rehearsal strategy, the characteristics of the rehearsal strategy varied with age. The third graders tended to repeat one or two items a number of times as each new stimulus was presented. In contrast, the older children showed a greater tendency to rehearse each newly presented word along with several previously presented items. Paralleling these variations in rehearsal techniques, recall performance improved with age, with the major developmental difference being the recall of items from the initial serial positions of the list. Recent work has shown that this change in the degree of rehearsal activity is directly related to developmental improvement in recall (Ornstein & Naus, 1978, in press).

The question, however, remains as to why there are these variations in the rehearsal process. One interpretation for the observance of the "passive" and "active" rehearsal techniques is that they represent quantitative rather than qualitative differences in the rehearsal process. The basis of this argument is that people have limited amounts of attentional resources which they can apply to any process. To the extent that a large portion of these resources are needed to rehearse one item, fewer resources will be available for the rehearsal of other items. If the effort required to rehearse an item can be supplanted by automatic processes, more attentional resources will be available for the rehearsal of other items. Our model of a spreading activation memory system expands upon this interpretation in the following way. As mentioned earlier, within a spreading activation memory system, when an item is presented, the node representing that item within memory becomes activated. The activation level of that node rises from its resting level to a level above its threshold value. When that concept is no longer being attended to, the activation level of the node will start to decay back to its resting level. A concept is available to consciousness, with some probability, when its activation level exceeds its threshold value. The higher the level of activation, the more probable it will be that the concept will be available to consciousness. Within this model, then, the rehearsal pattern will be dependent on the level of activation maintained by the node.

Given that rehearsal is used to keep information active in memory, the rate at which an item is rehearsed should vary depending on the tendency of a node to remain active independently of rehearsal. One might have to rely on rehearsal quite extensively to keep a node active that is not well known or integrated into some organizational structure; i.e., with such a concept, much of the resources available for rehearsal might be directed at keeping this concept active, leaving little attentional capacity available for the rehearsal of other concepts. This would produce a rehearsal pattern similar to the "passive" rehearsal strategy exhibited by the young children. To the extent that an item can stay active automatically, without having to rely heavily on rehearsal, more resources should be available to rehearse other items, as well as the item currently being presented. In such a situation, an "active" rehearsal strategy should be exhibited. The degree to which items will be rehearsed in isolation or in conjunction with other items would depend on the tendency of a concept to automatically maintain an active state.

Within this system, a number of factors independent of the rehearsal process (although interactive) will affect the length of time that a concept will remain active. One such factor is the degree to which a concept is interrelated with other concepts. When a node becomes activated and its activation level exceeds its threshold point, activation will then spread along the associative pathways to related nodes. With increases in either the level of activation of the original node or the strength of associative links, the amount of activation that will spread also increases. To the extent that the related nodes become activated and exceed their thresholds, and these nodes, in turn, have associative links to the original node, the original node would then also receive activation due to the automatic spread of activation. This returning activation would have the effect of counteracting the tendency to decay, allowing the node to stay active longer. Thus, variations in a node's tendency to stay active can be affected by the spread of activation independently of the rehearsal process. Increased interrelations among concepts would increase the length of time that a concept would remain active.

Characteristics of the nodes themselves (e.g., item specific vs. organizational factors) could also affect how long the node will remain active. In the previous examples, we have implied that all nodes had the same resting level. However, the resting level of a node might vary with the familiarity of an item—more familiar items have higher resting levels allowing them to get active faster, and thus, be more accessible. Such variations in nodes would also affect the length of time the node is to remain active. For example, if there were two nodes—A and B—and A had a resting level of $-.1$, B had a resting level of $-.2$, and the threshold levels of both were set to 0, then if A and B were both given the same amount of activation, node A would exceed the threshold level before node

B, would achieve a higher level of activation, and consequently would remain active for a longer period of time. In fact,within the McClelland and Rumelhart (1981) word perception model, nodes representing more familiar concepts were given higher resting levels than nodes representing less familiar concepts. This would allow more familiar concepts to automatically remain active longer than less familiar concepts. Such differences in learners' level of node activation may also explain individual differences in the rate of processing (Chi & Gallagher, 1982).

On the basis of this model, it would be hypothesized that rehearsal patterns would vary with differences in the accessibility of knowledge. Subjects memorizing a list of items that were very meaningful, and thus more accessible, would be more likely to exhibit an "active" rehearsal strategy than if they were asked to memorize items that were less meaningful. This hypothesis was recently tested in a study conducted by Ornstein and Naus (1984). In the first part of this study, an initial sample of third graders were asked to free generate as many words as they could in response to a target word. On the basis of this free generation data, Ornstein and Naus compiled two list of words—one composed of high-meaningful items (i.e., items for which the children were able to generate many items in response to) and the second composed of low-meaningful items (i.e., items for which the children generated few responses). In this case, then, high meaningful items would be more accessible than low meaningful items because they would be more interrelated with other items. An independent sample of third graders was then presented one of the two word lists to memorize. Once again, as in the Ornstein et al. (1975) experiment, the children were asked to rehearse aloud as each item was presented and then to recall the words in any order. Examination of the rehearsal patterns with the low-meaningful list revealed that these subjects tended to rehearse items in isolation; that is, they tended to use a "passive" rehearsal strategy. However, children presented with the high-meaningful list were much more likely to use an "active" rehearsal strategy, rehearsing the newly presented item along with several previously presented items. These differences in rehearsal patterns were correlated with amount recalled. Thus, the manner in which the children tended to rehearse the materials varied with the accessibility to that material.

In addition, we have suggested that deficiencies in accessibility can be counterbalanced by increases in cognitive effort. Although we are not aware of any experiments that explicitly varied effort, a study by Kunzinger and Witroyl (1984) might be considered relevant to this issue. In this study, differential incentive effects on rehearsal patterns and the relationship between rehearsal and subsequent free recall performance were investigated. Subjects were either in a constant incentive condition in which recall of any word was associated with a 5-cent incentive or in a differential incentive condition in which one half of the words was associated with 10 cents and the other half with 1 cent. Subjects in the differential incentive condition exhibited a greater tendency to "actively" rehearse items than subjects in the constant incentive condition. No direct training of rehearsal strategies was provided to any subject. It is assumed that the increased incentive associated with the 10-cent items would make it likely that the children would apply more cognitive effort to encode and maintain the activity level of the nodes. This increased effort, then, enabled the more active rehearsal strategy.

DISCUSSION

We began this chapter with the presentation of an initial premise: Learning-disabled children perform poorly because of deficiencies in strategic processing. We then went on to review some of the evidence that supports this premise. This premise should be accepted with caution, however. The term *learning-disabled* is used broadly to characterize a wide variety of disorders, characterizing many subpopulations of children. Most of the research reviewed in this chapter was conducted using children who were considered reading-disabled. Given the varied characterizations of children who are considered learning-disabled, the extent to which deficiencies in strategic processing should be used to characterize all these children should be questioned.

To the extent that deficiencies in strategic processing contribute to the poor performance of any subpopulation of disabled learners, we are proposing that accessibility to conceptual knowledge should be considered as a factor that might account for these deficiencies. We feel that strategies are processes that interact with conceptual knowledge rather than processes that just manipulate knowledge.

Making use of the distinction between the *availability* and the *accessibility* of knowledge (Mandler, 1967; Tulving & Pearlstone, 1966), we proposed that variations in the accessibility to relevant knowledge should affect the probability of people noticing the contexts in which many strategies should be used and the ease with which people can make use of given strategies. These effects should produce differences in the tendency to use various strategies.

We are offering the ideas presented in this chapter as a proposal and as a call for research. When knowledge is considered only in terms of availability it is easy to discard this factor as irrelevant. Future research needs to be aimed at assessing whether children who are less likely to spontaneously use strategies also have less accessible knowledge. The role that accessibility of knowledge plays in the execution of a strategy also needs to be further explored.

ACKNOWLEDGMENTS

Preparation of this manuscript was supported by funds from the Learning Research and Development Center at the University of Pittsburgh, which is funded in part by the National Institute of Education. We thank Victoria Hare, Jean Mandler, and Jackie Baker for helpful comments on earlier drafts of this chapter.

REFERENCES

Anderson, J. R. (1983). *The architecture of cognition.* Cambridge, MA: Harvard University Press.

Anderson, J. R., & Pirolli, P. L. (1984). Spread of activation. *Journal of Experimental Psychology: Learning, Memory, and Cognition, 10,* 791–798.

Bauer, R. H. (1977). Memory processes in children with learning disabilities: Evidence for deficient rehearsal. *Journal of Experimental Child Psychology, 24,* 415–430.

Bauer, R. H. (1979). Memory, acquisition, and category clustering in learning disabled children. *Journal of Experimental Child Psychology, 27,* 365–383.

Bauer, R. H. (1982). Information processing as a way of understanding and diagnosing learning disabilities. *Topics in Learning and Learning Disabilities, 2,* 33–45.

Bauer, R. H. (1984). Information processing in reading-disabled and nondisabled children. *Journal of Experimental Child Psychology, 37,* 271–281.

Brown, A. L., Bransford, J. D., Ferrara, R. A., & Campione, J. C. (1983). Learning, remembering, and understanding. In J. H. Flavell & E. M. Markman (Eds.), *Cognitive development: Vol. 2* of P. Mussen (Ed.), *Manual of child psychology.* New York: Wiley.

Campione, J. C., Brown, A. L., & Ferrara, R. A. (1982). Mental retardation and intelligence. In R. J. Sternberg (Eds.), *Handbook of human intelligence.* New York: Cambridge University Press.

Cavanaugh, J. C., & Perlmutter, M. (1982). Metamemory: A critical examination. *Child Development, 53,* 11–28.

Ceci, S. J. (1982). Extracting meaning from stimuli: Automatic and purposive processing of the language-based learning disabled. *Topics in Learning and Learning Disabilities, 2,* 46–53.

Ceci, S. J. (1984). A developmental study of learning disabilities and memory. *Journal of Experimental Child Psychology, 38,* 352–371.

Chi, M. T. H. (1985). Changing conceptions of sources of memory development. *Human Development, 28,* 50–56.

Chi, M. T. H. (in press). Interactive roles of knowledge and strategies in the development of organized sorting and recall. In S. Chipman, J. Siegel, & R. Glaser (Eds.). *Thinking and learning skills: Current research and open questions* (Vol. 2). Hillsdale, NJ: Lawrence Erlbaum Associates.

Chi, M. T. H., & Gallagher, J. D. (1982). Speed of processing: A developmental source of limitation. *Topics in Learning and Learning Disabilities, 2,* 23–32.

Collins, A. M., & Loftus, E. F. (1975). A spreading activation theory of semantic processing. *Psychological Review, 82,* 407–428.

Dallago, M. L. P., & Moely, B. E. (1980). Free recall in boys of normal and poor reading levels as a function of task manipulations. *Journal of Experimental Child Psychology, 30,* 62–78.

Flavell, J. H. (1971). First discussant's comments: What is memory development the development of? *Human Development, 14,* 272–278.

Flavell, J. H., & Wellman, H. M. (1977). Metamemory. In R. V. Kail, Jr., & J. W. Hagen (Eds.). *Perspectives on the development of memory and cognition* (pp. 3–33). Hillsdale, NJ: Lawrence Erlbaum Associates.

Kunzinger, E. L., & Witryol, S. L. (1984). The effects of differential incentives on second grade rehearsal and free recall. *Journal of Genetic Psychology, 144,* 19–30.

Lange, G. (1978). Organization-related processes in children's recall. In P. A. Ornstein (Ed.), *Memory development in children* (pp. 101–128). Hillsdale, NJ: Lawrence Erlbaum Associates.

Mandler, G. (1967). Verbal learning. In G. Mandler, P. Mussen, N. Kogan, & M. H. Wallach (Eds.), *New directions in psychology III.* New York: Holt, Rinehart, & Winston.

McClelland, J. L., & Rumelhart, D. E. (1981). An interactive activation model of context effects in letter perception: Part 1: An account of basic findings. *Psychological Review, 88,* 375–407.

Newell, A. (1979). One final word. In D. T. Tumas & F. Reif (Eds.), *Problem solving and education: Issues in teaching and research* (pp. 175–189). Hillsdale, NJ: Lawrence Erlbaum Associates.

Ornstein, P. A., & Naus, M. J. Rehearsal processes in children's memory. In P. A. Ornstein (Eds.), *Memory development in children* (pp. 69–100). Hillsdale, NJ: Lawrence Erlbaum Associates.

Ornstein, P. A., & Naus, M.J. (1984, April). *The influence of the knowledge base on the development of mnemonic strategies.* Paper presented at the Annual Meeting of the American Educational Research Association, New Orleans.

Ornstein, P. A., & Naus, M. J. (in press). Effects of the knowledge base on children's memory processing. In J. B. Sidowski (Ed.), *Conditioning, cognition, and methodology: Contemporary issues in experimental psychology.* Hillsdale, NJ: Lawrence Erlbaum Associates.

Ornstein, P. A., Naus, M. I., & Liberty, C. (1975). Rehearsal and organizational processes in children's memory. *Child Development, 46,* 818–830.

Palincsar, A. S., & Brown, A. L. (1984). Reciprocal teaching of comprehension-fostering and comprehension-monitoring activities. *Cognition and Instruction, 1,* 117–175.

Paris, S. G. (1978). Coordination of means and goals in the development of mnemonic skills. In P. A. Ornstein (Ed.), *Memory development in children* (pp. 129–156). Hillsdale, NJ: Lawrence Erlbaum Associates.

Paris, S. G. (in press). Theories and metaphors about learning strategies. In C. Weinstein, E. T. Goetz, & P. A. Alexander (Eds.), *Learning study strategies: Issues in assessment, instruction, and evaluation.* New York: Academic Press.

Rabinowitz, M. (1984). The use of categorical organization: Not an all-or-none situation. *Journal of Experimental Child Psychology, 38,* 338–351.

Torgesen, J. K. (1977). Memorization processes in reading-disabled children. *Journal of Educational Psychology, 69,* 571–578.

Torgesen, J. K., & Goldman, T. (1977). Verbal rehearsal and short-term memory in reading disabled children. *Child Development, 48,* 56–60.

Torgesen, J. K., & Houck, D. G. (1980). Processing deficiencies in children who perform poorly on the digit span test. *Journal of Educational Psychology, 72,* 141–160.

Tulving, E., & Pearlstone, Z. (1966). Availability and accessibility of information in memory for words. *Journal of Verbal Learning and Verbal Behavior, 5,* 381–391.

Wong, B. Y. L., Wong, R., & Foth, D. (1977). Recall and clustering of verbal materials among normal and poor readers. *Bulletin of the Psychonomic Society, 10,* 375–378.

Worden, P. E. (1983). Memory strategy instruction with the learning disabled. In M. Pressley & J. R. Levin, (Eds.), *Cognitive strategy research: Psychological foundations* (pp. 129–153). New York: Springer–Verlag.

Commentary: How Shall We Conceptualize the Language Problems of Learning-Disabled Children?

Stephen J. Ceci
Jacquelyn G. Baker
Cornell University

For most of us interested in understanding learning disabilities, the literature has become punishingly complex to interpret and integrate. Nowhere is this more apparent than in the study of micro-level cognitive processing abilities of LD children. Here, one is confronted with papers describing every kind of problem from the most basic deficits (e.g., phonetic coding of isolated phonemes, auditory short-term memory, syllabic awareness, etc.) to the most global deficits (e.g., reading connected discourse, listening comprehension, acquiring higher order rule systems, etc.). Putting aside for now questions about the reliability of some of these findings, what is one to make of the fact that LD children have been shown to be deficient in such a wide range of skills? How might one account for disabled childrens' pervasive deficits while still maintaining that their problems reflect the presence of a "specific learning disability"? After all, these same children who have been shown to be deficient across the board, are known to possess adequate intelligence and to be achieving at grade level in many academic areas. Can one *really* be deficient at everything from the most microlevel information-processing skills to the most macrolevel comprehension processes yet still perform adequately on many school-related tasks as well as on full scale measures of intelligence? A paradox would seem to exist between the consensual nature of learning disabilities (i.e., learning disabilities are presumed to reflect the presence of *specific* as opposed to *global* deficits) and the impression one obtains from a perusal of the empirical literature, documenting deficits in a wide range of micro and macrolevel skills. Some of this paradox may be explainable in terms of LDs' inferior overall level of intellectual functioning (e.g., McNellis argues in her chapter that although only 9% of the population score below 90 on IQ tests, nearly 35% of LDs who have participated in empirical studies have IQs below 90). However, most of us assume that children with learning disabilities have average or above-average academic potential (with the exception of the areas of intellectual functioning directly impeded by the disability). Thus their lower Full Scale IQs may be the result of the presence of the learning disability and not an indicant of their potential. Several of the chapters in this section have endorsed this position explicitly (e.g., Morrison). We shall have more to say about this later.

By focusing on the problems of children who experience specific reading disability, each of the chapters in this section has approached the topic in an ambitious and unique fashion. Spanning as they do the wide range of deficits shared by poor readers, all four chapters help us to answer several of the questions posed earlier. McNellis' contribution lies in her scrutiny of a single cognitive process that has been alleged by many researchers to be one of the most important deficits underlying poor reading, namely *selective attention*. Morrison and Spear and Sternberg have stepped back from data on single processes and attempt (with success, we think) to construct some theoretical scaffolding. Each of these contributions provides a framework that enjoys the support of a good deal of the empirical literature, though not all of it, as we shall argue later. Finally, Rabinowitz and Chi take still another approach to the problem of poor reading, focusing on the notion of the disabled child as strategically deficient. Furthermore, their simulation of the acquisition of word meaning is among the most recent in a line of sophisticated information-processing approaches. The value of this approach remains to be seen, but it definitely adds to researchers' arsenal of analytic tools to dissect the subprocesses of reading. We briefly review the high points of each chapter then provide our own analysis and synthesis.

For starters, McNellis has approached the problem of specific learning disabilities by calling into question the existing literature related to selective attention. Ingeniously, she is able to demonstrate that LD children, contrary to the claims often made about them, do not have a pervasive attentional deficit, at least not when one controls for their IQ, greater age variability, SES, race, sex, grade, and their lower baseline performance. Whatever other factors might underpin poor reading, McNellis has convinced us that an attentional deficit is not one of them. In fact, she has provided some of the most compelling evidence to date that *selective attention* may not even be a unitary construct. If she is correct, then the implications for both developmental and educational researchers are numerous.

Rabinowitz and Chi also examine the issue of learning disabilities in an interesting manner. They convincingly argue that some children are poor readers because of an inability to process information in a strategic manner. These authors have made an important contribution to the field of learning disabilities research by embedding the problems of LDs in currently popular information-processing concepts. By reference to Collins and Loftus' (1975) notions of "spreading activation," Rabinowitz and Chi make an interesting case for knowledge-based deficits in LDs. Far too many researchers assume that familiarity with stimuli is synonymous with knowledge; that is, if LDs and non-LDs can name stimuli with equal ease, then they have equivalent knowledge. As Rabinowitz and Chi remind us, this assumption of equivalent knowledge is never tested in an empirically adequate manner and there is good reason to doubt its validity. LDs' deficits may stem from either a lack of knowledge or a different representation of it. This is a refreshingly new approach, one that holds promise for understanding memory and comprehension deficits of LDs.

Morrison takes a still different approach in his chapter, neatly showing that poor readers, as a group, suffer from an inability to master irregular sound-symbol correspondences, which may be due to some more fundamental difficulty these children have learning complex rules. Morrison believes RDs are "cognitively intact," so the deficit in rule learning cannot be sufficiently pervasive to impair their performance on many nonreading tasks. According to this interpretation, RDs' difficulties in mastering complex word acquisition rules prevents them from automatizing word decoding and results in inadequate attentional reserves to engage in higher level analysis once words are identified (for further details, see Morrison & Manis, 1982). The developmental approach taken by Morrison and his colleagues is an extremely valuable feature of their work because it enables one to rule out certain explanations. Their framework, though not without challenge and rival frameworks, is the most empirically adequate of the "cognitive" frameworks that we have examined. Later, we offer an alternative viewpoint that we hope can account for much of Morrison's data as well as some data of other researchers. Our remarks are not meant to supplant the framework of Morrison and his colleagues but simply to recast it.

Finally, Spear and Sternberg have chosen to step back from their own data in order to provide an integration of the existing literature. The end result is a comprehensive framework for understanding the nature of poor reading that is sure to be regarded by researchers as a thought-provoking and *extremely* useful analysis. It is worth noting Spear and Sternberg's caution in interpreting the literature on reading deficit. It may be that poor readers are *not* deficient across-the-board. Their review establishes that many of the claims made about RDs' deficits either have not been replicated or have even been contradicted. Regardless whether one agrees with their conclusion, Spear and Sternberg have advanced the field in this thoughtful chapter by the sheer force of their awesome integration. This is quality thinking that we greatly enjoyed reading.

All the authors represented within this section have called into question the once popular notion that LDs are "all around" cognitively deficient (see Morrison and Spear and Sternberg for explicit statements). Despite this awareness that LDs are not depressed on all cognitive measures, however, the evidence is quite strong that children with specific reading disabilities *do* experience wide-ranging problems. Researchers are likely to reveal deficits among LDs whether they approach the problem from the bottom-up or from the top-down, that is, from the standpoint of documenting problems in the basic information-processing skills that underpin poor comprehension (e.g., phonetic coding) or from the standpoint of documenting problems in actually comprehending (e.g., drawing inferences).

Top-Down Versus Bottom-Up: The Wrong Question?   Spear and Sternberg conclude their chapter by suggesting that poor readers suffer from deficits that originate primarily at the primitive level of phonemic awareness and word decoding. According to their analysis, these deficits impede fluent reading (comprehension), which in turn impedes other primitive processes. Thus, true top-down deficits in areas such as comprehension, organization of long-term memory, and use of semantic context to speed word recognition, are initially unlikely to characterize RDs, except possibly as stated by Spear and Sternberg "for youngsters with more general types of language difficulties." As Spear and Sternberg suggested, deficits in basic processes can impede top-down processing, following prolonged reading failure.

It may very well be the case, however, that a purely bottom-up approach to the difficulties experienced by learning disabled children is only partially correct. Spear and Sternberg's framework focuses on the *reading* disabled child. Naturally, reading relies heavily on visual skills. In turn, Spear and Sternberg integrate findings that, for the most part, rely on studies that have assessed abilities using visual tasks. On the surface, this "bottom-up" position tends to support a more visual-perceptual explanation of reading disabilities. An alternative way of explaining the findings reviewed by Spear and Sternberg can be presented: Rather than argue that deficits exist specifically in bottom-up information-processing abilities, it can be argued that these skills are largely intact. The underlying problem, rather, can be attributed to RDs' faulty language processing skills. Studies of individual differences in both children (Berger & Perfetti, 1977; Curtis, 1980) and adults (Jackson & McClelland, 1979) have provided fairly clear evidence that both reading speed and comprehension are dependent on general visual *and* auditory language ability. From a developmental perspective poor readers may, from the start, experience language impairments (ranging in severity) which later impede their ability to derive meaning from linguistic stimuli. In this regard, it is important to bear in mind the subtle nature of many language impairments. As Herrman and his colleagues have shown (Chaffin & Herrman, 1984; Stasio & Herrmann, 1985), the knowledge of extremely subtle semantic contrasts often can account for verbal sorting and analogical reasoning performance even when subjects are unaware that they possess this knowledge (e.g., whether or not a contrast can be prefaced with a quantifier such as *very,* as in "hot : cold:: (a) tall : short, (b) living : dead, (c) single : married"). Although most of us do not consciously distinguish between antonyms that are continuous (hot:cold) versus those whose opposite member can be generated by its negation (living:dead), it is clear that we possess this knowledge and spontaneously employ it on word selection tasks (Stasio & Herrmann, 1985). When confronted with pairs of antonyms along a continuum like cold:hot, we tend to generate other continuous antonym pairs (i.e., those that can accept a quantifier like "very") rather than generate polar opposites like "alive:dead", which can only accept a quantifier in the metaphorical sense ("very alive"). Because of the subtleness of our language knowledge, deficits among children may go undetected with the result being that linguistic deficits get mistaken for cognitive ones.

For the most part, subtle measures of disabled readers' linguistic abilities have not yet been systematically examined (Perfetti, 1983). By assuming that such bottom-up factors as speed of processing of basic-level information are the critical components associated with reading disability, it is possible that past research efforts have been somewhat misguided. Certainly, a future incorporation of more sensitive visual and auditory measures within a developmental framework would provide a valuable service. Such evidence would go a long way (though perhaps not all the way) toward explaining poor readers' difficulties with phonetic coding, phonemic awareness, syllabic awareness, and the structure of the orthography. Anytime language is involved such children might find it difficult to access the orthographic, acoustic, and semantic representation of words. Such a view would allow us to account for some of the phenomena that so-called bottom-up views ignore, (e.g., RDs' difficulties with *listening* comprehension; Berger & Perfetti, 1977; Worden, Malmgren, & Gabourie, 1982).

It is known that children who have trouble reading are also likely to have trouble with other (nonreading) language-related tasks such as *vocabulary, syntactic complexity, acquiring the phonemic and syllabic structure of spoken language,* and so on. In our own work, we have examined the language-based deficits that accompany poor reading and have discovered something that many special education teachers have long known: it is the rule, rather than the exception, for poor readers also to have delayed language skills. Most of the children receiving Resource Room help in the schools we have visited also have speech and language problems that extend beyond reading per se. They have problems, for instance, answering questions based upon orally presented stories; they have poorer receptive vocabularies than their non-RD peers; and they often exhibit these language-related difficulties well before the onset of formal reading instruction, thus the possibility that reading failure may be causing the language problems is remote.

This view of reading disability has prompted us to refer to this group of children as "language/learning-disabled", or L/LDs (Ceci, Lea, & Ringstrom, 1980). We found that approximately three quarters of the poor readers also were exhibiting problems on nonreading tasks that required the processing of linguistic stimuli, such as oral vocabulary, listening comprehension, and grammatical complexity of spoken language. Once again, were it not for the fact that such children are easy to locate at very young ages, one could argue that these concomitant language difficulties are actually the result of poor reading rather than its cause (i.e., being unable to fluently decode words has deprived these children of the means of inducing higher order comprehension strategies).

There are three advantages of viewing RDs as having language processing problems as opposed to having top-down or bottom-up processing deficiencies. First, such a view fits the empirical description of these children, as just noted. Second, if RDs really had basic information-processing deficits or were generally inactive learners, how could they perform so well on IQ tests, especially the non verbal subtests? A deficit in some basic skill would be expected to result in difficulties in non linguistic areas, but that is not what one usually observes. Rather, the majority of RDs have *at least* average non verbal I.Q.s (Siegel & Heaven, 1986). And third, on those occasions when researchers have attempted to assess RDs' difficulties using the same basic process with both linguistic and non linguistic stimuli, they most often have found that the deficit was confined to the former (e.g., Byrne, & Shea, 1979; Ceci et al., 1980; see Vellutino, 1979; Vellutino & Scanlon, 1982, for review). In short, our argument boils down to the age old "chicken or egg?" question. Simply, do processing deficiencies limit language ability, or do language disabilities limit processing? We support the latter view. It seems more accurate to speak of these children as having language difficulties, anywhere from mild to severe, instead of searching for an explanation of their problems that is language-independent, e.g., bottom-up information-processing deficits.

This language-based view of RD is somewhat at variance with the zeitgeist; researchers have only just begun using the term RD in place of LD because of a dissatisfaction with the heterogeneity of groups of children covered by the latter label. There appears to be an implicit preference for RD because one can be sure about the phenomenon under investigation, unlike the situation that frequently occurs with LD research when children with undeveloped language skills (but appropriate math skills, for example) are lumped together with children who have undeveloped mathematics skills (but age-appropriate reading skills). Yet, by substituting RD for LD can one really obtain a much better understanding of educational disabilities? We think not. Classification on the basis of a reading-disabled/nondisabled dichotomy results in widespread confusion and uninter-pretable research findings, comparable to that which continues to plague the LD literature. To substantiate this, one needs only to glance through the RD literature. Regardless of the process or the task under scrutiny, measures of variability are almost always *much* greater for RD than for nondisabled readers. The end result is that children with qualitatively distinct patterns of linguistic and cognitive abilities (and poor reading skills) are placed within a single group. In an attempt to rectify this problem, there has been a recent movement towards subtyping of RD children. Richman and Lindgren (1980) have suggested that disabled children might better be understood by defining intellectual patterns prior to the identi-fication of a specific learning disability. In an examination of children who possessed a Verbal IQ at least 15 points lower than Performance IQ, they identified three groups of children. The first group consisted of children with a Specific Language Disability but adequate Abstract Reasoning skills, whereas the second group contained children with a Specific Learning Disability but good Sequencing/Memory skills. Finally, the third group included children experiencing a General Language Disability who possessed deficits in both Abstract Reasoning and Sequencing-Memory. Interestingly, when these patterns of intellectual performance were related to reading ability it was found that the first group of children was reading at grade level, whereas the second group was reading below grade level, and the third group tended to be severely reading disabled. Richman and Lindgren's findings suggest that the more pervasive the language disorder, the more severe the reading disability. Although these findings are certainly preliminary, they support the notion of an inextricable link between language and reading abilities.

Despite some similarities between the two frameworks, we think there is a real advantage in shifting from a bottom-up explanation to a language-based orientation. The most important reason is that it puts the emphasis where it belongs—on language. As Spear and Sternberg note, phonetic difficulties usually characterize young RDs, whereas comprehension deficits are much more likely to characterize older RDs. This simple fact seems to escape many researchers' notice. By the time most poor readers are adolescents they appear to have "cracked" the English rules of orthography, no longer reading in a halting, hesitating manner. For them, the basis of their low reading achievement scores is poor comprehension. They may have difficulty drawing remote inferences from text. (For example, an older RD child may be unable to infer that it was warm outside after reading a story in which someone was lightly dressed.) This interpretation is not meant to deny the fact that a small percentage of RDs do continue to have decoding difficulties well into adulthood. Their problems constitute a special case of reading failure that may be more perceptually based, though we hesitate to press this view very hard given the absence of data.

Therefore, we are struck by the following observation: The same children who are poor decoders at a young age become poor comprehenders at an older age. Although we agree that bottom-up performance is predictive of top-down performance, we do not regard the former as causal of the latter. As was already mentioned, these poor decoders frequently can be shown to possess poor language abilities even prior to the onset of their schooling. (Indeed, this is one of the best markers included in screening tests for preschoolers to predict later reading problems.) A language orientation to reading failure has the advantage of being able to explain why poor decoders become poor comprehenders (as well as why they often are poor at other language tasks that have nothing to do with reading, e.g., listening comprehension). Both decoding and comprehension involve transforming language into sounds and meaning. As Hunt (1985) has repeatedly demonstrated, low-verbal college students (those scoring in the bottom 25% on SAT verbal measures at the University of Washington), despite average or better phonetic decoding skills, are less efficient than high-verbal students on all aspects of language processing, from the most simple letter recognition tasks to the "deeper" aspects of comprehension such as recognizing anomalies. The children whom we call language/learning-disabled and whom we suspect are called reading disabled by others have anywhere from mild to pervasive difficulties with language processing. They have substantially lower scores on verbal subtests of I.Q. tests (*Information, Vocabulary, Analogies, Comprehension,* etc.) and often they are likely to be identified by kindergarten and first grade teachers as being verbally reticent. Important to note is that when these childrens' reading problems become serious enough to require special services and a multidisciplinary team evaluation, it has been our observation that they usually are shown to be deficient on the speech/language component of the evaluation.

We began this commentary by remarking on the punishingly complex literature covering the field by learning disabilities. The language orientation being put forward by us and others (Donohue, 1986; DeSoto & DeSoto, 1983; Perfetti, 1983; Vellutino, 1979, 1982) has some obvious advantages, as we have tried to show. There are, however, many examples of "poor readers" that do not conform to the description offered here; that is, it is possible to locate studies, several of which are reviewed by Spear and Sternberg and Morrison, in which RDs do not appear to be language-delayed.

This brings us to our final point, the need for researchers to carefully describe their subjects' I.Q.s, ages, and reading levels. This concern has been raised in all four chapters in this section as well as by numerous authors elsewhere (e.g., Keogh, 1986; Siegel & Heaven, 1986). It is important to know whether researchers are actually talking about similar populations when they use similar diagnostic labels. We doubt it. In many studies, including all our own, LD children were exhibiting sufficiently serious reading and language problems as to have been referred for evaluation and subsequently administered special services. Typically, this means that they were functioning at least a half year below expectancy (based on their IQ score) for *every* grade, after correction for regression of their IQ to the mean. For example, a poor reader with average IQ in fourth grade already may be reading 2 years below average. One can contrast this level of severity with those studies that select "poor readers" by going into a regular fourth-grade classroom and requesting the teacher to assign children to an average and a below-average group on the basis of reading grades. Comparing these two very different populations is not simply a matter of comparing apples and oranges, as the saying goes; it is more like comparing strawberries and onions!

The "message" here is simply that it is important to distinguish children who truly suffer from an inability to acquire reading, despite adequate intellectual resources and appropriate teaching and motivation from children who may be better characterized as having cultural or motivational/adjustment problems. We do not anticipate that this latter group of poor readers will be language impaired, naturally.

Summary.   Taken together, the four chapters presented within this section comprehensively span the range of abilities from selective attention and bottom-up processes to higher order rules, strategies, and knowledge. By all accounts, these four chapters provide an excellent empirical and theoretical foundation for understanding learning disabilities. As commentators, we have taken the liberty of having the last word. Our task has been a pleasurable one of "fine-tuning" ideas and frameworks that are both thoughtful and well-conceived. However, none of the ideas presented in these chapters can be considered incompatible with our view of learning disabilities as a language-based deficit. Elsewhere, it has been suggested that reading is comparable to a "psycholinguistic guessing game" (Gerber, 1981). We agree with this analogy. Indeed, at the beginning stages of reading, linguistic deficits possibly may masquerade as bottom-up deficiencies. Yet, as proficiency increases, the reader begins to draw increasingly more upon his or her knowledge about language and about the world in order to process information. The question that now remains is to what extent does linguistic knowledge relate to more general types of knowledge and abilities? Can the two be separated or are they inextricably bound together? These questions await answers. Answers that are certain to have implications for the remediation of a wide variety of learning disorders.

REFERENCES

Berger, N. S., & Perfetti, C. A. (1977). Reading skill and memory for spoken and written discourse. *Journal of Reading Behavior, 9,* 7–16.

Byrne, B., & Shea, P. (1979). Semantic and phonetic memory codes in beginning readers. *Memory and Cognition, 7,* 333–338.

Ceci, S. J., Lea, S. E. G., & Ringstrom, M. (1980). Coding characteristics of normal and learning disabled 10-year-olds: Evidence for modality-specific pathways to the cognitive system. *Journal of Experimental Psychology: Human Learning and Memory,*

Chaffin, R., & Herrman, D. (1984). The similarity and diversity of semantic relations. *Memory & Cognition, 12,* 134–141.

Collins, A., & Loftus, E. F. (1975). A spreading-activation theory of semantic processing. *Psychological Review, 82,* 407–428.

Curtis, M. E. (1980) Development of components of reading skill. *Journal of Educational Psychology, 72,* 656–669.

DeSoto, J. L., & DeSoto, C. B. (1983). Relationship of reading achievement to verbal processing abilities. *Journal of Educational Psychology, 75,* 116–127.

Donohue, M. (1986). Linguistic and communicative development in learning disabled children. In S. J. Ceci (Ed.), *Handbook of cognitive, social, and neuropsychological aspects of learning disabilities* (Vol. 1, pp. 263–289). Hillsdale, NJ: Lawrence Erlbaum Associates.

Gerber, A. (1981). Problems in the processing and use of language. In A. Gerber & D. N. Bryen (Eds.), *Language and learning disabilities.* Baltimore: University Park Press.

Hunt, E. (1985). Verbal ability. In R. J. Sternberg (Ed.), *Human abilities: An information-processing approach* (pp. 31–58). San Francisco: Freeman.

Jackson, M. D., & McClelland, J. L. (1979). Processing determinants of reading speed. *Journal of Experimental Psychology: General, 108,* 151–181.

Keogh, B. (1986). A marker system for describing learning disability samples. *In S. J. Ceci (Ed.), Handbook of cognitive, social, and neuropsychological aspects of learning disabilities* (Vol. 1, pp. 81–94). Hillsdale, NJ: Lawrence Erlbaum Associates.

Morrison, F. J., & Manis, F. R. (1982). Cognitive processes and reading disability: A critique and proposal. In C. J. Brainerd & M. I. Pressley (Eds.), *Verbal processes in children.* New York: Springer–Verlag.

Perfetti, C. A. (1983). Individual differences in verbal processes. In R. F. Dillon & R. R. Schmeck (Eds.), *Individual differences in cognition.* New York: Academic Press.

Richman, L. C., & Lindgren, S. D. (1980). Patterns of intellectual ability in children with verbal deficits. *Journal of Abnormal Child Psychology, 8,* 65–81.

Siegel, L. S., & Heaven, R. (1986). Defining and categorizing learning disabilities. In S. J. Ceci (Ed.), *Handbook of cognitive, social, and neuropsychological aspects of learning disabilities* (Vol. 1, pp. 95–121). Hillsdale, NJ: Lawrence Erlbaum Associates.

Stasio, T., & Herrmann, D. J. (1985). Relation similarity as a function of agreement between relation elements. *Bulletin of the Psychonomic Society, 23,* 5–8.

Vellutino, F. R. (1979). *Dyslexia: Theory and research.* Cambridge, MA: MIT Press.

Vellutino, F. R., & Scanlon, D. M. (1982). Verbal processing in poor and normal readers. In C. J. Brainerd & M. I. Pressley (Eds.), *Verbal processes in children* (pp. 189–265). New York: Springer–Verlag.

Worden, P. E., Malmgren, I., & Gabourie, P. 91982). Memory for stories in learning disabled adults. *Journal of Learning Disabilities, 15,* 145–152.

II

MACROLEVEL COGNITIVE ASPECTS OF LEARNING DISABILITIES

5 Patterns of Motivation and Reading Skills in Underachieving Children

Evelyn R. Oka
Scott G. Paris
University of Michigan

Unraveling the mysteries of learning disabilities is somewhat like searching for a cure for cancer. Both disabilities affect a significant number of people with often crippling consequences; both defy simple, uniform descriptions; and both can be detected before irrevocable damage is done. Although there may be a constitutional basis for both disabilities, e.g., neurological impairment, biochemical imbalance, or perceptual-motor dysfunction, environmental conditions can definitely contribute to the disabilities as well as to the remedies.

The analogy between learning disabilities and cancer can be elaborated with other similarities but we hasten to add that we do not subscribe to a medical model of learning disabilities. Learning disabilities are usually diagnosed after children enter school because a child's disability is based on a psychometric discrepancy between achievement and aptitude test scores. Thus, children who have average or above-average intelligence (e.g., scores above 85 on WISC-R) but are a year or more below their peers in school achievement, might be classified as learning disabled (LD). Underachievement most often occurs in reading although some children are identified as LD based on deficits in mathematics scores. It is important to recognize that the classification of children as LD depends on normative aptitude and achievement tests that are psychometric instruments designed to maximize discrimination among students, although the errors of measurement, regression effects, and relations among tests are rarely analyzed in these procedures (McLeod, 1979; Thorndike, 1963). Achievement tests are obviously content-dependent and relativistic. They also are correlated highly with standardized intelligence tests (but less than perfectly correlated or else there would be no discrepancy and no LDs). As a consequence, children identified as LD have at least "average" cognitive skills and knowledge but fail to perform at an average level in a particular academic area (e.g., reading) because of nonspecific factors or particular perceptual, cognitive, emotional, or motivational problems. Each of these candidate explanations (and others, such as cultural-familial deprivation) is undoubtedly correct for some children on some occasions. But they are also likely to interact and to change in importance as children progress through school and become reclassified by different relativistic criteria. Thus, any general statements about learning disabilities—whether diagnostic, descriptive, or prescriptive—must be accompanied by qualifiers or treated with skepticism.

We offer three solutions to these vexing problems. First, in order to circumvent controversies surrounding classification and etiology of LD, we describe directly the characteristics of children who vary in aptitude and reading achievement. This is an explicit recognition of the psychometric identification of an LD population and the relativistic bases of academic achievement. Second, we provide profiles of children's reading performance, attitudes, and metacognition together with measures of children's self-perceptions and motivation so that no single causal factor is presupposed by the research. Third, we try to interpret patterns of low academic achievement in a developmental framework of learning and motivation so that our understanding and prescriptions are based on a model of learning abilities that are shared by children. In this manner, individual differences in children's learning and achievement are embedded in general frameworks of development and schooling rather than in a medical model in which myriad factors are identified as potential obstacles to learning.

LEARNING DISABILITIES, READING, AND MOTIVATION

Most children identified as learning disabled are also poor readers. This is due in part to the use of achievement tests as criteria but also because identification of LD has been linked historically with verbal and cognitive processes even when the source of the disorder is perceptual (e.g., Wepman, Cruickshank, Deutsch, Morency, & Strother, 1975) or neurological (Myklebust & Johnson, 1967). Not all poor readers, though, are learning disabled. Some have generally low aptitude or general rather than specific educational handicaps. Downing and Leong (1982) estimate that approximately 10% to 12% of children with average or above-average intelligence have reading difficulties or specific reading disabilities. An examination of children's reading achievement relative to other measures of aptitude can reveal comparative differences among groups of children who might be labeled LD, poor readers, or underachievers with other children who might be labeled as average achievers, overachievers, or gifted students.

We are fortunate to be able to identify and compare characteristics of these various "categories" of children from a large set of data collected on children's reading skills (Paris, Cross, Jacobs, Oka, DeBritto, & Saarnio, 1984). The purpose of that study was to evaluate the effectiveness of a "metacognitive" curriculum in which teachers explained comprehension strategies to students and coached them to use the strategies independently. In conjunction with that project, we collected data on children's self-perceptions, motivation, and aptitude that supplemented information on children's reading achievement, comprehension skills, metacognition, and attitudes about reading (Oka, 1984). The result is a rich battery of tasks that provide cognitive and motivational profiles of third- and fifth-grade students.

There are several ways in which this set of data can help inform us about reading and learning disabilities. First, it is empirical. In this chapter we report data from over 600 children on more than a half dozen measures. Second, the tasks were designed to measure particular aspects of children's reading (i.e., standardized achievement test scores, use of strategies to supply missing words in text, awareness about reading skills and tasks, and attitudes toward reading). These important aspects of reading have all been implicated in learning disabilities (Baker, 1982; Brown, Armbruster, & Baker, 1986; Ryan, Ledger, Short, & Weed, 1982) but have not been assessed simultaneously in the same subjects. Third, the data set also includes measures of children's self-perceptions and motivation derived from Harter's (1981, 1983) research on perceived self-competence and intrinsic versus extrinsic orientations.

The collective measures provide a more comprehensive view of children's reading and learning because they combine assessments of cognitive skill and motivational will (Paris & Cross, 1983). Children's beliefs about themselves and their efforts to learn influence their effort, expectations, and affect (Nicholls, 1983; Weiner, 1979, 1983). A purely cognitive analysis of the skills used or not used by children does not reveal the reasons for their behavior. A motivational orientation that includes attributions, expectancies, and values helps us to understand children's interpretations of their behavior in school and why they may not persevere on tasks (Eccles, Adler, Futterman, Goff, Kaczala, Meece, & Midgley, 1983). Indeed, data from teachers, parents, and clinical assessments are valuable because they embed children's talents or disabilities into the context of their whole lives. Our report of combined cognitive and motivational measures is an improvement over searches for single factors that characterize exceptional children but it is still incomplete.

Our framework for understanding reading achievement and learning disabilities emphasizes context and function, that is, the role of the disability in the child's life, the importance attached to it, the influence that it has on self-esteem, and the pragmatic steps that are taken to avoid, disguise, or circumvent the difficulty. This adaptive view is consistent with self-efficacy theory (Bandura, 1982; Schunk, 1983) and self-worth theory (Covington & Beery, 1976). As White (1959) suggested in his theory of effectance motivation, self-efficacy involves interacting with the environment effectively and competently. The resulting "feeling" of efficacy motivates actions rather than the consequences of effort such as learning or reinforcement. In a similar vein, Bandura (1982) regards self-perceptions of efficacy as critical determinants of behavior, thoughts, and emotions because they influence people's choices of activities as well as the quality of their effort and persistence. Closely related to these views, Covington (1983) suggests that people are motivated to think, act, and achieve in ways that promote their feelings of esteem and pride, in short, their personal worth. These cognitive perspectives on motivation should enlighten our understanding of children's learning as motivated behavior, that is, abilities that are influenced by feelings of efficacy and worth rather than mere cognitive competencies.

In the following section we provide brief discussions of five important aspects of comprehension skills and motivation that influence reading and have particular relevance for low-achieving readers. Next we present data on each of these five aspects and describe the characteristic pattern of these variables for children of various achievement levels. In the last part of the chapter, we discuss adaptive motivation as a construct that reconciles children's perceptions of their abilities with their efforts. We discuss how children adjust their motivation according to (a) perceived control over the task, (b) value of the task and goals, (c) self-management of problem-solving strategies, and (d) personal interpretations of success and failure.

COMPONENTS OF READING RELATED TO LEARNING DISABILITIES

Comprehension Strategies

During the past 20 years, there has been considerable research on cognitive strategies that children use to aid memory, reading, attention, and problem solving. In general, researchers found that young children and novice problem solvers did not spontaneously recruit and use effective strategies that they were capable of employing with an adult's guidance (Paris & Lindauer 1982). This emphasis on production rather than mediation deficiencies (cf. Flavell, 1970) clearly suggested a tangible, remedial source of difficulty in children's thinking that had appeal to researchers in learning disabilities. In this framework, learning disabilities were not due to cognitive deficits but rather were based on differences in children's understanding or motivation to use appropriate strategies. Viewing learning-disabled children as nonstrategic led researchers to portray them as "inactive" (Torgesen, 1982) or "passive" learners (Hallahan & Kaufman, 1982). Although they may be more passive in typical learning situations, they may also be more confused, anxious, and threatened. Thus "passive learner" is only a descriptive starting point.

Torgeson (1982) states that between 1976 and 1981 there were 40 studies conducted on learning-disabled children's use of information-processing strategies: 78% of which investigated strategies to promote memory and attention. He concludes that "the research conducted thus far provides convincing evidence that learning disabled children as a group do not engage readily in certain organized, goal-directed strategies that aid performance on intellectual tasks" (p. 46). Although there have been relatively few studies of learning-disabled students' reading comprehension strategies, the available evidence reveals similar strategic inefficiency. For example, learning-disabled students in junior high and high school fail to read ahead and to use context as strategies for identifying missing words in text (DiVesta, Hayward, & Orlando, 1979; Ramanauskus, 1972).

Paris and Myers (1981) compared the comprehension strategies of fourth-grade good and poor readers who were matched by pairs on age, sex, and arithmetic achievement scores. The major difference between the two groups was that poor readers scored much below grade level on reading achievement tests whereas good readers were above grade level. The poor readers were less able to detect incongruous information inserted into passages while reading orally or when directed to underline parts of the story that did not make sense. They also used fewer aids to study text for later recall and they recalled less information in a more disorganized fashion.

The large number of studies of poor readers confirms the lack of strategic comprehension (Golinkoff, 1976; Ryan, 1981). Poor readers do not integrate word meanings well in sentences nor sentence meanings within paragraphs (Willows & Ryan, 1981). They also do not discriminate well between important and unimportant information in text nor make inferences as well as good readers (Smiley, Oakley, Worthen, Campione, & Brown, 1977). Although research has shown a strong correlation between poor comprehension strategies and children's identification as learning-disabled or poor readers, the reasons are unclear. Part of the disabled reader's difficulty in using sophisticated comprehension strategies may be due to poorer word recognition and decoding skills (Kavale, 1980). Alternatively, poor readers may not expend much effort or persist long on a difficult task. Or it may be that poor readers do not understand comprehension strategies, how they operate, or when to use them. We consider next this metacognitive hypothesis.

Metacognition, Reading, and Learning Disabilities

Metacognition generally refers to one's knowledge about cognition as well as self-regulation of one's thinking. The term has been used inconsistently in the literature to refer to many aspects of reported awareness and tacit knowing and rivals the definition of learning disabilities in fuzziness (Brown & Palincsar, 1982). Despite the conceptual murkiness of the construct, it has appealed to researchers in cognitive development and education because both lack of knowledge and self-controlled reasoning seem amenable to intervention. Furthermore, many researchers believe that the failure to use effective cognitive strategies is a manifestation of inadequate or erroneous metacognition (Hagen, Barclay & Newman, 1982; Wong, 1985). Thus, the research tactic of identifying metacognitive shortcomings in young or poor learners has helped to target specific weaknesses and to prescribe remediation.

Baker (1982) provides a succinct summary of nine "metacognitive deficits" in reading that are often observed in young and/or poor readers. We paraphrase them as follows:

1. Young readers focus on reading as decoding and fail to appreciate apprehension of meaning as the purpose of reading (Garner & Kraus, 1980; Myers & Paris, 1978).

2. Immature readers do not modify their reading behavior to meet different goals (Forrest & Waller, 1979).

3. Young children have difficulty identifying the main theme of a simple narrative (Smiley, Oakley, Worthen, Campione, & Brown, 1977), and learning-disabled children often require help in focusing on important information (Wong, 1979).

4. Low-achieving students may have difficulty recognizing the logical structure and relations embedded within stories (Owings, Peterson, Bransford, Morris, & Stein, 1980).

5. Poor readers do not effectively relate new information to prior knowledge (Sullivan, 1978).

6. Good readers attend better to syntactic and semantic constraints (Beebe, 1980).

7. Young children do not often evaluate text thoroughly for clarity, completeness, and consistency (Garner, 1980; Wagoner, 1983).

8. Poor readers have less knowledge about effective strategies for coping with comprehension difficulties and they are less likely to apply those strategies (Garner & Kraus, 1980; Paris & Myers, 1981).

9. Immature readers often cannot tell how well the material has been understood or if their answers to questions are correct (Forrest & Waller, 1979).

Most of this research has been conducted with children who have not been identified as learning disabled although many studies have tested poor readers. The strong implication from these studies is that learning-disabled children are unaware of many variables that influence reading and they do not understand how to plan, evaluate, and regulate their own thinking. Some of these metacognitive deficits may be characteristic of reading only and some may be more pervasive handicaps. More research is needed to determine if learning-disabled children have specific metacognitive deficits that accompany particular disabilities.

Attitudes About Reading

Learning strategies and metacognition supplement students' intellectual equipment for school but they do not insure optimal use. Children's beliefs about themselves and their motivations to excel contribute substantially to their academic achievement. As Licht (1983) notes, "LD children are characterized by high rates of off-task behavior, inattentiveness, poor concentration, and a lack of persistence, particularly when faced with difficult tasks" (p. 483). Although there are many possible reasons for these behaviors, it seems unlikely that they are due to simple passivity or lack of motivation. In the data to be presented, we focus on three aspects of motivation that are germane to reading handicaps so often observed in low-achieving children. These include attitudes, self-perceptions, and intrinsic motivation.

Some children love to read and some loathe it. Some believe they are good readers and some believe they are terrible. In their free time some children are always in the middle of a book, whereas others would rather pick up their rooms before picking up a book. These three characteristics of reading, feelings, beliefs, and behaviors, have been viewed as the basic components of attitudes toward reading (Epstein, 1980; Fishbein & Ajzen, 1975; Teale & Lewis, 1981). The cognitive dimension refers to children's conceptions and opinions about reading (such as "reading is important for getting a good job"). Affective reactions to reading are evaluations of reading often expressed as liking or disliking. The behavioral dimension of attitudes is the child's intention to read; it includes the predisposition to read as well as actual reading behavior. Reading attitudes are thus conceptualized as triadic interactions between cognitive, affective, and behavioral components. Positive and negative attitudes toward reading are learned and developed within the family environment, the school arena of success and failure, and through the influence of teacher attitudes (Alexander & Filler, 1976).

The relationship between attitudes and reading has been widely studied (Alexander & Filler, 1976; Engin, Wallbrown, & Brown, 1976; Hahn, 1977; Mathewson, 1976; McMillan, 1976, 1980) despite difficulties in its conceptualization and measurement. Generally, the evidence for a positive correlation between attitudes and achievement outweighs the counterevidence (Alexander & Filler, 1976; Kennedy & Halinski, 1975; Teale & Lewis, 1981). Attitudes, beliefs, and expectancies become more negative with failure; they provoke less effort and concentration, which in turn maintain the cycle of failure (Dweck & Bempechat, 1983). Learning-disabled children, in particular, seem pessimistic about their ability to improve their performance in school (Fincham & Barling, 1978; Pearl, Bryan, & Donahue, 1980). In a study of the reading attitudes of normal and disabled readers, Wallbrown, Vance, and Prichard (1979) observed that the disabled readers expressed greater reading difficulty, viewed reading group and instructional materials more negatively, and were less likely to view themselves as reading for instrisic value. The reading-disabled children's perceptions of reading as an unpleasant task may have helped to maintain their disability, which in turn helped to maintain their negative attitudes.

Perceived Self-competence

Harter (1978, 1981, 1983) proposed that perceived competence and positive affect mediate and sustain self-efficacy. Confidence promotes mastery behavior, whereas low self-perceptions and feelings of external control lead to anxiety and decreased motivation. However, children's perceptions of their own competence have a remarkably weak correlation with their actual performance. Young children tend to exaggerate their skills uniformly and self-perceptions of ability do not correlate significantly with teacher evaluations until about the third or fourth grade (Harter, 1981; Nicholls, 1978, 1979; Stipek, 1984). From that time, children's abilities to make accurate self-evaluations steadily improve until about the seventh grade (Harter, 1981; Nicholls, 1979). Upon entering junior high school, the pattern of increasing correlations between pupil ratings and both teacher ratings and achievement test scores is disrupted with correlations falling to the third grade level before continuing to rise in the eighth and ninth grade (Harter, 1981). The transition into junior high appears to jar existing skills and temporarily disable children's improving abilities to make realistic judgments. The demands of the new school environment coupled with the changes of adolescence are likely contributors to a temporary uncertainty over one's skills and abilities. In general, however, these findings indicate that children perceive their own abilities more accurately as they grow older. In becoming more realistic, however, many children forego predominantly positive self-perceptions and show a relative decline in their self-evaluations. They also adopt a "theory of intelligence" that views ability as fixed in contrast to earlier notions of "incremental intelligence" that provide for increases in ability as a result of effort (Dweck & Bempechat, 1983).

But self-perceptions are also influenced by the history of success and failure. Children who fail repeatedly despite trying hard may feel helpless and incompetent (Dweck, 1975; Nicholls, 1983). This negative view of one's abilities can influence future expectancies and effort as well as making performance on difficult tasks onerous and unpleasant. In general, research suggests that LD children are self-deprecatory and score lower than nondisabled children on measures of self-esteem and self-competence (Johnson, 1981; Winne, Woodlands, & Wong, 1983). Again, the critical issue is to determine how self-perceptions are related to a child's particular disability.

Intrinsic Motivation

Positive attitudes toward school learning and confidence in one's own abilities usually are associated with a sense of control (deCharms, 1976). Whether we call this intrinsic or mastery motivation, the focus is on engaging in tasks for one's own personal satisfaction until they are successfully completed. This positive source of motivation depends on correct interpretations of one's successes and failures so that responsibility is assumed for outcomes attributable to controllable factors.

Beliefs about why things happen have been appointed a major role in cognitive theories of motivation (Weiner, 1979, 1980). Attributional approaches to motivation propose a sequence of events that proceeds from an outcome identified as a success or failure to the formation of causal attributions to emotional reactions to future behavior (Weiner, 1979, 1983). The underlying assumption of attribution theory is that people search for reasons for why things happen to them. Causal beliefs are assumed to be the basis of action, mediating achievement motivation by influencing future expectancies, affect, and behavior.

A number of studies have examined the nature of causal attributions and their relation to achievement behavior across a variety of ages, skill levels, and achievement contexts. These studies indicate that attributions serve different functions depending on whether they account for success or for failure. Furthermore, depending on whether the cause is controllable, such as effort, determines whether or not future motivation is adversely affected. For example, when blame is assigned to external factors, Nicholls (1979) suggests that self-worth is preserved. When causal attributions to internal factors are made for failure, these thoughts may either facilitate or debilitate future performance. If the internal factor is controllable such as effort, blame is assigned to a factor that may be altered in the future. Thus, motivation is not necessarily impaired. When the internal attribution is uncontrollable, such as ability, the attribution may lead to helplessness, lack of persistence, and little expectation for future success. The allocation of credit functions in a similar manner to the assignment of blame. Self-worth is enhanced by internal attributions for success, particularly to ability. Conversely, allocating credit to external causes such as the help of others or task ease does not lead to an increase in feelings of self-worth.

Of course, a major problem is that LD children do not make adaptive attributions; they often credit external factors for success and blame their failures on low ability. Butkowsky and Willows (1980), for example, observed that reading-disabled children persisted less on difficult tasks, attributed their poor performance to low ability rather than effort, and had lower expectancies for future performance. LD children, thus, have an external locus of control (Fincham & Barling, 1978) more than an orientation toward task mastery and intrinsic standards.

In summary, research on cognitive development, learning-disabled children, and poor readers reveals that inappropriate motivation, metacognition, and cognitive strategies go hand in hand. Although we may isolate many cognitive skills that appear deficient in LD children it seems unlikely that such descriptions of deficits will inform us why children do not use better learning skills. A consideration of their knowledge about reading, attitudes, and self-perceptions can enlarge our understanding by including motivational and metacognitive beliefs that function over time to orient children positively or negatively to particular tasks such as reading. The data discussed in the following section is an attempt to provide more comprehensive, empirical information on these kinds of cognitive and motivational variables.

RESEARCH ON UNDERACHIEVEMENT IN READING

The data presented here examined the nature, frequency, and pattern of underachievement in reading among 332 third-grade and 337 fifth-grade children who participated in a larger instructional study. They were recruited from 11 schools in a metropolitan school district. A test battery that included measures of the following factors was administered at the end of the school year: reading comprehension skills, reading awareness, reading attitudes, and cognitive self-perceptions.

Reading comprehension was assessed in several ways, but only data on a cloze task and an error detection task are reported here. Children were given grade appropriate passages with words deleted throughout the text. They were instructed to fill in the blanks with the word that made the most sense for the passage. The resulting score is the total number of correctly identified missing words. The passages contained 13 blank slots yielding a range of possible scores from 0 to 13. The cloze task assesses comprehension strategies because children must be able to understand the surrounding text and strategically use relevant information from the context. As DiVesta et al. (1979) reported, skilled readers are more efficient in their use of context and use prior as well as subsequent text to facilitate comprehension.

The error detection task was designed to measure one aspect of comprehension monitoring, the ability to recognize inconsistencies in a passage and to make judgments about the comprehensibility of the passage. The children's task is to silently read grade appropriate passages containing semantic and syntactic anomalies and to identify the errors. The semantic anomalies were alterations that contradicted previous information in the text, were inaccurate referents, were illogical inferences, or contradicted children's prior knowledge. The syntactic anomalies were created by scrambling the word order within sentences. The task yields an error detection "efficiency score" that is a composite score of correct semantic and syntactic detections corrected for false alarms.

Children's awareness and understanding of reading was measured with the Index of Reading Awareness (Paris & Jacobs, 1984). Children answered 22 multiple-choice questions that assessed their awareness and understanding of the variables influencing reading. This included their knowledge of task goals, the planful use of strategies, and the effectiveness of those activities. The same 22-item version was given to both third and fifth graders. Each item had three alternatives with possible point values of 0, 1, or 2, depending on the response's strategic value for reading. Possible scores ranged from 0 to 44.

In order to measure reading attitudes, a scale was constructed that tapped children's beliefs, perceptions, and affect specifically about reading. The task consisted of seven statements such as "I really enjoy reading" and "If you are a good reader, it helps you learn lots of other things," to which children indicated their level of agreement. Children evaluated the statements on a 5-point Likert scale ranging from *disagree* (1) to *agree* (5). The mean of the items is computed to yield a composite score ranging from *negative attitudes* (1) to *positive attitudes toward reading* (5).

Children's self-perceptions of their academic abilities were measured with the cognitive subscale of the "Perceived Competence Scale for Children" (Harter, 1979, 1982). It contains items about how children judge the quality of their schoolwork and whether they have trouble doing assignments. The task consisted of seven brief descriptions of opposing characteristics. For example, one item says that "some kids often forget what they learn, but other kids can remember things easily." These descriptions were presented as being equally likely and that half the children are one way and that half the children are the other. The scale thus attempted to equate the attractiveness of both options by legitimizing either choice. In this forced-choice format, children first picked the description most similar to themselves and then decided whether the description was "really true" or "sort of true" for them. Thus, each item consisted of four possible responses, with scores ranging from 1 to 4. A mean score was computed that ranged from 1 (indicating negative cognitive self-perceptions) to 4 (indicating positive cognitive self-perceptions).

Subscales from "A Scale of Intrinsic versus Extrinsic Orientation in the Classroom" (Harter, 1980) were used to measure motivational variables. The mastery orientation subscale assesses the extent to which children view themselves as independent problem solvers as opposed to being dependent on the teacher to complete schoolwork. The Curiosity subscale was concerned with whether students do academic tasks out of an intrinsic interest and curiosity or in order to please the teacher. The scale had the same format as the Perceived Competence Measure and yielded scores ranging from 1 to 4. A composite Motivational score was computed based on the mean score of the Mastery Orientation and Curiosity subscales. A score of 4 represented intrinsic orientation, and a score of 1 an extrinsic orientation.

Achievement and Aptitude

For many children, their levels of achievement follow estimates of their aptitude. A substantial percentage of children do not follow this pattern, however, and are perplexing in their nonconforming pattern. Children whose academic performance is not governed by aptitude are puzzling at a cursory glance but form the optimal group to examine the influence of noncognitive or motivational factors on achievement. What are the prevailing influences on achievement for those children for whom IQ does *not* predict achievement? The two types of "inappropriate" achievers, Overachievers and Underachievers, are the focus of these analyses.

Underachievers and overachievers were identified on the basis of the discrepancy between verbal aptitude and reading achievement. A bivariate linear regression analysis was performed predicting reading achievement from children's verbal aptitude scores. Aptitude was assessed with the verbal subscale of the Cognitive Abilities Test (Thorndike & Hagen, 1978). The percentile scores were used, which ranged from 0 to 99. Reading achievement was measured with the comprehension subtest of the Gates–MacGinitie Reading Test (MacGinitie, 1978), which is a standardized measure of children's understanding of prose. Pearson product–moment correlations computed separately by grade revealed a significant relationship between reading comprehension and verbal aptitude scores: Grade 3, $r = .78$, $p < .01$; Grade 5, $r = .76$, $p < .01$. The strength of the relationship between reader group membership and IQ level thus appears developmentally robust. Residual scores, the difference between the scores actually obtained by the children and the predicted values, were computed next. The use of residual scores circumvent the need to specify arbitrary cut-off points for test scores and to adopt rigid criteria for the identification of discrepancies. It requires few assumptions concerning the relation between a particular score on one test and a particular score on another. The procedure yields a normal distribution of children and permits easy identification of children who markedly depart from predicted levels of achievement, irrespective of IQ. Children were thus divided into three achiever groups by partitioning them on the residual score at one standard deviation below the mean and one standard deviation above the mean. Thus, appropriate achievers consisted of children who deviated less than one standard deviation away from the mean residual score. The Underachievers were children with residual scores beyond one standard deviation below the mean residual score. The Overachievers were children who had residual scores beyond one standard deviation above the mean. The mean residual score was 0.00 for appropriate achievers, -1.60 for underachievers, and 1.60 for overachievers (the values are Z scores).

The first section of the results presents the distribution of over, under, and appropriate achievers in regular classrooms. In the next section we examine how the achievement groups performed on the battery of cognitive and affective measures. The last section of data presents the findings from multiple regression analyses used to predict reading achievement on the basis of the cognitive and motivational variables.

Achievement Category Frequencies

The classification of children into achievement groups based on residual scores resulted in similar distributions at both grade levels. As shown in Table 5.1, the majority of children were appropriate achievers. For the remaining children,

TABLE 5.1
Percentages of Children in Achievement Category by Grade

	Grade		
	Third	Fifth	Total
Underachievement	14	17	16
	(55)	(63)	(118)
Appropriate Achievement	70	68	69
	(272)	(252)	(524)
Overachievement	16	15	15
	(60)	(55)	(115)

Note: Numbers of children are shown in parentheses.

however, verbal aptitude was not predictive of actual reading achievement. Nearly a third of the children had scores that were at least one standard deviation above or below the mean residual score. Chi square analysis comparing achievement level categories as a function of grade were nonsignificant, indicating that the proportion of underachievers and overachievers is stable between the third and fifth grade.

Achievement level classification was also examined with regard to reader skill level. The reader skill groups were formed by partitioning subjects at the 33rd and 67th percentiles of the national norms of the Gates–MacGinitie Reading Comprehension subtest, a standardized measure of children's understanding of prose. The measure yields an Extended Scale Score, which is a continuous interval scale that indexes reading ability over a broad age range. The low group consisted of readers performing at or below the 33rd percentile, the mid group between the 33rd and the 67th percentiles, and the high group of readers performed at or above the 67th percentile. Reader skill level was significantly associated with achievement group $\chi^2(4) = 198.05$, $p < .001$. A Cramer's phi value of .36 was obtained. Grade level did not interact with reader skill level and the category percentages are thus presented for the total sample in Table 5.2. Examination of the statistics by row reveals that underachievers consist primarily of low- and mid-level readers. These findings indicate that a substantial number of children now reading at low- and mid-reader skill levels have the potential for improvement. In contrast, the overachieving children are nearly all high-level readers.

In summary, for the majority of children, IQ is highly predictive of levels of achievement. A small but consistent percentage of children, however, fail to achieve at higher levels, commensurate with their abilities. What accounts for the discrepant achievement of these children, as well as those who go beyond expected levels of performance? How is the "appropriate" achiever different from the "overachiever" and the "underachiever"? What are the cognitive and

TABLE 5.2
Percentages of Children in Each Achievement Category

	Reader Skill		
	Low	Mid	High
Underachievement	45	48	7
	(53)	(57)	(8)
Appropriate Achievement	13	35	52
	(71)	(182)	(271)
Overachievement	0	7	93
	(0)	(8)	(107)

Note: Numbers of children are shown in parentheses.

motivational patterns characterizing these children and how are they related to reading at different ages? These questions are examined in the next section.

Patterns of Performance

The relation between achievement group membership and performance on the test battery was examined with a 2 (grade) × 3 (achievement level) multivariate analysis of variance (MANOVA). The multivariate effect for the test battery was significant for both grade $F(9,655) = 129.51, p < .001$, and achievement group, $F(18,1310) = 74.9, p < .001$. Subsequent examination of the univariate F tests revealed that the grade main effect was significant for three of the nine tasks: Gates–MacGinitie comprehension subtest, $F(1,663) = 140.56, p < .001$; Cloze $F(1,633) = 27.71, p < .001$; and Reading Awareness $F(1,633) = 38.85$, $p < .001$. The fifth graders performed at higher levels than third graders on each of these measures demonstrating greater reading comprehension, use of reading strategies, and awareness of the variables influencing reading. As expected, no grade differences were obtained on the measure of verbal aptitude, the Cognitive Abilities Test. Children's verbal aptitude remains stable between the third and fifth grades. The error detection task also yielded no developmental differences. This was also expected given that grade appropriate passages were used. The absence of grade difference suggests that the tasks were equally difficult for each grade level. Among the motivational measures, no developmental differences were obtained. Children's attitudes toward reading, cognitive self-perceptions, accuracy of self-perceptions, and intrinsic motivation showed no change between Grades 3 and 5.

The univariate F tests revealed that the achievement group main effect was significant for all the tasks, except for verbal aptitude and reading awareness. Because an interaction was not obtained between the two factors, the combined results for Grades 3 and 5 are presented. The cell means and standard deviations are shown in Table 5.3.

The significant univariate ANOVAs were obtained for the Gates–MacGinitie comprehension test, $F(2,663) = 187.33$, $p < .001$; Cloze, $F(2,663) = 8.59$, $p < .001$; error detection, $F(2,663) = 3.82$, $p < .02$; reading attitudes, $F(2,663) = 13.66$, $p < .001$, cognitive self-perceptions, $F(2,633) = 4.34$, $p = .01$; and intrinsic motivation, $F(2,633) = 4.75$, $p = .009$. All three groups differed on these tasks with the overachieving children being more likely to be better readers and to use strategies more effectively. In the motivational domain, overachieving children were more likely to have positive attitudes toward reading, have high self-perceptions of competence, and be intrinsically motivated in school.

Differences in the Cognitive Abilities Test as a function of achievement level were not obtained, indicating that underachievers, appropriate achievers, and

TABLE 5.3
Means and Standard Deviations of Cognitive and Motivational
Measures by Achievement Level

	Underachievers (n = 106)	Appropriate Achievers (n = 464)	Overachievers (n = 99)
	M*	M*	M*
Tasks			
Verbal Aptitude	66.0 (23.0)	64.0 (23.0)	66.0 (22.7)
Reading Comprehension	469.2 (53.4)	520.9 (51.2)	585.2 (48.2)
Cloze	4.5 (2.2)	4.8 (2.1)	5.5 (1.8)
Error Detection	.9 (.6)	1.0 (.5)	1.1 (.5)
Reading Awareness	32.1 (4.8)	32.5 (4.6)	33.1 (4.4)
Reading Attitudes	3.7 (.7)	3.9 (.6)	4.2 (.6)
Cognitive Perceptions	2.9 (.7)	3.0 (.6)	3.1 (.6)
Intrinsic Motivation	2.9 (.5)	3.0 (.5)	3.1 (.5)

Note. Standard deviations are shown in parentheses.
*M indicates mean.

overachievers were comparable in verbal attitude. Differences in reading awareness were also not found among the achievement groups. Underachieving children were as likely as their appropriately and overachieving peers to be aware
of the variables that influenced reading.

Predicting Reading Achievement

In order to examine the relation between reading achievement and the cognitive
and motivational variables presented here, stepwise multiple regressions were
performed as a function of achiever group at each grade. The dependent measure
was the Gates–MacGinitie comprehension test and the predictors were: Cloze,
error detection, reading awareness, reading attitudes, cognitive self-perceptions,
and intrinsic motivation.

Three questions raised concerning the relation were: What is the relative
importance of these variables for reading comprehension?; Do developmental
differences occur in this pattern?; Are children of varying achiever groups characterized by different patterns of predictors?

The findings of the stepwise multiple regressions as a function of achievement category and grade are shown in Table 5.4. Among the underachieving
third graders the cloze significantly accounted for 52% of the variance in reading
comprehension. Awareness of the variables influencing reading and comprehension monitoring skills also contributed significantly to reading. Together these
three variables accounted for 65% of the variance in reading comprehension.
Comprehension and metacognitive skills were the predominant factor in underachiever's performance on the Gates–MacGinitie test.

The reading performance of appropriate third-grade achievers was explained
by motivational as well as comprehension and metacognitive variables. The cloze
was the best single predictor of reading, but it accounted for only 38% of the
variance compared to the 52% of the variance explained for underachievers. An
additional 7% of the variance was significantly accounted for by reading awareness, 6% by error detection, and 2% by cognitive self-perceptions. For appropriate achievers, reading was positively related to the effective use of
comprehension strategies, metacognitive knowledge about reading, and beliefs
about one's academic competence.

The best predictor of reading among overachieving third graders was the
attitudes toward reading task, accounting for 23% of the variance. Error detection
skills also contributed significantly to reading comprehension, explaining an
additional 15% of the variance. Thus, overachieving children's beliefs and feelings about reading and their comprehension monitoring skills are most predictive
of their reading performance. For this group of children, the effective use of
context, reading awareness, cognitive self-perceptions, and intrinsic motivation
were not predictive of their reading comprehension.

TABLE 5.4
Stepwise Multiple Regressions of the Gates–MacGinitie Reading
Test on Comprehension, Metacognitive, and Motivational Variables

Step	Variable	r^2	Partial r	Significance
	Grade 3: Underachievers, $n = 47$			
1	Cloze	.52	.72	.00
2	Reading Awareness	.60	.41	.00
3	Error Detection	.65	.35	.02
	Grade 3: Appropriate Achievers, $n = 233$			
1	Cloze	.38	.62	.00
2	Reading Awareness	.45	.32	.00
3	Error Detection	.51	.33	.00
4	Cognitive Self-perceptions	.53	.21	.00
	Grade 3: Overachievers, $n = 52$			
1	Reading Attitudes	.23	.48	.00
2	Error Detection	.38	.44	.00
	Grade 5: Underachievers, $n = 59$			
1	Error Detection	.32	.57	.00
2	Cloze	.43	.41	.00
3.	Cognitive Self-perceptions	.50	.34	.01
	Grade 5: Appropriate Achievers, $n = 231$			
1	Cloze	.33	.57	.00
2	Reading Attitudes	.42	.38	.00
3	Error Detection	.47	.38	.00
4	Reading Awareness	.50	.24	.00
5	Cognitive Self-perceptions	.52	.20	.00
	Grade 5: Overachievers, $n = 47$			
1	Cognitive Self-perceptions	.24	.49	.00
2	Reading Awareness	.33	.36	.02

The results of the multiple regression for the fifth graders were similar to that of the third-grade children with one important difference. The influence of motivational, attitudinal and self-perception variables on reading increased with age and experience. This can be seen in the results for the underachieving fifth graders. The three significant predictors included error detection (32%), Cloze, (9%), and cognitive self-perceptions (7%). The significant contribution of children's beliefs about their cognitive abilities over and above that of the Cloze and error detection reveals the emerging influence of motivational factors on reading.

The increasing influence of a greater variety of predictors was also observed among the appropriate achievers. Five variables significantly accounted for 52%

of the variance in reading comprehension and included the Cloze, reading attitudes, error detection, reading awareness, and cognitive self-perceptions.

The best single predictor of reading among overachieving fifth graders was the cognitive self-perceptions task accounting for 24% of the variance. Reading awareness significantly contributed an additional 9% of explained variance. The reading performance of overachieving fifth graders was positively related to motivational and metacognitive factors. Their views of their academic abilities and their metacognitive knowledge about reading were the best determinants of their reading skill. These findings reveal a differential pattern of predictors for reading achievement as a function of achievement group.

ACHIEVEMENT PROFILES

In order to integrate the findings of the data analysis, the following profiles of underachievers, appropriate achievers, and overachievers were formulated.

Underachievers

For these children, verbal aptitude predicts higher performance, yet they manage to evade appropriate achievement. With an IQ equivalent of 105 and reading achievement substantially below expected levels, these children most closely resemble the typical learning-disabled child. The children performed at significantly lower levels than the other groups on every measure in the test battery with the exception of reading awareness and verbal aptitude. Underachieving children were characterized by lower levels of comprehension and less effective use of reading strategies than their appropriate and overachieving peers. Underachievement in children was also accompanied by negative reading attitudes, lower self-perceptions of cognitive-competence, and an extrinsic orientation toward school.

The reading abilities of underachieving third graders were best predicted by reading awareness and comprehension skills. The set of motivational variables was generally unpredictive of reading performance for this group of children. In contrast, reading achievement among fifth-grade underachievers was positively related to comprehension monitoring, strategy use, and cognitive self-perceptions.

Appropriate Achievers

As described earlier, these children formed the largest subgroup and achieved at expected levels based on verbal aptitude. Their performance on the comprehension and motivational measures in the test battery fell at intermediate levels to the underachievers and overachievers. The pattern of predictors for reading among appropriate achievers spanned the comprehension, metacognitive, and motivational variables. Reading comprehension was positively related to variables that include strategy use, reading awareness, and cognitive self-perceptions.

Overachievers

The distinguishing features of overachievers in the third grade is their superior performance in comprehension skills and positive reading attitudes. At the fifth grade, these children were characterized primarily by higher self-perceptions of cognitive abilities and more positive reading attitudes than their appropriate and underachieving peers. Significant differences were not found in comprehension skills between the achiever groups among the older children. For these children, performance on the Gates–MacGinitie was most highly predicted by their self-perceptions of cognitive competence and their level of metacognitive knowledge.

These results suggest that cognitive skill differences underlying achiever levels diminish with age and experience. Whereas the overachievers in the third grade may in fact have better comprehension skills, these differences do not persist at the older age group. Rather, children's beliefs about their competence and their reading awareness appear to be more important determinants of actual achievement levels than cognitive skills among fifth graders. Thus, high self-perceptions, an awareness of how to best use one's skills, and a high value for reading may underlie their enhanced academic performance.

The data thus revealed different profiles of cognitive and motivational variables characterizing children of various achievement levels. Of special interest were children who departed from expected levels of achievement: overachievers and underachievers. High levels of reading awareness characterized the overachievers whereas underachievers exhibited low cognitive self-perceptions and negative attitudes toward reading. What accounts for children of comparable abilities to be differentiated as appropriate achievers, overachievers, and underachievers? We propose that children respond to their self-perceptions, attitudes, and skills in a manner that preserves self-worth. We call this functional balancing of personal perceptions and effort, adaptive motivation, which we discuss in the last section.

ADAPTIVE MOTIVATION

Coping is a central feature of a healthy adjustment to any environment. In the school setting, coping is especially salient because a relatively inflexible set of values, goals, and norms is imposed on children. Children respond to this situation in many ways; one common response is to adjust their levels of motivation. The data indicate that achievement motivation in school has different associated costs and benefits for children of different aptitude and achievement levels. Thus, adjusting one's level of motivation is a means of reconciling one's personal perceptions with the demands of the classroom.

We propose four "personalized dimensions" of motivation that underlie children's adaptive choices: (1) sense of control, (2) significant goals and values, (3) self-management skills, and (4) interpretations of success and failure. These personalized orientations toward achievement help children adjust their motivation in order to preserve self-worth. Thus, achievement motivation has a functional value of maintaining self-worth in the school context. These four dimensions of achievement motivation are discussed in the following sections.

Sense of Control

Beliefs about control have been incorporated in numerous motivational theories as important links to action (for review, see Stipek & Weisz, 1981). The belief–action linkage may best be illustrated with deCharms's (1976) theory of personal causation. He uses the term *origins* to denote people who experience a sense of control over the things that happen to them. They confidently select actions and direct their own lives. In contrast, *pawns* experience the world as an instrument of others' actions. They are characterized as having little self-confidence and believe that they do not initiate outcomes for their own lives. DeCharms's research involving underachievers in elementary through high school demonstrated that training students to function as origins can produce improvements in motivation and achievement. These effects of superior achievement were observed up to 5 years beyond training.

The debilitating effect of a perceived lack of control has been demonstrated in studies of learned helplessness (Seligman, 1975) and causal attributions (Frieze, 1980, Weiner, 1979). According to learned helplessness theory, repeated and prolonged failure leads to perceptions that outcomes are unrelated to an individual's actions. This results in a general expectation that all events that happen to a person are uncontrollable, which in turn produces passive behavior. Children who believe that they have no control over their achievement outcomes do not persist on tasks, do not expect to succeed on future attempts, and feel badly about themselves (Butkowsky & Willows, 1980). The belief that they lack control over their outcomes has negative consequences for feelings of self-worth as well as for achievement behaviors.

Significant Goals and Values

Learned helplessness and causal attribution concepts are useful approaches, but they do not consider how an event's importance may influence the resulting degree of helplessness. For example,, if a boy perceives that both scoring well on an exam and finding a healthy pet dog are beyond his control, learned helplessness theory would predict a passive response in both cases. The fact that getting a healthy pet dog may be more important to him would not influence the extent to which he shows helpless behavior toward the two goals. The importance of a goal's value is proposed to influence only the resulting self-esteem and affect, not behavior. Alternate views, however, assign values a pivotal role in achievement choices and behaviors (Eccles et al., 1983).

In a recently expanded model of achievement motivation, Wigfield and Eccles (1983) propose an interaction between values and achievement goal selection that answers the question: "Do I want to succeed?" They suggest that the value of a task is determined by three main factors. First, the activity's characteristics determine the value of engaging in the task. Second, the individual's needs, goals, and values contribute to the importance of the task. Third, the degree to which the task characteristics meet the individual's requirements influences whether a person will value doing the task. Activities that fulfill the needs, goals, and values of the individual take on the greatest importance and are most likely to be attempted. Activities that threaten self-concept or self-esteem can acquire a negative value and are likely to be avoided.

How is task value defined? Eccles, Adler, Futterman, Goff, Kaczala, and Midgley (1983) characterize subjective task value as having four main components: attainment value, intrinsic value, utility value, and anticipated costs. Attainment value refers to the importance of doing well. Intrinsic value or interest is the resulting satisfaction inherent in the task as opposed to rewards external to the task. A task has utility value if it is useful in reaching other goals and it is not an end in itself.

The subjective value of a task is also influenced by the cost of engaging in the task. If the task demands are excessive the task value may be diminished. Likewise, if the task value is sufficiently high, this may override even exceptional costs. Eccles et al. (1983) also allude to another kind of cost, that of NOT engaging in the task. There may be times when the costs of engaging in the task are high but less than the costs of not engaging in a task. For example, the student who does poorly in reading may nevertheless attempt to do the reading task because of the reprimands or losses that may follow from not doing the task.

Considering subjective task value as a function of the match between the individual's characteristics (needs, goals, values) and the task characteristics (demands, costs, benefits) provides a wide range of individual differences in the values children bring to academic tasks, depending on their backgrounds, past experiences, and self-perceptions. The relation between the value of a task outcome and performance was explored on a maze task with average, remedial, and failing 9- to 12-year-old boys (Johnson, 1981). Two value conditions were created. In one, children were told that the tasks were measures of school ability. In the other condition subjects were given a reward for their performance. Johnson found that neither the average nor the remedial students showed any difference in persistence between the two task value conditions. However, failing students worked significantly longer under the reward condition than under the academic incentive condition. These findings support the role of task value in influencing achievement behavior manifested by students. Thus, academics may have lost its value as an incentive for failing children (or possibly academic incentives never had value for the failing students). These results suggest that targets of intervention for some children may have to begin by addressing students' goals and imbuing academic goals with personal value and relevance.

Self-Management Skills

Motivated behavior may also depend on children's self-management skills, or the knowledge of how to apply particular skills effectively to achieve specific goals. Metacognition has been identified as a critical aspect of goal-directed behavior and strategy use (Brown, Armbruster, & Baker, 1986). The implications for achievement behavior concern children's abilities to evaluate the task, to form plans, and to regulate strategy use (Paris & Lindauer, 1982).

Evaluation involves children's skills in identifying task characteristics relevant to an activity. In writing a book report for example, it means recognizing the need to identify main ideas, the plot, and main characters, rather than isolated details and facts. A second aspect of self-management skills is being able to plan a course of action. Rather than stumbling blindly into a task, the child with adequate self-management skills knows that a sequence of actions must be executed in a deliberate manner. This may be as simple as knowing to read the book first in order to write a book report, or it may be as sophisticated as planning to summarize each chapter after it is read. A child who knows how to initiate an activity will be more motivated to begin the task than one who is uncertain of even the first step (Ryan, Ledger, Short, & Weed, 1982). Once goals have been set and steps taken toward it, students need to monitor and regulate their progress. This involves the revision of plans, the use of appropriate strategies, and vigilant monitoring/correcting of one's progress.

Interpretations of Success and Failure

Children's personal interpretations of success and failure comprise a fourth component of personalized achievement motivation. Viewing low achievement as adaptive in some cases, leads to a shift in focus from changing behaviors to changing the meaning of task involvement (Nicholls, 1979). If students have difficulty reading, they often avoid the task entirely. A conventional response is to get the student "back on task." A more promising approach may involve redefining success and failure as steps in learning and not terminal outcomes.

Failure is an ordinary occurrence in life. Although we may learn from our mistakes, rarely do we hear the virtue of learning from failure expounded. Especially in the minds of children there is no such thing as a constructive failure.

The goal is not to fail at all. For children, however, as novices in most academic activities, failure is an inevitable, if not a necessary part of learning. The key may be to teach children to redefine failure as a common and informative experience that leads to action, rather than to dead ends. For the poor reader, task involvement usually consists of negative information, such as "I'm bad at this, I don't like it, I have to work hard," that can errode self-worth and motivation. An emphasis on attributions prompts children to ask themselves how they performed and the reasons for their performance level. But it fails to direct children's attention to the next step of identifying adaptive ways of responding to failure. Not only should children ask themselves why they failed and how they did, but they should also look past their failures to subsequent goals. The same thing may naturally be said of success.

An adaptive response to failure is particularly important in view of theories that suggest failure is not only inevitable but also necessary for success (Clifford, 1980). Challenge, frustration, or anxiety may be necessary for achievement and they have each been incorporated into several theories of motivation (Amsel, 1972; Atkinson & Birch, 1978; Brehm, 1972). The critical problem is to identify when experiences of failure enhance achievement motivation.

In a study with female undergraduates, Wortman, Panciera, Shusterman, and Hibschuser (1976) found increased motivation after failure on a problem-solving task among subjects attributing their failure to ability. Wortman et al. reasoned that failure threatened perceived competence and prompted greater efforts to succeed in order to maintain self-worth. Thus, ability attributions for failure that imply a lack of competence may at times lead to action and achievement behaviors. On the other hand, ability attributions implying a lack of control may lead to passive behaviors and "learned helplessness."

Another attribution that may facilitate motivation after failure refers to how one performs a task. Attributing failure to ineffective strategies may have critically different implications for behavior than attributions to lack of ability. In a test of this hypothesis, Anderson and Jennings (1980) manipulated the attributions of college students on a persuasion task (convincing people to make blood donations) and had them experience failure initially on the task. Students who were led to believe that their strategies determined success or failure on the task were more likely to expect successes and to expect to improve with practice. They actually performed better than those who believed that ability was the main factor. Attributions to a controllable cause, such as strategy use, resulted in increased expectations for success even after failure. The strategy attribution group attended to strategic features and learned from their experiences.

This finding is particularly relevant for children's achievement in school. Unlike most of the prior research examining children's beliefs, this study further refines "effort" from a global construct to a more specific cause. This is especially useful for classroom tasks, because success depends not just on working hard, but on how one works. Thus, the child who puts in a great deal of time and effort and sees little return will expect little success in the future because effort expenditure is already high. However, if children recognize that their attempts are ineffective and that other more promising approaches exist, they are likely to keep trying and not reduce their future expectations. This also provides children with a means of maintaining self-concept and self-esteem. It offers nonthreatening opportunities for people to take chances and to invest themselves in a task without using up their options. Thus, a child may reason, "I tried hard, but I didn't use the headings and questions to help me to understand the story," and the expectation for success is maintained. This is particularly relevant for reading because a wide array of strategies exist to increase comprehension that may not be utilized by poor readers.

Perhaps the most compelling reason for redefining failure is to enable children to react adaptively to failure. Rather than focusing on the fact that they failed, it helps children to examine the reasons for failure. This can lead to identification of new ways to try to succeed. Low-achieving students would need to resort less to using low levels of motivation to cope with perceptions of past failures and projections of future failure. Thus, adaptive motivation may be replaced by "continuing motivation" (Maehr, 1976). Getting children to begin academic activities appears to be relatively easy, compared to the task of keeping them engaged. It may be that this aspect of motivation, which includes behaviors like persistence, pursuing tasks to completion, goal directed behaviors, and resisting distractions, may be an area that requires more specific attention and study. Thus, one of the main purposes of redefining failure is to enable children to continue in their endeavors and not allow their current setbacks to interfere with the attainment of their goals.

THE DYNAMICS OF ADAPTIVE MOTIVATION

Motivation may serve a functional role in school by preserving children's self-worth. Four personalized dimensions of achievement were described, which may help children to determine appropriate levels of adaptive motivation. In this section, the means by which this occurs is further explored.

Each of these dimensions is proposed to be motivational in character, either in a positive or negative way; that is, these dimensions have a valence. When a child shows high-positive valences on all four dimension (i.e., belief in a sense of control, high-task value, superior self-management skills, and a positive view of failure), high levels of motivation are likely to be observed. For the child who registers negative valences on each of these dimensions, motivation to achieve will probably be low. Indeed, this is an appropriate response when an activity is perceived as being beyond personal control, having little personal significance, self-management skills are absent, and failure is considered a debilitating and dead-end experience. Pursuit of an activity under these circumstances would be inconsistent with the maintenance of self-worth (Covington & Beery, 1976). To be highly motivated and to pursue a goal with these thoughts and feelings may in fact be indicative of pathological problems.

It is unlikely that children uniformly have positive or negative valences on all these dimensions. It is more often the case, that a combination of positive and negative valences exists. For example, children may view reading as a personally meaningful goal but believe that it is out of their control. They may show motivated behavior, if the extent to which they value reading is greater than the extent to which they regard it as unattainable. In other words, strong values for some components may override the weak values of others.

Environmental influences including family, school, and peer contexts overlay and influence an individual's thoughts and feelings about achievement. Other people provide incentives (both positive and negative), reinforcers, and values that can influence children's motivational tendencies. The developmental changes in the content and form of children's thoughts and feelings accompany changes in children's achievement environments.

The final motivational expression of all these forces is proposed to be reconciled in terms of self-worth. Our view is that children will pursue activities in which self-worth is confirmed to a greater extent than it is threatened. In the terminology of need achievement theories, goals may be selected where the desire to succeed is greater than the motive to avoid failure. For example, consider students who struggle to read stories and to answer accompanying questions. After this experience, some students may give up, yet others may pursue the task with even greater determination; that is, some become highly motivated whereas others become even less motivated. These divergent approaches to maintaining self-worth may be understood by examining the values held by the two types of students in this situation. Students who attach great value to reading (whether intrinsic, utility, etc.), believe it to be controllable, and have self-management abilities to apply their skills effectively, are likely to derive greater feelings of self-worth by continuing to display high levels of motivation. Given these components of achievement motivation, to show lower levels of motivation would be likely to erode self-worth by compromising one's values and giving up prematurely. The positive effect on self-worth may be further enhanced by the personal satisfaction gained through accomplishing (or simply attempting) a difficult task and eliciting positive social feedback from teachers, parents, and peers. In sum, the benefits derived from motivated behavior exceed its cost.

But this may not always be the case. The development of self-management skills is particulary important for children to be able to discern appropriate responses to failures. For example, some cases of failure would indicate the need to continue with the same behavior, others would indicate the need to modify one's strategies, whereas still others would suggest the need to change the level of one's goals. As Janoff-Bulman and Brickman (1980) suggest, it is not necessarily maladaptive to stop working on a task under certain conditions. They further propose that always persisting in the face of failure may in fact diminish one's well-being and adaptive functioning. In modifying one's view of failure, it is important to consider whether continuing motivation serves a personally meaningful and adaptive purpose and not just a means of being highly active, compliant, and involved in tasks.

For LD students who may find little value in reading activities, lack self-management skills, and believe it to be out of their control, a low level of motivation may be adaptive. Inaction may be further justified by emphasizing the unimportance of the task and personal irrelevance of negative reinforcers. These responses preserve self-worth by devaluing the activity and rejecting it as a personally meaningful goal.

These low levels of motivation are undoubtedly viewed as maladaptive from the teacher's perspective. From the LD student's point of view, however, displaying low-achievement motivation is preferable to the debilitating experience of trying hard in a no-win situation. To show highly motivated behavior would not only bring frustration and apparent wasted effort, but most condemning of all, confirmation of a lack of ability (Covington & Omelich, 1979). The dilemma of the poor student described by Covington and Omelich (1979) as the "double-edged sword" involves learning how to determine optimal levels of investment in a task. High levels of effort in the face of failure would suggest to the student a lack of ability with devastating consequences for self-worth (Covington & Beery, 1976). This is especially salient for LD children who are often in double jeopardy with diminished self-worth and academic achievement. Low levels of effort or inaction is, therefore, sometimes preferable to trying hard and revealing one's inadequacies. Variable levels of motivation thus serve as a means of coping with the demands and possible incongruities between the achievement context and the individual.

SUMMARY

The problem of academic underachievement is a persistent and multidimensional one. Rather than viewing it as a uniform problem, our research indicates the need to distinguish patterns of underachievement for children of varying abilities. A developmental shift in the importance of cognitive versus motivational factors for reading achievement was found. Comprehension skills were a powerful predictor of reading achievement among third graders, whereas the importance of comprehension skills was attenuated among fifth graders with whom motivational factors began to play a larger role. The performance of children who achieve at levels appropriate to their ability was primarily influenced by IQ. They performed at higher levels on all the cognitive and motivational measures corresponding to increases in aptitude and reading achievement. Their knowledge of strategic reading may allow them to use their existing skills more effectively and successfully. Underachievers were characterized by low self-perceptions of their cognitive abilities and negative attitudes toward reading. In summary, distinctive patterns of cognitive skills, attitudes, beliefs, and perceptions were found to underlie the academic attainments of children with different abilities.

The functional nature of motivation was proposed as an adaptive mechanism for coping in school. To the extent that pursuing an activity threatens self-worth, high levels of motivation would be less likely, low levels of motivation would be a more adaptive response. In dealing with underachievement we need to differentiate targets of intervention for children with different patterns of cognitive skills, abilities, and motivation. The adaptive value of low motivation is an obstacle to enhanced achievement motivation and must be addressed before academic gains, particularly among LD children, may be expected. Prospective targets of intervention include inducing a sense of control, making academic goals personally significant, insuring adequate self-management skills, and fostering a balanced view of success and failure.

REFERENCES

Alexander, J., & Filler, R. (1976). *Attitudes and reading.* Newark, DE: International Reading Association.

Amsel, A. (1972). Behavioral habituations, counterconditioning, and persistence. In A. Block & W. K. Prokasy (Eds.), *Classical conditioning II* (pp. 409–426). New York: Appleton–Century–Crofts.

Anderson, C. A., & Jennings, D. L. (1980). When experiences of failure promote expectations of success: The impact of attributing failure to ineffective strategies. *Journal of Personality, 48,* 393–407.

Atkinson, J. W., & Birch, D. (1978). *An introduction to motivation* (2nd ed.). New York: Van Nostrand.

Baker, L. (1982). An evaluation of the role of metacognitive deficits in learning disabilities. *Topics in Learning and Learning Disabilities, 2,* 27–36.

Bandura, A. (1982). Self-efficacy mechanism in human agency. *American Psychologist, 37,* 122–147.

Beebe, M.J. (1980). The effect of different types of substitution miscues on reading. *Reading Research Quarterly, 15,* 324–336.

Brehm, J. W. (1972). *Responses to loss of freedom: A theory of psychological reactance.* Morristown, NJ: General Learning Press.

Brown, A. L., Armbruster, B. B., & Baker, L. (1986). The role of metacognition in reading and studying. In J. Orasanu (Ed.), *Reading comprehension from research to practice* (pp. 49–76). Hillsdale, NJ: Lawrence Erlbaum Associates.

Brown, A. L., & Palincsar, A. S. (1982). Inducing strategic learning from texts by means of informed, self-control training. *Topics in Learning and learning Disabilities, 2*(1), 1–18.

Butkowsky, I. S., & Willows, D. M. (1980). Cognitive–motivational characteristics of children varying in reading ability: Evidence for learned helplessness in poor readers. *Journal of Educational Psychology, 72,* 408–422.

Clifford, M. (1980). Effects of failure: Alternative explanations and possible implications. In L. J. Fyans, Jr. (Ed.), *Achievement motivation, recent trends in theory and research* (pp. 96–113). New York: Plenum.

Covington, M., & Beery, R. (1976). *Self-worth and school learning*. New York: Holt, Rinehart & Winston.

Covington, M. V. (1983). Motivated cognitions. In S. Paris, G. Olson, & H. Stevenson (Eds.), *Learning and motivation in the classroom* (pp. 139–164). Hillsdale, NJ: Lawrence Erlbaum Associates.

Covington, M. V., & Omelich, C. L. (1979). Effort: Double-edged sword in school achievement. *Journal of Educational Psychology, 71*, 169–182.

deCharms, R. (1976). *Enhancing motivation: Change in the classroom*. New York: Irvington.

DiVesta, F. J., Hayward, K. G., & Orlando, V. P. (1979). Developmental trends in monitoring test for comprehension. *Child Development, 50*, 97–105.

Downing, J., & Leong, C. K. (1982). *Psychology of reading*. New York: MacMillan.

Dweck, C. S. (1975). The role of expectations and attributions in the alleviation of learned helplessness. *Journal of Personality and Social Psychology, 31*, 674–685.

Dweck, C. S., & Bempechat, J. (1983). Children's theories of intelligence: Consequences for learning. In S. G. Paris, G. M. Olson, & H. S. Stevenson (Eds.), *Learning and motivation in the classroom* (pp. 239–256). Hillsdale, NJ: Lawrence Erlbaum Associates.

Eccles, J., Adler, T. F., Futterman, R., Goff, S. B., Kaczala, C. M., & Midgley, C. (1983). Expectancies, values, and academic behaviors. In J. T. Spence (Ed.), *Perspectives on achievement and achievement motivation* (pp. 75–146). San Francisco: Freeman.

Engin, A., Wallbrown, F., & Brown, D. (1976). The dimensions of reading attitude for children in the intermediate grades. *Psychology in the Schools, 13*, 309–316.

Epstein, I. (1980). *Measuring attitudes toward reading*. Princeton, NJ: ERIC Clearinghouse on Tests, Measurements & Evaluation, ETS, ERIC/TM Report No. 73. (ERIC Document Reproduction Service No. ED 196 938).

Fincham, F., & Barling, J. (1978). Locus of control and generosity in learning disabled, normal achieving and gifted children. *Child Development, 49*, 530–533.

Fishbein, M., & Ajzen, I. (1975). *Belief, attitude, intention, and behavior*. Reading, MA: Addison–Wesley.

Flavell, J. H. (1970). Developmental studies of mediated memory. In H. W. Reese & L. P. Lipsett (Eds.), *Advances in child development and behavior* (Vol. 5, pp. 181–211). New York: Academic Press.

Forrest, D. L., & Waller, T. G. (1979, April). *Cognitive and metacognitive aspects of reading*. Paper presented at the biennial meeting of the Society for Research in Child Development, San Francisco.

Frieze, I. H. (1980). Beliefs about success and failure in the classroom. In J. H. McMillan (Ed.), *The social psychology of school learning* (pp. 39–78). New York: Academic Press.

Garner, R. (1980). Monitoring of understanding: An investigation of good and poor readers' awareness of induced miscomprehension of text. *Journal of Reading Behavior, 12*, 55–64.

Garner, R., & Kraus, C. (1980). *Monitoring of understanding among seventh graders: An investigation of good comprehender–poor comprehender differences in knowing and regulating reading behaviors*. Unpublished manuscript, University of Maryland, College Park, MD.

Golinkoff, R. (1976). A comparison of reading comprehension processes in good and poor comprehenders. *Reading Research Quarterly, 11*, 623–659.

Hagen, J. W., Barclay, C. R., & Newman, R. S. (1985). Metacognition, self-knowledge, and learning disabilities: Some thoughts on knowing and doing. *Topics in Learning and Learning Disabilities, 2*(1), 19–26.

Hahn, C. T. (1977). *Measuring attitudes toward reading, an annotated ERIC bibliography*. Princeton, NJ: ERIC Clearinghouse on Tests, Measurement, and Evaluation. (ERIC Document Reproduction Service No., ED 151 423).

Hallahan, D. P., & Kaufman, J. M. (1982). *Exceptional children: Introduction to special education* (2nd ed.). Englewood Cliffs, NJ: Prentice-Hall.

Harter, S. (1978). Effectance motivation reconsidered, toward a developmental model. *Human Development, 21*, 34–64.

Harter, S. (1979). *Manual for the Perceived Competence Scale for Children.* Denver, CO: University of Denver.

Harter, S. (1980). *A scale of intrinsic versus extrinsic orientation in the classroom, manual.* Denver, CO: University of Denver.

Harter, S. (1981). A model of mastery motivation in children: Individual differences and developmental change. In W. A. Colliers (Ed.), *Aspects of the development of competence: The Minnesota Symposium on Child Psychology* (Vol. 14, pp. 215–255). Hillsdale, NJ: Lawrence Erlbaum Associates.

Harter, S. (1982). The perceived competence scale for children. *Child Development, 53,* 87–97.

Harter, S. (1985). Competence as a dimension of self-evaluation: Toward a comprehensive model of self-worth. In R. Leahy (Ed.), *The development of the self.* New York: Academic Press.

Janoff-Bulman, R., & Brickman, P. (1980). Expectations and what people learn from failure. In N. T. Feather (Ed.), *Expectancy, incentive, and action* (pp. 207–237). Hillsdale, NJ: Lawrence Erlbaum Associates.

Johnson, D. S. (1981). Naturally acquired learned helplessness: The relation of school failure to achievement behavior, attributions, and self-concept. *Journal of Educational Psychology, 73,* 174–180.

Kavale, K. A. (1980). The reasoning abilities of normal and learning disabled readers on measures of reading comprehension. *Learning Disability Quarterly, 3,* 34–45.

Kennedy, L., & Halinski, R. (1975). Measuring attitudes: An extra dimension. *Journal of Reading, 18,* 518–522.

Licht, B. G. (1983). Cognitive–motivational factors that contribute to the achievement of learning disabled children. *Journal of Learning Disabilities, 16,* 483–490.

MacGinitie, W. G. (1978). *Gates-MacGinitie Reading Tests.* Boston: Houghton Mifflin.

Maehr, M. L. (1976). Continuing motivation: An analysis of a seldom considered educational outcome. *Review of Educational Research, 46,* 443–462.

Mathewson, G. C. (1976). The function of attitude in the reading process. In H. Singer & R. Ruddell (Eds.), *Theoretical models and processes of reading* (2nd ed., pp. 655–677). Newark, DE: International Reading Association.

Mcleod, J. (1979). Educational underachievement: Toward a defensible psychometric definition. *Journal of Learning Disabilities, 12,* 42–50.

McMillan, J. H. (1976). Factors affecting the development of pupil attitudes toward school subjects. *Psychology in the Schools, 13,* 322–325.

McMillan, J. H. (1980). Attitude development and measurement. In J. H. McMillan (Ed.), *The social psychology of school learning* (pp. 215–245). New York: Academic Press.

Myers, M., & Paris, S. G. (1978). Children's metacognitive knowledge about reading. *Journal of Educational Psychology, 70,* 680–690.

Myklebust, H. R., & Johnson, D. (Eds.). (1967). *Learning disabilities —Educational principles and practices.* New York: Grune & Stratton.

Nicholls, J. G. (1978). The development of the concepts of effort and ability, perception of academic attainment, and the understanding that difficult tasks require more ability. *Child Development, 49,* 800–814.

Nicholls, J. G. (1979). Development of perception of own attainment and causal attributions for success and failure in reading. *Journal of Educational Psychology, 71,* 94–99.

Nicholls, J. G. (1983). Conceptions of ability and achievement motivation: A theory and its implications for education. In S. Paris, G. Olson, & H. Stevenson (Eds.), *Learning and motivation in the classroom* (pp. 211–238). Hillsdale, NJ: Lawrence Erlbaum Associates.

Oka, E. R. (1984). *Metacognitive and motivational aspects of children's reading comprehension.* Unpublished doctoral dissertation, University of Michigan, Ann Arbor, MI.

Owings, R. A., Peterson, G. A., Bransford, J. D., Morris, C. D., & Stein, B. S. (1980). Spontaneous monitoring and regulation of learning: A comparison of successful and less successful fifth graders. *Journal of Educational Psychology, 72,* 250–256.

Paris, S. G., & Cross, D. R. (1983). Ordinary learning: Pragmatic connections among children's beliefs, motives, and actions. In J. Bisanz, G. Bisanz, & R. Kail (Eds.), *Learning in children* (pp. 137–169). New York: Springer–Verlag.

Paris, S. G., Cross, D. R., Jacobs, J. E., Oka, E. R., DeBritto, A. M., & Saarnio, D. A. (1984, April). *Improving children's metacognition and reading comprehension with classroom instruction.* Symposium conducted at the annual meeting of the American Educational Research Association, New Orleans.

Paris, S. G., & Jacobs, J. E. (1984). The benefits of informed instruction for children's reading awareness and comprehension skills. *Child Development, 55,* 2083–2093.

Paris, S. G., & Lindauer, B. K. (1982). The development of cognitive skills during childhood. In B. Wolman (Ed.), *Handbook of developmental psychology* (pp. 333–349). Englewood Cliffs, NJ: Prentice–Hall.

Paris, S. G., & Myers, M. (1981). Comprehension monitoring in good and poor readers. *Journal of Reading Behavior, 13,* 5–22.

Pearl, R., Bryan, T., & Donahue, M. (1980). Learning disabled children's attributions for success and failure. *Learning Disability Quarterly, 3,* 3–9.

Ramanauskas, S. (1972). Contextual constraints beyond a sentence on close responses of mentally retarded children. *American Journal of Mental Deficiency, 77,* 338–345.

Ryan, E. B. (1981). Identifying and remediating failures in reading comprehension: Toward an instructional approach for poor comprehenders. In T. G. Waller & G. E. MacKinnon (Eds.), *Advances in reading research.* New York: Academic Press.

Ryan, Ellen B., Ledger, G. W., Short, E. J., & Weed, K. A. (1982). Promoting the use of active comprehension strategies by poor readers. *Topics in Learning and Learning Disabilities, 2*(1), 53–60.

Schunk, D. H. (1983). Developing children's self-efficacy and skills: The roles of social comparative information and goal setting. *Contemporary Educational Psychology, 8,* 76–86.

Seligman, M. E. P. (1975). *Helplessness: On depression, development, and death.* San Francisco: Freeman.

Smiley, S. S., Oakley, D. D., Worthen, P., Campione, J. C., & Brown, A. L. (1977). Recall of thematically relevant material by adolescent good and poor readers as a function of written vs. oral presentation. *Journal of Educational Psychology, 69,* 381–388.

Stipek, D. J. (1984). Developmental aspects of achievement motivation in children. In R. Ames & C. Ames (Eds.), *Research on motivation in education: Vol. 1. Student motivation* (pp. 145–174). New York: Academic Press.

Stipek, D. J., & Weisz, J. R. (1981). Perceived personal control and academic achievement. *Review of Educational Research, 51*(1), 101–137.

Sullivan, J. (1978). Comparing strategies of good and poor comprehenders. *Journal of Reading, 21,* 710–715.

Teale, W., & Lewis, R. (1981). Nature and measurement of secondary school students' attitudes toward reading. *Reading Horizons, 21,* 94–102.

Thorndike, R. L. (1963). *The concepts of over- and underachievement.* New York: Bureau of Publications, Teachers College, Columbia University.

Thorndike, R. L., & Hagen, E. (1978). *Cognitive Abilities Test.* Boston: Houghton Mifflin.

Torgesen, J. K. (1982). The learning disabled child as an inactive learner: Educational implications. *Topics in Learning and Learning Disabilities, 2*(1), 45–52.

Wagoner, S. A. (1983). Comprehension monitoring: What it is and what we know about it. *Reading Research Quarterly, 28,* 328–346.

Wallbrown, F. H., Vance, H. H., & Prichard, K. K. (1979). Discriminating between attitudes expressed by normal and disabled readers. *Psychology in the Schools, 16,* 472–477.

Weiner, B. (1979). A theory of motivation for some classroom experiences. *Journal of Educational Psychology, 71,* 3–25.

Weiner, B. (1980). A cognitive (attribution)–emotion–action model of motivated behavior: An analysis of judgments of help-giving. *Journal of Personality and Social Psychology, 39,* 186–200.

Weiner, B. (1983). Some thoughts about feelings. In S. G. Paris, J. M. Olson, & H. M. Stevenson (Eds.), *Learning and motivation in the classroom* (pp. 165–178). Hillsdale, NJ: Lawrence Erlbaum Associates.

Wepman, J. M., Cruickshank, W. M., Deutsch, C. P., Morency, A., & Strother, C. R. (1975). Learning disabilities. In N. Hobbs (Ed.), *Issues in the classification of children* (Vol. 1). San Francisco: Jossey-Bass.

White, R. W. (1959). Motivation reconsidered: The concept of competence. *Psychological Review, 66,* 297–333.

Wigfield, A., & Eccles, J. (1983). *The development of achievement-related attributions: A critical review.* Unpublished manuscript, University of Michigan, Ann Arbor, MI.

Willows, D. M., & Ryan, E. B. (1981). Differential utilization of syntactic and semantic information by skilled and less skilled readers in the intermediate grades. *Journal of Educational Psychology, 73,* 607–615.

Winne, P. H., Woodlands, M. J., & Wong, B. Y. L. (1983). Comparability of self-concept among learning disabled, normal, and gifted students. *Journal of Learning Disabilities, 15,* 470–475.

Wong, B. Y. L. (1979). Increasing retention of main ideas through questioning strategies. *Learning Disabilities Quarterly, 2,* 42–47.

Wong, B. Y. L. (1985). Metacognition and learning disabilities. In D. L. Forrest-Pressley, C. E. MacKinnon, & T. G. Waller (Eds.), *Metacognition, cognition, and human performance, Vol. 2, Instructional practices* (pp. 137–180). Orlando, FL: Academic Press.

Wortman, C. B., Panciera, L., Shusterman, L., & Hibschuser, J. (1976). Attributions of causality and reactions to uncontrollable outcomes. *Journal of Experimental Social Psychology, 12,* 301–316.

6 Metacognition, Motivation, and Controlled Performance

John G. Borkowski
Mary Beth Johnston
Molly K. Reid
University of Notre Dame

During the past decade, significant advances have occurred in intelligence theory (Sternberg, 1981), instructional psychology (Resnick, 1982), and cognitive-behavior modification (Meichenbaum, 1977; Meyers & Craighead, 1984). These advances raised expectations that theoretically based intervention research would result in dramatically improved performance on training and transfer tasks for children with learning disabilities, mental retardation, and other special needs. In recent years, however, increasing evidence suggests that these expectations were not readily achieved (Borkowski & Cavanaugh, 1979; Campione & Brown, 1977; Hagan, Barclay, & Newman, 1982) and that current conceptualizations of intelligence and cognition, at least as translated into instructional research, provide only a partial understanding of the skills and processes needed to facilitate performance in special needs children. The problem is most clearly seen when the phenomena of strategy generalization is considered (Borkowski & Cavanaugh, 1979; Campione & Brown, 1977; Torgesen & Licht, 1983): Learning-disabled and mentally retarded children who are taught new learning strategies often do not use these strategies on transfer tasks similar to the training task (Kirk & Gallagher, 1979).

THE PROBLEM OF STRATEGY GENERALIZATION

A recent study by Gelzheiser (1984) illustrates the dilemma. Even after intensive training, based on insights from cognitive theory, LD children failed to transfer newly acquired skills. The goal of the intervention program was to teach LD children three important skills: (1) to employ study strategies to aid the recall of categorizable pictures (the training task), (2) to transfer these strategies to prose recall (the transfer task), and (3) to understand that recall would be more effective as a result of the transfer of skills. In short, Gelzheiser (1984) included in her intervention package components that had been successful in facilitating generalization in earlier studies (Hagan, Barclay, & Newman, 1982).

The subjects were learning-disabled and normal adolescents, assigned to various experimental or control conditions. The intervention involved extended training delivered in two phases, an information phase (two group sessions) and an individualized training phase (three sessions). During the information phase, students in the experimental conditions were taught to recognize different patterns of organization for different types of materials, in particular, to identify categorical organization. The LD students in a "rule condition" were taught to discriminate categories using examples of pictures, words, and two-word phrases; the LD students in an "example condition" were taught in a similar manner with the exception that prose examples (the eventual transfer test) were included in the training. All instructed students were taught four rules to use in studying categorically ordered information: sort before studying, study by grouping, name the group, and use clusters when recalling. They were also taught to discriminate tasks on which these rules would be applicable from tasks on which they would not be applicable (i.e., generalization was programmed). During the individualized training phase, students practiced using the rules on a variety of tasks, which increased in difficulty. Feedback was provided about the quality of their performance; information was given about the reasons why the use of the rules was important; and explicit directions on how to use the rules were faded across trials. What is unique about this intervention package is the integrated emphasis on lower level strategies, information about their value, and multiple examples of their applicability to different tasks. In short, training was thorough, insightful, and programmed for generalized success.

Despite the fact that Gelzheiser's (1984) intervention was theoretically and empirically driven, and unusually detailed, the results were rather disappointing. With respect to the training task, the strategy use and recall scores of the LD students in the experimental conditions were indistinguishable from those of the normal students in the control condition but superior to those of the LD students in the control condition. With respect to the strategy use scores on the transfer task (prose recall), strategy use by the instructed LD students was indistinguishable from that of uninstructed normal students but considerably better than that of the LD students in the control condition. In spite of their improved use of strategies, the recall of the LD students on the transfer task was unimpressive; in fact, only students in one of the LD instructed conditions, the "example condition," demonstrated prose recall greater than that of students in the LD control condition. Many LD children failed to transfer the skills to the prose recall task.

It is important to note that when recall scores of the instructed LD students who had consistently utilized all of the rules on the prose recall task were compared with recall for the instructed LD students who did not perform as instructed, the performance of the former group was considerably better than that of the latter. Apparently, some of the LD students profited considerably from the training whereas others did not. The results of Gelzheiser's (1984) study—perhaps the most extensive strategy training study conducted with LD students—are consistent with other results, which indicate that the generalization of strategies and skills is not readily achieved by most LD students (Hagan et al., 1982; Kirk & Gallagher, 1979).

In this chapter we propose a model that outlines potentially important factors influencing LD students' transfer of acquired strategies to novel tasks. In addition, we review the literature on generalization from the perspective of the model with a view toward delineating the nature of learning disabilities. Finally, we discuss recent theory-based instructional research that seems to facilitate more extensive transfer of strategies in LD adolescents and subsequent changes in their motivational states.

INDIVIDUAL DIFFERENCES IN STRATEGY TRANSFER

The most striking finding in the literature on the training and transfer of control processes is the persistent failure to find strategy generalization (Borkowski & Cavanaugh, 1979; Campione & Brown, 1977; Hagan et al., 1982). As we have seen in the Gelzheiser (1984) study, LD children thoroughly trained in the use of an effective study strategy often do not employ that strategy on new but similar tasks. Brown (1978) described this phenomenon as the "welding" of a strategy to a specific task. A child fails to recognize and understand a strategy's general applicability, preferring to use it only in isolated situations. This failure has been described as a failure in metacognition, a lack of awareness about the general utility and applicability of the newly acquired strategy (Flavell, 1978, 1979).

Hagen, Barclay, and Schwethelm (1982) presented a cognitive-development model of learning disabilities in which the child perceives and understands a task on the basis of constrained information. The constraints faced by an LD child can best be understood by considering the strategies and knowledge demanded by the task in order for a child to achieve optimal performance. The Hagen model places the theoretical burden primarily on cognitive skills: The child must have the requisite strategies and knowledge to complete the task. Also implicated, though in a subtle way, is motivation. The child must desire optimal performance and must try hard to achieve it. In a similar vein, Douglas (1980b) emphasized the importance of internal motivation and a clear understanding of the nature of one's own learning problem as prerequisites for effective training of both hyper-active and LD children.

It is important to emphasize that welding and its counterpart, generalization, are found among seemingly homogeneous groups of children who have received identical forms of strategy training. Two sets of data reflect the striking individual differences commonly observed in research on strategy transfer. Wanschura and Borkowski (1975) trained educable, mentally retarded children to use an elab-oration strategy with a paired-associate learning task. The training was thorough and intensive; as a consequence, all children in the experimental condition mas-tered the strategy.Two weeks after the final training session, an uninstructed transfer test was given using a similar task. Nineteen of 30 children showed perfect transfer. In contrast, the performance of the remaining children was comparable to that of the untrained children in the control condition. Why did children of the same MA and same level of strategy acquisition behave so differently during the test for strategy transfer? The key to understanding these differences found in mentally retarded children (and also possibly in LD children) lies in stable, long-standing individual differences in knowledge states about the operation of mental processes (metacognition) and in corresponding beliefs about their efficacy (motivation).

A second example, emphasizing the widespread variability in strategy use among children of the same diagnostic category, is found in a recent study by Belmont, Ferretti, and Mitchell (1982). At the onset of the experiment involving a serial-recall task, adolescents were instructed to recall the last few items in each list before recalling the initial items. In groups of normal and moderately retarded subjects, some individuals developed an effective "cumulative-rehearsal/fast-finish" study strategy, even though no instructions were given on how to study. The children who utilized this study strategy scanned the last three items in a seven-item list, then studied the first four items more intently using cumu-lative rehearsal. Regardless of intellectual level, those who spontaneously devel-oped the complex rehearsal strategy showed vastly superior recall to those who did not. Thus, a few adolescents—some normal, some mentally retarded—recognized that in order to perform effectively they needed to match recall requirements with an appropriate study strategy. This recognition often resulted in the invention of a complex strategy. But what accounts for large, within-group individual differences in strategy invention? This question is the focus of the remainder of the chapter.

On many complex problem-solving and memory tasks, deliberation often supplements speed as the chief determinant of good performance. In these con-texts, prior knowledge about learning and memory processes (metamemory) and associated beliefs about their value (motivation) become operative to produce efficient strategy-based performance (Borkowski, Reid, & Kurtz, 1984). These strategies—requiring deliberate, conscious, goal-directed activity—develop and change across trials; here, automatic processing is of limited usefulness (Sternberg, 1981). There is a special circumstance that calls for the conscious allocation of mental resources: strategy transfer. On transfer tasks, in which decisions are required about implementation, monitoring, and revision (Borkowski et al., 1984), deliberate strategy use becomes essential. It is in this context that the dynamic interplay between metamemory and motivation helps us understand more clearly the sources of individual differences in strategy use that characterize students with learning disabilities.

METACOGNITION AND MOTIVATION: A SYNTHESIS

Pressley, Borkowski, and O'Sullivan (1985) partitioned metamemory into a number of interactive, mutually dependent components. Each component has a unique developmental history, is differentially influenced by experience and instruction, and plays a distinctive role in explaining differences in learning and memory performance among normal, mentally retarded, and LD children. Some of the major components, listed in order of their developmental emergence, are the following: Specific Strategy Knowledge, General Strategy Knowledge, Relational Strategy Knowledge, and Metamemory Acquisition Procedures (Pressley et al., 1985).

Specific Strategy Knowledge

Metamemory, a component of metacognition (cf. Borkowski, Ryan, Kurtz, & Reid, 1983), has been defined as simple declarative and procedural knowledge about a wide range of memory phenomena and processes (Flavell, 1978, 1979). If metamemory is defined by a single instance of strategic knowledge (e.g., a child's demonstrated understanding about the role of organization in learning a clusterable list of words), the theoretical focus is on a component of metamemory called Specific Strategy Knowledge (Pressley et al., 1985). For instance, a child may know that organization into units will make a 24-item list easier to learn and/or that cumulative rehearsal within small groups of items is more efficient than rote, repetitive rehearsal. When several isolated bits of strategy-related knowledge accumulate, the child is said to possess a rich, mature metamemory. A cumulative index of metamemory can be obtained by ascertaining the range of information a child has about encoding and retrieval processes based on responses to a structured interview format (Borkowski et al., 1984). This knowledge becomes useful in acquiring new strategies for more complicated learning tasks.

Specific Strategy Knowledge includes the child's understanding of (a) a strategy's goals and objectives, (b) the tasks for which this procedural information is appropriate, (c) its range of applicability, (d) the learning gains expected from consistent use of the strategy, (e) the amount of effort associated with its deployment, and (f) whether the strategy is enjoyable or burdensome to use (e.g., elaborative imagery is fun whereas cumulative rehearsal requires hard work). When children possess a number of appropriate strategies together with corresponding knowledge about their various uses, they are in a position to make an "informed" judgment about strategy deployment on novel, transfer tasks. We assume that sophisticated learners—both children and adults—are in command of such information to varying degrees and that intelligent use of strategies cannot occur without it. The contents in Specific Strategy Knowledge accumulate slowly as the child matures, its development being paralleled by the hierarchical emergence of strategies (cf. Neimark, 1976).

We assume that Specific Strategy Knowledge is vital to efficient strategy use and that there is a dynamic bidirectionality between strategy use and Specific Strategy Knowledge. Not only does Specific Strategy Knowledge guide the deployment of individual strategies, but continued use of strategies results in an expansion and refinement of Specific Strategy Knowledge. In turn, enhanced knowledge improves future memory performance.

General and Relational Strategy Knowledge

As Specific Strategy Knowledge is acquired about multiple strategies (e.g., rehearsal, organization, and elaboration), two other components of metamemory emerge: General Strategy Knowledge and Relational Strategy Knowledge.

General Strategy Knowledge reflects a child's understanding that effort is required to apply strategies and that effort often produces success. With experience children come to learn that strategies, properly used, make learning easier and more efficient than nonstrategic learning. A unique property of General Strategy Knowledge—one not found in other components of metamemory—is its motivational character.

We believe that General Strategy Knowledge has energizing components; that is, general knowledge about the value of behaving strategically results in expectations about self-efficacy, which, in turn, can motivate children to confront challenging learning tasks. Of course, the positive, energizing property of General Strategy Knowledge influences only those children who believe they have the capacity and/or skills to take on learning challenges without undue fear of failure.

Relational Strategy Knowledge provides the child with a classification system for understanding the comparative values associated with a number of specific strategies. Relational information highlights the attributes of each strategy in the face of changing task demands and appears useful in strategy selection and revision decisions as these are necessary for completion of new tasks (Pressley et al., 1985). Little is known about Relational Strategy Knowledge in normal children; hence, it does not receive further attention in our analysis of the transfer problems of LD children.

Metamemory Acquisition Procedures

It is often necessary for children to learn techniques for producing their own information about new or underdeveloped strategies. This is because teachers often are not explicit or detailed in providing strategy instructions. Frequently, children are left to their own devices to discover how and when to use a strategy and often do so ineffectively. In such instances, Metamemory Acquisition Procedures assist children in learning more about low-level strategies and help them regulate those strategies. This higher order component of metamemory represents an important factor in the self-regulation of human behavior (Brown, 1978); thus, it is a causal factor in producing self-controlled behavior in young or developmentally delayed children (Campione, Brown, & Ferrara, 1982). We believe that Metamemory Acquisition Procedures are the hallmarks of human intelligence (Pressley et al., 1985).

Checking and monitoring a strategy's effectiveness leads to knowledge about its benefits and the difficulty involved in its implementation. More important, Metamemory Acquisition Procedures direct the child to "fill-in-gaps" in instructions so that he or she becomes able to fit a strategy to the unique requirements of the task. In the absence of explicit, detailed strategy instructions, this form of metamemory leads to the development of information contained in Specific Strategy Knowledge. This is a problem of discovering the format that best maps an available strategy to the task. Thus, Metamemory Acquisition Procedures become useful in making decisions about how and when to use a strategy or to switch to a new strategy when an earlier one proves ineffective. It is with a view towards ascribing some of the deficiencies commonly found with problem learners on complex, transfer tasks to Specific Strategy Knowledge, General Strategy Knowledge, and Metamemory Acquisition Procedures that we selectively review the literature on control processes and learning disabilities.

LEARNING DISABILITIES, TRANSFER, AND METAMEMORY DEFICITS

According to our model, Specific Strategy Knowledge, General and Relational Strategy Knowledge, and Metamemory Acquisition Procedures are required for normal, learning-disabled, or mentally retarded children to transfer strategies successfully. The model predicts that transfer failures may be due to deficits in one or more of these components, acting in combination with strategies per se and with automatic processes (Sternberg, 1981).

Some LD children have difficulty learning a new strategy. They may know less than other children about the to-be-learned strategy prior to its instruction. Hence, they fail to understand or appreciate fully its value for performing the task they confront. This type of deficiency in Specific Strategy Knowledge— insufficient information about the strategy's essential attributes—leads to the prediction that LD children are unlikely to transfer an instructed strategy even if they can perform it in rote fashion during training (Cavanaugh & Borkowski, 1979).

Some LD children may not appreciate the value of using an effortful, strategic approach to academic tasks, failing to understand that outcomes are sometimes under their personal control. The failure in General Strategy Knowledge should be accompanied by an attributional belief system that ascribes success to external factors such as luck or ease of the task and failure to internal factors such as a lack of ability. LD children, with their deficiencies in General Strategy Knowledge, should be less motivated to face the challenges posed by difficult transfer tasks.

Finally, most LD children do not know how to select, monitor, and revise strategies in order to successfully complete novel tasks; that is, they are deficient in a higher level of knowledge about memory, which we have called Metamemory Acquisition Procedures. This component of metamemory directs the implementation of lower level strategies and is probably a major correlate of learning disabilities (Douglas, 1980a).

Specific Strategy Use

LD children often fail to use strategic behaviors (Bauer, 1977; Torgesen, 1977), with LD children often falling 2 or 3 years behind their nonhandicapped peers on short-term memory tasks (Bauer, 1977, 1979; Hagen, 1971; Newman & Hagen, 1981; Torgesen, 1975, 1977; Torgesen & Goldman, 1977). The primary reason for memory defects in LD children is the failure to use organized, goal-directed strategies spontaneously (e.g., labeling, verbal rehearsal, clustering, and selective attention). When taught these strategies, their performance improves and resembles that of nonhandicapped students (Newman & Hagen, 1981; Tarver, Hallahan, Kauffman, & Ball, 1977; Torgesen, 1977). It should be noted that the well-known memory deficits have been attributed to failures in control processing, rather than to inadequate prior knowledge (metamemory) useful in acquiring strategies in the first place. Our model places great importance on the role of prior memory knowledge in explaining memory deficits in LD children.

Bauer (1977) compared rehearsal patterns of learning-disabled and normal children on an immediate and a delayed free recall task. He found that LD children had lower recall in the primacy position and inefficient rehearsal in both the primacy and recency positions on the delayed recall task. Normal children used rehearsal more frequently than LD children and, hence, were more effective at recall.

Torgesen (1977) investigated the recall and study behavior of fourth-grade good and poor readers and found similar results. Poor readers and good readers differed on their recall scores and on their study behavior. Although good readers approached the recall task in an active, organized way, poor readers did not use strategies effectively. Torgesen argued that the crucial factor in LD children's deficient performance on memory tasks is their failure to engage in goal-directed activity.

There is some suggestion in the literature that LD children may become more strategic following even minimal intervention. For instance, Wong (1979) studied the performance of fifth-grade normal and LD children under two experimental conditions. Students listened to a story as they read the text. For half of the students, the story was interspersed with questions about the most significant themes; for the other half, the story was read with no questions. Normal and LD children did not differ in their recall of thematically important units when questions were provided, whereas normal children recalled more of these units than LD students in the no-questions condition. When LD children were asked to generate their own retrieval cues, recall was just as good as when they were supplied with explicit cues. Thus, Wong demonstrated that, following prompting, LD children can engage in the inferential processing required to generate implied consequences. Bos and Filip (1982), using a similar procedure, concluded that LD children do not have specific deficiencies in comprehension monitoring; rather, they fail to select and utilize appropriate task-related strategies.

In summary, the findings on recall, study behavior, and reading with LD children led Hallahan and Kauffman (1982) to refer to LD children as passive learners lacking the strategies and skills needed for systematically approaching academic problems. LD children can be trained to employ strategies at least on simple tasks, with performance often approaching that of uninstructed nonhandicapped peers. Despite these gains following instruction, LD children lack the strategies required for performing well on novel complex tasks and the motivation to apply themselves diligently to such tasks (Covington, in press.)

Metamemorial Knowledge

Deficits in Specific Strategy Knowledge have seldom been implicated as reasons for the impoverished control processing of LD children. Borkowski and Kurtz (1984), however, argued that differences in the use of strategic behaviors such as those just described are related to inadequate metamemory development in some LD children. Trepanier (1981) compared LD and normal children on their knowledge about memory abilities, the ease of immediate versus delayed recall, memory estimation skills, and the allocation of study time. Each group was divided into young (ages 6 to 10) and old (ages 10 to 15) subgroups in order to examine developmental differences. The major difference between normal and LD children was on the memory estimation task; young LD children overestimated their own memory ability and inaccurately estimated the memory skills of their friends. Trepanier (1981) concluded that relative immaturity in metamemory development on selected tasks underlies the poorer performance of LD children.

Torgesen (1979) also found metamemorial immaturity in LD children. Using a metamemory questionnaire developed by Kreutzer, Leonard, and Flavell (1975), learning-disabled and nonhandicapped children were interviewed about how they would attempt to remember things. Torgesen found that LD children identified fewer alternative methods for remembering than nonhandicapped children.

Douglass (1981) used six of the Kreutzer et al. (1975) subtests (memory ability, immediate delay, study time, study plan, preparation object, and preparation event) and compared the performance of LD and normal children. Children were asked questions designed to assess their knowledge of serial recall and internal storage strategies. Both groups demonstrated familiarity with external storage strategies (e.g., note taking) but only normal children showed an understanding of internal storage strategies (e.g., cumulative rehearsal).

Loper, Hallahan, and Sanna (1980) compared learning-disabled and normal children's understanding of attention (meta-attention). Three variables influencing attention—interest, reward, and noise—were given high or low values, illustrated on picture cards, and presented in pairs to children for comparison judgments. For example, a child was shown a high-interest card and a low-noise card and asked in which situation it would be easier to attend. Normal children showed developmental effects for the interest and reward variables, with older children attaching greater importance to internal factors (interest) and less importance to external factors (reward). Younger children focused more on external factors (reward). Normal children also exhibited a positive relationship between achievement and awareness of attention. No such relationship was noted among the LD children. The LD children were then enrolled in a corrective reading program, which Loper et al. (1980) hypothesized would improve their knowledge about the relationship between attention and academic achievement. Although no such relationship existed in the pretreatment test, the interest variable was positively correlated at posttest with reading achievement, whereas the reward variable was negatively correlated. This finding is consistent with a theoretical framework provided by Douglas (1980b) that is germane to the problems inherent in teaching LD children: Understanding specific processing and motivational deficits is essential for effective remediation of learning deficits. A common characteristic of LD children is their poor task-oriented behavior (McKinney & Feagans, 1981). Inappropriate task orientation often involves poor attention, concentration, effort, and persistence. Integrating knowledge about the importance of attention (i.e., training meta-attention) into tests of other aspects of Specific Strategy Knowledge seems an important objective for future research.

Higher Level Metacognitive Skills

Monitoring skills are particularly essential in reading. Owings, Petersen, Bransford, Morris, and Stein (1980) requested that good and poor readers scan prose passages that differed in the extent to which they made sense. Two stories were presented; one contained predictable information (the hungry boy ate a hamburger) and the other contained subjects and predicates, which were mismatched (the hungry boy took a nap). Good readers were aware that the less sensible stories were more difficult to read, could explain why this was so, adjusted their study time according to the difficulty of the passages, and exhibited better recall. In contrast, poor readers were less able to evaluate mismatches in material and to regulate their study time. When asked to choose and alter a story, which did not make sense, all the children chose appropriately and altered the less sensible story so as to make it more meaningful. After minimal intervention, poor readers were not appreciably different from good readers.

Masson (1982) suggested that some LD children have a unique metacognitive deficit: Like younger children, they may be insensitive to their own failure to comprehend. McKean and Angell (1981) instructed good and poor readers to read or listen to standard stories and to stories that contained an obvious incongruity. Whereas good readers frequently identified the incongruities, poor readers did so only rarely. It appears, then, that LD students are less prepared to identify incongruous material. It follows that LD children will not be as successful as normal children in checking their own work for incongruities.

Smiley, Oakley, Worthen, Campione, and Brown (1977) asked good and poor readers to recall stories after reading or listening to them. In both conditions, good readers' recall was better than poor readers' recall. Good readers recalled more important rather than less important information. A similar pattern of recall, based on the units' structural importance, was not evident in the recall of poor readers. Furthermore, there was a strong, positive correlation between recall after reading and recall after listening, ($r = .85$). Smiley et al. (1977) concluded that poor readers lacked the metacognitive skills of good readers, especially in organizing story information. Poor readers had metacognitive deficits, which deleteriously affected both their reading and listening skills.

Motivation and Deficits in General Strategy Knowledge

Licht (1983) noted that motivational problems are among the most consistently reported characteristics of LD children. Several investigators (Douglas & Peters, 1979; Thomas, 1979; Torgesen, 1980) have suggested that these problems originate from failures experienced in the early school years. Licht (1983) described the sequence as follows: LD children experience academic failure (due to a variety of factors) beginning early in their school careers. This failure leads them to doubt their intellectual abilities and the effectiveness of effortful, strategic behavior in overcoming difficulties. As a result, LD children reduce their efforts, particularly when confronted with difficult tasks. This reduction in effort results in inadequate knowledge of the world and in a deficient repertoire of strategic behaviors.

We maintain that personal beliefs about the reasons for success and failure are a part of General Strategy Knowledge. Thus, cognitive deficits combine with motivational deficits to increase the likelihood of continued failures. This phenomenon resembles the "learned helplessness" syndrome (Dweck & Licht, 1980; Seligman & Maier, 1967; Seligman, Maier, & Geer, 1968). As "learned helplessness" is strengthened through repeated failure experiences, LD children come to view themselves as inept in a variety of academic settings. When they do experience success, they do not take credit for it, attributing success instead to external factors such as the ease of the task, the teacher, or luck.

The notion that failing repeatedly can cause children to doubt their abilities has support in the research literature. A number of investigators have manipulated success and failure in achievement situations and have found that repeated failure leads children to see themselves as lacking in ability and to lower their expectancies of future success as a result (Nicholls, 1975; Parsons & Ruble, 1977; Rholes, Blackwell, Jordan, & Walters, 1980). Although failure does not always have these debilitating effects, the kinds of failure experienced by LD children (i.e., those that occur frequently, over long periods, and across a variety of academic tasks and teachers) are the kinds most likely to precipitate the development of "helpless" beliefs (Torgesen & Licht, 1983).

The notion that children's beliefs about their abilities can affect their effortful behavior is based on the contention that certain beliefs imply that continued effort in the face of difficulty will be fruitful, whereas other beliefs imply that it will not. Licht (1983) argued that children who believe that their difficulties are surmountable through their efforts (a strong view about General Strategy Knowledge) will engage in achievement-oriented problem-solving behaviors. On the other hand, children who believe that their difficulties are due to factors beyond their control, particularly insufficient ability, will give up without trying and avoid challenging tasks. When confronted with difficult tasks, these children will demonstrate a deterioration in their effortful deployment of problem-solving strategies, resulting in a level of performance below their capabilities. In contrast, children who attribute difficulties to controllable factors, particularly inadequate effort, will tend to maintain effortful, strategic behavior even in the face of challenging tasks (Licht, 1983).

The notion that LD children hold beliefs that foster "learned helplessness" has been substantiated in several studies. Specifically, LD children score lower than their nonhandicapped peers on measures of self-esteem and perceptions of their abilities (Battle, 1979; Boersma & Chapman, 1981; Johnson, 1981). When confronted with difficult tasks, LD children attribute poor performance to insufficient ability more frequently than do their nonhandicapped peers (Butkowsky

& Willows, 1980) and to insufficient effort less frequently than do their non-handicapped peers (Kistner & Licht, 1983; Pearl, Bryan, & Donahue, 1980). When they experience success, LD children are less likely than nondisabled children to view it as a result of their ability (Butkowsky & Willows, 1980; Pearl, Bryan, & Herzog, 1983). LD children have lower expectations for future success than their peers and they demonstrate a greater decrement in expectancies following failure (Boersma & Chapman, 1981; Fincham & Barling, 1978). In general, LD children are pessimistic about their ability to influence outcomes in academic settings (Fincham & Barling, 1978; Hallahan, Gajar, Cohen, & Tarver, 1978; Pearl, Bryan, & Donahue, 1980).

Butkowsky and Willows (1980) investigated how good and poor readers interpret success and failure. Poor readers related failure to internal factors (ability, effort) and success to external factors (luck, difficulty of the task). Thus, these children saw both success and failure as out of their control. Good readers, on the other hand, attributed failure to a variety of factors and did not have lower expectancies because of it.

The maladaptive beliefs of children identified as reading disabled have been observed to generalize to other domains (Boersma & Chapman, 1981; Butkowsky & Willows, 1980; Pearl, 1982). Butkowsky (1982) compared poor, average, and above-average readers with respect to their perceptions of and responses to failures on reading and math tasks. The three groups were matched on IQ and previous achievement in math. Thus, if the disabled readers responded maladaptively to the math task, this could not be explained by more frequent failures in math. Butkowsky (1982) found that the reading-disabled children were more likely to show "helpless" beliefs and a lack of persistence than the other two groups, both on the reading and on the math tasks.

In summary, the existing literature implicates Specific Strategy Knowledge (especially knowledge about internally generated strategies and attentional processes), Metamemory Acquisition Procedures, and General Strategy Knowledge (especially its motivational derivatives) as interrelated problem areas common to different types of learning disabilities. Recent training studies have begun the process of unravelling the connections and combinations of components as they influence performance on a variety of training and transfer tasks.

INSTRUCTIONAL APPROACHES TO METACOGNITIVE–MOTIVATIONAL DEFICITS

There are a number of reasons why instructional research is useful for the study of metacognition in LD children: (a) training studies allow for the manipulation of treatment variables (e.g., knowledge about a specific strategy or about monitoring skills), yielding causal statements about the reasons for performance gains, provided of course that appropriate controls have been implemented; (b) they are conducive to arranging multiple experiences with the treatment variables. This is important because stable metacognitive knowledge seldom results from brief encounters with a strategy (Brown, 1978; Kurtz & Borkowski, 1984); (c) they allow for the development of complex treatment packages (e.g., combining Specific Strategy Knowledge and the motivational aspects of General Strategy Knowledge). These packages pay respect to the multidimensional nature of metacognitive theory and permit its assessment in ecologically valid settings.

The major disadvantage of the instructional approach is that it is difficult to disentangle the functional components of a complex package that may contain as many as three or four key ingredients. For instance, the important training study of Palinscar and Brown (1984), showing sizable gains in comprehension skills of poor readers, did not permit a specification of the relative contributions of the key variables in the training package—specific strategies (e.g., summarization), awareness of the impact of the strategies (metacognition), or implementation routines (e.g., monitoring skills). Despite the problems in analyzing complex treatment packages, the instructional approach holds promise for unravelling the metacognitive deficits associated with learning disabilities that develop over time in an interactive fashion.

A number of recent studies have attempted to combine the training of strategies with the assessment or manipulation of Specific Strategy Knowledge, General Strategy Knowledge (and beliefs about strategy efficacy), and Metamemory Acquisition Procedures. Although most of these studies have dealt with normal children, two recent studies focused on children with learning problems. We briefly mention the orientation and outcomes of studies with normal children as they pertain to the training of metacognitive skills and the importance of motivation as a substrate of metacognition. Against this background, we analyze several recent metacognitive training studies with LD children.

TRAINING MONITORING SKILLS IN
NON-LD CHILDREN

Ghatala, Levin, Pressley, and Lodico (1984) provided second-grade children with general training in monitoring the utility of strategies (e.g., "keep track of how well you're doing"), the affective consequences of strategy use (e.g., "it's fun to be strategic"), or no strategy-monitoring training. All children were then given a paired-associate learning task, first without strategy instructions and later with instructions to use either an effective strategy (verbal elaboration) or an ineffective strategy (counting letters in the stimulus and response words). Next, children learned another list using any method they desired; the purpose was to see if instructions in monitoring overcame the ineffective instructional set. The session ended following probes assessing the type of strategy used on the final list. Maintenance of the effective strategy was tested after 9 weeks to determine the durability of the monitoring instructions.

The most important aspect of the results of Ghatala et al. (1984) center on long-term strategy maintenance: Although monitoring and affective training conditions produced short-term maintenance of the effective strategy (elaboration), only monitoring training resulted in long-term maintenance; that is, children who were given strategy–utility training abandoned the ineffective strategy more frequently than children who were in the affective or no-training conditions. Responses to metamemory questions, assessing knowledge about the elaboration strategy, indicated that strategy efficacy (e.g., understanding that the elaboration was effective) was the reason for decisions about strategy choice only in the monitoring condition. The findings of Ghatala et al. (1984) strengthen the case for including monitoring instructions (i.e., Metamemory Acquisition Procedures) in multicomponent training packages aimed at producing durable strategy use.

A training study conducted in our laboratory showed an interesting relationship between strategy transfer and children's beliefs about the value of effort in deploying a strategy (Kurtz & Borkowski, 1984). Following a metamemory pretest, 60 first- and third-grade children were divided into three treatment groups that received task-specific strategy instructions appropriate for three memory problems (elaboration, organization, and memory-search strategies); general metacognitive information about subordinate and superordinate processing; or both strategy and metacognitive training. We were primarily interested in whether metacognitive training (including information about Metamemory Acquisition Procedures) would facilitate strategy transfer. As tests of strategy transfer, maintenance and generalization versions of three memory tasks were given followed by an assessment of children's perceptions of the causes for specific success and failure outcomes; that is, children were asked to give reasons for their performance on individual items in terms of effort, ability, luck, or ease of items.

As expected, the analyses of transfer data showed that strategy training was highly successful. Surprisingly, metacognitive training appeared to have no effect on subsequent metamemory scores or on strategy use with one exception: Metamemory and strategy use at transfer were significantly correlated only for children who received both metacognitive and strategy training. Apparently, children initially high in metamemory skills, profited more from the comprehensive training package, using newly learned metacognitive insights to aid the generalization of acquired strategies.

An interesting result emerged linking motivation to strategy transfer: Among strategy-trained children those who attributed success to effort were both more strategic and higher in metamemory than those who attributed task outcomes to noncontrollable factors such as ability or task characteristics. In contrast, children who did not receive strategy training showed no differences in strategy use across the attributional response categories representing controllable and uncontrollable causes for performance. Metamemory showed the same pattern as strategy scores:

Children skilled in metamemory knew that effort yielded success, provided they had recieved strategy training. This sequence suggests that changes in attributional responses occurred during strategy training and or transfer for children high in specific strategy knowledge.

Kurtz and Borkowski (1984) concluded that children with prior dispositions to attribute success to effort (i.e., those high in General Strategy Knowledge) and with mature metamemory knowledge (i.e., those high in Specific Strategy Knowledge) received greater cognitive and motivational boosts from strategy training than other children. Motivational and metacognitive processes interacted to influence the extent of strategy transfer. In contrast, children with poor meta-memories tended to attribute their learning outcomes to noncontrollable factors such as ability or task characteristics and generally failed to comprehend the potential usefulness of the instructed strategy. Because many LD children are deficient in metamemory and motivation, conclusions about interactive processes derived from the study of young, normal children provide guidelines for developing training packages appropriate for children with learning problems.

INSTRUCTIONAL RESEARCH WITH
PROBLEM LEARNERS

Douglas (1980b) suggested that it is important to combine cognitive, metacognitive, and motivational components in treatment packages designed for hyperactive and LD children. For Douglas, the cognitive–metacognitive–motivation sequences associated with the two disorders are similar, although the precipitating causes of hyperactivity and learning disabilities are different, with poor attention and inhibitory control being linked constitutionally to hyperactivity, and vulnerability to intrusions and early failure experiences linked to learning disability. Douglas (1980a) suggested that retraining programs for both childhood disorders should focus on three interrelated components: (a) helping the child understand the nature of the deficit and how training can help; (b) strengthening the child's motivation and capacity to deal with the problem-solving role via a set of general rules; (c) teaching specific problem-solving strategies.

In the terms of the model we presented earlier, Douglas's second step focuses on Metamemory Acquisition Procedures (giving the child rules that generate information about specific strategies) and General Strategy Knowledge (teaching that strategies produce success and that their implementation requires self-initiative and effort). Douglas's third step is aimed at instructing Specific Strategy Knowledge (procedures for focusing, listening, organizing, or studying). In a study that flowed from the model, Douglas, Parry, Marton, and Garson (1976) demonstrated that hyperactive children improved their level of impulsivity (MFFT), coping responses on a story completion test, and reading (taken from the Durrell

Analysis of Reading Difficulty) in comparison with matched, watching-list control children. It should be noted that in the Douglas et al. (1976) study, no attempt was made to determine the relative importance of the multiple factors in the training package. We turn now to more analytic examples of instructional research on metacognition, in which components are individually manipulated.

TRAINING ATTRIBUTIONS AND
READING STRATEGIES

Skilled readers possess sophisticated metacognitive knowledge (Baker & Brown, 1985). In contrast, LD children who are poor readers do not seem to understand the purpose of reading and the need to use strategies on complex reading tasks. They attribute reading problems to their "suspected" lack of ability rather than to a deficiency in the use of task-appropriate strategies.

Short and Ryan (1984) developed a training package designed to remediate some of the control problems common to poor readers. The instructions emphasized Specific Strategy Knowledge (story grammar strategies) and General Strategy Knowledge (including a focus on reshaping attributional beliefs about the reasons for reading failures). Story grammar training emphasized the use of five "wh" questions about setting and episode categories in order to improve comprehension: Who is the main character?; Where and when did the story take place?; What did the main character do?; How did the story end?; and How did the main character feel? Attribution training, in the form of self-statements ("try hard; you'll enjoy this story; you'll feel good if you do well"), was incorporated into the intervention program so as to enhance the likelihood of strategy use on the reading tasks. Training procedures emphasized the direct relationship between task-appropriate strategies and effort by incorporating self-statements about the importance of effort and its consequences for reading comprehension. The intent was to enable the poor readers to assume more active roles in learning and to recognize that the reading skills of good readers are due, in large part, to deliberate, conscious effort in deploying strategies.

The two main training components were taught to poor readers in a design that included three conditions: a training group, which received strategy and attribution training; a strategy group, which was given only strategy training; and a control group, which received only attribution training. Strategy maintenance was assessed on free and probed recall tests; strategy generalization was tested on a metareading task, which asked questions about the purposes of reading.

Strategy training produced dramatic gains in reading comprehension; only poor readers who received attribution training alone showed poorer performance than a comparison group of skilled readers. Partial support was obtained for generalization, with poor readers who received strategy training being similar to skilled readers on the metareading assessment test. Because strategy training, in combination with attribution training, improved comprehension by providing poor readers with metacognitive skills, their earlier deficiencies in reading appear to have resulted from a failure to employ existing story schema. It should be emphasized that the story grammar component was more effective than the attribution component. This is not surprising given the limited emphasis on attribution training within the overall package (Short & Ryan, 1984). We turn now to a study that focused more directly on attributional retraining.

Retraining Antecedent-Specific and Program-Specific Attributions

Reid and Borkowski (1984) recently developed and assessed a complex training package that included self-control strategies, lower level study strategies, antecedent attributions (e.g., beliefs about the reasons for past successes and failures in spelling, math, etc.) and program-specific attributions (e.g., beliefs about the reasons for success and failure on specific items on a strategy transfer test). A bidirectional hypothesis, linking metamemory and motivational states, was at the core of this training project that was designed to improve attributional style, metacognitive awareness, and self-control in hyperactive children, one-half of whom were also diagnosed as learning disabled. Before describing this study in more detail, additional information is needed to establish the theoretical tie between metamemory and attributional beliefs.

Attribution theory has provided a link between children's beliefs about the causes of success and failure and their failure expectations about performance (Weiner, 1979). Achievement expectations influence how much effort a child will expend on a future task, and the quality and persistence of responses following success or failure experiences. Shifts in expectations as a result of success and failure are closely tied to three dimensions of perceived causality: locus of causality, control, and stability. Locus refers to "backward looking beliefs" about a source or cause, which may be either internal or external. Ability and effort are examples of internal causality; luck and task difficulty are examples of external causality. Control is viewed as a separate dimension because some causes are under the individual's control and some are not. Effort is an internal controllable cause and ability an internal uncontrollable cause. A trait, such as patience, is often viewed as controllable, whereas inherited characteristics are viewed as uncontrollable. The third dimension of attribution theory, stability, refers to the degree to which a cause is perceived to be modifiable. Intelligence or task difficulty are examples of causes that are considered stable; mood or effort are examples of causes that are considered unstable.

Weiner (1979) contended that each of the three attribution dimensions is related to a behavioral consequence. For example, a child who attributes failure to mutable, unstable causes, such as bad luck or insufficient effort, is more likely to have an optimistic, future-oriented expectation about achievement than a child who attributes failure to the stable factors of ability or task difficulty. The bidirectional relationship between attributions (which we hypothesize are contained in General Strategy Knowledge) and metacognition is useful for understanding the devastating effects that a history of failure can have on the achievement expectations and style of learning displayed by LD children.

With respect to the motivational properties associated with general beliefs about strategy efficacy, we propose two categories for organizing relevant attributional constructs according to their histories: antecedent attributions are operative in a child over a long time frame and are presumed to be functional at the time a new intervention program is initiated, whereas program-generated attributions evolve from the immediate teaching procedures (Henker, Whalen, & Hinshaw, 1980). Antecedent attributions are influenced by the past records of achievement (success and failure) and the behavioral responses of parents, teachers, and peers. In addition, prior interventions have implicit message values (Whalen & Henker, 1976, 1980). For instance, the simple act of taking medication for behavioral control implies that the solution to a child's problems are outside of his or her own volition. In exploratory research, Henker and Whalen (1980) found that hyperactive children on medication tended to view their problems as physiologically based rather than attributable to either personal or social factors.

Program-generated attributions are a part of every strategy training routine (Henker & Whalen, 1980). In each formal therapeutic intervention there is a hidden informational content: the child's self-perceptions about whether the treatment will or will not be effective. Treatments that posit control within the child, such as Meichenbaum's (1977) self-control procedures, are believed to result in greater expectations for success than programs in which the control is outside the child (i.e., operant conditioning and stimulant medication).

Links between antecedent attributional beliefs and performance after failure have been found for children in achievement-oriented situations. In a study of "learned helplessness," Dweck (1975) identified two groups of children on the basis of attributional style: mastery-oriented and helpless children. Mastery-oriented students attributed their failure to the unstable cause of insufficient effort whereas the helpless students attributed unsuccessful performance to stable, nonremediable factors such as lack of ability or a physical problem. Despite identical pretest performance, when failure items were introduced helpless children showed a deterioration in persistence and in the quality of performance, whereas the mastery children did not.

There is evidence that antecedent attributions can be modified through attribution training. Dweck (1975) taught helpless children to take responsibility for failure and to attribute it to insufficient effort; training resulted in unimpaired performance following failure on a criterion situation, whereas a procedure that provided only success experiences led to changes of lesser magnitude.

According to our model, attempts to intervene in the cycle of learning disabilities should address specific strategy training (leading to Specific Strategy Knowledge), general-executive strategy training (producing improved Metamemory Acquisition Procedures), and attributional beliefs (building General Strategy Knowledge). Within our proposed model of metacognitive–motivational functioning, beliefs about the causes of success and failure are inseparable from metamemorial knowledge. Thus, metacognitive states (in the form of General Strategy Knowledge) become more than "information states" (Borkowski & Büchel, 1983). In addition to their cognitive aspect, they contain affective and motivational components (e.g., self-attributions about achievement) that can energize or hinder the use of a strategy or skill on a transfer task. The key to our analysis of strategy transfer is the following hypotheses: For newly acquired skills to generalize across time and setting, metamemorial awareness about strategic resources needs to be combined with appropriate self-attributions about the merits of strategic effort. The long-range consequence of a successful execution of this sequence across multiple tasks is the enhancement of self-esteem.

Intelligent children, who demonstrate successful strategy transfer, have a tendency to believe that effort determines successful recall (Kurtz & Borkowski, 1984). In contrast, we believe that many LD children do not understand the connection between effortful, strategic behavior and successful performance, and as a consequence, often fail on transfer tasks. If this scenario is correct, theoretically based interventions designed to improve metacognitive–motivation states are needed to enhance strategy transfer in LD children.

To begin to test the utility of our model, Reid and Borkowski (1984) assessed the influence of a combined Executive plus Attribution training condition that included self-control steps as well as attribution training on the maintenance, generalization, and long-term follow-up of strategic behaviors in children who had a variety of learning problems. The most complex experimental condition was compared with a condition that focused only on self-control behaviors but did not address, in a direct way, the child's inadequate understanding about the importance of effortful, strategic behavior. By training self-control in both experimental groups and manipulating the amount of attributional assistance in one of the treatments, we assessed the role of awareness about the value of effortful, strategic behavior on the transfer of skills to other tasks and settings. The key assessments included strategy transfer on laboratory tasks, strategy use in the classroom as reflected in grades and impulsive behavior, changes in attributional beliefs, and increases in strategic knowledge as indicated on a final metamemory test.

Second-, third-, and fourth-grade children labeled LD and/or hyperactive by their teachers (using the Conners scale) were assigned to one of three treatments. In the Executive condition, self-control and specific-strategy instructions were presented. Training in specific-memorization strategies followed the self-control instructions and included an interrogative-associative strategy for use on a paired-associate task and a clustering-rehearsal strategy for use on a sort recall readiness task. The self-control component was modeled, in many respects, after Padawer, Zupan, and Kendall's (1980) training procedures. Initially, the instructor demonstrated appropriate self-instructions; the child then copied the instructor's self-statements, rehearsing them aloud. Finally, the child shifted responses from overt verbalizations to covert statements. Training and practice in using the self-control routine were carried out with psychoeducational tasks.

The Executive plus Attribution condition received the same self-control steps and specific strategy training as the Executive group. In addition, children were given training designed to enhance antecedent and program-generated attributions. Failure occurred during the self-control instructions and was the occasion for training antecedent attributions. Whenever either the experimenter or the child made a mistake, a discussion stressing the importance of internal, controllable factors was introduced. The antecedent attributional training involved three aspects: a discussion dealing with beliefs about the causes of failure, an opportunity to successfully perform a previously failed item, and a reflection on beliefs about the causes of success.

Program-generated attributions were trained by providing feedback to the child about performance on the paired-associate and sort recall readiness tasks; that is, following these tasks, two examples were selected in which (a) the child used the strategy and accurately remembered the item, and (b) the child failed to use the strategy and the item was forgotten. Feedback about the relationships between strategy use and good recall, and a lack of strategy use and poor recall, was provided in order to develop a linkage between General Strategy Knowledge and attributional beliefs. A control condition was included in the design, in which only strategy training was given.

Generalization effects were assessed 3 weeks after training on measures of impulsive behaviors (teacher ratings), impulsivity–reflectivity (MFF2O), and strategy transfer (Cognitive Cuing and Picture Triad tests; see Cavanaugh & Borkowski, 1979). Long-term effects at a 9-month follow-up tested the use of strategic behaviors (as reflected by metamemory scores), attributional beliefs, impulsivity, and grades.

The data from the short-term generalization session showed wide-ranging changes in behavior, especially for children receiving attributional retraining embedded in the self-control and specific strategy training package: (a) strategy use was more prevalent on the transfer tests following training on the complex package; (b) attributional responses, reflecting beliefs about the reason for success and failure on the transfer tests as well as more enduring beliefs about past successes-failures on academic subjects, were altered in the Attribution–Executive condition; (c) teacher ratings of impulsivity improved for children given the most complex package. It should be emphasized that self-control training, without attention to attibutional beliefs, produced no improvements over those found in the strategy control condition. Results from the long-term follow-up showed that relatively permanent changes in metamemory and attributional beliefs persisted over the 9-month duration following training, with small improvements observed in impulsive behaviors in the classroom (Reid & Borkowski, 1984). These findings highlight the importance of attributional retraining in programs designed to change cognitive (strategy use) and metacognitive (self-control) processes. We hypothesize that attributional beliefs are tied tightly to metacognitive knowledge and serve an energizing function as children encounter complex, challenging tasks.

As setting variables, enhanced metamemorial and attributional development should increase the probability that the child will perform strategically in new, untrained situations (Borkowski & Büchel, 1983). Over time, new strategies and skills gained from a greater appreciation of strategy-related classroom experiences should enhance the child's repertoire of strategic skills and corresponding metacognitive awareness. If these relationshps between attributions and metamemory and between metamemory and strategic performance are tenable, then attributional boosts, indirectly and directly, should result in greater use of strategies over time. Furthermore, repeated strategy use is a prerequisite for the emergence of new beliefs about the utility of effortful, strategic behavior in the form of General Strategy Knowledge.

TRAINING CONTROL PROCESSES IN LEARNING-DISABLED CHILDREN: RESEARCH DIRECTIONS

Several decades of research have focused on the training of control processes in learning-disabled and mentally retarded children with less than satisfactory results. This is especially true if the goals of training are to produce generalized changes in ecologically valid settings (cf. Borkowski & Cavanaugh, 1979). It now appears that most of the research on lower level strategies has errored not because strategies are unimportant, but because of a failure to include executive routines and attributional reshaping in training packages.

The model we advance places motivation within a metacognition framework, with a clear reciprocal flavor. Attributional training makes it more likely that a child will understand the value of strategy-oriented effort. In turn, enhanced states of metamemorial awareness and attributional based motivation prepare the child to acquire, with greater understanding, and to use, with greater flexibility, teacher-assisted learning strategies. If this scenario is correct, the training of executive skills and the simultaneous reshaping of attributional beliefs should aid LD children to persist in using specific strategies in the short run. More important, children who have received metacognitive boosts should be disposed to acquire educationally relevant strategies in the classroom, resulting in improved grades and academic achievement in the long run.

It should be emphasized that metacognitive and motivational processes, individually or in combination, do not develop or change rapidly (Kurtz & Borkowski, 1984). Long-term training is required if durable and widespread changes in strategic behavior are to occur within the diverse population of LD children. Although the components of metacognition are not easy to teach, and simultaneously to control and measure, their emergence in the lives of LD children appears to assume differing developmental trajectories than for normal children (Douglas, 1980b). Hence, it is important to study the complexities that link the cognitive, metacognitive, and motivational processes of LD students over long periods of time, in both laboratory and classroom contexts. The availability of confirmatory, structural analyses (cf. Applebaum & McCall, 1983) makes possible the causal analyses of interactive factors that produce, maintain, or intensify learning disabilities. With both theoretical and analytic advances, we can hope to unravel the cognitive–intellectual correlates of learning disabilities and how they affect self-esteem, self-concept, and adjustment to crises across the life span.

ACKNOWLEDGMENTS

The writing of this chapter was supported in part by NIH Grant HD-17648. M. K. Reid was supported by NIH Training Grant HD-07184.

REFERENCES

Applebaum, M. I., & McCall, R. B. (1983). Design and analysis in developmental psychology. In P. H. Mussen (Ed.), *Handbook of child psychology* (4th ed., pp. 415–476). New York: Wiley.

Baker, L., & Brown, A. L. (1985). Metacognitive skills of reading. In P. D. Pearson (Ed.), *Handbook of reading research*. New York: Longman.

Battle, J. (1979). Self-esteem of students in regular and special classes.*Psychological Reports, 44*, 212–274.

Bauer, R. H. (1977). Memory processes in children with learning disabilities: Evidence for deficient rehearsal. *Journal of Experimental Child Psychology, 24*, 415–430.

Belmont, J. M., Ferretti, R. P., & Mitchell, D. (1982). Memorizing: A test of untrained mildly retarded children's problem solving. *American Journal of Mental Deficiency, 87*, 197–210.

Boersma, F. J., & Chapman, J. W. (1981). Academic self-concept, achievement expectations, and locus of control in elementary learning disabled children. *Canadian Journal of Behavioural Science, 13*, 349–358.

Borkowski, J. G., & Büchel, F. (1983). Learning and memory strategies in the mentally retarded. In M. Pressley & J. R. Levin (Eds.), *Cognitive strategy research: Psychological foundations* (pp. 103–128). New York: Springer-Verlag.

Borkowski, J. G., & Cavanaugh, J. C. (1979). Maintenance and generalization of skills and strategies by the retarded. In N. R. Ellis (Ed.), *Handbook of mental deficiency: Psychological theory and research* (pp. 569–618). Hillsdale, NJ: Lawrence Erlbaum Associates.

Borkowski, J. G., & Kurtz, B. E. (1984). Metacognition and special children. In J. B. Gholson & T. L. Rosenthal (Eds.), *Applications of cognitive developmental theory* (pp. 193–213). New York: Academic Press.

Borkowski, J. G., Reid, M. K., & Kurtz, B. E. (1984). Metacognition and mental retardation: Paradigmatic, theoretical, and applied perspective. In P. H. Brooks, R. Sperbe, & C. McCauley (Eds.), *Learning and cognition in the mentally retarded* (pp. 55–75). Hillsdale, NJ: Lawrence Erlbaum Associates.

Borkowski, J. G., Ryan, E. B., Kurtz, B. E., & Reid, M. K. (1983). Metamemory and metalinguistic development: Correlates of children's intelligence and achievement. *Bulletin of the Psychonomic Society, 21,* 393–396.

Bos, C., & Filip, D. (1982). Comprehension monitoring skills in learning disabled and average students. *Topics in Learning and Learning Disabilities, 2,* 79–85.

Brown, A. L. (1978). Knowing when, where & how to remember: A problem of metacognition. In R. Glaser (Ed.), *Advances in instructional psychology* (pp. 77–165). Hillsdale, NJ: Lawrence Erlbaum Associates.

Butkowsky, I. S. (1982, August). *The generality of learned helplessness in children with learning difficulties.* Paper presented at the meeting of the American Psychological Association, Washington, DC.

Butkowsky, I. S., & Willows, D. M. (1980). Cognitive–motivational characteristics of children varying in reading ability: Evidence for learned helplessness in poor readers. *Journal of Educational Psychology, 72,* 408–422.

Campione, J. C., & Brown, A. L. (1977). Memory and metamemory development in educable mentally retarded children. In R. V. Kail & J. W. Hagen (Eds.), *Perspectives on the development of memory and cognition* (pp. 376–406). Hillsdale, NJ: Lawrence Erlbaum Associates.

Campione, J. C., Brown, A. L., & Ferrara, R. A. (1982). Mental retardation and intelligence. In R. J. Sternberg (Ed.), *Handbook of human intelligence* (pp. 392–490). Cambridge, England: Cambridge University Press.

Cavanaugh, J. C., & Borkowski, J. G. (1979). The metamemory-memory "connection": Effects of strategy training and maintenance. *Journal of General Psychology, 101,* 161–174.

Covington, M. V. (in press). Achievement motivation, attributions, and exceptionality. In J. Borkowski & J. Day (Eds.), *Cognition and intelligence in special children.* Norwood, NJ: Ablex.

Douglas, V. I. (1980a). Higher mental processes in hyperactive children: Implications for training. In R. M. Knights & D. J. Bakker (Eds.), *Treatment of hyperactive and learning disordered children* (pp. 65–91). Baltimore: University Park Press.

Douglas, V. I. (1980b). Treatment and training approaches to hyperactivity: Establishing internal or external control. In C. K. Whalen & B. Henker (Eds.), *Hyperactive children: The social ecology of identification and treatment* (pp. 283–317). New York: Academic Press.

Douglas, V. I., Parry, P., Marton, P., & Garson, C. (1976). Assessment of a cognitive training program for hyperactive children. *Journal of Abnormal Child Psychology, 4,* 389–410.

Douglas, V. I., & Peters, K. G. (1979). Toward a clearer definition of the attentional deficit of hyperactive children. In G. Hale & M. Lewis (Eds.), *Attention and cognitive development* (pp. 173–247). New York: Plenum Press.

Douglass, L. C. (1981, April). *Metamemory in learning disabled children: A clue to memory deficiencies.* Paper presented at the meeting of the Society for Research in Child Development, Boston, MA.

Dweck, C. S. (1975). The role of expectations and attributions in the alleviation of learned helplessness. *Journal of Personality and Social Psychology, 45,* 165–171.

Dweck, C. S., & Licht, B. G. (1980). Learned helplessness and intellectual achievement. In J. Garber & M. E. P. Seligman (Eds.), *Human helplessness: Theory and application* (pp. 197–221). New York: Academic Press.

Fincham, F., & Barling, J. (1978). Locus of control and generosity in learning disabled, normal achieving, and gifted children. *Child Development, 49,* 530–533.

Flavell, J. H. (1978). Metacognitive development. In J. M. Scandura & C. J. Brainerd (Eds.), *Structural process theories of complex human behavior.* Alphen a.d. Rijn, The Netherlands: Sijtoff & Noordhoff.

Flavell, J. H. (1979). Metacognition and cognitive monitoring: A new area of cognitive–developmental inquiry. *American Psychologist, 34,* 906–911.

Gelzheiser, L. M. (1984). Generalization from categorical memory tasks to prose by learning disabled adolescents. *Journal of Educational Psychology, 76,* 1128–1138.

Ghatala, E. S., Levin, J. R., Pressley, M., & Lodico, M. (1984, March). *Metamemory acquisition in children: Effects of strategy-monitoring training.* Paper presented at the meetings of the American Educational Research Association, New Orleans, LA.

Hagen, J. W. (1971). Some thoughts on how children learn to remember. *Human Development, 14,* 262–271.

Hagen, J. W., Barclay, C. R., & Newman, R. S. (1982). Metacognition, self-knowledge, and learning disabilities: Some thoughts on knowing and doing. *Metacognition and Learning, 2,* 19–26.

Hagen, J. W., Barclay, C. R., & Schwethelm, B. (1982). Cognitive development of the learning disabled child. In N. R. Ellis (Ed.), *International review of research in mental retardation* (pp. 1–41). New York: Academic Press.

Hallahan, D., Gajar, A., Cohen, S., & Tarver, S. (1978). Selective attention and locus of control in learning disabled and normal children. *Journal of Learning Disabilities, 4,* 47–52.

Hallahan, D., & Kauffman, J. M. (1982). *Exceptional children* (2nd ed.). Englewood Cliffs, NJ: Prentice-Hall.

Henker, B., & Whalen, C. (1980). The many messages of medication: Hyperactive children's perceptions and attributions. In S. Sabinger, J. Antrobus, & J. Glick (Eds.), *The ecosystem of the "sick" child.* New York: Academic Press.

Henker, B., Whalen, C. K., & Hinshaw, S. P. (1980). The attributional contexts of cognitive motivational strategies. *Exceptional Educational Quarterly, 1,* 17–30.

Johnson, D. S. (1981). Naturally acquired learned helplessness: The relationship of school failure to achievement behavior, attributions and self-concept. *Journal of Educational Psychology, 73,* 174–180.

Kirk, S. A., & Gallagher, J. J. (1979). *Educating exceptional children.* (3rd ed.). Boston: Houghton Mifflin.

Kistner, J. A., & Licht, B. G. (1983). *Cognitive–motivational factors affecting academic persistence of learning disabled children.* Unpublished manuscript, Florida State University, Tallahassee.

Kreutzer, M. A., Leonard, C., & Flavell, J. (1975). An interview study of children's knowledge about memory. *Monographs of the Society for Research in Child Development, 40*(1, Serial No. 159).

Kurtz, B. E., & Borkowski, J. G. (1984). Children's metacognition: Exploring relations among knowledge, process, and motivational variables. *Journal of Experimental Child Psychology, 37,* 335–354.

Licht, B. G. (1983). Cognitive–motivational factors that contribute to the achievement of learning disabled children. *Journal of Learning Disabilities, 16,* 483–490.

Loper, A. B., Hallahan, D. P., & Sanna, S. O. (1980). Metaattention in learning disabled and normal children. *Learning Disabilities Quarterly, 5,* 29–36.

Masson, M. E. J. (1982). A framework of cognitive and metacognitive determinants of reading skill. *Topics in Learning and Learning Disabilities, 4,* 37–43.

McKean, S., & Angell, L. S. (1981). *Children's use of metacognitive knowledge about story structure in reading and listening comprehension.* Unpublished manuscript.

McKinney, J. D., & Feagans, L. (1981). *Learning disabilities in the classroom.* Final report to Bureau of Education for the Handicapped (Grant No. G00-76-0522-4). Washington, DC: U.S. Office of Education.

Meichenbaum, D. (1977). *Cognitive behavior modification.* New York: Plenum.

Meyers, A. W., & Craighead, W. E. (Eds.). (1984). *Cognitive behavior therapy with children.* New York: Plenum Press.

Neimark, E. D. (1976). The natural history of spontaneous mnemonic activity under conditions of minimal experimental constraint. In A. D. Pick (Ed.), *Minnesota symposia on child psychology* (Vol. 10, pp. 84–118). Minneapolis: University of Minnesota Press.

Newman, R. S., & Hagen, J. W. (1981). Memory strategies in children with learning disabilities. *Journal of Applied Developmental Psychology, 1,* 297–312.

Nicholls, J. G. (1975). Causal attributions and other achievement-related cognitions: Effects of task outcome, attainment value, and sex. *Journal of Personality and Social Psychology, 31,* 379–389.

Owings, R. A., Petersen, G. A., Bransford, J. D., Morris, C. D., & Stein, B. S. (1980). Spontaneous monitoring and regulation of learning: A comparison of successful and less successful fifth graders. *Journal of Educational Psychology, 72,* 250–256.

Padawer, W. J., Zupan, B. A., & Kendall, P. C. (1980). *Developing self-control in children: A manual of cognitive–behavioral strategies.* Minneapolis: University of Minnesota Press.

Palincsar, A. S., & Brown, A. L. (1984). Reciprocal teaching of comprehension-fostering comprehension-monitoring activities. *Cognition and Instruction, 1,* 117–175.

Parsons, J. E., & Ruble, D. N. (1977). The development of achievement-related expectancies. *Child Development, 48,* 1075–1079.

Pearl, R. (1982). LD children's attributions for success and failure: A replication with a labeled learning disabled sample. *Learning Disability Quarterly, 5,* 173–176.

Pearl, R., Bryan, T., & Donahue, M. (1980). Learning disabled children's attributions for success and failure. *Learning Disability Quarterly, 3,* 3–9.

Pearl, R. A., Bryan, T., & Herzog, A. (1983). Learning disabled and nondisabled children's strategy analyses under high and low success conditions. *Learning Disability Quarterly, 6,* 67–74.

Pressley, M., Borkowski, J. B., & O'Sullivan, J. T. (1985). Children's metamemory and the teaching of memory strategies. In D. L. Forrest-Pressley, G. E. MacKinnon, & T. G. Waller (Eds.), *Metacognition, cognition, and human performance* (pp. 111–153). New York: Academic Press.

Reid, M. K., & Borkowski, J. G. (1984). *A cognitive–motivational training program for hyperactive children.* Unpublished manuscript, University of Notre Dame, Notre Dame, IN.

Resnick, L. B. (1981). Instructional psychology. In M. Rosenzweig & L. Porter (Eds.), *Annual review of psychology* (Vol. 32, pp. 659–704). Palo Alto, CA: Annual Reviews.

Rholes, W. S., Blackwell, J., Jordan, C., & Walters, C. (1980). A developmental study of learned helplessness. *Developmental Psychology, 16,* 616–624.

Seligman, M. E. P. & Maier, S. F. (1967). Failure to escape traumatic shock. *Journal of Experimental Psychology, 74,* 1–9.

Seligman, M. E. P., Maier, S. F., Geer, J. H. (1968). Alleviation of learned helplessness in the dog. *Journal of Abnormal Psychology, 73,* 256–262.

Short, E. J., & Ryan, E. B. (1984). Metacognitive differences between skilled and less skilled readers: Remediating deficits through story grammar and attribution training. *Journal of Educational Psychology, 76,* 225–235.

Smiley, S. S., Oakley, D. D., Worthen, D., Campione, J. C., & Brown, A. L. (1977). Recall of thematically relevant material by adolescent good and poor readers as a function of written versus oral presentation. *Journal of Educational Psychology, 69,* 381–387.

Sternberg, R. J. (1981). The evolution of theories of intelligence. *Intelligence, 5,* 209–230.

Tarver, S. G., Hallahan, D. P., Kauffman, J. M., & Ball, D. W. (1977). Verbal rehearsal and selective attention in children with learning disabilities: A developmental lag. *Journal of Experimental Child Psychology, 22,* 375–385.

Thomas, A. (1979). Learned helplessness and expectancy factors: Implications for research in learning disabilities. *Review of Educational Research, 49,* 208–221.

Torgesen, J. K. (1975). Problems and prospects in the study of learning disabilities. In M. Hetherington & J. W. Hagen (Eds.), *Reivew of child development research* (Vol. 5, pp. 385–440). New York: Russell Sage Foundation.

Torgesen, J. K. (1977). Memorization processes in reading disabled chlidren. *Journal of Educational Psychology, 69,* 571–578.

Torgesen, J. K. (1979). Factors related to poor performance on memory tasks in reading disabled children. *Learning Disabilities Quarterly, 2,* 17–23.

Torgesen, J. K. (1980). Conceptual and educational implications of the use of efficient task strategies by learning disabled children. *Journal of Learning Disabilities, 13,* 364–371.

Torgesen, J., & Goldman, T. (1977). Rehearsal and short-term memory in reading disabled children. *Child Development, 48,* 56–60.

Torgesen, J. K., & Licht, B. G. (1983). The learning disabled child as an inactive learner: Retrospects and prospects. In J. D. McKinney & L. Feagans (Eds.), *Current topics in learning disabilities* (Vol. 1, pp. 3–31). Norwood, NJ: Ablex.

Trepanier, M. L. (1981, March). *Learning disabled children's understanding of their memory ability.* Paper presented at the meeting of the American Educational Research Association, Los Angeles.

Wanschura, P. B., & Borkowski, J. G. (1975). Long-term transfer of a mediational strategy by moderately retarded children. *American Journal of Mental Deficiency, 80,* 323–333.

Weiner, B. (1979). A theory of motivation for some classroom experiences. *Journal of Educational Psychology, 71,* 3–25.

Whalen, C. K., & Henker, B. (1976). Psychostimulants and children: A review and analysis. *Psychological Bulletin, 83,* 1113–1130.

Whalen, C. K., & Henker, B. (1980). *Hyperactive children: The social ecology of identification and treatment.* New York: Academic Press.

Wong, B. Y. L. (1979). The role of theory in learning disabilities research: Part I. An analysis of problems. *Journal of Learning Disabilities, 12,* 585–595.

7 Elaborative Learning Strategies for the Inefficient Learner

Michael Pressley
University of Western Ontario

Joel R. Levin
University of Wisconsin

This chapter is about the use of effective learning strategies by students who are inefficient learners. Our specific goal is to illustrate the significant learning advantages that such students would enjoy if they were to apply effective strategies. Before beginning, however, we should indicate exactly whom the term *inefficient learner* refers to here. Although much of the research to be discussed is based on learning-disabled (LD) children, we feel obliged to include more than this subset of students. One reason for not limiting our coverage to LD students is the fuzziness associated with defining "learning disabilities" (e.g., Hall & Humphreys, 1982; Shepard, Smith, & Vojir, 1983). A second reason is that the effects associated with many cognitive interventions are similar for LD and for other handicapped learners—educable mentally retarded (EMR) students, for example. Most notably, all categories of inefficient child learners generally fail to apply effective learning strategies spontaneously in situations where it would be beneficial to do so. When such strategies are made available to inefficient learners, their learning performance improves dramatically. Thus, inefficient learners perform below "normal" levels but can perform at higher levels if they are led to process information differently than they usually do. Most learners who perform below average for their age level would thus qualify as inefficient learners. We purposely cast this definition broadly because we believe—based on voluminous data, some of which is covered in this chapter—that there are many types of inefficient learners who can benefit from the learning strategies reviewed here.

We do not intend to offer an exhaustive summary of strategy-based treatments for inefficient learners. Instead we emphasize strategies for learning tasks with seemingly high ecological and educational validity. Thus, although there is some coverage of research on learning arbitrary items and associations, more extensive consideration is given to studies of vocabulary learning, fact learning, and prose learning. All these more educationally relevant learning tasks can be performed efficiently by applying variations of one class of strategies known as "elaboration." Because of the particular appropriateness of elaboration for real-world tasks, our review showcases this broad class of strategies.

Elaboration has been studied from several theoretical perspectives (e.g., Bransford, Stein, Vye, Franks, Auble, Mezynski, & Perfetto, 1982; Hyde & Jenkins, 1973; Jacoby & Craik, 1979; Rohwer, 1973). Much of the research on elaboration has occurred in the context of associative learning, including tasks frequently confronted by schoolchildren (such as vocabulary learning and the acquisition of social studies and science facts; see Levin, 1981a, and Pressley, 1982). Elaboration in these studies has involved placing two or more to-be-associated items in an "episode, process or relation involving both [or all] of them" (Rohwer, 1973). For example, to associate *cat* and *apple,* a learner using imagery elaboration might generate an interactive image of a cat *eating* an apple; a verbal elaboration of the same pair could be the sentence *The cat ate the apple.*

The mnemonic (memory-enhancing) *keyword method* (Atkinson, 1975), which is based on elaboration, can be employed for vocabulary learning, as well as for learning associated facts. For instance, to remember that the Spanish word *carta* means *postal letter,* a learner first notes some acoustic similarity between the foreign word and a concrete, familiar word in the learner's own native language (a keyword). *Cart* would be a good keyword for a native English speaker learning *carta.* The learner then links the keyword and meaning referents in an interactive relationship (e.g., imagining a postal letter in a shopping cart). In short, the keyword method involves what Levin (1983) refers to as the "three associative-mnemonic R's": (1) recoding an unfamiliar stimulus as a familiar proxy (in this case, recoding a vocabulary word as a keyword); (2) relating the recoded stimulus to the to-be-associated information (relating the keyword to the vocabulary word's meaning); which results in (3) a systematic means of retrieving the desired information from the re-presented original stimulus (retrieving the definition from the vocabulary word). Most learners benefit greatly from "imposed" keyword elaborations in the form of mnemonic illustrations; and in many situations, learners can be "induced" to generate their own facilitative keyword elaborations in the form of visual images or verbally produced sentences or phrases.[1] Although most of the work on associative mnemonics reviewed here involves the keyword

---

[1]The "imposed"/"induced" distinction was suggested by Levin (1972, 1976) to account for seemingly discrepant findings in the elaboration literature; Pressley, Levin, and Delaney (1982) provided extensive commentary on the conditions under which different mnemonic strategy variations are likely to be beneficial; and Pressley (1982) discussed in detail the development of elaboration skills during childhood and adolescence. In the final section of this chapter, we briefly consider the distinction as it applies to the inefficient learner.

method as just described, other mnemonic systems (such as the "pegword" method for remembering ordered associations) are considered briefly at appropriate points in the chapter. Such alternative mnemonic approaches are similar to the keyword method inasmuch as they include the "three R" components of recoding, relating, and retrieving.

Remembering the relationships in simple sentences has been the concern of Bransford, Franks, and colleagues in their recent work on elaboration (e.g, Bransford et al., 1982). These sentences contain ostensibly arbitrary relationships between subjects and predicates as, for example: *The hungry man got into his car, The tall man bought the crackers,* and *The old man bought the paint.* When learners elaborate these types of sentences in ways that provide good rationales for the particular actor/activity relationship (e.g., deciding that the hungry man is using the car *to go to a restaurant*), recall is increased on questions such as *Which man bought the crackers?; Which man bought the paint?;* and *Which man got into his car?* Bransford, Franks, and their associates refer to these types of rationales as "precise elaborations." They contrast with "imprecise elaborations" that do not permit understanding of the co-occurrences in the sentences (e.g., stating that the hungry man got into his car *and drove away*). The mechanism mediating learning in the situation studied by Bransford, Franks, and their colleagues is very similar to the mechanism mediating the associative connections studied in research on the mnemonic keyword method. Precise elaborations and associative mnemonic elaborations both involve the addition of meaningful contexts that incoporate the to-be-associated materials (or their recoded proxies) in order to facilitate subsequent information retrieval.

There is, moreover, another less restrictive definition of elaboration. Elaboration in this second sense means simply making any meaningful addition(s) to a set of to-be-remembered items (e.g., Hyde & Jenkins, 1973; Jacoby & Craik, 1979). Thus, for item recall or recognition, a learner can engage in relevant "semantic-processing" activities, such as generating synonyms for the stimulus items, or making evaluative or functional judgments related to semantic attributes of the stimuli (e.g., What is another word for X?, Do I like X? How is X used?). When the to-be-remembered information is contained in meaningful prose passages, a wide variety of semantic-processing activities can be performed by the learner. These include (among others) processing illustrations or constructing images that represent the content of the text; posing and answering questions about the text; and actively generating associations to and inferences from the text. Each of these prose-elaboration strategies are discussed later in the chapter.

To understand how the elaborative approaches reviewed here provide inefficient learners with the benefits of effective strategy use, it is important to understand the critical components of strategic processing. Understanding proficient learning also illuminates the vast processing differences between proficient and inefficient learners.

STRATEGY USE IN PROFICIENT LEARNERS

Effective strategy use involves strategies, knowledge about those strategies ("metastrategy" information), monitoring of strategy use, and the dynamic interaction among these three components (Pressley, Borkowski, & O'Sullivan, 1984, 1985). Expert strategy users possess a wide variety of beneficial strategies. With respect to learning and memory, these include rehearsal (repetition) strategies, organizational (typically, categorizing or grouping) strategies, and elaboration strategies. Each strategy in the expert's arsenal is accompanied by knowledge about the strategy, which includes knowledge of situations for which the strategy is appropriate, materials to which the strategy can be successfully applied, goals that the strategy can help to meet (e.g., means–end utility information), time constraints associated with strategy implementation, effort requirements, knowledge about personal satisfaction derived from use of the strategy, and information about how the strategy can be modified to suit one's needs. This metastrategy information is critical to effective strategy deployment, as is monitoring, which involves evaluating strategic actions as they are performed: Is the match between the ongoing strategy and task appropriate? Is the cognitive goal being achieved? What can be learned about the strategy's effects for the current strategic episode?

Strategies, metastrategy information, and monitoring are tightly tied in the sophisticated strategy user. When confronted with a problem that can be attacked strategically—especially a novel one—an optimally efficient learner will first analyze the task regarding goals, materials, time constraints, and other factors, and will then determine which strategy to use by comparing the current requirements against relevant metastrategy information. Such analysis presumably results in the selection of the strategy best suited to the task, materials, and processing constraints of the current situation. Once a strategy is invoked, the learner may either make progress with it or have difficulty with it. Proficient strategy users monitor effectiveness, enjoyment, and ease of strategy execution. This monitoring directs either continued use of the selected strategy or abandonment of it in favor of an alternative strategy. In other terms, strategy monitoring comprises the main mechanism of "troubleshooting" (see Norman & Schallice, 1980) and "on-line planning" (e.g., Rogoff & Gardner, 1984). Monitoring also produces new metastrategy information. For example, experiencing difficulty may be translated into durable knowledge that the strategy is not effective for a given task. Or, enjoying the current processing effort may be translated into knowledge that a particular strategy is "fun" in that situation.

Although researchers and theorists differ in their emphases and descriptions of particular components, virtually all recent formulations of effective strategy use include strategy, metastrategy, and monitoring components (e.g., Brown, 1980; Brown, Bransford, Ferrara, & Campione, 1983; Büchel, 1982; Flavell & Wellman, 1977; Paris, Lipson, & Wixson, 1983; Pressley, Borkowski, & O'Sullivan, 1984, 1985). Thus, the basic features of this portrait of effective strategy use are not controversial, and many aspects of it are supported by recent research conducted in our laboratories (e.g., Pressley, Levin, & Ghatala, 1984).

Before proceeding, a critical caveat needs to be interjected. Conventional wisdom has it that the proficient learners described in this section include such *populations* as college students and academically precocious ("gifted") grade schoolers. Most certainly, various *individuals* within these populations are proficient learners; and equally certainly, there is a *greater proportion* of proficient learners in these populations than in other less select populations (e.g., Pressley & Levin, 1977; Rohwer & Bean, 1973). Even so, it must be emphasized that: (a) there is considerable variability in the learning performance of individuals taken from these "proficient" populations; and (b) the learning performance of many individuals from these same populations can be substantially improved by an experimenter's provision of effective strategies. Thus, to assume that the strategies discussed in this chapter have implications only for handicapped learners (such as LD and EMR) is incorrect. There are many mature and able learners who are known to benefit from them as well. In sum, then, although the term *inefficient learner* is applied throughout the chapter primarily to the prototypical "slow learner," the complementary set does not consist exclusively of maximally efficient learners.

STRATEGY USE IN INEFFICIENT LEARNERS

Inefficient learners are inferior in all aspects of strategic functioning. Such learners use fewer strategies than do more proficient learners, and they use them less often and less effectively. Learning-disabilities researchers have been particularly interested in rehearsal and semantic-organizational strategies for list learning, where LD children have been found to use these strategies less frequently than do nondisabled learners (e.g., Bauer, 1977, 1979; Dallago & Moely, 1980; Newman & Hagen, 1981; Tarver, Hallahan, Kauffman, & Ball, 1976; Torgesen, Murphy, & Ivey, 1979). Inefficient learners are less likely to use effective strategies in more complex tasks as well, such as prose learning. For instance, they do not underline or take notes as extensively as do more proficient learners (e.g., Brown & Smiley, 1978), nor do they select helpful retrieval cues from text as efficiently (e.g., Wong, 1982a). Especially relevant to the present chapter (given its emphasis on elaboration strategies), inefficient learners do not spontaneously produce meaningful integrations of to-be-associated materials (e.g., Martin, 1978; Mastropieri, Scruggs, & Levin, 1983b, in press; Taylor & Turnure, 1979), and they do not go beyond the information given when processing materials containing relations than would be more meaningful if elaborated (e.g., Stein, Bransford, Franks, Owings, Vye, & McGraw, 1982).

Deficiencies in strategy production per se are exacerbated by deficiencies in knowledge about strategies. Inefficient learners lack critical knowledge about when, why, and how to use the strategies that they possess (e.g., Forrest-Pressley

& Waller, 1984; Gambrell & Heathington, 1981; Paris & Myers, 1981)—knowledge that is absolutely critical for conscious deployment of learning techniques.

Strategy regulation in inefficient learners also suffers from monitoring deficiencies. Failures both to monitor cognitive progress and to notice important task differences in learning problems have been reported in a number of situations (e.g., Bos & Filip, 1982; Capelli & Markman, 1982; Forrest-Pressley & Waller, 1984; Owings, Peterson, Bransford, Morris, & Stein, 1980; Paris & Myers, 1981; Wong, 1982b). Perhaps even more disturbing is that on those occasions when inefficient learners are aware that they are experiencing difficulty, they do not react as better learners do. Whereas proficient learners feel that strategy changes and increased effort are reasonable responses to task failure, inefficient learners often attribute failure to their abilities and, thus, are more likely to stop trying (e.g., Butkowsky & Willows, 1980; Cohen, 1983; Cullen & Boersma, 1982; Pearl, 1982; Pearl, Bryan, & Donahue, 1980; Pearl, Bryan, & Herzog, 1983; Tollefson, Tracy, Johnsen, Buenning, Farmer, & Barké, 1982). Given this defeatist tendency, it is not surprising that strategy switches (i.e., midcourse corrections) are much less frequent with inefficient learners than with better students (e.g., Garner & Reis, 1981).

Moreover, we suspect that there are other inefficiencies that have not yet been documented in the literature. For instance, Rohwer (1980) notes that well-intentioned educators often unwittingly teach strategies that do not work well. He goes on to hypothesize that better students likely come to realize that such strategies are often not what they are "cracked up" to be (i.e., better students monitor strategy efficacy, as mentioned previously). Having realized this, they abandon the teacher-recommended approaches (doing so surreptitiously, if need be, to avoid the wrath of their teachers). In contrast, poorer students are more likely to accept their teachers' opinions and persist in applying dysfunctional approaches. Ironically, then, the diligent inefficient learner may well acquire quite an extensive repertoire of strategies—but strategies that are ineffective.

STRATEGY-BASED REMEDIES FOR
INEFFICIENT LEARNERS

There are very few studies in which inefficient learners have been given systematic instruction in all three strategy components mentioned earlier (i.e., strategies, metastrategy information, and monitoring). Some of the ones that have are taken up later in the chapter. The most typical remediation study involves instructing inefficient learners in a particular strategy and then determining whether these instructed subjects perform at a higher level than learners not taught the strategy. Most research of this kind has involved simple rehearsal and organizational strategies applied to free- or serial-recall tasks. In general, it has proven possible to teach LD children and other inefficient learners to execute profitable encoding strategies (e.g., attentional, rehearsal, and categorization strategies); see, for example, Dallago and Moely (1980); Newman and Hagen (1981); Shuell (1983); Torgesen (1977); Torgesen and Goldman (1977); Torgesen, Murphy, and Ivey (1979); and Wong, Wong, and Foth (1977). Such studies have been discussed in numerous reviews of LD/non-LD comparisons, and so they need not be repeated here (see other chapters in this volume, as well as the recent chapter by Worden, 1983). It is interesting to note in passing that basic strategies (such as repetition rehearsal) that were originally studied in a simple item-learning context, are now being investigated in more complex prose-learning situations (e.g., Bender & Levin, 1978; Rose, Cundick, & Higbee, 1983; Worden, Malmgren, & Gabourie, 1982).

Elaboration and the Inefficient Learner

Mnemonic Elaboration Effects

It is well established that mnemonic elaboration facilitates the recall of arbitrarily paired nouns in populations of inefficient learners (Taylor & Turnure, 1979). A natural extension of this work was to determine whether mnemonic strategies would facilitate such learners' performance on more educationally valid associative tasks, such as vocabulary learning, fact learning, and prose learning. Motivation for attempting this extension followed from demonstrations that mnemonic methods can be successfully applied even by very young children (e.g., Pressley, Samuel, Hershey, Bishop, & Dickinson, 1981) and that tasks of the kind just mentioned are especially susceptible to mnemonic strategy facilitation (e.g., Levin, 1981a). There is documented evidence of the applicability of mnemonic strategies for students' acquisition of both foreign- and native-language vocabulary, for their remembering facts in content areas such as social studies and science, and for their recalling information contained in expository prose passages (Levin, in press). We summarize here research that has established that mnemonic methods can be very potent facilitators of learning for any task that has an associative component, with the discussion organized around the three types of content just cited: vocabulary acquisition, fact learning, and prose recall. Mnemonic strategies make all three tasks easier for inefficient learners, even when compared to educational interventions that are widely recommended in the curriculum-and-instruction literature. The illustrative studies considered here provide a general introduction to mnemonic strategy implementation and evaluation in inefficient learner populations (for additional discussion, see Mastropieri, Scruggs, & Levin, 1983a, 1984).

Vocabulary Acquisition.   When nonhandicapped elementary school students use the keyword method to learn vocabulary, they learn much faster than when left to their own devices (e.g., Pressley & Levin, 1978). Would the same be true of children with learning disabilities? In an initial investigation of this question, Berry (1982) taught fourth- and fifth-grade LD students the meanings of unfamiliar English vocabulary words such as *monocle, dahlia,* and *parchment.* Students in the mnemonic picture condition were shown illustrations in which a keyword proxy for the vocabulary item (e.g., *monkey* for *monocle, doll* for *dahlia, park* for *parchment*) interacted with the vocabulary item's definition. For *monocle,* a large monkey wore an eyepiece; for *dahlia,* a doll sniffed a flower; and for *parchment,* a park was littered with paper. Students who were presented such mnemonic pictures recalled far more definitions compared both to students who were given the vocabulary items, definitions, and corresponding illustrations (i.e., a picture of a monocle, a dahlia, or some parchment) and to students who were provided with the vocabulary items, their definitions, and meaningful sentences incorporating the vocabulary items.

In a subsequent study, Mastropieri, Scruggs, Levin, Gaffney, and McLoone (1985) compared the vocabulary learning of LD junior high school students under mnemonic and "direct" instruction (e.g., Carnine & Silbert, 1979). Direct-instruction approaches capitalize on the three "operant R's" of student active Responding, instructor-provided Reinforcement, and Repetition of the to-be-learned content (Scruggs, Mastropieri, Levin, & Gaffney, 1984). For vocabulary learning, this consists of repeated questioning of the student concerning each vocabulary word and its meaning, along with corrective feedback and cumulative review of the presented vocabulary items. Direct instruction is claimed to be particularly well-suited to LD students and other inefficient learners (e.g., Becker, Engelmann, Carnine, & Maggs, 1982). Mastropieri, Scruggs, Levin, Gaffney, and McLoone (1985, Experiment 1) found, however, that students who were shown mnemonic illustrations outperformed direct-instruction students by better than a 2½ to 1 margin (80% vs. 31% correct, on the average); direct instruction was inferior (69% vs. 47%) even when LD students had to generate their own mnemonic images internally (Experiment 2).[2]

The "induced" mnemonic imagery results in the Mastropieri, Scruggs, Levin, Gaffney, and McLoone (in press) study are interesting because not all subjects benefit from instructions to construct their own mnemonic images. For instance, young children experience difficulty executing a visual imagery mnemonic strategy (see Levin, 1976; Pressley, 1977). As a specific example, Pressley and Levin (1978) found that whereas *both* second and sixth graders could improve their learning of verbally presented vocabulary words when mnemonic illustrations were provided, only the sixth graders benefited from instructions to produce

---

[2]The differences in favor of mnemonic instruction are especially impressive inasmuch as direct-instruction students actually received 40% more exposure to the vocabulary definitions that were to be remembered. In particular, direct-instruction subjects studied the vocabulary items and their definitions throughout the entire study time allotted, whereas mnemonic subjects spent the initial part of that study time learning the keywords for the various vocabulary items.

their own mnemonic images. Like Pressley and Levin's (1978) nonhandicapped sixth-grade learners, then, LD junior high school students appear capable of executing a mnemonic imagery strategy without the need for experimenter-provided illustrations. At the same time, in neither of the just-mentioned studies were the participants required to generate their own keywords. Whether or not mnemonic facilitation would occur when both keyword and imagery generation are required of the learners is a question for further study (see also McGivern & Levin, 1983).

Scruggs, Mastropieri, and Levin (1985) extended the comparison of imposed mnemonic and direct-instruction vocabulary approaches to EMR junior high school students. A within-subjects crossover design was employed in the study, so that subjects learned a set of vocabulary items with each technique. Strategy order was counterbalanced across subjects. As in the LD study, the EMR students learned more vocabulary definitions under mnemonic instruction than under direct instruction. The across-order averages were 72% and 48% correct, respectively. There was no condition by order interaction, implying that subjects did not spontaneously transfer the initially acquired mnemonic strategy to the subsequent direct-instruction lesson.

Levin, Johnson, Pittelman, Hayes, Levin, Shriberg, and Toms-Bronowski (1984) provided additional evidence that the keyword method enhances the vocabulary learning of children who otherwise experience difficulty acquiring new vocabulary. The part of the study considered here was conducted in a school whose average achievement level was somewhat below the U.S. national norms. Fourth- and fifth-grade participants were assigned randomly to one of three experimental conditions. As *mnemonic picture* subjects learned the English vocabulary words, they viewed illustrations depicting keyword/definition referent interactions. In a *semantic-mapping* condition, learners studied the vocabulary items using a procedure recommended by curriculum theorists (Johnson & Pearson, 1978), namely to construct "maps" of the superordinate, subordinate, and coordinate relationships between the new words and words the student already knows. For example, in processing *angler, equestrian,* and *ornithologist,* students mapped them as members of the superordinate category *Sports and Hobbies. Stamp collector* and *gardener* were mapped as familiar instances from the same category. The third condition of the experiment involved *contextual analysis,* where students received instruction in inferring the meanings of the new words on the basis of semantic and syntactic contextual clues in paragraphs containing the items (Johnson & Pearson, 1978). Statistically higher definition recall occurred in the mnemonic picture condition than in either the semantic-mapping or contextual analysis conditions, with means of 69%, 49%, and 44%, respectively. Again, mnemonic instruction produced performance superior to that produced by popularly recommended alternative treatments.

There is other research documenting that inefficient learners profit—often considerably—from mnemonic instruction. For example, McGivern and Levin

(1983) reported that fifth graders with low verbal ability benefited from mnemonic vocabulary instruction. Consistent with results considered earlier, however, the benefits were relatively greater when the learners were provided with illustrations than when they had to generate their own internal images. In other research, the vocabulary learning of college students with lower ability has been facilitated by instructions to construct keyword mnemonics (McDaniel & Pressley, 1984; Pressley, Levin, Nakamura, Hope, Bispo, & Toye, 1980).

Fact Learning.   There are factual associations that children learn in school, such as facts about prime ministers and presidents, information about provinces and states, and the dates of particular historical events and the central figures in those events. Acquisition of these types of facts can be improved in nondisabled learners with mnemonic instruction (e.g., Jones & Hall, 1982; Levin, McCormick, & Dretzke, 1981; Levin, Shriberg, Miller, McCormick, & Levin, 1980; Pressley & Dennis-Rounds, 1980). Such interventions also enhance the fact acquisition of disabled learners.

Mastropieri, Scruggs, and Levin (1983b) demonstrated the effectiveness of mnemonic instruction for teaching LD junior high school students the hardness levels of minerals. In the *mnemonic* condition, students were shown illustrations that contained a keyword for the mineral's name (e.g., *box* for *bauxite*). The keyword referent interacted with a "pegword" referent corresponding to the hardness level (1–10), with pegwords derived from the "one-is-a-bun, two-is-a-shoe" mnemonic scheme (see, e.g., Paivio, 1971). For *bauxite* with a hardness level of *1*, mnemonic subjects saw a picture of a *box* full of *buns*. For *corundum* (No. *9*), a *car* (keyword) was pictured entangled in *vines* (pegword). Mnemonic subjects learned the mineral/hardness level associations more efficiently than subjects in two other conditions. Subjects in the *free-study* condition were left to their own devices to learn the associations. *Questioning* condition subjects were quizzed repeatedly on the mineral/hardness level associations. What was most impressive was the magnitude of the difference between the mnemonic condition and the two others. Mnemonic subjects learned 75% of the associations in the same total amount of time that free-study and questioning subjects learned 36% and 28% of the associations, respectively.

Mastropieri, Scruggs, and Levin (in press, Experiment 1) additionally evaluated the mnemonic strategy for teaching mineral hardness levels by comparing it with the previously discussed and highly regarded direct-instruction approach, which in this experiment included experimenter questioning, corrective feedback, and review, using flashcards and colored line drawings. In both the mnemonic and direct-instruction conditions, LD junior high school students were taught in small groups. Subjects in the mnemonic condition correctly recalled 80% of the hardness levels on the average, as compared to 50% in the direct-instruction condition. In a second experiment, these investigators extended the mineral/hardness level results to an EMR junior high school population, where students learned under both mnemonic and direct instruction in a crossover design. Again mnemonic instruction was superior (averages of 64% and 38% correct).

In yet another extension of this line of research, Scruggs, Mastropieri, Levin, and Gaffney (1984) taught LD junior high school students a set of three attributes for each of eight minerals. In addition to remembering a hardness level for each mineral, subjects had to remember a color and a common use. These two additional attributes were incorporated into the mnemonic pictures by illustrating the keyword referent in the indicated color and by adding a representation of the mineral's use. For example, to learn that *wolframite* has a hardness level of *4*, is *black* in color, and is commonly used in making *light bulbs,* mnemonic subjects studied an illustration where a *black wolf* was howling on stage *floor* (the pegword for *4*) illuminated by a row of *light bulbs.* Subjects who viewed such mnemonic pictures remembered substantially more facts from each of the attributable categories than did either direct-instruction or free-study subjects. The respective percentages correct were for hardness level (65%, 14%, and 33%), for color (82%, 33%, and 33%), and for use (61%, 25%, and 24%). Note, additionally, that for none of the attributes did direct instruction statistically surpass free study; in fact, it was somewhat *worse* for hardness level. Finally, the study included a second direct-instruction condition in which subjects were taught only half as many minerals as were taught in the other conditions. What is interesting is that across all attributes studied, mnemonic subjects mastered 69% of their 24-attribute list (an average of almost 17 attributes) in the same amount of time that the reduced-list direct-instruction subjects could master only 49% of their 12-attribute list (an average of slightly less than 6 attributes)!

Mastropieri, Scruggs, McLoone, and Levin (1984) recently completed a second multiple-attribute study. In that study, LD junior high school students were assigned to one of the three full-list conditions (mnemonic, direct instruction, free study) to learn three attributes for each of the eight minerals from the earlier study. In this case, however, the specific attribute values were replaced by dichotomous classifications (i.e., *hard/soft* for hardness level, *pale/dark* for color, and *home/industry* for use). Four minerals were associated with each of these dichotomous classifications in a taxonomic fashion. In the mnemonic condition, the illustrations incorporated either an old man or a baby (for hard or soft, respectively); keyword referents were either blackened in or not (for dark or pale, respectively); and each illustration was placed in either a living room or a factory setting (for home or industry, respectively). Thus, if *wolframite* were described as a *soft, dark* mineral used in the *home,* mnemonic subjects saw an illustration of a *blackened-in wolf* scaring a *baby* in a *living room* setting. In contrast, *calcite* (whose keyword is *cow,* and which was described as *soft, pale,* and used in *industry*) was depicted as a *baby* riding a *nonblackened-in cow* in a *factory* setting. Could LD students given such mnemonic illustrations both keep track of the multiple-attribute occurrences (e.g., four baby representations, four dark objects, and four home scenes) and decode them properly (e.g., a baby *symbolizes* a soft mineral)? With the "chance" level of dichotomous-attribute recall equal to 50%, the mean percentages were 95%, 64%, and 77% for mnemonic, direct instruction, and free study, respectively. Thus, once again disabled learners acquired science facts more efficiently with mnemonic pictures than with other approaches.

Prose Learning.   Pictorial mnemonic techniques facilitate the expository prose learning of nonhandicapped adolescent learners. This claim holds whether the target information is concrete or abstract, whether there are few or many facts to be recalled, whether the mnemonic pictures consist of actual illustrations or student-generated images, whether students read or listen to texts, and whether performance is gauged in terms of an initial test administered immediately following passage presentation or in terms of a retest administered a few days later (Levin, Shriberg, & Berry, 1983; McCormick & Levin, 1984; McCormick, Levin, Cykowski, & Danilovics, 1984; McGivern, Peters, Levin, & Pressley, 1984; Shriberg, 1982; Shriberg, Levin, McCormick, & Pressley, 1982).

In a recent study of particular relevance to the present chapter, Peters and Levin (1984) demonstrated that prose-learning gains occur when inefficient information processors are instructed to use mnemonic imagery as they read. Eighth graders whose reading comprehension scores were well below grade level (viz., at or below the 35th percentile nationally) were randomly assigned to mnemonic and no-strategy control conditions. Students read 12 short passages taken from Shriberg et al. (1982, Experiment 3). Each passage described the purported accomplishment of a fictious person whose surname could be directly recoded as a common occupation (e.g., *King = a king, Taylor = a tailor, Fidler = a fiddler*). For instance, one of the passages was the following:

> Animal owners all over the world are impressed that Charlene Fidler has taught her pet cat how to count. The cat can count to 20 without making any mistakes. Moreover, the remarkable cat can do some simple addition (p. 239)

Mnemonic subjects were taught first to convert the surname of each person to its corresponding occupation keyword (e.g., *Fidler = a fiddler*), and then to imagine the keyword referent in interaction with the stated major accomplishment (here, *owned a counting cat*). Control subjects were told simply to try their best to remember the accomplishments associated with the people.

Mnemonic subjects outperformed controls by a 3 to 1 margin (averages of 63% and 21% correct, respectively) on an immediate test of name/accomplishment recall. A large difference in favor of mnemonic subjects was also obtained on a delayed posttest given a week later (33% vs. 13%). Thus, once again, an induced mnemonic strategy proved potent with inefficient learners—in this case, with poor comprehenders reading expository prose passages.

Concluding Comments. Pictorial mnemonic techniques increase inefficient learners' acquisition of materials that have an associative component. We are almost certain that even more impressive mnemonic applications will be devised in the near future, applications that are especially likely to aid inefficient learners. For instance, Ehri, Deffner, and Wilce (1984) have succeeded in using mnemonic-based materials to teach pre-readers letter/sound associations. Work currently in progress in our laboratories is dealing with the issue of how to adapt mnemonics so that they promote learning of very large chunks of prose (Levin, 1982). For a discussion of many potential mnemonic applications with the retarded, see Taylor and Turnure (1979).

At the same time, mnemonics researchers do not expect that mnemonic strategies can do all things for all people (e.g., Higbee, 1978; Levin & Pressley, 1985). Their obvious benefits seem to be tied to occasions when the task is to remember associations that have an arbitrary quality (at least initially in the eyes of the learner). Still, because no technique devised has ever done all things for all people, this hardly constitutes a limitation. What mnemonic elaboration does do, however—namely, facilitate people's memory for factual information—it does incredibly well!

Precise Elaboration of Arbitrary Texts

In the early 1970s, Turnure and his associates (e.g., Buium & Turnure, 1977; Turnure, Buium, & Thurlow, 1976) hypothesized that not all paired-associate verbal elaborations are equally facilitative—especially with retarded learners. Turnure believed that the richer the elaboration, the greater the learning of the otherwise arbitrarily paired items embedded in the elaborations. For example, paragraph elaborations were hypothesized to be more powerful than single sentence elaborations. Although such extended elaborations did not always prove to be more potent than simpler elaborations, whenever differences occurred they were in favor of extended elaborations (e.g., Thurlow & Turnure, 1972; Turnure & Walsh, 1971). Recently, interest in extended elaborations has been rekindled; but rather than emphasizing simple noun-pair learning as Turnure did, researchers pursuing this problem in the 1980s are emphasizing its relevance to some types of prose learning. An important concern is explaining why certain extended elaborations facilitate the learning of arbitrary relationships embedded in sentences, whereas other extended elaborations have no positive effect.

As mentioned earlier in this chapter, Bransford, Franks, and their associates (e.g., Bransford, Stein, Vye, Franks, Auble, Mezynski, & Perfetto, 1982) have presented sentences and prose passages that vary in the explicitness of rationales for relationships presented in the text. A main hypothesis of these investigators is that proficient learners realize that arbitrary text is difficult to learn and, hence, they generate precise elaborations that render the text sensible and more memorable. In contrast, inefficient learners are much less likely to do this, and for either of two reasons. First, they may not possess the requisite knowledge to generate rationales for the text-specified relationships. Alternatively, they may fail to produce a precise elaboration strategy. Because the text in these studies consists of simple content (i.e., content for which even inefficient learners have adequate background knowledge), it has been possible largely to rule out the first possibility. This permits an evaluation of the second notion (namely, that a "production deficiency" exists), as well as a study of procedures for overcoming precise-elaboration production deficits.

Stein, Bransford, Franks, Owings, Vye, and McGraw (1982, Experiment 1) presented fifth graders sentences containing arbitrary relationships (i.e., the *man* sentences discussed previously). The children were told to read each sentence and then generate an ending that would help them understand and remember which man did what. Decoding assistance was provided by the experimenter as needed, so that differences between good and poor readers could not be explained by differences in what they could read. A cued recall test followed presentation of eight *man* sentences, with questions of the following form: "Which man _____?" (e.g., *Which man used the paint brush?*).

As predicted, above-average readers (as defined by in-school reading achievement) generated more precise elaborations than did average readers, who generated a higher proportion of precise elaborations than did poor readers. Within each reading-achievement level, sentences that were precisely elaborated were recalled better than sentences that were elaborated in an imprecise fashion (i.e., elaborations that did not reduce the arbitrariness of the relationship mentioned in the sentence).

In a follow up experiment, Stein, Bransford, Franks, Owing, Vye, and McGraw (1982, Experiment 2) provided a new sample of below-average readers with training in the generation of precise elaborations. These subjects first elaborated a set of 10 pretest sentences and took a cued recall test on them, following procedures similar to the ones in the first experiment. As in that experiment, the below-average readers here provided precise elaborations for a low proportion (30%) of the sentences, and their recall was low (40%). Training consisted of pointing out to the learners that the sentences they had just studied were hard to learn. Then an effort was made to get these subjects to evaluate the arbitrariness of the just-studied sentences. For example, the experimenter presented *The kind man bought the milk*, and students were asked: "Is there any reason to mention that a *kind* man bought the milk rather than a *tall* man or a *mean* man?" Subjects were encouraged to analyze in this fashion all sentences presented to them. The experimenter also prompted them to think of reasons why the particular man performed the particular action. They were encouraged to activate knowledge about the particular type of man, in order to understand why this person would perform the particular action. Training continued with each of the 10 pretest sentences. Cuing by the experimenter was faded as students assumed the role of spontaneously asking themselves relevant questions and generating precise relations.[3]

After training, the below-average readers were given the criterion sentences used in Experiment 1, following the procedures employed there. They precisely elaborated 84% of these sentences and recalled 90% of them. Thus, with training, the precise-elaboration production deficiency disappeared—although a no-training, practice-only control group would have strengthened the conclusion that students' greater use of precise elaboration was due to the training.

Franks, Vye, Auble, Mezynski, Perfetto, Bransford, Stein, and Littlefield (1982, Experiment 1) investigated an alternative to promoting precise elaborative activity, extending the research to longer prose passages. On the initial learning trial, fifth-grade subjects were presented one of two versions of a passage describing two exemplars of a given theme (e.g., two types of robots). For the *explicit* version of the *robot* passage, one of the robots was described as follows:

> Billy went to visit his father at work. He saw the new robots that his father had made. Billy first looked at the robot that paints houses. It had a bucket on top of its head in order to carry paint. The robot was carrying a roll of tape to put on the windows to protect them from paint. It also had a sign with the words "Wet Paint" written on it. (p. 415)

In contrast, *implicit* passages did not include reasons for the relationships specified in the test. Here is the implicit-passage description of the same robot:

> Billy went to visit his father at work. He saw the new robots that his father had made. Billy first looked at the robot that paints houses. It had a bucket on top of its head. The robot was carrying a roll of tape. It also had a sign with some words on it. (p. 415)

Students read the *robot* passage out loud, with the experimenter assisting in decoding as necessary. After reading, the students were told to study the passage until they knew the relationships specified in it (e.g., which properties went with each robot). Learners were then tested on this first passage. After the test, a second two-exemplar passage was presented (the implicit version was used for all subjects). Subjects were instructed to read and study the passage in preparation for a recall test.

---

[3]The correspondence between the Stein, Bransford, Franks, Owings, Vye, and McGraw (1982) work and work on paired-associate elaboration can be appreciated by comparing Stein et al.'s training operations with the "interrogative" approach of Turnure and his associates. These latter investigators have demonstrated that retarded children benefit more from verbal elaborations when they are forced to answer questions about the relationships specified in the elaborations—questions that require explanations of the relationships, to make them seem less arbitrary (Buium & Turnure, 1977; Turnure, Buium, & Thurlow, 1976).

Explicit texts were found to be easier to learn than implicit texts. However, above-average readers realized this and adjusted their study activity accordingly, studying implicit texts for a longer time and explicit texts for a shorter time than they had taken to read those texts originally. Below-average readers studied very differently, studying explicit texts longer than implicit texts. With explicit texts the recall difference between above- and below-average readers was small, but there was a large difference between these two reader groups for the implicit texts. Most critically, above-average readers had high recall regardless of text type; below-average readers learned explicit texts well, but implicit texts poorly. Below-average readers' second-trial study/recall of the implicit text was not affected by whether they had studied an explicit or an implicit text on the first trial, as Franks et al. (1982) had thought it might. In other words, these students showed no evidence of spontaneous transfer. Thus, both the study-time and recall data suggested that the better readers precisely elaborated the implicit texts, but that the poorer readers did not. More exposure to an explicit text initially was not sufficient to promote inefficient readers' precise elaboration of implicit texts on a second trial.

In a second experiment, Franks et al. (1982, Experiment 2) trained below-average readers to perform precise elaborations on imprecise texts of the kind included in the just-described experiment. The training procedures were very similar to those used by Stein, Bransford, Franks, Owings, Vye, and McGraw (1982, Experiment 2), which were described previously. Training had a similar positive effect in this experiment, increasing both study time and recall.

Concluding Comments.   These precise-elaboration results parallel outcomes in the mnemonic associative-learning literature (Pressley, 1982). And well they should, given that the same mechanism mediates mnemonic associative elaboration and precise elaboration (viz. creating a meaningful context for arbitrarily paired materials). Providing precise elaborations increases the learning of subjects who do not produce precise elaborations spontaneously, just as providing mnemonic elaborations increases the learning of subjects who do not produce their own elaborations. Just as mnemonic elaboration can be taught, so can precise elaboration.

The precise-elaboration studies as a group yield extensive data on differences in the processing of better and poorer students. Yet, it must be kept in mind that the texts developed here—as well as those in the mnemonic prose domain— where tailor-made for studying subjects' acquisition of seemingly arbitrary relationships. Although we accept the argument that text relationships sometimes are arbitrary (e.g., Anderson, 1984; Anderson & Armbruster, 1984; Beck, 1984; Bransford, 1984), there are many texts that are not so conspicuously devoid of precise elaborations. Also, rarely are real-world reading materials composed of subsections that are so mutually interfering (but see McCormick et al., 1984). Fortunately, others interested in elaboration have studied the process more broadly conceived (i.e., using less restrictive text materials). We now turn to that work.

General Elaboration of Prose

When learners go beyond the information given in text, they are elaborating it. Elaboration include references, reorganizations that are more meaningful to the learners, and integrations with learners' prior knowledge (e.g., through the generation of associations). How is such elaboration accomplished? Three prominent means are: (1) by viewing pictorial adjuncts to prose; (2) by answering questions and self-interrogation; and (3) by using a variety of "generative" approaches while processing text (e.g., Wittrock, 1974). The latter approach includes the two preceding ones, as well as paraphrasing, summarizing, and relating the text to one's prior knowledge (see also Levin & Pressley, 1981). We begin by discussing general pictures-in-prose effects, where "pictures" refer to both experimenter-provided illustrations and learner-generated visual images that represent the text content.

Representational Illustrations and Imagery.   As a preliminary to the discussion of general picture effects, it is necessary to contrast what is included here with the mnemonic picture approaches reviewed earlier. *Representational* illustrations and images are completely faithful to (overlapping with) the content of a prose passage. For example, representational illustrations for Dickens's *Christmas Carol* could include a picture of Scrooge confronting the Ghost of Christmas Past, and one of Tiny Tim on Bob Cratchet's shoulder. Although such pictures might also add to the text by revealing that the Ghost of Christmas Present was much taller than Scrooge, had long red hair, and wore clothing associated with upper class 19th-century life, it is important to note that what is pictured is consistent with, and follows from, the character relations specified in the prose.

In contrast, *transformational* or mnemonic pictures go far beyond the text content as presented. Being especially well suited to the acquisition of difficult-to-remember material (Levin, 1981b), they involve a transformation of initially unfamiliar text elements into a more familiar, concrete form. Because readers have no previously established image of Charlene Fidler, for example, memory for her famous counting cat is facilitated by first linking her name with an acoustically similar word representing a familiar concrete concept—a fiddler in this case. A fiddler is then placed prominently in the picture, interacting with the counting cat. Because a fiddler in no way figured into the original prose, some distortion of the relationships specified in the text is required in order to construct mnemonic pictures. Such mnemonic images or illustrations are helpful for remembering Charlene Fidler's claim to fame because they provide a direct retrieval route from Charlene *Fidler* to the *fiddler,* which is linked to the *counting cat* in the interactive picture.

Although the effects of both transformational illustrations and transformational imagery have been consistently positive and of impressive magnitude, the conclusions are not so straightforward when it comes to considering the effects of representational pictures (Levin, 1981b). In the first place, the benefits typically are not as large. Secondly, the success of representational pictures often depends on whether "pictures" are defined by actual illustrations or by self-generated images.

There is absolutely no doubt that providing representational illustrations to nonhandicapped child learners as they *listen* to narrative prose passages increases their recall of the pictured content (Levin, 1981b; Levin & Lesgold, 1978). This statement also applies to inefficient learners (e.g., Bender & Levin, 1978; Riding & Shore, 1974; Rohwer & Harris, 1975; Rohwer & Matz, 1975). Why such facilitation occurs is not precisely understood. Part, but not all, of the effect is due to simple repetition in the picture of the information presented in the prose (e.g., Levin, Bender, & Lesgold, 1976; Turner, 1984). The additional advantage associated with representational illustrations has been assumed to result from the to-be-learned information becoming more concrete and specific (Levin, 1981b). Moreover, if passages deal with abstract concepts, or if passages are vague with respect to content interrelationships, *interpretational* pictures (Levin, 1981b) can provide additional information not only that is consistent with the relationships specified in the text, but that is capable of clarifying them (e.g., Arnold & Brooks, 1976; Bransford & Johnson, 1972; Royer & Cable, 1976; Steingart & Glock, 1979).

Recent reviews of the literature also support the conclusion that imposed illustrations generally contribute to moderate recall increases for nonhandicapped learners *reading* prose passages (e.g., Haring & Fry, 1981; Levie & Lentz, 1982; Readence & Moore, 1981; Schallert, 1980). With inefficient readers, the small amount of data available are much more mixed, ranging from positive picture effects (e.g., DeRose, 1976) to no picture effects (e.g., Rohwer & Harris, 1975) to negative picture effects (e.g., Harber, 1983). A recurrent speculation is that illustrations distract inefficient readers from the printed text and, hence, their time spent dealing with the critical text content and relationships is reduced (see Harber, 1980, 1983, for the most recent version of this argument as applied to LD students).

We believe that the data and arguments bearing on inefficient readers' inability to benefit from illustrations while reading are unconvincing for a couple of reasons. First, in some of the studies cited as negative evidence, the illustrations provided bear little or no resemblance to the text content; that is, they do not qualify as representational pictures because they lack a text-overlapping quality (see Levin & Lesgold, 1978). In many studies, it is impossible to determine from the authors' descriptions whether the illustrations provided were or were not appropriately representational and, thus, picture failures may be due at least in part to inappropriate picture operationalizations. It is well known, for example, that when young children are presented narrative passages, the kind of pictures provided can dramatically affect whether or not learning benefits are observed (e.g., Digdon, Pressley, & Levin, 1985; Pressley, Levin, Pigott, LeComte, & Hope, 1983; Pressley, Pigott, & Bryant, 1982). Second, in studies where inefficient readers are being used to assess the effects of text-embedded illustrations, poor word-decoding abilities probably contribute greatly to the results obtained. Students who cannot decode cannot capitalize on pictures to improve their recall of what was not decoded (e.g., Bluth, 1972; Harber, 1983). See Levin (1973) and Rohwer and Harris (1975) for a similar argument concerning the insufficiency of pictures *by themselves* as text facilitators.

In short, with inefficient readers who lack adequate decoding skills, one cannot interpret the unsuccessful picture attempts as evidence against the benefits of pictures as reading comprehension adjuncts—a point that is elaborated in the discussion of self-generated imagery effects. When texts are appropriately geared to the reading level of the inefficient comprehender—as when nondisabled young children read primer passages—positive illustration effects have been documented. In summary, then, whether or not imposed illustrations can positively affect inefficient readers' comprehension is a question that requires additional experimental evaluation before definitive conclusions can be reached.

As far as self-generated visual imagery is concerned, nonhandicapped learners younger than 8 years of age do not benefit from instructions to construct internal imaginal representations of text content. Moreover, even with older nonhandicapped learners, representational imagery instructions do not produce effects as consistently positive or as large in magnitude as the effects associated with representational illustrations (see Levie & Lentz, 1982; and Levin, 1981b). Levin speculated that internally generated representational images result in weak and variable memory traces that do not add much to an already meaningfully interpreted text. This is in contrast to the presumed stronger, more reliable, traces produced by experimenter-provided illustrations.

On the other hand, for learners who do not spontaneously interpret text in a meaningful organized fashion, generating internal images of the within-text relationships might be expected to serve a particularly useful *organizational* function (Levin, 1981b). Levin (1973) assessed this notion by comparing the effects of an induced visual imagery strategy in two types of inefficient fourth-grade readers. One type exhibited below-average reading *comprehension* even though their reading *vocabulary* was in the normal range. Students with this profile of reading skills have been labeled *difference-poor* readers (Wiener & Cromer, 1967). Difference-poor readers presumably do not construct well-organized representations of a prose passage, even though they can decode it adequately. Levin (1973) reasoned that instructions to generate representational images might aid difference-poor readers, to the extent that the construction of such images involves organizing text information to reflect the meaning contained in the passage. Readers with more fundamental reading problems such as vocabulary deficiencies and/or decoding problems (Wiener & Cromer's, 1967, "deficit-poor" readers) would not be expected to benefit from an organizational reading strategy per se because they cannot adequately process the text even on a word-by-word basis.

In the conditions of the Levin (1973) study that are relevant here, the two types of poor readers read two 12-sentence narrative passages, with short-answer questions posed immediately after the completion of reading. The students were instructed either to read the passages while forming images of each sentence's content, or just to read the passages. As anticipated, the difference-poor readers benefited from the organizational imagery strategy, whereas the deficit-poor readers did not.

Replications and extensions of this work have been reported by Dillingofski (1980) and by Evans and Kerst (1983). In the latter study, for example, fifth-grade difference-poor readers again benefited from an induced imagery prose-learning strategy, whereas their deficit-poor counterparts did not. However, when deficit-poor readers were presented passages with simplified vocabulary, their reading performance was facilitated (especially when combined with induced imagery instructions). Such results are consistent with the assumption about the different sources of reading difficulty associated with the two reader types; that is, only when the passage vocabulary was within their respective word-recognition limits could the two different types of inefficient readers benefit from an organizational imagery strategy.

That LD students may also benefit from a representational imagery strategy for prose passages matched to their reading level is suggested by recent data reported by Rose, Cundick, and Higbee (1983). In that study, 8- to 10-year-old LD children who were given imagery instructions learned more from such passages than did control subjects who were told to try hard to remember what they read. Whether or not such findings are generalizable to similar populations and situations is uncertain, however, inasmuch as Bender and Levin (1978) and Warner and Alley (1981) found no evidence of prose-learning representational imagery facilitation with LD junior high school students and 10- to 16-year-old EMR students, respectively. The results of the latter two studies suggest that in some cases more than simple instructional manipulations are needed. In addition to vocabulary simplifications and other text modifications (e.g., Cromer, 1970; Evans & Kerst, 1983), learners could be given extensive systematic instruction in the application of strategies specially tailored to overcome their specific processing inefficiencies.

Questioning Strategies.   Asking people questions about what they are reading can improve their comprehension and recall of a prose passage. Questioning also plays a central role in a number of treatments that improve the prose processing of inefficient learners. Sometimes the questions are posed externally; other times the learners are taught to pose their own questions. A survey of recent research provides a catalog of both ways elaborative external questioning can be used to increase students' comprehension and of ways to increase students' elaborative *self-questioning* (see also Cook & Mayer, 1983).

There is a long history of placing questions in text and evaluating learning gains produced by those adjunct questions (e.g., Anderson & Biddle, 1975; Rothkopf, 1965), although most of this research has been conducted with adults. On the other hand, questioning effects have not been ignored entirely by researchers interested in children (see Pressley & Forrest-Pressley, 1985, for a review). There have been a number of studies comparing the use of questions that require verbatim or lower order recall and that of questions that require recall of higher order information—information that requires elaboration of information, including inferences and integrations (for an interesting recent example with adults, see Benton, Glover, & Bruning, 1983). Although there have been debates about the relative potency of lower and higher level questions (e.g., Winne, 1979), sensitive analysis of the available data favors higher level questioning, with small but consistent differences in favor of elaborative questioning (e.g., Redfield & Rousseau, 1981).

Several researchers have asked whether having inefficient learners answer elaborative questions about a prose passage improves their memory for its contents. Before touching on some illustrative studies, we offer three general concerns about research in this area. First, in many studies in which questions have been compared with no-questions control treatments, subjects in the questions condition have received more study time and/or exposure to the prose passage. We recognize that this is a problem that frequently occurs in a variety of research on processing adjuncts to text (see discussions by Faw & Waller, 1976; Levin, 1981b), and we do not mean to single out the questioning studies as being uniquely blameworthy. Nonetheless, such extra-time and extra-exposure confoundings cloud straightforward interpretations of these studies.

A second concern is that following questioning treatments or training, researchers have often made inferences about students' use of questioning strategies on the basis of students' recall data, rather than on the basis of more direct measures (such as behaviors indicative of self-questioning, changes in patterns of processing, and self-reports of strategy use). Reliance on these more direct measures would bolster conclusions about treatments changing learners' processing in the ways that the researchers presume. See Butterfield, Siladi, and Belmont (1980) for extensive commentary on the analytical gains associated with obtaining more direct measures of learners' processing.

Our third concern here is that in many studies questioning constitutes only part of a larger "package" of elaborative strategies. Thus, whether or not questioning is the strategy responsible for any obtained positive effects often cannot be discerned. Though tentatively tantalizing, such multicomponent strategy packages must be decomposed experimentally before the "active ingredients" can be pinpointed.

With these three concerns in mind, then, we mention some research studies that point to the potential of questioning as an effective prose-learning strategy for the inefficient learner. Wong's (1980) study is cited widely as supporting the position that questioning increases the elaborative processing and recall of text by LD students. In that study, the learners were presented sentences such as *My brother fell down on the playground.* When recall of the sentences was tested for by presenting the last noun of the sentence (i.e., *playground* for this example) and the implied consequence of the action (*skinned his knee*), second-grade LD children recalled 28% of the sentences and sixth-grade LD children recalled 39%. However, if the children answered the question "What do you think happened next?" as they studied the sentences, recall was considerably greater (72% for second graders and 76% for sixth graders). Questioning induced elaboration of the study sentences, elaboration that did not occur without questioning. This elaboration presumably resulted in greater compatibility of study and test cues in the questioning condition than in the no-questioning condition and, thus, increased recall.

Rickards and Hatcher (1978) also hypothesized that answering integrative higher order questions might increase the learning of inefficient learners. They reasoned that because poor comprehenders often read word by word and fail to organize and structure what they read, questions that require poor learners to interrelate passage details and ideas should promote comprehension and recall (see our previous discussion of "difference-poor" readers). To assess this hypothesis, fifth-grade readers with comprehension difficulties read an 800-word passage. The passage contained either questions that required relating passage details to a main theme of the passage ("higher order" questions), questions that required recall of only one specific detail ("verbatim" questions), or no questions (control). In general, overall learning (as evidenced by correct responses on a short-answer posttest) was facilitated only slightly by higher order questions (relative to both verbatim questions and no questions). The only strikingly positive result was that recall of one type of information was doubled by answering the higher order questions, namely, subordinate information that had to be used in answering the higher order questions presented during study.

Do modest benefits, such as those produced by Rickards and Hatcher (1978), suggest pessimism regarding the potential benefits of higher order questioning for inefficient learners? Not necessarily. The children in that study were required to respond to the higher order questions without the benefit of previous practice or training in how to do so effectively. Moreover, no measures were taken of whether the children actually could or did respond to such questions (or of *which* questions each student correctly answered). As a result, one cannot determine whether the only modest success was due to the ineffectiveness of the strategy or to the ineffectiveness of the strategy *implementation* procedures. Recent data indicate that grade-school children who are poor readers have difficulty answering integrative questions without specific instruction in how to find answers to such queries (Raphael & McKinney, 1982; Raphael, Wonnacott, & Pearson, 1981).

In these two studies, Raphael and her associates demonstrated that when poor comprehenders are taught that answering higher order questions requires integration across sentences or paragraphs, they can respond to such questions appropriately (thereby improving their comprehension of the text). In the remaining studies of this section, the students received a fair amount of practice answering elaborative questions before the critical dependent measures were taken; and as will be seen, questioning effects have been consistently positive in these instances.

Hansen and Pearson (1983) demonstrated that it is possible to increase fourth-grade poor readers' inferential comprehension by using a procedure that included questioning as a major component. This was operationalized by the teacher first probing the students about their knowledge of the world, and how such knowledge might relate to the subsequent text (see Levin & Pressley's, 1981, discussion of this type of "stage-setting strategy"). Then, specific questions about the text were provided. Consider, for example, a prototypical discussion before the presentation of a text about conservation (Hansen & Pearson, 1983):

> *Teacher*: What is it that we have been doing before we discuss each story?
> *Focus of responses:* We talk about our lives and we predict what will happen in the stories.
> *Teacher*: Why do we make these comparisons?
>
> *Focus of responses:* These comparisons will help us understand the stories.
>
> *Teacher:* Last week I asked you to think about a social studies lesson on Japan. Today, pretend that you are reading a science article about conservation. What might you be thinking about while you are reading the article?
>
> *Gist of responses:* Students relate personal experiences with conservation and explain how the experiences would be related to a text (e.g., students talked about how their families heat with wood to conserve oil, and they wanted to find out how the Japanese conserve oil). (p. 238)

The main goal of this pretext questioning was to help the poor readers develop a strategy for probing themselves about how the text might relate to information that they already possessed.

After the introduction that focused on the children's prior knowledge, passage-specific questions were posed. The students were again encouraged to think about the questions in terms of their own experiences, resulting in specific predictions about information that the passage might contain. After the children in this treatment condition read the text, they were given 10 inference questions for discussion, questions that required the use of information not explicitly stated in the text but that could be obtained by integrating the text with their prior knowledge. The discussion format used to present these inference questions provided plenty of modeling of inferential-answering procedures and feedback about adequacy of answers.

Control subjects read the same stories, following procedures suggested in teachers' manuals. Because comprehension training typically is not recommended by these sources (Durkin, 1981), the control subjects' pre-reading period was shorter than it was in the experimental condition. It consisted of brief previewing of the story by the teacher. After reading each training text, control subjects were presented eight verbatim ("literal") and two inference questions for discussion, reflecting the ratio of literal/inference questions usually included in reading instruction (e.g., Hodges, 1980). Thus, in comparison to the control condition, the experimental treatment differed in at least two important ways: Experimental subjects related their prior experiences to the text; they were given more extensive practice answering inference questions.

All the data collected in the study were consistent with the conclusion that the experimental treatment increased comprehension. For instance, after each training passage was read and discussed, there was a posttest containing both literal and inference questions. The recall of experimental subjects exceeded that of control subjects, with the effects more pronounced on the inference questions. At the conclusion of training, subjects in both conditions read two stories without prompting either to self-question or to relate the text to their prior knowledge. Again, experimental subjects recalled more text content than did control subjects, with the effects more pronounced on the inferential questions than on the literal questions. The data provided by Hansen and Pearson (1983) encourage the conclusion that the combined prior-knowledge and inferential-questioning training promoted a more active approach to students' text processing.

In comparison to the instructional procedures of Hansen and Pearson (1983), others have incorporated more explicit directions to learners to internalize interrogative processing. For example, Wong and Jones (1982) reported an ambitious effort to teach a self-questioning prose-learning strategy to eighth- and ninth-grade LD students. These investigators taught their experimental subjects how to ask themselves questions, and to respond to them as they read text and carried out self-instructions relevant to the text. They were first taught to ask themselves: "What are you studying this passage for?" Subjects were taught to find main ideas in the text, to underline them, and to think of good questions about those main ideas. They were also taught to remember the answers to their questions. As they proceeded through the text, students were instructed to think back to their previous questions and answers, and to see how each successive question and answer provided additional information. This aspect of training clearly encouraged integrative processing. Students who were taught this self-questioning procedure remembered more text content than did control subjects who read the passages without having been given any specific processing strategy.

The promise of combined self-interrogation and self-instruction strategies has been demonstrated in other laboratories as well. One of these was a study by

Palincsar and Brown (1984). The study involved seventh graders with comprehension, but not decoding, difficulties. Experimental subjects received extensive instruction over 20 days, instruction aimed at increasing comprehension. The subjects were taught to predict what might be coming in a story, as well as to summarize and pose questions about text. These skills were developed through one-to-one student/teacher interactions, in the form of a game in which the student and teacher took turns leading a dialogue. In these dialogues, a number of mechanisms were used to induce summarizing, questioning, predicting, and clarifying. Thus, when a new passage was presented, the learner was asked to predict passage content based on the title, as well as how the passage might relate to his/her prior knowledge. After presentation of the text, the student recalled the topic and several important points in the passage. As reading proceeded, the teacher and student would take turns asking questions, summarizing, and offering predictions and clarifications. The student was frequently prompted to guess what question a teacher might ask. Higher order inferential questioning was encouraged. Extensive modeling and feedback about appropriate questioning occurred throughout passage study. An important aspect of the treatment was that students were explicitly instructed to use their acquired strategies as they read.

In general, Palincsar and Brown's (1984) experimental subjects comprehended better after training than before, with their prose recall exceeding that of no-strategy control subjects. These comprehension gains also transferred to in-class reading: Comprehension of social studies and science materials read in class was better in the experimental children than in the control children. The control subjects in this study were given no special one-to-one attention, and neither were they exposed to the materials that the experimental subjects read during training. Thus, in addition to treatment-related effects, it is possible that the results are due in part to Hawthorne effects, practice effects, or both. Fortunately, in a very recently completed study, Palincsar (1984) obtained similar outcomes when controls were included to alleviate the Hawthorne and practice problems.

In summary, a variety of question-based interventions have been hypothesized to increase inefficient comprehenders' comprehension of text by increasing their elaboration of it (i.e., their integration of text with prior knowledge, their inferences about text propositions, and other efforts directed toward understanding within-text relationships). Although all the results cited in this section are consistent with concluding that question-based strategies are effective, additional research on questioning is needed for at least four reasons: (1) As was discussed earlier, some of the questioning treatments must be evaluated against more stringent control treatments, with more direct processing measures taken both during and after treatment administration; (2) comprehension instruction is usually neglected in the classroom, with poorer readers often receiving less systematic comprehension instruction than better readers (Pearson & Gallagher, 1983)! Additional research on questioning as a comprehension strategy would serve to showcase its potential value for the nonquestioning inefficient prose processor; (3) many comprehension strategies that are widely cited in the traditional curriculum and instruction literature, such as SQ3R (Robinson, 1961), contain questioning as a prominent component of the strategy. As educational psychologists who believe that empirical evaluation is a necessary component of strategy development (Levin & Pressley, 1983), we find it disturbing that approaches such as SQ3R have not been carefully evaluated (see Cook & Mayer, 1983, and Forrest-Pressley & Gillies, 1983, for detailed commentary on this point); (4) new and ambitious comprehension-training programs continue to be implemented that include questioning and self-questioning strategies very similar to the ones considered in this section. Space considerations permit description and discussion of only one of these programs here, but the example makes clear the real-world relevance of elaborative-questioning research.

The goal of the Kamehameha Early Education Program (KEEP) is to discover and evaluate ways of improving the educational achievement of Hawaiian children, a population known to be at risk for educational failure in terms of American standards of success. KEEP personnel have recently developed and evaluated a comprehension-oriented primary reading curriculum (Tharpe, 1982). At the heart of the program is elaborative questioning. When a text is introduced, the teacher asks children questions that activate memories of their own experiences with elements mentioned in the text. Then the teacher presents a question for the children to consider as they process the text. After reading is completed, the teacher continues asking questions, ranging from verbatim to higher order inquiries. Although no effort is made to teach children to internalize self-questioning or the processes that follow self-questioning (see Hansen & Pearson, 1983), the daily regimen of questioning reportedly has a long-term impact on cognitive functioning. Reading achievement is increased over levels associated with traditional reading instruction (Tharpe, 1982, Experiments 2 & 3), as well as over reading instruction with a decoding emphasis (Tharpe, 1982, Experiment 1). As with other elaborative-questioning research, additional evaluations are needed. Just *how* does the processing of KEEP children differ from the processing of students taught by traditional methods? Would the KEEP approach be even more potent if self-regulative questioning (e.g., Wong & Jones, 1982) were added to it?

Generative Approaches to Text Comprehension.   The final approach considered here involves a combination of elaborative strategies thought to stimulate active information processing on the part of the learner. Wittrock (e.g, Linden & Wittrock, 1981; Wittrock, 1981) argues that prose learning can be optimized by such "generative" activities as relating one's knowledge and experiences to text, by forming associations to text, and by deriving abstractions and inferences from text. Other generative activities include the construction of headings and subheadings, titles, questions, objectives, summaries, inferences, analyses, syntheses, metaphors, images, and paraphrases. Teachers or texts can encourage generative learning by providing elaborations that take these same forms (Wittrock, 1981). As should be clear from the studies reviewed in this chapter and elsewhere (e.g., Cook & Mayer, 1983; Levin & Pressley, 1981), the value of generative activities for all types of learners has received consistent empirical support.

Research reported by Wittrock points to the potential worth of generative-learning strategies in populations of inefficient learners (e.g., Doctorow, Wittrock, & Marks, 1978; Wittrock, 1981). As was mentioned in relation to other strategies described in this chapter, however, in many of these "generative activities" studies there is no attempt to isolate the specific strategies and strategy components that are the effective contributors to the success of multicomponent strategy packages. Nonetheless, a multicomponent generative approach may prove to be an effective way of dealing with the "inactive learner" (Torgesen, 1977); and various "strategy-training" programs have been implemented to enhance the learning performance of such populations as low-ability military recruits (Wittrock, 1984), as well as low-achieving college students (e.g., Dansereau, 1984; Snowman, Krebs, & Lockhart, 1980) and children in the Chicago public schools (Jones, 1984). Getting these individuals to use the various strategies properly (and in the proper sequence) may require that methods be developed to ensure adequate self-monitoring and self-regulation of the specific strategy components. We expand our thinking on the topics of self-monitoring and self-regulation in the final following section.

CLOSING COMMENTS

Strategy researchers have only begun the task of creating interventions for inefficient learners. The evidence presented here, however, provides abundant motivation for the continued development of effective learning strategies. Strategies often greatly assist the child with learning difficulties, and although comparisons with nonhandicapped learners were given little attention in this chapter, one comparison with such individuals should not go unmentioned: *Strategic interventions frequently raise the performance of handicapped learners to the level attained by nonhandicapped learners* (e.g., Franks et al., 1982; Levin, 1973; McGivern & Levin, 1983; Stein, Bransford, Franks, Owings, Vye, & McGraw, 1982; Wong, 1980). Thus, the "poor" learner need not be doomed to an intellectually impoverished state relative to his or her "normal" peers.

There are many potential dimensions on which the interventions reviewed in this chapter could be compared. One dimension that we consider important is the degree of external support required to provide benefits for the learner. Often children can be "induced" (Levin, 1972) through instruction to execute on their own strategies that they would not otherwise employ, such as when children are instructed to generate internal visual images that improve their learning (see also Pressley, Heisel, McCormick, & Nakamura, 1982). In contrast, children can be provided external mediators that mirror what they would have produced internally if they had used a strategy (Levin, 1972, dubbed this the "imposed" approach— short for "externally imposed" mediators). Providing illustrations is an imposed intervention. Finally, some of the approaches reviewed here were "partially imposed, partially induced." For instance, Wong and Jones (1982) provided learners with questions and statements that led to changes in text processing. One hypothesis that follows from developmental research is that the more capable the learner, the less external support required to produce efficient processing and good performance (Pressley, 1982; Rohwer, 1973). That there likely are individual differences in the "support" requirements of different inefficient learners creates some interesting challenges for strategy researchers. For instance, when can a strategy be induced, and with whom? Also, when is an imposed strategy effective if it cannot be induced (see, for example, Pressley, Forrest-Pressley, Elliott-Faust, & Miller, 1985)?

Most of the studies reported here did not deal with an espoused goal of many strategy interventionists—that of producing learners who employ strategies broadly, appropriately, and without external prompting (e.g., Brown, 1980). What does it take to produce this type of independent learner? It probably requires the mix of ingredients discussed at the beginning of the chapter: strategies, metastrategy information, and monitoring (see also Pressley, Forrest-Pressley, Elliott-Faust & Miller, 1985). Although we do not yet know how to produce this mix in inefficient learners, we have some hunches. Before offering them, however, we indicate some new research directions that may provide definitive information about how to produce independently efficient learners.

To date there has been little research on which aspects of strategy knowledge to emphasize during instructional training (O'Sullivan & Pressley, 1984; Pressley, Borkowski, & O'Sullivan, 1984, 1985), except that strategy durability is increased by adding strategy utility information to instruction (e.g., Kennedy & Miller, 1976). Even if we knew which aspects of metastrategy information to emphasize, work has only begun on how to add this information to instruction (e.g., O'Sullivan & Pressley, in press; Pressley, Levin, & Ghatala, 1984). Also, there are few studies of monitoring training (Elliott-Faust & Pressley, 1984; Ghatala, Levin, Pressley, & Lodico, 1984; Lodico, Ghatala, Levin, Pressley, & Bell, 1983; Markman & Gorin, 1981; Pressley, Ross, Levin, & Ghatala, 1984). Perhaps most distressing from the point of view of this chapter is that none of this research has focused on the inefficient learner.

More optimistically, there have been a few attempts to provide inefficient learners with instruction that lumps strategy instruction, knowledge about strategies, and monitoring into packages. Palincsar and Brown (1984) provided one such attempt. As the reader may recall, that procedure did lead to generalized improvements in comprehension (i.e., in the classroom as well as in the laboratory), as would be expected based on the model of efficient strategy use detailed in this chapter. The reader should note as well that relative to the amount of instruction provided in most other studies, very lengthy instruction was required to produce those generalized strategy gains.

That a lengthy intervention is needed to produce independent use of even simple strategies by inefficient learners can be appreciated further by considering a recent study by Gelzheiser (1984). Learning-disabled junior high school students were taught category-organizational strategies for list learning (i.e., sorting, studying by category, clustering during recall) in such a way that strategy use was transferred to the learning of prose that contained categorizable information. The training included a good deal of information about organizational strategies, with particular emphasis on the defining characteristics of tasks that are amenable to such strategies. A type of monitoring was also included, with frequent graphing of recall and the experimenter forcing the subject to note the connection between list recall and strategy use. The training included strategy application to different types of lists, and it extended over five 20-minute sessions. One hundred minutes of instruction were provided to produce successful transfer of a strategy from materials used during training to new materials, but ones that were "rigged" so that the strategy would be readily applicable to them. Additional work needs to be done before a claim can be made that it is possible to teach strategies in such a way that they will generalize across a wide range of materials.

Even though strategy interventionists do not know for sure how to train students so as to produce generalized and self-regulated use of strategies, there are educated guesses about how to do so based on extrapolations from related research, experimenter and teacher intuitions, and theoretical convictions—such as the belief that strategy training should include the three components mentioned throughout this chapter (see also Campione, Brown, & Ferrara, 1982). Deshler, Alley, Warner, and Schumaker (1981) developed such a list of educated guesses for the training of LD children. Their recommendations include, among others: (a) fully explaining the strategy, including each step of the procedure; (b) pointing out the advantages of applying the strategy; (c) modeling of the strategy by the teacher; (d) verbal and behavioral rehearsal of the strategy by the learner; (e) training with a variety of materials presented by (f) a variety of agents in (g) a variety of settings with (h) conditions varied greatly over the course of the training; (i) student assessment of how their performance improves when they use the strategy; and (j) explicitly telling the students to generalize the strategy to other situations. Given the recent explosion of interest in the question of how best to produce independently strategic learners (e.g., Brown et al., 1983; Campione et al., 1982; Pressley & Dennis-Rounds, 1980), we expect that the effects of these strategy-training recommendations (both alone and in combination) will be thoroughly researched in the next decade.

ACKNOWLEDGMENTS

The work represented here was funded by a grant to the first author from the Natural Sciences and Engineering Council of Canada and to the second author from the National Institute of Education through the Wisconsin Center for Education Research. The second author's work was facilitated by a Romnes Faculty Fellowship awarded by the Graduate School of the University of Wisconsin.

REFERENCES

Anderson, R. C. (1984). Role of the reader's schema in comprehension, learning and memory. In R. C. Anderson, J. Osborn, & R. J. Tierney (Eds.), *Learning to read in American schools: Basal readers and content texts.* Hillsdale, NJ: Lawrence Erlbaum Associates.

Anderson, R. C., & Biddle, W. B. (1975). On asking people questions about what they are reading. In G. Bower (Ed.), *The psychology of learning and motivation* (Vol. 9, pp. 90–132). New York: Academic Press.

Anderson, T. H., & Armbruster, B. B. (1984). Content area textbooks. In R. C. Anderson, J. Osborn, & R. J. Tierney (Eds.), *Learning to read in American schools: Basal readers and content texts.* Hillsdale, NJ: Lawrence Erlbaum Associates.

Arnold, D. J., & Brooks, P. H. (1976). Influence of contextual organizing material on children's listening comprehension. *Journal of Educational Psychology, 68,* 711–716.

Atkinson, R. C. (1975). Mnemotechnics in second-language learning. *American Psychologist, 30,* 821–828.

Bauer, R. H. (1977). Memory processes in children with learning disabilities. *Journal of Experimental Child Psychology, 24,* 415–430.

Bauer, R. H. (1979). Memory acquisition and category clustering in learning disabled children. *Journal of Experimental Child Psychology, 27,* 365–383.

Beck, I. L. (1984). Developing comprehension: The impact of the directed reading lesson. In R. C. Anderson, J. Osborn, & R. J. Tierney (Eds.), *Learning to read in American schools: Basal readers and content texts.* Hillsdale, NJ: Lawrence Erlbaum Associates.

Becker, W. C., Engelmann, S., Carnine, D. W., & Maggs, A. (1982). Direct instruction technology: Making learning happen. In P. Karoly & J. J. Steffen (Eds.), *Improving children's competence: Advances in child behavioral analysis and therapy* (Vol. 1, pp. 151–204). Lexington, MA: Heath.

Bender, B. G., & Levin, J. R. (1978). Pictures, imagery, and retarded children's prose learning. *Journal of Educational Psychology, 70,* 583–588.

Benton, S. L., Glover, J. A., & Bruning, R. H. (1983). Levels of processing: Effect of number of decisions on prose recall. *Journal of Educational Psychology, 75,* 382–390.

Berry, J. K. (1982). Unpublished doctoral research in progress. University of Wisconsin, Madison.

Bluth, L. F. (1972). *A comparison of the reading comprehension of good and poor readers in the second grade with and without illustrations.* Unpublished doctoral dissertation, University of Illinois, Champaign.

Bos, C. S., & Filip, D. (1982). Comprehension monitoring skills in learning disabled and average students. *Topics in Learning and Learning Disabilities, 2,* 79–86.

Bransford, J. D. (1984). Schema activation and schema acquisition: Comments on Richard C. Anderson's remarks. In R. C. Anderson, J. Osborn, & R. J. Tierney (Eds.), *Learning to read in American schools: Basal readers and content texts.* Hillsdale, NJ: Lawrence Erlbaum Associates.

Bransford, J. D., & Johnson, M. K. (1972). Contextual prerequisites for understanding: Some investigations of comprehension and recall. *Journal of Verbal Learning and Verbal Behavior, 11*, 717–726.

Bransford, J. D., Stein, B. S., Vye, N. J., Franks, J. J., Auble, P. M., Mezynski, K. J., & Perfetto, G. A. (1982). Differences in approaches to learning: An overview. *Journal of Experimental Psychology: General, 111*, 390–398.

Brown, A. L. (1980). Metacognitive development and reading. In R. J. Spiro, B. C. Bruce, & W. F. Brewer (Eds.), *Theoretical issues in reading comprehension* (pp. 453–481). Hillsdale, NJ: Lawrence Erlbaum Associates.

Brown, A. L., Bransford, J. D., Ferrara, R. A., & Campione, J. C. (1983). Learning, remembering, and understanding. In J. H. Flavell & E. M. Markman (Eds.), *Handbook of child psychology: Vol. 3. Cognitive development* (pp. 77–166). New York: Wiley.

Brown, A. L., & Smiley, S. S. (1978). The development of strategies for studying text. *Child Development, 49*, 1076–1088.

Büchel, F. P. (1982). Metacognitive variables in the learning of written text. In A. Flammer & W. Kintsch (Eds.), *Discourse processing* (pp. 352–359). Amsterdam: North–Holland.

Buium, N., & Turnure, J. E. (1977). A cross-cultural study of verbal elaboration productivity and memory in young children. *Child Development, 48*, 296–300.

Butkowski, I. S., & Willows, D. M. (1980). Cognitive–motivational characteristics of children varying in reading ability: Evidence for learned helplessness in poor readers. *Journal of Educational Psychology, 72*, 408–422.

Butterfield, E. C., Siladi, D., & Belmont, J. M. (1980). Validating theories of intelligence. In H. W. Reese & L. P. Lipsett (Eds.), *Advances in child development and behavior* (Vol. 15, pp. 95–162). New York: Academic Press.

Campione, J. C., Brown, A. L., & Ferrara, R. A. (1982). Mental retardation and intelligence. In R. J. Sternberg (Ed.), *Handbook of human intelligence* (pp. 392–490). Cambridge, England: Cambridge University Press.

Capelli, C. A., & Markman, E. M. (1982). Suggestions for training comprehension monitoring. *Topics in Learning and Learning Disabilities, 2*, 87–96.

Carnine, D., & Silbert, J. (1979). *Direct instruction reading*. Columbus, OH: Merrill.

Cohen, R. L. (1983). Reading disabled children are aware of their cognitive deficits. *Journal of Learning Disabilities, 16*, 286–289.

Cook, L. K., & Mayer, R. E. (1983). Reading strategies training for meaningful learning from prose. In M. Pressley & J. R. Levin (Eds.), *Cognitive strategy research: Educational applications* (pp. 87–131). New York: Springer–Verlag.

Cromer, W. (1970). The difference model: A new explanation for some reading difficulties. *Journal of Educational Psychology, 61*, 471–483.

Cullen, J. L., & Boersma, F. J. (1982). The influence of coping strategies on the manifestation of learned helplessness. *Contemporary Educational Psychology, 7*, 346–356.

Dallago, M. L. L., & Moely, B. E. (1980). Free recall in boys of normal and poor reading levels as a function of task manipulations. *Journal of Experimental Child Psychology, 30*, 62–78.

Dansereau, D. F. (1984, April). *Development and evaluation of computer-based learning strategy training modules*. Paper presented at the annual meeting of the American Educational Research Association, New Orleans.

DeRose, T. M. (1976). *The effects of verbally and pictorially induced and imposed strategies on children's reading comprehension*. Unpublished doctoral dissertation, University of Wisconsin, Madison.

Deshler, D. D., Alley, G. R., Warner, M. M., & Schumaker, J. B. (1981). Instructional practices for promoting skill acquisition and generalization in severely learning disabled adolescents. *Learning Disability Quarterly, 4*, 415–421.

Digdon, N., Pressley, M., & Levin, J. R. (1985). Preschoolers' learning when pictures do not tell the whole story. *Educational Communication and Technology Journal, 33,* 125–138.

Dillingofski, M. S. (1980). *The effects of imposed and induced visual imagery stategies on ninth-grade difference poor readers' literal comprehension of concrete and abstract prose.* Unpublished doctoral dissertation, University of Wisconsin, Madison.

Doctorow, M. J., Wittrock, M. C., & Marks, C. B. (1978). Generative processes in reading comprehension. *Journal of Educational Psychology, 70,* 109–118.

Durkin, D. (1981). Do basal manuals teach reading comprehension? In R. C. Anderson, J. Osborn, & R. J. Tierney (Eds.), *Learning to read in American schools: Basal readers and content texts* (pp. 29–38). Hillsdale, NJ: Lawrence Erlbaum Associates.

Ehri, L. C., Deffner, N. D., & Wilce, L. S. (1984). Pictorial mnemonics for phonics. *Journal of Educational Psychology, 76,* 880–893.

Elliot-Faust, D. J., & Pressley, M. (1984, April). *The "delusion of comprehension" phenomena in young children: An instructional approach to promoting listening comprehension monitoring capabilities.* Paper presented at the annual meeting of the American Educational Research Association, New Orleans.

Evans, R. A., & Kerst, S. M. (1983, April). *The effects of induced imagery and imposed synonyms upon prose comprehension.* Paper presented at the annual meeting of the American Educational Research Association, Montreal.

Faw, H. D., & Waller, T. G. (1976). Mathemagenic behaviors and efficiency in learning from prose. *Review of Educational Research, 46,* 691–720.

Flavell, J. H., & Wellman, H. M. (1977). Metamemory. In R. V. Kail, Jr., & J. W. Hagen (Eds.), *Perspectives on the development of memory and cognition* (pp. 3–33). Hillsdale, NJ: Lawrence Erlbaum Associates.

Forrest-Pressley, D. L., & Gillies, L. A. (1983). Children's flexible use of strategies during reading. In M. Pressley & J. R. Levin (Eds.), *Cognitive strategy research: Educational applications* (pp. 133–156). New York: Springer–Verlag.

Forrest-Pressley, D. L., & Waller, T. G. (1984). *Reading, cognition, and metacognition.* New York: Springer–Verlag.

Franks, J. J., Vye, N. J., Auble, P. M., Mezynski, K. J., Perfetto, G. A., Bransford, J. D., Stein, B. S., & Littlefield, J. (1982). Learning from explicit versus implicit texts. *Journal of Experimental Psychology: General, 111,* 414–422.

Gambrell, L. B., & Heathington, B. S. (1981). Adult disabled readers' metacognitive awareness about reading tasks and strategies. *Journal of Reading Behavior, 13,* 215–222.

Garner, R., & Reis, R. (1981). Monitoring and resolving comprehension obstacles: An investigation of spontaneous lookbacks among upper-grade good and poor comprehenders. *Reading Research Quarterly, 16,* 569–582.

Gelzheiser, L. M. (1984). Generalization of study rules for categorical memory tasks to prose by learning disabled adolescents. *Journal of Educational Psychology, 76,* 1128–1138.

Ghatala, E. S., Levin, J. R., Pressley, M., & Lodico, M. (1984, April). *Metamemory acquisition in children: Effects of strategy-monitoring training.* Paper presented at the annual meeting of the American Educational Research Association, New Orleans.

Hall, J. W., & Humphreys, M. S. (1982). Research on specific learning disabilities: Deficits and remediation. *Topics in Learning and Learning Disabilities, 2,* 68–78.

Hansen, J., & Pearson, P. D. (1983). An instructional study: Improving the inferential comprehension of good and poor fourth-grade readers. *Journal of Educational Psychology, 75,* 821–829.

Harber, J. R. (1980). Effects of illustrations on reading performance: Implications for further LD research. *Learning Disability Quarterly, 3,* 60–70.

Harber, J. R. (1983). The effects of illustrations on the reading performance of learning disabled and normal children. *Learning Disability Quarterly, 6,* 55–60.

Haring, M. J., & Fry, M. A. (1981, April). *A meta-analysis of the literature on pictures and reading comprehension.* Paper presented at the annual meeting of the International Reading Association, New Orleans.

Higbee, K. L. (1978). Some pseudo-limitations of mnemonics. In M. M. Gruneberg, P. E. Morris, & R. N. Sykes (Eds.), *Practical aspects of memory* (pp. 147–154). New York: Academic Press.

Hodges, C. A. (1980). Commentary: Toward a broader definition of comprehension instruction. *Reading Research Quarterly, 15,* 299–306.

Hyde, T. S., & Jenkins, J. J. (1973). Recall for words as a function of semantic, graphic, and syntactic orienting tasks. *Journal of Verbal Learning and Verbal Behavior, 12,* 471–480.

Jacoby, L. L., & Craik, F. I. M. (1979). Effects of elaboration on processing in encoding and retrieval: Trace distinctiveness and recovery of initial context. In L. S. Cermak & F. I. M. Craik (Eds.), *Levels of processing in human memory* (pp. 1–21). New York: Wiley.

Johnson, D. D., & Pearson, P. D. (1978). *Teaching reading vocabulary.* New York: Holt.

Jones, B. F., Friedman, L., & Cox, B. (1984, April). *Content-driven comprehension instruction.* Paper presented at the annual meeting of the American Educational Research Association, New Orleans.

Jones, B. F., & Hall, J. W. (1982). School applications of the mnemonic keyword method as a study strategy by eighth graders. *Journal of Educational Psychology, 74,* 230–237.

Kennedy, B. A., & Miller, D. J. (1976). Persistent use of verbal rehearsal as a function of information about its value. *Child Development, 47,* 566–569.

Levie, W. H., & Lentz, R. (1982). Effects of text illustrations: A review of research. *Educational Communication and Technology Journal, 30,* 195–232.

Levin, J. R. (1972). When is a picture worth a thousand words? In J. R. Levin (Ed.), *Issues in imagery and learning: Four papers* (Theoretical Paper No. 36). Madison: Wisconsin Research and Development Center for Cognitive Learning.

Levin, J. R. (1973). Inducing comprehension in poor readers: A test of a recent model. *Journal of Educational Psychology, 65,* 19–24.

Levin, J. R. (1976). What have we learned about maximizing what children learn? In J. R. Levin & V. L. Allen (Eds.), *Cognitive learning in children: Theories and strategies* (pp. 105–134). New York: Academic Press.

Levin, J. R. (1981a). The mnemonic '80s: Keywords in the classroom. *Educational Psychologist, 16,* 65–82.

Levin, J. R. (1981b). On functions of pictures in prose. In F. J. Pirozzolo & M. C. Wittrock (Eds.), *Neuropsychological and cognitive processes in reading* (pp. 203–228). New York: Academic Press.

Levin, J. R. (1982). Pictures as prose-learning devices. In A. Flammer & W. Kintsch (Eds.), *Discourse processing* (pp. 412–444). Amsterdam: North–Holland.

Levin, J. R. (1983). Pictorial strategies for school learning: Practical illustrations. In M. Pressley & J. R. Levin (Eds.), *Cognitive strategy research: Educational applications* (pp. 213–237). New York: Springer–Verlag.

Levin, J. R. (in press). Educational applications of mnemonic pictures: Possibilities beyond your wildest imagination. In A. A. Sheikh (Ed.), *Imagery and the educational process.* Farmingdale, NY: Baywood.

Levin, J. R., Bender, B. G., & Lesgold, A. M. (1976). Pictures, repetition, and young children's oral prose learning. *AV Communication Review, 24,* 367–380.

Levin, J. R., Johnson, D. D., Pittelman, S. D., Hayes, B. L., Levin, K. M., Shriberg, L. K., & Toms-Bronowski, S. (1984). A comparison of semantic- and mnemonic-based vocabulary-learning strategies. *Reading Psychology, 5,* 1–15.

Levin, J. R., & Lesgold, A. M. (1978). On pictures in prose. *Educational Communication and Technology Journal, 26,* 233–243.

Levin, J. R., McCormick, C. B., & Dretzke, B. J. (1981). A combined mnemonic pictorial strategy for ordered information. *Educational Communication and Technology Journal, 29,* 219–225.

Levin, J. R., & Pressley, M. (1981). Improving children's prose comprehension: Selected strategies that seem to succeed. In C. M. Santa & B. L. Hayes (Eds.), *Children's prose comprehension: Research and practice* (pp. 44–71). Newark, DE: International Reading Association.

Levin, J. R., & Pressley, M. (1983). Understanding mnemonic imagery effects: A dozen "obvious" outcomes. In M. L. Fleming & D. W. Hutton (Eds.), *Mental imagery and learning* (pp. 33–51). Englewood Cliffs, NJ: Educational Technology Publications.

Levin, J. R., & Pressley, M. (1985). Mnemonic vocabulary instruction: What's fact, what's fiction. In R. F. Dillon & R. R. Schmeck (Eds.), *Individual differences in cognition* (Vol. 2). New York: Academic Press.

Levin, J. R., Shriberg, L. K., & Berry, J. K. (1983). A concrete strategy for remembering abstract prose. *American Educational Research Journal, 20,* 277–290.

Levin, J. R., Shriberg, L. K., Miller, G. E., McCormick, C. B., & Levin, B. B. (1980). The keyword method in the classroom: How to remember the states and their capitals. *Elementary School Journal, 80,* 185–191.

Linden, M., & Wittrock, M. C. (1981). The teaching of reading comprehension according to the model of generative learning. *Reading Research Quarterly, 17,* 44–57.

Lodico, M. G., Ghatala, E. S., Levin, J. R., Pressley, M., & Bell, J. A. (1983). Effects of meta-memory training on children's use of effective learning strategies. *Journal of Experimental Child Psychology, 35,* 263–277.

Markman, E. M., & Gorin, L. (1981). Children's ability to adjust their standards for evaluating comprehension. *Journal of Educational Psychology, 73,* 320–325.

Martin, C. J. (1978). Mediational processes in the retarded: Implications for teaching reading. In N. R. Ellis (Ed.), *International review of research in mental retardation* (Vol. 9, pp. 61–84). New York: Academic Press.

Mastropieri, M. A., Scruggs, T. E., & Levin, J. R. (1983a). *Pictorial mnemonic strategies for special education.* Unpublished manuscript, Utah State University, Logan.

Mastropieri, M. A., Scruggs, T. E., & Levin, J. R. (1983b, August). *Transformational mnemonic strategies with learning disabled adolescents.* Paper presented at the annual meeting of the American Psychological Association, Anaheim, CA.

Mastropieri, M. A., Scruggs, T. E., & Levin, J. R. (1984). *Maximizing what exceptional students can learn: A review of research on mnemonic techniques.* Unpublished manuscript, Utah State University, Logan.

Mastropieri, M. A., Scruggs, T. E., & Levin, J. R. (in press). Direct instruction vs. mnemonic instruction: Relative benefits for exceptional learners. *Journal of Special Education.*

Mastropieri, M. A., Scruggs, T. E., Levin, J. R., Gaffney, J., & McLoone, B. (1985). Mnemonic vocabulary instruction with learning disabled students. *Learning Disability Quarterly, 8,* 299–309.

Mastropieri, M. A., Scruggs, T. E., McLoone, B., & Levin, J. R. (1984). *Facilitating the acquisition of science classifications in learning disabled students.* Unpublished manuscript, Utah State University, Logan.

McCormick, C. B., & Levin, J. R. (1984). A comparison of different prose-learning variations of the mnemonic keyword method. *American Educational Research Journal, 21,* 379–398.

McCormick, C. B., Levin, J. R., Cykowski, F., & Danilovics, P. (1984, April). *Mnemonic-strategy reduction of prose-learning interference.* Paper presented at the annual meeting of the American Educational Research Association, New Orleans.

McDaniel, M. A., & Pressley, M. (1984). Putting the keyword method in context. *Journal of Educational Psychology, 76,* 598–609.

McGivern, J. E., & Levin, J. R. (1983). The keyword method and children's vocabulary learning: An interaction with vocabulary knowledge. *Contemporary Educational Psychology, 8,* 46–54.

McGivern, J. E., Peters, E. E., Levin, J. R., & Pressley, M. (1984, April). *A further comparison of representational and transformational prose-learning imagery.* Paper presented at the annual meeting of the American Educational Research Association, New Orleans.

Newman, R. S., & Hagen, J. W. (1981). Memory strategies in children with learning disabilities. *Journal of Applied Developmental Psychology, 1,* 297–312.

Norman, D. A., & Schallice, T. (1980). *Attention to action: Willed and automatic control of behavior* (CHIP Tech. Rep. No. 99). La Jolla, CA: University of California.

O'Sullivan, J. T., & Pressley, M. (1984). Completeness of instruction and strategy transfer. *Journal of Experimental Child Psychology, 38,* 275–288.

Owings, R. A., Peterson, G. A., Bransford, J. D., Morris, C. D., & Stein, B. S. (1980). Spontaneous monitoring and regulation of learning: A comparison of successful and less successful fifth graders. *Journal of Educational Psychology, 72,* 250–256.

Paivio, A. (1971). *Imagery and verbal processes.* New York: Holt.

Palincsar, A. M. (1984, April). *Reciprocal teaching: Working within the zone of proximal development.* Paper presented at the annual meeting of the American Educational Research Association, New Orleans.

Palincsar, A. M., & Brown, A. L. (1984). Reciprocal teaching of comprehension-fostering and monitoring activities-monitoring. *Cognition and Instruction, 1,* 117–175.

Paris, S. G., Lipson, M. Y., & Wixson, K. K. (1983). Becoming a strategic reader. *Contemporary Educational Psychology, 8,* 293–316.

Paris, S. G., & Myers, M. (1981). Comprehension monitoring in good and poor readers. *Journal of Reading Behavior, 13,* 5–22.

Pearl, R. (1982). LD children's attributions for success and failure: A replication with a labeled LD sample. *Learning Disability Quarterly, 5,* 173–176.

Pearl, R., Bryan, T., & Donahue, M. (1980). Learning disabled children's attributions for success and failure. *Learning Disability Quarterly, 3,* 3–9.

Pearl, R., Bryan, T., & Herzog, A. (1983). Learning disabled and nondisabled children's strategy analyses under high and low success conditions. *Learning Disability Quarterly, 6,* 67–74.

Pearson, P. D., & Gallagher, M. C. (1983). The instruction of reading comprehension. *Contemporary Educational Psychology, 8,* 317–344.

Peters, E. E., & Levin, J. R. (1984, April). *Effects of a mnemonic imagery strategy on good and poor comprehenders' prose recall.* Paper presented at the annual meeting of the American Educational Research Association, New Orleans.

Pressley, M. (1977). Imagery and children's learning: Putting the picture in developmental perspective. *Review of Educational Research, 47,* 586–622.

Pressley, M. (1982). Elaboration and memory development. *Child Development, 53,* 296–309.

Pressley, M., Borkowski, J. G., & O'Sullivan, J. T. (1984). Memory strategy instruction is made of this: Metamemory and durable strategy use. *Educational Psychologist, 19,* 94–107.

Pressley, M., Borkowski, J. G., & O'Sullivan, J. T. (1985). Children's metamemory and the teaching of memory strategies. In D. L. Forrest-Pressley, G. E. MacKinnon, & T. G. Waller (Eds.), *Metacognition, cognition, and human performance* (pp. 111–153). New York: Academic Press.

Pressley, M., & Dennis-Rounds, J. (1980). Transfer of a mnemonic keyword strategy at two age levels. *Journal of Educational Psychology, 72,* 575–582.

Pressley, M., & Forrest-Pressley, D. L. (1985). Questions and children's cognitive processing. In A. Graesser & J. Black (Eds.), *Psychology of questions* (pp. 277–296). Hillsdale, NJ: Lawrence Erlbaum Associates.

Pressley, M., Forrest-Pressley, D. L., Elliott-Faust, D., & Miller, G. (1985). Children's use of cognitive strategies, how to teach cognitive strategies, and what to do if they can't be taught. In M. Pressley & C. J. Brainerd (Eds.), *Cognitive approaches to memory development.* New York: Springer–Verlag.

Pressley, M., Heisel, B. E., McCormick, C. B., & Nakamura, G. V. (1982). Memory strategy instruction. In C. J. Brainerd & M. Pressley (Eds.), *Progress in cognitive development research: Vol. 2. Verbal processes in children* (pp. 125–159). New York: Springer–Verlag.

Pressley, M., & Levin, J. R. (1977). Developmental differences in subjects' associative learning strategies and performance: Assessing a hypothesis. *Journal of Experimental Child Psychology, 24*, 431–439.

Pressley, M., & Levin, J. R. (1978). Developmental constraints associated with children's use of the keyword method of foreign language vocabulary learning. *Journal of Experimental Child Psychology, 26*, 359–372.

Pressley, M., Levin, J. R., & Delaney, H. D. (1982). The mnemonic keyword method. *Review of Educational Research, 52*, 61–92.

Pressley, M., Levin, J. R., & Ghatala, E. S. (1984). Memory strategy monitoring in adults and children. *Journal of Verbal Learning and Verbal Behavior, 23*, 270–288.

Pressley, M., Levin, J. R., Nakamura, G. V., Hope, D. J., Bispo, J. G., & Toye, A. R. (1980). The keyword method of foreign vocabulary learning: An investigation of its generalizability. *Journal of Applied Psychology, 65*, 635–642.

Pressley, M., Levin, J. R., Pigott, S., LeComte, M., & Hope, D. J. (1983). Mismatched pictures and children's prose learning. *Educational Communication and Technology Journal, 31*, 131–143.

Pressley, M., Pigott, S., & Bryant, S. L. (1982). Picture content and preschoolers' learning from sentences. *Educational Communication and Technology Journal, 30*, 151–161.

Pressley, M., Ross, K. A., Levin, J. R., & Ghatala, E. S. (1984, April). *Tapping what a child knows about a strategy.* Paper presented at the annual meeting of the American Educational Research Association, New Orleans.

Pressley, M., Samuel, J., Hershey, M. M., Bishop, S. L., & Dickinson, D. (1981). Use of a mnemonic technique to teach young children foreign language vocabulary. *Contemporary Educational Psychology, 6*, 110–116.

Raphael, T. E., & McKinney, J. (1982). *A developmental examination of children's question-answering behavior: An instructional study in metacognition.* Paper presented at the annual meeting of the National Reading Conference, Clearwater, FL.

Raphael, T. E., Wonnacott, C. A., & Pearson, P. D. (1981). *Heightening students' sensitivity to information sources: An instructional study in question-answer relationships.* Paper presented at the annual meeting of the National Reading Conference, Dallas.

Readence. J. E., & Moore, D. (1981). A meta-analytic review of the effect of adjunct pictures on reading comprehension. *Psychology in the Schools, 18*, 218–224.

Redfield, D. L., & Rousseau, E. W. (1981). Meta-analysis of experimental research in teacher questioning behavior. *Review of Educational Research, 51*, 237–245.

Rickards, J. P., & Hatcher, C. W. (1978). Interspersed meaningful learning questions as semantic cues for poor comprehenders. *Reading Research Quarterly, 13*, 538–553.

Riding, R. J., & Shore, J. M. (1974). A comparison of two methods of improving prose comprehension in educationally subnormal children. *British Journal of Educational Psychology, 44*, 300–303.

Robinson, F. P. (1961). *Effective study* (rev. ed.). New York: Harper & Row.

Rogoff, B., & Gardner, W. P. (1984). Developing cognitive skills in social action. In B. Rogoff & J. Lave (Eds.), *Everyday cognition: Its development in social context.* Cambridge, MA: Harvard University Press.

Rohwer, W. D., Jr. (1973). Elaboration and learning in childhood and adolescence. In H.W. Reese (Ed.), *Advances in child development and behavior* (Vol. 8, pp. 1–57). New York: Academic Press.

Rohwer, W. D., Jr. (1980). How the smart get smarter. *Educational Psychologist, 15*, 34–43.

Rohwer, W. D., Jr., & Bean, J. P. (1973). Sentence effects and noun-pair learning: A developmental interaction during adolescence. *Journal of Experimental Child Psychology, 15,* 521–533.

Rohwer, W. D., Jr., & Harris, W. J. (1975). Media effects on prose learning in two populations of children. *Journal of Educational Psychology, 67,* 651–657.

Rohwer, W. D., Jr., & Matz, R. (1975). Improving aural comprehension in white and in black children: Pictures versus print. *Journal of Experimental Child Psychology, 19,* 23–36.

Rose, M. C., Cundick, B. P., & Higbee, J. L. (1983). Verbal rehearsal and visual imagery: Mnemonic aids for learning-disabled children. *Journal of Learning Disabilities, 16,* 352–354.

Rothkopf, E. Z. (1965). Some theoretical and experimental approaches to problems in written instruction. In J. D. Krumboltz (Ed.), *Learning and the educational process* (pp. 193–221). Chicago: Rand McNally.

Royer, J. M., & Cable, G. W. (1976). Illustrations, analogies, and facilitative transfer in prose learning. *Journal of Educational Psychology, 68,* 205–209.

Schallert, D. L. (1980). The role of illustrations in reading comprehension. In R. J. Spiro, B. C. Bruce, & W. F. Brewer (Eds.), *Theoretical issues in reading comprehension* (pp. 503–524). Hillsdale, NJ: Lawrence Erlbaum Associates.

Scruggs, T. E., Mastropieri, & Levin, J. R. (1985). Vocabulary acquisition of retarded students under direct and mnemonic instruction. *American Journal of Mental Deficiency, 89,* 546–551.

Scruggs, T. E., Mastropieri, M. A., Levin, J. R., & Gaffney, J. (1984). *Facilitating the acquisition of science facts in learning disabled students.* Unpublished manuscript, Utah State University, Logan.

Shepard, L. A., Smith, M. L., & Vojir, C. P. (1983). Characteristics of pupils identified as learning disabled *American Educational Research Journal, 20,* 309–331.

Shriberg, L. K. (1982). *Comparison of two mnemonic encoding strategies in children's recognition and recall of abstract prose information.* Unpublished doctoral dissertation, University of Wisconsin, Madison.

Shriberg, L. K., Levin, J. R., McCormick, C. B., & Pressley, M. (1982). Learning about "famous" people via the keyword method. *Journal of Educational Psychology, 74,* 238–247.

Shuell, T. J. (1983). The effect of instructions to organize for good and poor learners. *Intelligence, 7,* 271–286.

Snowman, J., Krebs, E. W., & Lockhart, L. (1980). Improving recall of information from prose in high-risk students through learning strategy learning. *Journal of Instructional Psychology, 7,* 35–40.

Stein, B. S., Bransford, J. D., Franks, J. J., Owings, R. A., Vye, N. J., & McGraw, W. (1982). Differences in the precision of self-generated elaborations. *Journal of Experimental Psychology: General, 111,* 399–405.

Steingart, S. K., & Glock, M. D. (1979). Imagery and recall of connected discourse. *Reading Research Quarterly, 15,* 66–83.

Tarver, S. G., Hallahan, D. P., Kauffman, J. M., & Ball, D. W. (1976). Verbal rehearsal and selective attention in children with learning disabilities: A developmental lag. *Journal of Experimental Child Psychology, 22,* 375–385.

Taylor, A. M., & Turnure, J. E. (1979). Imagery and verbal elaboration with retarded children: Effects on learning and memory. In N. R. Ellis (Ed.), *Handbook of mental deficiency, psychological theory and research* (pp. 659–697). Hillsdale, NJ: Lawrence Erlbaum Associates.

Tharpe, R. G. (1982). The effective instruction of comprehension: Results and description of the Kamehameha early education program. *Reading Research Quarterly, 17,* 503–528.

Thurlow, M. L., & Turnure, J. E. (1972). Elaboration structure and list length effects on verbal elaboration phenomena. *Journal of Experimental Child Psychology, 14,* 184–195.

Tollefson, N., Tracy, D. B., Johnsen, E. P., Buenning, M., Farmer, A., & Barké, C. R. (1982). Attribution patterns of learning disabled adolescents. *Learning Disability Quarterly, 5,* 14–20.

Torgesen, J. K. (1977). Memorization processes in reading-disabled children. *Journal of Educational Psychology, 69,* 571–578.

Torgesen, J. K., & Goldman, T. (1977). Verbal rehearsal and short-term memory in reading-disabled children. *Child Development, 48,* 56–60.

Torgesen, J. K., Murphy, H., & Ivey, C. (1979). The effects of orienting task on the memory performance of learning disabled children. *Journal of Learning Disabilities, 12,* 396–401.

Turner, T. J. (1984). *The effects of illustration on memory for text.* Unpublished doctoral dissertation, University of Queensland, St. Lucia, Australia.

Turnure, J. E., Buium, N., & Thurlow, M. L. (1976). The effectiveness of interrogatives for promoting verbal elaboration productivity in young children. *Child Development, 47,* 851–855.

Turnure, J. E., & Walsh, M. K. (1971). Extended verbal mediation in the learning and reversal of paired-associates by EMR children. *American Journal of Mental Deficiency, 76,* 60–67.

Warner, M. M., & Alley, G. R. (1981). *Teaching learning disabled junior high students to use visual imagery as a strategy for facilitating recall of reading passages* (Research Rep. No. 49). Lawrence, KS: University of Kansas, Institute for Research in Learning Disabilities.

Wiener, M., & Cromer, W. (1967). Reading and reading difficulty: A conceptual analysis. *Harvard Educational Review, 37,* 620–643.

Winne, P. H. (1979). Experiments relating teachers' use of higher cognitive questions to student achievement. *Review of Educational Research, 49,* 13–50.

Wittrock, M. C. (1974). Learning as a generative process. *Educational Psychologist, 11,* 87–95.

Wittrock, M. C. (1981). Reading comprehension. In F. J. Pirozzolo & M. C. Wittrock (Eds.), *Neuropsychological and cognitive processes in reading* (pp. 229–259). New York: Academic Press.

Wittrock, M. C. (1984, April). *Research in reading comprehension.* Paper presented at the annual meeting of the American Educational Research Association, New Orleans.

Wong, B. Y. L. (1980). Activating the inactive learner: Use of questions/prompts to enhance comprehension and retention of implied information in learning disabled children. *Learning Disability Quarterly, 3,* 29–37.

Wong, B. Y. L. (1982a). Strategic behaviors in selecting retrieval cues in gifted, normal achieving and learning disabled children. *Journal of Learning Disabilities, 15,* 33–37.

Wong, B. Y. L. (1982b). Understanding learning disabled students' reading problems: Contributions from cognitive psychology. *Topics in Learning and Learning Disabilities, 2,* 43–50.

Wong, B. Y. L., & Jones, W. (1982). Increasing metacomprehension in learning-disabled and normally achieving students through self-questioning training. *Learning Disability Quarterly, 5,* 228–240.

Wong, B., Wong, R., & Foth, D. (1977). Recall and clustering of verbal materials among normal and poor readers. *Bulletin of the Psychonomic Society, 10,* 375–378.

Worden, P. E. (1983). Memory strategy instruction with the learning disabled. In M. Pressley & J. R. Levin (Eds.), *Cognitive strategy research: Psychological foundations* (pp. 129–154). New York: Springer–Verlag.

Worden, P. E., Malmgren, I., & Gabourie, P. (1982). Memory for stories in learning disabled adults. *Journal of Learning Disabilities, 15,* 145–152.

Commentary: The Four M's—Memory Strategies, Metastrategies, Monitoring, and Motivation

Patricia E. Worden
California State University at Fullerton

This commentary presents some thoughts about these three very interesting chapters: "Patterns of Motivation and Reading Skills in Underachieving Children," by Evelyn Oka and Scott Paris; "Metacognition, Motivation, and Controlled Performance" by John Borkowski, Mary Beth Johnston, and Molly Reid; "Elaborative Learning Strategies for the Inefficient Learner," by Michael Pressley and Joel Levin. The first thing to notice is that not one of these chapters uses the term "learning disabilities" in its title. The remarks begin with some comments on definitions of subject populations in research with disabled learners.

What Is Our Goal?

Lake Wobegon: Where all the women are strong, all the men are good looking, and all the children are above average.

—Garrison Keillor

The fact that all the children outside of Lake Wobegon are not above average is what motivates our studies. We are concerned about children whose school performance is below average, and we are particularly interested in children who have been labeled "learning disabled." Although being of average (or even above-average) intelligence, these children have a specific impairment (often having to do with reading) that prevents them from performing at their "true" ability level. According to this view it should be possible to reliably distinguish learning-disabled children from their peers who are simply consistently below average. Unfortunately, researchers and educators continue to disagree about how best to accomplish this. Farnham-Diggory (1986) discusses 14 ways of defining a learning-disabled sample, and reviews the sociopolitical, economic, and pragmatic reasons why definitional practice varies. She makes a case that "there is simply no reliable way" to classify a child as learning disabled. Others (Vellutino, this volume) make the contrasting argument that researchers *must* find a way to select precise subject samples, "if the object of one's inquiry is the understanding of learning disorder in otherwise normal children" (p. 331). Vellutino speaks for those who deplore the lax practices of researchers whose samples are contaminated by just plain below-average children and other elements of intellectual heterogeneity. It's true that when this happens the results are not definitive about the basic nature of specific learning disabilities, but that may not be the goal of the research.

According to the doctrine of specific deficits, Pressley and Levin's concept of the "inefficient learner" would be heresy. Nevertheless Pressley and Levin deliberately eschew the idea of restricting their research to rigidly and precisely constrained learning-disabled populations. They point out similarities in the ways specifically disabled learners, just plain below-average students, and educable mentally retarded students approach some learning problems, and Oka and Paris make the same point. Similarities are also found between learning-disabled subjects and their younger nondisabled peers. Purists may argue that this broad view of learners as more or less efficient (whether due to general ability differences, specific ability deficits, or developmental levels) is theoretically bankrupt. However, in my view the three target chapters are highly appropriate and informative, in spite of their unorthodox definitional approaches. The goal of the research, for these investigators, is primarily to identify appropriate means of remediation for learning difficulties, whatever the source.

Personally, I am not hopeful that the definitional problem will ever be solved to everyone's satisfaction. In the end we will best understand learning problems by considering converging research approaches, ranging from single case studies to studies of precisely selected subsamples to experiments with broadly defined heterogeneous groups. Therefore it would be a mistake to exclude the research covered in the three target chapters from our collection of knowledge about learning disabilities. While the controversy about the definitional problem rages on, these researchers have been harvesting some very useful and interesting data about inefficient learners' problems in academic tasks.

The Four M's

In a sense these researchers have taken an "expert systems" approach in the studies reviewed here. They have examined and catalogued the things that proficient learners do, and the goal of the research is to train inefficient learners to do these things. Note that this approach is rather agnostic about why inefficient learners have these deficits in the first place. The research focuses upon identifying critical component parts of the memory strategies, metastrategy information, and monitoring practices employed by so-called expert learners. The fourth M, motivation, represents the long-neglected affective component in learning. This approach presupposes that the coordination of these elements is at least as important for efficient learning as is possession of the individual components themselves. However, the interplay of the four M's in disabled learners is perhaps the least well understood aspect of this model.

Table C2.1 represents an attempt to organize the topics reviewed across all three chapters. It is intended only as an organizational device and in no sense should it be construed as anything but the sketchiest of models. Each set of authors will no doubt discover distortions caused by this attempt to accommodate all views. Nevertheless, Table C2.1 should be helpful for charting one's way through the concepts discussed in these chapters; it also reveals areas where concepts are a bit fuzzy and in need of more precise explication.

Overall, there was general consensus in these chapters about Memory Strategies (I), although this list is obviously incomplete; it focuses on topics showcased mainly in the Pressley and Levin chapter. My apologies to Oka and Paris, whose chapter is not, strictly speaking, about memory strategies but rather focuses on the task of reading comprehension. The main contribution in Oka and Paris's chapter is represented in the final element, motivation. Monitoring Practices (II) are listed next because monitoring is the process that adds meta-awareness to strategy execution and thus can result in Metastrategy Information (III). Although Borkowski, Johnston, and Reid consider monitoring practices to be part of metamemory acquisition procedures (belonging under IIIC.), monitoring can also be considered a separate process that may or may not increase metamemory knowledge (and Pressley and Levin seem to share this view). Monitoring practices also inform the motivational element and thus deserve a separate category. Finally, Motivation (IV) derives from what Borkowski, Johnston, and Reid call general strategy knowledge, or the understanding that an effortful strategic approach aids learning. This understanding interacts with a number of other affective and attributional factors that foster successful learning, as discussed by Oka and Paris, Each chapter is reviewed in turn.

If I Could Just Elaborate for a Moment . . .

The Pressley and Levin chapter presents a well-organized compendium of a huge body of research on mnemonic elaboration. In contrast to other memory strategies such as rehearsal and organizational procedures, elaborative techniques seem bafflingly indirect and even downright inefficient. Rehearsal, after all, is the ultimate form of "time on task," and organizational techniques exploit relationships inherent in the materials. Associative mnemonics such as the keyword and pegword methods, in contrast, require the learner to spend time memorizing *extra* things such as complex and outlandish images. Looked at this way, who would have guessed elaborative techniques would be so effective?

TABLE C2.1
Components of Successful Learning Employed by "Experts"

I. Memory Strategies
   A. Selective studying and attention
   B. Rehearsal
   C. Organizational-clustering
   D. Elaborative (Recoding, Relating, Retrieving)
      1. keyword
      2. peg word (ordered associations)
      3. prose elaborations
         a. precise elaborations
         b. constructing images
         c. processing illustrations
         d. posing and answering questions

II. Monitoring Practices
   A. On-line planning
   B. Evaluating
   C. Troubleshooting (identification of source of difficulty)
   D. Evaluating success in meeting goal

III. Metastrategy Information
   A. General knowledge about benefits of strategic approach
   B. Specific strategy knowledge
      1. appropriate situations
      2. appropriate materials
      3. goals the strategy can help to meet (means-end utility information)
      4. time constraints
      5. effort requirements
      6. personal satisfaction
   C. Metamemory acquisition procedures
      1. compensation for inadequate instructions
      2. strategy modification/switching
IV. Motivation
   A. Allocation of effort
      1. on-task behavior
      2. attentiveness
      3. concentration
      4. persistence
      5. completion
   B. Sense of control (attribution of success and failure)
      1. internal attributions
         a. ability
         b. effort
      2. external attributions
         a. luck
         b. task difficulty
   C. Estimate of stability/modifiability of problem
   D. Values and goals
      1. attainment value
      2. intrinsic value
      3. utility value
      4. anticipated costs
   E. Interpretations of success and failure

When this research was in its infancy it was feared that elaboration techniques had only limited application, namely, foreign language vocabulary learning (and even then its utility was limited because foreign language studies have declined so disgracefully in American education, and in any case the keyword method is a rotten way to learn correct pronunciation). It is encouraging, then, to note that mnemonic elaboration methods have now been studied with a wide variety of materials of increasing complexity and ecological validity: vocabulary learning (foreign language, native vocabulary); science facts (single and multiple attributes of minerals); social studies facts (prime ministers and presidents, provinces and states, dates and figures in history); information in expository passages. Unfortunately, as the complexity of the materials to be learned increases so does the uncertainty about the conditions under which elaborative strategies will prove effective.

It should be obvious that one area where mnemonic elaboration really shines is in vocabulary acquisition. Pressley and Levin and their colleagues have produced a staggering amount of research in this area. The effectiveness of the keyword technique in particular is indisputable and has been replicated time and time again. One issue that needs refinement however, concerns the amount of support necessary for a learning-disabled student to benefit from this strategy. Is there a certain age or ability level at which teachers could expect students to be able to generate their own elaborative mnemonics? For instance, McGivern and Levin (1983) found that low verbal ability fifth graders' benefits were "relatively greater" when provided with illustrations than when they had to generate their own images. On the other hand, Mastropieri, Scruggs, Levin, Gaffney, and McLoone (1985) found learning-disabled junior high students capable of executing a mnemonic imagery strategy without the need for experimenter-provided illustrations. Do these two findings indicate a shift in early adolescence from a requirement for external support to internal generation of mnemonic associations? Can learning-disabled students be taught to supply their own keywords as well as associative images? Pressley and Levin have discussed such issues for nondisabled students elsewhere (Pressley, Levin, & Delaney, 1982), but there are still questions about the special needs of disabled learners who attempt to use these methods.

Although most elaboration studies have focused on typical learning tasks of "middle-aged" children or adolescents, there is one study with much younger children that deserves special mention here. Ehri, Deffner, and Wilce (1984) studied ways of teaching prereaders letter–sound associations using pictorial mnemonics. Most alphabet-learning materials depict a target letter next to a picture of an object beginning with the appropriate letter sound ("D is for dog"). Ehri et al. found that a more effective approach was to create integrated pictures that depicted the letter as an integral part of the phonetically related picture. Thus, the lower case "f" was drawn as a droopy flower; the "l" was the stem of the lamp, and so forth. Although the technique clearly needs further development, this research is exciting because it represents a new approach that might be employed with very young children at risk for reading disabilities—those who have initial trouble acquiring letter–sound correspondences. For suggestions about how integrated picture mnemonics might be employed in computerized alphabet-learning programs as well as in picture books, see Worden, Kee, and Ingle (1985).

Fact learning represents the application of associative methods to more complex contents, and there is some interesting preliminary research in this area. In addition to impressive gains in the efficiency of learning paired associates (e.g., mineral names and hardness ratings), learning-disabled junior high students have demonstrated remarkable success in learning clusters of attributes (Mastropieri, Scruggs, McLoone, & Levin, 1985; Scruggs, Mastropieri, Levin, & Gaffney, 1985). Not only was there memory improvement, in comparison with standard instructional methods, but learning was accomplished more rapidly as well.

Moving up the complexity scale from multiple attributes to connected discourse, elaborative techniques to learn prose have also been studied. Peters and Levin (in press) recently evaluated a mnemonic imagery strategy for learning facts both in experimental passages (e.g., Charlene Fidler and her counting cat) and in actual prose passages, with promising results. Unfortunately, some experimental texts are really just lists of items embedded in sentences. Prose organizations are qualitatively different from lists in that even simple expository passages have elements that differ in importance (main ideas, subordinate concepts); narrative passages embody complex grammatical relations (Mandler & Johnson, 1977). Pressley and Levin are careful to point out the artificial nature of some of the materials tested, particularly in research on precise elaborations of textual materials. For instance, students have been found to benefit from instruction in inventing rationales for relating particular actor/activity relationships in sentences that do not directly express such relationships. Such materials are useful for discovering whether students can be trained to benefit from precise elaboration strategies, and under what conditions, but unless such strategies can be used with real-world materials (such as studied by Peters and Levin, in press) this research will be of limited value to educators.

Compared to the consistent advantages found for mnemonic elaborations with simple list-like materials, research on the effects of representational illustrations with prose materials is rather equivocal. Pressley and Levin point out that both the nature of the pictures and the strategies children use in processing them seem to be important for the success or failure of illustrations to aid memory. This is an issue of particular educational relevance because examinations of widely used basal readers (e.g., Beck, 1984) have shown that pictures in actual textbooks vary tremendously in both style and content. Similarly, much is yet to be discovered regarding the relationship between internally generated imagery and prose recall, who would benefit from learning such strategies, and with what materials.

In a lengthy section on questioning strategies and recall of prose passages, Pressley and Levin express a number of reservations about this research, although highlighting its great potential. They point out the extra-time and extra-exposure confoundings common in typical questioning strategy trained groups. They worry about indirect assessments of whether trained subjects actually use the questioning strategy that was instructed. In addition, as the complexity of the materials to be remembered increases, the tendency of researchers to bundle strategies increases. It should be obvious that such "shotgun" approaches preclude precise identification of the effective strategy element(s), as I have complained elsewhere (Worden, 1983). Finally, as always, we must be on the alert for signs of generalization, namely that students would or could benefit from employing the questioning strategy on their own with new texts. At any rate, the studies reviewed suggest that there are conditions under which inefficient learners could increase their memory and comprehension for prose materials by asking themselves integrative questions. The results are quite preliminary at this time, however, and this research should not be interpreted to mean that interrupting reading to ask questions is always a good idea. Beck (1984) notes a number of ways poorly placed and/or poorly focused questions can actually interfere with comprehension. Moreover, questions may be more effective for some kinds of memory tasks than others. For example, Wong and Jones (1982) only found that learning-disabled adolescents' answers to comprehension questions (cued recall) was improved by the self-questioning strategy; gist (free) recall was not improved.

At the end of their review, Pressley and Levin make the strong concluding statement that "strategic interventions frequently raise the performance of handicapped learners to the level attained by nonhandicapped learners" (p. 201). In spite of problems encountered when elaboration researchers stray into areas of complex strategies and materials, it should be obvious by now that mnemonic elaborative techniques have tremendous potential for certain educational tasks found difficult by inefficient learners. However, Pressley and Levin also make the point that findings of real-world value may require much greater effort than most researchers have been willing to invest in studies to date (e.g., longer and more elaborate training procedures, such as in Palinscar & Brown, 1984). It also seems obvious that no educational revolution will come unless future research concentrates more on the larger picture. In order to induce "expert" learning routines in inefficient learners, educators need to understand the relationships between execution of memory strategies (such as mnemonic elaboration) and metastrategy information, monitoring, and motivation. Pressley and Levin are only prepared to offer "hunches" about such relationships in this chapter, but *my* hunch is that they've got several studies in the works at this very moment.

Metastrategies and Generalization

Whereas Pressley and Levin devoted their chapter largely to showcasing the ways elaborative strategies can aid inefficient learners, Borkowski, Johnston, and Reid are particularly interested in the issue of generalization. Training inefficient learners to use a particular strategy is well and good, but true educational progress depends on whether the learner will then apply that strategy spontaneously and appropriately to new tasks. Borkowski, Johnston, and Reid point out that group data on strategy transfer can hide the fact that some of the subjects employ acquired strategies in new situations and others do not. What accounts for these individual differences? Borkowski, Johnston, and Reid draw our attention to the third component in Table C2.1, metastrategy information. They feel that knowledge about strategies is necessary for successful strategy application in new situations, and that successful strategy application leads to acquisition of knowledge about strategies. Thus the relationship between memory and metamemory is dynamic and bidirectional.

Metastrategy information is divided into several major components, and Borkowski, Johnston, and Reid devote most attention to the categories of specific strategy knowledge and metamemory acquisition procedures. It is the latter element that sometimes seems a bit confusing. Metamemory acquisition procedures are strategies for acquiring information about memory strategies. This definition makes sense in the abstract, but it is difficult, when presented with a specific behavior, procedure, or kind of knowledge, to decide whether it is a specific strategy, a monitoring procedure, or a strategy for acquiring new strategies. For instance, Borkowski, Johnston, and Reid state that "independence in problem solving, task perseverence in the face of challenge, and self-directed behaviors are signs of the operation of metamemory acquisition procedures" (p. 153). However, task perseverence sounds like a motivational element, self-directed behaviors show specific strategy knowledge, and it's not clear how independence in problem solving is necessarily a procedure for the acquisition of metamemory knowledge (it might reflect preexisting knowledge instead). As another example, Borkowski, Johnston, and Reid describe knowledge of the relationship between attention and learning as specific strategy knowledge, but knowledge about selective attention is considered a metamemory acquisition procedure. Clearly, some refinement of these categories is called for.

Still, the metamemory acquisition component makes an important contribution to our understanding of learning difficulties, particularly in classroom situations. Both the Borkowski, Johnston, and Reid and Pressley and Levin chapters remind us that teachers sometimes have difficulty instructing students in learning strategies. Often they make no strategy suggestions at all; sometimes they even suggest blatantly inappropriate strategies. In the seventh grade my daughter came home with a map of Africa to learn, plus instructions to purchase a set of colored pencils. The teacher had instructed the students to study by coloring each of the countries a distinct color. Outside of personal satisfaction, it's difficult to imagine what specific strategy knowledge this approach recruits. Needless to say, we decided to work out an alternate and more effective study strategy. We dispensed with the coloring (strategy rejection). The map was inappropriate for self-testing because each country had its name printed on it so we covered the names and xeroxed several copies (preparation of appropriate materials). We designed a repeated self-testing procedure to focus study on previously nonrecalled items and cooked up a number of wild associative mnemonics for particular countries (selection of specific strategies). Progress was noted on subsequent self-testing trials (appropriate attribution for success to the strategy, thus bolstering motivation), and the process was continued to the 100% criterion level (guaranteeing that goal and effort requirements were precisely met). Other potential strategies we rejected included flashcards as not useful for locating countries on a map (wrong goal), and an extremely elaborate system of numbering the countries, associating countries with numbers and numbers with locations (violation of time constraints and effort requirements). There is no need to belabor the point here, but I wonder what the other kids did? What about students whose parents aren't memory strategy experts?

How often are inappropriate strategies suggested by teachers? Teachers have been known to suggest that alphabetizing would aid memory, that spelling lists should be studied by merely looking at them, that notes could be memorized by copying them over, and college students have reported that the "coloring technique" was recommended in their anatomy classes. Indeed, Pressley and Levin fear that students might acquire "quite an extensive repertoire" of ineffective strategies suggested by well-intentioned teachers. This is obviously an empirical question, requiring detailed observations of actual classroom strategy instruction along the lines of Durkin's (1984) studies of reading instruction. A promising preliminary study was reported by Hart, Leal, Burney and Santulli (1985); they observed 69 K-6 teachers in language arts and mathematics lessons and tallied memory strategy suggestions. Each teacher was observed for five 30-minute periods, and in all 292 strategy suggestions were observed for the 69 teachers. In other words, each teacher made an average of 4.23 strategy suggestions in 2 ½ hours of instruction (but note also that there were wide individual differences . . .). This does not seem to be an overwhelming rate, but at least this is evidence that teachers do recognize the need to convey information about how to study effectively. More data are needed, however, about the appropriateness of the strategy suggestions, and it is interesting to note that Hart et al. observed only 15 examples of strategy suppression. To the extent that metamemory acquisition procedures involve strategy modification or switching, few examples of this skill are apparently taught directly in the classroom.

To return to the main theme of this chapter, generalization, Borkowski, Johnston, and Reid propose that transfer failures will occur when there is a combination of (a) deficits in automatic processing, (b) poor strategy execution, and (c) deficient metamemory. Practically nothing is said about (a), perhaps because so much has been said elsewhere about processing deficits in learning disabilities, and the authors wished to concentrate on (b) and (c). Indeed, lack of spontaneous strategy execution is considered to be perhaps the major problem for inefficient (or "passive") learners in this chapter. However, even though Borkowski, Johnston, and Reid point out that "LD children can be relatively easily trained to employ strategies, at least on simple tasks, with performance often approaching that of uninstructed nonhandicapped peers," (p. 155) is passivity really the only problem? The fact that disabled learners often fail to show evidence of strategic study does not necessarily prove they are merely passive learners (production deficient, in other parlance). Recently Guttentag (1984) asked the same question about younger versus older elementary children who were trained to use a simple cumulative rehearsal strategy to learn a list of words. By clever use of a simultaneous rapid finger-tapping task, Guttentag was able to estimate mental effort by looking at reductions in tapping rate under various memory conditions. Although it was clear that the second-grade children could be successfully trained to use the cumulative rehearsal strategy, their decrement in tapping rate suggested that use of this strategy required significantly more mental effort than it did for sixth-grade children. Guttentag speculated that younger children (and learning-disabled children, by extension) may exhibit a production deficiency not only because they don't know, understand, think, or want to perform a given strategy, but also because the strategy requires them to spend relatively large amounts of mental effort, compared to older (or nondisabled) children.

This relates directly to the issue of motivation. Borkowski, Johnston, and Reid review a number of studies (see also Licht, 1983) supporting the idea that disabled learners' early school failures lead them to doubt the effectiveness of effort in learning tasks. As they progress through school their reduced learning efforts result not only in continued school failure ("learned helplessness"), but also less opportunity to acquire metastrategy information. A key ingredient in this view is the attribution of failure by learning-disabled students to uncontrollable factors, such as low ability. Nondisabled students, in contrast, attribute difficulties to controllable factors such as effort, and they respond to difficult tasks with increased effort, whereas inefficient learners do not. Guttentag's (1984) study suggests a contrasting picture, however. Because learning strategies are so effortful for disabled learners there is not only less cognitive capacity available for acquiring metastrategy information, but strategy execution itself is aversive. Contrary to the view expressed by Borkowski, Johnston, and Reid, these students may well understand the role of effort in learning, but it is precisely because learning is so much more effortful for them than for their nondisabled classmates that they try to avoid using strategic behaviors. That strategies demand more resources in disabled learners may also explain why they may appear to exhibit lower effort on difficult tasks, whereas proficient learners are more free to respond to failures by selecting alternate and sometimes even more sophisticated strategies.

On the other hand, whatever the source, the difficulties encountered by disabled learners can have devastating emotional consequences, and Borkowski, Johnston, and Reid note that affective and motivational components can energize or hinder the use of a strategy or skill on a transfer task. For example, the notion of learned helplessness is useful to explain the tendency of learning-disabled children to exhibit inappropriate achievement attributions and low effort in areas on which they had not previously experienced failure, such as when poor readers were given math tasks, puzzles, a bowling game, and so forth (Licht, 1983). It also suggests why brief superficial attributional manipulations such as employed by Short and Ryan (1984) may be doomed to be ineffective. As Short and Ryan (1984) point out, it would be surprising indeed if three brief sessions using self-statements such as "praise yourself for a job well done; try hard; just think about how happy you will be when it comes time for the test and you're doing well" would potently counter antecedent attributions based upon years of unsuccessful school experiences. In contrast, the "attributional boost" procedures employed by Reid and Borkowski (1985) did seem to be effective, for both immediate and long-term performance. Actual incidents of failure were used as occasions to discuss the causes of failure, to induce the child to perform the failed task successfully using the correct strategy and to reflect upon controllable factors in success. It makes sense that this specific attributional training might be more beneficial than more general admonitions to "pat yourself on the back." Reid and Borkowski (1985) also found that the attribution-trained subjects achieved significantly higher generalization scores on some tests of strategy transfer. Thus this study shows a causal relationship between motivational factors and some forms of generalization.

Motivation and Coping

The chapter by Oka and Paris is most directly focused on the contribution of motivation to learning. It differs from the other two target chapters both in subject area (reading comprehension rather than memorization tasks) and approach (assessment rather than training studies). Nevertheless, the theme of motivation forges a strong tie between this chapter and the others.

Oka and Paris organize their chapter roughly along the lines of Table C2.1, in that they begin by reviewing a handful of exemplary studies documenting the difficulty disabled readers have in using sophisticated comprehension strategies. They next focus on the element of metastrategies by listing Baker's (1982) nine metacognitive deficits in reading. According to Table C2.1, though, these are not all strictly metacognitive problems (further illustrating the "fuzziness" in the concept of metacognition mentioned by Oka and Paris). According to the scheme we're using, metacognitive strategies would include Baker's categories of understanding that apprehension of meaning is a purpose of reading (goals the strategy can help meet), modifying reading behavior to meet different goals (a meta-memory acquisition procedure), and knowledge about strategies for coping with comprehension difficulties. However, identifying main themes, recognizing logical structure, relating new information to prior knowledge, attending to syntactic/semantic constraints, and evaluations of clarity, completeness, and consistency could all be thought of as strategies, rather than metastrategies. Ability to tell how well materials have been understood is a form of monitoring. Finally, likelihood of applying those strategies is a motivational element, under allocation of effort.

When Oka and Paris turn their attention to motivation they begin by reviewing research on how children's self-perceptions affect learning. It turns out that there is an interesting developmental progression in the accuracy of children's self-perceptions. Young children's perceptions of their own competence have a remarkably weak correlation with actual performance (or teacher evaluations) until about third or fourth grade (Harter, 1981). Before that, positive attitudes predominate, and overestimation of skills and abilities is common (Flavell & Wellman, 1977; Worden & Sladewski-Awig, 1982). However, self-perceptions are also influenced by one's history of success and failure. What isn't clear is whether there is a developmental increase in the impact of failure. The "learned helplessness" model implies that learning passivity exhibited by inefficient learners begins with the earliest experiences in failing, suggesting a certain urgency of intervention. However, the developmental improvement in the accuracy of self-perceptions suggests that the full impact of academic failure does not hit until middle elementary grades. In early stages of remediation, perhaps, basic skills should be stressed; in middle grades motivational elements require support too. Oka and Paris's data support this pedagogical suggestion.

The centerpiece of their chapter is an ambitious assessment of 669 third and fifth graders on a half a dozen measures related to reading achievement. Reading comprehension was tested with the cloze procedure and a test of error detection (using passages with semantic and syntactic anomalies). Awareness of reading was assessed with 22 multiple-choice items on knowledge of task goals, planful use of strategies, and effectiveness of those activities. Reading attitudes were tested with seven statements such as "I really enjoy reading." Self-perception was assessed with seven characteristics from the Perceived Competence Scale for Children (Harter, 1982). Intrinsic/Extrinsic classroom orientation was tested with four items from a scale created by Harter (1981).

Oka and Paris began their study by examining the degree to which ability predicted reading achievement in their sample. The Cognitive Abilities Test was highly correlated with the Comprehension subtest of Gates–MacGinitie Reading Test, $r = .78$. The difference between the scores actually obtained by the children and the predicted values was computed next. The distribution of residual scores from this analysis was partitioned at 1 $S.D.$ above and below the mean, resulting in groups of "overachievers" and "underachievers," respectively. This procedure identifies children who markedly depart from predicted levels of achievement, irrespective of IQ. Note that the discrepancy that produces extreme residual scores could result from any combination of high/low ability versus high/low reading achievement, but this was not the case. Oka and Paris found that low and average readers tended to show underachievement, whereas discrepant high-ability readers fall into the overachievement category. None of the low-skilled readers showed overachievement; only seven high readers showed underachievement.

On the initial 2 (grade) by 3 (achievement) manova, both main effects were significant, but no interaction was found. Univariate Fs revealed significant grade effects for Gates–MacGinitie comprehension, cloze, and reading awareness. Children's attitudes toward reading, cognitive self-perceptions, accuracy of self-perceptions, and intrinsic motivation showed no change between Grade 3 and 5. Achievement group effects were significant for all tasks, except verbal aptitude and reading awareness. These results are quite interesting but raise a couple of questions. First, it is of concern that some of the significant effects are based upon such miniscule differences (such as in the error detection efficiency scores of .9, 1.0 and 1.1). How meaningful are these given the whopping degrees of freedom (2,663) in a design with so many subjects? Second, no specific post hoc tests were reported, so we cannot pin down the loci of significant differences in particular achievement groups.

The major question of this study was the degree to which strategic, metastrategic, and motivational factors play a role in reading ability, as assessed in a multiple regression analysis. The dependent variable was the Gates–MacGinitie reading comprehension test; predictors were cloze, error detection, reading awareness, reading attitudes, cognitive self-perceptions and intrinsic motivation. At *third grade* reading proficiency was strongly predicted by reading strategies and metacognitive awareness in underachievers (.65 of the variance). Going up the achievement scale, skills became less important and less of the variance was explained. For overachievers, attitudes were most important, then error detection, and the whole package only accounted for .38 of the variance. The motivational element of cognitive self-perceptions only accounted for 2%, and only in average readers. For *fifth grade,* cognitive self-perceptions were important at all achievement levels, accounting for a whopping .24 of the variance in fifth-grade overachievers! For low-level children, metastrategic (reading awareness) information in the third-grade equation was replaced by this motivational component in the fifth-grade profile. Average achievers were relatively stable from third to fifth grade (only the reading attitudes factor was added to their equation). Overachievers' reading proficiency in fifth grade was predicted entirely by metacognitive (reading awareness) and motivational (cognitive self-perception) factors. I wonder if this is because overachievers are all reading so well by this time that reading skill per se is no longer an issue. They're like world-class athletes; they all have ample amounts of raw talent, and performance is more a matter of "heart" at this point. Do the results really reflect the emerging influence of motivational factors on reading, or do they reflect the diminishing influence of basic skills and metastrategies once a certain level of proficiency is attained?

Oka and Paris use the results of their regression analysis to create a profile of the underachiever. The underachieving group most resembles the traditionally defined learning-disabled population whose poor school achievement is based upon poor reading performance in spite of normal IQ. Underachieving children were characterized by "lower levels of comprehension and less effective use of reading strategies . . . negative reading attitudes, lower self-perceptions of cognitive competence, and an extrinsic orientation toward school" (p. 132). Unfortunately, such a thumbnail sketch of characteristics relative to those in average and above-average children distorts some of the actual findings. For instance, it's difficult to accept the description of the underachievers as having "negative reading attitudes," and an "extrinsic orientation" toward school. As Oka and Paris's Table 5.3 shows, even the underachievers' scores were in the positive range on these tests. In addition, note that the differences are particularly miniscule in some cases, especially on the measure of intrinsic motivation (2.9 vs. 3.0 vs. 3.1). It may be true that with nearly 700 subjects these differences are significant, but does a .2 difference really mean that underachievers have an extrinsic motivation toward school compared with the intrinsic motivation ascribed to overachievers?

In spite of these interpretive issues, the Oka and Paris study has made an important contribution to our understanding of how cognitive skills, attitudes, beliefs, and self-perceptions interact to form distinct patterns for different age and ability groups. In using the multiple regression approach, this study made the most progress of any of the target chapters in measuring the relative and joint contributions of basic abilities, metastrategies, monitoring, and motivation. For underachievers in particular, it was shown that awareness of one's own abilities is a significant contributing factor, but only for fifth-grade subjects. This suggests that younger children may be protected for a time by a sort of blithe ignorance about their learning difficulties, but that for older children remediation should address motivational issues as well as cognitive ones. Still, it is important to keep in mind the relatively small contribution of motivation in the disabled learners achievement equation (only 7% of the variance for fifth graders in this project). Further studies of this type should examine whether the importance of motivation varies when other tasks and predictors are investigated. Consider also the issue of determining when motivational factors are effects, and when they are causes. This question should prompt further training studies of the type discussed in the Borkowski, Johnston, and Reid chapter.

The final theme of the Oka and Paris chapter is coping. In order to understand the relationship between skills, motivation, and coping, they present four hypothetical "personalized dimensions" of motivation. The first, sense of control, is a common notion (also covered thoroughly in the Borkowski, Johnston, and Reid chapter), related to beliefs or attributions for success and failure to external or internal causes. The second, significant goals and values, is an important new contribution to this model. It's often taken for granted that school learning is necessarily a valued aspiration for all children, and it isn't. The third dimension, subjective task value (Eccles, Adler, Futterman, Goff, Kaczala, & Midgley, 1983), relates to questions such as: Is doing well important to me (attainment value)? Is personal satisfaction as important as external rewards (intrinsic value)? Is the task useful for achieving other goals too, or is it an end in itself (utility)? What is the cost of engaging (or not engaging) in the task? (The fourth "personalized" dimension of motivation, self-management skills, involves knowledge of how to apply particular skills effectively to achieve specific goals and has been described elsewhere in this review as a form of specific strategy knowledge, i.e., metastrategy information, rather than as an element of motivation).

Coping is a different concept from remediation in that it implies adjusting to the problem rather than curing it. Ordinarily, if students avoid reading or other academic tasks, a conventional response is to get the student "back on task." Oka and Paris feel that this may be a mistake: "It is not necessarily maladaptive to stop working on a task under certain conditions" (p. 134). In fact, Oka and Paris see low motivation as a healthy way of coping when children feel they have no control, the task has little personal significance, the child has no appropriate self-management skills, and failure is seen as a dead-end experience. In contrast to the "passive learner" view, it is recognized that disabled learners may actually expend more effort than their nondisabled classmates: "A child who puts in a great deal of time and effort and sees little return will expect little success in the future because effort expenditure is already high" (p. 138).

Oka and Paris recommend redefining success and failure as steps in learning and not as terminal outcomes. They feel that inefficient learners need to learn the virtue of failing, a common and informative experience that should lead to action, rather than inaction. Rather than using failure only to project future failure, children should be taught to react adaptively to failure, to identify the controllable factors in failure. It is interesting that this suggestion is embodied in the successful "attributional boost" method used by Reid and Borkowski (1985).

A couple of other sequelae flow from this line of reasoning. One is the assumption that "achievement environments" (provided by family, school, and peer contexts) can influence values. A child with learning difficulties may be showing a coping response if he or she selects a nonacademic context as a salient source of values, much to the consternation of teachers. At present there are few recommendations for dealing with this way of coping. An area where educators do have control, however, is in deciding whether a student should be placed in special classes or left in the "mainstream." To the extent that special classes provide greater opportunity to experience successful learning outcomes, this bolsters self-confidence. To the extent that special classes increase the child's awareness of his or her limitations, relative to peers, motivation may be damaged. This issue, of course, goes far beyond the limits of this commentary. Suffice it to say that educators need to weigh the motivational reactions of disabled learners to special class placement (or nonplacement), along with potential task-specific achievements.

The Goal Reconsidered

Collectively, these three chapters have charted the tremendous progress made in recent years in understanding how proficient learners succeed. Moreover, this understanding has prompted successful training studies and motivational interventions for problem learners with new hope of overcoming the generalization problem. At the beginning of this commentary it was noted that none of the authors limited their reviews strictly to children with specific learning disabilities. Much of the research did not employ the strict criteria for selection of learning-disabled subjects suggested by researchers who search for the elusive specific deficits. Vellutino (Vol. 1) states that, to some, such studies reflect "an alarming tendency to depart from certain of the rigorous standards that began to make the study of specific learning disability a legitimate and respectable area of inquiry" (p. 333).

Whether one considers the research reviewed in these chapters "alarming" or not stems from different views of the goal of the research. From a purely basic research perspective, many of the studies are deficient in various ways. A common problem, for example, is that a successful intervention often has several elements, and proper control groups have not been included to isolate the potent components. However, in contrast to studies of information processing in so-called average individuals, learning-disabilities research has an inherent educational mandate. An implied goal in all such studies is that something will be discovered that can help inefficient learners in educational settings. That the intervention is successful is worthy, even if for the moment we aren't entirely sure why.

As for the search for specific learning deficits, consider a woman I know who doesn't sing well, because she is "tone deaf." She "can't carry a tune in a bucket." However, she is well in the normal range on other aspects of musical knowledge and ability. She reads music and is otherwise music literate in that she enjoys, appreciates, and understands all kinds of music. In fact, she is well above average in her ability to play the piano. Is the analogy between learning disability and the specific musical deficit of tone deafness appropiate? No, for two reasons. First, tone deafness hasn't affected her other musical skills. It has just limited her arena of expression (she played organ for the church choir, but didn't sing in it). The nasty thing about a learning disability, as should be obvious from the target chapters, is its tendency to have a spreading effect, resulting in a variety of cognitive, behavioral, motivational, and emotional impacts that can bedevil the researcher and theoretician alike. Second, being unable to sing does not carry the same stigma as doing poorly in school, regardless of whether school problems are due to a specific disability or a generally low level of ability. This underscores the urgency for researchers to explore educational remedies, taking into account the four M's, and to seek treatments that are of practical use to educators. Our ultimate goal should include both the improvement of our knowledge base and of our educational system.

Finally, although the target chapters have generally taken an "expert systems" approach to the study of learning difficulties, it should be made clear that it is not an appropriate goal to seek a means of training all the children to be "above average," as they are in Lake Wobegon. Rather, given that each child has a range of potential achievement, our goal should be to discover how to help the child function as well as possible within that range.

REFERENCES

Baker, L. (1982). An evaluation of the role of metacognitive deficits in learning disabilities. *Topics in Learning and Learning Disabilities, 2,* 27–36.

Beck, I. (1984). Developing comprehension: The impact of the directed reading lesson. In R. C. Anderson, J. Osborn, & R. J. Tierney (Eds.), *Learning to read in American schools: Basal readers and content texts.* Hillsdale, NJ: Lawrence Erlbaum Associates.

Durkin, D. (1984). Do basal manuals teach reading comprehension? In R. C. Anderson, J. Osborn, & R. J. Tierney (Eds.), *Learning to read in American schools: Basal readers and content texts.* Hillsdale, NJ: Lawrence Erlbaum Associates.

Eccles, J., Adler, T. F., Futterman, R., Goff, S. B., Kaczala, C. M., & Midgley, C. (1983). Expectancies, values, and academic behaviors. In J. T. Spence (Ed.), *Perspectives on achievement and achievement motivation.* San Francisco: Freeman.

Ehri, L. C., Deffner, N. D., & Wilce, L. S. (1984). Pictorial mnemonics for phonics. *Journal of Educational Psychology, 76,* 880–893.

Farnham-Diggory, S. (1986). Time, now, for a little serious complexity. In S. J. Ceci (Ed.) *Handbook of cognitive, social, and neuropsychological aspects of learning disabilities* (Vol. 1, pp. 123–158). Hillsdale, NJ: Lawrence Erlbaum Associates.

Flavell, J. H., & Wellman, H. M. (1977). Metamemory. In R. Kail & J. Hagen (Eds.), *Perspectives on the development of memory and cognition* (pp. 1–34). Hillsdale, NJ: Lawrence Erlbaum Associates.

Guttentag, R. E. (1984). The mental effort requirement of cumulative rehearsal: A developmental study. *Journal of Experimental Child Psychology, 37,* 92–106.

Hart, S. S., Leal, L., Burney, L., & Santulli, K. A. (1985, April). *Memory in the elementary school classroom: How teachers encourage strategy use.* Paper presented at the biennial meetings of the Society for Research in Child Development, Toronto.

Harter, S. (1981). A model of mastery motivation in children: Individual differences and developmental change. In W. A. Collins (Ed.), *Aspects of the development of competence: The Minnesota symposium on child psychology* (Vol. 14). Hillsdale, NJ: Lawrence Erlbaum Associates.

Harter, S. (1982). The perceived competence scale for children. *Child Development, 53,* 87–97.

Licht, B. G. (1983). Cognitive–motivational factors that contribute to the achievement of learning disabled children. *Journal of Learning Disabilities, 16,* 483–490.

Mandler, J. M., & Johnson, N. S. (1977). Remembrance of things parsed: Story structure and recall. *Cognitive Psychology, 9,* 111–191.

Mastropieri, M. A., Scruggs, T. E., Levin, J. R., Gaffney, J., & McLoone, B. (1985). Mnemonic vocabulary instruction for learning disabled students. *Learning Disability Quarterly, 8,* 57–63.

Mastropieri, M. A., Scruggs, T. E., McLoone, B., & Levin, J. R. (1985). Facilitating learning disabled students' acquisition of science classifications. *Learning Disability Quarterly, 8,* 299–309.

McGivern, J. E., & Levin, J. R. (1983). The keyword method and children's vocabulary learning: An interaction with vocabulary knowledge. *Contemporary Educational Psychology, 8,* 46–54.

Palincsar, A. M., & Brown, A. L. (1984). Reciprocal teaching of comprehension-fostering and comprehension-monitoring activities. *Cognition and Instruction, 1,* 117–175.

Peters, E. E., & Levin, J. R. (in press). Effects of a mnemonic imagery strategy on good and poor readers' prose recall. *Reading Research Quarterly.*

Pressley, M., Levin, J. R., & Delaney, H. D. (1982). The mnemonic keyword method. *Review of Educational Research, 52,* 61–92.

Reid, M. K., & Borkowski, J. G. (1985, April). *Causal attributions of hyperactive children: Implications for training strategies and self-control.* Paper presented at the biennial meeting of the Society for Research in Child Development, Toronto.

Scruggs, T. E., Mastropieri, M. A., Levin, J. R., & Gaffney, J. (1985). *Facilitating the acquisition of science facts in learning disabled students. American Educational Research Journal, 22,* 575–586.

Short, E. J., & Ryan, E. B. (1984). Metacognitive differences between skilled and less skilled readers: Remediating deficits through story grammar and attribution training. *Journal of Educational Psychology, 76,* 225–235.

Wong, B. Y. L., & Jones, W. (1982). Increasing metacomprehension in learning-disabled and normally achieving students through self-questioning training. *Learning Disability Quarterly, 5,* 228–240.

Worden, P. E. (1983). Memory strategy instruction with the learning disabled. In M. Pressley and J. R. Levin, *Cognitive strategies: Developmental, educational, and treatment-related issues* (pp. 129–153). New York: Springer–Verlag.

Worden, P. E., Kee, D. W., & Ingle, M. J. (1985, April). *Parent–child alphabet learning with picture books vs. personal computers.* Paper presented at the biennial meetings of the Society for Research in Child Development, Toronto.

Worden, P. E., & Sladewski-Awig, L. (1982). Children's awareness of memorability. *Journal of Educational Psychology, 74,* 341–350.

III SOCIOEMOTIONAL ASPECTS OF LEARNING DISABILITIES

8 Affect and Cognition in Learning Disabilities

David Goldstein
Temple University
Irving Schwartz Institute for Children and Youth

William D. Dundon
Temple University

Over the past few decades the study of cognition has so dominated experimental and developmental psychology that the study of affect or emotion[1] has largely been ignored (Lewis & Michalson, 1983). As a consequence, the study of the interaction of these variables also has been ignored. Even when affect and cognition have been considered together, affect has been defined in cognitive terms (Izard, 1982). Only recently has the bidirectionality of affect and cognition begun to receive attention (e.g., Cairns & Valsiner, 1984).

We propose that the study of the interaction of affect and cognition can enrich our understanding of the behavior of LD children. In particular, we argue in this chapter that affect can play a central role in learning disabilities, functioning as a cause as well as a consequence of learning problems. We outline a framework that enables us to understand the role of affect in learning disabilities. In addition we offer some preliminary findings on the role of affect in the academic performance of LD children and discuss the remedial implications of the framework.

The idea that learning disabilities may be related to emotional factors is not a new one. Blanchard (1928), for example, argued that reading difficulties were

---

[1] There is no definitional consensus among researchers, although Simon (1982) offers a useful typology distinguishing three kinds of affect. Emotions that have an immediate survival function represent such phenomena as fear and surprise. Moods such as happiness or sadness have a more subtle effect but "influence and direct cognitive activities" (p. 335). Finally, valuations are cognitive evaluations of things or events, which can occur without a feeling component. In this chapter we use the terms affect, emotion, and mood interchangeably, but we are referring to mood in Simon's terms.

the result of "extreme negative feeling." Rabinovitch (1959) made a distinction between primary and secondary reading retardation; the former the result of basic processing deficits and the latter the result of emotional factors. Kirk (1962), who popularized the use of the term *learning disability,* proposed that learning disability resulted from "a possible cerebral dysfunction and/or emotional or behavioral disturbance" (p. 253).

In more recent years, however, the hypothesis that emotional factors contribute to learning disabilities has all but vanished from the literature. For example, the *Child Development Abstracts and Bibliography,* which covers virtually all of the major journals in psychology, education, and pediatrics, lists for the years 1982 and 1983 115 references under the heading of "learning disabilities," only one of which contains a category related to affect as a subheading. Smith's (1983) textbook on learning disabilities contains no index entry for affect or depression, and only 15 lines on "adverse emotional climate" in a 98-page section on "causes of learning disabilities."

Nowhere is the exclusion of affect from the literature on learning disabilities more marked than in the various definitions of learning disability adopted in recent years. The most widely cited definition, contained in PL 94–142, excludes from the category "learning-disabled" children whose school learning problems are "due primarily to . . . emotional disturbance" (Federal Register, 1977). The recent definition proposed by the National Joint Committee for Learning Disabilities, which was stimulated by widespread dissatisfaction with the definition of PL 94–142, states that "a learning disability may occur concomitantly with . . . social and emotional disturbance" but "is not the direct result of those conditions or influences" (Hammill, Leigh, McNutt, & Larsen, 1981, p. 336). Even the definition (in U.S. Office of Education, 1968) of the National Advisory Committee on Handicapped Children, chaired by Kirk in 1967 (5 years after his definition previously cited), stated explicitly that "Children with special learning disabilities . . . do not include learning problems which are due primarily to . . . emotional disturbance" (p. 34).

Although we would not dispute the argument that children whose learning problems can be clearly linked to "severe emotional disturbance" are better served by the diagnosis of "emotionally disturbed" (despite the considerable overlap between the diagnostic categories of learning disabled and emotionally disturbed; see Hallahan & Kauffman, 1977), we suggest that to exclude all emotional factors from the proposed causes of learning disabilities is to throw out the baby with the bath water. The possibility still exists that milder or more subtle forms of emotional distress may play a key role in the origin and maintenance of learning problems. Although some authors have suggested that emotional problems result from learning deficits and contribute to further learning problems, a situation that Kinsbourne and Caplan (1979, p. 16) label *the cycle of failure,* the possibility that emotional problems are the *underlying cause* of some children's learning failures has not been extensively explored in the literature.

One possible reason for the exclusion of emotional factors may be the absence of a framework within which one can meaningfully view the role of affect in learning disabilities. Therefore, one primary goal of this chapter is to propose such a framework. Following this proposal, we explore the role of affective factors in learning problems. In the course of this discussion, the problem of LD subgroups is briefly explored. Further, some data on a subgrouping scheme that incorporates affective factors is presented. Finally, the remedial implications of the overall framework are outlined.

A FRAMEWORK FOR THE STUDY OF AFFECT
AND COGNITION

Overview of Framework

Attention and Capacity

Two key concepts underlying this framework are attention and capacity. Attention is the process by which an individual receives and processes information (Rosenthal & Allen, 1978). Kahneman (1973) suggested that attention has two aspects—the selective and the intensive. Selective attention refers to the process whereby we take in only a limited amount of the information potentially available to us. The intensive aspect of attention is the effort needed to perform a task.

Capacity refers to the limited pool of energy available to individuals for the performance of mental activities or cognitive operations (Kahneman, 1973). The amount of capacity that an individual has available at any given time is not fixed but rather is variable. Both task and subject variables influence the amount of capacity that is available. Task variables include difficulty (e.g., reading the newspaper vs. reading Kant) and number of other tasks being performed at that point in time (e.g., trying to perform a complex motor skill while carrying on a lively conversation). Subject variables include arousal, motivation (e.g., hunger), personality variables (e.g., internal vs. external locus of control), and mood (e.g., joyful vs. depressed).[2] In particular, our working assumption is that negative mood (e.g., depression) lowers available capacity and consequently leads to reduced performance on effortful tasks among which are included most academic activities.

Human performance, then, is a function of the stimuli selected for input, the amount of effort demanded by the task at hand, and the available cognitive capacity. If the task selected requires more effort than the available capacity

---

[2]Whether or not age influences capacity is currently a matter of some debate. Neo-Piagetians such as Pascual-Leone (1970) have argued that capacity increases with age whereas cognitive psychologists such as Chi (1976) have argued that capacity is age invariant.

allows, performance will be poor. If the task requires little effort, performance will be good, even if capacity is relatively limited or temporarily reduced. Because capacity is variable, a task that requires considerable effort may be successfully performed at a time when capacity is greater and poorly performed at a time when capacity is reduced.

Automatic and Effortful Processes

Hasher and Zacks (1979) have used such a framework to argue that tasks may be placed on a continuum from automatic to effortful. Tasks that require effort use some of the individual's available capacity, interfere with ongoing activities (one cannot usually read a technical paper and watch television at the same time), require intention, benefit from practice and feedback, and show marked developmental trends. Most of the classroom activities that children engage in (and that psychologists study) are effortful tasks. Differences in education, in socioeconomic status, in culture, and in intelligence all have a profound impact on the ability to engage in effortful processing (Hasher & Zacks, 1984).

Tasks that can be performed without effort are referred to as automatic. Automatic-encoding operations are ones that use little capacity, do not interfere with other ongoing activities, and function continuously and well without the intention of the individual. Automatic processes are "basic" (see Flavell, 1977) in that they are expected to show minimal developmental trends across the entire life-span with maximal levels of proficiency already present early in life. Automatic processes are widely shared among people; differences in education, in socioeconomic status, in culture, and in intelligence all have little impact on the ability to encode an automatically processed attribute (Hasher & Zacks, 1984).

Certain fundamental aspects of experience are automatically encoded into memory (Hasher & Zacks, 1979, 1984); these include frequency of occurrence, spatial location, and temporal information. Frequency of occurrence, the most extensively studied of the automatic processes, refers to the number of times a particular event has occurred. For example, people are remarkably accurate at discriminating the number of times a particular picture has occurred in a lengthy series of pictures, despite the age or mood of the subject, amount of practice, prior instructions, or feedback about performance (Hasher & Zacks, 1984).

Although the encoding of frequency of occurrence, and possibly spatial and temporal information, is always automatic ("unlearned automatic processing"; Horton & Mills, 1984) and consequently requires no capacity, other tasks can require less effort over time as a function of practice. To take a simple example, learning to drive a manual transmission can be quite effortful at first and the driver may not be able to drive and listen to the radio or carry on a conversation at the same time without running the risk of stalling or grinding gears. With practice, however, the process of shifting gears becomes more automatic; that is, it requires less effort and thus frees cognitive capacity for other activities. Indeed, shifting gears may eventually require so little effort that the driver is scarcely aware of engaging in this activity. This type of automatic processing has been referred to as "learned automatic processing" (Horton & Mills, 1984). Whether learned or unlearned, what is important here is that automatic processing uses none of the individual's available capacity.

Implications of Framework for LD Children

Automatic and Effortful Processing

The first major implication of the framework is that on automatic tasks LD children should perform as well as non-LD children. Three recent studies have demonstrated that LD children perform as well on tasks of frequency estimation (unlearned automatic processing; Goldstein, Hasher, & Stein, 1983; Lund, Hall, Wilson, & Humphries, 1983) and semantic processing (learned automatic processing; Ceci, 1983) as non-LD children. By contrast, in the Ceci and Goldstein et al. studies, the LD children performed poorly relative to non-LD children on tasks requiring effort.

Taken together, these three papers provide strong support for the claim that LD children do not differ from non-LD children in automatic processing of at least two types of information but do differ in effortful processing. These findings are important for at least two reasons. First, in so far as automatic processing represents the "hard-wiring" of our information-processing capabilities (Hasher & Zacks, 1979), LD children appear to be as intact as normal children. This view stands in sharp contrast to the historical view of LD children that emphasized neurological impairment (e.g., Cruickshank, 1977). Second, because information must be selectively attended to in order for the concomitant automatic processing to occur, the performance of LD children in these three reports indicates rather convincingly that these children are not suffering from an inability to attend to task-relevant stimuli. This view stands in sharp contrast to the currently popular view of LD children that emphasizes a (selective) attention deficit (e.g., Hallahan & Reeve, 1980; Smith, 1983, chap. 5). Indeed, recent evidence has cast considerable doubt upon the utility of the view that LD children have a deficit in selective attention (e.g., Cairns & Valsiner, 1984). Rather, we propose that LD children have an attentional deficit in the sense that they have difficulties with *intensive* attention (i.e., effort).

The second major implication of this framework is that LD children are deficient relative to non-LD children only on tasks that require effort. In fact, from our perspective much of the recent experimental literature on LD children can be interpreted as demonstrations of this point.

Factors Leading to Reduced Performance

We turn now to a central question of this chapter: If LD children show difficulties with effortful tasks, what factors are responsible? In the following section we briefly review evidence in support of four possible sources of these difficulties. The first two problem areas assume that LD children have normal amounts of capacity but use it inefficiently. They are thought to be deficient in the use of cognitive strategies and/or metacognitive abilities. The other two problem areas assume that these children have reduced capacity compared to non-LD children. The source of this deficit may be permanent (i.e., structural) or temporary (i.e., a functional deficit due to affective problems).

Normal Capacity With Strategic Deficits.   The relatively successful performance of non-LD children on effortful tasks is based in part upon their use of efficient learning strategies such as rehearsal, category clustering, and mnemonics (e.g., Kail, 1979). Torgesen (1980), among others, has suggested that the failure of LD children to use strategies is a primary source of their learning problems. There is a large literature documenting the poor performance of LD children on tasks that require the use of strategies, including rehearsal (Bauer, 1977), organization (Kosteski, Goldstein, & Hasher, 1979), and elaboration (Loe, 1978). Whereas these studies have helped to document the many ways in which LD children demonstrate inferior performance on effortful tasks relative to non-LD children, most of these studies fail to suggest *why* LD children have these difficulties. One possibility is that LD children are unaware that a particular strategy is required.

Normal Capacity With Metacognitive Deficits.   It is possible that LD children are potentially capable of using strategies but are unaware of the need for their use (Goldstein, Hasher, & Kosteski, 1980). Knowledge of how to use one's cognitive capabilities is an aspect of metacognition (Brown, 1975). Three recent studies demonstrate that at least some LD children have deficient metacognitive skills, particularly in the area of memory.

Torgesen (1979) compared a group of good readers and a group of poor readers with memory difficulties on a series of questions designed to assess knowledge of memory and memory strategies. The poor readers with memory difficulties demonstrated inferior knowledge in a variety of areas, such as the use of rehearsal, and the ability to generate possible retrieval strategies. Torgesen concluded that poor readers with memory deficits may not have limited learning capabilities but rather fail to manage or utilize their capabilities in an efficient and planful manner. These results were largely replicated by Trepanier and Casale (1983) and by Goldstein and Golding (1984) using samples of diagnosed LD children. In the latter study, however, only LD children with a specific memory deficit (indexed by retarded or borderline performance on the WISC-R Digit Span subtest) demonstrated metamemorial deficits relative to non-LD controls; LD children with Digit Span performance in the normal range had metamemory skills equal to those of non-LD children.

Thus, it appears that at least some LD children have cognitive deficits that are related to inadequate knowledge of how to use effort. It remains to be seen whether deficits in areas other than memory can be linked to deficits in metacognition.

Structurally Reduced Capacity.   In addition to difficulties exerting effort on strategic tasks because of a lack of metacognitive awareness, LD children may have problems with strategic and other types of effortful tasks because of insufficient cognitive capacity.

The capacity deficits from which LD children suffer are of two possible types. First, some LD children may have structural capacity deficits due to neuropsychological impairment. This view, closely related to the traditional view of LD children as having a minimal brain dysfunction, has been advocated most recently as one of limited information-processing capacity (e.g., Kershner, 1983). Because of prenatal, perinatal, or neonatal insult or through inherited deficiencies (e.g., Pennington, Bender, Puck, Salbenblatt, & Robinson, 1982), LD children may be permanently limited in available capacity and therefore either incapable of performing many effortful tasks or slow to develop the necessary behaviors (e.g., Kinsbourne & Caplan, 1979). In our view, although some LD children may have this type of difficulty (see Torgesen & Houck, 1980), its prevalence in the LD population has been greatly overestimated, in part because of the medical orientation that has until recently dominated the LD field.

Functionally Reduced Capacity.   A second possible type of capacity deficit, and the one central to our thesis, is a functional deficit that is temporary (and consequently remediable) rather than permanent. This type of functional reduction in available cognitive capacity is mediated by affective factors. This notion, already briefly discussed, is now treated in some detail.

AFFECTIVE FACTORS IN LEARNING DISABILITIES

There are many affective variables that may influence learning such as happiness, sadness (Masters, Barden, & Ford, 1979), self-esteem, and anxiety (Patten, 1983). Currently there is no consensus as to how these variables operate, although capacity can be reduced in at least two ways: (1) The relationship between arousal and capacity is presumed to be curvilinear with some optimal level of arousal yielding maximum capacity (Kahneman, 1973). Emotional variables that result in underarousal or overarousal would reduce available capacity (Weingartner, Cohen, Murphy, Martello, & Gerdt, 1981); (2) affective variables may excite irrelevant, interfering cognitions that would drain available capacity (Bower, 1981).

In this section we focus on the role of depression in LD children. Within our framework it is hypothesized that depression might reduce capacity by lowering arousal and/or by stimulating task irrelevant cognitions. In either case, depression can lead to poor school performance in LD children. There is a growing literature that indicates that depression is related to school achievement in non-LD children (e.g., Pozanski, 1982) and in children referred for school problems (Weinberg, Rutman, Sullivan, Penick, & Dietz, 1973) as well as a growing literature on adults showing the relationship between depression and performance on tasks requiring cognitive effort (Weingartner et al., 1981).

There are to date, however, no published reports showing that LD children are more depressed than non-LD children and that this depression is related to their school learning problems. In the following sections, we summarize some studies from our research program that address these issues.

Are LD Children More Depressed Than Non-LD Children?

The Children's Depression Inventory (CDI; Kovacs, 1980/1981) is a research instrument that has been recently designed to assess the severity of depressive symptoms in children. It is adapted from the widely used Beck Depression Inventory for adults and consists of 27 questions that deal with issues such as feelings of sadness, self-hatred, trouble sleeping, having fun, doing well in school, and so on.

Goldstein and Paul (1983) administered the CDI to 82 children with learning and behavioral problems at the Irving Schwartz Institute for Children and Youth. This setting serves LD children from predominantly black neighborhoods in Philadelphia. The mean CDI score for this sample was 13.78. This was significantly higher than the mean of 9.27 reported by Kovacs (1980/81) for a sample of 875 Canadian children and a mean of 7.59 for 226 third- and fifth-grade children from the Philadelphia area (Henderson, 1983). The black children within Henderson's sample had a mean score of 8.5 and 6.7 for the third and fifth graders, respectively. Goldstein, Dundon, and Wasik (1984) obtained a mean of 23.4 for a sample of 11 children from a Philadelphia public school classroom for the "emotionally disturbed." These children were from the same ethnic and economic background as the Irving Schwartz Institute sample. It appears then that the LD children were more depressed than non-LD children but not as depressed as emotionally disturbed children.

Depression and Achievement in LD Children

The demonstration that LD children are, as a group, more depressed than non-LD children, led Goldstein and Paul (1983) to the question of how depression was related to classroom achievement in reading and math. These investigators divided their sample into four subgroups, only two of which are of interest here. The two subgroups were based upon the presence or absence of "socioemotional disturbance" (SED) in conjunction with learning disabilities. In Pennsylvania, socioemotional disturbance refers to a cluster of symptoms including poor interpersonal relations, inappropriate behavior or feelings, a pervasive mood of unhappiness or depression, and psychosomatic complaints. Thus, the two subgroups were designated as the "LD" group, consisting of children with only a diagnosis of LD and no signs of socioemotional disturbance, and the "LD/ SED" group consisting of children with both a diagnosis of LD and SED.

The LD and LD/SED groups in this study did not differ significantly in average score on the CDI (14.9 vs. 12.5) but differed dramatically in the extent to which depression was related to reading and math achievement. For the LD group, the correlations between depression and reading and depression and math were $-.03$ and $-.21$, respectively (neither correlation was significant). For the LD/SED group, the respective correlations were $-.82$ and $-.53$ (both significant).

Within the LD/SED group it was hypothesized that depression plays a causal role in the underachievement of these children (see also Goldstein, Paul, & Sanfilippo-Cohn, 1985). Although we must await the results from cross-lagged panel and path analyses before any conclusions can be drawn, results from another study support the hypothesis that the learning failure of such a subgroup of children is mediated by affective variables.

Affect As the Basis for Subgroups of LD Children

It is widely recognized that LD children constitute a heterogeneous population, and progress in the field requires the ability to identify homogeneous subgroups. Within our framework we would predict that a subgroup of children would have reduced capacity due to affective variables, a reduction that should be temporary and subject to remediation. This prediction found partial support in the Goldstein and Paul (1983) study. We sought to examine this issue more closely.

We investigated the validity of four subgrouping schemes by comparing their ability to predict achievement. Use of achievement scores seemed the most valid approach because underachievement is the most characteristic feature of these children. Additionally, we gathered longitudinal data so that we could examine achievement differences at specific points in time as well as different patterns of achievement over time.

Four subgrouping schemes were examined. Three of them were based upon the use of WISC-R data as suggested in the literature (Kaufman, 1979; Rugel, 1974) by considering (a) verbal IQ—performance IQ discrepancies, (b) amount of subtest scatter, and (c) the presence or absence of the Bannatyne profile of subtest scores. The fourth scheme (described in detail later) was based in part on the presence or absence of affective factors.

All the students included in the study attended the Irving Schwartz Institute and came from predominantly black families[3]. A diagnosis, based upon

---

[3]Leinhardt, Seewald, and Zigmund (1982) have reported no differences between black and white LD children in average IQ, level of achievement, and conformity to diagnostic criteria. Therefore, we see no reason to limit the generality of our findings to children such as those in our present sample.

DSM-II or ICD-9 criteria, was provided for each child by the Institute's multidisciplinary diagnostic team during the first few months of the child's attendance at the school. This diagnosis served as the basis for the subgrouping. In addition, data from the WISC-R, the Woodcock Reading Test, and the KeyMath Diagnostic test (all individually administered) were gathered.

Although the Irving Schwartz Institute serves LD children, we have observed that many of them do not fit a strict definition of LD necessary for research. Therefore, we selected only those who did not exhibit severe emotional problems, who had a full-scale IQ of at least 80, and who were performing below 75% of their expected achievement level, based upon age and IQ. One hundred and fifty-nine subjects remained for study, 125 boys and 34 girls.

Table 8.1 presents the diagnostic categories used to form the affectively based subgroups. All the children were diagnosed as LD, but one subgroup (LD/OH) had an organic and/or hyperactive component, another (LD/SED) had a significant socioemotional component, whereas the third (LD) showed no evidence of these other components. Based upon our framework, we would characterize the LD group as having normal but inefficiently used capacity, the LD/OH group as having structurally reduced capacity, and the LD/SED group as having functionally reduced capacity, due to affective factors.

Regression analyses were performed using the subgrouping schemes to predict reading and math achievement at each of five times of measurement (representing the scores upon entering the school and 4 subsequent years). Two or more subgrouping schemes could then be statistically compared to see which best accounted for the achievement variance. However, none of these comparisons

TABLE 8.1
Diagnostic Categories From DSM-II And ICD #9 Used to Form
Diagnostic Subgrouping Scheme

Subgroup	Diagnostic Category
LD	Specific learning disturbance[a]
	Specific delays in development[b]
LD/SED	Adjustment reaction of childhood[a,b]
	Withdrawn reaction[a]
	Disturbance of emotions[b]
	Disturbance of conduct[b]
	Depressive disorder[b]
	Other behavior disorders[a]
LD/OH	Hyperkinetic reaction[a]
	Nonpsychotic OBS[a,b]
	Hyperkinetic syndrome of children[b]

[a] = DSM - II.
[b] = ICD #9.

could be made because none of the schemes based upon the WISC-R significantly predicted achievement. Although the WISC-R profiles may have been validated using other criteria (e.g., Dudley-Marling, Kaufman, & Tarver, 1981), we were unable to offer support for these systems using longitudinal achievement data.

The affective approach to subgrouping did lead to significant results, however. There was significant prediction of math achievement at the second and fifth times of measurement, representing the completion of 1 and 4 years of schooling, and significant prediction of reading achievement at the second, third, fourth, and fifth times of measurement. Due to different dropout rates each year as well as other factors, the number of subjects differed at each time of testing. Therefore, we selected subjects who had complete longitudinal data at times two, three, and four (i.e., after completing 1, 2, and 3 years of school). The three subgroups did not differ from each other in age, IQ, or initial level of achievement.

A three (subgroups) by three (times of measurement) ANOVA was performed separately on the arithmetic and reading scores. For arithmetic there were significant main effects for testing times and subgroups. The interaction was not significant. The Tukey HSD post hoc test indicated that all groups improved significantly each year. More importantly, the LD and LD/OH group did not differ from each other but both differed from the LD/SED group. This last group had significantly greater performance at each time of measurement.

The findings were similar for reading achievement except that the interaction term was also significant. A post hoc F-test was used to determine which patterns of results differed. The pattern of reading achievement for the LD group was significantly different from the LD/SED subgroup ($p < .001$). The LD/OH group did not differ from either of the other groups (see Fig. 8.1).

The rather impressive gains made by the LD/SED group are consistent with our view that these children were initially failing because of affective factors. During the course of their schooling at the Irving Schwartz Institute, their emotional problems were treated both in the classroom and in individual therapy sessions. Basically, we are suggesting that an improvement in affect led to increased capacity and a subsequent improvement in achievement.

The poor educational progress of the LD group suggests that their learning problems are due to factors other than affective ones. At this point we can only speculate that these children have normal capacity but are inefficient information processors. This hypothesis is further complicated because the LD/OH group did not differ significantly from the LD group in reading or math and did not differ from the LD/SED group in reading. We are currently attempting to replicate this study and investigate the underlying processes of these subgroups.

These data, although still of a preliminary nature, provide further support for our hypothesis that affective variables may be usefully considered in the study of LD children both for understanding the origins of their academic difficulties and for the remediation of their difficulties. It is to the latter issue that we now turn.

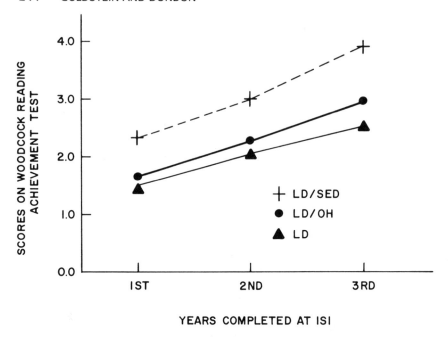

FIG. 8.1 Patterns of reading achievement for LD, LD/SED, and LD/OH subgroups.

REMEDIAL CONSIDERATIONS

Increase Available Capacity

Given that depression reduces the capacity available for classroom activities, one potentially effective remedial strategy for at least a subgroup of LD children would be to increase the amount of cognitive capacity that is available to the child for school tasks by ameliorating depression. We suggest two basic types of approaches: a short-term approach based upon mood induction techniques and a long-term approach based upon psychotherapeutic intervention.

Mood induction techniques involve reading short passages that encourage the subject to think about either happy, sad, or neutral content. Masters et al., (1979) manipulated both mood and tempo (think of something that makes you feel like jumping up and down vs. just sitting down). On a shape discrimination task these manipulations affected the performance of 4-year-olds in the expected directions.

Graves and Lahey (1983) gave mood-induction instructions to 4–6-year-old, economically disadvantaged, black, preschool children. The child was asked to "remember something that happened to you that made you feel . . . so happy that you wanted to jump up and down (positive mood induction); like just sitting (neutral mood); so sad that you just wanted to sit and frown (negative mood)."

These instructions were read between pretests and posttests of a letter discrimination task (a good predictor of reading achievement). Positive and negative mood inductions produced significantly different changes in both accuracy and latency of responses relative to neutral mood induction. Pilot data collected with LD children at the Irving Schwartz Institute using the positive and neutral mood induction procedures of Graves and Lahey lead to significantly better letter discrimination performance under the positive condition (Goldstein et al., 1984).

A promising long-term approach to increasing available capacity is psychotherapy. Although inducing a positive mood may have short-term effects, there is no reason to suppose that a brief "pep talk" will result in lasting improvement. Rather, psychotherapeutic techniques that enable the child to provide his or her own "pep talk" offer the promise of long-term improvement. Although we know of no project in which this approach has been systematically adopted and evaluated, similar techniques have been used by researchers interested in training cognitive and behavioral self-monitoring skills (e.g., Meichenbaum, 1977). Perhaps extending these techniques to affective variables may prove helpful for LD children.

Use Available Capacity More Efficiently

The major approach to increasing the efficient use of available capacity is to increase the efficiency of effortful processing. There are two ways in which this goal could be met: For short-term gains, the LD child can be provided with a strategy for more efficient processing whereas for long-term gains, the LD child could be trained in the use of strategies.

A large amount of research has been conducted recently on the effects of providing strategies for LD children. In an early study, Torgesen and Goldman (1977) found that poor readers used the strategy of naming and verbal rehearsal less than good readers and consequently had poorer recall. When the poor readers were instructed in the use of the strategy, however, they no longer differed from the good readers in strategy usage and recall. Other techniques that have been shown to improve performance of LD children include: imposing organization on material to be learned in Piagetian memory tasks (Trepanier & Liben, 1979), blocking of words into categories in standard free recall tasks (Kosteski et al., 1979), and encouraging the child to continue trying before a second opportunity at free recall (Goldstein et al., 1984).

A better long-term approach to the goal of increased efficiency on effortful tasks is to train the child in the use of strategies. A recent 12-week training study conducted at the Irving Schwartz Institute demonstrated the efficacy of elaboration training for the learning, maintenance, and generalization of paired-associate learning skill; although as a result of the extensive training period, control children also acquired the skills, suggesting that specific training procedures may be less important than providing LD children with structured and frequent opportunities to develop the kinds of learning skills that non-LD children seem to acquire on their own (Sanfilippo-Cohn, 1984).

CONCLUDING REMARKS

In this chapter we have attempted to demonstrate the utility of an attention-capacity framework for considering the interaction of affective and cognitive variables in learning disabilities. An understanding of previously neglected affective factors can contribute to the identification of LD subgroups and lead to potentially valuable remedial approaches. Yet, we must caution that a framework is not equivalent to a fully articulated theory, and much work needs to be done before many of the broad statements outlined earlier can become useful hypotheses.

Depression is the particular aspect of affect highlighted in this chapter, although our analysis could be readily extended to other mood states and emotions, such as anger and anxiety. We have presented some preliminary data that suggest that for a subgroup of LD children depression is the underlying cause of their learning problems. Yet, if subsequent research lends additional support to this hypothesis an interesting question arises: Are the children in the LD/SED subgroup really learning-disabled children? Although some might suggest that they are not, we offer two arguments in favor of retaining the LD placement for these children. First, because these children do not fit the criteria for a diagnosis of emotionally disturbed, excluding them from the LD category forces us to either neglect them altogether or place them in a new category, such as "minimal affect dysfunction." We do not see the value in either alternative. Second, from the perspective of our framework, the problem is not that this subgroup might fail to fit the present definition of learning disabilities, but rather that the present definition (and the underlying view of LD that sustains it) is inadequate. In particular, the inadequacy arises from the current neglect of the role that depression and other affective factors play in learning problems.

Remedial techniques are readily suggested by our framework and may be of more use to teachers than other approaches that emphasize presumed organically based deficits. In the final analysis, multiple-factor approaches should prove to be more useful in understanding and treating LD children than the plethora of single factor approaches that has evolved over the past few decades. Our framework offers a context for multiple factor approaches and provides a vehicle for collaboration among the many disciplines and orientations that are found in the LD field. For example, a particular child with neonatal trauma, a depressed mother, and poor nutrition may enter school as a depressed child with both remediable and permanent capacity deficits. Clearly, a number of approaches originating in several disciplines would be required to assist this child. A framework that enabled each discipline to see its role and the role of others would be welcomed indeed.

Finally, we must emphasize that all children have limited attentional resources and develop more rapid and more efficient processing skills as they grow (Kail & Bisanz, 1982). In that sense, we do not conceptualize LD children as different in kind from non-LD children. Rather, within the context of this framework we see LD children as having more of the same kinds of difficulties that younger, non-LD children encounter. Therefore, we remain optimistic about the prospects for success in helping these children overcome their learning difficulties.

ACKNOWLEDGMENTS

The authors acknowledge the substantial contributions to this chapter made by Melissa Bell, Lynn Hasher, Gilda Paul, Silvia Sanfilippo-Cohn, Steve Stancroff, and Barbara Wasik. We are grateful to John Rubinsohn and the students and staff of the Irving Schwartz Institute for Children and Youth for their continuing support and cooperation.

REFERENCES

Bauer, R. H. (1977). Memory processes in children with learning disabilities: Evidence for deficient rehearsal. *Journal of Experimental Child Psychology, 24*, 415–430.

Blanchard, R. R. (1928). Reading disabilities in relation to maladjustment. *Mental Hygiene, 12*, 772–788.

Bower, G. H. (1981). Mood and memory. *American Psychologist, 36*, 129–148.

Brown, A. L. (1975). The development of memory: Knowing, knowing about knowing, and knowing how to know. In H. W. Reese (Ed.), *Advances in child development and behavior* (Vol. 10, pp. 103–152). New York: Academic Press.

Cairns, R. B., & Valsiner, J. (1984). Child psychology. *Annual Review of Psychology, 35*, 553–578.

Ceci, S. J. (1983). Automatic and purposive semantic processing characteristics of normal and language/learning-disabled children. *Developmental Psychology, 19*, 427–439.

Chi, M. (1976). Short-term memory limitations in children: Capacity or processing deficits? *Memory and Cognition, 4*, 559–572.

Cruickshank, W. M. (1977). *Learning disabilities in home, school, and community*. Syracuse: Syracuse University Press.

Dudley-Marling, C. G., Kaufman, N. J., & Tarver, S. (1981). WISC and WISC-R profiles of learning disabled children: A review. *Learning Disability Quarterly, 4*, 307–319.

Federal Register. (1977, December). Department of Health, Education, and Welfare. *Office of Education: Part III.*

Flavell, J. H. (1977). *Cognitive development*. Englewood Cliffs, NJ: Prentice–Hall.

Goldstein, D., Dundon, W., & Wasik, B. (1984). *Evaluation of the therapeutic educational program of the Irving Schwartz Institute for Children and Youth.* Unpublished manuscript.

Goldstein, D. & Golding, J. (1984). *Memory and metamemory processes in learning disabled and nondisabled children.* Unpublished manuscript, Temple University, Philadelphia, PA.

Goldstein, D., Hasher, L., & Kosteski, D. (1980, August). *Automatic and effortful memory processes in learning disabled children.* Paper presented at the meeting of the American Psychological Association, Montreal.

Goldstein, D., Hasher, L., & Stein, D. (1983). Processing of occurrence rate and item information by children of different ages and abilities. *American Journal of Psychology, 96,* 229–241.

Goldstein, D., & Paul, G. G. (1983, May). *Depression and achievement in learning disabled children.* Paper presented at the meeting of the Jean Piaget Society, Philadelphia.

Goldstein, D., Paul, G. G., & Sanfilippo-Cohn, S. (1985). Depression and achievement in subgroups of children with learning disabilities. *Journal of Applied Developmental Psychology.*

Graves, K. J., & Lahey, B. B. (1983). The effects of induced affective states on letter discrimination in disadvantaged preschool children. *Journal of Applied Developmental Psychology, 3,* 149–154.

Hallahan, D. P., & Kauffman, J. M. (1977). Labels, categories, behaviors: ED, LD, and EMR reconsidered. *Journal of Special Education, 11,* 139–149.

Hallahan, D. P., & Reeve, R. E. (1980). Selective attention and distractibility. In B. K. Keogh (Ed.), *Advances in special education* (Vol. 1, pp. 141–181). Greenwich, CT: JAI Press.

Hammill, D. D., Leigh, J. E., McNutt, G., & Larsen, S. C. (1981). A new definition of learning disabilities. *Learning Disability Quarterly, 4,* 336–342.

Hasher, L., & Zacks, R. T. (1979). Automatic and effortful processes in memory. *Journal of Experimental Psychology: General, 108,* 356–388.

Hasher, L., & Zacks, R. T. (1984). Automatic processing of fundamental information: The case of frequency of occurrence. *American Psychologist, 39,* 1372–1388.

Henderson, J. G. (1983). *An assessment of the effects of depression upon effortful and automatic processes in reading.* Unpublished doctoral dissertation, Temple University, Philadelphia, PA.

Horton, D. L., & Mills, C. B. (1984). Human learning and memory. *Annual Review of Psychology, 35,* 361–394.

Izard, C. E. (1982). Comments on emotion and cognition: Can there be a working relationship? In M. S. Clark & S. T. Fiske (Eds.), *Affect and cognition: The seventeenth annual Carnegie Symposium on Cognition* (pp. 229–240). Hillsdale, NJ: Lawrence Erlbaum Associates.

Kahneman, D. (1973). *Attention and effort.* New York: Prentice-Hall.

Kail, R. (1979). *The development of memory in children.* San Francisco: W. H. Freeman.

Kail, R., & Bisanz, J. (1982). Information processes and cognitive development. In H. W. Reese (Ed.), *Advances in child development and behavior* (Vol. 17, pp. 45–81). New York: Academic Press.

Kaufman, A. S. (1979). *Intelligent testing with the WISC-R.* New York: Wiley.

Kershner, J. R. (1983). Laterality and learning disabilities: Cerebral dominance as a cognitive process. *Topics in Learning and Learning Disabilities, 3,* 66–74.

Kinsbourne, M., & Caplan, P. J. (1979). *Children's learning and attentional problems.* Boston: Little, Brown.

Kirk, S. A. (1962). *Educating exceptional children.* Boston: Houghton-Mifflin.

Kosteski, D. M., Goldstein, D., & Hasher, L. (1979). *Organizational strategies in the memory of learning-disabled and non-disabled children.* Paper presented at the meeting of the Eastern Psychological Association, Philadelphia.

Kovacs, M. (1980/1981). Rating scales to assess depression in school-aged children. *Acta Paedopsychiatrica, 46,* 305–315.

Leinhardt, G., Seewald, A. M., & Zigmond, N. (1982). Sex and race differences in learning disabilities classrooms. *Journal of Educational Psychology, 74,* 835–843.

Lewis, M., & Michalson, L. (1983). *Children's emotions and moods: Developmental theory and measurement.* New York: Plenum.

Loe, D. C. (1978). Verbal elaboration: Implications for learning disabilities. *Academic Press, 13,* 301–304.

Lund, A. M., Hall, J. W., Wilson, K. P., & Humphreys, M. S. (1983). Frequency judgment accuracy as a function of age and school achievement (learning disabled versus non-learning-disabled) patterns. *Journal of Experimental Child Psychology, 35,* 236–247.

Masters, J. C., Barden, R. C., & Ford, M. E. (1979). Affective states, expressive behavior, and learning in children. *Journal of Personality and Social Psychology, 37,* 380–390.

Meichenbaum, D. (1977). *Cognitive-behavior modification: An integrative approach.* New York: Plenum.

Pascual-Leone, J. (1970). A mathematical model for the transition rule in Piaget's developmental stages. *Acta Psychologica, 32,* 301–345.

Patten, M. D. (1983). Relationships between self-esteem, anxiety, and achievement in young learning disabled students. *Journal of Learning Disabilities, 16,* 43–45.

Pennington, B. F., Bender, B., Puck, M., Salbenblatt, J., & Robinson, A. (1982). Learning disabilities in children with sex chromosone anomalies. *Child Development, 53,* 1182–1192.

Poznanski, E. (1982). The clinical characteristics of childhood depression. In L. Grinspoon (Ed.), *Psychiatry 1982: Annual review* (pp. 296–307). Washington, DC: American Psychiatric Press.

Rabinovitch, R. D. (1959). Reading and learning disabilities. In S. Arieti (Ed.), *American handbook of psychiatry* (pp. 857–869). New York: Basic Books.

Rosenthal, R. H., & Allen, T. W. (1978). An examination of attention, arousal, and learning dysfunctions of hyperkinetic children. *Psychological Bulletin, 85,* 689–715.

Rugel, R. P. (1974). WISC subtest scores of disabled readers: A review with respect to Bannatyne's recategorization. *Journal of Learning Disabilities, 7,* 48–55.

Sanfilippo-Cohn, S. (1984). *The effects of strategy training on the learning disabled.* Unpublished doctoral dissertation, University of Pennsylvania, Philadelphia, PA.

Simon, H. A. (1982). Comments. In M. S. Clark & S. T. Fiske (Eds.), *Affect and cognition: The seventeenth annual Carnegie Symposium on Cognition* (pp. 333–342). Hillsdale, NJ: Lawrence Erlbaum Associates.

Smith, C. R. (1983). *Learning disabilities: The interaction of learner, task, and setting.* Boston: Little, Brown.

Torgesen, J. K. (1979). Factors related to poor performance on memory tasks in reading disabled children. *Learning Disability Quarterly, 2,* 17–23.

Torgesen, J. K. (1980). Implications of the LD child's use of efficient task strategies. *Journal of Learning Disabilities, 13,* 364–371.

Torgesen, J. K., & Goldman, T. (1977). Verbal rehearsal and short-term memory in reading disabled children. *Child Development, 48,* 56–60.

Torgesen, J. K., & Houck, D. G. (1980). Processing deficiencies in learning disabled children who perform poorly on the Digit Span Test. *Journal of Educational Psychology, 72,* 141–160.

Trepanier, M. L., & Casale, C. M. (1983). Metamemory development in learning disabled children. In W. M. Cruickshank & E. Task (Eds.), *Academics and beyond* (pp. 182–193). Syracuse: Syracuse University Press.

Trepanier, M. L., & Liben, L. S. (1979). The operative basis of performance on Piagetian memory tasks: Evidence from normal and learning disabled children. *Developmental Psychology, 15,* 668–669.

U.S. Office of Education. (1968). *First annual report, National Advisory Committee on Handicapped Children.* Washington, DC: U.S. Department of Health, Education, & Welfare.

Weinberg, W., Rutman, J., Sullivan, L., Penick, E., & Dietz, S. (1973). Depression in children referred to an educational diagnostic center: Diagnosis and treatment. *Journal of Pediatrics, 83,* 1065.

Weingartner, H., Cohen, R. M., Murphy, D. L., Martello, J., & Gerdt, C. (1981). Cognitive processes in depression. *Archives of General Psychiatry, 38,* 42–67.

9 Psychosocial Aspects of Learning Disabilities

Maribeth Montgomery Kasik
Governors State University

David A. Sabatino
Patricia Spoentgen
University of Wisconsin-Stout

The history of research on learning disabilities has demonstrated that with each new finding, additional unanswered questions have been raised. One explanation is that the recency of the field creates much needed information. Another hypothesis is that learning disabilities represent a secondary handicapping condition— a condition secondary to what may be a difference in how environmental information is processed. The history and the impact of the study of information-processing behaviors on learning have been reviewed and rereviewed (Mann, 1980). The resulting research to date has repeatedly and steadfastly indicated that even the well-researched topical areas can be organized into three component aspects for clarity. These aspects are the learning-disabled child in response to the task being presented, the environment in which the task is presented, and the expectations for social competence by teachers and significant others.

The review to follow has selected a few of the well-researched psychological behaviors commonly associated with learning disabilities and has examined them in light of the task being presented, the physical environment, type of placement, and the social competence expected from their interaction with other persons. This chapter attempts to limit the literature review to the last 10 years. In fact, the emphasis is on work reported in the literature since 1980. The principle behavioral areas reviewed in the first section are arousal, attentional behaviors, and hyperactivity. In the second section of the chapter, beginning with 1975 (the year Public Law 94-142 mandated services to all handicapped children), the focus becomes the educational environment. In that section the impact of classroom variables such as lighting, the type of placement, and seating arrangement are discussed.

The third section attempts to examine the awareness of teachers toward the condition of learning disabilities by reviewing their attitudes and styles of instructional and personal (attitudinal) interaction. The section ends with a summary of social competency theory, examining that research to date.

The reader should be aware that in a limited number of pages, reflecting selected topics and areas, it is difficult to draw definitive conclusions. However, many interesting trends are noteworthy. The very definition of what may be included in the psychosocial study of learning disabilities continues to expand dramatically with new research efforts. For that reason, the psychosocial behaviors reviewed are primarily those that are most commonly observed in the school environment.

PSYCHOSOCIAL BEHAVIORS

The psychosocial behaviors displayed by children and youth with learning disabilities appear to be highly "setting sensitive." Although this is a fairly simple point, it has far reaching implications. Although the severely mentally or physically handicapped children are disabled in practically all settings, the mildly handicapped may perform quite functionally in some environments, with handicapped behaviors not being apparent. However, when placed in a different environment, devastating behaviors may result. The mildly handicapping conditon known as learning disabilities tends to manifest itself primarily and most observably in the school environment. The term *6-hour retardate*, used by the 1969 President's Committee on Mental Retardation, is illustrative of this point. It refers to the educable or mildly mentally retarded child who may function quite successfully in the home and social environment; the child's handicapping behaviors are evident only when confronted with the rigors of the school day.

This setting specificity of behaviors may result in a lack of understanding between the school and the parents. An excellent example of this appears in an article by Klein, Altman, Dreizen, Friedman, and Powers (1981), which focuses on dysfunctional parental attitudes toward childrens' learning and behavior in school. They point out that the school requires students to develop an acceptable level of behavioral response in terms of attentiveness, school performance and accomplishment, and nondisruptive behavior. When the learning-disabled student's behavioral response is inappropriate in school, a negative parental attitude is set into motion. This is typified by an attitudinal and communication breakdown between school and home. Frequently, the parents blame the school, and the school blames the home for the child's inappropriate behavior. The resulting conflict between these adult groups only serves to increase the student's inappropriate responses. Much of the learning-disabled student's behavioral (and possibly educational) difficulty is seen as the result of a negative communication system established between the home and the school. If not dealt with in a more productive way, this complicated interaction among parents, teacher, and child may exacerbate the child's inappropriate behavior.

Most of the available research has dealt primarily with elementary school-age children (Lerner, 1981), with teachers' observations of behaviors presented being the single, most voluminous data base (McKinney & Feagens, 1983). Very little attention has been paid to preschool, secondary aged, or postschool aged learning disabled. One exception to this trend is a study by Meyers and Messerer (1981) that compared adult adjustment of 12 learning-disabled students with 9 behaviorally disordered students and 23 nonhandicapped control group subjects 3 years following high school graduation. Results indicated that in comparison to nondisabled adults, learning-disabled adults had specific adjustment difficulties in the areas of vocational activities, social adjustments, and daily living skills. In some respects it was difficult to distinguish learning-disabled adults from adults who as students were classified as behaviorally disordered.

Although the data on behaviors at the time of school entry is sparse, the results of the few available studies indicate that at the point of entrance, two behaviors stand out as characteristic of the learning-disabled child (Pelham 1981). These maladaptive behaviors are attentional problems and hyperactivity.

Arousal and Attentional Behaviors

Forness and Esveldt (1975) recorded behavioral interactions, attending behaviors, and disruptive and aggressive social behaviors with 24 6- to 11-year-old under-achieving boys during reading and math. The attending behaviors of the learning disabled were significantly lower than for the nonlearning-disabled children. Bryan (1974) observed that learning-disabled boys in kindergarten, first-, second-, fourth-, and sixth-grade classrooms were less attentive than the non-learning disabled. McKinney, Mason, Perkerson, and Clifford (1975) developed an observational instrument (SCAN) that sampled 14 mutually exclusive categories of behaviors. Richey and McKinney (1978) observed 15 learning-disabled and 15 nonlearning-disabled boys in third- and fourth-grade classrooms with this instrument (SCAN). Distractability was the only behavior that significantly differentiated the two groups of students.

More recently, Feagans and McKinney (1981) used SCAN to observe 58 pairs of children (learning disabled and nonlearning disabled) in first, second, and third grades. Learning-disabled children in contrast to comparison groups were more likely to display off-task behaviors and had a higher level of individual contact with the teacher. The later finding is seemingly one worthy of much additional research. It could be hypothesized that not all the increased teacher attention is positively directed.

These results were replicated by McKinney and Feagans (1983) with a sample of 63 learning-disabled and 63 nonlearning-disabled 6- and 7-year-old children. In another study McKinney, McClure, and Feagans (1982) observed 22 pairs of children (learning disabled and nonlearning disabled) in which 11 pairs were divided by sex. The SCAN observational system was used and replicated previous findings of less task-oriented behavior and more teacher interaction. Sex differences were not found.

Two decades of research have supported the idea that learning-disabled students display attentional deficits in the classroom. Although nonattending may be manifested in a variety of specific behaviors, they are clearly seen to be counterproductive in the learning environment.

Harris and King (1982) examined the relationship among academic, socio-psychological, and personality variables in a sample of 242 children who were classified into groups as follows: behavior disorders, learning disabilities, learning and behavioral disorders, and no problem. They found that the level of academic success among the groups seemed to be the serious point of differentiation. The cause for the absence of academic success in the learning-disabled group may be postulated as an off-task behavioral response to academic learning. This, in turn, tends to reduce peer acceptability of the learning-disabled group. In short, many behaviors that are chronically disruptive or norm violating are acceptable to peers when the student displaying them is performing well academically in at least one or two subjects. The learning-disabled student who is failing everything academically also appears to fail socially; the result is that he/she may be at the bottom of both peer and teacher's sociometric rating.

The Harris and King (1982) study opens many doors for some rather surprising new postulates. Learning-disabled children may, or may not, have secondary behavioral problems. There can be diagnostic differentiation between learning-disabled and behavioral disordered students when children in the later group are achieving academically. Attending behaviors may be the critical discriminating variable diagnostically and in terms of a remedial menu. In short, the attending dimension may be one of the most identifiable characteristics of the learning-disabled students' classic syndrome.

Hyperactivity

Recently there has been a rebirth of interest in neuropsychology as it relates to hyperactivity and an increased diagnostic interest in learning disabilities. Gaddes (1981) rebuked the field for failing to be concerned with neurological implications noting that hyperactivity is a common symptom of learning disabilities, and its etiology may be primary (i.e., the direct result of brain injury or infection) or secondary to the frustrations resulting from academic failure or inept parental treatment. He claims that a detailed neuropsychological assessment is the most useful procedure for producing a differential diagnosis of organic versus psychosocial etiology. If the behavior is completely based in psychosocial frustrations and there is evidence of very little neurological involvement, then the child's learning problems are not truly in the learning-disabilities category but are secondary to his or her hyperactivity (Gaddes, 1981). Gaddes' concerns are being echoed nationally, and a new round of neuropsychological theory and research appears to be forthcoming.

Because the learning-disabled child exists in a highly contaminated environment, environmental effects must be factored in response to a multitude of sociobiological and psychological considerations. Two variables that have received attention are diet and drugs. Several researchers (Feingold, 1975; Levy, Dumbrell, Hobbs, Ryan, Witton, & Woodhill, 1978; Smith, 1976; Swanson & Kinsbourne, 1980; Trites, Tryphonas, & Ferguson, 1980; Weis, 1980; Williams, Cram, Tausig, & Weissler, 1978) have attempted to explain the relationship of allergic reactions and nutritional regimes to either a specific or general type of behavioral response given a specific learning environment. An area not addressed that may need to be researched in the immediate future is that of eating disorders and nutrition.

The Influence of the Educational Environment

In response to Public Law 94-142, which made it mandatory that every child be placed in the least restrictive environment, a variety of educational environments was examined to facilitate the learning-disabled child's array of unique instructional requirements. Unfortunately, this law was not adequately carried out in all states and local educational agencies. On the continuum of services required by law, there exist programs that in title only meet the mandates required by federal law. It is possible that upon closer inspection, special education delivery services may not yet be inclusive enough to meet the unique learning and behavioral characteristics of this group of students. Most assuredly another decade shall bring greater specificity in research on the effects of many aspects of the learning environment. This is evidenced by (a) the growing number of learning-disabled adolescents being identified for the first time in high schools (Lerner, 1981), (b) the greater incidence of mild learning-disabled students requiring comprehensive special education services for multihandicapping conditions (Miller & Davis 1982), and (c) the overlaps between behavior disordered and learning-disabled groups and the newly established consideration of career and vocational education for this population (Sabatino, 1983; White & Wimmer, 1982).

In examining the environment in which learning-disabled children are attempting to excel academically, the differences in types of programming available should be distinguished. Simply stated, it can be reasoned that some tasks are learned more effectively and efficiently in certain environments. McKinney and

Feagans (1983) report that learning-disabled elementary students exhibit a "relatively stable pattern of classroom behavior that distinguishes them from average achieving students and contributes to their difficulties in school learning" (p. 366). Unidentified learning-disabled children who remain in the regular classroom will continue to experience many frustrations as they interact within an environment beyond their control (depending, of course, on the severity of their problem). Some of the factors in the educational environment that may pose problems to the learning-disabled student that is addressed by the authors are lighting, type of setting, seating arrangement, and specific behavioral characteristics, which may be magnified by an inapropriate workplace.

Lighting

The major purpose of classroom lighting is to produce an environment in which students are able to accomplish visual work with minimal discomfort and distraction (D'Alonzo, 1983). Researchers have examined classroom lighting and among their findings are the following: With typical ceiling fixtures, the light levels at the sides of a room are 50% of that in the center (Sampson, 1970). A room with fluorescent lighting is less than one tenth as bright as the area under a tree on a sunny day (Hellman, 1982). The emission of soft x-ray and radio frequencies from fluorescent lighting and television may create hyperactivity in children (Ott, 1976). Therefore, activities demanding illumination such as paper and pencil work should be conducted 4 or more feet from the walls. Hellman provides a comprehensive review of the research literature on the effect of lighting and light on humans and states researchers in photobiology and related fields are discovering new and unexpected connections between light, health, and human response to specific stimuli. A recent Russian study (Hellman, 1982) describes the "effect of irradiation by ultraviolent erythema lamps on the working ability of school children" (p. 23). It concludes that the irradiated pupils had a faster reaction time to light and sound, experienced less fatigue of the visual receptor, and improved working capacity as evidenced by increased attention and easiness of arousal.

   O'Leary, Rosenbaum, and Hughes (1978) noted most of the experimental treatment programs have not included scientific investigation of environmental influences, with research to date failing to produce impressive or consistent results. They conducted a scientific study where classroom lighting conditions were manipulated in a laboratory school for 8 weeks, with observers unaware of the change in lighting conditions. On odd numbered weeks the classroom was illuminated by standard cool white fluorescent lighting systems. During even numbered weeks the classroom was illuminated with a daylight simulating fluorescent system with controls for the purported emission of soft x-rays and radio frequencies. The result revealed no differences in the effects of the two lighting conditions.

It would appear by the limited research on the effects of lighting that it is an important factor that needs to be considered when planning the workplace for the learning-disabled child. However, even though current research is limited and contradictory, the extent of neglect can be witnessed in the real world. Here, stages, dining halls, and closets have become the makeshift classroom for the learning disabled. These environments are rarely adequately illuminated.

Type of Setting

It is possible that a child with a mild learning disability may be able to cope and interact better in an environment *not* structured to his/her needs than will a child with moderate or severe difficulties. Future research models need to examine a range of services offered within a range of environments and how these interact with the degree of severity of the child's disability. For example, if a self-contained program is needed and the child remains in a resource program, the student may respond negatively to the inappropriate placement. Maybe this explains why most learning-disabled students receive a combination of resource room and regular classroom instruction. The working hypothesis applied by the practitioner might be that a combined special and regular class may be a safer approach to placement than either one in isolation. Working hypotheses such as these are frequently little more than poor compromises in the absence of solid data (Montgomery-Kasik, 1983). One explanation for this practice is that educators are still unsure of the "best placement" and tend, as a result, to make the most comfortable placement (often in a legal sense). Perhaps the result is generalizing the environment to all the child's needs but specific to none of them.

The most commonly used classroom environments for special education are: Hewett's (1968) engineered classroom, Haring and Phillips's (1962) structured classroom (both of which place emphasis on structured environment and the teaching-learning process by arranging the floor plan to suit a specific purpose), and Newcomer's (1980) open classroom model, which encourages children to explore and experience through flexibility and self-direction (Marsh, Price, & Smith, 1983).

Technically it is impossible to examine the response of a learning-disabled child to a particular environment without considering the length of time per school year (or per day) spent in that particular environment. Of consideration is the amount of time spent in the special education classroom—a "resource room" setting where the student will spend any amount of time up to 50% of a given school day—or in a "self-contained" program where the student may spend more than 50% of the school day. The relationship between the amount of time in these two settings is an actual variable to be recorded. Although these two settings may be similar in physical structure, the time structure and curriculum have been observed to be quite different (Montgomery-Kasik, 1983).

Unfortunately, much of the literature of the last 15 years does not examine environmental considerations. However, the evidence to date suggests most identified learning-disabled students receive a majority of their education in the regular classroom with supportive "help" from an itinerant specialist or resource room teacher (Glass, Christiansen, & Christiansen, 1982). The resource room setting continues to be the most popular form of service delivery in the 1980s for the learning disabled. Behavior of learning-disabled students in resource rooms has been found to differ from that of learning-disabled students in regular classrooms with regard to attending behavior and dependence. The difference in behaviors in each setting is related to achievement. Montgomery-Kasik (1983) in reviewing research on resource rooms noted that student attending behaviors were positively correlated with academic achievement, while teacher interaction was negatively correlated with attending behaviors (on task). Her review indicated that distractibility and dependency in the regular classroom were negatively correlated with academic achievement while passive teacher responses were positively correlated.

These researchers conducted another study that found that LD students were more frequently positively reinforced than negatively reinforced in the regular classroom. Comparison of these two studies indicates doubt regarding "appropriate learning style" within the regular classroom (McKinney & Feagans, 1983). Ito (1980) evaluated the long-term effects of resource room programs on learning-disabled children's reading achievement. It was found that the group with the shortest stay in the resource room made significant gains.

Terry, Kretsch, and Rawlings (1981) studied the effects of environmental manipulation on second- and third-grade learning-disabled students in a self-contained classroom setting designed to improve on-task behavior. This study included modifications of: environmental arrangements, curriculum, instruction, and classroom management. The results suggest that students show improvement on task and study behavior measures as well as on general classroom functioning measures.

Marsh, Price, and Smith (1983) raise additional questions yet to be answered about the learning-disabled students' learning environment:

1. How different from the regular classroom would the resource room be if one of the classroom models were implemented?
2. Would behavioral expectations differ greatly from a regular classroom?
3. Could the students handle the change?
4. Could the strategies be suggested to the regular teacher?
5. Is there any chance for implementation in the regular classroom?
6. How does the school administration feel?

The current research indicates that a full range of placement options for the learning disabled is still lacking. Most learning-disabled students are in the regular classroom receiving resource room help. There is an absence of data comparing physical structure and curriculum differences among the placement alternatives.

When considering the educational workplace, educators must also take into consideration special characteristics of the learning-disabled child, which determine differences in a special educational setting from the so-called regular educational setting. Bryan and McGrady (1972), replicating earlier findings of Myklebust, Boshes, Olson, and Cole (1969) and using the same teacher rating scale on a large sample of learning-disabled children, described learning-disabled children as less socially adept, less task oriented, less verbally facile, and less organized and responsible with school work in comparison to nondisabled children. Bryan (1978) stated that these studies "support the hypothesis that learning disabled children experience difficulties in social development, interpersonal relationships and perceiving and understanding others affective states" (p. 60–61). In addition, teachers, peers, or strangers often make negative evaluations of learning-disabled children. According to Bryan (1978), "the source of difficulty for learning disabled childrens' interpersonal problems seem to rest in the comprehension of nonverbal communication, their affective involvements with others, and their expressive language ability—what they say and how they say it" (p. 60). Tarver (1982) added that the adaptive behavior of the learning-disabled child in the regular classroom differs from their normally achieving peers; these differences are associated with academic competencies and not with social affective competencies.

Ross (1980) believed the learning-disabled child's level of selective attention is another important consideration for educational placement. He contended that the hyperactivity characteristic of learning-disabled children may be due to a child's attending to the wrong stimulus, requiring a controlled environment. For example, body movements are natural, and are appropriate responses to pressure on ones buttocks, body strain, bladder pressure, a growling stomach, an itchy foot, and so forth. However, body movements in response to these stimuli are inappropriate when the student is expected to read, write, or do seatwork. Ross (1980) added:

Distractability may be no more than a child attending to stimuli in the room other than those the teacher has specified. Therefore, problems identified as hyperactivity or distractibility are expressions of problems in not selectively attending to the right stimuli (yet those two terms are not interchangeable). (p. 224)

The range of undertakings to increase attending behaviors and reduce distractibility runs the gamut of behavioral, cognitive, social, and academic therapies. Twenty years ago it was thought that the means to gaining selective attention was to modify the learning environment. The early efforts attempted to eliminate distractors in the classroom (Cruickshank, Bentzen, Ratzeberg, &

Tannhauser, 1961). Following those years, came the period when all curricula were examined for saliency. One of the seeming shortcomings of these environmental and curriculum approaches is their lack of transfer to other environments or to other curricula.

Operant conditioning strategies also seemed to suffer from a problem of task/ environment transfer. Control of time on task through extrinsic reinforcers showed positive results, at least during the course of many research studies. In order to obtain transfer, a search for intrinsic motivators was undertaken. The early 1970s generated several hundred operant studies in which the type of reinforcer became the independent variable. A shortcoming of several of these studies was that although highly specific (targeted) attentional behaviors increased, there was little or no mention of particular improvement in academic achievement.

McKinney and Feagans (1983) concluded that our present knowledge of the classroom adaptation of learning-disabled students is based on observations of child behavior and/or teacher–child interactions. They remind us that studies of children or teachers alone do not provide direct knowledge of the classroom processes that influence variation in behavior and mediate its relationship to academic progress. Classroom achievement depends not only on cognitive skills but also on certain behaviors that are adaptive to the demands of the classroom environment. Ecological research reviewed by McKinney and Feagans (1983) suggests that variation in the sequence of events in classrooms and in different types of learning activities shape student behavior in different settings (Gump, 1975, Kovnin & Doyle, 1975).

Barkley (1981) provides another view that states that research to date has not provided any convincing evidence of the efficiency of the reduced stimulation programs. Similar research on the use of study cubicles for highly distractable and inattentive children has not brought forth any evidence to suggest that cubicles are beneficial to improving the classroom behavior, academic productivity, or accuracy of learning-disabled children. Barkley (1981) concluded that there probably exist certain classes of high-appeal distractors (such as jewelry, colors, lighting, clutter, etc.) that are more likely to draw hyperactive children off task than they are to distract normal children. However, a program that focuses solely on the reduction of distractors is quite unlikely to bring about any substantial improvement in the behavior or academic performance of hyperactive children (p. 395). Most of the research before 1980 contrasted learning-disabled hyperactive children with nonhandicapped children. More recently, Copeland and Weissbrod (1983) compared hyperactive learning-disabled with a small group ($N = 10$) of nonhyperactive learning-disabled children. An extensive battery of research measures were administered, which attempted to ascertain intellectual functioning, cognitive tempo, conservation, and cognitive style in terms of how information was processed. The results were a bit startling. Hyperactive and nonhyperactive children performed similarly on all but one task. Nonhyperactive learning-disabled children seemed to exercise a more mature cognitive learning style than their hyperactive counterparts. These findings suggest that hyperactivity is a continuum of behavior, not a singularly identifiable symptom in the learning-disabilities syndrome. Gaddes (1980) added that when there is no evidence of any organic cause of the child's hyperactivity, it may be increasingly more common to hypothesize that the problem is a purely psychological and social one.

Characteristics common to the field and definition of learning disabilities that do not provide any new or unknown revelation to aid diagnosis but should be considered in planning the learning environment are:

1. Hyperactivity.
2. Perceptual motor impairments (gross and fine).
3. Emotional outbursts.
4. Distractibility.
5. Impulsivity.
6. Memory deficits.
7. Comprehension deficits.
8. Neurological functioning.
9. Interpersonal relationships.
10. Self-concept.

If the learning-disabled child is to demonstrate learning, the workplace may need to reflect a student's particular learning style. The effective educator will synthesize as much as possible about the characteristics of the learner and identify strengths, weaknesses, motivations, and reinforcements in order to construct the most appropriate learning environment for the learner. The educator must realize that the environment cannot be uniform for all learning-disabled students any more than the regular classroom is the same for all normal learners. The educational environment is subject to change.

Seating Arrangement

Seating arrangements remain the most widely investigated environmental consideration. Early research examined the impact of seating on grades. Recent research is examining its effects on the students' academic achievement and attitude toward school (Johnson, 1984). Axelrod, Hall, and Tams (1979) demonstrated that the arrangement of tables and desks in the classroom could directly affect the amount of outburst and disruptive behavior in traditional educational settings. The traditional seating arrangement—straight rows and columns facing the instructor at the front of the room—is still the most common (Johnson, 1984). Becker, Sommer, Bee, and Oxley (1974) studied students' selection of seating and found that students who select seats near the front of the room have more positive attitudes toward school, receive better grades, and participate more in discussion. Stires (1980) found that students seated in the middle of the classroom received better grades and had better attitudes than those sitting on the sides. An extension of these findings suggest the hypothesis that mainstreamed learning-disabled students rarely sit in the front or center of the classroom if the seating is unstructured. Even more interesting could be a hypothesis addressing the possible interaction between attitudinal/behavioral variables and seating arrangement that influence learning disabilities or, indeed, are influenced by learning disabilities.

The educational environment (classroom design and ecology, curriculum, instruction, time, behavior management) and its interaction with the unique learning behaviors of the learning disabled then have been hypothesized to be significant considerations in the education of the learning disabled. Yet, further research needs to be conducted beyond informal teacher observations and teacher rating scales to provide a foundation for implementation of quality services for the learning-disabled population. As it now stands, there is marginal justification, at best, for a *specialized* environment; and yet, the presence of *specialized* environment seems so very logical.

THE LEARNING-DISABILITIES TEACHER: ATTITUDES AND INTERACTIONS

Structural changes in the learning-disabled students' workplace are often easier to make than changes in attitudes and behaviors of teachers working with them. Although changes in physical structure are immediately apparent, changes in attitude may be viewed as unobtrusive manifestations in the students' academic and social behavior. Much of the current literature reports attitudes of regular educators toward special education students mainstreamed into their classrooms. Little current research has examined both the attitudes of teachers toward their learning-disabled students and their interaction with these students within the school setting. The common space shared by learning-disabilities teachers and learning-disabled students and the resulting interactions may decide the future of the learning-disabled student. This section reviews selected studies that examine learning-disabilities teachers' attitudes toward the students they teach.

In a survey of regular education teachers, Ysseldyke, Pianta, Christenson, Wang, and Algozzine (1982) reported that teachers who had referred a student for psychoeducational evaluation most often believed that the causes of the student's problems were within the child or the child's home. Further, the instructional interventions these teachers used before resorting to referral involved changes in materials or physical setting. Regular education teachers rarely are trained specifically to meet the needs of special education students. Of late, many states are beginning to require coursework in special education for regular teacher certification, but for most regular educators their knowledge of special education techniques comes to them through infusion of ideas into their regular curriculum (Montgomery-Kasik, 1983).

Thurlow and Ysseldyke (1982) sampled 127 learning-disabilities teachers on the characteristics of learning-disabled students. "Extreme variability" was reported in the teachers' beliefs about learning-disabled students and approaches to instruction. Few differences were found between the beliefs of teachers with 1 to 2 years of special education experience and the beliefs of teachers with 10 or more years of experience (p. 5). The 127 teachers sampled worked with approximately 1,600 students during a typical day, usually within a resource room setting. The teachers were well educated; over 60% had earned degrees beyond bachelors. Approximately 60% had taught special education for at least 5 years. The teachers demonstrated a lack of confidence in their contribution to serving the learning-disabled student. According to Thurlow and Ysseldyke (1982), the teachers believed learning-disabled students could be characterized by their processing and memory difficulties, attentional difficulties and distractibility, poor academic achievement, and a variety of other characteristics. The characteristic that typified the learning-disabled student receiving highest agreement was that of processing and memory difficulties (p. 19).

Teachers, regardless of their actual number of years in the field, attributed their knowledge of characteristics of learning-disabled students and what works in teaching them, to their personal experience. This finding is consistent with the earlier conclusions of sociological studies of the teaching profession (Lortie, 1975) where teachers attributed their teaching abilities to trial and error learning in the classroom. Although one might expect that if experience underlies teachers' knowledge and abilities to teach, the beliefs of more experienced and less experienced teachers would differ. This was not the case.

Podemski and Marsh (1981) described a systems framework for assessing attitudes toward learning-disabled students. Their three-level framework shows each level being the locus of attitude development that, in turn, affects attitude development at the other levels. Level I describes attitudes that affect the goals of the system. Level II describes attitudes that pervade the organizational structure of the school. Level III describes attitudes within the student environment. This study includes interaction between the learning-disabled student and the learning-disability specialist. It reports that because teacher–student interactions characterize the student environment, the attitudes at this level reflect the type of instruction students receive as well as the success of instruction. Pokemski and Marsh (1981) offered the following points:

> 1) Placement of the learning disabled child in the regular class creates a new dynamic among all children as well as between the regular teacher and the learning disabled child,

2) Interaction between learning disabled and non-learning disabled children serves to change the attitude of the non-learning disabled child toward their learning disabled peer,

3) Regular classroom teachers must reflect upon their own attitudes toward learning disabled children and the significance of such attitudes for educational challenges created by the presence of such children in the classroom,

4) In many settings the requirements for the least restrictive environment also creates a new dynamic between regular and special education personnel,

5) These teachers must recognize how their attitudes contribute to or distract from the success of educational services for the learning disabled, and

6) Learning disabilities specialists may realize that protective concern for the learning disabled will interfere with successful integration and create potential for resentment from regular teachers. (p. 221–222)

DeLoach, Earl, Brown, Poplin, and Warner (1981) conducted a study of learning-disability teachers' perceptions of the characteristics of severely learning-disabled students. This study reported that a high prevalence of students in the learning-disabled classrooms were perceived to be nonlearning disabled. DeLoach reported that there appears to be considerable support for using the judgment of learning-disabilities teachers in the diagnosis of learning disabilities, but that the specific factors considered by learning-disabilities teachers when making clinical judgments about the source of student learning problems have not been identified. Results from their study indicate that teachers do not view students presently being served in learning-disabilities classrooms as representing a homogenous group. This study supported the concept of a heterogenous learning-disability population within which a subgroup of specific learning disabilities (SLD) can be identified.

Harris and King (1982) examined the relationships among teachers' perceptions of academic and social problems. They sought to determine if differences existed among groups of children selected by teachers as experiencing learning problems, behavior problems, both learning and behavior problems, or no problems of a learning or behavioral nature. Harris and King's (1982) results supported teachers' "ability to discriminate between children with no problems and those with behavior problems and children with learning and/or behavior problems. Children with learning problems and those with learning and behavior problems were less clearly distinguished from each other" (p. 457).

Historically, teachers have demonstrated a preference for the types of students and subjects they desire to teach through the selection of their college major. With the advent of mainstreaming, teachers are now responsible for a wider spectrum of students in their classrooms and thus are no longer able to select the type of student with whom they wish to work simply by selection of a major.

Approximately 20 years ago, Wittmer (1982) reported that educable mentally retarded children are more "acceptable" to teachers than are brain-injured, mentally retarded. The difference is the distractibility and hypersensitivity commonly displayed by brain-damaged children. Shortel, Iano, and McGettigan (1972) found that teachers preferred learning-disabled to emotionally disturbed children and felt less favorable toward the educable mentally retarded.

Wittmer (1982) conducted a survey study to determine if the attitudes of undergraduate students in special education learning-disabilities courses differ from the attitudes of teachers who have a minimum of 1 year of experience teaching in a learning-disabilities classroom. Her results indicate a statistically significant difference on only 9 of 147 variables. Wittmer attributes these findings to the small sample size.

D'Alonzo (1983) reported that special educators as a group tend to characterize themselves as individuals interested in doing "good" things for people who generally have had very few good things happen to them. His premise is that doing good for the handicapped makes special educators feel good. Some regular educators argue that they choose to teach normal students because they do not feel comfortable working with individuals who have handicaps.

Vandiver and Vandiver (1981) hypothesized that teachers would favor main-streaming learning-disabled students over educable mentally retarded or emotionally disturbed and emotionally disturbed over educable mentally retarded children. Furthermore, they suggested that teachers who had direct experience teaching mainstreamed exceptional students would be more willing to accept handicapped students than those without such experience. The results indicated that teachers favored emotionally disturbed and learning-disabled over educable mentally retarded children and learning-disabled over emotionally disturbed children regardless of the severity of the disability.

In an unpublished study, Montgomery-Kasik (1983) compared the attitudes of 100 undergraduate special education majors and 100 regular education majors by administering two attitude instruments—the Rokeach Value Survey (Rokeach, 1967) and the Minnesota Teacher's Attitude Survey (Cook, Leed, & Calles, 1975). Statistical analysis indicated a significant difference in the attitudes of those students entering into special education as opposed to those entering regular education. Regular education majors indicated preferences for working with nonhandicapped students with comfort level being a significant factor in their decision.

In the literature and research available, reports on attitudes of regular educators toward mainstreamed special education students abound. Research attention has also been focused on teacher expectancy and learning-disabled students' achievement. Research on attitudes of the learning-disabilities teacher toward the learning-disabled student and their classroom interactions is not as abundant. Little has been done to document the validity of teachers' attitudes or techniques of the attitudes reported. Teachers do not view all students in learning-disabilities classes as similar. Most teachers prefer working with mildly handicapped students or the learning-disabled population over educably mentally retarded or emotionally disturbed. These students' attitudes toward teaching the handicapped can be traced back to a teacher's beginnings in special education when he or she first makes the decision to teach either "normal" or handicapped students.

SELF-REGULATIVE BEHAVIORS: THE SOCIOPSYCHOLOGICAL RESPONSE TO LEARNING DISABILITIES

A few years ago, cognitive psychologists (Siegler, 1978) began to redirect their attention from the amount and type of information-processing behaviors, to the strategies with which these behaviors were utilized. Qualification and quantification of the information-processing deficit did not prove to be particularly fruitful. Belmont and Butterfield (1977) attempted to understand atypical development in children by examining the self-regulative or metacognitive development displayed in a wide range of learn behavior and learned behaviors such as memory (Brown, 1978), problem solving (Stone & Day, 1978), a full range of academic achievements (Stone & Wertsch, 1984), and more recently sociopsychological functioning (Schumaker & Hazel, 1984).

Vygotsky (1981) placed the study of social behaviors into an origin-and-consequences related structure that concludes in self-regulatory skills:

> We could formulate the general genetic law of cultural development as follows: Any function in the child's cultural development appears twice, or on two planes. First it appears on the social plane, and then on the psychological plane. First it appears between people as an interpsychological category, and then within the child as an intrapsychological category. This is equally true with regard to voluntary attention, logical memory, the formation of concepts and the development of volition.

In a sense of modern remedial management, Stone and Wertsch (1984) developed a reasonable hypothesis that views the LD child's development as a pattern of self-regulative strategies learned in the interaction process. This hypothesis suggests that specific information-processing deficits in LD populations interfere with their ability to profit fully from remedial interactions. In short, the nature of the cognitive deficit may not be as important as (a) how residual capacities are realized and utilized, and (b) the type of sociopsychological (behavioral) response LD children receive for success or failure and the type of interpersonal interaction that takes place.

Certainly, the 1970s will be remembered as the era highlighting the social differences that LD children perceive between themselves and others, the differences their peers perceive and the possible influence these self-perceptions and perceptions of others have on academic and social learning. The conclusion seems to be that social skills and self-esteem of the LD child are affected, which in turn affects how others view the LD child. The net result is a profile of LD students as having poorly developed social skills. The difficulty with this research is the wide and vague interpretation as to what constitutes social skills and the fact that all social skills may be socially relative to any given situation.

The research to date on remediating social skill deficits tends to show that antecedents and consequences may be arranged so as to increase the occurrence of desirable self-regulating practices while decreasing the use of undesirable social behaviors (Schumaker & Hazel, 1984). Only a limited number of studies have been conducted in this area. Although the results of some studies have shown that self-recording of behaviors (e.g., Broden, Hall, & Mitts, 1971) and self-evaluation of behaviors (e.g., Kaufman & O'Leary, 1972) are useful for producing decreases in classroom disruptiveness, none of the studies in this area has focused on LD individuals and the behavioral excesses specifically indentified for LD individuals within social interactions (e.g., negative statements). Because some evidence suggests that LD individuals can learn to use self-control procedures (Hallhan, Lloyd, Kosiewicz, Kauffman, & Graves, 1979; Seabaugh & Schumaker, 1981), such procedures may conceivably be useful in this regard; however empirical work needs to be conducted before more definitive conclusions can be drawn.

Additionally, little is known about the lasting effects of identified interventions. Finally, according to some authors, the critical feature behind the LD individual's social competence is whether they become internally motivated to use or avoid certain social behaviors (Adelman & Taylor, 1982; Deshler, Schumaker, & Lenz, 1984). At this time, it is unclear whether the application of external contingencies or the arrangement of antecedent events can change LD individuals' internal motivation to perform social behaviors over long periods of time. Additional research is needed to examine these issues.

SUMMARY

It is possible that one of the major contributions that psychology has provided society at large is an awareness of how selected critical psychological variables are strengthened or reduced in the perception of one person or in that of others. If we were to trace the history of what we have researched in the area of learning disabilities, it would become obvious that most of the early research was directed at a study of those psychological variables that defined the condition. With good reason, of course, the initial critical question being asked by the disciplines involved, and society in general, was: How do we discriminate these persons with learning disabilities from all others?

That work began in the mid-1950s when learning disabilities as a diagnostic entity had not been differentiated from brain injury. The crucial aspects were to identify the psychoneurological determinants, which could be used in refining a diagnosis. The psychosocial implications for research had grown by the mid-1960s to include sociological variables. The search was still an attempt to lend diagnostic clarity to the differentiation of this population, with scattered references to the impact of socioeconomic and a few interpersonal interactive variables that might be predictors of remedial success.

It has been postulated repeatedly that remedial efforts directed at modifying basic psychological processes or increasing academic achievement growth would, in turn, significantly alter a wider array of psychological variables. Some of these psychological variables were reviewed in this chapter and are much more aptly described as psychosocial variables. The major breakthroughs in new knowledge were in reverse of what had been initially hypothesized. Thus, by the mid-1970s the conclusion that could be drawn safely was that the most pronounced means of altering social or academic growth of so-called learning-disabled populations was to convince them they were not learning-disabled and that they need not fall victim to the psychosocial behaviors commonly associated with this condition. Well-designed studies on the effects of remediation repeatedly bore out this observation.

From that point in time until now, several major new directions have been forged in expanding the role that selected psychosocial variables play in the academic and social development of learning-disabled children.

The trends that can be established from the work reviewed in this chapter are that:

1. Learning-disabled children tend to show that the earlier they are identified and the longer they are alienated in stress-related environments, the poorer their views of themselves become. They tend to see themselves as others see them: poorly organized in response to life's demands (the demands of peers, school, or home), unable to interpret social cues meaningfully, unable to verbally respond to the pressures they feel.

2. The physical environment of the school does not influence those behaviors associated with learning disabilities, as was once believed. Hyperactivity, impulsivity, memory, and self-concept are not seemingly altered under stable, constant environmental conditions in the classroom.

3. The type of class the student is placed in (i.e., self-contained, regular class, resource room) does seem to result in at least raising or lowering self-concept, which in turn influences many other psychosocial behaviors.

4. One of the most promising variables to be studied to date is teacher–parent interaction. The attitudes of those people influencing learning-disabled children's performance on academic and social factors seemingly become a looking glass; they provide the feedback (or fail to provide corrective feedback) in many cases. The results are the development of faulty interpersonal relationship skills and a serious limiting of what the child is expected to achieve.

If the research to date were to be indicative of a guideline with implications toward directing a behavioral change in these areas, the most precise single conclusion may be that this population needs extraordinary measures of psychosocial support. In the presence of an emotionally protective environment offering realistic expectations, learning-disabled children do perform better than those who find themselves in less adequate attitudinal environments. Conclusively, they need more structure in their physical environment, a more highly structured learning setting, and more emotional support than do their nonlearning disabled peers. Hence, there is need for an attitude of psychosocial nuturance from those who interact with them.

REFERENCES

Adelman, H., & Taylor, L. (1982). Enhancing the motivation and skills needed to overcome interpersonal problems. *Learning Disability Quarterly, 5,* 438–446.

Axelrod, S., Hall, R., & Tams, A. (1979). Comparison of two common seating arrangements. *Academic Therapy, 15*(1), 29–36.

Barkley, R. A. (1981). *Hyperactive children: A handbook for diagnosis and treatment.* New York: Guilford Press.

Becker, F., Sommer, R., Bee, J., & Oxley, B. (1974). College classroom ecology. *Sociometry, 12,* 504–521.

Belmont, J., & Butterfield, E. (1977). The instructional approach to developmental research. In R. V. Kail & J. W. Hagen (Eds.), *Perspectives on the development of memory and cognition.* Hillsdale, NJ: Lawrence Erlbaum Associates.

Broden, M., Hall, R. V., & Mitts, B. (1971). The effect of self-recording on the classroom behavior of two eighth-grade students. *Journal of Applied Behavior Analysis, 4,* 191–199.

Brown, A. L. (1978). Knowing when, where and how to remember: A problem of metacognition. In R. Glaser (Ed.), *Advances in instruction psychology.* Hillsdale, NJ: Lawrence Erlbaum Associates.

Bryan, T. (1974). Peer popularity of learning disabled children. *Journal of Learning Disabilities, 7,* 261–268.

Bryan, T. H. (1978). Social relationships and verbal interaction of learning disabled children. *Journal of Learning Disabilities, 11,* 58–66.

Bryan, T. S., & McGrady, H. J. (1972). The use of a teacher rating scale. *Journal of Learning Disabilities, 5,* 199–206.

Cook, W., Leeds, C., & Callis, R. (1975). *Minnesota Teacher Aptitude Inventory.* New York: The Psychological Corporation.

Copeland, A., & Weissbrod, C. (1983). Cognitive strategies used by learning disabled children: Does hyperactivity always make things worse? *Journal of Learning Disabilities, 16*(8), 473–477.

Cruickshank, W. A., Bentzen, F., Ratzeberg, & Tannhauser, M. (1961). *A teaching method for brain-injured and hyperactive children.* Syracuse, NY: Syracuse University Press.

D'Alonzo, B. J. (1983). *Educating adolescents with learning and behavior problems.* Rockville, MD: Aspen Systems Corporation.

DeLoach, T. F., Earl, J. M., Brown, B. S., Poplin, M. S., & Warner, M. M. (1981). LD teachers perceptions of severely disabled students. *Learning Disabilities Quarterly, 4*(4), 343–358.

Deshler, D. D., Schumaker, J. B., & Lenz, B. K. (1984). Academic and cognitive interventions for LD adolescents: Part I. *Journal of Learning Disabilities, 17,* 108–117.

Feagans, L., & McKinney, J. D. (1981). The pattern of exceptionality across domains in learning disabled children. *Journal of Applied Behavior Analysis, 1*, 313–328.

Feingold, B. F. (1975). *Why your child is hyperactive*. New York: Random House.

Forness, S. R., & Esveldt, K. C. (1975). Classroom observation of children with learning and behavior problems. *Journal of Learning Disabilities, 8*, 49–52.

Gaddes, W. (1981). Neuropsychology, fact or mythology, educational help or hinderance? *School Psychology Review, 10*(3), 322–329.

Gaddes, W. H. (1980). *Learning disabilities and brain function*. New York: Springer–Verlag.

Glass, R. M., Christiansen, J., & Christiansen, J. L. (1982). *Exceptional students in the regular classroom*. Boston: Little, Brown.

Gump, P. V. (1975). Ecological psychology and children. In E. M. Hetherington (Ed.), *Review of child development research* (5), 322. Chicago: University of Chicago Press.

Hallahan, D. P., Lloyd, J., Kosiewicz, M. M., Kauffman, J. M., & Graves, A. W. (1979). Self-monitoring of attention as a treatment for a learning disabled boy's off-task behavior. *Learning Disability Quarterly, 2*, 24–34.

Haring, N. G., & Phillips, E. L. (1962). *Educating emotionally disturbed children*. New York: McGraw–Hill.

Harris, W. J., & King, D. R. (1982). Achievement, sociometric status, and personality characteristics of children selected by their teachers as having learning and/or behavior problems. *Psychology in the Schools, 19*(10), 452–457.

Hellman, H. (1982, February). Guiding light. *Psychology Today*, pp. 22–28.

Hewett, F. (1968). *Educating the emotionally disturbed child in the classroom*. Boston: Allyn & Bacon.

Ito, H. R. (1980). Long term effects of resource room programs on learning disabled children's reading. *Journal of Learning Disabilities, 6*(13), 36–40.

Johnson, J. (1984). *The effects of seating location on school related variables*. Unpublished manuscript, University of Wisconson-Stout, Menomonie, WI.

Kaufman, K. F., & O'Leary, K. D. (1972). Reward, cost, and self-evaluation procedures for disruptive adolescents in a psychiatric hospital school. *Journal of Applied Behavior Analysis, 5*, 293–309.

Kovnin, J. S., & Doyle, P. H. (1975). Degree of continuity of a lesson's signal system and the task involvement of children. *Journal of Educational Psychology, 67*, 159–164.

Lerner, J. (1981). *Learning disabilities: Theories, diagnosis and teaching strategies* (3rd ed.). Boston, NY: Houghton Mifflin.

Levy, F., Dumbrell, S., Hobbs, G., Ryan, M., Witton, N., & Woodhill, J. M. (1978). Hyperkinesis and diet: A double blind crossover trial with a tartazine challenge. *Medical Journal of Australia, 1*, 61–64.

Lortie, D. C. (1975). *Schoolteacher: A sociological study*. Chicago: University of Chicago press.

Mann, L. (1980). *On the trail of process*. New York: Grune & Stratton.

Marsh, G. E., Price, B. J., & Smith, T. E. (1983). *Teaching mildly handicapped children: A generic approach to comprehensive teaching*. St. Louis: C. V. Mosby.

Meyers, G. & Messerer, J. (1981). *The social and vocational adjustment of learning disabled/behavior disordered adolescents after high school: A pilot study*. (*ERIC*, ED213-245).

McKinney, J. D., Mason, J., Perkerson, F., & Clifford, M. (1975). Relationship between classroom behavior and academic achievement. *Journal of Educational Psychology, 67*, 198–203.

McKinney, J. D., McClure, S., Feagans, L. (1982). Classroom behavior of learning disabled children. *Learning Disability Quarterly, 5*, 45–52.

Miller, T. L., & Davis, F. E. (1982). *The mildly handicapped student*. New York: Grune & Stratton.

Montgomery Kasik, M. (1983). *Analysis of the professional preparation of the resource room teacher* (Doctoral dissertation, Southern Illinois University at Carbondale, 1983).

Myklebust, H., Boshes, B., Olson, D., & Cole, C. (1969). *Minimal brain damage in children. Final report* (U.S.P.H.S. Contract No. 108-65-142). Evanston, IL: Northwestern University Publications.

Newcomer, P. L. (1980). *Understanding and teaching emotionally disturbed children.* Boston: Allyn & Bacon.

O'Leary, K. D., Rosenbaum, A., & Hughes, P. C. (1978). Fluorescent lighting: A purported source of hyperactive behavior. *Journal of Abnormal Child Psychology, 6,* 285–289.

Ott, J. N. (1976). *Health and light.* New York: Pocket Books.

Pelham, W. E. (1981). Attention deficits in hyperactive and learning disabled children. *Exceptional Education Quarterly, 2,* 13–23.

Podemski, R. S., & Marsh, G. E. (1981). A systems framework for assessing attitudes toward the learning disabled. *Learning Disabilities Quarterly, 4,* 217–223.

President's Committee on Mental Retardation and Bureau of Education of the Handicapped. (1969). *The six-hour retarded child.* Washington, DC: U.S. Government Printing Office.

Richey, D. D., & McKinney, J. D. (1978). Classroom behavior patterns in learning disabled children. *Journal of Learning Disabilities, 11,* 38–43.

Rokeach, M. (1967). *Rokeach value survey, (RVS).* New York: Free Press.

Ross, A. (1980). *Psychological disorders of children: A behavioral approach to theory, research and therapy* (2nd ed.). New York: McGraw–Hill.

Sabantino, D. A. (1983). Genesis of a desire: Prologue. In S. Miller & P. Schloss. *Career-vocational education for handicapped youth.* Rockville, MD: Aspen Systems Corporation.

Sampson, E. (1970). *Contrast rendition in school lighting.* New York: Educational Facilities Laboratories.

Schumaker, J., & Hazel, J. (1984). Social skills assessment and training for the learning disabled: Who's on first and what's on second? Part II. *Journal of Learning Disabilities, 17*(8), 492–499.

Seabaugh, G., & Schumaker, J. (1981). *The effects of self-regulation training of LD and NLD adolescents* (Research Rep. No. 37). Lawrence, KS: University of Kansas Institute for Research in Learning Disabilities.

Shotel, J. R., Iano, R. P., & McGettigan, J. F. (1972). Teachers attitudes associated with the integration of handicapped children. *Exceptional Children, 38,* 677–682.

Siegler, R. (Ed.). (1978). *Children's thinking: What develops?* Hillsdale, NJ: Lawrence Erlbaum Associates.

Smith, L. (1976). *Your child's behavior chemistry.* New York: Random House.

Stires, L. (1980). Classroom seating location, students grades and attitude: Environment or self selection. *Environment, 12*(2), 241–254.

Stone, C., & Day, M. (1978). Levels of availability of a formal operational strategy. *Child Development, 49,* 1054–1065.

Stone, C., & Wertsch, J. (1984). A Social interactional analysis of learning disabilities remediation. *Journal of Learning Disabilities, 17*(4), 194–99.

Swanson, J. M., & Kinsbourne, M. (1980). Food dyes impair performance in hyperactive children on a laboratory learning test. *Science, 207,* 1485–1487.

Tarver, S. (1982). Characteristics of learning disabilities. In T. L. Miller & E. E. Davis (Eds.), *The mildly handicapped student.* New York: Grune & Stratton.

Terry, B. J., Kretsch, M. S., & Rawlings, D. (1981, February). *Effects of environmental manipulation, curriculum change and implementationn of a token system on on-task behavior of second and third grades in a learning disabilities classroom.* Paper presented at the CEC Conference on the Exceptional Black Child, New Orleans.

Thurlow, M. L., & Ysseldyke, J. (1982, January). *Teacher's beliefs about LD students.* Washington, DC: Minneapolis Institute for Research on LD. Office of Special Education and Rehabilitation Services, Unpublished U.S. Department of Education Report p. 67.

Trites, R. L., Tryphonas, H., & Ferguson, H. B. (1980). Diet treatment for hyperactive children with food allergies. In R. Knights & D. Bakker (Eds.), *Treatment of hyperactive and learning disordered children*. Baltimore: University Park Press.

Vandiver, P. L., & Vandiver, S. C. (1981). Teachers attitudes toward mainstreaming exceptional students. *Journal for Special Educators, 17*, 381–388.

Vygotsky, L. S. (1981). The genesis of higher mental functions. In J. V. Wertsch (Ed.), *The concept of activity in soviet psychology*. Armonk, NY: M. E. Sharpe.

Weiss, B. (1980). In rebuttal. *American Journal of Diseases in Children, 134*, 1126–1127.

White, W. J., & Wimmer, B. D. (1982). The cognitively impaired. In T. F. Harrington (Ed.), *Handbook of career planning for special needs students* (pp. 101–128). Rockville, MD: Aspen Systems Corporation.

Williams, J. I., Cram, P. M., Tausig, F. T., & Weissler, E. (1978). Relative effects of drugs & diet on hyperactive behavior. An experimental study. *Pediatrics, 61*, 811–817.

Wittmer, D. D. (1982). *Attitudes about learning disabilities: A comparison between experienced teachers and future teachers*. Unpublished master's thesis, Southern Illinois University, Carbondale, IL.

Ysseldyke, J., Pianta, R., Christenson, S., Wang, J., & Algozzine, B. (1982). Institutional constraints and external pressures influencing referral decisions. *Psychology in the Schools, 19*(3), 341–345.

10 Social Cognitive Factors in Learning-disabled Children's Social Problems

Ruth Pearl
University of Illinois at Chicago

The disturbing finding that many learning-disabled children experience problematic peer relationships is by now well known. The question of why these students are susceptible to problems in their relationships with others is a topic important to those with theoretical interests in understanding the range of ramifications associated with having a learning disability, as well as to those concerned with ameliorating the social difficulties of these children. Prominent among the hypotheses advanced as to the cause of learning-disabled children's social problems is the suggestion that these children may process social information in ways that lead them to respond to others differently, and perhaps less appropriately, than do nondisabled children.

This chapter reviews the current status of the social cognition hypothesis. Because the research relating to this issue is limited in both quantity and scope, this chapter is necessarily more speculative than conclusive. Areas of social cognitive functioning that might profitably be examined are suggested, and research and interpretive issues that confront investigators in this area are outlined. Because these topics presuppose knowledge about the nature of learning-disabled children's social problems, the chapter begins with a summary of research that characterizes these children's social status and behavior.

LEARNING-DISABLED CHILDREN'S SOCIAL STATUS AND BEHAVIOR

Using a variety of sociometric measures, numerous studies have found learning-disabled children to be comparatively less popular, more rejected, more ignored, or rated less positively than the typical nondisabled child (e.g., Bruininks, 1978a,

1978b; Bryan, 1974a, 1976; Donahue & Prescott, 1983; Garrett & Crump, 1980; Prilliman, 1981; Scranton & Ryckman, 1979; Sheare, 1978; Siperstein, Bopp, & Bak, 1978; Siperstein & Goding, 1983). Studies of adults' impressions of and attitudes toward learning-disabled children indicate that parents and teachers similarly consider learning-disabled children to possess a variety of negative and bothersome characteristics (e.g., Bryan & McGrady, 1972; Doleys, Cartelli, & Doster, 1976; Garrett & Crump, 1980; Owen, Adams, Forrest, Stolz, & Fisher, 1971; Touliatos & Lindholm, 1980). Thus, learning-disabled children appear to be more likely than other children to be judged unfavorably by the individuals important in their lives.

Other studies have sought to determine whether learning-disabled children's social behavior differed from that of other children, thereby being either a possible cause of or reaction to the low regard in which learning-disabled children are held. In these studies, learning-disabled children did not appear to be withdrawn or isolated; in fact, they generally participated in social interactions as frequently as other children (Bryan, 1974b; Bryan & Wheeler, 1972; McKinney, McClure, & Feagans, 1982; Schumaker, Wildgen, & Sherman, 1982). However, in other respects, their behavior often contrasted with that of their peers, although in seemingly inconsistent ways. In some instances, the learning-disabled children appeared somewhat hostile (Bryan & Bryan, 1978; Bryan, Wheeler, Felcan, & Henek, 1976), whereas in other cases they seemed more passive and deferential (Bryan, Donahue, & Pearl, 1981). Learning-disabled children also appeared in these studies to be less skillful than peers in maintaining and dominating a conversation (Bryan et al., 1981; Bryan, Donahue, Pearl, & Sturm, 1981; Donahue & Bryan, 1982; Donahue & Prescott, 1983). Hence, learning-disabled children's behavior was found to be discrepant from that of other children, although the exact nature of the discrepancy seemed often to be situationally dependent (Pearl, Bryan, & Donahue, 1983).

THE SOCIAL COGNITION HYPOTHESIS

The evidence that learning-disabled children are likely to have different and less satisfactory social relationships than nondisabled children has led, not surprisingly, to the question of why these children should be so vulnerable to problems in the social arena. Learning-disabled children, after all, are presumably identified on academic grounds. Numerous explanations have been generated as possible sources of the children's social problems. These include the stigmatizing effect of low-academic achievement or of being labeled learning disabled, behavioral deficiencies, and a lack of social motivation on the part of these children. Although these possibilities have all received some attention, the explanation that seems to have aroused the most interest is the notion that learning-disabled children may have problems in various aspects of social cognition, which handicap them in their interactions with others.

Social cognition is the term used to refer to the knowledge and cognitive activities employed by individuals in dealing with the social world. Interest in this area has grown enormously since the resurgence of interest in cognitive psychology that occurred in the 1970s. A wide range of subjects have been studied under this rubric, including such diverse topics as one's concepts about friendship (e.g., Bigelow, 1977), perception of nonverbal behavior (e.g., Wood, 1978), knowledge about routine events (e.g., Schank & Abelson, 1977), and attributions about the causes of behavior (e.g., Weiner, 1972). Thus the field of social cognition actually encompasses a variety of interrelated and overlapping areas.

Although investigators concerned with social adjustment among nondisabled children have been interested in the role played by social cognitive skill (e.g., Urbain & Kendall, 1980), the role played by social cognitive functioning has particularly intrigued those studying social relationships of learning-disabled children. The major appeal of what is abbreviated in this chapter as "the social cognition hypothesis" is that it posits that the underlying disorder that causes children to be disabled in the academic domain, "a disorder in one or more of the basic psychological processes involved in understanding or using language" (U.S. Office of Education, 1977, p. 65083), may also make them disabled in the social domain. Thus, the rationale for examining social cognition in learning-disabled students has most frequently been the hypothesis that these children's disordered psychological processes may interfere with the understanding of subjects in the social as well as the academic realm. Nevertheless, findings that social cognitive problems exist for these children do not necessarily substantiate the notion that these are simply another manifestation of the children's learning disability. The interpretation of social cognitive differences is an issue that is discussed later in this chapter.

One major limitation of the current body of literature on the social cognitive abilities of learning-disabled students is that this research has largely been conducted without the guidance of a comprehensive theoretical framework. This was perhaps inevitable because, given the newness of the field, research even on nondisabled populations has tended to focus on only isolated aspects of social cognitive skill suggested to be important by investigators' particular theoretical interests and orientations. Comprehensive models that delineate how social cognitive knowledge and self-perceptions influence what social information is gathered, and what different information-processing skills are involved in the gathering of social information, have only recently been forthcoming.

As a result, research on learning-disabled children has examined a miscellany of areas, and any attempt to meaningfully organize the studies produces rather arbitrary groupings. This caveat made, studies on learning-disabled students' social cognition can be grouped into three broad areas. First, studies have examined learning-disabled children's comprehension of various displays of socially important information. Second, studies have examined learning-disabled children's role-taking abilities; that is, their ability to infer another's feelings, thoughts, or visual perspective when their own perspective is different. Third, studies have examined learning-disabled children's social knowledge.

In the following sections, this research is described. Although these studies make a clear contribution by initiating the evaluation of whether social cognitive problems exist for learning-disabled children, a number of issues that beg consideration are also apparent. These issues are discussed subsequently.

SOCIAL PERCEPTION

The question of whether learning-disabled children are as accurate as nondisabled children in the inferences they make when viewing socially important displays has been investigated in a variety of studies. Researchers have examined learning-disabled students' understanding of nonverbal emotional expressions, social situations depicted in drawings, and complex social interactions. Learning-disabled children were suspected to be at risk for misconstruing these social displays primarily because many learning-disabled children have been found to have attentional or perceptual deficits (Hallahan & Kaufmann, 1976) that could interfere with the children's fully comprehending a situation. However, as is suggested later, some mistakes made on these tasks could be due to differences in the children's social knowledge rather than to perceptual or attentional difficulties.

The first study examining perception of nonverbal behavior by learning-disabled students was done by Wiig and Harris (1974) who videotaped a young woman pantomiming the emotions of anger, embarrassment, fear, frustration, joy, and love. The woman was videotaped above the waist and so a variety of body cues were in view. Adolescent subjects were asked to circle on a response sheet the emotion depicted in each of the segments. Not only did the learning-disabled students make more errors than the nondisabled students, their errors were more often the result of a confusion of negatively and positively balanced emotions, e.g., a confusion of embarrassment and joy.

In a similar study, Bryan (1977) showed third- through fifth-grade children a version of the Profile of Nonverbal Sensitivity (PONS; Rosenthal, Hall, DiMatteo, Rogers, & Archer, 1979). This test involves showing subjects a series of filmed scenarios in which an adult female expresses either positive or negative affects in combination with submissive or dominant expressions. In the scenarios, either the face of the woman or only her upper torso are in view. For some scenarios, only the audio portion of the film was presented. For other scenarios, the audio portion was rendered uninterpretable; thus only the video portion was clear. After viewing each scenario, the subject was required to indicate which of two descriptions applied to the scene. For example, one choice involved selecting between the alternatives "Jane likes the pretty flowers" and "Jane is sorry for what she did." The results of this study indicated that the learning-disabled children were less accurate than the nondisabled children in responding to both the audio and visual channels. However, when the PONS was administered to 9- to 12-year-old boys who were given incentives to pay close attention to the scenes, no differences were found between learning-disabled and nondisabled subjects (Stone & LaGreca, in press).

Learning-disabled students have been found to be less skilled than nondisabled peers in their understanding of nonverbal behavior in several unpublished doctoral dissertations (Emery, 1975; Puckett, 1980; Thomas, 1979; all reported in Maheady & Maitland, 1982) although in two studies, when auditory as well as visual cues were present, no differences were detected (Maheady, 1981; Maitland, 1977; both reported in Maheady & Maitland, 1982). In addition, in a study of children's understanding of feedback from a listener indicating noncomprehension, learning-disabled and nondisabled children in third through eighth grade did not differ in their comprehension of expressions indicating puzzlement (Pearl, Donahue, & Bryan, 1981).

Group differences in the understanding of pictorially depicted social situations were examined in two studies through the use of the Test of Social Inference (Edmonson, deJung, Leland, & Leach, 1974). In this test, 30 different pictures of common social situations are presented. Answers to a series of standard questions asked about each picture are scored according to whether they indicate comprehension of the situation depicted. Gerber and Zinkgraf (1982) administered the Test of Social inference to children aged 7 through 10 years old. The learning-disabled children in their sample scored lower than the nondisabled children.

Bruno (1981) similarly found that learning-disabled students, aged 9 through 11 ½ years old, made fewer correct inferences about the Test of Social Inference situations. Moreover, the learning-disabled children made, on average, more outright errors in their interpretation of the pictures, apparently because they often responded to irrelevant details in the pictures. Additional questions which probed the children's inferences about antecedent and subsequent occurrences revealed no differences between learning-disabled and nondisabled children's answers about precipitating events. However, the learning-disabled children were more likely to predict illogical consequences to the scenes than were the nondisabled children.

Comprehension of videotaped social interactions was examined in two studies. In one, four scenes from television soap operas were shown to sixth through eighth graders (Pearl & Cosden, 1982). In each segment, two individuals, one male and one female, discussed an emotion-laden topic (that is, one of them moving out of the area, their feelings toward each other, their feelings about a third person, and their own feelings of insecurity). The real feelings of the characters were often presented only through indirect or subtle facial, behavioral, or verbal cues. The subjects were asked five multiple-choice questions about each segment, probing their comprehension of the situations. The learning-disabled children consistently made more errors than the nondisabled students.

The second study, however, reported no group differences in social comprehension. Maheady (reported in Maheady & Maitland, 1982) showed 7 through 12-year-old and adolescent males the Social Interpretation Test (Archer & Akert, 1977). In this test, subjects are shown twenty sequences of social interaction and are asked an interpretive question about each scene. The learning-disabled children did at least as well on this task as the nondisabled children.

These studies, then, although indicating that learning-disabled children often misinterpret social displays, also suggest that there are circumstances under which differences between groups are less likely to occur. One possibility suggested by this body of research is that the learning-disabled/nondisabled differences are attenuated when the children are highly motivated to pay attention, or if redundant or attention-grabbing cues are present. Thus, it may be that learning-disabled children have the ability to decipher the meaning of social displays but are less accurate only when they attend to them less carefully. However, because most studies have not fully explored the impact of task demands on the children's performance, acceptance of this conclusion is premature. The importance of task demands is considered in a later section of this chapter.

ROLE-TAKING STUDIES

In the studies described in the previous section, the subjects were given unimpeded views of the social displays. In contrast, role-taking tasks examine individuals' understanding of another person's point of view precisely when they themselves have a different point of view. The issue of interest is whether the individuals are able to ignore their own experience in making inferences about the experience of the other person. Role taking has been examined in affective, cognitive, and perceptual domains. Affective role taking refers to the ability to understand another's emotions; cognitive role taking refers to the ability to understand another's thoughts; and perceptual role taking refers to the ability to understand another's physical perspective.

Interest in learning-disabled children's role-taking skills seems to be an out-growth of the attention paid by developmental psychologists to the growth of role-taking skills among nondisabled children. This attention was stimulated by Piaget's suggestion that young children are egocentric, trapped in their own point of view. Role-taking studies seek to track the development of children's understanding that others may not share their view. An additional rationale for studying role taking in learning-disabled children has been that if learning-disabled children fail to employ task-appropriate strategies on cognitive tasks (Torgesen, 1980), they may also fail to use appropriate strategies (that is, role taking) in social situations (Wong & Wong, 1980).

Dickstein and Warren (1980) examined the role-taking abilities of 5- through 8-year-olds on cognitive, affective, and perceptual tasks. Each task comprised 10 questions. Five questions required only that the children answer from their own perspective; this allowed an evaluation of the child's understanding of directions. The other five questions, the role-taking questions, required the children to take into account the viewpoint of someone whose perspective differed from their own. Responses required the child to point to one of three objects.

The cognitive role-taking questions required the child to predict another's thoughts when they possessed different information than that known by the child. One example is: "Andy told his Dad he was going to draw a lion in art class. When Andy got to school, his teacher told him he could draw a zebra, a giraffe, or a lion. Andy decided to draw a giraffe instead, and brought the picture home in his school bag. Point to the one Daddy will think Andy drew in art class."

The affective role-taking questions required that the child predict another's feelings when they differed from those of the child. For example, if the child had indicated in response to a previous question that he or she liked to take baths, the experimenter would say, "Sally doesn't like to take baths. Sally's Mom tells Sally that it is time to take a bath. Point to the face that shows how Sally feels."

Dickstein and Warren's (1980) perceptual role-taking task was somewhat different from the typical perceptual role-taking task. Whereas most perceptual role-taking tasks measure children's ability to assess another's view when the person's vantage point differs from that of the child, Dickstein and Warren's task assessed the children's understanding that another might not have access to the visual information they had. Two dolls were set up to "look" at identical sets of toys mounted on a turntable. The dolls initially faced the same toy on their set of toys. The children were told that each doll would see where the other doll was looking. Then the dolls were placed back to back, with the children told that now "neither doll can see what the other doll is looking at." The experimenter then quietly rotated the display of the first doll so that the doll faced a new toy. The child was asked to point out the toy that the second doll would think the first doll was looking at. Thus, a correct answer required the child to know that the doll would be likely to make an egocentric error. In a sense then, this task required cognitive role taking as well as perceptual role taking.

The results indicated that, at each age, the learning-disabled children performed less well than the nondisabled children who, by the age of 8, performed almost perfectly on these tasks. To see if older learning-disabled children would reach this level of performance, additional groups of 9- and 10-year-old learning-disabled children were administered the tasks. These children showed no improvement in role-taking ability over the scores achieved by the learning-disabled 8-year-olds.

The cognitive and affective role-taking tasks given by Dickstein and Warren (1980) were adapted in a study by Bruck and Hébert (1982), with children aged 7 through 10 years old. This study also found lower role-taking abilities among the learning-disabled children.

Third-, and fourth-grade children's cognitive and perceptual role-taking abilities were examined by Horowitz (1981). To assess perceptual role taking, children were asked to identify which of eight photographs showed a doll's view of a model of a mountain (Piaget, 1956). The cognitive role-taking measure required the child to first create a story about a picture and then to retell the story from the point of view of each of the characters. The children's performance was rated according to how well the children were able to shift focus while maintaining consistency between the different story versions. Analyses indicated that although learning-disabled children received lower scores than nondisabled students on the cognitive role-taking task, the group differences disappeared when IQ scores were used as a covariate. On the mountain task, however, the learning-disabled children performed more poorly than the nondisabled students even with the effects of IQ controlled.

Wong and Wong (1980) showed third and fourth graders three cartoon series from Chandler's (1973) cognitive role-taking task. Each series showed a character involved in an event which influenced the character to react emotionally to what otherwise would have been an innocuous occurrence. For example, a boy who ran home after breaking a window reacted to a knock on the door with fear. The subjects were asked first to tell the story depicted by pretending they were the character, and then to tell the story from the point of view of a second character who had been introduced after the precipitating event. Thus, in the example described, the second character would not have known that the boy had broken the window. At issue was whether the subject would realize that the second character was not privy to the whole story. The results indicated that although there were no differences between learning-disabled and nondisabled boys in their ability to take on the second person's perspective, the learning-disabled girls were less successful than the normally achieving girls in adopting the bystander's point of view.

Two other studies also found no differences between learning-disabled and nondisabled boys in cognitive role taking. These studies both used a role-taking measure developed by Flavell and his colleagues (Flavell, Botkin, Fry, Wright, & Jarvis, 1968), a task similar to that used by Wong and Wong (1980). Ackerman, Elardo, and Dykman (1979) found no differences among learning-disabled, hyperactive, and normal boys between the ages of 7 and 10. Fincham (1979) found no differences between learning-disabled and normally achieving 8- and 9-year-old boys.

Other studies have used tasks where role-taking skills are needed for a successful performance. Referential communication tasks, for example, have been used to examine whether learning-disabled students are as proficient as other children in providing clues that allow a listener to identify a particular referent. To give good clues on these tasks requires, along with semantic and syntactic skills, that the clue-giver evaluate the listener's background knowledge and view of the situation. In two studies using referential communication tasks, learning-disabled children were found to give less informative clues to their listeners than did nondisabled children (Noel, 1980; Spekman, 1981). In these studies, it appeared that the results were less likely to be due to problems in expressive language than to role-taking deficits (Donahue, Pearl, & Bryan, 1983).

Learning-disabled children's tactfulness was examined in another study (Pearl, Donahue, & Bryan, in press). Tact, the "delicate perception of the right thing to say or do without offending" (Guralnik, 1973), requires, among other skills, the ability to take on the perspective of the listener enough to realize the impact a statement is likely to have. Learning-disabled and nondisabled first through fourth graders' tactfulness was assessed on a task requiring the children to role play what they would say in five different situations in which they had to give negative feedback to a peer. An example is the following situation:

> Suppose you want to play a game of checkers. You walk up to two friends and ask them if either wants to play with you. Both say they want to play. You choose one of them. You have to tell them of your choice. What would you say to the boy (girl) you did not choose?

The other situations required the child to tell the friend that he or she could not come along with the child's family to get an ice-cream cone, that the friend was not chosen for a desired part in the class play, that the child did not want to watch the friend's choice of television program, and that the friend could not go with the child to the movies. The children's statements were scored according to the degree to which there was an attempt to make the news less hurtful or insulting to the listener. The results indicated that the learning-disabled children were less tactful than the nondisabled children.

Although some support for the hypothesis that learning-disabled children have problems with role taking can be found in these studies, there is enouch inconsistency in the results to indicate that clarification of learning-disabled children's strengths and weaknesses in this area awaits further analysis. Some of the factors that need to be more systematically examined are considered in a later section.

SOCIAL KNOWLEDGE

A small number of studies have assessed whether learning-disabled children differ from other children in their basic knowledge about social situations or skills. For example, Bachara (1976) examined learning-disabled boys' assumptions about the emotions experienced by children in different situations. The boys were told stories, some accompanied by pictures, in which a child underwent an experience that would have been likely to make him happy, sad, mad, or afraid. The learning-disabled boys, whose ages ranged from 7 to 12, were less accurate than the nondisabled boys in choosing a face depicting the appropriate emotion. Although interpretation of the results of this study is complicated by the fact that accurate responding required social perception skills as well as social knowledge, the findings do suggest the possibility that some learning-disabled children may be less knowledgeable about the likely impact of different events on individuals' emotions.

Other studies have not found that elementary school learning-disabled children differ from classmates in their social knowledge. Bryan and Sonnefeld (1981) found no differences in learning-disabled and nondisabled children's beliefs about what tactics would be most desirable for ingratiating peers, parents, or teachers in different situations. Stone and LaGreca (in press) found that learning-disabled boys, age 9 to 12, did not differ from nondisabled boys in the steps they went through while role playing the act of making friends with a new boy in school. Bursuck (1983) asked third- and fourth-grade low-achieving and learning-disabled boys to describe what they should do in different hypothetical situations in which they were involved in either interpersonal conflict or in initiating or maintaining an interaction. The strategies chosen by the learning-disabled boys were not rated as significantly more positive, negative, or withdrawn than those of the low-achieving boys.

However, the fact that differences in knowledge were not found in these studies does not necessarily mean that there aren't differences in knowledge about other socially important areas or differences even in these areas that might have been detected by other measures. Further, whether, and how well, this knowledge is actually applied may well distinguish learning-disabled children from their peers. For instance, Stone and LaGreca (in press) found that despite the fact that learning-disabled and nondisabled children did not differ on the making friends role-playing task, adults observing their performance rated them as being less socially skilled.

RESEARCH AND INTERPRETIVE ISSUES

For the most part, these studies support the notion that at least some social cognitive problems may exist in the population of learning-disabled children. Thus, these studies lay an important foundation for further research in that they indicate that the social cognition hypothesis remains viable and should be further pursued. However, if in the future we are going to be able to say more than just that some learning-disabled children may have some types of social cognitive problems, it is important to now think through a number of issues that have become apparent. These both raise questions about how meaningful and important past findings are, and questions about the interpretation of any social cognitive differences that are found. Obviously, then, deliberation about these issues is desirable before more research is done in this area.

Specifically, consideration needs to be given to the following issues: the interpretation of performance on social cognitive tasks; the issue of which learning-disabled children are studied; the types of social cognitive skills assessed; the interpretation of any discovered social cognitive deficits; the relationship of social cognitive deficits to social problems; and finally, the question of the importance of remediation of social cognitive deficits.

Interpretation of Performance on Social Cognitive Tasks

Probably because research on social cognition of learning-disabled students is of such recent origin, complexities in such social cognitive activities as role taking have yet to be fully acknowledged. For example, Flavell (1985) pointed out that one cannot assume that individuals possessing the ability to make an inference necessarily always use this ability. Unless individuals feel the need to engage in an inferential act, they may not make an inference, even if they have the ability to do so if compelled. Thus, to solve a role-taking problem, a child must not only have the ability to role take in that particular situation, he or she must also recognize the situation as one where role taking is needed.

This distinction between the ability to role take and the recognition of appropriate occasions for role taking has not been adequately unraveled. Children who fail role-taking problems may do so because they lack role-taking skills or because they don't recognize the need to engage in role taking. Children who solve role-taking problems may do so because they spontaneously role take at appropriate times or because, by being presented with what clearly is a role-taking problem, they are reminded that they should do so. Thus, a number of different social cognitive activities are actually tapped by role-taking tasks.

Others have pointed out that simply distinguishing role-taking tasks by broad content areas (for example, whether they tap cognitive, affective, or perceptual domains) may not sufficiently describe variations among role-taking tasks. Role-taking tasks vary not only in their subject matter but also in their structure; that is, even within a single domain tasks vary in such things as the number of elements in the problem that must be simultaneously considered. These factors influence the types of cognitive operations required for solving a problem (Higgins, 1981; Shantz, 1983). Thus to find, for example, that learning-disabled children do well on an affective role-taking task but not a cognitive role-taking task is difficult to interpret without knowing whether the structural demands of the different tasks were equivalent.

Further, within a domain the difficulty of discerning another's viewpoint is certainly affected by the subject's familiarity with that particular viewpoint. For example, a young child may successfully detect another's feelings of sadness but not another's feeling of wariness. In other words, an individual's social knowledge limits the types of inferences he or she is likely to make.

In addition, failure on role-taking tasks can in some cases be due, not to an inability to deal with the content or structure of the task, but to children's inability to prevent their own viewpoint from interfering with judgment. Although one of the requirements of a role-taking task is that the subject have a different view than the target person, what this definition does not take into account is that the salience of one's own point of view can vary over situations. Further, one can have a different point of view for different reasons. The subject and the target person may have different views because the situational factors they experience are different, or because they possess different characteristics (Higgins, 1981). Evaluation of the impact of differing types of point of view possessed by subjects on their ability to role take has not been systematically explored in the developmental literature, much less the research on learning-disabled children.

Other questions have been raised regarding tasks used to measure social perception. Tasks involving pictured situations have been criticized as unrealistic in their two-dimensional, state portrayals. Other tasks which present social information through only audio or visual channels have been criticized on the grounds that, in actual situations, both sources of information are usually available (Maheady & Maitland, 1982). Thus, this argument goes, even if deficiencies on such tasks are found, whether the subject suffers from any real-life disadvantage can be questioned. Although this is a good point, it should also not be overstated; in many instances, socially relevant information not only is not redundantly presented through two channels, it is actually masked. For example, with development comes the realization that in some cases it is not socially desirable to display one's emotions (for example, showing embarrassment at being one of the last picked for a team; Saarni, 1979). In this instance, attention to extremely subtle cues may be the only way to correctly perceive the target person's affect.

Another limitation of social perception tasks is that failure on these tasks, like on role-taking tasks, could occur for a number of different reasons. The subjects may have had trouble discriminating the relevant cues from the wealth of social information available in the displays. Or, the subjects may have detected these features as well as other individuals but may not have gone on to make inferences about what they indicated. Yet another possibility is that the subjects made inferences, but incorrect ones. This could stem from a lack of social knowledge about what different cues tend to mean, or because of consistent positive or negative biases (for example, an assumption that others have malevolent attitudes). Further, as with the role-taking tasks, not all inferences are of equal complexity. For example, children may be able to make correct inferences concerning an unspecified part of a story line, but not about a character's hidden motivation.

Thus, now that there is information suggesting that many learning-disabled children have social perception problems, or social perception problems in certain situations, research is still needed to specify why and when these problems emerge.

Learning-Disabled Samples

One of the most widely discussed issues among learning disability researchers is the question of how to select and describe the group that serves as a study's learning-disabled sample. This is an issue because of the diverse procedures used by school districts to identify learning disabilities and because of the heterogeneity of problems included under the classification of learning disabilities. The reason for concern, of course, is the question of whether the results of one investigation are applicable to a different group of learning-disabled children.

Most of the studies that have examined social cognitive skills in the learning disabled have had as their aim the goal of determining whether this population, in general, seems likely to have social cognitive problems. The samples have been drawn from the learning-disabled population in a number of ways. The majority of studies have used school labeled learning-disabled children, a procedure that usually leaves unspecified the particular criteria used by a school district for identifying learning disabilities. Other studies have used experimenter determined criteria to identify children whose characteristics conform to those in the definition of learning disabilities, a procedure that makes clear the factors used to determine learning-disability status but may possibly not identify the same children that would be identified by a more thorough process. Still other studies have drawn their sample from out-of-school clinic facilities where children are either being tested or are receiving help for learning-disability problems. These children may therefore have different or more severe problems than the typical learning-disabled child.

To help mitigate the shortcomings of these procedures, most investigators, to varying degrees, try to report as much information about the sample as possible. This should be continued, using, whenever possible, widely known measures that can serve as marker variables (Keogh, Major-Kingsley, Omori-Gordon, & Reid, 1982) by which a sample's characteristics can be compared to those of other samples.

Because past social cognition studies have intended merely to establish whether learning-disabled children in general seem vulnerable to social cognitive problems, the use of what are probably somewhat heterogeneous samples of learning-disabled students has not been totally inappropriate. However, within the field of learning disabilities there is currently great interest in determining whether there are identifiable subgroups within the learning-disabled population. The call for examining subgroups of learning-disabled children often ignores the fact that learning-disabled children can be classified in different ways depending on the purpose of the classification (Keogh, 1983). There are at least three ways to classify learning-disabled children into subgroups that could aid our understanding of learning-disabled children's social cognitive skills.

First, evaluating the social cognitive skills of children divided into subgroups according to nonsocial criteria (for example, whether they suffer from a math or reading disability) would provide fuller information on the social ramifications of different types of disabilities and might suggest hypotheses about what specific cognitive deficits are related to various problems in social cognitive functioning. Second, evaluating the correlates of subgroups of learning-disabled children who experience different types of social cognitive problems could lead to more precise hypotheses about the antecedents and consequences of these problems. Third, comparing the social cognitive skills of learning-disabled children who are rejected or ignored by peers with those of learning-disabled children who are accepted by peers could indicate how important these skills really are to the children's social relationships.

These three methods of subgrouping would be likely to lead to different, but complementary and useful, information. As in other areas of learning-disability research, then, research on social cognitive skills of learning-disabled children would profit if greater attention was paid to the characteristics of the children studied.

Types of Social Cognitive Skills Assessed

As was apparent in the brief review of past research, only limited areas of social cognitive functioning in learning-disabled students have been studied. Although it certainly would not advance the field to simply study a new random assortment of topics, a thoughtful expansion of the areas investigated could aid our knowledge of how learning-disabled children process social information. In particular, new approaches developing in the field of social psychology may be useful in providing insights in to the processes of learning-disabled children.

For example, our knowledge of how learning-disabled children gather socially important information would be enriched by an examination of whether these children differ from others in the way they extract information from sequences of behavior. Newtson (1973) suggested that viewers gain information from identifying "breakpoints" in streams of behaviors that define and summarize significant actions. Where these breakpoints are perceived to occur is a function both of the stimulus that is observed and of the observer's cognitive set (Newtson, 1980). Hence, individuals can differ in their identification of significant breakpoints. In turn, differences in the number of breakpoints identified can alter the information gained from a behavioral sequence (Newtson, 1973). A comparison of learning-disabled and other children's choice of breakpoints might help explain why these children differ in their interpretation of certain situations.

Yet another potentially useful conception for helping to determine learning-disabled children's social knowledge is that of "scripts." Scripts are "a coherent sequence of events expected by the individual, involving him either as a participant or an observer" (Abelson, 1976, p. 33). The classic example is the restauraunt script. When one enters a restaurant, a particular sequence of events is expected to follow. We expect to be seated, be given a menu, order, be served our food, get a bill, leave a tip, pay the bill, and leave. These expectations about events guide our understanding and behavior and free us from the need to consciously reflect on every aspect of the situations we experience (Langer, 1978).

There are several ways the conception of scripts could provide useful information about learning-disabled children. First, learning-disabled children may differ from nondisabled children in their acquisition of scripts. For example, it may be that problems in social perception lead the children to develop less accurate scripts or develop scripts at a slower pace than other children. Difficulties in social perception could also interfere with the children's ability to recognize the optional elements in a script, with the result that they attend less than they should to parts of the scripted situation that may vary.

In addition, it is possible that learning-disabled children differ from other children in the content of their scripts. For instance, they may have different scripts for what follows a greeting from another child. Learning-disabled children, based on their experiences, may anticipate a less friendly interaction than do other children. Because the scripts that are salient to an individual seem to influence their social behavior (e.g., Wilson & Capitman, 1982), knowing what the children's expectations are could be important information.

Another approach that could provide relevant information would be to assess learning-disabled children's attributions for social success and failure. Children's interpretation of the causes of their experiences have been found to be related to subsequent social behavior (Goetz & Dweck, 1980), and so an examination of learning-disabled children's social attributions might be revealing. Learing-disabled children's achievement attributions have been examined (e.g., Pearl, 1982; Pearl, Bryan, & Donahue, 1980), but their attributions about events in the social domain have received little attention (Sobol, Earn, Bennett, & Humphries, 1983). Other approaches that examine whether the children's knowledge and feelings about their capabilities and status affect their processing of social information could also be enlightening.

However, it is important to reiterate that investigations of new areas will be useful only if they bring new theoretical approaches to the understanding of social cognitive problems or if they specify how certain aspects of social cognitive functioning relate to other aspects. Simply finding new measures on which learning-disabled children perform poorly will not be likely to increase our understanding of learning disabled children's difficulties.

Interpretation of Social Cognitive Deficits

If social cognitive problems are substantiated among the learning-disabled population, the question remains as to *why* this group is deficient in this area. It cannot be assumed that social cognitive deficits are necessarily just another manifestation of the children's learning disabilities. There are a number of other plausible reasons why learning-disabled children might have problems in this domain.

First, it may be the case that some of the apparent social cognitive deficits are really associated with general intellectual deficiencies rather than with learning disabilities in particular. To rule out this possibility, most studies have equated learning-disabled and nondisabled groups on IQ or have statistically controlled for group differences in intelligence. However, not all studies have done so. It is critical that studies purporting to find deficiencies associated with learning disabilities rule out the possibility that these are simply related to general intellectual status. Others have suggested that certain problems found in learning-disabled groups may really be due to the fact that learning disabilities are often confounded with hyperactivity (LaGreca, 1983).

However, even in methodologically sound studies, it is not necessarily the case that social cognitive deficits are a product of the children's learning disabilities, as indeed many of the researchers have pointed out. One alternative explanation is that the learning-disabled children's social cognitive skills are less developed as a result of the different types of social interactions they experience That is, as a consequence of their social problems, they may not interact with other children in the way necessary to promote optimal social cognitive development. In other words, the social relationship problems experienced by the children may prevent them from having the types of interactions required for normal social cognitive development.

Another possibility is that the learning-disabled children appear to be lacking in social cognitive skills not because the social cognitive processes they employ are any less developed than those of other children their age, but because their aberrant social experiences have led them to make inferences that are discrepant from those typically made. For example, the children may engage in the process of role taking to the same degree as others but make inaccurate inferences as a result of their atypical experiences. Hence, even if the learning-disabled children employ sophisticated social cognitive skills, this may be masked if they end up making inferences that are similar in content to those made by children with less developed social cognitive skills.

The last two possibilities would mean that social cognitive problems are only coincidentally associated with having a learning disability. Determination of the reason or reasons for learning-disabled children's social cognitive problems could have both theoretical and practical implications.

Relationship of Social Cognitive Deficits to Social Problems

Even if learning-disabled children are deficient in social cognitive skills, it does not automatically follow that these deficiencies are directly producing the children's social problems. It could be, after all, that social cognitive deficits are no more related to learning-disabled children's social status or behavior than are deficits in any other area. Except for two studies, the research examining learning-disabled children's social cognitive skills has not actually evaluated whether these skills bear a direct relationship to the children's social problems. Thus the crux of the social cognition hypothesis, that social cognitive problems interfere with learning-disabled children's peer relationships, has not been addressed in most of the studies conducted. This is understandable because these studies were aimed at the preliminary concern of establishing whether social cognitive deficits were even a viable possibility as a cause of the children's problems. However, now that there is enough support for the notion that learning-disabled children may be lacking in certain social cognitive areas, it is time to examine if, and how, these deficiencies are associated with the children's social competence.

The two studies that did examine this question did not find impressive support for the social cognition hypothesis. Stone and LaGreca (in press) found that scores on the PONS measure of nonverbal comprehension were unrelated to either teachers' ratings of aggressive and withdrawn behavior or to the children's performance on a task in which they had to role play friendship-making skills. Bruck and Hébert (1982) examined learning-disabled children's performance on role-taking tasks and parents' and teachers' ratings of the child's peer interactions. Only weak evidence of an association between the factors was found.

Although these failures to substantiate the social cognition hypothesis certainly do not disprove it, they suggest that a more specific formulation of the hypothesis might be called for. For instance, it may well be the case that not all the social cognitive skills measured are equally critical. There may also be age changes in the importance of certain of these skills; some social cognitive deficits might be debilitating to children of one age-group but not another. Further, these skills undoubtedly bear different relationships to different measures of social status and behavior. It may be that performance on the social cognition measures assessed in the Stone and LaGreca (in press) and Bruck and Hébert (1982) studies would be related to a measure of the children's sociometric status, for example.

If a clear understanding of the importance of social cognitive abilities to learning-disabled children is to emerge, researchers need to start identifying which particular social cognitive skills are related to specific measures of social acceptance and competence.

Remediation of Social Cognitive Deficits

Finally, if social cognitive deficits are found among learning-disabled students, does it necessarily mean that these deficits should be remediated? Although it is hard to argue that anyone is better off with social cognitive deficits, the costs and benefits of training social cognitive skills need to be carefully evaluated and monitored. For one thing, as was stated earlier, it has not even yet been clearly established that learning-disabled children's social problems are at all the consequence of social cognitive deficits. Although this is more the result of the paucity of studies in this area than of any evidence weakening the social cognitive hypothesis, it still means that advocates of social cognitive training are relying more on faith than on data.

Another reason for closely monitoring social cognitive training is that attempts to make learning-disabled children like others may inadvertently cause more harm than good. For example, the meaning of various social cues may vary according to the status of the interpreter; a smile from a popular child to an unpopular learning-disabled child may not mean the same thing as a smile to another popular child. Until more about such things is known, interventions should be cautious and conservative or risk exacerbating the children's problems. Further, even if learning-disabled children have ameliorable social cognitive problems, it may sometimes be more efficacious to structure the environment to accommodate children's limitations on social cognition or to try to make the class as a whole more accepting of individual differences than to target attention on an individual child.

These admonitions are not meant to imply that interventions should not be attempted, merely that their successfulness and importance should be tested, not assumed. Carefully executed training studies that assess the impact of teaching social cognitive skills to learning-disabled children deficient in these skills could make an important contribution to our understanding of this area.

SUMMARY

Enough evidence now exists to suggest that some learning-disabled children may have deficits in some social cognitive processes that may interfere with some aspects of their relationships with others. By thoughtfully considering the issues that are now apparent in this area, future research should provide a more conclusive conclusion.

REFERENCES

Abelson, R. P. (1976). Script processing in attitude and decision making. In J. S. Carroll & J. W. Payne (Eds.), *Cognition and social behavior* (pp. 33–45). Hillsdale, NJ: Lawrence Erlbaum Associates.

Ackerman, P. T., Elardo, P. T., & Dykman, R. A. (1979). A psychosocial study of hyperactive and learning disabled boys. *Journal of Abnormal Child Psychology, 7,* 91–99.

Archer, D., & Akert, R. M. (1977). Words and everything else: Verbal and nonverbal cues in social interpretation. *Journal of Personality and Social Psychology, 35,* 443–449.

Bachara, G. H. (1976). Empathy in learning disabled children. *Perceptual and Motor Skills, 43,* 541–542.

Bigelow, B. J. (1977). Children's friendship expectations: A cognitive developmental study. *Child Development, 48,* 246–253.

Bruck, M., & Hébert, M. (1982). Correlates of learning disabled students' peer interaction patterns. *Learning Disability Quarterly, 5,* 353–362.

Bruininks, V. L. (1978a). Actual and perceived peer status of learning disabled students in mainstream programs. *Journal of Special Education, 12,* 51–58.

Bruininks, V. L. (1978b). Peer status and personality of learning disabled and nondisabled students. *Journal of Learning Disabilities, 11,* 29–34.

Bruno, R. M. (1981). Interpretation of pictorially presented social situations by learning disabled and normal children. *Journal of Learning Disabilities, 14,* 350–352.

Bryan, J. H., & Sonnefeld, L. J. (1981). Children's social desirability ratings of ingratiation tactics. *Learning Disability Quarterly, 4,* 287–293.

Bryan, T., Donahue, M., & Pearl, R. (1981). Learning disabled children's peer interactions during a small-group problem solving task. *Learning Disability Quarterly, 4,* 13–22.

Bryan, T., Donahue, M., Pearl, R., & Sturm, C. (1981). Learning disabled children's conversational skills: The "TV talk show." *Learning Disability Quarterly, 4,* 260–270.

Bryan, T., & McGrady, H. (1972). Use of a teacher rating scale. *Journal of Learning Disabilities, 5,* 199–206.

Bryan, T., & Wheeler, R. (1972). Perception of learning disabled children: The eye of the observer. *Journal of Learning Disabilities, 5,* 484–488.

Bryan, T. H. (1974a). Peer popularity of learning disabled children. *Journal of Learning Disabilities, 7,* 621–625.

Bryan, T. H. (1974b). An observational analysis of classroom behaviors of children with learning disabilities. *Journal of Learning Disabilities, 7,* 26–34.

Bryan, T. H. (1976). Peer popularity of learning disabled children: A replication. *Journal of Learning Disabilities, 9,* 307–311.

Bryan, T. H. (1977). Children's comprehension of non-verbal communication. *Journal of Learning Disabilities, 10,* 501–506.

Bryan, T. H., & Bryan, J. H. (1978). Social interactions of learning disabled children. *Learning Disability Quarterly, 1,* 33–39.

Bryan, T. H., Wheeler, R., Felcan, J., & Henek, T. (1976). "Come on dummy": An observational study of children's communications. *Journal of Learning Disabilities, 9,* 661–669.

Bursuck, W. D. (1983). Sociometric status, behavior ratings, and social knowledge of learning disabled and low-achieving students. *Learning Disability Quarterly, 6,* 329–337.

Chandler, M. J. (1973). Egocentrism and antisocial behavior: The assessment and training of social perspective-taking skills. *Developmental Psychology, 9,* 326–332.

Dickstein, E. B., & Warren, D. R. (1980). Roletaking deficits in learning disabled children. *Journal of Learning Disabilities, 13,* 378–382.

Doleys, D., Cartelli, L., & Doster, J. (1976). Comparison of patterns of mother–child interaction. *Journal of Learning Disabilities, 9,* 371–375.

Donahue, M., & Bryan, T. H. (1982). *Conversational skills and modeling in learning disabled children.* Paper presented at the Boston University Conference on Language Development, Boston.

Donahue, M., Pearl, R., & Bryan, T. (1983). Communicative competence in learning disabled children. In I. Bialer and K. Gadow (Eds.). *Advances in learning and behavioral disabilities* (Vol. 2, pp. 49–84). Greenwich, CT: J.A.I. Press.

Donahue, M., & Prescott, B. (1983). *Young learning disabled children's conversational episodes in dispute episodes with peers.* Chicago, IL: Chicago Institute for the Study of Learning Disabilities, University of Illinois at Chicago.

Edmonson, B., Dejung, J., Leland, H., & Leach, E. (1974). *The test of social inference.* New York: Educational Activities.

Emery, J. E. (1975). Social perception processes in normal and learning disabled children. *Dissertation Abstracts International, 36,* 1942b–1943b.

Fincham, F. (1979). Conservation and cognitive role-taking ability in learning disabled boys. *Journal of Learning Disabilities, 12,* 34–40.

Flavell, J. H. (1985). *Cognitive development.* Englewood Cliffs, NJ: Prentice-Hall.

Flavell, J. H., Botkin, P. T., Fry, C. L., Wright, J. W., & Jarvis, P. E. (1968). *The development of role-taking and communication skills in children.* New York: Wiley.

Garrett, M. K., & Crump, W. D. (1980). Peer acceptance, teacher references, and self-appraisal of social status among learning disabled students. *Learning Disability Quarterly, 3,* 42–48.

Gerber, P. J., & Zinkgraf, S. A. (1982). A comparative study of social-perceptual ability in learning disabled and nonhandicapped students. *Learning Disability Quarterly, 5,* 374–378.

Goetz, T. E., & Dweck, C. S. (1980). Learned helplessness in social situations. *Journal of Personality and Social Psychology, 39,* 246–255.

Guralnik, D. B. (1973). *Webster's new world dictionary of the American language.* World Publishing Company.

Hallahan, D. P., & Kaufmann, J. M. (1976). *Introduction to learning disabilities: A psychobehavioral approach.* Englewood Cliffs, NJ: Prentice-Hall.

Higgins, E. T. (1981). Role-taking and social judgment: Alternative developmental perspectives and processes. In J. H. Flavell & L. Ross (Eds.), *Social cognitive development* (pp. 119–153). Cambridge: Cambridge University Press.

Horowitz, E. C. (1981). Popularity, decentering ability, and role-taking skills in learning disabled and normal children. *Learning Disability Quarterly, 4,* 23–30.

Keogh, B. F. (1983). Classification, compliance, and confusion. *Journal of Learning Disabilities, 16,* 25.

Keogh, B. K., Major-Kingsley, S., Omori-Gordon, H., & Reid, H. P. (1982). *A system of marker variables for the field of learning disabilities.* Syracuse: Syracuse University Press.

LaGreca, A. M. (1983, August). *Social competence in learning disabled children: Directions for the future.* Paper presented at the meetings of the American Psychological Association, Anaheim, CA.

Langer, E. J. (1978). Rethinking the role of thought in social interaction. In J. H. Harvey, W. Ickes, & R. F. Kidd (Eds.), *New directions in attribution research* (Vol. 2, pp. 35–58). Hillsdale, NJ: Lawrence Erlbaum Associates.

Maheady, L. (1981). *The interpretation of social interactions by learning disabled, socially/emotionally disturbed, educable mentally retarded and nondisabled children.* Unpublished doctoral dissertation, University of Pittsburgh, Pittsburgh, PA.

Maheady, L., & Maitland, G. (1982). Assessing social perception abilities in learning disabled students. *Learning Disability Quarterly, 5,* 363–370.

Maitland, G. E. (1977). *The perception of facial and vocal expressions of emotions by learning disabled, emotionally disturbed, and normal children.* Unpublished doctoral dissertation, University of Virginia, Charlottesville, VA.

McKinney, J. D., McClure, S., & Feagans, L. (1982). Classroom behavior of learning disabled children. *Learning Disability Quarterly, 5,* 45–52.

Newtson, D. (1973). Attribution and the unit of perception of ongoing behavior. *Journal of Personality and Social Psychology, 28,* 28–38.

Newtson, D. (1980). An interactionist perspective on social knowing. *Personality and Social Psychology Bulletin, 6,* 520–531.

Noel, M. N. (1980). Referential communication abilities of learning disabled children. *Learning Disability Quarterly, 3,* 70–75.

Owen, R. W., Adams, P. A., Forrest, T., Stolz, L. M., & Fisher, S. (1971). Learning disorders in children: Sibling studies. *Monographs of the Society for Research in Child Development, 36* (4, Serial No. 144).

Pearl, R. (1982). Learning disabled children's attributions for success and failure: A replication with a labeled learning disabled sample. *Learning Disability Quarterly, 5,* 183–186.

Pearl, R., Bryan, T. H., & Donahue, M. (1980). Learning disabled children's attributions for success and failure. *Learning Disability Quarterly, 3,* 3–9.

Pearl, R., Bryan, T., & Donahue, M. (1983). Social behaviors of learning disabled children: A review. *Topics in Learning and Learning Disabilities, 3,* 1–14.

Pearl, R., & Cosden, M. (1982). Sizing up a situation: Learning disabled children's understanding of social interactions. *Learning Disability Quarterly, 5,* 371–373.

Pearl, R., Donahue, M., & Bryan, T. (1981). Children's responses to nonexplicit requests for clarification. *Perceptual and Motor Skills, 53,* 919–925.

Pearl, R., Donahue, M., & Bryan, T. (in press). The development of tact: Children's strategies for delivering bad news. *Journal of Applied Developmental Psychology.*

Piaget, J. (1956). *The child's conception of space.* New York: Norton.

Prillaman, D. (1981). Acceptance of learning disabled students in the mainstream environment: A failure to replicate. *Journal of Learning Disabilities, 14,* 344–346.

Puckett, D. (1980). *An investigation of nonverbal sensitivity of academically talented, average, and learning disabled male students.* Unpublished doctoral dissertation, Memphis State University, Memphis, TN.

Rosenthal, R., Hall, J. A. DiMatteo, M. R., Rogers, P. L., & Archer, D. (1979). *Sensitivity to nonverbal communication: The PONS Test.* Baltimore: John Hopkins University Press.

Saarni, C. (1979). Children's understanding of display rules for expressive behavior. *Developmental Psychology, 15,* 424–429.

Schank, R. C., & Abelson, R. (1977). *Scripts, plans, goals, and understanding,* Hillsdale, NJ: Lawrence Erlbaum Associates.

Schumaker, J. B., Wildgen, J. S., & Sherman, J. A. (1982). Social interaction of learning disabled junior high students in their regular classrooms: An observational analysis. *Journal of Learning Disabilities, 15,* 355–358.

Scranton, T., & Ryckman, D. (1979). Sociometric status of learning disabled children in an integrative program. *Journal of Learning Disabilities, 12,* 402–407.

Shantz, C. U. (1983). Social cognition. In J. H. Flavell & E. M. Markman (Eds.), *Cognitive development: Vol. 3. Handbook of child psychology.* New York: Wiley.

Sheare, J. B. (1978). The impact of resource programs upon the self-concept and peer acceptance of learning disabled children. *Psychology in the Schools, 15,* 406–412.

Siperstein, G. N., Bopp, M. J., & Bak, J. J. (1978). Social status of learning disabled children. *Journal of Learning Disabilities, 11,* 98–102.

Siperstein, G. N., & Goding, M. J. (1983). Social integration of learning disabled children in regular classrooms. In I. Bialer & K. Gadow (Eds.), *Advances in learning and behavioral disabilities* (Vol. 2, pp. 227–263). Greenwich, CT: J.A.I. Press.

Sobol, M. P., Earn, B. M., Bennett, D., & Humphries, T. (1983). A categorical analysis of the social attributions of learning disabled children. *Journal of Abnormal Child Psychology, 11,* 217–228.

Spekman, N. (1981). A study of the dyadic verbal communication abilities of learning disabled and normally achieving fourth and fifth grade boys. *Learning Disability Quarterly, 4,* 139–151.

Stone, W. L., & LaGreca, A. M. (in press). Comprehension of nonverbal communication: A reexamination of the social competencies of learning disabled children. *Journal of Abnormal Child Psychology.*

Thomas, C. H. (1979). *An investigation of the sensitivity to nonverbal communication of learning disabled and normal children.* Unpublished dictoral dissertation, University of Virginia, Charlottesville, VA.

Torgesen, J. (1980). Conceptual and educational implications of the use of efficient task strategies by learning disabled children. *Journal of Learning Disabilities, 13,* 364–371.

Touliatos, J., & Lindholm, B. W. (1980). Dimensions of problem behavior in learning disabled and normal children. *Perceptual and Motor Skills, 50,* 145–146.

U.S. Office of Education. (1977). Assistance to states for education of handicapped children. Procedures for evaluating specific learning disabilities. *Federal Register, 42,* 65082–65085.

Urbain, E. S., & Kendall, P. C. (1980). Review of social-cognitive problem-solving interventions with children. *Psychological Bulletin, 88,* 109–143.

Weiner, B. (1972). Attribution theory, achievement motivation, and the educational process. *Review of Educational Research, 42,* 203–215.

Wiig, E. H., & Harris, S. P. (1974). Perception and interpretation of nonverbally expressed emotions by adolescents with learning disabilities. *Perceptual and Motor Skills, 38,* 239–245.

Wilson, T. D., & Capitman, J. A. (1982). Effects of script availability on social behavior. *Personality and Social Psychology Bulletin, 8,* 11–19.

Wong, B. Y., & Wong, R. (1980). Role-taking skills in normal achieving and learning disabled children. *Learning Disability Quarterly, 3,* 11–18.

Wood, M. E. (1978). Children's developing understanding of other people's motives for behavior. *Developmental Psychology, 14,* 561–562.

Commentary: Socioemotional Factors in Learning Disabilities

Elaine Walker
Cornell University

This section on socioemotional factors addresses one of the most important, yet complex, issues relevant to learning disabilities. As the chapter by Goldstein and Dundon points out, diagnosticians and educators have struggled with the distinction between learning and emotional disorders. Recent definitions of learning disability have attempted to resolve the issue by making reference to emotional disturbance either as an exclusion criterion or as a secondary concomitant. The implicit assumption is that this criterion will serve to increase homogeneity within the diagnostic category by excluding those individuals who are manifesting learning problems as a *consequence* of emotional disorder. These individuals, presumably, are not suffering from a learning disability in the "pure" sense.

Our knowledge regarding the role of socioemotional factors in learning disabilities is limited. Yet, it is clear that a substantial proportion of learning-disabled youngsters also suffer from diagnosable emotional disorders, and many others manifest behavior, both within and outside the classroom, that is classified as problematic. There is no doubt in the minds of most researchers, clinicians, and educators that disabilities in the domains of cognition and emotion are correlated. But there is considerable controversy regarding the predominant causal direction in the relationship.

The primary reason that the issue of emotional problems in learning-disabled children is such a complex one is that we have so little understanding of the relation between emotion and cognition. Although the notion that functioning within the domain of emotion can influence processes in the cognitive domain, and vice versa, seems intuitively reasonable, we know very little about the nature of these interactional influences. Both the chapters by Pearl and by Goldstein and Dundon discuss the question in a very direct manner. There are at least three possible models. The first approach assumes that emotional disturbances cause learning problems. Thus, disturbances in emotional state may produce specific impairments in learning in a child with average or above-average intelligence. Second, it is possible that learning disabilities cause emotional problems. The frustrating academic experiences associated with having a learning disability may produce symptoms of emotional maladaptation. Alternatively, as Pearl suggests, learning problems may extend to the social domain; learning-disabled children may be impaired in the capacity to process the sequential social information embedded in interpersonal interactions. This would be expected to retard social-cognitive development and, consequently, increase the risk for emotional disorder. Finally, the correlation between disorders of emotion and learning may be due to a third, mediating factor. For example, environmental stressors may produce disturbances in both emotional and cognitive development.

The chapter by Goldstein and Dundon illustrates the first approach; namely, the assumption that emotional factors influence learning ability. The authors first introduce the notion of controlled versus automatic information processing. There is strong evidence supporting the existence of these two processing capacities in normals, and the controlled/automatic distinction offers a new perspective on atypical cognition. As Goldstein and Dundon point out, there is substantial support for the notion that controlled, but not automatic, processes are impaired in at least some learning-disabled children. These authors suggest several possible determinants of controlled processing deficits in learning disability; an inability to use relevant cognitive strategies (e.g., rehearsal, clustering, etc.), lack of awareness of the need for strategies, structurally reduced capacity, and functionally reduced capacity. It is the latter determinant, namely, functionally reduced capacity, that is of greatest interest to these researchers. They speculate on ways that affective factors, particularly depression, might act to reduce available cognitive capacity. They present data from their own research on depression in learning-disabled youngsters to support their position. These data indicate that, as a group, learning disabled-children are more depressed than nondisabled children. Moreover, the presence of depression in learning-disabled children appears to be associated with superior academic performance and greater improvement in performance over time. They attribute this improvement to therapeutic interventions that reduce depression.

Of course, there are alternative interpretations for Goldstein and Dundon's data. For example, the presence of depression in learning-disabled youngsters may reflect a greater discomfort with poor academic performance, and this discomfort may serve to as a source of motivation. However, the fact remains that Goldstein and Dundon clearly demonstrate an association between self-reported depression and the nature of cognitive functioning.

The chapter by Pearl emphasizes the second approach to the relation between socioemotional factors and learning disabilities. She reviews the rapidly accumulating body of literature on social cognitive functions in learning-disabled children and concludes that there is evidence that at least some of these children manifest social-cognitive deficits. The literature suggests that these deficits are most pronounced in the area of nonverbal social cue processing or interpretation. Deficits seem to be less apparent when cues are presented in multiple modalities.

Research by Spivack, Platt, and Schure (1976) and by others has demonstrated that social cognitive abilities are correlated with adjustment in nonlearning-disabled youngsters. It is easy to imagine how the specific social-cognitive deficits discussed by Pearl could be translated into problems in socioemotional adjustment for learning-disabled children. For example, the failure to perceive or accurately label nonverbal cues of emotion may reduce the child's capacity to predict the likely outcome in sequences of interpersonal behavior. This, in turn, might result in more frustrating social experiences and more inappropriate social behavior in learning-disabled children.

The children discussed by Pearl would meet standard criteria for learning disability because any socioemotional problems they might manifest would be viewed as secondary to their learning problems. In contrast, the subgroup of children upon which Goldstein and Dundon focus their attention would not technically meet the standard criteria; their learning problems are viewed as secondary to their emotional maladjustment. Yet, it is likely that the groups described by both authors are represented in the general population of children classified as learning disabled. Moreover, the processes they describe may be simultaneously operative in the same children. Thus, some children may suffer from a learning deficit that impairs their ability to process information of both an academic and social nature. The stressors associated with this impairment may produce a depressed mood state that further interferes with learning. Alternatively, a child with no initial learning deficits may develop an emotional disorder that interferes with learning. Over time, there may be a cumulative detrimental effect on basic learning skills that, in turn, contributes to further depression. Of course, in addition to these two subtypes, it is apparent that there are children who meet the criteria for learning disability yet show no signs of emotional maladjustment. It would seem likely that this latter group is comprised of children who either have competencies in other areas that serve as a source of self-esteem or are receiving exceptional social support from their environment.

The chapter by Kasik, Sabatino, and Spoentgen emphasizes the potential role of the environment in mitigating or exacerbating the deficits of learning-disabled youngsters. On the social level, the feedback provided by parents and teachers is an important determinant of the child's conceptualization of his/her learning disability. If the adults in the child's environment communicate negative expectations, problematic behaviors may increase. Similarly, peers may be more intolerant of behavioral transgressions in children who are experiencing academic difficulties, and this may serve to deflate the self-esteem of learning-disabled youngsters. On the level of the physical learning environment, special educational interventions aimed at remediating the child's deficits may inadvertently increase stigmatization. This, in turn, may result in increased self-deprecation and concomitant behavior problems. Thus, the environmental factors discussed by Kasik, Sabatino, and Spoentgen are potentially important determinants of the child's emotional state.

Our general lack of knowledge regarding the relation between emotion and cognition is at least partially due to the tendency to conceptualize them as orthogonal domains of functioning. Thus separate theories of affective and cognitive processes emerged, and, until recently, there has been little overlap between the groups of researchers pursuing these two topics. We now see increasing numbers of investigators attempting to bridge the theoretical gap between emotion and cognition (e.g., Hamilton, 1983; Speilberger & Sarason, 1977).

The chapters in this section represent the efforts of scholars in the field of learning disabilities to conceptualize the relation between emotional factors and cognitive functions. The roots of this line of investigation can be traced to early research on arousal and performance (see Eysenck, 1976, for a review of this literature). Repeated demonstrations that "state" and "trait" arousal levels have implications for cognitive functions led to the formulation of the inverted "U" model of the relation between arousal and performance. Unfortunately, the ambiguity surrounding the concept of arousal may have been responsible for the decline in this area of research in the 1970s.

The recent revival of research on emotion and cognition coincides with an increased precision in the definition of concepts and a greater complexity of models of emotion and cognition (e.g., Buck, 1984; Heilman & Satz, 1983). The unitary concept of arousal level has given way to more specific and discrete dimensions of emotion. At the same time, contemporary models of human information processing distinguish among various stages and types of information processing. Thus, the stage has been set for a new era of investigation into the links between emotional and cognitive functions. This new research may also elucidate connections among behavioral, emotional, and cognitive factors.

A recent article by Zentall and Zentall (1983) illustrates this new line of theorizing and investigation. These authors present a model of autism and hyperactivity, which views the behavioral and cognitive characteristics of these disorders as manifestations of deviant states of autonomic arousal. They argue that the extreme behaviors of children with these two disorders are compensatory and serve the function of either attenuating or enhancing sensory input. Similarly, the cognitive deficits of these children are shown to be specific to certain contexts and stimulus characteristics, and to be amenable to different interventions.

In summary, our understanding of learning disabilities is likely to be enhanced by a greater appreciation of the complex interplay between emotional state and cognitive function. Knowledge of the links between affect and cognition may provide a framework for future efforts at subtyping learning disabilities on the basis of etiology. Thus, this line of research may have applied as well as theoretical implications.

REFERENCES

Buck, R. (1984). *The communication of emotion*. London: Guilford Press.

Eysenck, M. (1976). Arousal, learning and memory. *Psychological Bulletin, 83*, 75–90.

Hamilton, V. (1983). *The cognitive structures and processes of human motivation and personality*. New York: Wiley.

Heilman, K., & Satz, P. (1983). *Neuropsychology of emotion*. London: Guilford Press.

Speilberger, C., & Sarason, I. (1977). *Stress and anxiety*. New York: Halsted.

Spivack, G., Platt, J., & Schure, M. (1976). *The problem solving approach to adjustment*. San Francisco: Jossey–Bass.

Zentall, S., & Zentall, T. (1983). Optimal stimulation: A model of disordered activity and performance in normal and deviant children. *Psychological Bulletin. 94*, 446–471.

IV NEUROPSYCHOLOGICAL ASPECTS OF LEARNING DISABILITIES

11

Natural Histories in Learning Disabilities: Neuropsychological Difference/Environmental Demand

Jane M. Holmes
Children's Hospital, Boston

The concept of the natural history of a disorder implies some knowledge of the expected course of that disorder. Such knowledge in turn implies prediction of outcome. The ability to predict at least some aspects of the course of a disorder is a major part of a physician's role in managing a case. This has not, perhaps, been so clearly recognized by psychologists who are trained either to measure performance at specific points in time or to provide psychotherapeutic services that typically proceed on a highly individualized basis.

The neuropsychologist's role in the management of the child with learning problems (and here I emphasize *neuro*psychologist as opposed to the more traditional psychometrically trained psychological assessor who is likely to emphasize information-processing deficits and/or specific academic problem areas) is very much akin to that of the physician. However, in the case of learning disabilities, I argue that the natural history is not determined only (or largely) by parameters internal to the patient, but—importantly—derives from the interaction between a child's given style of thinking and regular patterns of changing demand in the educational process and in the environment generally. Why is such a concept important? Most significantly, it allows a clinician to begin to predict potential problem areas for a specific child, problem areas that can then hopefully be circumvented or at least minimized to avoid the painful and repeated failures that damage self-esteem, erode self-confidence, and reduce a child's willingness to get involved in the educational process at all.

THE CONCEPT OF LEARNING DISABILITY

Before discussing further this interaction between the individual child and the demands placed upon him by a changing environment, let us examine briefly the construct of *learning disability* with which we are working. I take the position that *learning disability* implies the coexistence in one individual of more or less age-appropriate performance in some skills and noticeably lower performance in others. Intraindividual differences can thus be considered the hallmark of learning disabilities.[1]

Let me give an example of the type of "imbalance" in available skills that can be understood as potentially creating a risk factor for learning problems. Take, for example, the child who is eventually diagnosed as having "covert" or "subtle" language disability as the cognitive substrate for academic difficulties. This is the type of child who is typically not recognized by family or even teachers as having specific language problems: In general conversational settings he or she manages to interact linguistically more or less effectively with both peers and adults. Examined in the context of a multidisciplinary evaluation (as is widely practiced in many learning-disabilities clinics today), the child demonstrates age-appropriate general knowledge, motor skills, and ability to deal with visuo-constructional materials. In contrast, he or she scores at a level below age-expectancy on specific language tasks. If the child is, for example, 10 years old and has "8-year-old" skills in specific language domains, he or she is hardly likely to be seen as someone unable to use language. What the evaluation that identifies this discrepancy does, however, is to identify a "vulnerable spot" in the child, a vulnerable spot that is like a weak link in a chain: Under the impact of increasing stress, this is the point at which the child can be expected to "break."

The concept of intraindividual differences in available skills is widely recognized in the learning-disabilities literature. It underlies, for example, the "subtyping" issue in dyslexia (see Boder, 1973; Denckla, 1977; Mattis, French & Rapin, 1975) and in learning disabilities in general (see Rourke & Strang, 1983). Depending on one's discipline (education, neurology, psychology), it is approached in terms of the deficit topic (reading disabled, math disabled, etc.), in terms of

---

[1]I am specifically excluding "mental retardation" from the category of *learning disability* although technically there is no reason why a low-IQ child could not demonstrate intraindividual differences in his skills—and, indeed, many do. However, it can be argued that even where, for example, an "extra" language disability can be identified for such a child, the overall low functioning nonetheless usually needs to be the basic premise for educational intervention—because this is the primary substrate for the child's dealings with the world. The (understandable, if ill-advised) wish of many parents with a low-functioning youngster to have him or her characterized as "learning disabled" is one of serious concern for practicing clinicians: requiring a low-functioning child to learn in the same format as a youngster with more normally-distributed abilities, but with a specific deficit therein, is very likely to affect adversely the low-functioning child's ability to reach his own potential.

concepts derived from the study of the aphasias and related disorders (dyslexic, dyscalculic, dysnomic, etc.), and/or in terms of the presumed underlying information-processing deficit (auditory–perceptual, visuospatial, etc.)

From the viewpoint of neuropsychology, the "intraindividual difference" concept reflects the differential contributions of different brain systems to overall human behavior as derived from the study of brain–behavior relationships in adult humans and other animals (see Hecaen & Albert, 1978).

THE NEUROPSYCHOLOGICAL MODEL

At the present time neuropsychological models for use with children must be viewed with caution (Fletcher & Taylor, 1984). The relationships between brain and behavior outlined for the adult can be applied to the behavior of the child only with due reference to the developmental stage (both neurological and cognitive/social) of the child—and with full recognition that one is proceeding on a more or less "circumstantial evidence" basis. With these caveats, the general model within which I am working can be described as a "3-axis model." The critical axes are: (a) the *left/right* axis—that is, the complementary but different information-processing capacities of the two cerebral hemispheres; (b) the *posterior/anterior* axis—that is, the sensory versus motor distinction at the neurological level and the higher order associative, encoding, storage (or general "input") modalities versus the organization, control, and modulation capacities of the "output" system as described at the neuropsychological level; (c) the *up/down* axis—that is, the organizational capacities of frontal brain systems and their complex and far-reaching interactions with the subcortical systems that are involved in the maintenance and regulation of attention and the actual executive functions involved in specific behaviors (Luria, 1973). The impact of developmental progress is seen not only at the neurological level ("basic" motor and sensory systems—hemispheric association areas—frontal/prefrontal systems; Van Der Vlugt, 1979), but also what is thought to be differential neuropsychological response to increasingly available neural mechanisms (see Rourke, Bakker, Fisk, & Strang, 1983, chap. 3). The effects of developmental change in the clinical context must also be assessed in light of potential damage to the system (Rudel, 1979; Van Der Vlugt, 1979).[2]

Working in a clinical context with children this "3-axis-plus-developmental-progression" model has proved very valuable (see Denckla, 1979a) and appears

---

[2]Note that this "3-axis" model is a necessarily simple representation of our knowledge of brain-behavior relationships at the present time. The "poles" of the axes must not be understood as representing single and discrete functional units but should be viewed as functional *systems* interacting in a highly complex and diversified fashion not only with respect to each other within the brain, but also being subtly modulated by the environment within which the behaviors they mediate take place.

to work—with appropriate modifications—for different levels of brain–behavior relationships. It appears that one's neuropsychological status or "thinking style" can be a product of *brain difference*—individual variation in "talents" versus "untalents,"[3] of *brain dysfunction*—a "software" or "wiring" (functional) deficit, or of *brain damage*—a "hardware" (or structural) deficit; although there are some clear differences between these in terms of performance variables, a common underlying model of integrative brain functioning does appear to work for these different levels of brain "difference."[4]

THE CLINICAL PROBLEM

Let us take now a specific example of the type of child we may have to deal with. We have a small person (usually a young man) in the third grade—only reading at the primer/first-grade level. Teaching staff wonder if he is "dyslexic"— and he may well get such a diagnostic label applied to him. But he is a lucky young man: He has friends; he is a good sportsman; his mother and father are comfortable together; he does not have a younger sibling coming up quickly behind him; he has a good classroom teacher; and extra remedial services can be offered by his school in a small-group setting. So he plugs away. At the end of the fifth grade, he can just about read orally at the fifth-grade level. And people say he is "cured." But what is he cured of? His "dyslexia." Not exactly clear. The best one can say, perhaps, is that he has been cured of his "inability-to-read-at-grade-level" . . . for now. He has not, presumably, been cured of what it was that contributed to the reading problem in the first place—his brain, or his thinking/learning style.

Now what happens? Our young man's learning style (allowing for maturational change) remains the same. But the world does not! He now has to make the transition to junior high school. The critical fourth-grade shift from learning-to-read to reading-to-learn starts to take effect: It is now not enough for him to be able to decode words, his laboriously acquired decoding skills must be sufficiently automatized to permit fluent and efficient access to new information from the material that is read. So what happens? All too frequently nobody recognizes the impact of this striking increase in demand—and our young man fails again. His underlying vulnerability vis-à-vis written language skills is not such as can

---

[3]Denckla M. B. (1978): Personal communication.

[4]In this regard it has been of some interest to me in recent years to follow a number of children with documented evidence of early and specific brain damage who, later in their educational career, are being provided with classic learning disabilities remedial support and thus treated as a "learning-disabled child" without the present teaching staff necessarily being aware that the child can accurately be described as "brain-damaged." This has been praticularly noteworthy when the neuropsychological reevaluation has been requested because someone thinks that the child's learning problem can be entirely explained on emotional grounds!

take on the increased demand in this area without continuing academic support. Had the stress been recognized, the support could have been provided. Once a child is flagged, that little red flag dictates careful monitoring of his performance *throughout his school career*. The "risk factor" that he carries might not be manifest again (if he is lucky) but the risk is always there.[5]

The role of the neuropsychologist working with youngsters with learning disabilities can essentially be characterized as responding to two aspects of the foregoing anecdote: (1) to determine the individual youngster's pattern of thinking skills, and (2) to help parents and educators recognize which stress points in one's educational (and social) career are most likely to interact adversely with a given child's thinking style. The clinician's role not only as a diagnostician, but also as a "case manager," now reveals another necessary component to our model. The "learner-oriented" approach that is at the heart of neuropsychological diagnostic method is seen in light of *what is to be learned*. Such a (now interactive) model can not only help elucidate the critical "stress points" in a child's developmental career, but—for a neuropsychologist who is as much interested in how the brain works as how learning disabilities can be managed—has the added advantage of being entirely consistent with recent neuropsychological research in highlighting the crucial interaction (in both directions!) of a brain and its environment (see Allen, 1983).

NEUROPSYCHOLOGICAL PROFILES

Within the general framework of our "3-axis" model then, we identify three groups of individuals at risk for specific learning problems. Neuropsychologically, these groups can be described as *left hemisphere impaired, right hemisphere impaired,* and *frontal system impaired.*

Before we go any further, a word of caution about these labels. It is very important to recognize that, when using a label like *left hemisphere impaired,* one is *not* thereby implying (necessarily) that the individual in question has a recognizable "hole in the head" in the left hemisphere. Nor is one implying in any way that *all* (presumed) left-hemisphere-mediated skills are unavailable, nor that those left-hemisphere-mediated skills that do appear to be affected are *totally* disrupted or lacking. *Left hemisphere impairment* is used here as a shorthand to characterize the fact that, for this particular individual, some of the skills that are presumed to depend for their mediation on the integrity of left hemisphere

---

[5]The importance of this point cannot be easily overestimated. Given the present state of our knowledge, it is usually unavoidable that a child fail once in order to be recognized as having difficulties and thus obtain appropriate educational services. For a child to fail twice in order to continue to get those services is little short of criminal—and is a shocking indictment of our educational system as a whole.

brain systems are *relatively less efficient* than other skills presumed to depend on the integrity of other brain systems. Similarly, *right hemisphere impairment* is used to describe the difficulties experienced by a child who has *relatively less efficient* skills thought to depend on the integrity of right hemisphere brain systems—and *frontal system impairment* denotes *relatively less efficient* (or mature) executive and organizational skills in a child whose knowledge and thinking is otherwise appropriate for age, experience, and so forth.

Recognizing the use of such shorthand labels then, let us examine some of the implications of such patterns of *relative imbalance* of skills as they are manifest by one type of child as opposed to another. Note that we are—given that our overall professional discipline is psychology—interested not simply in the academic manifestations of the child's "thinking pattern," but we are equally interested in the child's adjustment in other (social) aspects of his life. For our initial description of the impact of the child's neuropsychological profile in his school and social life, we make a distinction between earlier and later school experience where "early" is intended to refer roughly to the elementary school years and the latency period in a child's development and "late" is intended to grossly characterize the later junior high and high school experience.

Examination of Table 11.1 reveals that the child with insecure oral language-processing skills is at significant risk for efficient acquisition of those basic written language skills that depend heavily on oral language facility and the ability (related to aspects of language processing) to maintain ordered elements in a series, which appears to be crucial for the development of arithmetic facts. Note that the present formulation does not specify exactly where the deficit may occur. Some children have tremendous difficulty in appreciating the concept of

TABLE 11.1
The Left Hemisphere-Impaired Child

Neuropsychological Construct *Psychological Construct*	*left hemisphere impaired* *language (and language-related) processing* *difficulty*	
	Early	Late
Academic	basic skills ↓ • reading • writing • spelling • math facts	written assignments ↓ • reading • writing
Social	skills usually adequate (but note degree of language difficulty)	at risk for • withdrawal • acting out • peer group language interaction

the *phoneme* (a "cortical abstraction," not a learned construct), which will immediately render them at risk for major problems with sound–symbol relationships
as manifest in the orthography. A child may also have problems in maintaining
the serial order of elements (at the level of sounds, words, or ideas)—likely to
get him into great difficulty with various aspects of written language skills. Yet
again, difficulty may not appear at the basic sound–symbol or ordering level of
language elements but may be seen a little later when the child has trouble in
understanding and remembering what is read. Note that the child has difficulty
with the aforementioned skills, not only because this is his "vulnerable area,"
but also because these skills are exactly what are demanded by the education
system in the early grades. If, of course, the child had not had to go to school
and learn to read he would not have demonstrated a reading problem!

What is demanded by the educational process in the higher grades is the
completion of written language assignments. These include both reading increasingly complex text to derive information therefrom, and being able to produce
written synopses or explications of that text to demonstrate to a teacher that the
material has been appropriately understood. The child whose underlying language-
processing systems are somewhat (or significantly) insecure typically finds himself overwhelmed by the sheer amount of the language processing load at this
point in time (and specific recommendations thus involve systematic breaking
down of the "load").

In the social domain, the child with subtle language-processing problems is
usually able to function adequately (although, obviously, children with significant
language-processing problems can have major socioemotional difficulties as a
consequence thereof). It is, however, not sufficient to accept this comment at
face value. Good clinical method in neuropsychology (as, presumably, elsewhere) requires that one ask oneself how it is that a youngster with discontinuities
in language processing that get him into significant trouble in formal academic
skills, finds himself able to cope more effectively in the open-ended give-and-
take of spontaneous conversation with peers. The answer highlights the variety
of compensatory supports for language-processing discontinuities in such a context. They include the availability of gesture, of intonation, of quick repetition
and paraphrase where necessary, of context-dependent references, and so forth.
They also include, however, the fact that effective social interaction in the small
boys who make up the bulk of children referred for learning problems does not
depend heavily on elaborate linguistic interaction: Small boys play sports together,
climb trees, ride bicycles, and so forth—all physical activities that can be undertaken very comfortably with a minimum of complex language.

As youngsters get older, however, other factors begin to come into play. The
child with the subtle discontinuities in language often has difficulty with the very
frequent "in-group" languages that are developed within the adolescent population as part of their normal developmental moves for autonomy and indivi-
dualization from the adult group. I have recently seen in my clinical practice a

variety of young adolescents who "don't quite catch" individual shifts in language use developed by a particular group—with the result that they begin to feel that other youngsters are laughing at them and may actively withdraw from the group to avoid this feeling of rejection. Other youngsters with language-processing difficulties have demonstrated other behaviors: significant withdrawal from both social and family life in a youngster whose abnormal electroencephalographic status (left hemisphere) was associated with a need for four or five repetitions of information before he understood exactly what was required; he explained to the examiner that it was easier to avoid people altogether than to have them get increasingly irritated at his need for multiple repetitions in conversation! Another young man whose problem was one of expressing efficiently and with sufficient force exactly what he wanted to say seemed to feel that if he could not express his angers, frustrations, and general opinions at the world in a verbal fashion, he would demonstrate all of these feelings in a physical fashion by lashing out in all directions whenever provoked.

These last-mentioned behaviors seem reasonably interpreted as direct reactions to the nature of the language-processing problem. Children with these difficulties do also, however, have their problems compounded as a function of the differing expectations of the environment and changes in their status in other aspects of life. A common example is the young man with a history of oral and written language problems in the early grades who has been able to maintain his self-esteem and confidence because of good social and sports abilities. At the point, however, when academic skills are beginning to be doubly stressed by the amount of written language he is required to handle at the higher grades, the support for his emotional well-being that sports abilities had provided in the past is being eroded: It is now no longer sufficient to kick the ball accurately and far, he is expected to handle strategy and tactics, both of which are typically given in verbal form—which may be degraded by the fact that it is yelled across a football field or an already echoing hockey rink. A child who has difficulty processing language under normal conversational conditions is not likely to be helped by any further degradation in the language medium. This young man's life may become very difficult: At the same time as the increasing demand on written language skills is overstressing his academic abilities, the previous self-esteem and confidence derived from sports is being threatened—and all the (potentially stressful) developmental changes of adolescence must begin. The impact of the underlying "neuropsychology" extends far beyond his academic problems alone.

Let us now look at the second group of youngsters within this same format: The group here is that which, in neuropsychological terms, is characterized as being relatively less efficient in skills thought to depend on the integrity of right hemisphere brain systems (see Table 11.2).

The psychological constructs hypothesized to underlie the problem experienced by the child with relative right hemisphere impairment warrant some discussion. Again, it is important to recognize that the notion *right hemisphere*

TABLE 11.2
The Right Hemisphere-Impaired Child

| Neuropsychological Construct | | right hemisphere impaired |
Psychological Construct		organization and social processing difficulty
	Early	Late
Academic	good enough	written language assignments ↓ • abstracting information from written texts • producing coherent narrative
Social	socially inconsistent; unaware of socially relevant cues; can be dramatically anomalous in behavior ⎯⎯⎯⎯⎯⎯⎯⎯⎯⎯⎯⎯⎯⎯⎯→	

impairment does not imply absence of *all* the skills thought to depend on the integrity of the right hemisphere systems. In our clinics we clearly see children who have organizational problems without social perceptual difficulties—although I remember no case of the converse. Difficulties in organization appear to reflect the right hemisphere brain systems' role in the appreciation of the overall configurations of elements and a sense of the "whole."[6] The "social perceptual" difficulty described as a component of the *right hemisphere-impaired* profile appears also to be related to the ability to appreciate the relationships between elements—here the emotionally relevant cues related to the configuration of an intonation pattern, the configuration of a facial expression, the configuration of a bodily stance, and so forth. The right hemisphere's role in emotional responding, although not yet fully understood, has now been well documented for both adults with acquired brain lesions (DeKosky, Heilman, Bowers, & Valenstein, 1980; Gainotti, 1972; Ross & Mesulam, 1979) and in adults with learning disabilities (Weintraub & Mesulam, 1983).

Within our model as represented here, the early *academic* demand for the development of basic written language skills does not typically stress the *right hemisphere-impaired* child. These youngsters are much more likely to show up in specialist clinics around the junior high school level when they are required to get information from complex text and produce written assignments. Unlike the subtly language-impaired child, their difficulty is not simply one of language

---

[6]Note that this is a somewhat different use of *organization* than that typically associated with frontal brain system capacity; "organization" in this latter case presumably involves not only the ability to see the big picture but also to "put out" behaviors, integrating both awareness of the whole (right hemisphere mediated) and of the individual elements of behavior in series (left hemisphere mediated). In our clinic, "organization and output" is used to (grossly) characterize frontal system functioning.

overload but rather reflects a lack of appreciation for the main theme or guiding principle of a text. They have great difficulties with coherent note taking or outlining of assignments and offer rambling and repetitive written work. (A child who demonstrated an extreme example of this wrote a "paragraph" for the examiner that was the same, linguistically accurate, sentence repeated six times!) This is the youngster who may show up very nicely on a standardized reading instrument such as the *Gilmore Oral Reading* test (Gilmore & Gilmore, 1968)— for example, up to about the fourth-grade level both *Accuracy* and *Comprehension* scores progress in tandem; at the point, however, where comprehension skills begin to be assessed on the basis of inferential reasoning, rather than on simple recall of facts, this youngster's *Comprehension* scores may fall whereas his *Accuracy* scores continue to make more or less appropriate progress.

Socially, these youngsters run the gamut from no specific difficulty through mild but not particularly noticeable problems to gross anomalies of behavior that suggest a lack of coherent contact with reality (which may have some of the characteristics of psychotic behavior but which, typically, does not quite "feel right" to clinicians experienced with psychotic children). These children are all too frequently seen, initially at least, by psychiatrically oriented clinicians and may undergo psychotherapy without particular progress before the possibility of an underlying cognitive deficit as a limiting factor to the psychotherapeutic input is recognized. Where such a cognitive deficit can be identified in such aberrant social behavior, it seems reasonable to characterize the existence of a *social learning disability*—which arguably entails a more overtly teaching approach to the whole problem of social behavior. Indeed, these children are exactly those who are most likely to benefit from "social tutoring" (Denckla, 1979b). This can often be undertaken by a sensitive teacher who sees aberrant interactions within the classroom context and can immediately react to them in a quiet but effective fashion. Group therapy contexts are also valuable—where actual behaviors can be discussed and dealt with "on the spot." Not surprisingly, given their problem in appreciating the cues on which normal social interaction is based, these youngsters often have difficulty in responding to the more traditional once-a-week "talking therapy" approach to psychological intervention (in spite of their highly verbal style) in that they may not be able to encode accurately enough for efficient storage and later recall those behaviors that a psychotherapist might find most useful to discuss with them.

The third group of youngsters is that subsumed under the neuropsychological label *frontal system impairment* (see Table 11.3). This group includes those individuals who have been characterized in previous years as belonging to the "hyperactive child syndrome" and who have recently been redescribed as having an "attentional deficit disorder" (Diagnostic and Statistical Manual of Mental Disorders, 1980)—the relabeling de-emphasizes the overactivity of the body in favor of what might be called "overactivity of the mind." As a group these youngsters appear to have less-than-adequate control of their output systems

TABLE 11.3
The Frontal System-Impaired Child

Neuropsychological Construct	*frontal system impaired*	
Psychological Construct	*poor modulation of behavior*	
	Early	Late
Academic	learning to learn ↓	disorganization; difficulty with
	attention ↓	independent work
Social	disinhibited; poorly modulated ————————————→	
		(gets less acceptable with increasing age)

generally—where "output systems" is understood to encompass the whole range of organizational, executive and regulatory functions that are thought to depend on the integrity of the frontal brain mechanisms and their extensive connections.

The primary difficulty here appears to be difficulty in appropriate modulation of behavior (for age). This can range from grossly hyperactive behavior to relatively subtle discontinuities of focusing and attending in children of clearly superior ability. These are the children who may well be brought to medical attention prior to the onset of the school experience because of difficulties with behavioral control. These youngsters are, arguably, not really ready for the school experience at the age at which they are expected to attend within our system of education. Especially where there is a "late birthday," they are children who would benefit from starting as late as possible and are often children who do better when given more early experience in the so-called transitional grade classrooms. They may have specific difficulties in certain academic tasks but need not. They do, however, have difficulty in dealing with the whole concept of learning to learn in the standard classroom format. Ideally, they need extra structuring and support and frequently do better in the smallest classroom with the best teacher/student ratio that can be offered. They typically have a history of "good years" and "bad years" that closer questioning reveals to be related to the nature of the individual teacher's style at any given point: Such children respond best to a firm, "cheerleading" approach in an individual who is highly organized but flexible (Denckla & Heilman, 1979). (The flexibility appears to be as important as the structuring: My clinical experience has demonstrated rather clearly that the highly formalized but somewhat rigid structure that is characteristic of parochial schools works no better for these youngsters than a too informal, "open classroom" type of setting.) As they proceed through the grades these youngsters continue to have difficulty with disorganization and get into trouble in any situation where independent work is called for. They often create major problems for themselves by being the type of individual who can work perfectly well as long as the teacher is at their shoulder but who cannot maintain focus or concentration where there is not this extra support available. (Teachers in particular often find this type of behavior very difficult to cope with and are hard put not to offer a diagnosis of "moral turpitude": He "won't do it"—rather than, perhaps, he "can't do it.")

Socially, these youngsters often have great difficulty with the peer group. Where the subtly language-impaired youngster has a tendency to distance himself from the group and the *right hemisphere-impaired* youngster tends to be left alone by the group, these youngsters can be actively rejected by their peer group. They typically do well with adults (note the importance of getting information about their *peer* relationships); they tend to choose as companions older children who can provide, like adults, a little extra support, organization, and structure or they will play with younger children whose abilities for self-control and appropriate modulation of behavior may be more on a par with theirs. They have a strong tendency to try and get attention even if it means doing so by negative means. In social interactions they frequently do not know when to stop, they are too loud, and can be simply too friendly when it is not called for. Not surprisingly, they are often very unhappy "loners" who really do not understand the nature of their exclusion from the group.

HISTORIES IN LEARNING DISABILITIES

Presenting patterns of difficulty manifest by learning-disabled children with different neuropsychological profiles in the aforementioned format highlights the way in which a learner-oriented, neuropsychological approach to learning problems brings together what have more traditionally been the domains of school or educational psychologists on the one hand (*academic* problems) and clinical psychologists on the other (*social* problems). The *early/late* distinction brings in developmental psychology also—albeit in an as yet rather limited fashion. Identification of the two points in time subsumed under *early* and *late*, however, has another important consequence: It permits one to begin to look at *histories*— and, eventually, to characterize the natural history of learning profiles of different types.

In examining the role of *histories* in the diagnosis and management of youngsters with learning problems, let us consider the nature of the clinical team that is involved in the diagnosis and management of such children. (I am talking here about the *professional* clinical team; it is, of course, important for a practicing clinician dealing with learning disabilities to recognize that the *total* treatment team for such a child must include, not only the psychologist, the teacher and/or the physician, but also the child himself and his parents or guardians and family.) At the point where specialist help is sought, two specific individuals, or groups thereof, are involved in the diagnosis of a child with learning problems. These are classroom teachers and clinic-based learning-disability specialists— either psychologists or physicians.

There is frequently a considerable degree of tension between educators and clinicians when dealing with individual children with learning issues. Teachers are wary of medical personnel who seem to have little appreciation of the day-to-day problems of classroom management and clinicians may have a tendency to feel that their consultative role allows them to make somewhat sweeping "final statements." For the child's overall well-being, however, this type of tension must be dissipated because the teacher and the diagnostic clinician are, in fact, in a complementary relationship with respect to their view of the child, and information from both sides of the equation will be crucial to the clinical outcome. The critical differences in the approaches of these two groups of people, however, need to be recognized so that their complementarity can be appreciated. One could characterize it thus: Teachers work with the *trees* of the problem, whereas the psychologist in his or her diagnostic role can be seen as dealing with the *forest*.

One can easily appreciate the "trees" of the problem. Teachers work on an hour-to-hour, day-to-day basis with individual children in situations which can be fraught with emotional struggle and great frustration. It can be very difficult indeed to stand back and get a view of the child's problem from a more objective standpoint. It is also difficult for any teacher (however well intentioned and however interested) to follow a child's progress from grade to grade. Even if progress can be appreciated from grade to grade within a school, the structure of a school system's real estate—which responds to the different competencies of children of different developmental stages—makes it all but impossible to follow a child's progress as he moves from building to building (or campus to campus).

For the clinician, however, the situation is very different. Like all clinicians, the psychologist dealing with the child with learning disabilities deals in *histories*. One sees Johnny at the age of 14 and takes a history. The history-taking elicits information about the child at different ages. A comparable history is taken from Fred at 7, and Michael at 9, and Peter at 12, and so forth. The neuropsychological assessment, of which the histories are a part, identifies groups of children with (grossly) similar learning styles (Denckla, 1979b; Rourke, 1982). Within these groups the history taking begins to demonstrate regular patterns of difficulty across the educational process. For the clinician, the *history* begins to operate not only backward, but also forward, in time: The general form of the educational system being the same for all, the 7-year-old with a given history and (after assessment) with a given neuropsychological profile is at risk for the same types of problems that are repeatedly described in the ("older") histories of youngsters seen at 14, 15, and older ages.

ENVIRONMENTAL "STRESS POINTS"

Let us now look at the educational system that is "the same for all"—in its more general aspects and examine the nature of the *demand* imposed by it at different ages, demand that causes some youngsters to fail. These demands are also a part of *what is to be learned* by our *learner* in the interactive model of brain–behavior relationships that we are advocating. They include now, however, not only specific academic subject matter (learning to read, to add and subtract, to do calculus, to compose poetry, to program a computer, etc.), but also "lessons" that seem more closely allied to our maturational level and its associated competency in behavioral modulation and control (which is typically thought of as more "social" than "academic"). Table 11.4 presents an initial characterization of the major stress points in a child's progress through school.

Examination of these stress points in light of the types of children characterized earlier allows one to predict which type of child might get into trouble at which point in time. A child with the attentional deficit disorder profile, for example, will be expected to have trouble at the kindergarten level; a subtly language-impaired youngster might have difficulty at either the first grade or the fourth-grade level, or both; the child with the right hemisphere-mediated organizational difficulty is likely to get into trouble at the fourth-grade and the junior high level—as well as, probably, at the high school level also.

The advantage of looking at the relationship between the child and the demand from this point of view is, I think, that the role of *prediction* is easier to see. The child who appears in one's office at the age of 6 with the organizational and output difficulties thought to reflect relatively less efficient frontal system functioning is likely to need careful monitoring throughout school not only because of his difficulty in conforming to the usual classroom demands and "learning to learn" efficiently, but also because, even if he manages to cope in the elementary school where there is a single classroom teacher in an organized environment, he is at significant risk for failing to cope again at the junior high level where not only is organization of (more demanding) academic subject matter required, but so is organizing oneself, that is, getting from classroom to classroom and teacher to teacher during the course of the day and getting one's homework done at night. This brings up the fact that operating across these stress points, as a child gets older, is a decreasing amount of adult support in response to the expected developmental increase in the ability to monitor and organize oneself.

TABLE 11.4
The Major Stress Points

Kindergarten	learning to *learn*
Grade 1	learning to *read*
Grade 4	learning to *read* → *reading to learn*
Junior High School	learning to *organize* your learning
High School	learning to read ⎫ learning to organize ⎬ *on your own* learning to learn ⎭
College	*doing it* on your own

Not all children seem able to take optimal advantage of this developmental change with its attendant reduction in support.

THE ROLE OF PREDICTION

Integrating the learner-oriented neuropsychological approach to learning problems with the developmental nature of the changing demand introduces a longer-term clinical view of the "problem" than typically taken by the learning-disabilities specialist whose focus is on the nature of the topic to be learned. Knowledge of the risk factors that can attend a given neuropsychological profile and of the demands imposed by the environment provides a framework within which to predict potential future problem areas for a given child. The clinical neuropsychologist's role is then naturally that of a "case manager"—again, more akin to the role of the physician than to the traditional role of the psychological assessor. The clinician can work with the child with learning problems and his or her family over the course of the school experience, anticipating the increasing demands of higher grades as they are likely to impinge on this child's progress, and—with careful discussion among parents, teacher, and the child her or himself— suggesting plans to increase or modify educational, parental, and/or therapeutic support as and when necessary to obviate or minimize the failure that is so destructive of overall well-being.

Thus far, we have viewed *demand* as referring to the educational context as a whole. However, the clinical model of "learner versus demand" also permits a much finer analysis of the nature of *demand* in a specific clinical interaction. This has, for me, been particularly important in the clinical management of the high school individual or the adult. For example, earlier in a child's career the nature of the demand is simply to make it into the junior high school—as expected for everyone. At the high school level, however, the nature of the demand is much more a function of the individual's vocational aspirations and/or the societal expectations to which he must respond. If one is dealing with youngsters of high overall ability who wish to (and should) go to college in spite of their learning disability, then good clinical management requires the clinician to think carefully about how to achieve that longer term goal. A youngster with learning disabilities who wishes to go to college and is capable of functioning at that level relatively comfortably (albeit with some extra help) may need to start thinking about the college application process up to 2 years before other youngsters in his grade are doing so. He may need the time to balance out required coursework so as to avoid having two very difficult (for him) courses running concurrently. He needs to know exactly what is required for college entrance in the college of his choice—to avoid "wasting energy" on coursework which is not relevant for his ultimate goals, energy he needs elsewhere. He may consider carefully the nature of the colleges to which he should apply and may even need to consider the advantages (or otherwise) of a postgraduate high school year. In conjunction with all these general environmental considerations, he may also need specific recommendations from the clinician in study techniques or other remedial supports that are specifically directed towards the nature of his thinking style.

It is at this point that the whole concept of *environmental demand* may need to be extended somewhat! *Demand* in the sense just discussed is not perhaps the best word—*goal* might be better—to characterize not only the demands imposed by the environment but also aspirations one has for oneself. Younger children have little option but to respond to the forces imposed from "outside" in the form of developmental change or school organization, and clinical management of a child with learning disabilities who is still in the lower grades must equally respond to these. Later, however, the role of the neuropsychologist in counselling the individual with a history of learning problems can proceed on a much more individualized basis: The neuropsychologist provides the diagnosis of the individual's thinking style, the individual provides the goals to be attained—and together clinician and patient work towards a practicable solution (with, always, the possibility that appropriate clinical management may require one to delineate the unrealistic nature of the goals—or the potentially overwhelming price to be paid to meet them).

FINALE

The neuropsychological emphasis on the learning individual and his brain—seen against the backdrop of developmental change—highlights the crucial interaction of individual and environment that is the basis of clinical observation and knowledge. Application of neuropsychological models to children with learning problems—incorporating knowledge of brain differentiation, developmental change and environmental demand—can provide a more integrated, longer term view of clinical management of learning-disabled children. The emphasis on the interaction between the learner and what is to be learned derived from this population must inform more and better developmental neuropsychological models; it offers a potentially powerful tool for better understanding (and management) of behavior not only in developmental neuropsychology, however, but also in psychological, neurological, and psychiatric domains generally.

ACKNOWLEDGMENT

I thank Antonette Johnson for speedy preparation of this manuscript.

REFERENCES

Allen, M. (1983). Models of hemispheric specialization. *Psychological Bulletin, 93,* 73–104.

American Psychiatric Association. (1980). *Diagnostic and statistical manual of mental disorders* (3rd ed.). Washington, DC: Author.

Boder, E. (1973). Developmental dyslexia: A diagnostic approach based on three atypical reading-spelling patterns. *Developmental Medicine & Child Neurology, 15,* 663–687.

DeKosky, S. T., Heilman, K. M., Bowers, D., & Valenstein, E. (1980). Recognition and discrimination of emotional faces and pictures. *Brain & Language, 9,* 206–214.

Denckla, M. B. (1977). Minimal brain dysfunction and dyslexia: Beyond diagnosis by exclusion. In M. E. Blaw, I. Rapin, & M. Kinsbourne (Eds.), *Topics in child neurology* (pp. 243–262). New York: Spectrum.

Denckla, M. B. (1979a). Minimal brain dysfunction. In J. S. Chall & A. F. Mirsky (Eds.), *Education and the brain* (pp. 223–268). Chicago: University of Chicago Press.

Denckla, M. B. (1979b). Childhood learning disabilities. In K. M. Heilman & E. Valenstein (Eds.), *Clinical neuropsychology* (pp. 535–573). Oxford: Oxford University Press.

Denckla, M. B., & Heilman, K. M. (1979). The syndrome of hyperactivity. In K. M. Heilman & E. Valenstein (Eds.), *Clinical neuropsychology* (pp. 574–597). Oxford: Oxford University Press.

Fletcher, J. M., & Taylor, H. G. (1984). Neuropsychological approaches to children: Towards a developmental neuropsychology. *Journal of Clinical Neuropsychology, 6,* 39–56.

Gainotti, G. (1972). Emotional behavior and hemispheric side of lesion. *Cortex, 8,* 41–55.

Gilmore, J. V., & Gilmore, E. C. (1968). *The Gilmore Oral Reading Test.* New York: Harcourt Brace Jovanovich.

Hecaen, H., & Albert, M. L. (1978). *Human neuropsychology.* New York: Wiley.

Luria, A. R. (1973). *The working brain.* London: Penguin.

Mattis, S., French, J. H., & Rapin, I. (1975). Dyslexia in children and young adults: Three independent neuropsychological syndromes. *Developmental Medicine & Child Neurology, 17,* 150–163.

Ross, E. D., & Mesulam, M-M. (1979). Dominant language functions of the right hemisphere: Prosody and emotional gesturing. *Archives of Neurology, 36,* 144–148.

Rourke, B. P. (1982). Central processing deficiencies in children: Toward a developmental neuropsychological model. *Journal of Clinical Neuropsychology, 4,* 1–18.

Rourke, B. P., Bakker, D. J., Fisk, J. L., & Strang, J. D. (1983). *Child neuropsychology.* New York: Guilford.

Rourke, B. P., & Strang, J.D. (1983). Subtypes of reading and arithmetical disabilities: A neuropsychological analysis. In M. Rutter (Ed.), *Developmental neuropsychiatry* (pp. 473–488). New York: Guilford.

Rudel, R. G. (1979). Neuroplasticity: Implications for development and education. In J. S. Chall & A. F. Mirsky (Eds.), *Education and the brain* (pp. 269–307). Chicago: University of Chicago Press.

Van Der Vlugt, H. (1979). Aspects of normal and abnormal neuropsychological development. In M. S. Gazzaniga (Ed.), *Handbook of behavioral neurobiology (Vol. 2), Neuropsychology* (pp. 99–117). New York: Plenum.

Weintraub, S., & Mesulam, M-M. (1983). Developmental learning disabilities of the right hemisphere. *Archives of Neurology, 40,* 463–468.

12 Learning Disability With and Without Attention Deficit Disorder

Elizabeth H. Aylward
Dennis Whitehouse
John F. Kennedy Institute for Handicapped Children
Johns Hopkins University

In 1971, Dykman and his colleagues outlined a theory that proposed that the difficulties experienced by the learning-disabled child in the learning situation are explained by "organically based deficiencies in attention" (Dykman, Ackerman, Clements, & Peters, 1971). A great deal of research supports the notion that learning-disabled children, as a group, do differ from normal controls on a variety of attention measures. Several reviews of the literature (Keogh & Margolis, 1976; Routh, 1979; Samuels & Edwall, 1981; Tarver & Hallahan, 1974) present evidence for LD–control group differences on vigilance, reaction time, distractibility, and arousal, as well as on other factors presumably related to the construct of attention (e.g., overactivity, field dependence/independence, impulsivity, etc.). As clinicians, however, we are more interested in the concomitant symptoms exhibited by the *individual* learning-disabled child than in the *group* differences which distinguish LDs from controls. Like most other investigators we find an impressive overlap between the conditions of hyperactivity, learning disability, and attention deficit disorder. However, we are equally impressed by the fact that there seem to be many children with learning disabilities who do not exhibit attention deficits and many children with attention deficit disorder (with or without hyperactivity) who do not show definite learning disabilities. The focus of this chapter is, therefore, an attempt to disentangle the research findings on these two developmental disabilities.

As is often noted, there has been a long-standing confusion regarding the terms hyperactivity, attention deficit disorder, learning disability, minimal brain damage, and so forth. In fact, Levine, Brooks, and Shonkoff (1980) list 48 terms for these and related syndromes which are often used synonymously. Although there are no definite figures regarding the prevalence of ADD within the LD population, Lambert and Sandoval (1980) provide data which definitely indicate that hyperactivity and LD are not synonymous. Only about half of hyperactive subjects also met criteria for learning disability; 20% of a randomly selected population of nonhyperactive school-age children were diagnosed as LD. Safer and Allen (1976), after reviewing research on the topic, estimate that approximately 30% of hyperactive children are learning disabled, whereas approximately 40% of LD children are hyperactive. As a result of these and other data, many studies are now attempting to define learning disabilities in a more specific manner. They include in their LD samples only those children who exhibit significant deficit in some area or areas of academic achievement which cannot be explained by lack of intellectual ability, impaired sensory functioning, major emotional disorders, environmental deprivation, or lack of opportunity to learn.

Because of the relative recency of "attention deficit disorder" (ADD) as a diagnostic category (American Psychiatric Association, 1980), research on this disability has included less well-defined populations. According to DSM III (American Psychiatric Association, 1980), a child must meet criteria for inattention (e.g., failure to finish things he or she starts, failure to listen, easy distractibility, difficulty in concentrating and/or sticking to a play activity) and criteria for impulsivity (e.g., acting before thinking, shifting from one activity to another, difficulty in organization, need for supervision, frequent calling out in class, and difficulty awaiting turns) to be diagnosed as having ADD. For a diagnosis of ADD with hyperactivity, the child must also run or climb excessively, have difficulty sitting still or staying seated, move excessively during sleep, and/or act as if "driven by a motor" (American Psychiatric Association, 1980, p. 44). As noted by the manual, these behaviors must be reported by the parents or the school; because "signs of the disorder may be absent when the child is in a new or one-to-one situation" (p. 43) the clinician often observes no evidence for ADD.

Research is just beginning to appear that compares nonhyperactive LD children with hyperactive LD children (e.g., Dykman, Ackerman, & Oglesby, 1979, 1980; McIntyre, Murray, & Blackwell, 1981). To the authors' knowledge, only one study has been published so far which distinguishes between subjects with learning disabilities and those with attention deficit disorder (Dykman, Ackerman, & McCray, 1980).

The following review attempts to identify those aspects of attention deficit that characterize the learning-disabled population. By including discussion of studies on attention in hyperactive children, as well as discussion of those studies that have attempted to distinguish between hyperactive and nonhyperactive LD children, we hope to be able to come to some conclusions regarding the aspects of attention which are deficient in the ADD/hyperactive population but are not *necessarily* concomitant deficiencies of learning disability per se.[1]

In previous reviews of the research on attention and learning disability, attempts have been made to characterize attention by identifying its component parts. For example, Samuels and Edwall (1981) distinguished between arousal, alertness, vigilance, capacity, and selective attention. Tarver and Hallahan (1974) discussed studies of distractibility, hyperactivity, impulsivity, intersensory integration, and vigilance. Keogh and Margolis (1976) described studies involving coming to attention, decision making, and maintaining attention. The following review focuses on studies that have compared LDs and controls on the following factors related to attention: vigilance, reaction time, distractibility, autonomic arousal, and coritical arousal. This analysis of attention was formulated by Rosenthal and Allen (1978) in a review of attention deficits in hyperkinetic children. By using the same analysis we can easily compare the findings on LD children with those on hyperactive children.[2] It is important to note here that several investigators have attempted to study attention in LD children by using complex tasks such as Pribram's (1967) problem-solving task requiring attention focused inward (Ackerman, Oglesby, & Dykman, 1981; Dykman, Ackerman, & McCray, 1980; Dykman et al., 1979) or short-term auditory memory tasks (Bauer, 1979; Torgesen & Houck, 1980). Because of inconsistent findings using these tasks, lack of replication, and difficulty in determining exactly what cognitive processes are being tapped by the tasks, little reference is made to those studies using complex procedures whose connection to attention is uncertain.

VIGILANCE

LD Versus Control Comparisons. As Rosenthal and Allen (1978) explain, a vigilance task requires continuous sustained attention in order to detect an infrequent stimulus. On auditory and visual vigilance tasks, Noland and Schuldt (1971), Anderson, Halcolmb, and Doyle (1973), and Dainer, Klorman, Salzman, Hess, Davidson, and Michael (1981) found that LDs had fewer correct detections

---

[1]It is important to note that the studies reviewed were screened for their use of the term learning disability. In sections which compare LD to control subjects, studies are included for review *only* if they described their subjects as LD or reading disabled (not MBD, hyperactive, slow learners, underachievers, etc.) *or* if they gave a description of their subject selection procedures which indicate that the subjects met the commonly accepted criteria of LD (i.e., normal intelligence; academic performance significantly below what would be predicted for IQ; no uncorrected sensory deficit; no major emotional disorders; adequate educational opportunity, etc.).

[2]Rosenthal and Allen (1978) also included a section on brain chemistry in their analysis of attention in hyperkinetic children. Because there are no studies, to the authors' knowledge, which focus on measures of brain chemistry during attention tasks with subjects identified as primarily LD, no section on this topic is included in this presentation.

and more false alarms than controls. Rugel, Cheatam, and Mitchell (1978) and
Rugel and Rosenthal (1974) also found poorer vigilance performance in LDs
than in controls. As with Noland and Schuldt, Rugel et al. (1978) found that
performance decrement did not distinguish the two groups. On a more complex
auditory vigilance task where subjects had to indicate whether pairs of Morse
Code signals were identical, Van Camp (1980) found no LD-control differences.
Another vigilance matching task used by Keogh and Margolis (1976) required
subjects to cross out numbers in a booklet as they were read from a tape. LD
subjects were found to make more errors of omission and commission and had
a greater degree of response decrement over time than normal achievers. Thus,
results from vigilance tasks with LD subjects indicate that, at least for simple
auditory and visual vigilance tasks, LD subjects have poorer performance but
no greater response decrements than controls. Results for more complex vigilance
tasks (that presumably demand cognitive skills other than attention) are less clear
cut.

Hyperactive Versus Control Comparisons.   Rosenthal and Allen (1978) conclude from their review of the literature that hyperactive children, like LD
children, show poorer detection of correct signals and more false alarms than
normals. Because conclusions based on data from hyperactive subjects are similar
to those based on data from LD subjects, it seems plausible that the deficit seen
in vigilance among LD subjects may be due to the hyperactive-LD subjects
included in the sample and may not reflect a *necessary* concomitant of LD per se.

Hyperactive LD Versus Nonhyperactive LD Comparisons.   Ackerman, Dykman, and Peters (1977), Anderson et al. (1973), and Dykman, Walls, Suzuki,
Ackerman, and Peters (1970) addressed the issue of vigilance within a population
of hyperactive and nonhyperactive LD boys. In these studies, LD boys were
classified as hyperactive, hypoactive, or normoactive. The hyperactive children
are described by Dykman et al. (1970) as "distractible, impulsive, easily exhaus-
tible, and lacking an ability to concentrate" (p. 768). Most also showed excessive, poorly focused movements, and some were excessively talkative. The
hypoactives "had, in general, characteristics opposite to those of hyperactives:
they were unusually slow in motor action, speech, thought, and/or affect" (p. 768).
Subjects who were not clearly hyperactive or hypoactive were classified
"normoactive."
    Anderson et al. (1973) used observation and school reports to divide their
LD subjects into the three activity groups. On a visual vigilance task, they found
that the hyperactive LDs made fewer correct detections and more false alarms
than the hypoactive or normoactive LDs. The hypoactive LDs demonstrated
some attention deficit in this task, but not as much as the hyperactive LDs; the
performance of the normoactive LDs was near correct. The authors, Anderson
et al. (1973), conclude that "at a functional level, the assessment of a child as

learning disabled does not automatically presume that he has an attentional deficit" (p. 538).

In a study by Dykman et al. (1970), vigilance was assessed during a complex visual search task with and without distraction. A composite error score (hits, false alarms, premature and late release of key) across the distraction and no-distraction conditions revealed no differences between the normoactive LD subjects and the controls. Both the hyperactive and hypoactive LDs, however, made significantly more errors than controls. Because error rates were not reported separately for the distraction versus no distraction conditions, it is not possible to determine whether the group differences were due to differences in vigilance or in distractibility.

Ackerman et al. (1977) followed Dykman et al.'s (1970) group of subjects at age 14 on the same tasks. At this older age, the hyperactive and normoactive LDs made more procedural errors (failure to depress or release key, depressing key during interstimulus interval) than hypoactives or controls. Thus, the hyperactive LDs were consistent across age as showing more deficits in the vigilance task, whereas the normoactive and hypoactive LDs differed from controls only at one of the two testing times. Ackerman et al. used this and other data to suggest that the hyperactive LDs may be suffering from actual brain dysfunction whereas other LD types may be experiencing a developmental lag in the maturation of attentional mechanisms.

On a more complex vigilance task that required subjects to check off numbers in a booklet as they were read from a tape, Keogh and Margolis (1976) found no differences between hyperactive and nonhyperactive LDs (classified according to a teacher rating scale). The authors suggest that lack of significant differences may be due to an overselection of hyperactive pupils in the LD classes (thereby making the relatively nonhyperactive LD children still more hyperactive than normals) or to the fact that some of the hyperactive LD subjects were taking medication to control hyperactivity.

Although results from the four studies comparing hyperactive and nonhyperactive LDs on vigilance performance have not been in total agreement, the hyperactive LD subjects showed more consistent deficits than the other LD groups. Performance of normoactive LDs was generally equal to that of controls. Thus, it can be concluded that vigilance may be a component of attention that does not necessarily distinguish the individual LD subject from the normal achiever; only if the LD child is also hyperactive will he or she show deficits in vigilance.

REACTION TIME

LD Versus Control Comparisons.   The amount of time taken by a subject to react to a target stimulus is often used to measure attention. The greater the attention, it is presumed, the faster the subject is able to respond. Results from research on reaction time do not, however, allow any definite conclusions regarding differences between LDs and normals. Rugel and Rosenthal (1974), using a simple reaction-time task requiring the subject to press a key in response to a visual and auditory stimulus found slower speeds among LDs. Likewise, Sobotka and May (1977) found slower reaction times for LDs than for controls on a task requiring a response to dim flashes of light. In a similar task using a visual target stimulus, Noland and Schuldt (1971) found no reaction time differences between LDs and controls.

Using a slightly more complex task, Pihl and Niaura (1982) required subjects to release a key when a target light appeared. No main effect was found for LD versus control reaction time; however, the reaction times of the LD subjects increased across trials to a greater degree than those of controls. On a more complex choice reaction-time task which required the subject to make a decision regarding the stimulus (e.g., circle versus square; horizontal versus vertical lines) as quickly as possible, Pelham (1979) found longer reaction times, as well as more errors in the LD group than in the control group.

Thus, three of the five studies reviewed found slower reaction times among the LDs; the others found no group differences. Of the two studies that investigated response decrement, one found significant LD-control group differences and one did not. The difficulty level or duration of the task employed did not appear to explain these contradictory findings.

Hyperactive Versus Control Comparisons.   In reviewing studies of hyperactive children on reaction time tasks, Rosenthal and Allen (1978) conclude that at least on simple reaction time tasks, hyperactives had slower reaction times than controls. When tasks became more complex (e.g., choice reaction time or serial reaction time tasks), results were less clear-cut. They also present some evidence that hyperactive children show more intraindividual variation in simple reaction times and show more response decrement than controls.

Hyperactive LD Versus Nonhyperactive LD Comparisons.   Dykman et al. (1970), using a vigilance task with and without distraction, measured reaction times of hyperactive, normoactive, and hypoactive LDs and controls. LDs, as a group, had slower reaction times than controls. For subjects between 8 and 10 years, hypoactive LDs were significantly slower than the other LD groups; at 10 to 12 years, normoactive LDs were the slowest group. In following this same group of subjects at age 14, Ackerman et al. (1977) found that the LD groups did not differ from controls or from one another on the no-distraction portion of the vigilance task.

McIntyre et al. (1981) compared hyperactive LDs, nonhyperactive LDs and non-LD hyperactive boys with controls on a more complex reaction time task requiring subjects to identify the location of target letter in an array as quickly as possible. Reaction times of non-LD hyperactive boys did not differ from controls; both LD groups (hyperactive and nonhyperactive) had slower reaction times than controls. This difference may, of course, be due to the task, because the LD boys, being less familiar with letter stimuli, processed them more slowly.

Conclusions.   Combining findings from the studies comparing LDs and controls with those studies comparing hyperactive LDs with nonhyperactive LDs, it can be concluded that LDs, as a group, do not consistently show slower reaction times than controls. At least on simple reaction-time tasks, hyperactive subjects generally *are* slower than controls. Thus, one might predict hyperactive LDs, but not nonhyperactive LDs, to show slower reaction times than controls in those studies that subgroup the LD subjects. There is, however, no consistent evidence for this hypothesis. In fact, Dykman et al. (1970) found that it was the hypoactive and normoactive LDs (at younger and older ages, respectively) who showed the slowest reaction times. It is important to note here that the findings reviewed earlier focus on reaction time without consideration of accuracy. It is possible that the impulsivity often considered characteristic of hyperactives prevents the demonstration of reaction-time differences between hyperactivity LDs and nonhyperactive LDs. This, however, would not be consistent with the often replicated finding of slower reaction times among hyperactive subjects.

DISTRACTIBILITY

LD Versus Control Comparisons.   In a review of attention deficits in LD, hyperactive, and brain damaged children, Tarver and Hallahan (1974) conclude that the effects of distracting stimuli on these children depend on the nature of the distractors. Those that are internally related to the central task (e.g., irrelevant written material presented on the same page as written material to be remembered; verbal material presented in a different voice from verbal material to be reported) have a more distracting effect than those stimuli that are external to the task (e.g., a loud "hooter" sounded during a visual task; flashing peripheral lights during a visual choice task).

On visual tasks with embedded visual distractors some studies have shown that LD subjects are more susceptible to distraction than normals (Sabatino & Yssledyke, 1972; Willows, 1974, 1978). Others failed to demonstrate LD-control differences. Using a picture-naming task where the distractor was the inappropriate color of the pictures, Alwitt (1966) found no more distraction for the LDs than for the controls, although both groups performed poorer under the distraction condition. On a speeded classification task with simple stimuli relevant to the task and complex stimuli containing irrelevant information, Pelham (1979) found no greater distractibility in LDs than in controls.

Several studies have examined distractibility using a central–incidental recall paradigm. In this task the subjects are presented with information to which they are told to attend. This material is accompanied by incidental information that the subject is told to ignore. After material is presented, subjects are asked to recall both sets of information. In a review of studies using this paradigm with normal children, Hagen and Kail (1975) conclude that performance on the central task increases through the primary grades whereas performance on the incidental task remains constant until about age 12 when it decreases. As the child's cognitive abilities mature, it is assumed, he or she learns to attend only to that information which will help solve the task at hand. Thus, a child who performs well on the central task and poorly on the incidental task can be presumed to have attended selectively, whereas the child who performs poorly on the central task and relatively well on the incidental task can be presumed to have been distracted by the incidental stimuli.

Of the studies using the central–incidental task paradigm designed by Hagen (1967), only Pelham (1979) found no significant differences between the performance of LDs and controls on the central task. The rest (Hallahan, Kauffman, & Ball, 1973; Pelham & Ross, 1977; Tarver, Hallahan, Kauffman, & Ball, 1976) found that LDs had poorer performance on the central task than controls. Using a card-sorting task with cards containing central and incidental stimuli, Deikel and Friedman (1976) also found that LDs performed poorer than controls on the central task. Vrana and Pihl (1980) found poorer performance by the LDs on the central task only when central and incidental stimuli were clustered together, not when they were presented at opposite sides of the card. Thus, most studies support the inferior ability of LD subjects on a central recall task. This finding alone cannot, however, support the hypothesis of greater susceptibility to distraction among LDs, because this deficit could be due to cognitive processes other than attention (e.g., memory, impulsivity, etc.). Only by examining the LDs' performance on the incidental task can conclusions be drawn regarding distractibility. Unfortunately, data from the incidental task are less clear-cut than data from the central task. Hallahan et al. (1973), Pelham (1979), and Vrana and Pihl (1980) found no differences between LDs and controls on the incidental tasks. Deikel and Friedman (1976) and Pelham and Ross (1977) found greater incidental recall among LDs than among controls.

Tarver, Hallahan, Cohen, and Kauffman (1977), incorporating data from Tarver et al. (1976), examined developmental changes in performance on the central-incidental task among LD subjects. On the central portion of Hagan's (1967) task, older LD subjects (13- and 15-year-olds) performed significantly better than younger subjects. On the incidental task, the 15-year-old LDs performed significantly poorer than younger LDs (8- to 13-year-olds). Tarver et al. (1977) concluded that the older LD subjects had, by 15 years, caught up with normal children in showing a pattern of decreasing attention to incidental stimuli and that "the selective attention deficits of children with learning disabilities represent a developmental lag rather than a permanent deficit" (p. 32). If the

Tarver et al. (1977) conclusion is correct, one would expect studies with younger LD subjects to show consistently poorer performance by the LDs than by the controls on the incidental task. Studies just reviewed, all of which examined subjects younger than 15 years of age, do not consistently support the Tarver et al. conclusion. Furthermore, the differences among the findings of these studies cannot be explained by the ages of the subjects used.

Thus, results from studies using visual central-incidental tasks support the hypothesis of poorer central task performance by the LD groups but do not consistently support the hypothesis of more susceptibility to distraction among LD subjects. Studies have also examined the effects of embedded *auditory* distraction on LD subjects. Cherry and Kruger (1983) presented auditory distraction (white noise, speech backward, and speech forward) on a task where subjects were required to point to pictures named by a taped voice. On this task, LDs had poorer performance than controls under all distraction conditions, but not under the no-distraction condition. On a task that required subjects to repeat spoken passages presented in one ear under conditions of either no distraction or distraction (a competing passage presented simultaneously in the other ear), Hebben, Whitman, Milberg, Andresko, and Galpin (1981) also found LD subjects to be more susceptible to distraction than controls. However, Pelham (1979), using the same procedure with digits rather than spoken passages, found no differences between LDs and controls on susceptibility to the distraction.

Only one study (Pelham, 1979) has examined distractibility in LD subjects using an auditory version of the central–incidental recall task. On the central task, controls performed better than LD subjects; no significant group differences were found on incidental task performance. Thus, results from studies involving embedded auditory distraction, like those involving embedded visual distraction, are inconsistent. It is by no means conclusive, then, that LD subjects are more susceptible to distraction, either visual or auditory, than are normal controls.

As noted earlier, Tarver and Hallahan (1974), after reviewing studies whose populations included underachievers, minimally brain damaged, brain damaged, and hyperactive children as well as reading retarded and learning-disabled subjects, concluded that these children were distracted by the embedded but not by the external, distracting stimuli. When limited to studies whose subjects are more specifically defined as learning disabled, however, this conclusion is not so consistently supported. Patton, Routh, and Offenbach (1981) used videotapes of classroom activities as a distractor during math and reading tasks. Although this external distractor was effective in producing poorer performance among both nonhyperactive LD subjects and normal controls, the groups did not differ on their susceptibility to it. Vrana and Pihl (1980), as described earlier, found poorer performance by the LD subjects on a central task only when central and incidental stimuli were clustered together, not when they were presented at opposite sides of a card. In a study involving external distraction similar or dissimilar to the central task, Cermak, Goldberg-Warter, Deluca, Cermak, and Drake (1981) required subjects to recall word triads (presented visually or auditorily) after a distraction or nondistraction delay period. Distraction was presented in the same modality (visual or auditory) and consisted of a task requiring either phonemic, semantic, or nonverbal analysis. Cermak et al. found that when the distracting material was quite different from the material to be remembered (i.e., the nonverbal analysis distraction condition), LD children did as well as controls. When the distracting material was similar to the memoranda (i.e., the phonemic and semantic analysis distraction conditions), the LDs' performance was significantly worse than the controls'. Thus, results from studies using external distracting stimuli, like those using embedded distracting stimuli, are not totally consistent but do suggest more susceptibility among LDs to related or embedded versus unrelated or external distraction.

Hyperactive Versus Control Comparisons.   Unlike Tarver and Hallahan (1974), Rosenthal and Allen (1978) concluded from their review of the literature that hyperactive subjects do not show more susceptibility to distraction than normals. In order to explain this surprising absence of differences, they suggest that extraneous stimuli may actually arouse the hyperactive subject (who, it has been proposed, may be underaroused). Thus, the "distracting" stimuli may have a normalizing effect on the hyperactive subject rather than a decremental effect. Rosenthal and Allen note that most of the studies reviewed involved external stimuli as distractors. In agreement with Tarver and Hallahan (1974), they suggest that distractibility might be better assessed if the task involved the child inhibiting attention to irrelevant stimuli embedded within the central task.

Nonhyperactive LD Versus Hyperactive LD Comparisons.   In a study comparing hyperactive, hypoactive, and normoactive LDs with controls, Dykman et al. (1970) required subjects to press a key in response to the onset of a red light and to release the key in response to the onset of a white light. Under a differentiation task (which can be thought of as a visual distraction condition), the subject again had to respond to the red and white lights but had to ignore a green light. In the third condition, an auditory distractor (a loud "hooter") was also introduced. During the distraction conditions (conditions 2 and 3), LDs as a group, had slower reaction times than controls. For subjects under 10 years of age, hypoactive LDs had slower reaction times than controls under both distractor conditions; hyperactive LDs were slower than controls in the third (auditory/visual distraction) condition. For subjects over 10 years, only normoactive LDs were slower than controls under both distractor conditions.

When Ackerman et al. (1977) followed this group of subjects at age 14, the normoactives again showed slower response latencies than the other groups under the differentiation (visual distraction) condition, but only on release of the key (not on key depress). In the auditory/visual distraction condition, hyperactives were slower than controls (as they had been at 10 years) and normoactives had slower press latencies than controls. In terms of error scores, none of the LD groups differed from controls on the two distraction tasks.

Doyle, Anderson, and Halcomb (1976) also examined differences between hyperactive, hypoactive, and normoactive LDs on a vigilance task with visual distraction. The subject was required to press a button any time a red and green light were lit together. To the lower left of the lights was a visual display of colors and numbers, which the subject was told to ignore. LDs as a group performed significantly worse than controls on both correct detection and false alarms. They also demonstrated more eye contact with the distraction stimulus. Comparing the three LD groups, Doyle et al. found no differences on the correct detection score but found that the hyperactive LDs had significantly more false alarms than the hypoactive or normoactive LDs and had more erratic performance over time. On measures of frequency and duration of eye contact with the visual distraction, hyperactive LDs again were grossly different from the other LD groups; hypoactives were practically indistinguishable on these measures from controls. Doyle et al. conclude that most of the attention deficits observed in LD subjects can be attributed to those LDs who are also hyperactive.

Conclusions.   Neither studies with learning-disabled subjects nor studies with hyperactive subjects lead one to a definite conclusion that these populations are more susceptible to distraction than normals, whether the distractor is embedded or external to the task. Data is fairly consistent in revealing poorer performance among LDs on the central portion of a central–incidental task. This deficit could, however, be related to many factors other than distractibility. Data from the incidental portion of the tasks do not consistently reveal more susceptibility to distraction among the LDs. Inconsistencies among the data from distractibility studies cannot be easily explained by possible differences among hyperactive versus nonhyperactive LDs. Results from these studies were equally conflicting.

Thus, until more consistent data are available, it is not now possible to draw a conclusion that LDs, as a group, or specific subgroups among the LD population are more susceptible to distraction than normals. This finding is surprising, because one of the main complaints of teachers regarding most hyperactive and many LD children is their distractibility. Perhaps the laboratory tasks designed to tap the contruct of distractibility are not as sensitive as the teacher's critical eye. Hallahan (1975) found that at least one task used to measure distractibility, Hagen's (1967) central–incidental task, is not correlated with observations of behaviors generally considered signs of inattention (e.g., attention shifts, out of seat, inappropriate manipulation of objects, change of position, touching others). Furthermore, the types of distractors often used in laboratory measures (e.g., flashing lights, embedded words) most certainly cannot be assumed to be as interesting (i.e., as worthy of attention) to the subjects as the stimuli occurring naturally in the classroom situation. Thus, it is possible that greater susceptibility to distraction among LD students might be found if more ecologically valid measures were used.

AUTONOMIC AROUSAL

LD Versus Control Comparisons. Dykman, Ackerman, Holcomb, and Boudreau (1983) provide a thorough review of autonomic measures of attention in LD students. As they point out, the autonomic measures most often used include heart rate, skin resistance or skin conductance, galvanic skin response, skin potential, and respiration, and the majority of psychophysiological studies of LD children have examined the topics of arousal, orienting, and attention. From studies of basal levels of heart rate and skin conductance, that is, from studies of arousal—Ackerman et al. (1977), Boydstun, Ackerman, Stevens, Clements, Peters, and Dykman (1968), Johnson and Keffe (1972), and Rugel and Rosenthal (1974)—Dykman et al. (1983) conclude that LD children, under baseline conditions, are at least as aroused if not more aroused than normal subjects.

Autonomic measures taken during orientation to a novel stimulus have been studied by Dykman et al. (1971), by Hunter et al. (1972), and by Rugel and Rosenthal (1974). In the Dykman et al. study, no significant differences were seen in number of LDs versus controls whose skin resistance response indicated orientation to the novel tones. The controls who responded, however, showed larger changes in skin resistance in response to the stimuli than those LDs who responded. Also, LD subjects continued to respond to the non-novel tones longer than the controls, suggesting slower habituation during the orientation task. Rugel and Rosenthal (1974), measuring GSR to an auditory–visual stimulus, found no significant differences in responsiveness or habituation between LDs and controls. Hunter et al. (1972) compared LDs and controls on measures of skin conductance in response to a repeated auditory stimulus. LDs consistently showed less change in skin conductance in response to the stimuli; changes in skin conductance decreased across trials at the same rate for both groups. On heart rate measures, Hunter et al. found increases over the orienting trials for both groups but no significant differences between LDs and controls in magnitude, shape, or habituation of the heart rate orienting response. Thus, results from orientation tasks suggest that controls may show somewhat more electrodermal responsivity to novel stimuli; habituation rates probably do not distinguish LDs from controls on the passive orientation tasks.

On simple reaction-time tasks where the subject was required to respond to the onset of a target stimulus, two studies have demonstrated faster habituation among LD subjects. Rugel and Rosenthal (1974) required subjects to press a key whenever a visual/auditory stimulus occurred. As in the passive orientation condition, no differences were seen between LDs and controls in GSR across trials. However, habituation was faster for LDs than for controls, suggesting a deficit in sustained attention among the LDs. Hunter et al. (1972) required subjects to press a button in response to an auditory tone. As in their passive orientation task, skin conductance response was less for LDs than controls. Furthermore, LDs habituated faster to the response task than controls. Hunter et al. interpreted these data as reflecting the LD child's inability to "stay with" the task. On a similar task, Rugel et al. (1978) failed to find differences between LDs and controls in habituation of skin conductance changes in response to auditory stimuli that had to be identified. Surprisingly, skin conductance for both LDs and controls rose as the response task progressed. The authors suggest this may be a reflection of discomfort created by increasing underarousal. Results from the Hunter et al. (1972) and Rugel et al. (1978) studies suggest that on tasks which require a response from the subject, LD subjects are less able to sustain attention than controls.

Hyperactive Versus Control Comparisons.   Rosenthal and Allen (1978) reviewed findings on studies of autonomic arousal in hyperactive subjects. On basal levels of skin conductance and heart rate, they conclude, hyperactive children do not differ from normal children. In studies examining phasic orienting responses to loud tones, skin conductance responses and the cardiac deceleration component of the orienting response were found to be smaller in hyperactives than in controls. Rosenthal and Allen (1978) conclude that the hyperactive children "produce smaller orienting and sustained responses to stimuli than do normal children" (p. 700). Several studies have found that hyperactive children show more rapid habituation of skin conductance responses than normals, but Rosenthal and Allen suggest that these findings are confounded by the hyperactive subjects' lower initial level of responding.

Hyperactive LD Versus Nonhyperactive LD Comparisons.   Delamater, Lahey, and Drake (1981) compared hyperactive LDs and nonhyperactive LDs who were classified according to a teacher rating scale. On basal measures of skin conductance, frequency of nonspecific skin conductance response, or heart rate, the two groups did not differ. The groups also did not differ on skin conductance amplitude or latency in response to tones during a habituation task or on a discrimination task. Delamater et al. (1981) conclude that hyperactive and nonhyperactive subgroups of learning-disabled children may have a similar biological substrate.

Ackerman et al. (1977) and Dykman et al. (1971) compared hyperactive, hypoactive, and normoactive LDs with controls on cardiac deceleration responses to auditory stimuli. In summarizing this research, Ackerman et al. (1977) and Dykman et al. (1983) suggested a two component orienting response to nonthreatening novel tones. The first component, heart rate deceleration, reflects registration of the stimulus; the second component, heart rate acceleration, reflects an evaluation of the stimulus. Results from both primary level and adolescent LDs revealed hyperactive LDs as having the largest initial deceleration, followed by normoactive LDs, controls, and hypoactive LDs. The greatest subsequent acceleration was seen in controls, followed by hyperactive, normoactive, and hypoactive LD subjects. Dykman et al. (1983) interpreted these data as suggesting that the hyperactive LD subjects orient most strongly, are most attracted to novelty, and are "seekers of external stimulation," whereas the hypoactive LDs are more inhibitory or passive and more difficult to arouse.

Conclusions.   Studies comparing LDs with controls have found fairly consistent evidence that LDs show lower electrodermal responsivity to novel stimuli and, possibly, higher basal levels of autonomic arousal and faster habituation on vigilance tasks requiring the subject to make a response. No consistent group differences were found on habituation during passive orienting tasks or on level of arousal during a vigilance task requiring a response. Among studies comparing hyperactives and controls, results are fairly consistent in suggesting no differences in basal levels of arousal. Hyperactives show less autonomic responsivity in passive orienting tasks and possibly more rapid habituation. The similarities between the LD and hyperactive groups are supported by research comparing hyperactive LDs and nonhyperactive LDs that failed to find reliable group differences. Perhaps subtle differences in autonomic arousal between the two syndromes can be identified if one considers various phases of the orienting response, as did Ackerman et al. (1977).

CORTICAL AROUSAL

In a review of research on EEGs with clinic populations, Dykman, Holcomb, Oglesby, and Ackerman (1982) identified several abnormalities in the EEGs of LD and hyperactive subjects. As Dykman et al. (1971) pointed out, these abnormalities in EEG are relevant to a discussion of attentional factors in learning disability because "the brain mechanisms that control EEG frequency and amplitude are exactly those mechanisms important in attention" (p. 85). Despite the relatively large number of studies supporting the hypothesis of abnormalities in cortical measures presumably related to attention, Dykman et al. (1982) saw a need for studies that examine EEG frequency components from LD children specifically engaged in tasks manipulating attention. Our review here focuses primarily on those studies of cortical arousal during attention-related tasks.

LD Versus Control Comparisons.   Dykman et al. (1971) compared LD subjects with normal controls on contingent negative variation, the slow negative potential that develops during the prepatory period between a warning stimulus and a target stimulus in a reaction-time task. During the preparatory period, LD subjects showed lower cortical excitability than controls. Using a similar procedure, Cohen (1971) found that only 16 of the 42 LD subjects produced a normal contingent negative variation, whereas all the 65 normal subjects did so. In contrast to these two studies, Dainer et al. (1981) found no differences between nonhyperactive LDs and controls on contingent negative variation during a continuous performance task.

Sobotka and May (1977) compared LDs and normals on a task requiring subjects to make a response to dim flashes of light interspersed with bright flashes. Visual evoked responses to the bright flashes were recorded. Visual and evoked response data demonstrated significantly greater parietal and occipital amplitudes in the LD subjects than in the controls. These results are inconsistent with those from a study by Conners (1970) in which the same task was used. In a comparison of good and poor readers, Conners found attenuation of amplitude in the parietal visual evoked responses of the LD subjects. Interestingly, both investigators interpret their data as support for the hypothesis of possible attention deficits in the LD subjects. Sobotka and May (1977) suggested that the inconsistency in results may possibly be due to different methods used to measure amplitude or to different definitions of dyslexia.

In support of Conners (1970), Preston, Guthrie, and Childs (1974) recorded visual evoked responses to flashes of light and word stimuli for LD and control subjects. When the data from stimulus types were combined, the LD subjects were found to have substantially lower visually evoked response amplitudes than a group of normal subjects of the same age and a group of normal subjects of the same reading ability. Preston et al. (1974) interpreted their findings as suggesting neurological deficiency in the disabled group or, possibly, less attentiveness among the LDs. (These two interpretations are, of course, not mutually exclusive.) It is important to note that abnormal VER patterns should not be assumed to imply a global neurological deficit. Attentional problems may be the result of fairly localized brain dysfunction.

Musso and Harter (1976) employed a visual discrimination task that required subjects to respond to a relevant stimulus and withhold response to an irrelevant stimulus. Subjects were LD children whose reading difficulties were attributed to visual perceptual problems (the VRD group) or auditory perceptual problems (the ARD group). The amplitude difference of visual evoked responses to relevant versus irrelevant stimuli was greater for the VRD group than for normals, suggesting *more* selective attending among the VRD children. Musso and Harter (1976) interpreted these findings as evidence that the VRD subjects "compensated for their deficiency by greater selective attention in the visual discrimination task" (p. 302). Visual evoked response data indicated that both ARD and VRD groups had significantly longer latencies than normals, interpreted as suggesting that the LDs process sensory information at a slower rate than normals.

Dainer et al. (1981) compared nonhyperactive LDs and normal subjects on a continuous performance task which required the child to first watch passively a series of letters; then to watch the letter series and press a switch whenever an *X* was detected; and finally, to watch the letter series and press a switch whenever an *X* was preceded by a *B*. Evoked potential differences between the LDs and controls were prominant only for the most complex task (the B–X version). On this task, controls showed higher amplitude of the late positive componant (LPC) of the evoked potential in response to the relevant stimuli. Across trials of this task, the amplitude of the response decreased for LDs but increased for controls. The LDs also displayed longer LPC latencies than normals on the tasks requiring a response. Like other investigators in this area, Dainer et al. (1981) interpreted their data as supporting the hypothesis that "LD children are characterized by a deficit in sustained attention" (p. 90).

Thus, three studies (Conners, 1970; Dainer et al., 1981; Preston, et al., 1974) found lower VER amplitudes for the LD subjects, whereas two (Musso & Harter, 1978; Sobotka & May, 1977) suggest *more* responsivity among LD subjects.

Hyperactive Versus Control Comparisons.   Data from studies of tonic, or background EEG suggest that hyperkinetics have lower overall cortical arousal (Rosenthal & Allen, 1978). Evoked potential studies comparing hyperactive subjects with controls, like those comparing LDs with controls, have come up with discrepant results. Most investigators, Rosenthal and Allen noted, interpret their results as suggesting a delay in cortical maturation among the MBD subjects.

Hyperactive LD Versus Nonhyperactive LD Comparisons.   Dykman et al. (1982) compared EEGs of hyperactive, LD, and hyperactive-LD (mixed) subjects with controls during a complex visual search task developed by Pribram (1967). The 480 waveforms derived across subjects, sites, and trials were subjected to a principal components analysis. One resulting component, which had primary loading between 16 and 20 Hz and secondary loading between 7 and 10 Hz, discriminated between the four subject groups. The LD group had a significantly lower loading on the component than the controls or mixed group; the hyperactive-control contrast was marginal. The authors (Dykman et al., 1982) concluded that the clinical groups differed "from controls and to a lesser degree from each other in certain aspects of electrocortical activity" (p. 682).

Conclusions.   Studies comparing both LDs and hyperactive subjects with controls have generally found group differences on at least some measures of cortical arousal. These differences have not, however, been consistent and have not always been in the same direction. As Dykman, Holcomb, Oglesby, and Ackerman (1982) noted, "the principal difficulty inherent in all EEG studies of LD and hyperactive children concerns the question of what is actually being measured" (p. 683). Although studies examining EEGs of LDs and hyperactive subjects have been successful in identifying certain abnormalities in cortical arousal, they do not allow us to identify the CNS structural abnormalities responsible for the group differences in cortical arousal between LD children with and without hyperactivity. Whatever abnormalities have been found in the EEGs of LD and hyperactive subjects, investigators have generally interpreted them as reflecting attentional deficits.

DISCUSSION

There is a large body of literature that argues against the supposition that the LD population is a homogeneous group (e.g., Applebee, 1971; Denkla, 1972; Harris, 1982). Investigators have discussed several methods of subgrouping LD children in order to better understand eitologies, characteristics, and optimal treatment strategies—for example, familial versus nonfamilial LDs (Rugel & Mitchell, 1977; Rugel & Rosenthal, 1974), auditory versus visual dyslexics (Myklebust, 1965, 1978), higher Verbal IQs versus higher Performance IQs (e.g., Cermak, Goldberg, Cermak, & Drake, 1980; Kinsbourne & Warrington, 1966), older versus younger dyslexics (Sabatino & Hayden, 1970; Satz & Van Nostrand); and dysphonetic versus dyseidetic LDs (Boder, 1971, 1973). Some of these methods of subgrouping have resulted in more meaningful distinctions among LD subjects than others. The intent of this chapter was to examine one more way in which LD subjects might be subgrouped in order to better understand the attentional deficits often assumed to be a universal characteristic of this disorder.

As is often the case, our review has produced more questions than answers. Even studies which used fairly narrowly defined populations of LD subjects provide conflicting results. In brief, we can summarize our conclusions regarding attention deficits in LD children as follows: LD children have poorer performance than controls on simple vigilance tasks; they do not differ consistently from controls on reaction time and do not appear to be more susceptible to distracting stimuli. LDs show lower autonomic responsivity to novel stimuli and faster autonomic habituation during orienting tasks which require a response, but not during passive orienting. No consistent differences are demonstrated between LDs and controls on measures of cortical arousal during attention tasks.

Based primarily on a review by Rosenthal and Allen (1978), we can draw similar conclusions about attention in hyperactive children: Like the LD children, hyperactives show poorer performance than controls on vigilance tasks, they may not be more susceptible to distracting stimuli than controls and show no consistent differences from controls on measures of cortical arousal during attention tasks. Unlike LD children, the hyperactives had slower reaction times than controls (at least on simple signal-detection tasks) and possibly more response decrement on reaction time tasks than controls. Thus results from the studies of LD subjects (which generally did not exclude hyperactive-LD subjects) were quite similar to those from studies of hyperactive subjects. This could be interpreted as indicating that (a) hyperactive children show the same types of attention deficits as learning-disabled subjects, or (b) the attention deficits found among the LD groups were due to the hyperactive-LD subjects included within the groups. It was hoped that the studies which examined hyperactive versus nonhyperactive LDs would shed some light on these possible interpretations. Unfortunately, results from these studies were quite inconsistent. It appears that the second interpretation can explain the similarity between hyperactives' and LD subjects' poor performance on vigilance tasks—that is nonhyperactive LDs generally had more correct detections and fewer false alarms than the hyperactive LDs. The studies comparing nonhyperactive LDs and hyperactive LDs unfortunately do not provide us with conclusive evidence to explain other similarities and differences among the LD versus hyperactive groups.

Our lack of clear-cut results may be due to the fact that we were restricted by the nature of the research conducted so far to an examination of attention in hyperactive versus nonhyperactive LDs, instead of being able to compare LDs with and without ADD. Although hyperactivity and ADD are overlapping conditions (like hyperactivity and LD), they are not synonymous. This is especially true at older ages, when children who once met the criteria for hyperactivity no longer display the behaviors necessary for that diagnosis but still suffer from attention deficits (Komm, 1982). There still appears a need, therefore, for studies that examine the LD population from a perspective that takes into account the heterogeneity of the population on factors related to attention. Differences between LD subjects with ADD and those without ADD might be expected to include differential WISC–R scatter, especially among the ACID subtests (Arithmetic, Coding, Information, and Digit Span) which are presumed to be influenced by distractibility; differences in perceptual asymmetries, as measured by dichotic listening and hemiretinal tests (Aylward, 1984), differential responsivity to medication (Dykman, Ackerman, & McCray, 1980) or other interventions, and/or prognoses. Results from a pilot study with our clinic population and findings from other investigators (e.g., Rugel & Mitchell, 1977) also suggest that the LD subjects without attentional problems may be more likely to have an etiology based on genetic inheritance than those LD subjects without accompanying attentional problems. Investigation of these and other factors in LD subjects with and without ADD may be fruitful in helping us better understand these disorders.

REFERENCES

Ackerman, P., Dykman, R., & Peters, J. (1977). Teenage status of hyperactive and nonhyperactive learning disabled boys. *American Journal of Orthopsychiatry, 47,* 577–596.
Ackerman, P., Oglesby, D., & Dykman, R. (1981). A contrast of hyperactive, learning disabled, and hyperactive-learning disabled boys. *Journal of Clinical Child Psychology, 10,* 168–172.

Alwitt, L. (1966). Attention in a visual task among non-readers and readers. *Perceptual and Motor Skills, 23,* 361–362.

American Psychiatric Association. (1980). *Diagnostic and statistical manual of mental disorders* (3rd ed.). Washington, DC: Author.

Anderson, R., Halcomb, C., & Doyle, R. (1973). The measurement of attention deficits. *Exceptional Children, 39,* 534–538.

Applebee, A. (1971). Research in reading retardation: Two critical problems. *Journal of Child Psychiatry, 12,* 91–113.

Aylward, E. (1984). Lateral asymmetry in subgroups of dyslexic children. *Brain and Language, 22,* 221–231.

Bauer, R. (1979). Recall after a short delay and acquisition in learning disabled and nondisabled children. *Journal of Learning Disabilities, 12,* 596–607.

Boder, E. (1971). Developmental dyslexia: Prevailing diagnostic concepts and a new diagnostic approach. In H. Mykelbust (Ed.), *Progress in learning disabilities* (Vol. 2, pp. 292–321). New York: Grune and Stratton.

Boder, E. (1973). Developmental dyslexia: A diagnostic approach based on three atypical reading–spelling patterns. *Developmental Medicine and Child Neurology, 14,* 663–687.

Boydston, J., Ackerman, P., Stevens, D., Clements, S., Peters, J., & Dykman, R. (1968). Physiologic and motor conditioning and generalization in children with minimal brain dysfunction. *Conditional Reflex, 3,* 81–104.

Cermak, L., Goldberg, J., Cermak, S., & Drake, C. (1980). The short-term memory ability of children with learning disabilities. *Journal of Learning Disabilities, 13,* 20–24.

Cermak, L., Goldberg-Warter, J., Deluca, D., Cermak, S., & Drake, C. (1981). The role of interference in the verbal retention ability of learning disabled children. *Journal of Learning Disabilities, 14,* 291–295.

Cherry, R., & Kruger, B. (1983). Selective auditory attention abilities of learning disabled and normal achieving children. *Journal of Learning Disabilities, 16,* 202–205.

Cohen, J. (1971). *A new psychological approach to the diagnostic evaluation of children.* Personal communication cited in Dykman, Ackerman, Clements, & Peters, 1971.

Conners, C. (1970). Cortical visual evoked response in children with learning disorders. *Psychophysiology, 7,* 418–428.

Dainer, K., Klorman, R., Salzman, L., Hess, D., Davidson, P., & Michael, R. (1981). Learning-disordered children's evoked potentials during sustained attention. *Journal of Abnormal Child Psychology, 9,* 79–94.

Deikel, S., & Friedman, M. (1976). Selective attention in children with learning disabilities. *Perceptual and Motor Skills, 42,* 675–678.

Delamater, A., Lahey, B., & Drake, L. (1981). Toward an empirical subclassification of "learning disabilities": A psychophysiological comparison of "hyperactive" and "nonhyperactive" subgroups. *Journal of Abnormal and Child Psychology, 9,* 65–77.

Denkla, M. (1972). Clinical syndromes in learning disabilities. The case for "splitting" vs. "lumping." *Journal of Learning Disabilities, 5,* 401–406.

Doyle, R., Anderson, R., & Halcomb, C. (1976). Attention deficits and the effects of visual distraction. *Journal of Learning Disabilities, 9,* 59–65.

Dykman, R., Ackerman, P., Clements, S., & Peters, J. (1971). Specific learning disabilities: An attentional deficit syndrome. In H. Myklebust (Ed.), *Progress in learning disabilities* (Vol. 2, pp. 56–93). New York: Grune and Stratton.

Dykman, R., Ackerman, P., Holcomb, P., & Boudreau, Y. (1983). Physiological manifestations of learning disability. *Journal of Learning Disabilities, 16,* 46–53.

Dykman, R., Ackerman, P., & McCray, D. (1980). Effects of methylphenidate on selective and sustained attention in hyperactive, reading-disabled, and presumably attention-disordered boys. *The Journal of Nervous and Mental Disease, 168,* 745–752.

Dykman, R., Ackerman, P., & Oglesby, D. (1979). Selective and sustained attention in hyperactive, learning-disabled, and normal boys. *The Journal of Nervous and Mental Disease, 167,* 288–297.

Dykman, R., Ackerman, P., & Oglesby, D. (1980). Correlates of problem solving in hyperactive, learning disabled, and control boys. *Journal of Learning Disabilities, 13,* 309–318.

Dykman, R., Holcomb, P., Oglesby, D., & Ackerman, P. (1982). Electrocortical frequencies in hyperactive, learning-disabled, mixed, and normal children. *Biological Psychiatry, 17,* 675–685.

Dykman, R., Walls, R., Suzuki, T., Ackerman, P., & Peters, J. (1970). Children with learning disabilities: Conditioning, differentiation, and the effect of distraction. *American Journal of Orthopsychiatry, 40,* 766–781.

Hagen, J. (1967). The effect of distraction on selective attention. *Child Development, 38,* 685–694.

Hagen, J., & Kail, R. (1975). The role of attention in perceptual and cognitive development. In W. Cruickshank & D. Hallahan (Eds.), *Perceptual and learning disabilities in children: Vol. 2. Research and theory* (pp. 165–192). Syracuse: Syracuse University Press.

Hallahan, D. (1975). Distractibility in the learning disabled child. In W. Cruickshank & D. Hallahan (Eds.), *Perceptual and learning disabilities in children: Vol. 2. Research and theory* (pp. 195–218). Syracuse: Syracuse University Press.

Hallahan, D., Kauffman, J., & Ball, D. (1973). Selective attention and cognitive tempo of low achieving and high achieving sixth grade males. *Perceptual and Motor Skills, 36,* 579–583.

Harris, A. (1982). How many kinds of reading disability are there? *Journal of Learning Disabilities, 15,* 456–460.

Hebben, N., Whitman, R., Milberg, W., Andresko, M., & Galpin, R. (1981). Attentional dysfunction in poor readers. *Journal of Learning Disabilities, 5,* 287–290.

Hunter, E., Johnson, L., & Keefe, F. (1972). Electrodermal and cardiovascular responses in nonreaders. *Journal of Learning Disabilities, 5,* 187–197.

Keogh, B., & Margolis, J. (1976). Learn to labor and to wait: Attentional problems of children with learning disorders. *Journal of Learning Disabilities, 9,* 276–286.

Kinsbourne, M., & Warrington, E. (1966). Developmental factors in reading and writing backwardness. In J. Money (Ed.), *The disabled reader: Education of the dyslexic child* (pp. 59–71). Baltimore: The Johns Hopkins Press.

Komm, R. (1982). He's "LD"—I mean he's "ADD." *Academic Therapy, 17,* 431–435.

Lambert, N., & Sandoval, J. (1980). The prevalence of learning disabilities in a sample of children considered hyperactive. *Journal of Abnormal Child Psychology, 8,* 33–50.

Levine, M., Brooks, R., & Shonkoff, J. (1980). *A pediatric approach to learning disorders.* New York: Wiley.

McIntyre, C., Murray, M., & Blackwell, S. (1981). Visual search in learning disabled and hyperactive boys. *Journal of Learning Disabilities, 14,* 156–162.

Musso, M., & Harter, M. (1976). Contingent negative variation, evoked potential, and psychophysical measures of selective attention in children with learning disabilities. In D. Otto (Ed.), *Multidisciplinary perspectives in event-related brain potential research* (pp. 300–302). Washington, DC: U.S. Environmental Protection Agency.

Myklebust, H. (1965). *Development and disorders of written language: Picture story language test.* New York: Grune and Stratton.

Myklebust, H. (1978). Toward a science of dyslexiology. In H. Myklebust (Ed.), *Progress in learning disabilities* (Vol. 4, pp. 1–39). New York: Grune and Stratton.

Noland, E., & Schuldt, J. (1971). Sustained attention and reading retardation. *The Journal of Experimental Education, 40,* 73–76.

Patton, J., Routh, D., & Offenbach, S. (1981). Televised classroom events as distractors for reading-disabled children. *Journal of Abnormal Child Psychology, 9,* 355–370.

Pelham, W. (1979). Selective attention deficits in poor readers? Dichotic listening, speeded classification, and auditory and visual central and incidental learning tasks. *Child Development, 50,* 1050–1061.

Pelham, W., & Ross, A. (1977). Selective attention in children with reading problems: A developmental study of incidental learning. *Journal of Abnormal Child Psychology, 5,* 1–8.

Pihl, R., & Niaura, R. (1982). Learning disability: An inability to sustain attention. *Journal of Clinical Psychology, 38,* 632–634.

Preston, M., Guthrie, J., & Childs, B. (1974). Visual evoked responses (VERs) in normal and disabled readers. *Psychophysiology, 11,* 452–457.

Pribram, K. (1967). Memory and the organization of attention. In D. Lindsley & A. Rumsdaine (Eds.), *Brain function and learning* (pp. 79–122). Berkeley: University of California Press.

Rosenthal, R., & Allen, T. (1978). An examination of attention, arousal, and learning dysfunctions of hyperkinetic children. *Psychological Bulletin, 85,* 689–715.

Routh, D. (1979). Activity, attention, and aggression in learning disabled children. *Journal of Clinical Child Psychology, 8,* 183–187.

Rugel, R., Cheatam, D., & Mitchell, A. (1978). Body movement and inattention in learning-disabled and normal children. *Journal of Abnormal Child Psychology, 6,* 325–337.

Rugel, R., & Mitchell, A. (1977). Characteristics of familial and nonfamilial disabled readers. *Journal of Learning Disabilities, 10,* 308–313.

Rugel, R., & Rosenthal, R. (1974). Skin conductance, reaction time and observational ratings in learning-disabled children. *Journal of Abnormal Child Psychology, 2,* 183–192.

Sabatino, D., & Hayden, D. (1970). Variation in information processing behaviors. *Journal of Learning Disabilities, 3,* 404–412.

Sabatino, D., & Ysseldyke, J. (1972). Effect of extraneous "background" on visual–perceptual performance of readers and nonreaders. *Perceptual and Motor Skills, 35,* 323–328.

Safer, D., & Allen, R. (1976). *Hyperactive children: Diagnosis and management.* Baltimore: University Park Press.

Samuels, S., & Edwall, G. (1981). The role of attention in reading with implications for the learning disabled student. *Journal of Learning Disabilities, 14,* 353–361.

Satz, P., & Van Nostrand, G. (1973). Developmental dyslexia: An evaluation of a theory. In P. Satz & J. Ross (Eds.), *The disabled learner: Early detection and intervention* (pp. 121–148). Rotterdam: Rotterdam University Press.

Sobotka, K., & May, J. (1977). Visual evoked potentials and reaction time in normal and dyslexic children. *Psychophysiology, 14,* 18–24.

Tarver, S., & Hallahan, D. (1974). Attention deficits in children with learning disabilities: A review. *Journal of Learning Disabilities, 7,* 560–569.

Tarver, S., Hallahan, D., Cohen, S., & Kauffman, J. (1977). The development of visual selective attention and verbal rehearsal in learning disabled boys. *Journal of Learning Disabilities, 10,* 491–500.

Tarver, S., Hallahan, D., Kauffman, J., & Ball, D. (1976). Verbal rehearsal and selective attention in children with learning disabilities: A developmental lag. *Journal of Experimental Child Psychology, 22,* 375–385.

Torgesen, J., & Houck, G. (1980). Processing deficiencies of learning-disabled children who perform poorly on the digit span test. *Journal of Educational Psychology, 72,* 141–160.

Van Camp, S. (1980). An analysis of auditory attending skills. *Journal of Learning Disabilities, 13,* 223–227.

Vrana, F., & Pihl, R. (1980). Selective attention deficit in learning disabled children: A cognitive interpretation. *Journal of Learning Disabilities, 13,* 387–391.

Willows, D. (1974). Reading between the lines: Selective attention in good and poor readers. *Child Development, 45,* 408–415.

Willows, D. (1978). Individual differences in distraction by pictures in a reading situation. *Journal of Educational Psychology, 70,* 837–847.

13 Event-Related Potentials of RDs During Memory Scanning

Phillip J. Holcomb
The Salk Institute

Peggy T. Ackerman
Roscoe A. Dykman
University of Arkansas for Medical Sciences

Although infrequently mentioned, perhaps the most basic premise in modern cognitive psychology is that mental operations are the result of the flow of information between subsystems in the human brain. It is further assumed that with careful experimental manipulation the nature and working of these subsystems can be revealed. The promise of this "information-processing" approach has attracted a number of researchers from areas outside mainstream cognitive psychology. Clinical investigators interested in patients with cognitive deficits have frequently found the techniques of information processing rewarding. For example, in the area of learning disabilities, considerable research has been dedicated to isolating deficient systems/processes (see Sternberg & Wagner, 1982). The information-processing approach also has appealed to researchers studying brain correlates of cognition. Those interested in scalp-recorded brain marco potentials or event-related potentials have found the information-processing paradigm particularly well suited for their research (Donchin, 1979).

Following Donders (1969), who proposed that the duration of different thought processes could be deduced by subtracting the time required for performing a simple task from the time required for a more complex task, Sternberg (1969) formulated a model that divides information processing into four stages: encoding, serial search/comparison, decision, and response execution. Sternberg's model was based on data collected in a systematic series of experiments using a recognition memory paradigm that has been referred to as the short-term memory scanning or Sternberg Task.

In the primary variation of this procedure, subjects are presented with from one to five digits or letters (referred to as the memory set) followed by a single digit or letter (referred to as the probe). A different memory set can be given prior to each trial (varied set procedure) or one constant set can be given (for memorization) prior to a block of trials (fixed set procedure). In either case the subject's task is to indicate whether the probe item is or is not a member of the memory set by rapidly pressing one of two response buttons. Sternberg (1969) reported that probe reaction time (RT) increased at a constant rate with the size of the memory set regardless of the position of the probe in the set and was the same for yes and no responses. He then reasoned that subjects must be comparing the probe with a stored representation of the memory set, one item at a time (serial search), and that they must also be comparing the probe with all items regardless of whether a match was found on an earlier item (exhaustive search). An exhaustive search explanation is supported by the lack of a difference between no and yes RTs, as yes RTs at larger set sizes would tend to be faster than no responses if subjects terminated upon finding a match. That the search process is serial as opposed to parallel is supported by RT increasing at a constant rate with increases in memory set size. If the search were parallel, that is, if more than one memory-set item was compared to the probe at one time, then searching larger set sizes would not produce an orderly increase in RT.

In an ingenious set of experiments, Sternberg (1969) demonstrated that the zero intercept of the RT-set-size function (see Fig. 13.3) represents the combined times of the encoding, decision, and response execution stages (i.e., the sum time of the processes that remain invariant over the various set sizes). He also demonstrated that the slope of the RT-set size function represents the speed of the memory scanning/comparison operation, each successive increase in set size adding a constant (the time to compare the probe to one more memory item) to total RT.

The original appeal of Sternberg's model was the supposition that operations that affect the same stage of processing have interactive effects on RT whereas operations that affect different stages have additive effects (so-called Additive Factors Model). Although strict adherence to the Additive Factors Model is no longer considered tenable (e.g., see McClelland, 1979; Taylor, 1976), the number of investigators using the Sternberg task suggest the basic paradigm is still viable. In particular, many researchers interested in development and individual differences have used the Sternberg task to contrast various groups of subjects.

The Effects of Development in the Sternberg Task

An important question in cognitive development research has been which stages of processing are affected at what times during maturation. In the Sternberg task this translates to: Between which developmental periods do the slope of the RT-set size function (scan rate) or the zero intercept differ? Differences in slope are

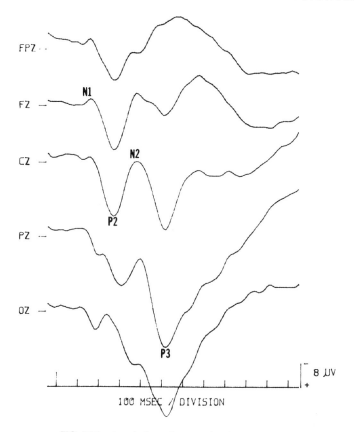

FIG. 13.1. A typical set of event-related potentials from 5 midline scalp locations in one subject (8 years old). These waveforms are averaged from approximately 30 presentations of a low probability visual event (the letters "DTM") to which the subject had to press a button. Stimulus onset is the first and largest vertical mark on the time scale. The components N1, P2, N2 and P3 are labeled to facilitate their identification in later graphs.

generally taken to implicate changes in processes requiring central attentional resources (although this may depend on the variation of the task used and the amount of practice given—see following), whereas intercept differences are taken to imply encoding or response organization processes are changed.

Hoving, Maier, and Konick (1970) compared kindergarten, fourth-grade, and college students and found only intercept differences between the groups, which suggests that scanning time is relatively invariant in this period whereas either encoding, decision, or execution processes become more efficient with increasing age. Anders and Fozard (1973), however, found both slope and intercept differences between young (mean age = 21 years) and old adults (mean age = 55 years). Search speed was approximately twice as fast per item for young adults as for older adults, and older adults also had higher zero intercepts. Together these studies suggest a dichotomy in processing development; that is, scanning rates appear to optimize early (6 years old) and to decrease sometime in middle age, whereas encoding and/or response processes develop more slowly, reach a peak in the 20s, and then decay with older age.

Several subsequent studies have supported the Hoving et al. finding. Harris and Fleer (1974), Silverman (1974), Maisto and Baumeister (1975), and Keating and Bobbitt (1978) all found no slope but substantial zero intercept differences when comparing children to young adults. However, Naus and Ornstein (1977) reported a significant difference between the slopes of third- and sixth-grade children engaged in the Sternberg task. A subsequent study by Baumeister and Maisto (1977) also produced a slope difference between age-groups of children (preschool vs. third vs. fifth grade), but only when memory-set items were random line drawings. In a follow-up experiment, when young children were given a strategy for recoding the random figures, the slope of their scanning function decreased to that of older children. Using digits, Herrmann and Landis (1977) also found slope differences between young (2nd grade) and older children (7th and 12th grades). In a second experiment they eliminated the possibility that maintaining a larger memory set might have interfered more with young children's scanning than older children's by showing a zero slope for all subjects in a task where the probe only had to be named. In summary, four studies have reported no or nonsignificant slope differences with age and three have reported steeper slopes for young children than for older children.

Herrmann and Landis (1977) suggested that the critical variable relative to slope effects between young and older children (i.e., differences in scanning rate) is amount of practice. In all four reports with no slope differences, subjects were given extensive practice prior to experimental sessions. In fact, in the Baumeister and Maisto (1977) study, young children were given more practice than older subjects. In the three studies that obtained slope differences, fewer practice trials were given prior to experimental sessions. It seems then that younger children benefit more from extensive practice, at least in terms of scanning efficiency, than older children.

One reason young children appear to benefit more from practice may derive from the way subjects perform the scanning/comparison process. Schneider and Shiffrin (1977) showed that extensive practice with a limited set of alternative items produces rapid, interference-free performance, whereas less practice with a wider range of items results in slower (capacity-limited) performance. The former condition has been referred to as "automatic detection" and the latter "controlled processing." It may be that young and older subjects do not differ substantially in their automatic detection of probes but do differ when controlled processing is called for (e.g., when less practice has been given). A number of studies demonstrate that older children and young adults make better use of attentional strategies involved in controlled processing than do younger children (see Dempster, 1981). However, a number of innate and learned automatic behaviors do not appear to differ as a function of age (Hasher & Zacks, 1979).

Individual Differences

Several investigators have used the Sternberg task to compare subjects of different mental abilities. The questions of interest are generally the same as in the developmental studies: that is, which measures (slopes or intercepts), and, therefore, which information-processing stages, differ with mental ability? Harris and Fleer (1974) contrasted three age-groups of normally intelligent subjects (mean ages = 8, 16, and 24 years) with two educable mentally retarded (MR) groups (familial/cultural and encephalopaths, mean age = 16 years). As discussed earlier, the three normal groups differed only in their zero intercepts (i.e., they had similar RT slopes). However, both MR groups had steeper RT slopes than did the controls. Only the encephalopathic MR group had a higher zero intercept than controls (they also showed the biggest slope difference). Dugas and Kellas (1974) also reported substantial slope and zero intercept differences between fourth- and fifth-grade normally intelligent subjects and mental age-matched MRs (CA = 16.9 years). Normal subjects scanned memory twice as fast per item as did the MR subjects. Silverman (1974), on the other hand, found no differences in slope between normally intelligent subjects and cultural/familial MRs but did report a higher zero intercept for the MRs. McCauley, Kellas, Dugas, and DeVellis (1976) compared high (mean = 125) and low (mean = 87) IQ normal subjects and reported both slope (high IQ faster/item than low IQ) and zero intercept (high IQ faster zero intercept) differences. Interestingly, when subjects were asked to rehearse the memory set during the memory-set-probe interval (a varied-set procedure was used), the high IQ subjects benefited more (slope decreased more) than did lower IQ subjects. Keating and Bobbitt (1978) divided normal subjects into high and low ability based on the standard and advanced Progressive Matrices (Raven 1965). Young high-ability subjects (9 years old) had significantly faster search rates (slopes) than did young low-ability subjects, although this ability level difference was not apparent for older subjects (13 and 17 years old).

Note that only Silverman (1974) failed to find slope differences between differing ability levels. But, only he used a fixed-set procedure. In the fixed-set procedure, memory sets are stored in long-term memory (as opposed to short-term memory in the varied set). Also, only one set size is presented within a block of trials. Both of these conditions would seem to make the fixed-set task much easier to perform. Silverman's absence of slope difference may have been due to the MRs not being taxed enough. Also, Silverman paid his MR subjects, but not his normals. At least one study showed that rewards decrease the slope of the RT function (Banks & Atkinson, 1974).

Finally, three studies have examined normally intelligent but academically troublesome children using memory-scanning tasks. Sprague and Sleator (1977) contrasted hyperactive children off and on 2-dose levels of methylphenidate in a task quite similar to the Sternberg paradigm. Stimuli were simple pictures with set sizes somewhat larger than the typical Sternberg task (3, 9, and 15 items). The varied-set procedure was used. Sprague and Sleator's data reveal that moderate doses of methylphenidate (.3 mg/kg) resulted in faster scanning rates than did placebo or high doses (1.0 mg/kg).

Sergeant (1981) used two auditory variations of the Sternberg task to contrast hyperactive and normal children. He hoped to show that selective attention deficits in hyperactive children are manifested in the slope of the RT/set size function, scanning or comparison rate being a process requiring central attentional resources. A fixed-set auditory experiment with set sizes of 2, 3, and 4 letters showed hyperactive and somewhat hyperactive subjects (mean age = 10 years) to have significantly longer RTs than controls. This effect did not interact with response type or memory-set size (i.e., it was a zero intercept difference) indicating that the locus of the group difference was in the encoding or response organization stages and not in the scanning operation. In a second experiment using set sizes of 1, 2, and 3 letters, Sergeant (1981) was unable to reveal differences between hyperactive subjects low and high in activity rating or hyperactive subjects rated as variable or consistent task applicators.

Maisto and Sipe (1980) employed the same paradigm (i.e., fixed set with considerable practice) used by Maisto and Baumeister (1975) to contrast normal children with age-matched reading-disabled (RD) children. As in the earlier Maisto and Baumeister (1975) work, Maisto and Sipe reported no slope differences between the two groups, but they did report a significant difference in the zero intercept, particularly when the probe was degraded with an overlying checkerboard. Inasmuch as RD subjects were much more hindered by the degraded probe, these investigators concluded that RDs do not have a central scanning (retrieval and comparison processes) problem but rather have a deficit in encoding operations. Encoding deficits have been implicated in the problems of RD subjects by other investigators using different paradigms (see Sternberg & Wagner, 1982).

Event-Related Potentials

The stimulus-locked portion of the human electroencephalogram (EEG) is commonly referred to as the event-related potential (ERP). If a number of ERPs recorded under similar stimulus conditions are averaged together, only that portion of the EEG specifically responsive to the stimulus will be enhanced, whereas nonstimulus related activity, or "noise," will be attenuated because it is random with respect to the stimulus. The positive (plotted in the downward direction) and negative (plotted up) fluctuations of the averaged ERP are referred to as components (unless otherwise noted, all ERPs referred to in this chapter are based on averages from between 10 and 100 identical trials). Components are labeled either by the latency of their peak poststimulus onset (e.g., P300 is a positive component at circa 300 msec) or the relative position of their peak in the waveform (e.g., P3 is the third positive component); both amplitude (in microvolts) and latency (in msec poststimulus onset) of the peak of components can be measured. ERPs are generally recorded from several standardized positions on the scalp, each referenced to a common neutral location such as the earlobes or the mastoid muscle (see Fig. 13.1 for typical ERPs from five midline scalp locations). Multiple electrode sites give the investigator information about the distribution of ERP components and how this distribution changes when independent variables are manipulated. This type of information can theoretically help in locating the origin of specific components in the brain.

Generally speaking, those components prior to 300 msec poststimulus onset are thought to reflect "exogenous" factors; that is, they respond to the physical characteristics of the stimulus such as modality, intensity, shape or tone (Donchin, 1979). Late ERP components, those 300 msec or more poststimulus onset, are considered "endogenous"; that is, they respond to subjective variables such as the probability of the stimulus, the value of the stimulus, and stimulus novelty (Donchin, 1979). This chapter is concerned primarily with the endogenous P3 component, which occurs with a latency somewhere between 280 and 800 msec poststimulus onset.

P3 amplitude has been demonstrated to vary with a subject's expectedness of a stimulus (see Pritchard, 1981, for a review of P3). Highly expected events result in small P3s and unexpected events result in large P3s. The relevance of an event to the subject also affects P3 amplitude, with extremely relevant events producing large P3s (Johnston & Holcomb, 1980). This latter finding has also been interpreted within a selective attention model, highly relevant events being those that are typically selectively attended to (Becker & Shapiro, 1980).

The latency of P3 (that is, the point in time where the component reaches its peak) has been shown to reflect the timing of processes underlying stimulus evaluation or decision time (e.g., Donchin, 1979). McCarthy and Donchin (1980) presented evidence that P3 latency and RT measure the duration of the same set of subprocesses with the exception of response selection and execution, which only RT seems to index. Duncan-Johnson (1981) corroborated this finding using a variation of the Stroop task.

With regard to development, Courchesne (1978, 1983) showed P3 latency gradually decreases from young childhood (7–8 years) to adolescence and further decreases from adolescence to young adulthood. Others (Ford, Roth, Mohs, Hopkins, & Kopell, 1979) showed that the reverse trend occurs for older adults (>55 years); that is, their P3 latency tends to become greater.

ERPs in the Sternberg Task

Because of both the similarities and slight differences in what P3 latency and RT appear to measure, the combined use of these dependent variables is ideally suited for aiding in the disentanglement of the various stages of information processing.

Gomer, Spicuzza, and O'Donnell (1976) used the fixed-set Sternberg task (1, 2, 4 and 6 letter memory sets) in normal adults (21 to 37 years) while recording ERPs from the vertex (center of the head). Their results indicate that the slope and zero intercept of the RT and P3 latency functions were different. RT was about 90 msec later than P3 (330 msec intercept) and had a much steeper slope. The smaller (faster) zero intercept in the P3 latency results probably reflects the absence of the response selection and execution components. The shallower slope for P3 latency, however, suggests that P3 may not be measuring the full set of processes involved in memory scanning or, alternatively, that some process other than scanning that affects RT slope does not influence P3 latency.

At least four additional studies (Adam & Collins, 1978; Ford et al., 1979, 1982; Pfefferbaum et al., 1980) used the Sternberg task in combination with ERP techniques. All these studies employed the varied-set procedure, and three (Ford et al., 1979; Ford, Pfefferbaum, Tinklenberg, & Kopell, 1982; and Pfefferbaum, Ford, Roth, & Kopell, 1980) looked at age differences between young and older adults. The general trend has been for less steep P3 latency slopes than RT slopes and for an earlier latency P3 zero intercept. In young versus older adults, there has usually been a slope and zero intercept difference in RT (as in Anders & Fozard, 1973) but only a zero intercept difference in P3 latency (the presence of an RT and absence of P3 slope effect can be seen from the increase in P3 latency to RT as a function of set size—see Pfefferbaum et al., 1980). These studies have also reported a breakdown with age in the P3 latency— RT correlation.

Only one study has compared RD and normal children in the Sternberg task, and no study using this task has collected ERPs in children. The goal of the research to be presented here was to integrate the ERP and Sternberg techniques for use with normal and RD children. Previous work in our laboratory has shown that RD children, like hyperactives, have difficulty with selective attention in effortful tasks (Dykman, Ackerman, & Oglesby, 1979). In the Sternberg task attentional deficits should translate into steeper RT and P3 slopes for RD than normal children, if attentional resources are required to scan the memory set. To make sure that subjects used effortful attention, the procedure employed here was made somewhat more difficult than the standard Sternberg task by having set sizes of 1, 3, and 5 items and by including all consonants as potential memory-set members. Other reports (Maisto & Sipe, 1980; Sternberg & Wagner, 1982) have suggested RDs to be deficient in their ability to encode stimuli. This deficiency should be revealed by longer latency P3 and RT zero intercepts in the RD group than controls, although such differences would not eliminate the possiblity that response variables are involved.

METHODS

Subjects

Forty-eight grade-school boys with IQs (WISC-R) greater than 90 served as subjects. Twenty-four were diagnosed as having a reading disability (RD) and 24 were normal readers (controls). Twelve of the controls and 10 of the RDs were between 8^0 and 9^{11} and 12 of the controls and 14 of the RDs were between 10^0 and 11^{11}. None had significant uncorrected visual or hearing problems, neurological problems, or other childhood psychiatric diagnoses on the DSM-III with the exception of attentional deficits without hyperactivity (see Results).

Criteria for the RD classification were a mean standard score on the reading and spelling subtests of the Wide Range Achievement Test (WRAT) of less than 90, a discrepancy of at least 10 points between this WRAT mean and WISC-R Verbal or Performance IQ, and a report from the teacher of a reading ability at least 1 year behind that expected for the subject's age. Criteria for inclusion in the control group were a WRAT reading–spelling mean score greater than 90 and a teacher report of no significant reading or behavioral problems. Classification data for the two groups are reported in Table 13.1.

TABLE 13.1
Classification Data
(Group Means Followed by Standard Deviations in Parentheses)

	Age(months)		IQ[a]		Wrat[b]		Add Index[c]	
Young Control	109.00	(6.25)	112.83	(5.92)	113.67	(9.95)	3.25	(3.02)
Old Control	131.08	(5.81)	117.92	(7.10)	115.25	(13.57)	1.08	(2.47)
Young RD	114.30	(4.74)	100.90	(7.81)	83.55	(4.39)	19.30	(5.42)
Old RD	134.43	(8.79)	102.64	(7.50)	81.82	(5.92)	13.14	(6.26)

[a]WISC Full Scale IQ
[b]Mean of Wide Range Achievement Test Reading and Spelling standard scores (1965 norms).
[c]Eleven-item Attentional Deficit Disorder Index. Each item scored from 0 (not at all a problem) to 3 (very much a problem); maximum score = 33. (Items available from authors on request.)

Apparatus

A Varian V-77/400 minicomputer was used to manage the experiment (collect behavioral and ERP data, present stimuli, and summarize data). Visual stimuli were presented on a Burroughs Self-Scan plasma display. Responses were measured by two microswitches placed on either arm of the subject's chair. A Grass model 7D polygraph fitted with 7P511 amplifiers (.1 to 40 Hz, 3 db bandpass) was used to amplify the EEG and electrooculogram (EOG). All data were stored on digital tape during each intertrial interval.

Stimuli

Visual stimuli were selected from the 21 consonants in the English alphabet. An auditory tone (60 db, 1000 Hz) was used as a warning stimulus. All letters were displayed as capitals in the center of the viewing field and subtended .5 degrees of vertical and from .5 to 3 degreees of horizontal visual angle.

Procedure

Subjects were seated in a comfortable lounge chair in a sound-attenuated electrostatically shielded chamber. They were affixed with Ag/AgCl disk electrodes at FPz, Fz, Cz, Pz, and Oz, referenced to linked earlobes. These electrode sites are all located along the midline of the scalp starting at a point just above the bridge of the nose on the forehead to a point 180° away on the back of the head and represent placements over occipital cortex (Oz), parietal cortex (Pz), parietofrontal cortex (Cz), frontal cortex (Fz), and fronto-polar cortex (FPz). A headband and surgical tape held the scalp electrodes in place. An eye movement/blink electrode, used to measure the EOG, was placed below and to the left of the left eye and was referenced to the FPz site (electrical signals resulting from blinking and eye movements contaminate the ERP if they occur during the ERP epoch).

All subjects participated in 20 practice trials followed by 180 experimental trials in the varied-set version of the Sternberg task. A rest break (approximately 5 minutes) was given after trial 120 of the experimental session. Set size was varied between 1, 3, and 5 items in a pseudo-random fashion with the restriction that no set size could occur more than twice in a row. For set sizes 3 and 5, all the letters were presented simultaneously, but the position of the probe on positive trials was varied equally between each position. In-set and out-of-set probes were also equally probable. To minimize confusion between the memory set and probe, the probe was always enclosed in double quotation marks. Each trial proceeded as follows: (a) a memory set presented for either 500 msec (set size 1), 1500 msec (set size 3), or 3500 msec (set size 5); (b) a 550 msec blank interval; (c) a 250 msec warning tone; (d) a 600 msec blank interval; (e) a 250 msec probe; (f) a 4500 msec intertrial interval.

During the practice session, subjects were instructed to examine the memory-set stimuli and rapidly indicate if the subsequently presented probe was (yes) or was not (no) a member of the set by pressing the appropriate response button. The "yes" button was paired with the dominant hand. They were told to avoid body movements and to make as few errors as possible. To minimize motor artifact contaminating the ERP, subjects were instructed to keep their index fingers resting on the two response buttons (buttons required only .5 cm travel and 73 grams force to be activated). RT was measured from the onset of the probe.

Subjects who did not understand the task after 20 trials were coached through a second set of 20 practice trials. All subjects were able to perform after 40 practice trials.

Data Analysis

Starting 50 msec preprobe onset, 1200 msec of EEG and EOG data (100 Hz sample rate) were recorded on each trial along with RT and the subject's response. Averate RTs from correct response trials and the number of correct responses for each set size and response type were computed from the initial 120 trials. Average ERPs were computed from trials where the subject made correct responses and did not produce significant eye or movement artifact. Because approximately 20 artifact-free ERP trials are needed to obtain a good signal to noise ratio, all 180 trials were used to calculate average waveforms. Preliminary analyses on the behaivoral data did not reveal any reliable differences between the first 120 and last 60 trials. Separate ERPs were formed for yes and no responses for each of the 3 set sizes and 5 electrode sites ($2 \times 3 \times 5 = 30$ waveforms/subject). Only results from electrode sites Cz, Pz, and Oz are presented here as these sites produced the most reliable P3 components.

Using an interactive computer program, all ERPs were searched for the largest positive component between 350 and 900 msec poststimulus onset. Both the amplitude in microvolts and latency in msec for the peak of this component in each ERP were calculated. Amplitude was measured relative to the average voltage for the 50 msec preprobe onset. Mixed design analyses of variance (BMDP2V) were used to contrast the two groups (RD vs. controls) and the two ages (8^0 to 9^{11} vs. 10^0 to 11^{11}) as well as the within-subject variables of set size (1 vs. 3 vs. 5 items) and response type (yes vs. no). In the case of ERPs, separate analyses were performed at each electrode site (Cz vs. Pz vs. Oz). The Geisser–Greenhouse (1959) epsilon correction factor was used in calculating p levels for repeated measures with greater than two levels.

Latency corrected P3 amplitude values were also calculated (Woody, 1967). This procedure involved shifting each single trial ERP on a subject-by-subject basis (at each electrode site) so that the peak of all P3s, across trials, lined up at 600 msec. Specifically, a two-iteration filter was employed with the noncorrected average as the original template. After each pass, the new average was used as the template. Points between 300 and 900 msec were used to compute single trial/template cross products. Waveforms were lead/lagged 130 msec in both directions. The rationale for using this type of procedure is to remove trial-by-trial variations in the latency of the P3. If this variability is substantial, then the average ERP resulting from the sum of the single trials will tend to have a broad and flat P3 component (i.e., the amplitude of P3 in the average will not reflect the true amplitude of P3 in the individual single trial). Variability in component latency could result from an experimental condition (e.g., memory-set size or group membership) adding an inconsistent amount of time to the processes underlying the generation of that component in one or more conditions. To explore this possibility, latency-corrected P3 amplitudes were contrasted with P3 amplitudes calculated from the normal average ERPs. For obvious reasons, latency-corrected ERPs were not analyzed for changes in P3 latency. (For a more detailed discussion of this procedure, see Ford et al., 1982.)

RESULTS

Behavioral Data

The RD children had more attentional problems, based upon a behavioral rating form completed by each subject's teacher (Table 13.1), than did controls, $F = 85.04(1,46)p < .0001$. The RDs also had significantly lower Full Scale IQs than did controls, $F = 41.77(1,46)p < .0001$ (see Table 13.1).

One of the assumptions made by Sternberg (1969) and by other researchers interested in RT is that subjects respond in an error-free or nearly error-free manner. Error rates in the current experiment exceeded 10% for all groups except the older controls (overall mean = 16.6%). Therefore, analyses on the number of correct responses in each experimental category were performed. There were significant group, $F = 9.78(1,44)p < .003$ (Control = 87% vs. RD = 78%), age, $F = 17.38(1,44)p < .0001$ (old = 89% vs. young = 77%), set size, $F = 38.23(2,88)p < .0001$, and response type, $F = 10.7(1,44)p < .002$ (81% for yes vs. 85% for no) main effects. The linear trend for the set size variable accounted for 90% of the variance. There was also an interaction between group and set size, $F = 4.55(2,88)p < .015$. Controls were more accurate than RDs at all three set sizes, but more so at set sizes 3 and 5 than at set size 1 (Fig. 13.2A). To better evaluate the interaction in Fig. 13.2A, an AOV was performed on the slope of the accuracy/set size function. RDs had significantly more negative slopes ($-.73$) than did controls ($-.39$), $F = 5.47(1,44)p < .024$. There were no significant differences in the number correct zero intercept.

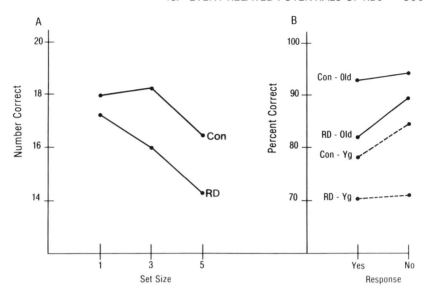

FIG. 13.2. (A) Mean number of correct responses for all 24 controls (CON) and all 24 reading disabled (RD) subjects in each of the 3 memory set size conditions. (B) Mean percentage of correct responses for older controls (CON-OLD), older reading disabled (RD-OLD), younger controls (CON-Yg), and younger reading disabled (RD-Yg) for yes and no responses.

In the overall number correct analysis there was also an interaction between group, age, and response type, $F = 4.47(1,44)p < .04$ (Fig. 13.2B). Young controls and older RDs were considerably more accurate on no responses than yes responses, whereas old controls and young RDs were only slightly more accurate on "no's." To gain a better understanding of the apparent "no" response bias, the total number of no and yes responses for each age and group were analyzed. There was an overall significant difference in the number of no and yes responses (60 no and 53 yes), $F = 15.14(1,44)p < .0003$, and an interaction between the number of nos/yeses, age and group, $F = 4.34(1.44)p < .043$. Young controls and older RDs responded "no" an average of 11 and 9 (respectively) times more than they did "yes," whereas older controls and young RDs responded "no" on average only 3 more times than "yes."

An AOV on the RT data revealed a main effect of age, $F = 6.09(1,44)p < .018$ (older faster than younger), set size, $F = 199.18(2,88)p < .0001$ (set size 1 faster than set size 3 faster than set size 5), and response type, $F = 34.4(1,44)p < .0001$ (yes faster than no). There were no significant or nearly significant interactions (all $Fs < 1$). Orthogonal polynomial analysis indicated that the linear trend for the memory set variable accounted for 94% of the variance. Although the quadratic trend accounted for only 6% of the variance, this too was highly significant, $F = 49.34(1,44)p < .0001$ (Fig. 13.3).

Analysis of variance was also used to contrast the zero intercepts and slopes of the RT set size function. The intercept analysis produced significant age, $F = 7.99(1,44)p < .007$ (old = 1080 vs. young = 1257 msec) and response type, $F = 26.81(1,44)p < .0001$ (yes = 1093 vs. no = 1233 msec) main effects, and no significant interactions. The slope analysis produced no significant differences.

ERPs

Presentation of the brainwave results are divided into four sections: visual inspection of waveforms; analysis of P3 latency; analysis of P3 amplitude; and analysis of latency-corrected P3 amplitudes.

As there were no visible differences in the ERPs between the two ages for either group, the age variable was summed over in computing ERPs for Fig. 13.4. The components visible in the waveforms plotted in Fig. 13.4 can be divided into those that are apparent at all sites and those that are restricted to one site.

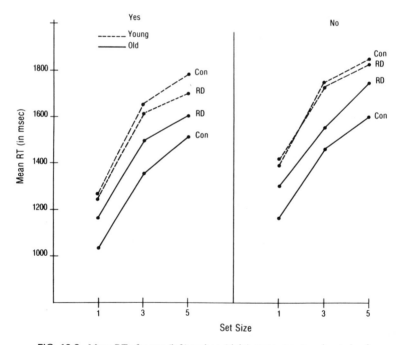

FIG. 13.3. Mean RTs for yes (left) and no (right) responses at each set size for controls (CON) and reading disabled (RD) subjects divided into younger and older age groups.

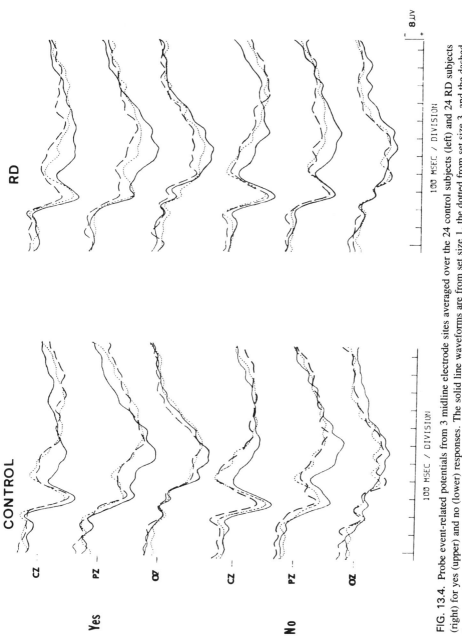

FIG. 13.4.   Probe event-related potentials from 3 midline electrode sites averaged over the 24 control subjects (left) and 24 RD subjects (right) for yes (upper) and no (lower) responses. The solid line waveforms are from set size 1, the dotted from set size 3, and the dashed from set size 5. Stimulus onset is the first and largest vertical mark on the time scale. P3 can be seen most clearly as the broad positive process which peaks between 500 and 600 msec post-stimulus onset at Pz in set size 1 waveforms.

The first component clearly discernible in Fig. 13.4 is the small negative blip that occurs between 150 and 200 msec poststimulus onset at the Cz site. This activity probably represents the occurrence of the frequently reported N1 component (Hillyard, Hink, Schwent, & Picton, 1973). N1 is followed immediately by a large positive complex, P2, which peaks at about 270 msec at Cz and Pz, but not Oz. A negative going (although negative going, this component does not in many cases cross the baseline into the negative region) component, N2, which is visible at the same sites as P2, peaks at between 350 and 450 msec. (Note that N2 is quite attenuated at Pz—possibly by the large ensuing positive component.) P3 can be seen as the large and broad positive component, which follows N2 at the Cz and Pz sites. P3 can also be seen in the Oz record where, as with Pz, it is the largest ERP component. P3 spans the epoch between 400 and 800 msec at all sites.

Further discussion is limited to the P3 region of the ERP. P3 appears to be more well defined, larger in amplitude, and earlier in peak latency when the memory set contained only one item (for yes and no responses), as opposed to when it contained three or five items. It is not apparent whether P3 differs in latency at set sizes 3 and 5.

"Yes" response probes have higher amplitude and earlier P3s than no response probes at Pz and Oz. Although in the Pz waveforms, P3 looks to be slightly larger for controls, it is roughly equivalent for the groups at the other two sites.

P3 Latency Analysis

As with RT, the raw latencies of the P3 component were analyzed as well as the slope and zero intercept values. The memory-set size and response type variables were significant at all three sites (all $p < .0001$). Linear trends accounted for 78% (Cz), 80% (Pz), and 82% (Oz) of the variance in the set size variable (all p's $< .0001$). As with RT, the quadratic trend, although accounting for less variance, was also significant at all three sites ($p < .01$).

At Pz and Oz the set size and response type interaction differed between the groups resulting in a significant three-way effect, $F = 3.14(2,88)p < .049$ and $F = 3.32(2,88)p < .043$, respectively (see Fig. 13.5A). The controls had earlier P3 peaks in all conditions except the no-response category at set size 5. At Cz the group variable entered into an interaction with the response type variable, $F = 6.81(1,44)p < .012$. Controls had earlier P3s than RDs at Cz but this difference was much greater in the yes condition (Fig. 13.5B).

AOVs on the zero intercepts of the P3 latency/set size function revealed significant group, $F = 8.49(1,44)p < .0056$, and response type, $F = 15.07(1,44)p < .0003$, effects. Controls had significantly earlier zero intercepts (530 msec) than did RDs (592 msec). Yes intercepts (533) were earlier than no intercepts (588). The P3-slope latency analysis produced a group, $F = 6.05(1,44)p < .018$, and group by response type interaction, $F =$

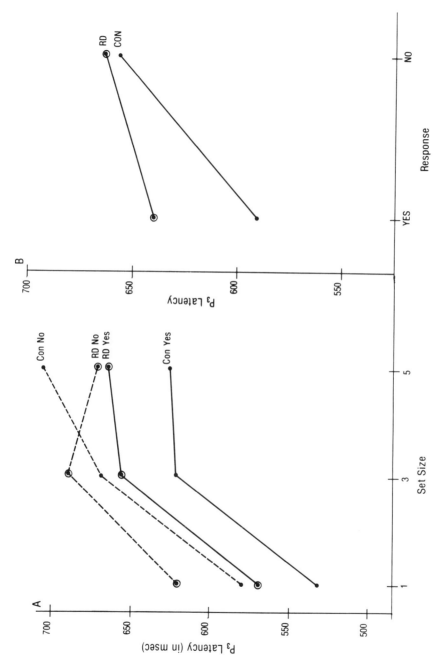

FIG. 13.5. (A) Mean P3 latency at the Pz electrode site for controls (CON) and reading disableds (RD) in the two age groups (dashed = young, solid = old) for yes and no responses at the 3 different set sizes. (B) Mean P3 latency at the Cz site for controls (CON) and reading disableds (RD) for yes and no responses.

4.68)1,44)$p < .036$. Controls had steeper P3 latency slopes (29 msec) than RDs (17.5 msec), but most notably on no (32.5 vs. 10.3 msec) as opposed to yes (26 vs. 25 msec) responses.

P3 Amplitude

AOVs on the P3 amplitude data produced significant results only at the Pz and Oz electrode sites. At Pz both the memory-set size, $F = 8.84(2,88)p < .0004$, and response type, $F = 13.79(1,44)p < .0006$, variables produced reliable effects. P3 decreased in amplitude as set size increased and was larger for yes than no responses. These same trends held for the Oz site ($F = 20.1(2,88)p < .0001$ and $F = 15.76(1,44)p < .0003$), but in addition, the set size variable produced a significant interaction with the group variable, $F = 3.24(2,88)p < .045$. At Oz, the subjects in the RD group experienced a greater decrease in P3 amplitude as the memory-set size got larger than did controls. This effect is more apparent in analyzing the set size/P3 amplitude slope function. RDs had significantly more negative slopes at Pz and Oz than did controls. (-1.62 microvolts vs. $-.39$ microvolts) $F = 4.61(1,44)p < .037$.

Latency-Corrected P3 Amplitude (Woody Filter)

ERPs resulting from latency correction in the time band of P3 are plotted in Fig. 13.6. Most obvious is that components earlier than P3 have been virtually eliminated by the latency shifting operation (due to their being freed from stimulus locking). In these waveforms, P3 is narrower and larger in amplitude than in the uncorrected average (part of this increase is due to lining all P3s up at precisely 600 msec). It also appears that the differences between the set sizes is much smaller.

P3 amplitudes from these ERPs were analyzed exactly the same as the more traditionally calculated P3 amplitudes. The response type variable was significant only at Oz, $F = 16.28(1,44)p < .0002$, with yes P3s being larger than no P3s. This variable was significant at all three sites in the uncorrected analysis. The set size variable was significant only at Pz, $F = 6.81(2,88)p < .0019$; it too was significant at all three sites in the uncorrected analysis. The group × set size interaction dropped out.

In comparing latency-corrected with traditional P3 amplitudes, it is apparent that latency correcting resulted in a substantial increase in overall P3 amplitude (24.66 microvolts vs. 16.6 microvolts), $F = 415.99(1,44)p < .0001$.

DISCUSSION

Somewhat surprisingly, neither the slopes, intercept, nor overall reaction time differentiated RD from normal children in our version of the Sternberg task. These findings must be tempered, however, by the greater than typical error

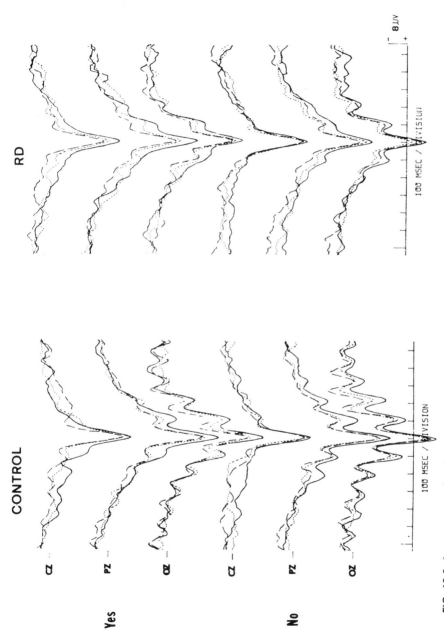

FIG. 13.6. Latency corrected probe event-related potentials from 3 electrode sites averaged over the 24 control (CON) subjects (left) and 24 reading disabled (RD) subjects (right) for yes (upper) and no (lower) responses. The solid line is for set size 1 waveforms, the dotted line for set size 5. P3s from all subjects have been arbitrarily lined up at 600 msec in this figure.

rates (mean = 16.6%) for all but the older control subjects. Pachella (1974) has pointed out that under certain circumstances subjects can "trade off" accuracy for speed. In the Sternberg task, high-error rates (greater than 10%) in more taxing conditions may indicate that in some cases subjects were responding impulsively or in a random or biased fashion, rather than to the demands of the task. Random responses time locked to the presentation of the probe could be expected to result in an overall faster and flatter RT/memory-set size function and to reduce or remove differences between groups (particularly when only one group adopts the impulsive strategy). Fig. 13.2 shows that RD subjects' accuracy decreased more over set sizes than did controls (group × set size interaction), indicating that at set sizes 3 and 5 they were trading accuracy for greater response speed. Put another way, had RD subjects been somehow required to make a higher percentage of correct responses at the larger 2 set sizes, then they probably would have had to respond more slowly than they (or the controls) did.

One possible explanation of the high-error rates is the brief interval that separated trials (4.5 sec). Although during pilot runs, this duration seemed adequate, the occasional very long duration of responses at set sizes 3 and 5 (as great as 4 sec) implies that some subjects did not have enough time to make accurate decisions and to prepare for the next trial. If rather than risk getting too far behind, subjects opted either to guess at the correct response or use a classification strategy other than full serial comparison, then their RTs would be faster, but only at the expense of making more mistakes.

Other strategies that subjects might have used include global familiarity (i.e., the subject asks himself, "Have I seen this stimulus recently?") and partial search or partial encoding. One appeal of a familiarity strategy is that it does not necessarily require the subject to maintain the memory set in working or short-term memory. He only has to encode the set and then assign a plus (yes) or minus (no) valence to the probe in terms of how familiar it seems. This strategy would produce fast decisions because comparisons of memory-set items with the probe are unnecessary, but it would also result in a substantial increase in errors as interference from other recent memory sets intrudes to influence probe valence. A number of theorists have proposed models that involve familiarity judgments in recognizing stimuli previously stored (e.g., Atkinson & Juola, 1973; also see Gillund & Shiffrin, 1984). However, most of these models are concerned with recognition of items from memory sets larger, and therefore more difficult to search and maintain, than in the standard Sternberg task. It could be argued that because of its complexity our task influenced subjects to behave as though they were in a more difficult recognition experiment.

A partial search or encoding explanation suggests that on some trials, possibly because of the lack of time or low motivation, subjects either did not encode or maintain the full memory set in working memory and/or did not search the entire list during comparison. Presumably, increases in set size would tend to emphasize all of these possibilities with an attendant increase in errors.

The significant quadratic trends in RT suggest that subjects treated set size 3 and 5 trials in a qualitatively different way from set size 1 trials (Fig. 13.4). A serial search model predicts that RT should be a linear function of set size, each item adding a fixed amount of time to the comparison process. In this study, RT increased much more (all groups) going from set size 1 to 3 than from 3 to 5, which implies that a serial search was not used by all subjects.

Although "yes" responses were faster overall than "no" responses, the pattern was not different over the 3 set sizes (i.e., the response type × memory-set interaction was not significant), which suggests that subjects used the same favored strategy whether a probe was in or out of the memory set. (Remember Sternberg interprets parallel functions as evidence for an exhaustive search model.) Interestingly, subjects were more accurate on no than yes responses (particularly the younger controls and older RDs—Fig. 13.2B). But, this effect may reflect a "no" response bias. A no bias would result in more correct no responses but also in more no responses when a yes is correct. This conclusion was born out by an analysis of the absolute number of no and yes responses. Subjects in both groups and ages responded "no" more often than "yes," but this bias was most pronounced in the younger controls and older RDs. One explanation for this bias is that when in doubt subjects responded no. It seems reasonable that doubtful trials would also be those with the slowest responses, which could have contributed to the larger no than yes RTs seen here and in other studies (e.g., Ford et al., 1979).

There were significant differences in RT and number of correct responses between the two age-groups. The RT effect can be seen most clearly in the intercept of the RT/set size function. Younger subjects had considerably longer latencies than older subjects. There was, however, no indication of a difference in the shape of the set size function (i.e., slope) for either RT or errors between the two ages.

Herrmann and Landis (1977) suggested that well-practiced young subjects show similar search rates to older subjects, but that lack of practice slows young children's responses at larger set sizes more than it does older children's and adults'. In the Introduction section it was suggested that more practiced subjects in the Sternberg task might rely on automatic detection in searching the memory set and that younger and older subjects do not differ substantially in their ability to use this type of processing. Subjects in the current experiment were probably intermediate, among the studies reviewed, in the amount of practice received (20 to 40 trials), and therefore it might be predicted that some or all subjects used automatic attention. However, given the difficulty of the task and the overall poor level of performance, it is doubtful that any subject was using automatic detection even by the end of the session. In fact, by design this version of the Sternberg task was intended to require the investment of attentional resources (controlled attention) so that differences in search rate would be apparent between ages and clinical groups. It is, therefore, surprising that at least the age slope differences were not obtained. The only explanation we can offer is that the age differences between the two groups (8^0 to 9^{11} vs. 10^0 to 11^{11}) were relatively small and error rates were higher than expected.

P3 latencies showed no significant age effects. As in the case of no RT slope difference between the ages, this finding was probably because of the narrow spacing of the groups. Many subjects in both age bands were closer in age to members in the other age band than in their own. Previously reported maturational differences in P3 latency in children have been between groups farther apart in age (Courchesne, 1978).

Unlike RT, the P3 latency/set size function significantly differentiated the two groups, although only in the interaction with response type. There was a significant increase in P3 latency as set size became larger for both yes and no responses in control subjects, but RDs showed this increase only on yes responses. On no responses, RDs' P3 latencies actually decreased from set size 3 to set size 5. It could be that the latency of P3 for RDs was unreliably assessed at set size 5 for "no" trials. However, if this were true, then the variance in the P3 latencies (across subjects) would be expected to be greater for this condition. In fact, RD subjects' P3 variances for "no" responses at set size 5 are less than the comparable variance for controls. A plausible explanation of the yes–no difference in RD subjects is that there was a breakdown in the relationship between P3 latency and the timing of decisional processes in RD subjects in this condition. The lack of a similar trend in the RT and number correct analyses supports this conclusion (Fig. 13.2 and 13.4). In their most recent study comparing young and older adults, Ford et al. (1982) suggested that the P3 latency dissociation from behavioral measures they observed in older subjects "may provide a way of assessing the early and, therefore, small but significant loss in ability to cope with cognitive demands" (p. 320).

To evaluate the relationship between P3 latency and RT in this study, correlations were computed for each group and age across the two within-subject variables (set size and response type). P3-RT correlations were small and nonsignificant (range $+.11$ to $+.16$) for all but the older controls ($r = .55$, $n = 72$, $p < .001$). It will be remembered that it was also the older controls that performed with less than 10% errors.

Further comparison of P3 latencies and RTs reveals a striking difference in the time between the two measures. P3 is 672 msec earlier than RT at set size 1, 918 msec at set size 3, and 1039 msec at set size 5. In the original Ford et al. (1979), study, which used young and old adults, P3-RT differences ranged from 300 to just over 600 msec, roughly half those reported here. The major disparity between the experiments is in RT; Ford et al.'s P3 latencies were only slightly earlier than ours. If the RT-P3 differences are to be accepted, then the response selection/execution processes that are inherent in RT, but not P3 latency, must be responsible (McCarthy & Donchin, 1980). It seems unlikely, however, that response variables could account for as much (or more) time as all of the preceding stages together. More probable is that P3 latency most often reflects a relatively early decisional process on which subjects were frequently unwilling to base a response. On a great many trials, subjects may instead have chosen to reevaluate the probe and memory set after the ERP epoch was over.

If the aberrant point (set size 5 "no" response) in the RD P3 latency data is ignored, the difference between groups appears to be a zero intercept effect with controls having a 62 msec advantage. The yes responses across the 3 set sizes and the no responses across set sizes 1 and 3 are virtually parallel at all 3 electrode sites. This finding is in agreement with the RT results of Maisto and Sipe (1980), who found only an intercept difference between RD and control subjects.

For most subjects, the task required constant attention and effort, especially at the larger set sizes. The P3 amplitude results reflect this task difficulty. Israel, Chesney, Wickens, and Donchin (1981) showed P3 amplitude to be inversely related to processing load, the greater the load the smaller the peak. P3 here was not as large as in other tasks (Holcomb et al., 1985) and decreased in amplitude as set size increased, particularly for the RD group. This indicates that increases in set size introduced a disproportionately greater load on RD subjects than controls. However, because the maneuver of latency correcting the single trials removed P3 amplitude differences between the two groups, much of the load effect was apparently in the variability it introduced in the trial-by-trial latency of P3 (that in turn affected the relative amplitude of the peak).

One interpretation of the P3 amplitude difference in memory load between RDs and controls is that it reflects the inability of RD subjects to use attentional resources in more demanding situations. Other investigators have pointed out that RD children are less able (or willing) to allocate attentional control in situations that require it (e.g., Ceci, 1983). That this sample of RD cihldren had attentional problems is supported by the more adverse ratings they received from their teachers in classroom attentional behavior (see Table 13.1). However, whether these real-world ratings relate to our laboratory measures of attention is unknown and will require further study. It probably is not going too far beyond the data, however, to speculate that an inability to allocate sufficient attentional resources would adversely affect one's ability to perform complex cognitive tasks such as reading, spelling, and arithmetic.

All the RD/control group effects (behavioral and ERP) should be viewed within the context of the differences observed in full scale WISC-R IQs. Post hoc, the relationship between IQ and the other study variables was explored with analysis of covariance. In short, all the major group differences (accuracy slopes, P3 latency zero intercepts, and P3 amplitude slopes) were reduced when IQ was removed from the model. Only the P3 amplitude slopes remained significant at conventional levels, $F = 3.93(1,43)p < .05$, although both of the other measures (accuracy and P3 latency) were still in the predicted direction. It appears then that although some aspect of IQ contributed to the differences between the two groups, reading ability was also important.

In summary, this version of the Sternberg task proved to be too difficult for all but the older control subjects. There was evidence that the RD group traded accuracy for speed, particularly at larger set sizes. Had these subjects been somehow required to make fewer errors, it is possible that there would have been differences between the two groups in scanning rate. In the ERP latency results, only the "no" condition at set size 5 suggested a group difference in scanning rate, and that contrary to expectations. Others (Ford et al., 1982) have suggested that a breakdown between P3 latency and RT might be a good measure of cognitive dysfunction. This issue needs further exploration in RD subjects.

The major ERP latency effect was in the zero intercept, with controls having significantly earlier P3 peaks than RDs. Such a result has been previously interpreted to suggest differences in encoding abilities (Maisto & Sipe, 1980), although in this experiment the possibility of differences in response processes cannot be eliminated as they also tend to influence the zero intercept. Changes in the amplitude of P3, which were attributed to variability in the trial by trial latency of P3, were also shown to differentiate the two groups at the larger set sizes, thus indicating that the increased demands of more memory set items hindered RDs more than controls. Future studies of RD children using Sternberg's procedure should guard against high-error rates although keeping processing load as high as possible. Reward and/or response cost might be helpful in this regard.

ACKNOWLEDGMENTS

This research was supported by NIMH grant MH34409 and by the Marie Wilson Howells Memorial Fund of the Department of Psychiatry.

REFERENCES

Adam, N., & Collins, G. I. (1978). Late components of the visual evoked potential to search in short-term memory. *Electroencephalography and Clinical Neurophysiology, 44,* 147–156.

Anders, R. T., & Fozard, J. L. (1973). Effects of age upon retrieval from primary and secondary memory. *Developmental Psychology, 9,* 411–415.

Atkinson, R. C., & Juola, J. F. (1973). Factors influencing speed and accuracy of word recognition. In S. Kornblum (Ed.), *Attention and performance IV* (pp. 583–612). New York: Academic Press.

Banks, W., & Atkinson, R. (1974). Accuracy and speed strategy in scanning active memory. *Memory and Cognition, 2,* 629–636.

Baumeister, A. A., & Maisto, A. A. (1977). Memory scanning by children: Meaningfulness and mediation. *Journal of Experimental Child Psychology, 24,* 97–107.

Becker, D. E., & Shapiro, D. (1980). Directing attention toward stimuli affects the P300 but not the orienting response. *Psychophysiology, 17,* 391–385.

Ceci, S. (1983). Automatic and purposive semantic processing characteristics of normal and language/learning disabled (L/LD) children. *Developmental Psychology, 19,* 427–439.

Courchesne, E. (1978). Neurophysiological correlates of cognitive development: Changes in long-latency event-related potentials from childhood to adulthood. *Electroencephalography and Clinical Neurophysiology, 45*, 468–482.

Courchesne, E. (1983). Cognitive components of the event-related brain potential: Changes associated with development. In A. W. K. Gaillard & W. Ritter (Eds.), *Tutorials in ERP research: Endogenous components* (pp. 329–344). Amsterdam: North Holland.

Dempster, F. N. (1981). Memory span: Sources of individual and developmental differences. *Psychological Bulletin, 89*, 63–100.

Donchin, E. (1979). Event-related brain potentials: A tool in the study of human information processing. In H. Begleiter (Ed.), *Evoked brain potentials and behavior* (pp. 13–88). New York: Plenum Press.

Donders, F. C. (1969). Over de snelkerd van psychische processen. Onderzoekingen gedaan in het Physiologisch Laboratorium der Altrechtsche Hoogeschool, 1868–1869, Tweede reeks, II, 92–120. (W. G. Koster, Trans.) In W. G. Koster (Ed.), Attention and performance II. *Acta Psychology, 30*, 412–421.

Dugas, J. L., & Kellas, G. (1974). Encoding and retrieval processes in normal children and retarded adolescents. *Journal of Experimental Child Psychology, 17*, 177–185.

Duncan-Johnson, C. (1981). P300 latency: A new metric of information processing. *Pschophysiology, 18*, 207–215.

Dykman, R. A., Ackerman, P. T., & Oglesby, D. M. (1979). Selective and sustained attention in hyperactive, learning disabled and normal boys. *Journal of Nervous and Mental Disease, 167*, 288–297.

Ford, J., Roth, W., Mohs, R., Hopkins, W., & Kopell, B. (1979). Event-related potentials from young and old adults during a memory retrieval task. *Electroencephalography and Clinical Neurophysiology, 47*, 450–459.

Ford, J. M., Pfefferbaum, A., Tinklenberg, J. R., & Kopell, B. S. (1982). Effects of perceptual and cognitive difficulty on P3 and RT in young and old adults. *Electroencephalography and Clinical Neurophysiology, 54*, 311–321.

Geisser, S., & Greenhouse, S. W. (1959). On methods in the analysis of profile data. *Psychometrika, 24*, 95–112.

Gillund, G., & Shiffrin, R. M. (1984). A retrieval model for both recognition and recall. *Psychological Review, 91*, 1–67.

Gomer, F. E., Spicuzza, R.J., & O'Donnell, R. D. (1976). Evoked potential correlates of visual item recognition during memory-scanning tasks. *Physiological Psychology, 4*, 61–65.

Harris, G. J., & Fleir, R. E. (1974). High speed memory scanning in mental retardates: Evidence for a central processing deficit. *Journal of Experimental Child Psychology, 17*, 452–459.

Hasher, L., & Zacks, R. (1979). Automatic and effortful processing in memory. *Journal of Experimental Psychology: General, 108*, 356–388.

Herrmann, I. J., & Landis, T. T. (1977). Differences in the search rate of children and adults in short-term memory. *Journal of Experimental Child Psychology, 23*, 151–161.

Hillyard, S. A., Hink, R., Schwent, V., & Picton, T. (1973). Electrical signs of selective attention in the human brain. *Science, 182*, 177–180.

Holcomb, P. J., Ackerman, P. T., & Dykman, R. A. (1985). Cognitive event-related potentials in children with attention and reading deficits. *Psychophysiology, 22*, 656–667.

Hoving, K. L., Maier, R. E., & Konick, D. S. (1970). Recognition reaction time and size of the memory set: A developmental study. *Psychonomic Science, 21*, 247–248.

Israel, J. B., Chesney, G. C., Wickens, C. D., & Donchin, E. (1981). P300 and tracking difficulty: Evidence for multiple resources in dual-task performance. *Psychophysiology, 17*, 259–273.

Johnson, V. S., & Holcomb, P. J. (1980). Probability learning and the P3 component of the visual evoked potential in man. *Psychophysiology, 17*, 396–400.

Keating, D. P., & Bobbitt, B. R. (1978). Individual and developmental differences in cognitive-processing components of mental ability. *Child Development, 49,* 155–167.

Maisto, A. A., & Baumeister, A. A. (1975). A developmental study of choice reaction time: The effect of two forms of stimulus degradation on encoding. *Journal of Experimental Child Psychology, 20,* 456–464.

Maisto, A. A., & Sipe, S. (1980). An examination of encoding and retrieval processes in reading disabled children. *Journal of Experimental Child Psychology, 30,* 223–230.

McCarthy, G., & Donchin, E. (1980). A metric for thought: A comparison of P300 latency and reaction time. *Science, 211,* 77–80.

McCauley, C., Kellas, G., Dugas, J., & DeVellis, R. (1976). Effects of serial rehearsal training on memory search. *Journal of Educational Psychology, 68,* 474–481.

McClelland, J. L. (1979). On the true relation of neutral processes: An explanation of systems of processes in cascade. *Psychological Review, 86,* 287–329.

Naus, M.J., & Ornstein, P. A. (1977). Developmental differences in the memory search of categorized lists. *Developmental Psychology, 13,* 60–68.

Pachella, R. G. (1974). Interpretation of reaction time in information processing research. In B. Kantowitz (Ed.), *Human information processing: Tutorial in performance and cognition* (pp. 41–82). Hillsdale, NJ: Lawrence Erlbaum Associates.

Pfefferbaum, A., Ford, J. M., Roth, W. T., & Kopell, B. S. (1980). Age differences in P3-reaction time associations. *Electroencephalography and Clinical Neurophysiology, 49,* 257–265.

Pritchard, W. (1981). The psychophysiology of P300. *Psychological Bulletin, 89,* 506–540.

Raven, J. C. (1965). *Advanced progressive matrices.* London: Lewis.

Schneider, W., & Shiffrin, R. M. (1977). Controlled and automatic human information processing: I. Detection, search and attention. *Psychological Review, 84,* 1–66.

Sergeant, J. A. (1981). *Attentional studies in hyperactivity.* Unpublished doctoral dissertation, Rijksuniversiteit te Groningen, Lennoxtown, Holland.

Silverman, W. P. (1974). High speed scanning of nonalphanumeric symbols in cultural-familially retarded and nonretarded children. *American Journal of Mental Deficiency, 79,* 44–51.

Sprague, R. L., & Sleator, E. K. (1977). Methylphenidate in hyperkinetic children: differences in dose effects on learning and social behavior. *Science, 198,* 1274–1276.

Sternberg, R. J., & Wagner, R. K. (1982). Automatization failure in learning disabilities. *Topics in Learning and Learning Disabilities, 2,* 1–11.

Sternberg, S. (1969). Memory-scanning: mental processes revealed by reaction-time experiments. *American Scientist, 4,* 421–457.

Taylor, D. A. (1976). Stage analysis of reaction time. *Psychological Bulletin, 83,* 161–191.

Woody, C. D. (1967). Characteristics of an adaptive filter for the analysis of variable latency in neuroelectric signals. *Medical and Biological Engineering, 5,* 539–553.

Commentary: Brain Function and Learning Disabilities

Karl Pribram
Diane McGuinness
Stanford University

The task of reviewing these chapters of the book provides us with an opportunity to highlight some general problems regarding the relationship between brain function and learning disorders. The chapters are written by authors dedicated to research in this important area of investigation, authors who on the whole represent some of the better work in the field. At the same time, these authors do not address the issues to which we wish to call attention.

And we, the reviewers, do not completely agree in our emphasis on the relative importance of brain factors as causal agents in the production of learning disorders. There is no essential disagreement between us, but Pribram is more interested in relating individual differences in performance to the differences in development and competence of various brain systems, whereas McGuinness prefers to emphasize the normality of such variation.

Critical to any understanding of the relationship of brain factors to learning disorders is the scope of the population under examination. Often when one deals with individual differences there is a small sample of the population that is at the extreme of the distribution. Much can be learned from that sample regarding those making up the remainder of the distribution. At the same time there is the danger that when the application is rendered the remainder are labeled abnormal when in fact almost any physical or psychological dimension shows such a distribution.

McGuinness reviewed the evidence for such misapplication in a volume entitled *When Children Don't Learn* (McGuinness, 1985). The point we wish to make may best be illustrated here by an example totally removed from the field of learning disabilities. Size is a dimension of human physical development and competence. There is sexual dimorphism in size, and norms for the two sexes

369

differ. Should that sex difference be ignored, certain people might be classified as abnormally short or abnormally tall when in fact they fall well within the range of distribution of this dimension for their sex. Furthermore, some people actually do fall outside those distributions: They are dwarfs and acromegalics. From studying such people we have learned about the relationship of pituitary, sex, and other hormones in the regulation of normal growth. But we do not, except perhaps in jest, address our short friends as dwarfs or the tall ones as acromegalics, despite the fact that the same regulatory hormonal factors are responsible for our friends' shortness and tallness.

Unfortunately in the field of learning disorders, such labeling goes beyond an occasional jest. Someone who is slow to learn to read or has limited reading competence is declared brain "damaged." Some of the individuals who are so labeled do indeed have brain damage, and we can learn from studying them which parts of the brain are involved in reading and how the brain functions to make reading possible. But many others fall within the normal distribution of individual differences in language skills, especially when sex differences in distribution are taken into consideration. In a similar fashion, three-dimensional spatial skills are differentially at risk for the sexes and may show an essentially normal distribution within each sex. Socially appropriate activity is even more sensitive to the sex dimension. Are we therefore to conclude that a large proportion of all males are brain-"damaged?" Privately females may well think this is so when they view politicians engaged in rhetoric on the nuclear arms race, but unfortunately territorial posturing is a function of normal brain processes in most male mammals.

Our review of the three chapters in this section must assume that the investigators are attempting to deal with that small fraction of the learning-disabled within whom brain damage may have occurred—a portion of the population that corresponds to dwarfism or acromegaly. But this is not made clear in the chapters, and they suffer accordingly. Although Holmes's account of neuropsychological analysis and her conclusions often fit with our intuitions (especially those of Pribram), her descriptions of symptoms (social, configural, contextual, linguistic) are insufficiently precise to allow any realistic testing of the relationship of learning problems to the functions of specific brain systems. This vagueness in description becomes especially embarrassing when Holmes attributes "social learning disabilities" to the right hemisphere (when in fact such disorders may well involve decoding verbal signals, especially their prosodics, which appear to be related to the left frontal cortex and the underlying basal ganglia.

The same lack of precision plagues the classification "hyperactivity." Some children are fidgity, others are acting out in response to stress, some are distractible in what are to them boring situations (such as the vigilance or continuous performance type tasks so often employed in "diagnosis"), and still others are simply boys whose temperament (an active searching out by prehension rather than by verbal comprehension) makes them unfit for the standard classroom environment. McGuinness finds it unlikely that such a potpourri of symptoms could be attributed to any single brain system. Pribram, on the other hand, finds it intriguing to speculate, as has Holmes, that the frontal systems of the forebrain may well lag in development in boys, with the result that context-sensitive behaviors of all sorts are affected. Such developmental differences between the sexes are known to occur (Goldman, Crawford, Stokes, Galkin, and Rosvold, 1974). Also, the incidence of bed-wetting is much more common in boys than in girls, and all of us who have seen patients with meningiomas or other foreign objects pressing on the frontal lobes have observed the great difficulty with incontinence experienced by such patients and their caretakers; circumstantial evidence, of course, but suggestive.

However, this does not make all such boys (and the few girls) abnormal, nor are their frontal lobes abnormal. Individual differences in development of different brain systems should not be viewed in any different light than the differential time course of development of the lower and upper jaws of boys during puberty. Holmes does not make the most of this possibility (of differential development) when she correctly notes that the fact that the "demand" characteristics of current school curricula often are limited to getting into the next higher level of the school system. Recently, some school districts have started experimental schools based on "outcomes." These are set out by subject matter and progress chronologically. Different children can pass along these routes at different rates. The outcomes are specific, such as being able to punctuate, capitalize, read, and remember prose of a specific level of difficulty and length. Most children with learning problems, given concrete objectives such as these, and given access to remedial techniques that are reliable would never appear in the clinic.

Some of the remedial techniques that are available are those used by Lindamood and Lindamood (1983) for reading/spelling,[1] by Davidson (1979) for mathematics, and by O'Leary and O'Leary (1977) for behavioral problems. Relating individual differences to differences in brain system development and competence is of fundamental interest and can lead to the development of "cognitive prostheses." When such prostheses are already available, they should be used.

Holcomb, Ackerman, and Dykman have produced some of the best research on inappropriately active children. The group with whom they work has all the criteria just noted, which can reveal whether brain damage is present. They distinguish clearly between learning disabilities and inappropriate activity and often use tests that have differential diagnostic value as demonstrated in experimental or clinical brain lesion populations.

In their chapter, Holcomb, Ackerman, and Dykman provide further evidence of dissociation between altered activity and reading disorders. The Sternberg

---

[1]See Howard (1982) for field research results.

task is used to measure reaction times and event-related brain electrical activity. What makes the results of the study difficult to interpret is the same fact that makes the study interesting: a group of children who may well have some real brain damage. This is reflected in the fact that the clinical population showed an IQ some 10 to 15 points lower than the controls and also displayed marked attention disorders. When an ANOVA controlled for IQ, essentially all behavioral group effects disappeared. Further, when the brain electrical potential latencies in the P300 range were lined up, all group differences disappeared despite the IQ differences.

What are we to conclude? McGuinness suggests that the results of the experiments cannot tell us whether IQ, attentional, or reading problems are responsible for the differences—in short, that the experimental results are inconclusive. Pribram, on the other hand, recalls a clinical dictum he learned from Alexander Romanovitch Luria. Examining a patient with a large frontal lesion, Pribram had remarked that the damage was so extensive that little could be learned with regard to localization. Luria replied that it is just in such cases in which damage is extensive that localizing symptoms appear, because the remainder of the brain cannot compensate for the defect.

Applied to the results of the group studied by Holcomb, Ackerman, and Dykman, Pribram suggests, in keeping with the spirit of their presentation, that in fact the low IQ serves as a background against which localizing symptoms are enhanced. Further, the change in latency of the P300 attributable to lower IQ, altered attention, or delayed reading is also an important finding, which allows for possible further analysis. Is the P300a perchance related to attentional disorders and the P300b to lower IQ? The event-related brain potential may well be just the tool necessary to answer the question posed by McGuinness, and the group studied by Holcomb, Ackerman, and Dykman the ideal setting in which to ask the question.

Finally, the chapter by Aylward and Whitehouse is a most welcome review of the literature on children with inappropriate activity (as compared to learning disorders). There are only two areas in which we wish the authors had been a bit more critical. Often they initially appear to accept the interpretations put forward in the papers they review only to note considerably later—often in the concluding remarks—that the data do not support the conclusions.

Also, Aylward and Whitehouse are often uncritical in evaluating the results of findings with autonomic or brain electrical indicators of function. By and large, but with significant exceptions such as the neurometrics of John and his group (John & Thatcher, 1977), there is to date no reliable evidence that such indicators can distinguish between subpopulations of children except those that are mentally retarded. Nonetheless, the Aylward and Whitehouse review performs a much needed service in that it allows the reader to peruse that literature and draw his/her own conclusions as to reliability and validity.

In closing, we wish to thank the contributors for their efforts in their research and in presenting results in this very difficult but important area of investigation. At the same time, we hope they will join us in eradicating the notion that all persons who are not in the very center of language, spatial, and appropriate activity distributions are therefore abnormal. We have come a long way since all sinistrals were thought to be sinister. Can't we come the remainder of the way and allow for individual differences in other manifestations of brain function?

REFERENCES

Davidson, P. S. (1979, May). Neurobiological research and its implications for mathematics education. *The Virginia Mathematics Teacher*.

Goldman, P. S., Crawford, H. T., Stokes, L. P., Galkin, T. W., & Rosvold, H. E. (1974). Sex dependent behavioral effects of cerebral cortical lesions in the developing Rhesus monkey. *Science, 186,* 540–542.

Howard, M. (1982). Utilizing oral-motor feedback in auditory conceptualization. *Journal of Education and Neuropsychology, 2,* 24–35.

John, E. R., & Thatcher, R. W. (1977). *Functional neuroscience, Vol. 1. Neurometrics: Clinical applications of quantitative electrophysiology*. New York: Halsted.

Lindamood, C. H., & Lindamood, P.C. (1983). *Auditory discrimination in depth*. Allex, TX: Developmental Learning Materials.

McGuinness, D. (1985). *When children don't learn* New York: Basic Books.

O'Leary, K. D., & O'Leary, S. G. (1977). *Classroom management: The successful use of behavior modification*. Elmsford, NY: Pergammon.

Author Index

A

Abelson, R., 275, 293
Ackerman, P., 15, 26, 63, 65, 79, 280, 291, 321, 322, 323, 324, 326, 330, 332, 333, 334, 338, 339, 350, 367
Adam, M., 350, 366
Adams, J., 69, 78
Adams, P. A., 274, 293
Adelman, H., 267, 269
Adler, T. F., 227, 229
Akert, R. M., 278, 291
Alegria, J., 15, 16, 20, 26, 29, 60
Algozzine, B., 262, 272
Allen, M., 307, 319
Allen, R., 322, 341
Allen, T. W., 65, 81, 235, 249, 323, 324, 326, 330, 333, 341
Alley, G. R., 194, 203, 205, 212
Allington, R. L., 8, 26
Alwitt, L. F., 67, 79, 80, 327, 341
Anders, R. T., 345, 350, 366
Anderson, J. R., 86, 101
Anderson, R. C., 190, 204
Anderson, R. P., 68, 79, 323, 324, 331, 339
Anderson, T. H., 190, 195, 204
Andresko, M., 329, 340
Andrews, J. M., 67, 81
Angell, L. S., 157, 172
Applebaum, M., 169

Applebee, A., 337, 339
Archer, D., 276, 278, 293
Armbruster, B. B., 190, 204
Arnold, D. J., 192, 204
Atkinson, R. C., 176, 204, 347, 362, 366
Auble, P. M., 176, 189, 205
Aylward, E., 338, 339

B

Bachara, G. H., 281, 291
Badcock, D., 58
Bak, J. J., 274, 293
Baker, L., 163, 169, 223, 229
Bakker, B. P.,
Bakker, J. D., 305, 319
Ball, D. W., 71, 79, 81, 154, 173, 179, 211
Banks, W. A., 347, 366
Barclay, C. R., 147, 148, 171
Barden, R. C., 239, 249
Barke, C. R., 180, 211
Barkley, R. A., 260, 269
Barling, J., 159, 171
Barnes, M. A., 61
Baron, J., 10, 26, 58, 62
Barron, R. W., 12, 26, 58
Battle, J., 158, 169
Bauer, D. W., 58
Bauer, R. H., 17, 18, 26, 58, 84, 85, 101, 155, 169, 179, 204, 238, 247, 323, 339

Baumeister, A. A., 346, 348, 366, 368
Bean, J. P., 179, 211
Beck, I., 15, 29, 61, 190, 204, 218, 219, 229
Becker, D. E., 349, 366
Becker, F., 261, 269
Becker, W. C., 182, 204
Bee, J., 261, 269
Bell, J. A., 202, 208
Bell, L. C., 12, 27
Bell-Berti, F., 60
Belmont, J. M., 150, 169, 195, 205, 266, 269
Bender, B. G., 181, 192, 194, 204, 239, 249
Bender, L., 68
Benton, S. L., 195, 204
Bentzen, F., 259, 269
Berdiansky, B., 58
Berger, N. S., 106, 107, 111
Berko, J., 58
Berry, J. K., 182, 185, 204, 208
Bertelsch, P., 60
Bertelson, P., 15, 29
Beverly, S. E., 20, 27
Biddle, W. B., 190, 195, 204
Bigelow, B. J., 275, 291
Bisanz, G. L., 58
Bishop, S. L., 181, 210
Bispo, J. G., 184, 210
Blackwell, J., 158, 172
Blackwell, S., 322, 326, 340
Blanchard, R. R., 233, 247
Bluth, L. F., 193, 204
Bobbitt, B. R., 346, 347, 368
Boder, E., 304, 337, 339
Boersma, F. J., 158, 169, 180, 205
Bopp, M. J., 274, 293
Borkowski, J. G., 147, 149, 150, 151, 154,
    155, 159, 161, 162, 164, 166, 167, 168,
    169, 170, 171, 177, 202, 209, 227
Bos, C., 155, 170, 180, 204
Boshes, B., 259, 271
Botkin, P. T., 280, 292
Boudreau, Y., 332, 339
Bower, G. H., 239, 247
Bowers, D., 311, 319
Bowyer, P. M., 15, 27, 60
Boydstun, J., 332, 339
Bradley, L., 59
Bransford, J. D., 9, 27, 84, 59, 101, 157,
    172, 176, 177, 178, 179, 180, 187, 188,
    190, 192, 201, 205, 211
Broden, M., 267, 269

Brooks, P. H., 192, 204
Brooks, R., 321, 340
Brown, A. L., 8, 17, 30, 84, 85, 87, 101,
    102, 147, 149, 153, 157, 159, 170, 172,
    178, 179, 199, 202, 203, 205, 209, 219
Brown, B. S., 264, 269
Bruck, M., 280, 289, 291
Bruininks, V. L., 273, 291
Bruning, R. H., 195, 204
Bruno, R. M., 277, 291
Bryan, J. H., 64, 70, 79, 274, 291
Bryan, T. H., 159, 172, 180, 209, 253, 259,
    264, 269, 274, 276, 277, 281, 282, 291
Bryant, P. E., 15, 27, 59
Büchel, F., 166, 168, 169, 178, 205
Buck, R., 298, 299
Buenning, M., 180, 211
Buium, N., 187, 189, 205
Burney, L., 222, 229
Bursuck, W. D., 282, 291
Butkowsky, I. S., 158, 19, 170, 180, 205
Butterfield, E. C., 195, 205, 266, 269
Byrne, B., 19, 20, 27, 59, 108, 111

C

Cable, G. W., 192, 211
Cairns, R. B., 233, 237, 247
Calfee, R. C., 12, 15, 27, 59, 62
Calles, R., 265, 269
Cambell, S., 67, 79
Camperell, K., 9, 29, 61
Campione, J. C., 8, 17, 30, 84, 85, 101, 147,
    149, 153, 157, 170, 172, 178, 203, 205
Canter, A., 68, 69, 78, 79
Capelli, C. A., 180, 205
Caplan, P. J., 234, 239, 248
Capps, C., 15, 30
Carey, L., 15, 29, 60
Carnine, D., 182, 204, 205
Carroll, J. B., 59
Cartelli, L., 274, 291
Carter, B., 15, 28, 60
Cavanaugh, J. C., 101, 147, 148, 154, 167,
    168, 170
Ceci, S. J., 13, 14, 21, 24, 27, 84, 59, 101,
    107, 108, 111, 237, 247, 365, 366
Cermak, L., 330, 337, 339
Cermak, S., 330, 339
Chabot, R. J., 60
Chaffin, R., 106, 111

Chall, J. S., 23, 27
Chandler, M. J., 280, 291
Chapman, J. W., 158, 169
Chapman, R. S., 12, 27, 59, 62
Cheatam, D., 324, 341
Cherry, R., 329, 339
Chesney, G. C., 365, 367
Chi, M. T. H., 84, 99, 101, 104, 105, 112, 235, 247
Childs, B., 335, 341
Christenson, S., 262, 272
Christiansen, J. L., 258, 270
Christiansen, J., 258, 270
Clements, S. D., 63, 79, 321, 322, 339
Clifford, M., 253, 270
Cohen, J., 74, 75, 79
Cohen, P., 74, 75, 79
Cohen, R. L., 180, 205
Cohen, R. M., 239, 249
Cohen, S. B., 71, 81, 159, 171, 328, 341
Cole, C., 259, 271
Coles, G., 66, 68, 79
Collins, A. M., 86, 101, 104, 111
Collins, G. I., 350, 366
Connors, 335, 336, 339
Cook, L. K., 195, 200, 201, 205
Cook, W., 265, 269
Copeland, A. P., 71, 79, 260, 269
Cosden, M., 277, 293
Courchesne, E., 349, 364, 367
Covington, M. V., 155, 170
Cowen, R. J., 69, 79
Craighead, W. E., 147, 172
Craik, F. I. M., 176, 177, 207
Cram, P. M., 255, 272
Crause, M. B., 62
Crawford, H. T., 371, 373
Cromer, W., 8, 27, 193, 194, 205, 212
Cronbach, L., 75, 79
Cronnell, B., 58
Crowder, R. G., 19, 27
Cruickshank, W. M., 237, 247, 259, 269
Crump, W. D., 274, 292
Cullen, J. L., 180, 205
Cundick, B. P., 181, 194, 211
Curtis, M. E., 106, 111
Cykowski, F., 185, 208

D

D'Alonzo, B. J., 256, 269
Dainer, K., 323, 335, 336, 339

Dallago, M. L. P., 17, 27, 85, 101, 179, 181, 205
Danilovics, P., 185, 208
Dansereau, D. F., 201, 205
Das, J. P., 58
Davids, A., 67, 81
Davidson, B. J., 61
Davidson, P. S., 371, 373
Davidson, P., 59, 323, 339
Davis, J., 74, 79
Dawson, M. M., 71, 79
Day, M., 266, 271
Deffner, N. D., 187, 206, 217, 229
Deikel, S., 328, 339
Dejung, J., 277, 292
DeKosky, S. T., 311, 319
Delaney, H. D., 217, 230
DeLoach, T. F., 264, 269
Deluca, D., 330, 339
Dempster, F. N., 347, 367
Denkla, M. P., 15, 21, 27, 304, 305, 306, 312, 313, 315, 319, 337, 339
Denney, D. R., 67, 79
Dennis-Rounds, J., 203, 209
DeRose, T. M., 192, 205
DeSetto, L., 11, 30
Deshler, D. D., 203, 205, 267, 269
DeSoto, I. L., 110, 111
DeSoto, L. B., 110, 111
DeVellis, R., 347, 368
Dickinson, D., 181, 210
Dickstein, E. B., 279, 280, 291
Diekel, S. M., 70, 79
Digdon, N., 193, 206
DiLillo, V., 59
Dilingofski, M. S., 194, 206
DiMatteo, M. R., 276, 293
Doctorow, M. J., 201, 206
Doehring, D. G., 59
Doleys, D., 274, 291
Donchin, E., 343, 349, 365, 367
Donohue, M., 110, 111, 159, 172, 180, 209, 274, 277, 281, 292, 293
Doster, J., 274, 291
Douglas, V. I., 67, 71, 79, 149, 154, 156, 157, 162, 163, 169, 170
Doyle, P. H., 260, 270
Doyle, R. B., 68, 79, 323, 324, 331, 339
Drake, C., 330, 339
Dretzke, B. J., 184, 208
Drumbrell, S., 255, 270

Dudley-Marling, C. G., 243, 247
Dugas, J. L., 347, 367, 368
Duncan-Johnson, C., 349, 367
Dundon, W., 240, 248
Durkin, D., 9, 27, 198, 206, 221, 229
Dweck, C. S., 158, 165, 171
Dykman, R. A., 15, 26, 63, 65, 79, 280, 291, 322, 323, 324, 325, 326, 327, 330, 332, 333, 334, 336, 338, 339, 350, 367

E

Earl, J. M., 264, 269
Eccles, J., 227, 229
Edmondson, B., 277, 292
Edwall, G., 64, 81, 321, 341
Ehri, L. C., 68, 79, 59, 187, 206, 217, 229
Elardo, P. T., 280, 291
Elkins, 64, 80
Elliott-Faust, D., 202, 206, 209
Emery, J. E., 277, 292
Engelmann, S., 25, 27, 182, 204
Eskins, S., 67, 79
Esveldt, K. C., 253, 270
Evans, R. A., 194, 206
Eysenck, M., 298, 299

F

Fabian, J. J., 68, 79
Farmer, A., 180, 211
Farnham-Diggory, S., 213, 229
Faw, H. D., 195, 206
Feagans, L., 156, 172, 253, 254, 256, 260, 270, 274, 293
Federal Register, 234, 247
Feingold, B. F., 255, 270
Felcan, J., 274, 291
Ferguson, H. B., 255, 272
Ferrara, R. A., 84, 85, 101, 153, 170, 178, 203, 205
Ferretti, R. P., 150, 169
Fiedorowicz, A. M., 59
Filip, D., 155, 170, 180, 204
Fincham, F., 159, 171, 280, 292
Finger, E., 11, 12, 13, 14, 29
Firth, I., 12, 27, 59
Fischer, F. W., 15, 19, 28, 29, 60, 62
Fisher, S., 274, 293
Fisk, J. L., 305, 319
Flavell, J. H., 85, 101, 149, 156, 171, 178, 206, 224, 229, 280, 283, 292

Fleir, R. E., 346, 347, 367
Fleisher, L. S., 59
Ford, J., 349, 350, 354, 364, 367
Ford, M. H., 239, 249
Forness, S. R., 253, 270
Forrest, T., 274, 293
Forrest-Pressley, D., 9, 27, 179, 180, 195, 200, 202, 206, 209
Foth, D., 85, 102, 181, 212
Fowler, C. A., 19, 20, 29, 30, 60, 62, 59
Fox, B., 15, 27
Fozard, J. L., 345, 350, 366
Franks, J. J., 176, 177, 179, 187, 188, 189, 190, 201, 205, 211
French, J., 60, 304, 319
Friedman, M. P., 70, 79
Friedman, M., 328, 339
Fry, C. L., 280, 292
Fry, M. A., 59, 192, 207
Furby, L., 75, 79
Futterman, R., 227, 229

G

Gabourie, I., 16, 31, 107, 112, 181, 212
Gaddes, W., 254, 255, 261, 270
Gaffney, J., 182, 185, 208, 211, 217, 230
Gainotti, G., 311, 319
Gajar, A. H., 71, 80, 159, 171
Galkin, T. W., 371, 373
Gallagher, J., 99, 101, 147, 148, 171
Gallagher, M. C., 199, 209
Galpin, R., 329, 340
Gandara, P., 5, 28
Gardner, W. P., 178, 210
Garner, R., 9, 27, 59, 180, 206
Garrett, M. K., 274, 292
Garson, C., 162, 170
Gebben, G., 72, 81
Geer, J. H., 158, 172
Gelzheiser, L. M., 147, 148, 171, 202, 206
Gerber, A., 111
Gerber, P. J., 277, 292
Gerdt, C., 239, 249
Ghatala, E., 160, 161, 171, 179, 202, 210
Gibson, E. J., 73, 79, 59
Gibson, J. J., 59
Gillies, L. A., 200, 206
Gillund, G., 362, 367
Gilmore, E. C., 312, 319
Gilmore, J. V., 312, 319
Giordani, B., 11, 29, 61

Glass, R. M., 258, 270
Gleitman, L., 15, 29, 61
Glock, M. D., 192, 211
Glover, J. A., 195, 204
Glushko, R. J., 59
Goding, M. J., 274, 293
Goff, S. B., 227, 229
Goldberg-Warter, J., 330, 339
Golding, J., 238, 248
Goldman, P. S., 371, 373
Goldman, R. L., 69, 79
Goldman, S. R., 12, 27, 29, 61
Goldman, T., 18, 30, 154, 173, 181, 212,
    245, 249
Goldman, T., 84, 102
Goldstein, D., 237, 238, 240, 241, 245, 248,
    249
Golinkoff, R., 15, 28, 68, 81
Gomer, F. E., 350, 367
Goodman, K. S., 7, 28
Gorin, L., 202, 208
Goyen, J., 60
Graves, K. J., 244, 245, 248
Gump, P., 260, 270
Guralnik, D. B., 281, 292
Guthrie, J. T., 59, 62, 335, 341
Guttentag, R., 68, 80, 222, 229

H

Hagen, J. W., 71, 72, 147, 148, 149, 154,
    171, 179, 181, 209, 328, 340, 331
Haith, M. M., 68, 80
Halcomb, C. G., 66, 79, 323, 324, 331, 339
Halfgott, J., 60
Hall, J. A., 276, 293
Hall, J. W., 5, 20, 28, 60, 175, 184, 207,
    237, 249
Hall, M., 69, 80
Hall, R. V., 267, 269
Hallahan, D., 64, 71, 79, 81, 154, 155, 156,
    159, 171, 173, 179, 211, 234, 237, 247,
    248, 267, 270, 276, 292, 321, 327
Hamilton, V., 298, 299
Hammill, D. D., 12, 28, 234, 248
Hansen, C. L., 17, 28
Hansen, J., 197, 206
Hanson, D., 59
Harber, J. R., 192, 193, 206
Hardin, V. B., 69, 79
Haring, M. J., 192, 207
Haring, N. G., 258, 270

Harris, A., 337, 340
Harris, G. J., 346, 347, 367
Harris, K. S., 60
Harris, W. J., 192, 193, 211, 254, 264, 270,
    276, 294
Hart, S. S., 222, 229
Harter, M., 335, 336, 340
Harter, S., 224, 229
Harvey, N., 69, 79
Hasher, L., 236, 237, 247, 347, 367
Hatcher, C. W., 196, 210
Hayden, B. S., 69, 78
Hayden, D., 337, 341
Hayes, B. L., 183, 207
Hazel, J., 266, 267, 271
Heaven, R., 108, 110, 112
Hebben, N., 329, 340
Hebert, M., 280, 289, 291
Hecaen, H., 305, 319
Heddle, M., 60
Heilman, K., 298, 299
Heilman, M., 311, 313, 319
Heisel, B. E., 202, 210
Helfgott, J., 16, 28
Hellman, H., 256, 270
Henderson, J. G., 240, 248
Henek, T., 274, 291
Henker, B., 165, 171, 173
Herrmann, D., 106, 111, 112, 346, 363, 367
Hershey, M. M., 181, 210
Herzog, A., 180, 209
Hess, D., 323, 339
Hewett, F., 256, 270
Higbee, J. L., 181, 194, 211
Higbee, K. L., 187, 207
Higgins, E. T., 283, 284, 292
Hillyard, S. A., 358, 367
Hink, R., 358, 367
Hinshaw, S. P., 165, 171
Hobbs, G., 255, 270
Hodges, C. A., 198, 207
Hogaboam, T., 11, 12, 13, 14, 19, 27, 28,
    29, 60, 61
Holcomb, P., 332, 334, 336, 339, 349, 367
Holmes, D. R., 11, 28
Hope, D. G., 184, 210
Hopkins, W., 349, 350, 354, 364, 367
Horowitz, E. C., 280, 292
Horton, D. L., 236, 237, 248
Houck, D. G., 18, 30, 85, 102, 239, 249,
    323, 341
Hoving, K., 345, 367

Howell, E. A., 62
Hsu, C., 11, 30, 62
Hughes, C., 15, 29, 61
Hughes, P. C., 256, 271
Humphreys, M. S., 5, 20, 28, 60, 175, 237, 249
Hunt, E., 108, 112
Hunter, E., 332, 333, 340
Hyde, T. S., 176, 177, 207

I

Iano, R. S., 265, 271
Ingle, M. J., 218, 230
Israel, J. B., 365, 367
Ito, H. R., 258, 270
Ivey, C., 179, 181, 212
Izard, C. E., 233, 248

J

Jackson, M. D., 106, 112
Jacobs, V. W., 68, 79
Jacoby, L., 176, 177, 207
Jarvis, P. E., 280, 292
Jenkins, J. J., 176, 177, 207
Jenkins, J. R., 59
Johnson, D. J., 4, 28
John, E. R., 372, 373
Johnsen, E. P., 180, 211
Johnson, C. S., 59
Johnson, D. D., 183, 207
Johnson, D. S., 158, 171
Johnson, J., 261, 270
Johnson, L., 332, 340
Johnson, M. K., 192, 205
Johnson, N. S., 17, 28, 218, 229
Johnston, V. S., 349, 367
Jones, B. F., 184, 201, 207
Jones, W., 198, 200, 202, 212, 219, 230
Jordan, C., 158, 172
Juola, J. F., 60, 362, 366

K

Kaczala, C. M., 227, 229
Kahneman, D., 65, 80, 235, 239, 248
Kail, R. V., 71, 72, 80, 238, 248, 328, 340
Kaman, M., 11, 30
Kandel, G. K., 62
Karp, J., 69, 81

Katz, L., 60
Katz, R. B., 19, 28
Kauffman, J. M., 71, 81, 154, 155, 173, 179, 211, 234, 241, 243, 247, 248, 276, 292, 328, 340, 341
Kaufman, K. F., 267, 270
Keating, D. P., 346, 347, 368
Kee, D. W., 218, 230
Keen, R. H., 60
Keffe, F., 332, 340
Kellas, G., 347, 367, 368
Kendall, P. C., 167, 172
Kennedy, B. A., 202, 207
Kenney, T. J., 69, 80
Keogh, B., 5, 28, 64, 80, 110, 112, 285, 292, 321, 323, 325, 340
Kershner, J. R., 239, 248
Kerst, S. M., 194, 206
King, D. R., 254, 264, 270
Kinsbourne, M., 234, 239, 248, 255, 271, 337, 340
Kirk, S. A., 4, 28, 64, 80, 147, 148, 171, 234, 248
Kistner, J. A., 159, 171
Kitamura, S., 11, 30, 62
Kliegl, R., 61
Klorman, R., 323, 339
Koehler, J. A., 58
Komm, R., 338, 340
Konick, D. S., 345, 367
Koppell, B., 64, 80, 349, 350, 354, 364, 367
Kosteski, D. M., 238, 245, 248
Kovacs, M., 240, 248
Kovnin, J. S., 260, 270
Krebs, E. W., 201, 211
Kretsch, M. S., 258, 271
Kreutzer, M. A., 156, 171
Krueger, L. E., 60
Kruger, B., 329, 339
Kukish, K. S., 68, 81
Kunzinger, E. L., 99, 101
Kurz, B. E., 150, 151, 155, 161, 162, 166, 170

L

Laberge, D., 4, 9, 10, 22, 25, 28, 60
LaGreca, A. M., 277, 282, 289, 294
Lahey, B. B., 244, 245, 248
Lambert, N., 322, 340
Landis, T. T., 346, 363, 367

Lane, D. M., 71, 80
Lange, G., 92, 101
Larsen, S. C., 234, 248
Laskey, E. Z., 70, 80
Lea, S. E. G., 107, 111
Leach, E., 277, 292
Leal, L., 222, 229
Lee, S., 11, 30, 62
Leed, C., 265, 269
Leigh, J. E., 234, 248
Leland, H., 277, 292
Lentz, R., 192, 193, 207
Lenz, B. K., 267, 269
Leonard, C., 156, 171
Lerner, J., 253, 255, 270
Lesgold, A., 9, 17, 29, 61, 192, 207
Levie, W. H., 192, 193, 207
Levin, H., 59
Levin, J. R., 8, 28, 160, 171, 176, 179, 181,
    182, 183, 184, 185, 186, 187, 191, 192,
    193, 194, 197, 200, 201, 202
Levin, K. M., 183, 207
Levine, M., 321, 340
Levy, F., 255, 270
Lewis, M., 233, 248
Liben, L. S., 245, 249
Liberman, A. M., 60
Liberman, I. Y., 10, 11, 12, 15, 16, 19, 20,
    24, 28, 29, 60, 62, 59
Liberty, C., 97, 102
Licht, B. G., 147, 157, 158, 159, 171, 173,
    222, 229
Lindamood, C. J., 15, 27, 371, 373
Lindamood, P. C., 15, 27, 371, 373
Lindauer, B. K., 9, 29
Linden, M., 200, 208
Lindgren, S. D., 108, 109, 112
Lindolm, B. W., 274, 294
Lipson, M. Y., 178, 209
Litcher, J. H., 16, 28
Littlefield, J., 189, 206
Lockhart, L., 201, 211
Lodico, M., 160, 171, 206, 208
Loe, D. C., 238, 249
Loftus, E. F., 86, 101, 104, 111
Loper, A. B., 156, 171
Lorsback, T. C., 14, 30
Lortie, D. C., 263, 270
Lovegrove, W. J., 58, 60
Lucker, G. W., 11, 30, 62
Lund, A. M., 237, 249

Luria, A. R., 305, 319
Lyle, J. G., 60

M

Maggiore, R., 69, 71, 81
Maggs, A., 182, 204
Maheady, L., 277, 278, 284, 292
Maier, R. E., 345, 367
Maier, S. F., 158, 172
Maisto, A. A., 346, 350, 366, 368
Maitland, G., 277, 278, 284, 292
Major-Kingsley, 5, 28, 64, 80, 285, 292
Malmgren, I., 16, 31, 107, 112, 181, 212
Mancini, G., 58
Mandler, G., 87, 100, 101
Mandler, J. M., 17, 28, 218, 229
Manis, F. R., 10, 11, 28, 29, 60, 61, 105,
    112
Mann, L., 251, 270
Mann, V. A., 16, 19, 20, 24, 28, 60
Margolis, J., 64, 80, 321, 323, 325, 340
Mark, L. S., 19, 29, 62
Markman, E. M., 180, 202, 205, 208
Marks, C. B., 201, 206
Marsh, G. E., 258, 263, 270, 271
Martello, J., 239, 249
Martin, C. J., 179, 208
Marton, P., 162, 170
Mason, J. M., 60
Mason, M., 60
Massaro, D. W., 60
Masson, M. E. J., 157, 171
Masters, J. C., 239, 244, 249
Mastropieri, M. A., 179, 181, 182, 183, 184,
    208, 211, 217, 218, 230
Mattis, S., 60, 304, 319
Matz, R., 192, 211
May, J., 326, 335, 336, 341
Mayer, R. E., 195, 200, 201, 205
McCall, R., 169
McCarthy, G., 349, 364, 368
McCaughey, M. W., 60
McCauley, C., 347, 368
McClelland, J. L., 99, 89, 101, 106, 112,
    344, 368
McCloone, B., 182, 185, 208, 217, 230
McClure, S., 253, 254, 258, 260, 270, 274,
    293
McCormick, C. B., 12, 29, 184, 185, 190,
    201, 208

McCray, D., 322, 323, 338, 339
McDaniel, M. A., 184, 208
McGettigan, J. F., 265, 271
McGivern, J. E., 183, 201, 208, 209
McGrady, H. J., 259, 269
McGrady, H., 274, 291
McGraw, W., 188, 201, 211
McGuinness, D., 369, 373
McIntyre, C., 322, 326, 340
McIntyre, J. S., 59
McKean, S., 157, 172
McKeever, W. F., 11, 28
McKinney, J. D., 156, 172, 196, 210, 253, 254, 258, 260, 270, 274, 293
McNellis, K. L., 73, 77, 80, 103, 104
McNutt, C., 234, 248
Meichenbaum, D., 147, 165, 172, 245, 249
Messerer, J., 253, 270
Mesulam, M. M., 311, 319
Meyers, A. W., 147, 172
Meyers, G., 253, 270
Mezynski, K. J., 176, 189, 205
Michael, R., 323, 339
Michalson, L., 233, 248
Midgley, C., 227, 229
Milberg, W., 329, 340
Miller, D. J., 202, 207
Miller, G., 202, 209
Mills, C. B., 236, 237, 248
Mitchel, A., 324, 337, 338, 341
Mitchel, D., 150, 169
Mitts, B., 267, 269
Moely, B. E., 17, 27, 85, 101, 179, 181, 205
Mohs, R., 349, 350, 354, 364, 367
Mondani, M. S., 70, 80
Montgomery-Kasik, M., 256, 258, 263, 265, 270
Moore, D., 192, 210
Moore, W. A., 69, 81
Morais, J., 15, 16, 20, 26, 29, 60
Morris, C. D., 157, 172, 180, 209
Morrison, F., 10, 11, 29, 60, 61, 104, 105, 112
Muehl, S., 59
Mulberg, W., 69, 80
Murphy, D. L., 239, 249
Murphy, H., 179, 181, 212
Murray, M., 322, 326, 340
Musso, M., 335, 336, 340

Myers, M., 180, 209
Myklebust, H. R., 4, 28, 259, 271, 337, 340

N

Nagy, I., 11, 29, 61
Nakamura, G. V., 17, 31, 184, 201, 210
Naus, M. J., 61, 92, 97, 99, 102, 346, 368
Neimark, E., 152, 172
Newcomer, P. L., 12, 29, 258, 271
Newell, A., 84, 101
Newman, R. S., 147, 148, 154, 171, 179, 181, 209
Niaura, R., 326, 341
Nichols, J. G., 158, 172
Noel, M. N., 280, 293
Noland, E., 323, 324, 326, 340
Norman, D. A., 178, 209

O

O'Donnell, R. E., 350, 367
O'Leary, K. D., 256, 267, 270, 271, 371, 373
O'Leary, S. G., 371, 373
O'Sullivan, J. T., 151, 172, 177, 202, 209
Oaken, R., 8, 29
Oakley, D. D., 8, 17, 30, 157, 172
Offenbach, S., 329, 340
Oglesby, D. M., 65, 79, 322, 323, 334, 336, 338, 340, 350, 367
Olson, D., 259, 271
Olson, R. K., 61
Oltman, P., 69, 81
Omori-Gordon, 5, 28, 64, 80, 285, 292
Orlando, C., 60
Ornstein, P. A., 61, 92, 97, 99, 102, 346, 368
Orton, S. T., 4, 29
Osser, R., 59
Ott, J. M., 256, 271
Owen, R. W., 274, 293
Owings, R. A., 157, 172, 180, 187, 188, 201, 209, 211
Oxley, B., 261, 269

P

Pace, A. J., 68, 80
Pachella, R. G., 362, 368
Pack, M., 239, 249
Padawer, W. J., 167, 172
Palincsar, A. S., 102, 160, 172, 199, 202, 209, 219, 230
Pany, D., 59

Paris, S. G., 9, 29, 84, 102, 178, 180, 209
Parry, P., 162, 170
Parsons, J. E., 158, 172
Pascual-Leone, J., 235, 249
Patel, P. G., 59
Patten, J., 329, 340
Patten, M. D., 239, 249
Paul, G., 240, 241, 249
Pavlidis, G. T., 61
Pearl, R., 159, 172, 180, 209, 274, 277, 281, 293
Pearlstone, Z., 87, 100, 102
Pearson, P. D., 9, 29, 61, 183, 196, 197, 199, 206, 207, 209, 210
Pelham, W. E., 64, 70, 71, 72, 78, 81, 253, 271, 326, 327, 328, 329, 340, 341
Pennington, B. F., 239, 249
Perfetti, C. A., 4, 8, 11, 12, 13, 14, 15, 17, 19, 20, 22, 27, 28, 29, 60, 61, 106, 107, 110, 112
Perfetto, G. A., 176, 205
Perlmutter, M., 101, 189, 206
Peter, B., 69, 81
Peters, E. E., 185, 209, 218, 230
Peters, J. E., 63, 79, 321, 322, 339
Peters, K. G., 65, 71, 79, 157, 170
Petersen, G. A., 157, 172, 180, 209
Pfefferbaum, A., 350, 368
Phillips, E. L., 258, 270
Piaget, J., 280, 293
Pianta, R., 262, 272
Pick, A., 59
Picton, T., 358, 367
Pignot, E., 16, 20, 26
Pihl, R., 326, 328, 329, 341
Piralli, P. L., 86, 101
Pittelman, S. D., 183, 207
Platt, J., 297, 299
Podemski, R. S., 263, 271
Poplin, M. S., 264, 269
Powell, J. S., 4, 30
Prescott, B., 274, 292
Pressley, M., 151, 152, 153, 160, 171, 172, 176, 179, 182, 183, 184, 186, 187, 191, 193, 195, 197, 200, 201, 202, 203
Preston, M., 335, 336, 341
Price, B. J., 258, 270
Prilliman, D., 274, 293
Pritchard, W., 349, 368
Puckett, D., 277, 293

Q, R

Quay, L., 71, 81
Rabinovitch, R. D., 234, 249
Rabinowitz, M., 102, 105, 112
Rader, N., 73, 79
Randall, D., 67, 81
Raphael, T. E., 196, 210
Rapin, I., 60, 304, 314, 319
Raskin, E., 69, 81
Ratzeberg, J., 259, 269
Raven, J. C., 347, 368
Rawlings, D., 258, 271
Readence, J. E., 192, 210
Redfield, D. L., 195, 210
Reeve, R. E., 71, 79, 237, 248
Reid, H. P., 5, 28, 64, 80, 285, 292
Reid, M. K., 150, 151, 164, 166, 168, 170, 172, 223, 227, 230
Reis, R., 9, 27, 180, 206
Resnick, L. B., 147, 172
Rholes, W. S., 158, 172
Richman, B., 59
Richman, L. C., 108, 109, 112
Rickards, J. P., 196, 210
Riding, R. J., 192, 210
Ries, R., 59
Ringstrom, M. D., 107, 111
Roberge, L. P., 16, 28
Robinson, A., 239, 249
Robinson, F. P., 200, 210
Rogers, P. L., 276, 293
Rogoff, B., 178, 210
Rohwer, W. D., 176, 179, 180, 192, 193, 202, 210, 211
Rokeach, M., 265, 271
Rose, M. C., 181, 194, 211
Rosenbaum, A., 256, 271
Rosenthal, R. H., 65, 81, 235, 249, 276, 293, 323, 324, 326, 330, 332, 333, 336, 337, 341
Rosinski, R. R., 68, 81
Rosner, J., 15, 29, 61
Ross, A. O., 71, 81, 259, 271, 328, 341
Ross, E. D., 311, 319
Ross, K. A., 202, 210
Rosvold, H. E., 371, 373
Roth, S., 4, 8, 22, 29
Roth, W., 349, 350, 354, 364, 367
Rothkopf, E. Z., 195, 211

Rourke, B., 61, 305, 315, 319
Rousseau, E. W., 195, 210
Routh, D. K., 15, 27, 321, 324, 329, 340, 341
Royer, J. M., 192, 211
Rozin, P., 15, 29, 61
Ruble, D., 158, 172
Rublevich, B., 60
Rudel, R. G., 15, 21, 27, 305, 313, 319, 324, 326, 341
Rugel, R. P., 241, 332, 333, 336, 337, 341, 249
Rumelhart, D. E., 99, 89, 101
Rutledge, L., 67, 81
Rutter, M., 61
Ryan, E. B., 62, 151, 163, 164, 172, 170, 223, 230
Ryan, M., 255, 270
Ryckman, D., 274, 293

S

Saarni, C., 284, 293
Sabatino, D. A., 68, 81, 255, 271, 327, 337, 341
Safer, D., 322, 341
Salzman, L., 323, 339
Sampson, E., 256, 271
Samuel, J., 181, 210
Samuels, S. J., 4, 9, 10, 12, 22, 25, 28, 29, 30, 60, 64, 81, 321, 341
Sandoval, J., 322, 340
Sanfilippo-Cohn, S., 241, 246, 248, 249
Sanna, S. O., 156, 171
Santa, C. M., 61
Santostephano, S., 67, 81
Santulli, K. A., 222, 229
Sarason, I., 298, 299
Satz, P., 298, 299, 337, 341
Scanlon, D. M., 108, 112
Schadler, M., 60
Schallert, D., 192, 211
Schank, R. C., 275, 293
Schiff, D., 69, 80
Schneider, W., 346, 368
Schuldt, J., 323, 324, 326, 340
Schumaker, J. B., 203, 205, 266, 267, 269, 274, 293
Schure, M., 297, 299
Schwantes, F. M., 61

Schwent, V., 358, 367
Schwethelm, B., 149, 171
Scott, N. A., 69, 81
Scranton, T., 274, 293
Scruggs, T. E., 179, 181, 182, 183, 184, 185, 208, 211, 217, 218, 230
Seabaugh, G., 267, 271
Seidenberg, M. S., 61
Seifert, M., 59
Seligman, M. E. P., 158, 172
Semel, M. S., 62
Sergeant, J. A., 348, 368
Shallice, T., 178, 209
Shankweiler, D., 10, 11, 12, 15, 19, 20, 24, 28, 29, 60, 62, 59
Shantz, C. U., 283, 293
Shapiro, D., 349, 366
Shea, P., 19, 20, 27, 59, 108, 111
Sheare, J. B., 274, 293
Shepherd, L. A., 175, 211
Sherman, J. A., 274, 293
Shiffrin, R. M., 346, 362, 367, 368
Shonkoff, J., 321, 340
Shore, J. M., 192, 210
Short, E. J., 163, 164, 172, 223, 230
Shotel, J. R., 265, 271
Shriberg, L. K., 183, 185, 207, 208
Shuell, T. J., 181, 211
Siegel, L. S., 62, 108, 110, 112
Siegler, R., 266, 271
Siladi, D., 195, 205
Silbert, J., 182, 205
Silverman, M., 67, 81
Silverman, W. P., 346, 347, 367
Simon, D. P., 15, 29, 61
Simpson, G. B., 14, 30
Sipe, S., 348, 350, 368
Siperstein, G. N., 274, 293
Sladewski-Awig, L., 224, 230
Slaghuis, W., 60
Sleator, E. K., 348, 368
Smead, W. S., 12, 30
Smiley, S. S., 8, 17, 30, 157, 172, 179, 205
Smith, C. R., 234, 237, 249
Smith, F., 7, 30
Smith, G. A., 62
Smith, L., 255, 271
Smith, M. L., 175, 211
Smith, T. E., 74, 79, 258, 270
Snowling, M. J., 62
Snowman, J., 201, 211

Sobol, M. P., 293
Sobotka, K., 326, 335, 336, 341
Solbenblatt, J., 239, 249
Sommer, R., 261, 269
Sonnefeld, L. J., 282, 291
Spear, L., 13, 25, 30, 104, 105, 109, 112
Speilberger, C., 298, 299
Spekman, N., 280, 294
Spellacy, F., 69, 81
Spicuzza, R. J., 350, 367
Spivak, G., 297, 299
Sprague, R. L., 348, 368
Spring, C., 15, 30
Stanley, G., 62
Stanovich, K. E., 4, 8, 15, 22, 30, 58, 62
Stasio, T., 106, 112
Steger, J. A., 11, 30, 62
Stein, B. S., 9, 27, 59, 157, 172, 176, 179,
    180, 187, 188, 189, 190, 201, 205, 209,
    211
Stein, D., 237, 248
Steingart, S. K., 192, 211
Steinheiser, F., 62
Stephenson, C. B., 74, 79
Sternberg, R. J., 4, 9, 13, 22, 25, 30, 62,
    104, 105, 109, 112, 147, 151, 153, 173,
    343, 344, 348, 350, 368
Stevenson, H. W., 11, 24, 30, 62
Stigler, J. W., 11, 30, 62
Stires, L., 262, 271
Stokes, L., 371, 373
Stolz, L. M., 274, 293
Stone, C., 266, 271
Stone, W. L., 277, 282, 289, 294
Strange, J., 305, 319
Strawson, C., 10, 26
Stroop, J. R., 67, 81
Sturm, C., 274, 291
Suzuki, T., 324, 340
Swanson, J. M., 255, 271

T

Talmadge, M., 69, 80
Tanenhaus, M. K., 61
Tannhauser, M., 259, 269
Tarver, S. G., 64, 69, 71, 81, 154, 159, 171,
    173, 179, 211, 243, 247, 259, 271, 321,
    327, 328, 329, 330, 340, 341
Tausig, F. T., 255, 272
Taylor, A. M., 179, 181, 187, 211

Taylor, B. M., 9, 30
Taylor, D. A., 344, 368
Taylor, G. A., 60
Taylor, L., 267, 269
Taylor, M. B., 9, 30
Terry, B. J., 258, 271
Tharpe, R. G., 200, 211
Thatcher, R. W., 372, 373
Thomas, A., 157, 173
Thomas, C. H., 277, 294
Thurlow, M. L., 187, 211, 263, 271
Tinklenberg, J. R., 350, 367
Tinzmann, M. B., 20, 28, 60
Tobin, H., 70, 80
Tollefson, N., 180, 211
Toms-Bronowski, S., 183, 207
Torgesen, J. K., 17, 18, 30, 84, 85, 102, 147,
    154, 155, 157, 158, 173, 179, 181, 201,
    212, 238, 239, 245, 249, 278
Touliatos, J., 274, 294
Toye, A. R., 184, 210
Tracy, D. B., 180, 211
Trepanier, M. L., 155, 156, 173, 245, 249
Trieman, R., 62
Triphonas, H., 255, 272
Trites, R. L., 59, 255, 272
Tulving, E. E., 87, 100, 102
Turnure, J. E., 179, 181, 187, 189, 205, 211
Tutko, T. A., 70, 80

U, V

U.S. Office of Education, 234, 249, 275, 294
Valenstein, E., 311, 319
Valsiner, J., 233, 237, 247
Van Der Vlugt, H., 305, 319
VanCamp, S., 324, 341
Vandiver, P. L., 265, 272
Vandiver, S. C., 265, 272
Vellutino, F. R., 4, 5, 11, 12, 19, 30, 62,
    108, 110, 112, 214
Venezky, R. L., 12, 27, 59, 62
Vogel, S. A., 62
Vojir, C. P., 175, 211
VonNostrand, G., 337, 341
Vrana, F., 328, 329, 341
Vye, N. J., 9, 27, 59, 176, 188, 189, 201,
    205, 206, 211
Vytgotsky, L. S., 266, 272

W

Wagner, R. K., 9, 30, 62, 343, 348, 350, 368
Walford, G., 62
Waller, T. G., 9, 27, 62, 180, 195, 206
Walls, R., 324, 340
Walsh, M. K., 187, 212
Walters, C., 158, 172
Wang, J., 262, 272
Wanschura, P. B., 150, 173
Warner, M. M., 194, 203, 205, 212, 264, 269
Warren, D. R., 279, 290, 291
Warrington, E., 337, 340
Wasik, B., 240, 248
Waters, G. S., 61
Weber, R. M., 8, 30
Weinberg, W., 239, 249
Weiner, B., 164, 173
Weiner, M., 8, 29, 193, 194, 212
Weingartner, H., 239, 249
Weintraub, S., 311, 319
Weiss, B., 255, 272
Weissbrod, C., 260, 269
Weissler, E., 255, 272
Weld, G. L., 71, 81
Wellman, H. N., 101, 178, 206, 224, 229
Werfelman, M., 19, 28
Wertsch, J., 266, 271
West, R. F., 8, 30, 62
Whalen, C. K., 165, 171, 173
Wheeler, R., 274, 291
Whitman, R. D., 69, 80, 329, 340
Wickens, C. D., 365, 367
Wicklund, D. A., 60
Wiig, E. H., 62, 276, 294
Wilce, L. S., 68, 79, 187, 206, 217, 229
Wilgen, J. S., 274, 293
Williams, J. I., 9, 16, 30, 255, 272

Willows, D. M., 159, 170, 180, 205, 327, 341
Wilson, K. P., 20, 28, 100
Wilson, K. P., 237, 249
Wisniewski, N. M., 71, 79
Witkin, H., 69, 81
Witryol, S. L., 99, 101
Wittmer, D. D., 264, 265, 272
Witton, N., 255, 270
Wittrock, M. C., 191, 200, 201, 208, 212
Wixson, K. K., 178, 209
Wolford, G., 20, 30, 62
Wong, B. Y. L., 8, 17, 31, 85, 102, 155, 173, 179, 180, 181, 196, 198, 200, 201, 202, 212, 219, 230, 278, 280, 294
Wong, R., 85, 102, 181, 212, 278, 280, 294
Wonnacott, C. A., 196, 210
Wood, M. E., 275, 294
Woodhill, J., 255, 270
Woody, C. D., 353, 368
Worden, P. E., 5, 9, 16, 18, 31, 84, 87, 102, 107, 112, 181, 212, 218, 219, 224, 230
Worthen, D., 8, 17, 30, 157, 172
Wright, J. W., 280, 292

Y

Ysseldyke, J. E., 68, 81, 262, 263, 271, 272, 327, 341
Yule, W., 61

Z

Zacks, R. T., 236, 237, 247, 347, 367
Zentall, S., 298, 299
Zentall, T., 298, 299
Zingraf, S. A., 277, 292
Zupan, B. A., 167, 172

Subject Index

A

Academic performance, 125, 240, *see also* Achievement
Academic skills, 308, 310, 311, 313, 314
Achievement, 11, 22, 34, 63, 115, 116, 121, 125, 126, 127, 128, 130, 132, 133, 134, 135, 136, 137, 139, 140, 223, 225, 226, 241, 243, 254, 258, 265, 266, 268, 274, 322
Acromegalics, 370
Additive factors model, 344
Adjustment reaction of childhood, 242
Adolescence, 310
Aggression, 253
Alertness, 323, *see also* Attention
Analogies, 48, *see also* Reasoning
Aphasia, 305
Aptitude, 125, 128, 133, 140
Associative learning, 176
Attention, 63–81, 92, 181, 220, 235–236, 251, 256, 266, 321, 323, 337–338, 365
  arousal, 64, 65, 66, 77, 235, 239, 251, 256, 298, 321, 323, 330, *see also* Autonomic arousal and Electrical activity of the brain
  capacity, 97, 98, 222, 235, 236, 237, 238, 239, 241, 243, 244, 245, 246, 247, 256, 296, 323, 365

Attention (*cont.*)
  deficits, 63, 64, 65, 66, 67, 77, 253, 254, 263, 276, 321, 325, 327, 337, 338, 350, 351, 365
  selection, 37, 64, 67, 68, 70, 71, 72–77, 78, 104, 220, 235, 237, 259, 323, 328, 335, 341, 349, 350
  sustained, 37, 323
  vigilance, 64, 66, 77, 321, 323–325, 326, 334, 337, 338, 370
Attention deficit disorder, 63, 77, 312, 313, 321, 322, 323, 338, 372, *see also* Attention deficits
Attribution theory, 123, 164
Attributional training, 165, 167–168, 223, 227
Auditory Analysis Test, 39
Auditory perceptual deficits, 335
Autism, 298
Automatic processing, 6, 9, 12, 13, 21, 22, 23, 24, 45, 48, 58, 86, 97, 98, 105, 151, 153, 221, 236–237, 296, 346, 363
  frequency of occurence, 236
  spatial location, 236
  temporal information, 236
Autonomic arousal, 332–334, *see also* Cortical arousal
Axes model [of LD], 305

B

Bannatyne profile, 241
Basal ganglia, 370
Behavioral disturbance, 253, 254, 255
Bender Visual Motor Gestalt Test, 68, 72
Bender Visual Motor Gestalt Test (Background
    Interference Procedure), 68, 73, 75,
    76, 77
Biochemical imbalance, 115
Bottom-up processing, 5, 20, 21, 22, 24, 106,
    108, see also Language, Reading,
    and Memory
Brain damage, 83, 234, 254, 264, 265, 267,
    305, 311, 325, 329, 335, 370, 371

C

Categorization, 181
Causal attribution, 134
Children Depression Inventory, 240
Children Embedded Figures Test [CEFT], 69
Classroom behavior, 256
Classroom environment, 255–256, 257, 259,
    260, 268
Classroom environment (seating arrangement),
    261–262
Cognitive Abilities Test, 126, 128, 129, 225
Cognitive behavior modification, 147, 150,
    153, 168
Cognitive deficits, 35, 238, 343, 366
Computer simulation, 89
Conceptual knowledge, 86, 95, 100
Conduct disorder, 242
Coping skills, 133, 140
Cortical arousal, 334–337, see also Electrical
    brain activity
Cross-modal integration, 37
Cultural-familial deprivation, 116

D

Daily living skills [in LDs], 253
Decoding skills, 2, 12, 306
Depression, 234, 235, 239, 240, 242, 244,
    246, 296
Development of LD, 105, 315
Developmental delays, 242
Developmental differences, 128, 139, 328–
    329, 346
Developmental disabilities, 321

Developmental lag, 325, 328
Distractibility, 67, 74, 253, 256, 258, 259,
    261, 263, 264, 321, 322, 323, 324,
    325, 327–332, 337, 338
Distractibility
    auditory, 329, see also Attention
    visual, 329, see also Attention
DSM II, 242
DSM III, 63, 242, 322
Dwarfism, 370
Dyscalculia, 304, 305
Dyslexia, 305, 306, 335, 337
Dysnomia, 305

E

Education, 236, see also Schooling
Effortful performance, 235
Effortful processing, 6, 9, 13, 45, 154, 155,
    236–237, 245, 296, 346, 350, 365
Effortful tasks, 238, 239
Elaborative encoding, 8, 45, 161, 176, 177,
    179, 213, 215, 217, 218, 219, 245
Elaborative encoding (mnemonic keyword
    method), 176, 177, 181–182, see
    also learning strategies
Elaborative questioning, 194–200
Electrical brain activity, 372
    EEG electrode sites, 334, 336, 337, 352,
        365
    EEG, 65, 66, 310, 346, 348, 352, 353
    electrooculogram, (EOG), 352, 353
    event related potentials (ERPs), 343, 348–
        349, 350, 352, 353, 354, 356, 357,
        358, 360, 365
    evoked potentials, 335–336
    N1, 358
    N2, 358
    P2, 358
    P3, 349–351, 353–354, 356, 358–360, 361,
        363, 365, 366
    P300, 349, 372
    scalp-recorded macro potentials, 343
Electrooculogram [EOG], see Electrical brain
    activity
Embedded Figures Test [EFT], 69, 73, 76
Emotional disturbance, 3, 116, 234, 240, 241,
    242, 265, 295, 296, 297, 322
Emotional factors [in LDs], 233, 234, 235,
    239, 241, 243, 246
Emotional responsivity, 311

Environmental demands, 314–315, 318
Environmental deprivation, 3, 322
Extrinsic reinforcers, 260

F

Fact learning, 184–186
Failure, 158, 164–165, 223, 225, 227, 254
Field dependence, 69, 321
Frono-polar cortex [FPz], 352
Frontal cortex
  dysfunction, 307, 308, 312, 316
  Fz, 352, 370, 305, 371, 372

G

Galvanic skin response, 332
Gates-MacGintie Reading Test, 126, 127, 128,
  129, 130, 133, 225
Genetic abnormalities, 239
Gilmore Oral Reading test, 312
Goal-oriented behavior, 86
Grammatical relations, 218
Graphemic processing, 42, 47
Group therapy, 312

H

Habituation [in LDs], 332, 333, 334
Hagen's Incidental Learning Paradigm, 71, 72,
  76, 78, 149
Hemispheric differences, 305
Heterogeneity [in LDs], 35
Hyperactivity, 14, 63, 64, 65, 69, 150, 162,
  165, 166, 242, 251, 253, 254–255,
  256, 259, 260–261, 268, 298, 312,
  313, 321, 322, 323, 324–325, 326–
  327, 329, 330–331, 333–334, 336,
  337–338, 348, 350, 351, 370
Hypoactivity, 324, 325, 326, 330–331, 333–
  334

I

ICD-9, 242
Imagery, 191–194, 217, 218
Impulsivity, 162, 167, 168, 261, 268, 321,
  322, 323, 324, 327
Incontinence, 371
Index of Reading Awareness, 124
Index of Selective Attention Efficiency, 71, 76

Inefficient learners, 175, 177, 179, 180, 181,
  182, 183, 184, 186, 187, 188, 192,
  193, 194, 195, 199, 200, 201, 202,
  203, 214, 218, 219, 225
Inferential processing, 155
Information processing, 36–37, 119, 235, 237,
  239, 243, 251, 260, 266, 298, 343
  decision processes, 343, 344, 345, 365
  developmental trends, 345–347
  encoding, 151, 343, 344, 345, 348, 350,
    362, 366
  parallel search, 344
  partial encoding, 362
  partial search, 362
  serial search, 19, 343, 344, *see also*
    Memory
  visual, 6, 83
Intelligence, 11, 64, 116, 147, 153, 164, 213,
  236, 296, 322, *see also* IQ and
  WISC-R
  componential model, 21
Intersensory integration, 323
Intra-individual differences, 304, 305
IQ, 4, 7, 9, 13, 16, 34, 36, 40, 42, 45, 51,
  64, 67, 68, 69, 74, 77, 103, 104,
  108, 109, 110, 125, 126, 127, 132,
  140, 225, 226, 241, 242, 243, 337,
  347, 351, 354, 365, 372, *see also*
  WISC-R and Intelligence
ISA links, 88, *see also* spreading activation

K

Kamehameha Early Education Program
  [KEEP], 200
Key Math Diagnosis Test, 242
Knowledge accessibility, 86–91, 93, 94, 95,
  96, 99, 100

L

Language aquisition, 10, 39
Language deficits, 35
Language processing, 6, 7, 39–42, 106, 107,
  110
  bottom-up, 5, 12, 13–15
  top-down, 5, 12–13
  disabilities, 304, 311, 314, 316
  language learning, 12, 13, 107, 110
Learned automatic processing, 237
Learned helplessness, 134, 137, 222, 223, 225

Learning strategies, 8, 9, 16, 73, 83, 100, 104, 118, 121, 123, 124, 128, 130, 132, 133, 136, 137, 140, 151, 153, 154, 155, 160, 161, 163, 175–212, 214, 215, 218, 221, 222, 223, 224, 225, 226, 238, 245, 278, 296, 362, *see also* Memory and Elaborative coding
  contextual, 91–96
Left hemisphere, 310
  dysfunction, 307
Letter discrimination, 42
Letter recognition, 42
Lexical access, 12
Localization, 372
Locus of control
  in LDs, 123, 134
    external, 164, 225, 226
    internal, 164, 225, 226

M

Mainstreaming, 264
Marker variables [in LDs], 4, 110, 166
Math achievement, 34, 35, 119, 240, 241, 242, 243
Memory, 10, 11, 34, 45, 48, 65, 84, 85, 150, 151, 152, 161, 214, 215, 218, 219, 220, 222, 223, 238, 266, 268, 327, 365
  bottom-up processing, 5, 17, 18–20
  capacity, 9, 38, 323, 345, 346, *see also* Attention capacity
  long term, 6, 11, 15–17, 347
  recall, 8, 17, 84, 85, 92, 95, 96, 97, 99, 119, 147–148, 149, 150, 151, 154, 155, 156, 157, 166, 167, 177, 180, 192, 195, 196, 198, 203, 219, 245
  recognition, 11, 177, 343, 362
  semantic, 83, 84, 86
  short term, 6, 16, 17, 18–20, 21, 37, 38–39, 154, 323, 343, 347
  top-down processing, 5, 15–18
Memory deficits, 35, 154, 261, 263
Memory strategies (in LDs), 2, 17, 22
Meningiomas, 371
Mental retardation, 2, 24, 175, 179, 214, 238, 252, 264, 265, 347
Metacognition, 87, 96, 116, 117, 119, 120, 123, 124, 130, 131, 132, 133, 136, 150, 151, 157, 159, 160, 161, 213, 223, 225, 238, 239, 266

Metamemory, 39, 150, 151, 152, 154, 155, 156, 161, 162, 168, 221, 238
Metamemory (aquisition procedures), 151, 153, 154, 159, 160, 161, 162
Metastrategy information, 178, 180, 202, 219, 220, 222, 223, 224, 225, 226, 227
Methylphenidate, 348
Minimal brain damage, 239, 321, 329, 336
Minnesota Teacher's Attitude Survey, 265
Mnemonics, 215, 217, 218, 219, 221, *see also* Learning strategies
Monitoring skills, 214, 215, 220, 224, 226
Mood induction techniques, 244, 255
Morphology, 41
Motivation, 115, 116, 117, 118, 121–122, 123, 124, 125, 128, 130, 131, 132, 133, 149, 150, 151, 154, 155, 156, 157–159, 160, 162, 165, 166, 168, 169, 213, 214, 219, 220, 221, 222, 223, 224, 225, 226, 227, 235, 260, 261, 267, 296
Multihandicapping condition, 255

N

N1, *see* Electrical brain activity
N2, *see* Electrical brain activity
Neonatal insult, 239
Neurological functioning, 261
Neurological impairment, 115, 237, 239, 335
Neuropsychological assessment, 254
Neuropsychological theory, 254
Normoactivity, 324, 325, 326, 330–331, 333–334

O

Occipital cortex [Oz], 352, 353, 358, 359, 360
Operant conditioning, 260
Oral language processing, 308
Orthography, 9–10, 22, 23, 24, 309
Overachievement, 126, 127, 129, 130, 132, 133, 225, 226
Overactivity, 321
Overarousal, 239

P

P2, *see* Electrical brain activity
P3, *see* Electrical brain activity[P3]
P300, *see* Electrical brain activity

Parietal Cortex [Pz], 335, 352, 353, 358, 359, 360
Parieto-frontal cortex [Cz], 352, 353, 358
Peer relationships, 314, *see also* Social skills and adjustment
Perceived Competence Scale for Children, 125
Perception, 37, 42
Perceptual deficits, 10, 276
Perceptual speed, 24
Perceptual-motor dysfunction, 115, 261
Perinatal insult, 239
Phoneme, 309
Phonemic abilities, 14–15, 19, 20–21, 39–41
Phonemic processing, 42, 330
Phonetic coding, 9, 18–20, 21, 37, 110, 217
Physical handicap, 252
Piagetian memory tasks, 245
Pituitary gland, 370
Prenatal insult, 239
Primacy effect, 154
Problem-solving, 150, 162, 220
Production deficiency [in LDs], 188
Professional orientation towards treatment [of LDs], 314–315
Proficient learners, 178–179
Profile of Nonverbal Sensitivity [PONS], 276, 277, 289
Progressive Matrices, 347
Pronunciation, 47, 49, 50, 51, 52, 217
Prose learning, 186, 198
Pseudoword naming, 42, 43
Psychiatric disturbance [in LDs], 312
Psychosocial behaviors, 252
Psychotherapeutic intervention, 243, 244, 245

R

Reaction time [of LDs], 65, 68, 73, 77, 354–355, 360, 362–366
Reading
    achievement, 4, 19, 39, 40, 116, 117, 119, 130–132, 140, 200, 225, 240, 241, 242, 245, 250
    bottom-up processing, 7
    comprehension, 2, 5, 6, 7, 8, 9, 16, 21, 22, 23, 24, 39, 45–47, 58, 95, 119, 124, 126, 128, 130, 131, 132, 133, 138, 140, 141, 193, 194, 197, 198, 199, 215, 219, 223, 225, 226, 312
    contextual sensitivity, 7, 9, 10, 20, 22, 24, 45, 119

Reading (*cont.*)
    decoding, 5, 6, 7, 9, 20, 21, 22, 24, 193, 199, 200
    graphic properties, 42–43
    interactive compensatory models, 21
    meaning based facilitation, 12
    orthographic properties, 42, 43, 47
    phonological properties, 42, 45, 48
    top-down processing, 6–10
Reading abilities, 42–45, 76, 223, 225, 365
Reading difficulties, 36, 233–234
Reading disabilities, 2–25, 33–54, 100, 105, 106, 108, 110, 123, 218, 304, 329, 348, 350–351, 353, 354, 355, 356, 357, 358, 359, 360, 362, 363, 364, 365, 366, 371
Reading retardation [primary], 234
Reading retardation [secondary], 234
Reasoning [analogical], 24
Reasoning [inferential], 119, 312
Recency effect, 154
Referential communication, 280
Rehearsal, 17, 18, 38–39, 47, 84, 85, 92, 97, 98, 99, 100, 150, 151, 152, 154, 155, 156, 167, 178, 179, 180, 181, 222, 238, 245, 296, *see also* Learning strategies
Remediation [synthetic-phonetic approach], 9, *see also* Schooling remediation
Residualized Gain Scores, 74
Retrieval cues, 8
Reversal errors, 42
Right hemisphere, 370
Right hemisphere (dysfunction), 307, 308, 310–311, 314, 316
Rokeach Value Survey, 265
Role-taking, 278–281, 283, 284
Rule aquisition, 41
Rule conditionality, 47, 48, 50
Rule consistency, 47–48, 49, 55, 56
Rule learning, 57, 105

S

SCAN, 253, 254
Scholastic Aptitude Tests [SATs], 110
Schooling, 8, 16, 226, 243, 313
    elementary school, 35, 39, 40, 181, 222, 253, 281, 308
    experimental, 371
    high school, 119, 253, 255, 308, 317

Schooling (cont.)
  junior high school, 119, 122, 182, 183,
      184, 185, 194, 203, 217, 308, 311,
      316, 317
  learner-oriented approach, 307, 317
  open classrooms, 313
  parochial, 313
  remediation, 9, 83, 180–191, 225, 226,
      227, 241, 243, 244, 246, 267, 268,
      371
  resource room, 2, 257, 258
  special ed, 9, 227, 245, 247, 259, 262,
      263, 265, 266, 297
  structured classrooms, 257
  transitional grade classrooms, 313
Selective listening, 69–70, see also Attention
Self-esteem, 117, 122, 135, 138, 139, 140,
      141, 169, 239, 266, 297
Self-management skills, 136, 139, 140, 141,
      227
Self-monitoring skills, 201, 202, 245
Self-perception, 116, 117, 118, 122, 123, 124,
      130, 131, 132, 133, 135, 141, 165,
      220, 221, 224, 225, 226, 275, 282
Self-regulative behaviors, 201, 203, 266–267
Semantic processing, 20, 39, 177, 179, 225,
      281, 330
Sensory impairment, 3
Sentence boundary cue utilization [in LDs], 11
Serial processing, 37, 38, 47, 366
Serial recall, see Information processing
Serial-ordering deficits, 35
Sex differences, 369, 371
Sinistrality, 373
Social adjustment, 275
Social competence [in LDs], 251, 253, 259,
      267
Social comprehension, 277
Social interaction, 273, 274
Social Interpretation Test, 278
Social knowledge, 276, 281–282, 284
Social learning disability, 312, 376
Social motivation, 274
Social perception, 276–278, 284, 285, 311
Social skills and adjustment, 267, 307, 308,
      310, 311, 312, 313, 314, see also
      Peer relationships
Social withdrawal, 308, 310
Social-cognition, 296, 273, 283, 285, 286,
      289, 290

Social-cognition hypothesis, 273, 274–276,
      282, 289
Social-cognitive deficits, 283, 289, 290, 297
Socio-economic status [of LDs], 104, 236
Socioemotional disturbance [SED], 240–241,
      242, 243, 244, 246, 297, see also
      Emotional disturbance
Sound-symbol relationships, 48, 50, 105, 309
Spatial skills, 370
Speading activation (associative links), 88, 89,
      91, 92, 93, 98
Speech [sound structure], 14–15
Spreading activation, 84, 86, 88, 89, 90, 97,
      98
Spreading activation (resting state), 89, 97, 98
Spreading activation (threshold point), 89, 91,
      92, 93, 97, 98
Statistical redundancy [of letters], 43
Sternberg task, 344–347, 348, 350, 354–356,
      360, 362–366
Strategic processing, 83–86
Strategy aquisition, 8, 17, 150, 151, see also
      Learning strategies and Elaborative
      encoding
Strategy knowledge
  general, 151, 152–153, 154, 158, 159, 160,
      162, 163, 165, 166, 167, 168
  specific, 151–152, 153, 154, 155, 156, 159,
      160, 162, 163, 220, 223, 227
Strategy training, 8, 17, 24, 85, 92, 93, 95,
      147, 148, 150, 159–162, 163–169,
      180–191, 196, 201, 203, 219, 222,
      245, see also Learning strategies
Strategy transfer, 149–151, 154, 166, 219–
      220, 222, 223
Stroop task, 67, 72, 73, 74, 76
Subtypes [of LD], 108, 235, 241, 242, 264
Symtomatology [of LDs], 370, 371
Syntactic development, 39, 41–42
Syntactic skills, 225, 281

T

Teachers attitudes [towards LDs], 262–266
Temperament, 370
Test of Social Inference, 277
Text oraganization, 8
Text processing, 198, 200, 202
Text scanning, 8

Top-down processing, 5, 19, 20, 21, 23, 24, 106, 108, *see also* Language, Reading, and Memory
Transformational imagery, *see* Mnemonics and Learning strategies

U

Under-achievement, 67, 70, 115, 116, 124, 126, 127, 129, 130, 132, 133, 134, 138, 140, 213, 225, 226, 241, 253, 329
Underarousal, 239

V

Verbal abilities, 17, 109, 110
Verbal deficit theory, 3
Visual processing, 10–11, 42
Visual processing deficits, 37–38, 69, 335
Visual search task, 325

Vocabulary aquisition, 181–184
Vocational activities [in LDs], 253

W

Wide Range Achievement Test [WRAT], 40
WISC-R, 12, 115, 238, 241, 242, 243, 337, 338, 351, 365, *see also* Intelligence and IQ
Withdrawal, 242
Woodcock Reading Test, 242
Word consistency, 48, 49, 51, 52, 55, 56
Word familiarity, 43
Word frequency, 51
Word knowledge, 53
Word learning, 42
Word perception, 99
Word recognition, 6–7, 9, 11–12, 20, 21, 22, 119
Word-decoding skills, 41, 42, 45, 47, 51, 53, 55, 57
Written language processing, 308, 309, 310, 311